THE ENCYCLOPÆDIA BRITANNICA
ELEVENTH EDITION

VOLUME XV SLICE III

Japan (part) to Jeveros

I0429400

After the abolition of the shōgunate and the resumption of administrative functions by the Throne, one of the first acts of the newly organized government was to invite the foreign representatives to Kiōto, where they *Japan's Claim for Judicial Autonomy.* had audience of the mikado. Subsequently a decree was issued, announcing the emperor's resolve to establish amicable relations with foreign countries, and "declaring that any Japanese subject thereafter guilty of violent behaviour towards a foreigner would not only act in opposition to the Imperial command, but would also be guilty of impairing the dignity and good faith of the nation in the eyes of the powers with which his majesty had pledged himself to maintain friendship." From that time the relations between Japan and foreign states grew yearly more amicable; the nation adopted the products of Western civilization with notable thoroughness, and the provisions of the treaties were carefully observed. Those treaties, however, presented one feature which very soon became exceedingly irksome to Japan. They exempted foreigners residing within her borders from the operation of her criminal laws, and secured to them the privilege of being arraigned solely before tribunals of their own nationality. That system had always been considered necessary where the subjects of Christian states visited or sojourned in non-Christian countries, and, for the purpose of giving effect to it, consular courts were established. This necessitated the confinement of foreign residents to settlements in the neighbourhood of the consular courts, since it would have been imprudent to allow foreigners to have free access to districts remote from the only tribunals competent to control them. The Japanese raised no objection to the embodiment of this system in the treaties. They recognized its necessity and even its expediency, for if, on the one hand, it infringed their country's sovereign rights, on the other, it prevented complications which must have ensued had they been entrusted with jurisdiction which they were not prepared to discharge satisfactorily. But the consular courts were not free from defects. A few of the powers organized competent tribunals presided over by judicial experts, but a majority of the treaty states, not having sufficiently large interests at stake, were content to delegate consular duties to merchants, not only deficient in legal training, but also themselves engaged in the very commercial transactions upon which they might at any moment be required to adjudicate in a magisterial capacity. In any circumstances the dual functions of consul and judge could not be discharged without anomaly by the same official, for he was obliged to act as advocate in the preliminary stages of complications about which, in his position as judge, he might ultimately have to deliver an impartial verdict. In practice, however, the system worked with tolerable smoothness, and might have remained long in force had not the patriotism of the Japanese rebelled bitterly against the implication that their country was unfit to exercise one of the fundamental attributes of every sovereign state, judicial autonomy. From the very outset they spared no effort to qualify for the recovery of this attribute. Revision of the country's laws and reorganization of its law courts would necessarily have been an essential feature of the general reforms suggested by contact with the Occident, but the question of consular jurisdiction certainly constituted a special incentive. Expert assistance was obtained from France and Germany; the best features of European jurisprudence were adapted to the conditions and usages of Japan; the law courts were remodelled, and steps were taken to educate a competent judiciary. In criminal law the example of France was chiefly followed; in commercial law that of Germany; and in civil law that of the Occident generally, with due regard to the customs of the country. The jury system was not adopted, collegiate courts being regarded as more conducive to justice, and the order of procedure went from tribunals of first instance to appeal courts and finally to the court of cassation. Schools of law were quickly opened, and a well-equipped bar soon came into existence. Twelve years after the inception of these great works, Japan made formal application for revision of the treaties on the basis of abolishing consular jurisdiction. She had asked for revision in 1871, sending to Europe and America an important embassy to raise the question. But at that time the conditions originally calling for consular jurisdiction had not undergone any change such as would have justified its abolition, and the Japanese government, though very anxious to recover tariff autonomy as well as judicial, shrank from separating the two questions, lest by prematurely solving one the solution of the other might be unduly deferred. Thus the embassy failed, and though the problem attracted great academical interest from the first, it did not re-enter the field of practical politics until 1883. The negotiations were long protracted. Never previously had an Oriental state received at the hands of the Occident recognition such as that now demanded by Japan, and the West naturally felt deep reluctance to try a wholly novel experiment. The United States had set a generous example by concluding a new treaty (1878) on the lines desired by Japan. But its operation was conditional on a similar act of compliance by the other treaty powers. Ill-informed European publicists ridiculed the Washington statesmen's attitude on this occasion, claiming that what had been given with one hand was taken back with the other. The truth is that the conditional provision was inserted at the request of Japan herself, who appreciated her own unpreparedness for the concession. From 1883, however, she was ready to accept full responsibility, and she therefore asked that all foreigners within her borders should thenceforth be subject to her laws and judiciable by her law-courts, supplementing her 241application by promising that its favourable reception should be followed by the complete opening of the country and the removal of all restrictions hitherto imposed on foreign trade, travel and residence in her realm. "From the first it had been the habit of Occidental peoples to upbraid Japan on account of the barriers opposed by her to full and free foreign intercourse, and she was now able to claim that these barriers were no longer maintained by her desire, but that they existed because of a system which theoretically proclaimed her unfitness for free association with Western nations, and practically made it impossible for her to throw open her territories completely for the ingress of foreigners." She had a strong case, but on the side of the European powers extreme reluctance was manifested to try the unprecedented experiment of placing their people under the jurisdiction of an Oriental country. Still greater was the reluctance of those upon whom the experiment would be tried. Foreigners residing in Japan naturally clung to consular jurisdiction as a privilege of inestimable value. They saw, indeed, that such a system could not be permanently imposed on a country where the conditions justifying it had nominally disappeared. But they saw, also, that the legal and judicial reforms effected by Japan had been crowded into an extraordinarily brief period, and that, as tyros experimenting with alien systems, the Japanese might be betrayed into many errors.

The negotiations lasted for eleven years. They were begun in 1883 and a solution was not reached until 1894. Finally European governments conceded the justice of Japan's case, and it was agreed that from July 1899 Japanese **Recognition by the Powers.**tribunals should assume jurisdiction over every person, of whatever nationality, within the confines of Japan, and the whole country should be thrown open to foreigners, all limitations upon trade, travel and residence being removed. Great Britain took the lead in thus releasing Japan from the fetters of the old system. The initiative came from her with special grace, for the system and all its irksome consequences had been originally imposed on Japan by a combination of powers with Great Britain in the van. As a matter of historical sequence the United States dictated the terms of the first treaty providing for consular jurisdiction. But from a very early period the Washington government showed its willingness to remove all limitations of Japan's sovereignty, whereas Europe, headed by Great Britain, whose preponderating interests entitled her to lead, resolutely refused to make any substantial concession. In Japanese eyes, therefore, British conservatism seemed to be the one serious obstacle, and since the British residents in the settlements far outnumbered all other nationalities, and since they alone had newspaper organs to ventilate their grievances—it was certainly fortunate for the popularity of her people in the Far East that Great Britain saw her way finally to set a liberal example. Nearly five years were required to bring the other Occidental powers into line with Great Britain and America. It should be stated, however, that neither reluctance to make the necessary concessions nor want of sympathy with Japan caused the delay. The explanation is, first, that each set of negotiators sought to improve either the terms or the terminology of the treaties already concluded, and, secondly, that the tariff arrangements for the different countries required elaborate discussion.

Until the last of the revised treaties was ratified, voices of protest against revision continued to be vehemently raised by a large section of the foreign community in the settlements. Some were honestly apprehensive as to the**Reception given to the Revised Treaties.**issue of the experiment. Others were swayed by racial prejudice. A few had fallen into an insuperable habit of grumbling, or found their account in advocating conservatism under pretence of championing foreign interests; and all were naturally reluctant to forfeit the immunity from taxation hitherto enjoyed. It seemed as though the inauguration of the new system would find the foreign community in a mood which must greatly diminish the chances of a happy result, for where a captious and aggrieved disposition exists, opportunities to discover causes of complaint cannot be wanting. But at the eleventh hour this unfavourable demeanour underwent a marked change. So soon as it became evident that the old system was hopelessly doomed, the sound common sense of the European and American business man asserted itself. The foreign residents let it be seen that they intended to bow cheerfully to the inevitable, and that no obstacles would be willingly placed by them in the path of Japanese jurisdiction. The Japanese, on their side, took some promising steps. An Imperial rescript declared in unequivocal terms that it was the sovereign's policy and desire to abolish all distinctions between natives and foreigners, and that by fully carrying out the friendly purpose of the treaties his people would best consult his wishes, maintain the character of the nation, and promote its prestige. The premier and other ministers of state issued instructions to the effect that the responsibility now devolved on the government, and the duty on the people, of enabling foreigners to reside confidently and contentedly in every part of the country. Even the chief Buddhist prelates addressed to the priests and parishioners in their dioceses injunctions pointing out that, freedom of conscience being now guaranteed by the

2

constitution, men professing alien creeds must be treated as courteously as the followers of Buddhism, and must enjoy the same rights and privileges.

Thus the great change was effected in circumstances of happy augury. Its results were successful on the whole. Foreigners residing in Japan now enjoy immunity of domicile, personal and religious liberty, freedom from official interference, and security of life and property as fully as though they were living in their own countries, and they have gradually learned to look with greatly increased respect upon Japanese law and its administrators.

Next to the revision of the treaties and to the result of the great wars waged by Japan since the resumption of foreign intercourse, the most memorable incident in her modern career was the conclusion, first, of an *entente*, and, *Anglo-Japanese Alliance.* secondly, of an offensive and defensive alliance with Great Britain in January 1902 and September 1905, respectively. The *entente* set out by disavowing on the part of each of the contracting parties any aggressive tendency in either China or Korea, the independence of which two countries was explicitly recognized; and went on to declare that Great Britain in China and Japan in China and Korea might take indispensable means to safeguard their interests; while, if such measures involved one of the signatories in war with a third power, the other signatory would not only remain neutral but would also endeavour to prevent other powers from joining in hostilities against its ally, and would come to the assistance of the latter in the event of its being faced by two or more powers. The *entente* further recognized that Japan possessed, in a peculiar degree, political, commercial and industrial interests in Korea. This agreement, equally novel for each of the contracting parties, evidently tended to the benefit of Japan more than to that of Great Britain, inasmuch as the interests in question were vital from the former power's point of view but merely local from the latter's. The inequality was corrected by an offensive and defensive alliance in 1905. For the scope of the agreement was then extended to India and eastern Asia generally, and while the signatories pledged themselves, on the one hand, to preserve the common interests of all powers in China by insuring her integrity and independence as well as the principle of equal opportunities for the commerce and industry of all nations within her borders, they agreed, on the other, to maintain their own territorial rights in eastern Asia and India, and to come to each other's armed assistance in the event of those rights being assailed by any other power or powers. These agreements have, of course, a close relation to the events which accompanied or immediately preceded them, but they also present a vivid and radical contrast between a country which, less than half a century previously, had struggled vehemently to remain secluded from the world, and a country which now allied itself with one of the most liberal and progressive nations for the purposes of a policy 242 extending over the whole of eastern Asia and India. This contrast was accentuated two years later (1907) when France and Russia concluded *ententes* with Japan, recognizing the independence and integrity of the Chinese Empire, as well as the principle of equal opportunity for all nations in that country, and engaging to support each other for assuring peace and security there. Japan thus became a world power in the most unequivocal sense.

Japan's Foreign Wars and Complications.—The earliest foreign war conducted by Japan is said to have taken place at the beginning of the 3rd century, when the empress Jingō led an army to the conquest of Korea. But as the *War with Korea.* event is supposed to have happened more than 500 years before the first Japanese record was written, its traditional details cannot be seriously discussed. There is, however, no room to doubt that from time to time in early ages Japanese troops were seen in Korea, though they made no permanent impression on the country. It was reserved for Hideyoshi, the taikō, to make the Korean peninsula the scene of a great over-sea campaign. Hideyoshi, the Napoleon of Japan, having brought the whole empire under his sway as the sequel of many years of incomparable generalship and statecraft, conceived the project of subjugating China. By some historians his motive has been described as a desire to find employment for the immense mob of armed men whom four centuries of almost continuous fighting had called into existence in Japan: he felt that domestic peace could not be permanently restored unless these restless spirits were occupied abroad. But although that object may have reinforced his purpose, his ambition aimed at nothing less than the conquest of China, and he regarded Korea merely as a stepping-stone to that aim. Had Korea consented to be put to such a use, she need not have fought or suffered. The Koreans, however, counted China invincible. They considered that Japan would be shattered by the first contact with the great empire, and therefore although, in the 13th century, they had given the use of their harbours to the Mongol invaders of Japan, they flatly refused in the 16th to allow their territory to be used for a Japanese invasion of China. On the 24th of May 1592 the wave of invasion rolled against Korea's southern coast. Hideyoshi had chosen Nagoya in the province of Hizen as the home-base of his operations. There the sea separating Japan from the Korean peninsula narrows to a strait divided into two channels of almost equal width by the island of Tsushima. To reach this island from the Japanese side was an easy and safe task, but in the 56-mile channel that separated Tsushima from the peninsula an invading flotilla had to run the risk of attack by Korean war-ships. At Nagoya Hideyoshi assembled an army of over 300,000 men, of whom some 70,000 constituted the first fighting line, 87,000 the second, and the remainder formed a reserve to be subsequently drawn on as occasion demanded. The question of transport presented some difficulty, but it was solved by the simple expedient of ordering every feudatory to furnish two ships for each 100,000*koku* of his fief's revenue. These were not fighting vessels but mere transports. As for the plan of campaign, it was precisely in accord with modern principles of strategy, and bore witness to the daring genius of Hideyoshi. The van, consisting of three army corps and mustering in all 51,000 men, was to cross rapidly to Fusan, on the south coast of the peninsula, and immediately commence a movement northward towards the capital, Seoul, one corps moving by the eastern coast-road, one by the central route, and one by the western coast-line. Thereafter the other four corps, which formed the first fighting line, together with the corps under the direct orders of the commander-in-chief, Ukida Hideiye, were to cross, for the purpose of effectually subduing the regions through which the van had passed; and, finally, the two remaining corps of the second line were to be transported by sea up the west coast of the peninsula, to form a junction with the van which, by that time, should be preparing to pass into China over the northern boundary of Korea, namely, the Yalu River. For the landing place of these reinforcements the town of Phyong-yang was adopted, being easily accessible by the Taidong River from the coast. In later ages Japanese armies were destined to move twice over these same regions, once to the invasion of China, once to the attack of Russia, and they adopted almost the same strategical plan as that mapped out by Hideyoshi in the year 1592. The forecast was that the Koreans would offer their chief resistance, first, at the capital, Seoul; next at Phyong-yang, and finally at the Yalu, as the approaches to all these places offered positions capable of being utilized to great advantage for defensive purposes.

On the 24th of May 1592 the first army corps, under the command of Konishi Yukinaga, crossed unmolested to the peninsula; next day the castle of Fusan was carried by storm, which same fate befell, on the 27th,**Landing In Korea and Advance of the Invaders.**another and stronger fortress lying 3 miles inland and garrisoned by 20,000 picked soldiers. The invaders were irresistible. From the landing-place at Fusan to the gates of Seoul the distance is 267 miles. Konishi's corps covered that interval in 19 days, storming two forts, carrying two positions and fighting one pitched battle *en route*. On the 12th of June the Korean capital was in Japanese hands, and by the 16th four army corps had assembled there, while four others had effected a landing at Fusan. After a rest of 15 days the northward advance was resumed, and July 15th saw Phyong-yang in Japanese possession. The distance of 130 miles from Seoul to the Taidong had been traversed in 18 days, 10 having been occupied in forcing the passage of a river which, if held with moderate resolution and skill, should have stopped the Japanese altogether. At this point, however, the invasion suffered a check owing to a cause which in modern times has received much attention, though in Hideyoshi's days it had been little considered; the Japanese lost the command of the sea.

The Japanese idea of sea-fighting in those times was to use open boats propelled chiefly by oars. They closed as quickly as possible with the enemy, and then fell on with the trenchant swords which they used so skilfully.**Fighting at Sea.**Now during the 15th century and part of the 16th the Chinese had been so harassed by Japanese piratical raids that their inventive genius, quickened by suffering, suggested a device for coping with these formidable adversaries. Once allow the Japanese swordsman to come to close quarters and he carried all before him. To keep him at a distance, then, was the great desideratum, and the Chinese compassed this in maritime warfare by completely covering their boats with roofs of solid timber, so that those within were protected against missiles, while loop-holes and ports enabled them to pour bullets and arrows on a foe. The Koreans learned this device from the Chinese and were the first to employ it in actual warfare. Their own history alleges that they improved upon the Chinese model by nailing sheet iron over the roofs and sides of the "turtle-shell" craft and studding the whole surface with *chevaux de frise*, but Japanese annals indicate that in the great majority of cases solid timber alone was used. It seems strange that the Japanese should have been without any clear perception of the immense fighting superiority possessed by such protected war-vessels over small open boats. But certainly they were either ignorant or indifferent. The fleet which they provided to hold the command of Korean waters did not include one vessel of any magnitude; it consisted simply of some hundreds of row-boats manned by 7000 men. Hideyoshi himself was perhaps not without misgivings. Six years previously he had endeavoured to obtain two war-galleons from the Portuguese, and had he succeeded, the history of the Far East might have been radically different. Evidently, however, he committed a blunder which his countrymen in modern times have conspicuously avoided; he drew the sword without having fully investigated his adversary's resources. Just about the time when the van of the Japanese army was entering Seoul, the Korean admiral, Yi Sun-sin, at the head of a fleet of 80 vessels, attacked the Japanese squadron which lay at anchor near the entrance to Fusan harbour, set 26 of the vessels on fire and dispersed the rest. Four other engagements ensued in rapid succession. The last and most important took place shortly after the Japanese troops had seized Phyong-yang. It 243resulted in the sinking of over 70 Japanese vessels, transports and fighting ships combined, which formed the main part of a flotilla carrying reinforcements by sea to the van of the invading army. This despatch of troops and supplies by water had been a leading feature of Hideyoshi's plan of campaign, and the destruction of the flotilla to which the duty was entrusted may be said to have sealed the fate of the war by isolating the army in Korea from its home base. It is true that Konishi Yukinaga, who commanded the first division, would have continued his northward march from Phyong-yang without delay. He argued that China was wholly unprepared, and that the best hope of ultimate victory lay in not giving her time to collect her forces. But the commander-in-chief, Ukida Hideiye, refused to endorse this plan. He took the view that since the Korean provinces were still offering desperate resistance, supplies could not be drawn from them, neither could the troops engaged in subjugating them be freed for service at the front. Therefore it was essential to await the consummation of the second phase of Hideyoshi's plan, namely, the despatch of reinforcements and munitions by water to Phyong-yang. The reader has seen how that second phase fared. The Japanese commander at Phyong-yang never received any accession of strength. His force suffered constant diminution from casualties, and the question of commissariat became daily more difficult. It is further plain to any reader of history—and Japanese historians themselves admit the fact—that no wise effort was made to conciliate the Korean people. They were treated so harshly that even the humble peasant took up arms, and thus the peninsula, instead of serving as a basis of supplies, had to be garrisoned perpetually by a strong army.

The Koreans, having suffered for their loyalty to China, naturally looked to her for succour. Again and again appeals were made to Peking, and at length a force of 5000 men, which had been mobilized in the Liaotung*Chinese Intervention.*peninsula, crossed the Yalu and moved south to Phyong-yang, where the Japanese van had been lying idle for over two months. This was early in October 1592. Memorable as the first encounter between Japanese and Chinese, the incident also illustrated China's supreme confidence in her own ineffable superiority. The whole of the Korean forces had been driven northward throughout the entire length of the peninsula by the Japanese armies, yet Peking considered that 5000 Chinese "braves" would suffice to roll back this tide of invasion. Three thousand of the Chinese were killed and the remainder fled pell-mell across the Yalu. China now began to be seriously alarmed. She collected an army variously estimated at from 51,000 to 200,000 men, and marching it across Manchuria in the dead of winter, hurled it against Phyong-yang during the first week of February 1593. The Japanese garrison did not exceed 20,000, nearly one-half of its original number having been detached to hold a line of forts which guarded the communications with Seoul. Moreover, the Chinese, though their swords were much inferior to the Japanese weapon, possessed great superiority in artillery and cavalry, as well as in the fact that their troopers wore iron mail which defied the keenest blade. Thus, after a severe fight, the Japanese had to evacuate Phyong-yang and fall back upon Seoul. But this one victory alone stands to China's credit. In all subsequent encounters of any magnitude her army suffered heavy defeats, losing on one occasion some 10,000 men, on another 4000, and on a third 39,000. But the presence of her forces and the determined resistance offered by the Koreans effectually saved China from invasion. Indeed, after the evacuation of Seoul, on the 9th of May 1593, Hideyoshi abandoned all idea of carrying the war into Chinese territory, and devoted his attention to obtaining honourable terms of peace, the Japanese troops meanwhile holding a line of forts along the southern coast of Korea. He died before that end had been accomplished. Had he lived a few days longer, he would have learned of a crushing defeat inflicted on the Chinese forces (at Sö-chhön, October 30, 1598), when the Satsuma men under Shimazu Yoshihiro took 38,700 Chinese heads and sent the noses and ears to Japan, where they now lie buried under a tumulus (*mimizuka*, ear-mound) near the temple of Daibutsu in Kiōto. Thereafter the statesmen to whom the regent on his death-bed had entrusted the duty of terminating the struggle and recalling the troops, intimated to the enemy that the evacuation of the peninsula might be obtained if a Korean prince repaired to Japan as envoy, and if some tiger-skins and*ginseng* were sent to Kiōto in token of amity. So ended one of the greatest over-sea campaigns recorded in history. It had lasted 6½ years, had seen 200,000 Japanese troops at one time on Korean soil, and had cost something like a quarter of a million lives.

From the recall of the Korea expedition in 1598 to the resumption of intercourse with the Occident in modern times, Japan enjoyed uninterrupted peace with foreign nations.*Contrast between Foreign Relations in Medieval and Modern Times.*Thereafter she had to engage in four wars. It is a striking contrast. During the first eleven centuries of her historical existence she was involved in only one contest abroad; during the next half century she fought four times

5

beyond the sea and was confronted by many complications. Whatever material or moral advantages her association with the West conferred on her, it did not bring peace.

The first menacing foreign complication with which the Japanese government of the Meiji era had to deal was connected with the traffic in Chinese labour, an abuse not yet wholly eradicated. In 1872, a Peruvian ship, the *The "Maria Luz" Complication.*"Maria Luz," put into port at Yokohama, carrying 200 contract labourers. One of the unfortunate men succeeded in reaching the shore and made a piteous appeal to the Japanese authorities, who at once seized the vessel and released her freight of slaves, for they were little better. The Japanese had not always been so particular. In the days of early foreign intercourse, before England's attitude towards slavery had established a new code of ethics, Portuguese ships had been permitted to carry away from Hirado, as they did from Macao, cargoes of men and women, doomed to a life of enforced toil if they survived the horrors of the voyage. But modern Japan followed the tenets of modern morality in such matters. Of course the Peruvian government protested, and for a time relations were strained almost to the point of rupture; but it was finally agreed that the question should be submitted to the arbitration of the tsar, who decided in Japan's favour. Japan's attitude in this affair elicited applause, not merely from the point of view of humanity, but also because of the confidence she showed in Occidental justice.

Another complication which occupied the attention of the Tōkyō government from the beginning of the Meiji era was in truth a legacy from the days of feudalism. In those days the island of Yezo, as well as Sakhalin *The Sakhalin Complication.*on its north-west and the Kurile group on its north, could scarcely be said to be in effective Japanese occupation. It is true that the feudal chief of Matsumae (now Fuku-yama), the remains of whose castle may still be seen on the coast at the southern extremity of the island of Yezo, exercised nominal jurisdiction; but his functions did not greatly exceed the levying of taxes on the aboriginal inhabitants of Yezo, the Kuriles and southern Sakhalin. Thus from the beginning of the 18th century Russian fishermen began to settle in the Kuriles and Russian ships menaced Sakhalin. There can be no doubt that the first explorers of Sakhalin were Japanese. As early as 1620, some vassals of the feudal chief of Matsumae visited the place and passed a winter there. It was then supposed to be a peninsula forming part of the Asiatic mainland, but in 1806 a daring Japanese traveller, by name Mamiya Rinzo, made his way to Manchuria, voyaged up and down the Amur, and, crossing to Sakhalin, discovered that a narrow strait separated it from the mainland. There still prevails in the minds of many Occidentals a belief that the discovery of Sakhalin's insular character was reserved for Captain Nevelskoy, a Russian, who visited the place in 1849, but in Japan the fact had then been known for 43 years. Muravief, the great Russian empire-builder in East Asia, under whose orders Nevelskoy acted, quickly appreciated the necessity of acquiring Sakhalin, which commands the estuary of the Amur. 244After the conclusion of the treaty of Aigun (1857) he visited Japan with a squadron, and required that the strait of La Pérouse, which separates Sakhalin from Yezo, should be regarded as the frontier between Russia and Japan. This would have given the whole of Sakhalin to Russia. Japan refused, and Muravief immediately resorted to the policy he had already pursued with signal success in the Usuri region: he sent emigrants to settle in Sakhalin. Twice the shōgunate attempted to frustrate this process of gradual absorption by proposing a division of the island along the 50th parallel of north latitude, and finally, in 1872, the Meiji government offered to purchase the Russian portion for 2,000,000 dollars (then equivalent to about £400,000). St Petersburg, having by that time discovered the comparative worthlessness of the island as a wealth-earning possession, showed some signs of acquiescence, and possibly an agreement might have been reached had not a leading Japanese statesman—afterwards Count Kuroda—opposed the bargain as disadvantageous to Japan. Finally St Petersburg's perseverance won the day. In 1875 Japan agreed to recognize Russia's title to the whole island on condition that Russia similarly recognized Japan's title to the Kuriles. It was a singular compact. Russia purchased a Japanese property and paid for it with a part of Japan's belongings. These details form a curious preface to the fact that Sakhalin was destined, 30 years later, to be the scene of a Japanese invasion, in the sequel of which it was divided along the 50th parallel as the shōgun's administration had originally proposed.

The first of Japan's four conflicts was an expedition to Formosa in 1874. Insignificant from a military point of view, this affair derives vicarious interest from its effect upon the relations between China and Japan, *Military Expedition to Formosa.*and upon the question of the ownership of the Riūkiū islands. These islands, which lie at a little distance south of Japan, had for centuries been regarded as an apanage of the Satsuma fief. The language and customs of their inhabitants showed unmistakable traces of relationship to the Japanese, and the possibility of the islands being included among the dominions of China had probably never occurred to any Japanese statesman. When therefore, in 1873, the crew of a wrecked Riūkiūan junk were barbarously treated by the inhabitants of northern Formosa, the Japanese government

6

unhesitatingly assumed the responsibility of seeking redress for their outrage. Formosa being a part of the Chinese Empire, complaint was duly preferred in Peking. But the Chinese authorities showed such resolute indifference to Japan's representations that the latter finally took the law into her own hands, and sent a small force to punish the Formosan murderers, who, of course, were found quite unable to offer any serious resistance. The Chinese government, now recognizing the fact that its territories had been invaded, lodged a protest which, but for the intervention of the British minister in Peking, might have involved the two empires in war. The final terms of arrangement were that, in consideration of Japan withdrawing her troops from Formosa, China should indemnify her to the extent of the expenses of the expedition. In sending this expedition to Formosa the government sought to placate the Satsuma samurai, who were beginning to show much opposition to certain features of the administrative reforms just inaugurated, and who claimed special interest in the affairs of the Riūkiū islands.

Had Japan needed any confirmation of her belief that the Riūkiū islands belonged to her, the incidents and settlement of the Formosan complication would have constituted conclusive evidence. Thus in 1876 she did not *The Riūkiū Complication.* hesitate to extend her newly organized system of prefectural government to Riūkiū, which thenceforth became the Okinawa prefecture, the former ruler of the islands being pensioned, according to the system followed in the case of the feudal chiefs in Japan proper. China at once entered an objection. She claimed that Riūkiū had always been a tributary of her empire, and she was doubtless perfectly sincere in the contention. But China's interpretation of tribute did not seem reducible to a working theory. So long as her own advantage could be promoted, she regarded as a token of vassalage the presents periodically carried to her court from neighbouring states. So soon, however, as there arose any question of discharging a suzerain's duties, she classed these offerings as insignificant interchanges of neighbourly courtesy. It was true that Riūkiū had followed the custom of despatching gift-bearing envoys to China from time to time, just as Japan herself had done, though with less regularity. But it was also true that Riūkiū had been subdued by Satsuma without China stretching out a hand to help her; that for two centuries the islands had been included in the Satsuma fief, and that China, in the sequel to the Formosan affair, had made a practical acknowledgment of Japan's superior title to protect the islanders. Each empire positively asserted its claims; but whereas Japan put hers into practice, China confined herself to remonstrances. Things remained in that state until 1880, when General Grant, visiting the East, suggested the advisability of a compromise. A conference met in Peking, and the plenipotentiaries agreed that the islands should be divided, Japan taking the northern group, China the southern. But on the eve of signature the Chinese plenipotentiary drew back, pleading that he had no authority to conclude an agreement without previously referring it to certain other dignitaries. Japan, sensible that she had been flouted, retired from the discussion and retained the islands, China's share in them being reduced to a grievance.

From the 16th century, when the Korean peninsula was overrun by Japanese troops, its rulers made a habit of sending a present-bearing embassy to Japan to felicitate the accession of each shōgun. But after the fall of *The Korean Complication.* the Tokugawa shōgunate, the Korean court desisted from this custom, declared a determination to have no further relations with a country embracing Western civilization, and refused even to receive a Japanese embassy. This conduct caused deep umbrage in Japan. Several prominent politicians cast their votes for war, and undoubtedly the sword would have been drawn had not the leading statesmen felt that a struggle with Korea, involving probably a rupture with China, must fatally check the progress of the administrative reforms then (1873) in their infancy. Two years later, however, the Koreans crowned their defiance by firing on the boats of a Japanese war-vessel engaged in the operation of coast-surveying. No choice now remained except to despatch an armed expedition against the truculent kingdom. But Japan did not want to fight. In this matter she showed herself an apt pupil of Occidental methods such as had been practised against herself in former years. She assembled an imposing force of war-ships and transports, but instead of proceeding to extremities, she employed the squadron—which was by no means so strong as it seemed—to intimidate Korea into signing a treaty of amity and commerce, and opening three ports to foreign trade (1876). That was the beginning of Korea's friendly relations with the outer world, and Japan naturally took credit for the fact that, thus early in her new career, she had become an instrument for extending the principle of universal intercourse opposed so strenuously by herself in the past.

From time immemorial China's policy towards the petty states on her frontiers had been to utilize them as buffers for softening the shock of foreign contact, while contriving, at the same time, that her relations with them should *War with China.* involve no inconvenient responsibilities for herself. The aggressive impulses of the outside world were to be checked by an unproclaimed understanding that the territories of these states partook of the inviolability of

7

China, while the states, on their side, must never expect their suzerain to bear the consequences of their acts. This arrangement, depending largely on sentiment and prestige, retained its validity in the atmosphere of Oriental seclusion, but quickly failed to endure the test of modern Occidental practicality. Tongking, Annam, Siam and Burma were withdrawn, one by one, from the fiction of dependence on China and independence towards all other countries. But with regard to Korea, China proved more tenacious. The 245possession of the peninsula by a foreign power would have threatened the maritime route to the Chinese capital and given easy access to Manchuria, the cradle of the dynasty which ruled China. Therefore Peking statesmen endeavoured to preserve the old-time relations with the little kingdom. But they could never persuade themselves to modify the indirect methods sanctioned by tradition. Instead of boldly declaring Korea a dependency of China, they sought to keep up the romance of ultimate dependency and intermediate sovereignty. Thus in 1876 Korea was suffered to conclude with Japan a treaty of which the first article declared her "an independent state enjoying the same rights as Japan," and subsequently to make with the United States (1882), Great Britain (1883) and other powers, treaties in which her independence was constructively admitted. China, however, did not intend that Korea should exercise the independence thus conventionally recognized. A Chinese resident was placed in Seoul, and a system of steady though covert interference in Korea's affairs was inaugurated. The chief sufferer from these anomalous conditions was Japan. In all her dealings with Korea, in all complications that arose out of her comparatively large trade with the peninsula, in all questions connected with her numerous settlers there, she found herself negotiating with a dependency of China, and with officials who took their orders from the Chinese representative. China had long entertained a rooted apprehension of Japanese aggression in Korea—an apprehension not unwarranted by history— and that distrust tinged all the influence exerted by her agents there. On many occasions Japan was made sensible of the discrimination thus exercised against her. Little by little the consciousness roused her indignation, and although no single instance constituted a ground for strong international protest, the Japanese people gradually acquired a sense of being perpetually baffled, thwarted and humiliated by China's interference in Korean affairs. For thirty years China had treated Japan as a contemptible deserter from the Oriental standard, and had regarded her progressive efforts with openly disdainful aversion; while Japan, on her side, had chafed more and more to furnish some striking evidence of the wisdom of her preference for Western civilization. Even more serious were the consequences of Chinese interference from the point of view of Korean administration. The rulers of the country lost all sense of national responsibility, and gave unrestrained sway to selfish ambition. The functions of the judiciary and of the executive alike came to be discharged by bribery only. Family interests predominated over those of the state. Taxes were imposed in proportion to the greed of local officials. No thought whatever was taken for the welfare of the people or for the development of the country's resources. Personal responsibility was unknown among officials. To be a member of the Min family, to which the queen belonged, was to possess a passport to office and an indemnity against the consequences of abuse of power. From time to time the advocates of progress or the victims of oppression rose in arms. They effected nothing except to recall to the world's recollection the miserable condition into which Korea had fallen. Chinese military aid was always furnished readily for the suppression of these risings, and thus the Min family learned to base its tenure of power on ability to conciliate China and on readiness to obey Chinese dictation, while the people at large fell into the apathetic condition of men who possess neither security of property nor national ambition.

As a matter of state policy the Korean problem caused much anxiety to Japan. Her own security being deeply concerned in preserving Korea from the grasp of a Western power, she could not suffer the little kingdom to drift into a condition of such administrative incompetence and national debility that a strong aggressor might find at any moment a pretext for interference. On two occasions (1882 and 1884) when China's armed intervention was employed in the interests of the Min to suppress movements of reform, the partisans of the victors, regarding Japan as the fountain of progressive tendencies, destroyed her legation in Seoul and compelled its inmates to fly from the city. Japan behaved with forbearance at these crises, but in the consequent negotiations she acquired conventional titles that touched the core of China's alleged suzerainty. In 1882 her right to maintain troops in Seoul for the protection of her legation was admitted; in 1885 she concluded with China a convention by which each power pledged itself not to send troops to Korea without notifying the other.

In the spring of 1894 a serious insurrection broke out in Korea, and the Min family appealed for China's aid. On the 6th of July 2500 Chinese troops embarked at Tientsin and were transported to the peninsula, where they went *The Rupture with China.*into camp at Ya-shan (Asan), on the south-west coast, notice of the measure being given by the Chinese government to the Japanese representative at Peking, according to treaty. During the interval immediately preceding these events, Japan had been rendered acutely sensible of China's arbitrary and unfriendly interference in Korea. Twice the efforts of the Japanese government to obtain redress for unlawful and ruinous commercial prohibitions had been thwarted by the Chinese representative in Seoul; and an ultimatum addressed from Tōkyō to the Korean government had elicited from the viceroy Li in Tientsin a thinly veiled threat of Chinese armed opposition. Still more provocative of national indignation was China's procedure with regard to the murder of Kim Ok-kyun, the leader of progress in Korea, who had been for some years a refugee in Japan. Inveigled from Japan to China by a fellow-countryman sent from Seoul to assassinate him, Kim was shot in a Japanese hotel in Shanghai; and China, instead of punishing the murderer, conveyed him in a war-ship of her own to Korea to be publicly honoured. When, therefore, the Korean insurrection of 1894 induced the Min family again to solicit China's armed intervention, the Tōkyō government concluded that, in the interests of Japan's security and of civilization in the Orient, steps must be taken to put an end to the misrule which offered incessant invitations to foreign aggression, and checked Korea's capacity to maintain its own independence. Japan did not claim for herself any rights or interests in the peninsula superior to those possessed there by China. But there was not the remotest probability that China, whose face had been contemptuously set against all the progressive measures adopted by Japan during the preceding twenty-five years, would join in forcing upon a neighbouring kingdom the very reforms she herself despised, were her co-operation invited through ordinary diplomatic channels only. It was necessary to contrive a situation which would not only furnish clear proof of Japan's resolution, but also enable her to pursue her programme independently of Chinese endorsement, should the latter be finally unobtainable. She therefore met China's notice of a despatch of troops with a corresponding notice of her own, and the month of July 1894 found a Chinese force assembled at Asan and a Japanese force occupying positions in the neighbourhood of Seoul. China's motive for sending troops was nominally to quell the Tonghak insurrection, but really to re-affirm her own domination in the peninsula. Japan's motive was to secure such a position as would enable her to insist upon the radically curative treatment of Korea's malady. Up to this point the two empires were strictly within their conventional rights. Each was entitled by treaty to send troops to Korea, provided that notice was given to the other. But China, in giving notice, described Korea as her "tributary state," thus thrusting into the forefront of the discussion a contention which Japan, from conciliatory motives, would have kept out of sight. Once formally advanced, however, the claim had to be challenged. In the treaty of amity and commerce concluded in 1876 between Japan and Korea, the two high contracting parties were explicitly declared to possess the same national status. Japan could not agree that a power which for nearly two decades she had acknowledged and treated as her equal should be openly classed as a tributary of China. She protested, but the Chinese statesmen took no notice of her protest. They continued to apply the disputed appellation to Korea, and they further asserted their assumption of sovereignty in the peninsula by seeking to set limits to the number of troops sent by Japan, as well as to the sphere of their employment. Japan then proposed that 246the two empires should unite their efforts for the suppression of disturbances in Korea, and for the subsequent improvement of that kingdom's administration, the latter purpose to be pursued by the despatch of a joint commission of investigation. But China refused everything. Ready at all times to interfere by force of arms between the Korean people and the dominant political faction, she declined to interfere in any way for the promotion of reform. She even expressed supercilious surprise that Japan, while asserting Korea's independence, should suggest the idea of peremptorily reforming its administration. In short, for Chinese purposes the Peking statesmen openly declared Korea a tributary state; but for Japanese purposes they insisted that it must be held independent. They believed that their island neighbour aimed at the absorption of Korea into the Japanese empire. Viewed in the light of that suspicion, China's attitude became comprehensible, but her procedure was inconsistent, illogical and unpractical. The Tōkyō cabinet now declared its resolve not to withdraw the Japanese troops without "some understanding that would guarantee the future peace, order, and good government of Korea," and since China still declined to come to such an understanding, Japan undertook the work of reform single-handed.

The Chinese representative in Seoul threw his whole weight into the scale against the success of these reforms. But the determining cause of rupture was in itself a belligerent operation. China's troops had been sent originally for **Outbreak of Hostilities.** the purpose of quelling the Tonghak rebellion. But the rebellion having died of inanition before the landing of the troops, their services were not required. Nevertheless China kept them in Korea, her declared reason for doing so being the presence of a Japanese military force. Throughout the subsequent negotiations the Chinese forces lay in an entrenched camp at Asan, while the Japanese occupied Seoul. An attempt on China's part to send reinforcements could be construed only as an unequivocal

9

declaration of resolve to oppose Japan's proceedings by force of arms. Nevertheless China not only despatched troops by sea to strengthen the camp at Asan, but also sent an army overland across Korea's northern frontier. At this stage an act of war occurred. Three Chinese men-of-war, convoying a transport with 1200 men encountered and fired on three Japanese cruisers. One of the Chinese ships was taken; another was so shattered that she had to be beached and abandoned; the third escaped in a dilapidated condition; and the transport, refusing to surrender, was sunk. This happened on the 25th of July 1894, and an open declaration of war was made by each empire six days later.

From the moment when Japan applied herself to break away from Oriental traditions, and to remove from her limbs the fetters of Eastern conservatism, it was inevitable that a widening gulf should gradually grow between **Remote Origin of the Conflict.** herself and China. The war of 1894 was really a contest between Japanese progress and Chinese stagnation. To secure Korean immunity from foreign—especially Russian—aggression was of capital importance to both empires. Japan believed that such security could be attained by introducing into Korea the civilization which had contributed so signally to the development of her own strength and resources. China thought that she could guarantee it without any departure from old-fashioned methods, and by the same process of capricious protection which had failed so signally in the cases of Annam, Tongking, Burma and Siam. The issue really at stake was whether Japan should be suffered to act as the Eastern propagandist of Western progress, or whether her efforts in that cause should be held in check by Chinese conservatism.

The war itself was a succession of triumphs for Japan. Four days after the first naval encounter she sent from Seoul a column of troops who routed the Chinese entrenched at Asan. Many of the fugitives effected their escape to **Events of the War.** Phyong-yang, a town on the Taidong River, offering excellent facilities for defence, and historically interesting as the place where a Japanese army of invasion had its first encounter with Chinese troops in 1592. There the Chinese assembled a force of 17,000 men, and made leisurely preparations for a decisive contest. Forty days elapsed before the Japanese columns converged upon Phyong-yang, and that interval was utilized by the Chinese to throw up parapets, mount Krupp guns and otherwise strengthen their position. Moreover, they were armed with repeating rifles, whereas the Japanese had only single-loaders, and the ground offered little cover for an attacking force. In such circumstances, the advantages possessed by the defence ought to have been well-nigh insuperable; yet a day's fighting sufficed to carry all the positions, the assailants' casualties amounting to less than 700 and the defenders losing 6000 in killed and wounded. This brilliant victory was the prelude to an equally conspicuous success at sea. For on the 17th of September, the very day after the battle at Phyong-yang, a great naval fight took place near the mouth of the Yalu River, which forms the northern boundary of Korea. Fourteen Chinese war-ships and six torpedo-boats were returning to home ports after convoying a fleet of transports to the Yalu, when they encountered eleven Japanese men-of-war cruising in the Yellow Sea. Hitherto the Chinese had sedulously avoided a contest at sea. Their fleet included two armoured battleships of over 7000 tons displacement, whereas the biggest vessels on the Japanese side were belted cruisers of only 4000 tons. In the hands of an admiral appreciating the value of sea power, China's naval force would certainly have been led against Japan's maritime communications, for a successful blow struck there must have put an end to the Korean campaign. The Chinese, however, failed to read history. They employed their war-vessels as convoys only, and, when not using them for that purpose, hid them in port. Everything goes to show that they would have avoided the battle off the Yalu had choice been possible, though when forced to fight they fought bravely. Four of their ships were sunk, and the remainder escaped to Wei-hai-wei, the vigour of the Japanese pursuit being greatly impaired by the presence of torpedo-boats in the retreating squadron.

The Yalu victory opened the over-sea route to China. Japan could now strike at Talien, Port Arthur, and Wei-hai-wei, naval stations on the Liaotung and Shantung peninsulas, where powerful permanent fortifications, built after plans prepared by European experts and armed with the best modern weapons, were regarded as almost impregnable; They fell before the assaults of the Japanese troops as easily as the comparatively rude fortifications at Phyong-yang had fallen. The only resistance of a stubborn character was made by the Chinese fleet at Wei-hai-wei; but after the whole squadron of torpedo-craft had been destroyed or captured as they attempted to escape, and after three of the largest vessels had been sunk at their moorings by Japanese torpedoes, and one by gun-fire, the remaining ships surrendered, and their brave commander, Admiral Ting, committed suicide. This ended the war. It had lasted seven and a half months, during which time Japan put into the field five columns, aggregating about 120,000 of all arms. One of these columns marched northward from Seoul, won the battle of Phyong-yang, advanced to the Yalu, forced its way into Manchuria, and moved towards Mukden by Feng-hwang, fighting several minor engagements, and conducting the greater part of its operations amid deep snow in midwinter. The second column diverged westwards from the Yalu, and, marching through southern Manchuria, reached Hai-cheng, whence it advanced to the capture of Niuchwang and Ying-tse-kow. The third landed on the Liaotung peninsula, and, turning southwards, carried Talien and Port Arthur by assault. The fourth moved up the Liaotung peninsula, and, having seized Kaiping, advanced against Ying-tse-kow, where it joined hands with the second column. The fifth crossed from Port Arthur to Wei-hai-wei, and captured the latter. In all these operations the total Japanese casualties were 1005 killed and 4922 wounded—figures which sufficiently indicate the inefficiency of the Chinese fighting. The deaths from disease totalled 16,866, and the total monetary expenditure was £20,000,000 sterling.

The Chinese government sent Li Hung-chang, viceroy of Pechili and senior grand secretary of state, and Li Ching-fong, to discuss terms of peace with Japan, the latter being represented by Marquis (afterwards Prince) Itō and **Conclusion of Peace.** Count Mutsu, prime minister and minister for foreign affairs, respectively. A treaty was signed at Shimonoseki on the 17th of April 1895, and subsequently ratified by the sovereigns of the two empires. It declared the absolute independence of Korea; ceded to Japan the part of Manchuria lying south of a line drawn from the mouth of the river Anping to the mouth of the Liao, through Feng-hwang, Hai-cheng and Ying-tse-kow, as well as the islands of Formosa and the Pescadores; pledged China to pay an indemnity of 200,000,000 taels; provided for the occupation of Wei-hai-wei by Japan pending payment of the indemnity; secured some additional commercial privileges, such as the opening of four new places to foreign trade and the right of foreigners to engage in manufacturing enterprises in China, and provided for the conclusion of a treaty of commerce and amity between the two empires, based on the lines of China's treaties with Occidental powers.

No sooner was this agreement ratified than Russia, Germany and France presented a joint note to the Tōkyō government, recommending that the territories ceded to Japan on the mainland of China should not be permanently **Foreign Interference.** occupied, as such a proceeding would be detrimental to peace. The recommendation was couched in the usual terms of diplomatic courtesy, but everything indicated that its signatories were prepared to enforce their advice by an appeal to arms. Japan found herself compelled to comply. Exhausted by the Chinese campaign, which had drained her treasury, consumed her supplies of warlike material, and kept her squadrons constantly at sea for eight months, she had no residue of strength to oppose such a coalition. Her resolve was quickly taken. The day that saw the publication of the ratified treaty saw also the issue of an Imperial rescript in which the mikado, avowing his unalterable devotion to the cause of peace, and recognizing that the counsel offered by the European states was prompted by the same sentiment, "yielded to the dictates of magnanimity, and accepted the advice of the three Powers." The Japanese people were shocked by this incident. They could understand the motives influencing Russia and France, for it was evidently natural that the former should desire to exclude warlike and progressive people like the Japanese from territories contiguous to her borders, and it was also natural that France should remain true to her alliance with Russia. But Germany, wholly uninterested in the ownership of Manchuria, and by profession a warm friend of Japan, seemed to have joined in robbing the latter of the fruits of her victory simply for the sake of establishing some shadowy title to Russia's goodwill. It was not known until a later period that the German emperor entertained profound apprehensions about the "yellow peril," an irruption of Oriental hordes into the Occident, and held it a sacred duty to prevent Japan from gaining a position which might enable her to construct an immense military machine out of the countless millions of China.

Japan's third expedition over-sea in the Meiji era had its origin in causes which belong to the history of China (*q.v.*). In the second half of 1900 an anti-foreign and anti-dynastic rebellion, breaking out in Shantung, spread **Chinese Crisis of 1900.** to the metropolitan province of Pechili, and resulted in a situation of extreme peril for the foreign communities of Tientsin and Peking. It was impossible for any European power, or for the United States, to organize sufficiently prompt measures of relief. Thus the eyes of the world turned to Japan, whose proximity to the scene of disturbance rendered intervention comparatively easy for her. But Japan hesitated. Knowing now with what suspicion and distrust the development of her resources and the growth of her military strength were regarded by some European peoples, and aware that she had been admitted to the comity of Western nations on sufferance, she shrank, on the one hand, from seeming to grasp at an opportunity for armed display, and, on the other, from the solecism of obtrusiveness in the society of strangers. Not until Europe and America made it quite plain that they needed and desired her aid did she send a division (21,000) men to Pechili. Her troops played a fine part in the subsequent expedition for the relief of Peking, which had to be approached in midsummer under very trying conditions. Fighting side by side with European and American soldiers, and under the eyes of competent military critics, the Japanese acquitted themselves in such a manner as to establish a high military reputation. Further, after the relief of Peking they withdrew a moiety of their forces, and that step, as well as their unequivocal co-operation with Western powers in the subsequent negotiations, helped to show the injustice of the suspicions with which they had been regarded.

From the time (1895) when Russia, with the co-operation of Germany and France, dictated to Japan a cardinal alteration of the Shimonoseki treaty, Japanese statesmen seem to have concluded that their country must one day *War with Russia.*cross swords with the great northern power. Not a few European and American publicists shared that view. But the vast majority, arguing that the little Eastern empire would never invite annihilation by such an encounter, believed that sufficient forbearance to avert serious trouble would always be forthcoming on Japan's side. Yet when the geographical and historical situation was carefully considered, little hope of an ultimately peaceful settlement presented itself.

Japan along its western shore, Korea along its southern and eastern, and Russia along the eastern coast of its maritime province, are washed by the Sea of Japan. The communications between the sea and the Pacific Ocean are practically two only. One is on the north-east, namely, Tsugaru Strait; the other is on the south, namely, the channel between the extremity of the Korean peninsula and the Japanese island of the nine provinces. Tsugaru Strait is entirely under Japan's control. It is between her main island and her island of Yezo, and in case of need she can close it with mines. The channel between the southern extremity of Korea and Japan has a width of 102 m. and would therefore be a fine open sea-way were it free from islands. But almost mid-way in this channel lie the twin islands of Tsushima, and the space of 56 m. that separates them from Japan is narrowed by another island, Iki. Tsushima and Iki belong to the Japanese empire. The former has some exceptionally good harbours, constituting a naval base from which the channel on either side could easily be sealed. Thus the avenues from the Pacific Ocean to the Sea of Japan are controlled by the Japanese empire. In other words, access to the Pacific from Korea's eastern and southern coasts and access to the Pacific from Russia's maritime province depend upon Japan's goodwill. So far as Korea was concerned this question mattered little, it being her fate to depend upon the goodwill of Japan in affairs of much greater importance. But with Russia the case was different. Vladivostok, which until recent times was her principal port in the Far East, lies at the southern extremity of the maritime province; that is to say, on the north-western shore of the Japan Sea. It was therefore necessary for Russia that freedom of passage by the Tsushima channel should be secured, and to secure it one of two things was essential, namely, either that she herself should possess a fortified port on the Korean side, or that Japan should be bound neither to acquire such a port nor to impose any restriction upon the navigation of the strait. To put the matter briefly, Russia must either acquire a strong foothold for herself in southern Korea, or contrive that Japan should not acquire one. There was here a strong inducement for Russian aggression in Korea.

Russia's eastward movement through Asia has been strikingly illustrative of her strong craving for free access to southern seas and of the impediments she had experienced in gratifying that wish. An irresistible impulse had driven her oceanward. Checked again and again in her attempts to reach the Mediterranean, she set out on a five-thousand-miles march of conquest right across the vast Asiatic continent towards the Pacific. Eastward of Lake Baikal she found her line of least resistance along the Amur, and when, owing to the restless perseverance 248of Muravief, she reached the mouth of that great river, the acquisition of Nikolayevsk for a naval basis was her immediate reward. But Nikolayevsk could not possibly satisfy her. Situated in an inhospitable region far away from all the main routes of the world's commerce, it offered itself only as a stepping-stone to further acquisitions. To push southward from this new port became an immediate object to Russia. There lay an obstacle in the way, however; the long strip of sea-coast from the mouth of the Amur to the Korean frontier—an area then called the Usuri region because the Usuri forms its western boundary—belonged to China, and she, having conceded much to Russia in the matter of the Amur, showed no disposition to make further concessions in the matter of the Usuri. In the presence of menaces, however, she agreed that the region should be regarded as common property pending a convenient opportunity for clear delimitation. That opportunity came very soon. Seizing the moment (1860) when China had been beaten to her knees by England and France, Russia secured final cession of the Usuri region, which now became the maritime province of Siberia. Then Russia shifted her naval base on the Pacific from Nikolayevsk to Vladivostok. She gained ten degrees in a southerly direction.

From the mouth of the Amur, where Nikolayevsk is situated, to the southern shore of Korea there rests on the coast of eastern Asia an arch of islands having at its northern point Sakhalin and at its southern Tsushima, the keystone of the arch being the main island of Japan. This arch embraces the Sea of Japan and is washed on its convex side by the Pacific Ocean. Immediately after the transfer of Russia's naval base from Nikolayevsk to Vladivostok, an attempt was made

12

to obtain possession of the southern point of the arch, namely, Tsushima. A Russian man-of-war proceeded thither and quietly began to establish a settlement, which would soon have constituted a title of ownership had not Great Britain interfered. The Russians saw that Vladivostok, acquired at the cost of so much toil, would be comparatively useless unless from the sea on whose shore it was situated an avenue to the Pacific could be opened, and they therefore tried to obtain command of the Tsushima channel. Immediately after reaching the mouth of the Amur the same instinct had led them to begin the colonization of Sakhalin. The axis of this long narrow island is inclined at a very acute angle to the Usuri region, which its northern extremity almost touches, while its southern is separated from Yezo by the strait of La Pérouse. But in Sakhalin the Russians found Japanese subjects. In fact the island was a part of the Japanese empire. Resorting, however, to the Usuri fiction of joint occupation, they succeeded by 1875 in transferring the whole of Sakhalin to Russia's dominion. Further encroachments upon Japanese territory could not be lightly essayed, and the Russians held their hands. They had been trebly checked: checked in trying to push southward along the coast of the mainland; checked in trying to secure an avenue from Vladivostok to the Pacific; and checked in their search for an ice-free port, which definition Vladivostok did not fulfil. Enterprise in the direction of Korea seemed to be the only hope of saving the maritime results of the great Trans-Asian march.

Was Korea within safe range of such enterprises? Everything seemed to answer in the affirmative. Korea had all the qualifications desired by an aggressor. Her people were unprogressive, her resources undeveloped, her self-defensive capacities insignificant, her government corrupt. But she was a tributary of China, and China had begun to show some tenacity in protecting the integrity of her buffer states. Besides, Japan was understood to have pretensions with regard to Korea. On the whole, therefore, the problem of carrying to full fruition the work of Muravief and his lieutenants demanded strength greater than Russia could exercise without some line of communications supplementing the Amur waterway and the long ocean route. Therefore she set about the construction of a railway across Asia.

The Amur being the boundary of Russia's east Asian territory, this railway had to be carried along its northern bank where many engineering and economic obstacles presented themselves. Besides, the river, from an early stage in its course, makes a huge semicircular sweep northward, and a railway following its bank to Vladivostok must make the same détour. If, on the contrary, the road could be carried over the diameter of the semicircle, it would be a straight and therefore shorter line, technically easier and economically better. The diameter, however, passed through Chinese territory, and an excuse for extorting China's permission was not in sight. Russia therefore proceeded to build each end of the road, deferring the construction of the Amur section for the moment. She had not waited long when, in 1894, war broke out between China and Japan, and the latter, completely victorious, demanded as the price of peace the southern littoral of Manchuria from the Korean boundary to the Liaotung peninsula at the entrance to the Gulf of Pechili. This was a crisis in Russia's career. She saw that her maritime extension could never get nearer to the Pacific than Vladivostok were this claim of Japan's established. For the proposed arrangement would place the littoral of Manchuria in Japan's direct occupation and the littoral of Korea in her constructive control, since not only had she fought to rescue Korea from Chinese suzerainty, but also her object in demanding a slice of the Manchurian coast-line was to protect Korea against aggression from the north; that is to say, against aggression from Russia. Muravief's enterprise had carried his country first to the mouth of the Amur and thence southward along the coast to Vladivostok and to Possiet Bay at the north-eastern extremity of Korea. But it had not given to Russia free access to the Pacific, and now she was menaced with a perpetual barrier to that access, since the whole remaining coast of east Asia as far as the Gulf of Pechili was about to pass into Japan's possession or under her domination.

Then Russia took an extraordinary step. She persuaded Germany and France to force Japan out of Manchuria. It is not to be supposed that she frankly exposed her own aggressive designs and asked for assistance to prosecute them. Neither is it to be supposed that France and Germany were so curiously deficient in perspicacity as to overlook those designs. At all events these three great powers served on Japan a notice to quit, and Japan, exhausted by her struggle with China, had no choice but to obey.

The notice was accompanied by an *exposé* of reasons. Its signatories said that Japan's tenure of the Manchurian littoral would menace the security of the Chinese capital, would render the independence of Korea illusory, and would constitute an obstacle to the peace of the Orient.

By way of saving the situation in some slight degree Japan sought from China a guarantee that no portion of Manchuria should thereafter be leased or ceded to a foreign state. But France warned Japan that to press such a demand would offend Russia, and Russia declared that, for her part, she had no intention of trespassing in Manchuria. Japan, had she been in a position to insist on the guarantee, would also have been in a position to disobey the mandate of the three powers.

13

Unable to do either the one or the other, she quietly stepped out of Manchuria, and proceeded to double her army and treble her navy.

As a reward for the assistance nominally rendered to China in this matter, Russia obtained permission in Peking to divert her Trans-Asian railway from the huge bend of the Amur to the straight line through Manchuria. Neither Germany nor France received any immediate recompense. Three years later, by way of indemnity for the murder of two missionaries by a mob, Germany seized a portion of the province of Shantung. Immediately, on the principle that two wrongs make a right, Russia obtained a lease of the Liaotung peninsula, from which she had driven Japan in 1895. This act she followed by extorting from China permission to construct a branch of the Trans-Asian railway through Manchuria from north to south.

Russia's maritime aspirations had now assumed a radically altered phase. Instead of pushing southward from Vladivostok and Possiet Bay along the coast of Korea, she had suddenly 249leaped the Korean peninsula and found access to the Pacific in Liaotung. Nothing was wanting to establish her as practical mistress of Manchuria except a plausible excuse for garrisoning the place. Such an excuse was furnished by the Boxer rising in 1900. Its conclusion saw her in military occupation of the whole region, and she might easily have made her occupation permanent by prolonging it until peace and order should have been fully restored. But here she fell into an error of judgment. Imagining that the Chinese could be persuaded or intimidated to any concession, she proposed a convention virtually recognizing her title to Manchuria.

Japan watched all these things with profound anxiety. If there were any reality in the dangers which Russia, Germany and France had declared to be incidental to Japanese occupation of a part of Manchuria, the same dangers must be doubly incidental to Russian occupation of the whole of Manchuria—the security of the Chinese capital would be threatened, and an obstacle would be created to the permanent peace of the East. The independence of Korea was an object of supreme solicitude to Japan. Historically she held towards the little state a relation closely resembling that of suzerain, and though of her ancient conquests nothing remained except a settlement at Fusan on the southern coast, her national sentiment would have been deeply wounded by any foreign aggression in the peninsula. It was to establish Korean independence that she waged war with China in 1894; and her annexation of the Manchurian littoral adjacent to the Korean frontier, after the war, was designed to secure that independence, not to menace it as the triple alliance professed to think. But if Russia came into possession of all Manchuria, her subsequent absorption of Korea would be almost inevitable. For the consideration set forth above as to Vladivostok's maritime avenues would then acquire absolute cogency. Manchuria is larger than France and the United Kingdom lumped together. The addition of such an immense area to Russia's east Asiatic dominions, together with its littoral on the Gulf of Pechili and the Yellow Sea, would necessitate a corresponding expansion of her naval forces in the Far East. With the one exception of Port Arthur, however, the Manchurian coast does not offer any convenient naval base. It is only in the splendid harbours of southern Korea that such bases can be found. Moreover, there would be an even stronger motive impelling Russia towards Korea. Neither the Usuri region nor the Manchurian littoral possesses so much as one port qualified to satisfy her perennial longing for free access to the ocean in a temperate zone. Without Korea, then, Russia's east Asian expansion, though it added huge blocks of territory to her dominions, would have been commercially incomplete and strategically defective.

If it be asked why, apart from history and national sentiment, Japan should object to a Russian Korea, the answer is, first, because there would thus be planted almost within cannon-shot of her shores a power of enormous strength and insatiable ambition; secondly, because, whatever voice in Manchuria's destiny Russia derived from her railway, the same voice in Korea's destiny was possessed by Japan as the sole owner of railways in the peninsula; thirdly, that whereas Russia had an altogether insignificant share in the foreign commerce of Korea and scarcely ten bona-fide settlers, Japan did the greater part of the over-sea trade and had tens of thousands of settlers; fourthly, that if Russia's dominions stretched uninterruptedly from the Sea of Okhotsk to the Gulf of Pechili, her ultimate absorption of north China would be as certain as sunrise; and fifthly, that such domination and such absorption would involve the practical closure of all that immense region to Japanese commerce and industry as well as to the commerce and industry of every Western nation except Russia. This last proposition did not rest solely on the fact that to oppose artificial barriers to free competition is Russia's sole hope of utilizing to her own benefit any commercial opportunities brought within her reach. It rested also on the fact that Russia had objected to foreign settlements at the marts recently opened by treaty with China to American and Japanese subjects. Without settlements, trade at those marts would be impossible, and thus Russia had constructively announced that there should be no trade but Russian, if she could prevent it.

Against such dangers Japan would have been justified in adopting any measure of self-protection. She had foreseen them for six years, and had been strengthening herself to avert them. But she wanted peace. She wanted to develop her material resources and to accumulate some measure of wealth, without which she must remain insignificant among the nations. Two pacific devices offered, and she adopted them both. Russia, instead of trusting time to consolidate her tenure of Manchuria, had made the mistake of pragmatically importuning China for a conventional title. If then Peking could be strengthened to resist this demand, some arrangement of a distinctly terminable nature might be made. The United States, Great Britain and Japan, joining hands for that purpose, did succeed in so far stiffening China's backbone that her show of resolution finally induced Russia to sign a treaty pledging herself to withdraw her troops from Manchuria in three instalments, each step of evacuation to be accomplished by a fixed date. That was one of the pacific devices. The other suggested itself in connexion with the new commercial treaties which China had promised to negotiate in the sequel of the Boxer troubles. In these documents clauses provided for the opening of three places in Manchuria to foreign trade. It seemed a reasonable hope that, having secured commercial access to Manchuria by covenant with its sovereign, China, the powers would not allow Russia arbitrarily to restrict their privileges. It seemed also a reasonable hope that Russia, having solemnly promised to evacuate Manchuria at fixed dates, would fulfil her engagement.

The latter hope was signally disappointed. When the time came for evacuation, Russia behaved as though no promise had ever been given. She proposed wholly new conditions, which would have strengthened her grasp of Manchuria instead of loosening it. China being powerless to offer any practical protest, and Japan's interests ranking next in order of importance, the Tōkyō government approached Russia direct. They did not ask for anything that could hurt her pride or injure her position. Appreciating fully the economical status she had acquired in Manchuria by large outlays of capital, they offered to recognize that status, provided that Russia would extend similar recognition to Japan's status in Korea, would promise, in common with Japan, to respect the sovereignty and the territorial integrity of China and Korea, and would be a party to a mutual engagement that all nations should have equal industrial and commercial opportunities in Manchuria and the Korean peninsula. In a word, they invited Russia to subscribe the policy enunciated by the United States and Great Britain, the policy of the open door and of the integrity of the Chinese and Korean empires.

Thus commenced a negotiation which lasted five and a half months. Japan gradually reduced her demands to a minimum. Russia never made the smallest appreciable concession. She refused to listen to Japan for one moment about Manchuria. Eight years previously Japan had been in military possession of Manchuria, and Russia with the assistance of Germany and France had expelled her for reasons which concerned Japan incomparably more than they concerned any of the three powers—the security of the Chinese capital, the independence of Korea, the peace of the East. Now, Russia had the splendid assurance to declare by implication that none of these things concerned Japan at all. The utmost she would admit was Japan's partial right to be heard about Korea. And at the same time she herself commenced in northern Korea a series of aggressions, partly perhaps to show her potentialities, partly by way of counter-irritant. That was not all. Whilst she studiously deferred her answers to Japan's proposals and protracted the negotiations to an extent which was actually contumelious, she hastened to send eastward a big fleet of war-ships and a new army of soldiers. It was impossible for the dullest politician to mistake her purpose. She intended to yield nothing, but to prepare such a parade of force that her obduracy would 250command submission. The only alternatives for Japan were war or total and permanent effacement in Asia. She chose war, and in fighting it she fought the battle of free and equal opportunities for all without undue encroachment upon the sovereign rights or territorial integrity of China or Korea, against a military dictatorship, a programme of ruthless territorial aggrandizement and a policy of selfish restrictions.

The details of the great struggle that ensued are given elsewhere (see RUSSO-JAPANESE WAR). After the battle of Mukden the belligerents found themselves in a position which must either prelude another stupendous effort on *The Results of the War.*both sides or be utilized for the purpose of peace negotiations. At this point the president of the United States of America intervened in the interests of humanity, and on the 9th of June 1905 instructed the United States' representative in Tōkyō to urge that the Japanese government should open direct negotiations with Russia, an exactly corresponding note being simultaneously sent to the Russian government through the United States' representative in St Petersburg. Japan's reply was made on the 10th of June. It intimated frank acquiescence, and Russia lost no time in taking a similar step. Nevertheless two months elapsed before the plenipotentiaries of the belligerents met, on the 10th of August, at Portsmouth, New Hampshire, U.S.A. Russia sent M. (afterwards Count) de Witte and Baron Rosen; Japan, Baron (afterwards Count) Komura, who had held the portfolio of

15

foreign affairs throughout the war, and Mr. (afterwards Baron) Takahira. In entering this conference, Japanese statesmen, as was subsequently known, saw clearly that a great part of the credit accruing to them for their successful conduct of the war would be forfeited in the sequel of the negotiations. For the people of Japan had accustomed themselves to expect that Russia would assuredly recoup the expenses incurred by their country in the contest, whereas the cabinet in Tōkyō understood well that to look for payment of indemnity by a great state whose territory had not been invaded effectively nor its existence menaced must be futile. Nevertheless, diplomacy required that this conviction should be concealed, and thus Russia carried to the conference a belief that the financial phase of the discussion would be crucial, while, at the same time, the Japanese nation reckoned fully on an indemnity of 150 millions sterling. Baron Komura's mandate was, however, that the only radically essential terms were those formulated by Japan prior to the war. She must insist on securing the ends for which she had fought, since she believed them to be indispensable to the peace of the Far East, but she would not demand anything more. The Japanese plenipotentiary, therefore, judged it wise to marshal his terms in the order of their importance, leaving his Russian colleague to imagine, as he probably would, that the converse method had been adopted, and that everything preliminary to the questions of finance and territory was of minor consequence. The negotiations, commencing on the 10th of August, were not concluded until the 5th of September, when a treaty of peace was signed. There had been a moment when the onlooking world believed that unless Russia agreed to ransom the island of Sakhalin by paying to Japan a sum of 120 millions sterling, the conference would be broken off; nor did such an exchange seem unreasonable, for were Russia expelled from the northern part of Sakhalin, which commands the estuary of the Amur River, her position in Siberia would have been compromised. But the statesmen who directed Japan's affairs were not disposed to make any display of earth-hunger. The southern half of Sakhalin had originally belonged to Japan and had passed into Russia's possession by an arrangement which the Japanese nation strongly resented. To recover that portion of the island seemed, therefore, a legitimate ambition. Japan did not contemplate any larger demand, nor did she seriously insist on an indemnity. Therefore the negotiations were never in real danger of failure. The treaty of Portsmouth recognized Japan's "paramount political, military and economic interests" in Korea; provided for the simultaneous evacuation of Manchuria by the contracting parties; transferred to Japan the lease of the Liaotung peninsula held by Russia from China together with the Russian railways south of Kwang-Cheng-tsze and all collateral mining or other privileges; ceded to Japan the southern half of Sakhalin, the 50th parallel of latitude to be the boundary between the two parts; secured fishing rights for Japanese subjects along the coasts of the seas of Japan, Okhotsk and Bering; laid down that the expenses incurred by the Japanese for the maintenance of the Russian prisoners during the war should be reimbursed by Russia, less the outlays made by the latter on account of Japanese prisoners—by which arrangement Japan obtained a payment of some 4 millions sterling—and provided that the contracting parties, while withdrawing their military forces from Manchuria, might maintain guards to protect their respective railways, the number of such guards not to exceed 15 per kilometre of line. There were other important restrictions: first, the contracting parties were to abstain from taking, on the Russo-Korean frontier, any military measures which might menace the security of Russian or Korean territory; secondly, the two powers pledged themselves not to exploit the Manchurian railways for strategic purposes; and thirdly, they promised not to build on Sakhalin or its adjacent islands any fortifications or other similar military works, or to take any military measures which might impede the free navigation of the straits of La Pérouse and the Gulf of Tartary. The above provisions concerned the two contracting parties only. But China's interests also were considered. Thus it was agreed to "restore entirely and completely to her exclusive administration" all portions of Manchuria then in the occupation, or under the control, of Japanese or Russian troops, except the leased territory; that her consent must be obtained for the transfer to Japan of the leases and concessions held by the Russians in Manchuria; that the Russian government would disavow the possession of "any territorial advantages or preferential or exclusive concessions in impairment of Chinese sovereignty or inconsistent with the principle of equal opportunity in Manchuria"; and that Japan and Russia "engaged reciprocally not to obstruct any general measures common to all countries which China might take for the development of the commerce and industry of Manchuria." This distinction between the special interests of the contracting parties and the interests of China herself as well as of foreign nations generally is essential to clear understanding of a situation which subsequently attracted much attention. From the time of the opium war (1857) to the Boxer rising (1900) each of the great Western powers struggled for its own hand in China, and each sought to gain for itself exclusive concessions and privileges with comparatively little regard for the interests of others, and with no regard whatever for China's sovereign rights. The fruits of this period were: permanently ceded territories (Hong-

Kong and Macao); leases temporarily establishing foreign sovereignty in various districts (Kiaochow, Wei-hai-wei and Kwang-chow); railway and mining concessions; and the establishment of settlements at open ports where foreign jurisdiction was supreme. But when, in 1900, the Boxer rising forced all the powers into a common camp, they awoke to full appreciation of a principle which had been growing current for the past two or three years, namely, that concerted action on the lines of maintaining China's integrity and securing to all alike equality of opportunity and a similarly open door, was the only feasible method of preventing the partition of the Chinese Empire and averting a clash of rival interests which might have disastrous results. This, of course, did not mean that there was to be any abandonment of special privileges already acquired or any surrender of existing concessions. The arrangement was not to be retrospective in any sense. Vested interests were to be strictly guarded until the lapse of the periods for which they had been granted, or until the maturity of China's competence to be really autonomous. A curious situation was thus created. International professions of respect for China's sovereignty, for the integrity of her empire and for the enforcement of the open door and equal opportunity, 251coexisted with legacies from an entirely different past. Russia endorsed this new policy, but not unnaturally declined to abate any of the advantages previously enjoyed by her in Manchuria. Those advantages were very substantial. They included a twenty-five years' lease—with provision for renewal—of the Liaotung peninsula, within which area of 1220 sq. m. Chinese troops might not penetrate, whereas Russia would not only exercise full administrative authority, but also take military and naval action of any kind; they included the creation of a neutral territory in the immediate north of the former and still more extensive, which should remain under Chinese administration, but where neither Chinese nor Russian troops might enter, nor might China, without Russia's consent, cede land, open trading marts or grant concessions to any third nationality; and they included the right to build some 1600 m. of railway (which China would have the opportunity of purchasing at cost price in the year 1938 and would be entitled to receive gratis in 1982), as well as the right to hold extensive zones on either side of the railway, to administer these zones in the fullest sense, and to work all mines lying along the lines. Under the Portsmouth treaty these advantages were transferred to Japan by Russia, the railway, however, being divided so that only the portion (521½ m.) to the south of Kwang-Cheng-tsze fell to Japan's share, while the portion (1077 m.) to the north of that place remained in Russia's hands. China's consent to the above transfers and assignments was obtained in a treaty signed at Peking on the 22nd of December 1905. Thus Japan came to hold in Manchuria a position somewhat contradictory. On the one hand, she figured as the champion of the Chinese Empire's integrity and as an exponent of the new principle of equal opportunity and the open door. On the other, she appeared as the legatee of many privileges more or less inconsistent with that principle. But, at the same time, nearly all the great powers of Europe were similarly circumstanced. In their cases also the same incongruity was observable between the newly professed policy and the aftermath of the old practice. It was scarcely to be expected that Japan alone should make a large sacrifice on the altar of a theory to which no other state thought of yielding any retrospective obedience whatever. She did, indeed, furnish a clear proof of deference to the open-door doctrine, for instead of reserving the railway zones to her own exclusive use, as she was fully entitled to do, she sought and obtained from China a pledge to open to foreign trade 16 places within those zones. For the rest, however, the inconsistency between the past and the present, though existing throughout the whole of China, was nowhere so conspicuous as in the three eastern provinces (Manchuria); not because there was any real difference of degree, but because Manchuria had been the scene of the greatest war of modern times; because that war had been fought by Japan in the cause of the new policy, and because the principles of the equally open door and of China's integrity had been the main bases of the Portsmouth treaty, of the Anglo-Japanese alliance, and of the subsequently concluded *ententes* with France and Russia. In short, the world's eyes were fixed on Manchuria and diverted from China proper, so that every act of Japan was subjected to an exceptionally rigorous scrutiny, and the nations behaved as though they expected her to live up to a standard of almost ideal altitude. China's mood, too, greatly complicated the situation. She had the choice between two moderate and natural courses: either to wait quietly until the various concessions granted by her to foreign powers in the evil past should lapse by maturity, or to qualify herself by earnest reforms and industrious development for their earlier recovery. Nominally she adopted the latter course, but in reality she fell into a mood of much impatience. Under the name of a "rights-recovery campaign" her people began to protest vehemently against the continuance of any conditions which impaired her sovereignty, and as this temper coloured her attitude towards the various questions which inevitably grew out of the situation in Manchuria, her relations with Japan became somewhat strained in the early part of 1909.

Having waged two wars on account of Korea, Japan emerged from the second conflict with the conviction that the policy of maintaining the independence of Korea must be modified, and that since the identity of Korean and *Japan in Korea after the War with Russia.*Japanese interests in the Far East and the paramount character of Japanese interests in Korea would not permit Japan to leave Korea to the care of any third power, she must assume the charge herself. Europe and America also recognized that view of the situation, and consented to withdraw their legations from Seoul, thus leaving the control of Korean foreign affairs entirely in the hands of Japan, who further undertook to assume military direction in the event of aggression from without or disturbance from within. But in the matter of internal administration she continued to limit herself to advisory supervision. Thus, though a Japanese resident-general in Seoul, with subordinate residents throughout the provinces, assumed the functions hitherto discharged by foreign representatives and consuls, the Korean government was merely asked to employ Japanese experts in the position of counsellors, the right to accept or reject their counsels being left to their employers. Once again, however, the futility of looking for any real reforms under this optional system was demonstrated. Japan sent her most renowned statesman, Prince Ito, to discharge the duties of resident-general; but even he, in spite of profound patience and tact, found that some less optional methods must be resorted to. Hence on the 24th of July 1907 a new agreement was signed, by which the resident-general acquired initiative as well as consultative competence to enact and enforce laws and ordinances, to appoint and remove Korean officials, and to place capable Japanese subjects in the ranks of the administration. That this constituted a heavy blow to Korea's independence could not be gainsaid. That it was inevitable seemed to be equally obvious. For there existed in Korea nearly all the worst abuses of medieval systems. The administration of justice depended solely on favour or interest. The police contributed by corruption and incompetence to the insecurity of life and property. The troops were a body of useless mercenaries. Offices being allotted by sale, thousands of incapables thronged the ranks of the executive. The emperor's court was crowded by diviners and plotters of all kinds, male and female. The finances of the throne and those of the state were hopelessly confused. There was nothing like an organized judiciary. A witness was in many cases considered*particeps criminis*; torture was commonly employed to obtain evidence, and defendants in civil cases were placed under arrest. Imprisonment meant death or permanent disablement for a man of small means. Flogging so severe as to cripple, if not to kill, was a common punishment; every major offence from robbery upward was capital, and female criminals were frequently executed by administering shockingly painful poisons. The currency was in a state of the utmost confusion. Extreme corruption and extortion were practised in connexion with taxation. Finally, while nothing showed that the average Korean lacked the elementary virtue of patriotism, there had been repeated proofs that the safety and independence of the empire counted for little in the estimates of political intriguers. Japan must either step out of Korea altogether or effect drastic reforms there. She necessarily chose the latter alternative, and the things which she accomplished between the beginning of 1906 and the close of 1908 may be briefly described as the elaboration of a proper system of taxation; the organization of a staff to administer annual budgets; the re-assessment of taxable property; the floating of public loans for productive enterprises; the reform of the currency; the establishment of banks of various kinds, including agricultural and commercial; the creation of associations for putting bank-notes into circulation; the introduction of a warehousing system to supply capital to farmers; the lighting and buoying of the coasts; the provision of posts, telegraphs, roads and railways; the erection of public buildings; the starting of various industrial enterprises (such as printing, brick-making, forestry and coal-mining); the laying out of model farms; the beginning of cotton cultivation; the 252building and equipping of an industrial training school; the inauguration of sanitary works; the opening of hospitals and medical schools; the organization of an excellent educational system; the construction of waterworks in several towns; the complete remodelling of the central government; the differentiation of the court and the executive, as well as of the administration and the judiciary; the formation of an efficient body of police; the organization of law courts with a majority of Japanese jurists on the bench; the enactment of a new penal code; drastic reforms in the taxation system. In the summer of 1907 the resident-general advised the Throne to disband the standing army as an unserviceable and expensive force. The measure was doubtless desirable, but the docility of the troops had been over-rated. Some of them resisted vehemently, and many became the nucleus of an insurrection which lasted in a desultory manner for nearly two years; cost the lives of 21,000 insurgents and 1300 Japanese; and entailed upon Japan an outlay of nearly a million sterling. Altogether Japan was 15 millions sterling out of pocket on Korea's account by the end of 1909. She had also lost the veteran statesman Prince Ito, who was assassinated at Harbin by a Korean fanatic on the 26th of October 1909. Finally an end was put to an anomalous situation by the annexation of Korea to Japan on the 29th of August 1910. (See further KOREA.)

IX.—DOMESTIC HISTORY

Cosmography.—Japanese annals represent the first inhabitant of earth as a direct descendant of the gods. Two books describe the events of the "Divine age." One, compiled in 712, is called the *Kojiki (Records of Ancient Matters)*; the other, compiled in 720, is called the *Nihongi (Chronicles of Japan)*. Both describe the processes of creation, but the author of the *Chronicles* drew largely upon Chinese traditions, whereas the compilers of the *Records* appear to have limited themselves to materials which they believed to be native. The *Records*, therefore, have always been regarded as the more trustworthy guide to pure Japanese conceptions. They deal with the creation of Japan only, other countries having been apparently judged unworthy of attention. At the beginning of all things a primordial trinity is represented as existing on the "plain of high heaven." Thereafter, during an indefinite time and by an indefinite process, other deities come into existence, their titles indicating a vague connexion with constructive and fertilizing forces. They are not immortal: it is explicitly stated that they ultimately pass away, and the idea of the cosmographers seems to be that each deity marks a gradual approach to human methods of procreation. Meanwhile the earth is "young and, like floating oil, drifts about after the manner of a jelly-fish." At last there are born two deities, the creator and the creatress, and these receive the mandate of all the heavenly beings to "make, consolidate and give birth to the drifting land." For use in that work a jewelled spear is given to them, and, standing upon the bridge that connects heaven and earth, they thrust downwards with the weapon, stir the brine below and draw up the spear, when from its point fall drops which, accumulating, form the first dry land. Upon this land the two deities descend, and, by ordinary processes, beget the islands of Japan as well as numerous gods representing the forces of nature. But in giving birth to the god of fire the creatress (Izanami) perishes, and the creator (Izanagi) makes his way to the under-world in search of her—an obvious parallel to the tales of Ishtar and Orpheus. With difficulty he returns to earth, and, as he washes himself from the pollution of Hades, there are born from the turbid water a number of evil deities succeeded by a number of good, just as in the Babylonian cosmogony the primordial ocean, Tiamat, brings forth simultaneously gods and imps. Finally, as Izanagi washes his left eye the Goddess of the Sun comes into existence; as he washes his right, the God of the Moon; and as he washes his nose, the God of Force. To these then he assigns, respectively, the dominion of the sun, the dominion of the moon, and the dominion of the ocean. But the god of force (Sosanoo), like Lucifer, rebels against this decree, creates a commotion in heaven, and after having been the cause of the temporary seclusion of the sun goddess and the consequent wrapping of the world in darkness, kills the goddess of food and is permanently banished from heaven by the host of deities. He descends to Izumo on the west of the main island of Japan, and there saves a maiden from an eight-headed serpent. Sosanoo himself passes to the under-world and becomes the deity of Hades, but he invests one of his descendants with the sovereignty of Japan, and the title is established after many curious adventures. To the sun goddess also, whose feud with her fierce brother survives the latter's banishment from heaven, the idea of making her grandson ruler of Japan presents itself. She despatches three embassies to impose her will upon the descendants of Sosanoo, and finally her grandson descends, not, however, in Izumo, where the demi-gods of Sosanoo's race hold sway, but in Hiūga in the southern island of Kiūshiū. This grandson of Amaterasu (the goddess of the sun) is called Ninigi, whose great-grandson figures in Japanese history as the first human sovereign of the country, known during life as Kamu-Yamato-Iware-Biko, and given the name of Jimmu tennō (Jimmu, son of heaven) fourteen centuries after his death. Japanese annalists attribute the accession of Jimmu to the year 660 B.C. Why that date was chosen must remain a matter of conjecture. The *Records of Ancient Matters* has no chronology, but the more pretentious writers of the *Chronicles of Japan*, doubtless in imitation of their Chinese models, considered it necessary to assign a year, a month, and even a day for each event of importance. There is abundant reason, however, to question the accuracy of all Japanese chronology prior to the 5th century. The first date corroborated by external evidence is 461, and Aston, who has made a special study of the subject, concludes that the year 500 may be taken as the time when the chronology of the *Chronicles* begins to be trustworthy. Many Japanese, however, are firm believers in the *Chronicles*, and when assigning the year of the empire they invariably take 660B.C. for starting-point, so that 1909 of the Gregorian calendar becomes for them 2569.

Prehistoric Period.—Thus, if the most rigid estimate be accepted, the space of 1160 years, from 660 B.C. to A.D. 500, may be called the prehistoric period. During that long interval the annals include 24 sovereigns, the first 17 of whom lived for over a hundred years on the average. It seems reasonable to conclude that the so-called assignment of the sovereignty of Japan to Sosanoo's descendants and the establishment of their kingdom in Izumo represent an invasion of

19

Mongolian immigrants coming from the direction of the Korean peninsula—indeed one of the *Nihongi's* versions of the event actually indicates Korea as the point of departure—and that the subsequent descent of Ninigi on Mount Takachiho in Hiūga indicates the advent of a body of Malayan settlers from the south sea. Jimmu, according to the *Chronicles*, set out from Hiūga in 667 B.C. and was not crowned at his new palace in Yamato until 660. This campaign of seven years is described in some detail, but no satisfactory information is given as to the nature of the craft in which the invader and his troops voyaged, or as to the number of men under his command. The weapons said to have been carried were bows, spears and swords. A supernatural element is imported into the narrative in the form of the three-legged crow of the sun, which Amaterasu sends down to act as guide and messenger for her descendants. Jimmu died at his palace of Kashiwa-bara in 585 B.C., his age being 127 according to the *Chronicles*, and 137 according to the *Records*. He was buried in a kind of tomb called *misasagi*, which seems to have been in use in Japan for some centuries before the Christian era—"a highly specialized form of tumulus, consisting of two mounds, one having a circular, the other a triangular base, which merged into each other, the whole being surrounded by a moat, or sometimes by two concentric moats with a narrow strip of land between. In some, perhaps in most, cases the misasagi contains a large vault of great unhewn stones without mortar. The walls of this vault converge gradually towards the top, which is roofed in by enormous slabs of stone weighing 253many tons each. The entrance is by means of a gallery roofed with similar stones." Several of these ancient sepulchral mounds have been examined during recent years, and their contents have furnished information of much antiquarian interest, though there is a complete absence of inscriptions. The reigns of the eight sovereigns who succeeded Jimmu were absolutely uneventful. Nothing is set down except the genealogy of each ruler, the place of his residence and his burial, his age and the date of his death. It was then the custom—and it remained so until the 8th century of the Christian era—to change the capital on the accession of each emperor; a habit which effectually prevented the growth of any great metropolis. The reign of the 10th emperor, Sūjin, lasted from 98 to 30 B.C. During his era the land was troubled by pestilence and the people broke out in rebellion; calamities which were supposed to be caused by the spirit of the ancient ruler of Izumo to avenge a want of consideration shown to his descendants by their supplanters. Divination—by a Chinese process—and visions revealed the source of trouble; rites of worship were performed in honour of the ancient ruler, his descendant being entrusted with the duty, and the pestilence ceased. We now hear for the first time of vigorous measures to quell the aboriginal savages, doubtless the Ainu. Four generals are sent out against them in different directions. But the expedition is interrupted by an armed attempt on the part of the emperor's half-brother, who, utilizing the opportunity of the troops' absence from Yamato, marches from Yamashiro at the head of a powerful army to win the crown for himself. In connexion with these incidents, curious evidence is furnished of the place then assigned to woman by the writers of the *Chronicles*. It is a girl who warns one of the emperor's generals of the plot; it is the sovereign's aunt who interprets the warning; and it is Ata, the wife of the rebellious prince, who leads the left wing of his army. Four other noteworthy facts are recorded of this reign: the taking of a census; the imposition of a tax on animals' skins and game to be paid by men, and on textile fabrics by women; the building of boats for coastwise transport, and the digging of dikes and reservoirs for agricultural purposes. All these things rest solely on the testimony of annalists writing eight centuries later than the era they discuss and compiling their narrative mostly from tradition. Careful investigations have been made to ascertain whether the histories of China and Korea corroborate or contradict those of Japan. Without entering into detailed evidence, the inference may be at once stated that the dates given in Japanese early history are just 120 years too remote; an error very likely to occur when using the sexagenary cycle, which constituted the first method of reckoning time in Japan. But although this correction suffices to reconcile some contradictory features of Far-Eastern history, it does not constitute any explanation of the incredible longevity assigned by the *Chronicles* to several Japanese sovereigns, and the conclusion is that when a consecutive record of reigns came to be compiled in the 8th century, many lacunae were found which had to be filled up from the imagination of the compilers. With this parenthesis we may pass rapidly over the events of the next two centuries (29 B.C. to A.D. 200). They are remarkable for vigorous measures to subdue the aboriginal Ainu, who in the southern island of Kiūshiū are called Kuma-so (the names of two tribes) and sometimes earth-spiders (*i.e.*cave-dwellers), while in the north-eastern regions of the main island they are designated Yemishi. Expeditions are led against them in both regions by Prince Yamato-dake, a hero revered by all succeeding generations of Japanese as the type of valour and loyalty. Dying from the effects of hardship and exposure, but declaring with his last breath that loss of life was as nothing compared with the sorrow of seeing his father's face no more, his spirit ascends to heaven as a white bird, and when his son, Chūai, comes to the throne, he causes cranes to be placed in the moat surrounding his palace in memory of his illustrious sire.

The sovereign had partly ceased to follow the example of Jimmu, who led his armies in person. The emperors did not, however, pass a sedentary life. They frequently made progresses throughout their dominions, and on these occasions a not uncommon incident was the addition of some local beauty to the Imperial harem. This licence had a far-reaching effect, since to provide for the sovereign's numerous offspring—the emperor Keikō (71-130) had 80 children—no better way offered than to make grants of land, and thus were laid the foundations of a territorial nobility destined profoundly to influence the course of Japanese history. Woman continues to figure conspicuously in the story. The image of the sun goddess, enshrined in Ise (5 B.C.), is entrusted to the keeping of a princess, as are the mirror, sword and jewel inherited from the sun goddess; a woman (Tachibana) accompanies Prince Yamato-dake in his campaign against the Yemishi, and sacrifices her life to quell a tempest at sea; Saho, consort of Suinin, is the heroine of a most tragic tale in which the conflict between filial piety and conjugal loyalty leads to her self-destruction; and a woman is found ruling over a large district in Kiūshū when the Emperor Keikō is engaged in his campaign against the aborigines. The reign of Suinin saw the beginning of an art destined to assume extraordinary importance in Japan—the art of wrestling—and the first champion, Nomi no Sukune, is honoured for having suggested that clay figures should take the place of the human sacrifices hitherto offered at the sepulture of Imperial personages. The irrigation works commenced in the time of Sūjin were zealously continued under his two immediate successors, Suinin and Keikō. More than 800 ponds and channels are described as having been constructed under the former's rule. We find evidence also that the sway of the throne had been by this time widely extended, for in 125 a governor-general of 15 provinces is nominated, and two years later, governors (*miyakko*) are appointed in every province and mayors (*inaki*) in every village. The number or names of these local divisions are not given, but it is explained that mountains and rivers were taken as boundaries of provinces, the limits of towns and villages being marked by roads running respectively east and west, north and south.

An incident is now reached which the Japanese count a landmark in their history, though foreign critics are disposed to regard it as apocryphal. It is the invasion of Korea by a Japanese army under the command of the empress **Invasion of Korea.** Jingo, in 200. The emperor Chūai, having proceeded to Kiūshiū for the purpose of conducting a campaign against the Kuma-so, is there joined by the empress, who, at the inspiration of a deity, seeks to divert the Imperial arms against Korea. But the emperor refuses to believe in the existence of any such country, and heaven punishes his incredulity with death at the hands of the Kuma-so, according to one account; from the effects of disease, according to another. The calamity is concealed; the Kuma-so are subdued, and the empress, having collected a fleet and raised an army, crosses to the state of Silla (in Korea), where, at the spectacle of her overwhelming strength, the Korean monarch submits without fighting, and swears that until the sun rises in the west, until rivers run towards their sources, and until pebbles ascend to the sky and become stars, he will do homage and send tribute to Japan. His example is followed by the kings of the two other states constituting the Korean peninsula, and the warlike empress returns triumphant. Many supernatural elements embellish the tale, but the features which chiefly discredit it are that it abounds in anachronisms, and that the event, despite its signal importance, is not mentioned in either Chinese or Korean history. It is certain that China then possessed in Korea territory administered by Chinese governors. She must therefore have had cognisance of such an invasion, had it occurred. Moreover, Korean history mentions twenty-five raids made by the Japanese against Silla during the first five centuries of the Christian era, but not one of them can be identified with Jingo's alleged expedition. There can be no doubt that the early Japanese were an aggressive, enterprising people, and that their nearest over-sea neighbour suffered much from their activity. Nor can there be any reasonable doubt that the Jingo tale contains a large germ of truth, and is at least an echo of the relations that existed between Japan and Korea in the 3rd and 4th centuries. The records of the 69 years comprising 254 Jingo's reign are in the main an account of intercourse, sometimes peaceful, sometimes stormy, between the neighbouring countries. Only one other episode occupies a prominent place: it is an attempt on the part of Jingo's step-brothers to oppose her return to Yamato and to prevent the accession of her son to the throne. It should be noted here that all such names as Jimmu, Sūjin, Chūai, &c., are posthumous, and were invented in the reign of Kwammu (782-806), the fashion being taken from China and the names themselves being purely Chinese translations of the qualities assigned to the respective monarchs. Thus Jimmu signifies "divine valour"; Sūjin, "deity-honouring"; and Chūai, "sad middle son." The names of these rulers during life were wholly different from their posthumous appellations.

Chinese history, which is incomparably older and more precise than Korean, is by no means silent about Japan. Long notices occur in the later Han and Wei records (25 to 265). The Japanese are spoken of as dwarfs (*Wa*), and **Earliest Notices in Chinese History.** their islands, frequently called the queen country, are said to be mountainous, with soil suitable for growing grain, hemp, and the silkworm mulberry. The climate is so mild that vegetables can be grown in winter and summer; there are neither oxen, horses, tigers, nor leopards; the people understand the art of weaving; the men tattoo their faces and bodies in patterns indicating differences of rank; male attire consists of a single piece of cloth; females wear a gown passed over the head, and tie their hair in a bow; soldiers are armed with spears and shields, and also with bows, from which they discharge arrows tipped with bone or iron; the sovereign resides in Yamato; there are stockaded forts and houses; food is taken with the fingers but is served on bamboo trays and wooden trenchers; foot-gear is not worn; when men of the lower classes meet a man of rank, they leave the road and retire to the grass, squatting or kneeling with both hands on the ground when they address him; intoxicating liquor is much used; the people are long-lived, many reaching the age of 100; women are more numerous than men; there is no theft, and litigation is infrequent; the women are faithful and not jealous; all men of high rank have four or five wives, others two or three; wives and children of law-breakers are confiscated, and for grave crimes the offender's family is extirpated; divination is practised by burning bones; mourning lasts for some ten days and the rites are performed by a "mourning-keeper"; after a funeral the whole family perform ablutions; fishing is much practised, and the fishermen are skilled divers; there are distinctions of rank and some are vassals to others; each province has a market where goods are exchanged; the country is divided into more than 100 provinces, and among its products are white pearls, green jade and cinnabar. These annals go on to say that between 147 and 190 civil war prevailed for several years, and order was finally restored by a female sovereign, who is described as having been old and unmarried; much addicted to magic arts; attended by a thousand females; dwelling in a palace with lofty pavilions surrounded by a stockade and guarded by soldiers; but leading such a secluded life that few saw her face except one man who served her meals and acted as a medium of communication. There can be little question that this queen was the empress Jingo who, according to Japanese annals, came to the throne in the year A.D. 200, and whose every public act had its inception or promotion in some alleged divine interposition. In one point, however, the Chinese historians are certainly incorrect. They represent tattooing as universal in ancient Japan, whereas it was confined to criminals, in whose case it played the part that branding does elsewhere. Centuries later, in feudal days, the habit came to be practised by men of the lower orders whose avocations involved baring the body, but it never acquired vogue among educated people. In other respects these ancient Chinese annals must be credited with remarkable accuracy in their description of Japan and the Japanese. Their account may be advantageously compared with Professor Chamberlain's analysis of the manners and customs of the early Japanese, in the preface to his translation of the *Kojiki*.

"The Japanese of the mythical period, as pictured in the legends preserved by the compiler of the *Records of Ancient Matters*, were a race who had long emerged from the savage stage and had attained to a high level of barbaric skill. The Stone Age was forgotten by them—or nearly so— and the evidence points to their never having passed through a genuine Bronze Age, though the knowledge of bronze was at a later period introduced from the neighbouring continent. They used iron for manufacturing spears, swords and knives of various shapes, and likewise for the more peaceful purpose of making hooks wherewith to angle or to fasten the doors of their huts. Their other warlike and hunting implements (besides traps and gins, which appear to have been used equally for catching beasts and birds and for destroying human enemies) were bows and arrows, spears and elbow-pads—the latter seemingly of skin, while special allusion is made to the fact that the arrows were feathered. Perhaps clubs should be added to the list. Of the bows and arrows, swords and knives, there is perpetual mention, but nowhere do we hear of the tools with which they were manufactured, and there is the same remarkable silence regarding such widely spread domestic implements as the saw and the axe. We hear, however, of the pestle and mortar, of the fire-drill, of the wedge, of the sickle, and of the shuttle used in weaving. Navigation seems to have been in a very elementary state. Indeed the art of sailing was but little practised in Japan even so late as the middle of the 10th century of our era, subsequent to the general diffusion of Chinese civilization, though rowing and punting are often mentioned by the early poets. To what we should call towns or villages very little reference is made anywhere in the *Records* or in that part of the *Chronicles* which contain the account of the so-called Divine Age. But from what we learn incidentally it would seem that the scanty population was chiefly distributed in small hamlets and isolated dwellings along the coast and up the course of the larger streams. Of house-building there is frequent mention. Fences were in use. Rugs of skins and rush-matting were occasionally brought in to sit on, and we even hear once or twice of silk rugs being used for the same purpose by the noble and wealthy. The habits of personal cleanliness which so pleasantly distinguish the modern Japanese from their neighbours, in continental Asia, though less fully developed than at present would seem to have existed in the germ in early times, as we read more than once of bathing in rivers, and are told of bathing women being specially attached to the person of a certain Imperial infant. Lustrations, too, formed part of the religious practices of the race. Latrines are mentioned several times. They would appear to have been situated away from the houses and to have been generally placed over a running stream, whence doubtless the name for latrine in the archaic dialect—*kawaya* (river-house). A peculiar sort of dwelling-place which the two old histories bring prominently under our notice is the so-called parturition house—a one-roomed hut without windows, which a woman was expected to build and retire into for the purpose Of being delivered unseen. Castles are not distinctly spoken of until a time which coincides, according to the received chronology, with the first century B.C. We then first meet with the curious term rice-castle, whose precise signification is a matter of dispute among the native commentators, but which, on comparison with Chinese descriptions of the early Japanese, should probably be understood to mean a kind of palisade serving the purpose of a redoubt, behind which the warriors could ensconce themselves. The food of the early Japanese consisted of fish and of the flesh of the wild creatures which fell by the hunter's arrow or were taken in the trapper's snare. Rice is the only cereal of which there is such mention made as to place it beyond a doubt that its cultivation dates back to time immemorial. Beans, millet and barley are indeed named once, together with silkworms, in the account of the Divine Age. But the passage has every aspect of an interpolation in the legend, perhaps not dating back long before the time of the eighth-century compiler. A few unimportant vegetables and fruits, of most of which there is but a single mention, are found. The intoxicating liquor called *sake* was known in Japan during the mythical period, and so were chopsticks for eating food with. Cooking pots and cups and dishes—the latter both of earthenware and of leaves of trees—are also mentioned; but of the use of fire for warming purposes we hear nothing. Tables are named several times, but never in connexion with food: they would seem to have been used exclusively for the purpose of presenting offerings on, and were probably quite small and low—in fact, rather trays than tables, according to European ideas. In the use of clothing and the specialization of garments the early Japanese had reached a high level. We read in the most ancient legends of upper garments, skirts, trowsers, girdles, veils and hats, while both sexes adorned themselves with necklaces, bracelets and head ornaments of stones considered precious—in this respect offering a striking contrast to their descendants in modern times, of whose attire jewelry forms no part. The material of their clothes was hempen cloth and paper—mulberry bark, coloured by being rubbed with madder, and probably with woad and other tinctorial plants. All the garments, so far as we may judge, were woven, sewing being nowhere mentioned. From the great place which the chase occupied in daily life, we are led to suppose that skins also were used to make garments of. There is in the *Records* at least one passage which favours this supposition, 255and the *Chronicles* in one place mention the straw rain-coat and broad-brimmed hat, which still form the Japanese peasant's effectual protection against the inclemencies of the weather. The tendrils of creeping plants served the purposes of strings, and bound the warrior's sword round his waist. Combs are mentioned, and it is evident that much attention was devoted to the dressing of the hair. The men seem to have bound up their hair in two bunches, one on each side of the head, while the young boys tied theirs in a top-knot, the unmarried girls let their locks hang down over their necks, and the married women dressed theirs after a fashion which apparently combined the two last-named methods. There is no mention in any of the old books of cutting the hair or beard except in token of disgrace; neither do we gather that the sexes, but for the matter of the head-dress, were distinguished by a diversity of apparel and ornamentation. With regard to the precious stones mentioned above as having been used as ornaments for the head, neck and arms, we know from the specimens which have rewarded the labours of archaeological research in Japan that agate, crystal, glass, jade, serpentine and steatite were the most used materials, and carved and pierced cylindrical shapes the commonest forms. The horse—which was ridden, but not driven—the barn-door fowl and the cormorant used for fishing, are the only domesticated creatures mentioned in the earlier traditions, with the doubtful exception of the silkworm. In the later portions of the *Records* and *Chronicles* dogs and cattle are alluded to, but sheep, swine and even cats were apparently not yet introduced."

As the prehistoric era draws to its end the above analyses of Japanese civilization have to be modified. Thus, towards the close of the 3rd century, ship-building made great progress, and instead of the small boats hitherto in use, a vessel 100 ft. long was constructed. Notable above all is the fact that Japan's turbulent relations with Korea were replaced by friendly intercourse, so that she began to receive from her neighbour instruction in the art of writing. The date assigned by the*Chronicles* for this important event is A.D. 285, but it has been proved almost conclusively that Japanese annals relating to this period are in error to the extent of 120 years. Hence the introduction of calligraphy must be placed in 405. Chinese history shows that between 57 and 247 Japan sent four embassies to the courts of the Han and the Wei, and this intercourse cannot

23

have failed to disclose the ideograph. But the knowledge appears to have been confined to a few interpreters, and not until the year 405 were steps taken to extend it, with the aid of a learned Korean, Wang-in. Korea herself began to study Chinese learning only a few years before she undertook to impart it to Japan. We now find a numerous colony of Koreans passing to Japan and settling there; a large number are also carried over as prisoners of war, and the Japanese obtain seamstresses from both of their continental neighbours. One fact, related with much precision, shows that the refinements of life were in an advanced condition: an ice-house is described, and we read that from 374 (? 494) it became the fashion to store ice in this manner for use in the hot months by placing it in water or *sake*. The emperor, Nintoku, to whose time this innovation is attributed, is one of the romantic figures of Japanese history. He commenced his career by refusing to accept the sovereignty from his younger brother, who pressed him earnestly to do so on the ground that the proper order of succession had been disturbed by their father's partiality—though the rights attaching to primogeniture did not receive imperative recognition in early Japan. After three years of this mutual self-effacement, during which the throne remained vacant, the younger brother committed suicide, and Nintoku reluctantly became sovereign. He chose Naniwa (the modern Osaka) for his capital, but he would not take the farmers from their work to finish the building of a palace, and subsequently, inferring from the absence of smoke over the houses of the people that the country was impoverished, he remitted all taxes and suspended forced labour for a term of three years, during which his palace fell into a state of ruin and he himself fared in the coarsest manner. Digging canals, damming rivers, constructing roads and bridges, and establishing granaries occupied his attention when love did not distract it. But in affairs of the heart he was most unhappy. He figures as the sole wearer of the Japanese crown who was defied by his consort; for when he took a concubine in despite of the empress, her jealousy was so bitter that, refusing to be placated by any of his majesty's verses or other overtures, she left the palace altogether; and when he sought to introduce another beauty into the inner chamber, his own half-brother, who carried his proposals, won the girl for himself. One other fact deserves to be remembered in connexion with Nintoku's reign: Ki-no-tsuno, representative of a great family which had filled the highest administrative and military posts under several sovereigns, is mentioned as "the first to commit to writing in detail the productions of the soil in each locality." This was in 353 (probably 473). We shall err little if we date the commencement of Japanese written annals from this time, though no compilation earlier than the *Kojiki* has survived.

Early Historical Period.—With the emperor Richū, who came to the throne A.D. 400, the historical period may be said to commence; for though the chronology of the records is still questionable, the facts are generally accepted as credible. Conspicuous loyalty towards the sovereign was not an attribute of the Japanese Imperial family in early times. Attempts to usurp the throne were not uncommon, though there are very few instances of such essays on the part of a subject. Love or lust played no insignificant part in the drama, and a common method of placating an irate sovereign was to present a beautiful damsel for his delectation. The veto of consanguinity did not receive very strict respect in these matters. Children of the same father might intermarry, but not those of the same mother; a canon which becomes explicable on observing that as wives usually lived apart from their husbands and had the sole custody of their offspring, two or more families often remained to the end unconscious of the fact that they had a common sire. There was a remarkable tendency to organize the nation into groups of persons following the same pursuit or charged with the same functions. A group thus composed was called *be*. The heads of the great families had titles—as *omi,muraji, miakko, wake*, &c.—and affairs of state were administered by the most renowned of these nobles, wholly subject to the sovereign's ultimate will. The provincial districts were ruled by scions of the Imperial family, who appear to have been, on the whole, entirely subservient to the Throne. There were no tribunals of justice: the ordeal of boiling water or heated metal was the sole test of guilt or innocence, apart, of course, from confession, which was often exacted under menace of torture. A celebrated instance of the ordeal of boiling water is recorded in 415, when this device was employed to correct the genealogies of families suspected of falsely claiming descent from emperors or divine beings. The test proved efficacious, for men conscious of forgery refused to undergo the ordeal. Deprivation of rank was the lightest form of punishment; death the commonest, and occasionally the whole family of an offender became serfs of the house against which the offence had been committed or which had been instrumental in disclosing a crime. There are, however, frequent examples of wrong-doing expiated by the voluntary surrender of lands or other property. We find several instances of that extreme type of loyalty which became habitual in later ages—suicide in preference to surviving a deceased lord. On the whole the successive sovereigns of these early times appear to have ruled with clemency and consideration for the people's welfare. But there were two notable exceptions—Yuriaku (457-479) and Muretsu (499-506). The former slew men ruthlessly in fits of passion or resentment, and the latter was the Nero of Japanese history, a man who loved to witness the agony of his fellows and knew no sentiment of mercy or remorse. Yet even Yuriaku did not fail to promote industrial pursuits. Skilled artisans were obtained from Korea, and it is related that, in 462, this monarch induced the empress and the ladies of the palace to plant mulberry trees with their own hands in order to encourage sericulture. Throughout the 5th and 6th centuries many instances are recorded of the acquisition of landed estates by the Throne, and their occasional bestowal upon princes or Imperial consorts, such gifts being frequently accompanied by the assignment of bodies of agriculturists who seem to have accepted the position of serfs. Meanwhile Chinese civilization was gradually becoming known, either by direct contact or through Korea. Several immigrations of Chinese 256or Korean settlers are on record. No less than 7053 householders of Chinese subjects came, through Korea, in 540, and one of their number received high rank together with the post of director of the Imperial treasury. From these facts, and from a national register showing the derivation of all the principal families in Japan, it is clearly established that a considerable strain of Chinese and Korean blood runs in the veins of many Japanese subjects.

The most signal and far-reaching event of this epoch was the importation of the Buddhist creed, which took place in 552. A Korean monarch acted as propagandist, sending a special envoy with a bronze image of the Buddha and *Introduction of Buddhism.*with several volumes of the Sutras. Unfortunately the coming of the foreign faith happened to synchronize with an epidemic of plague, and conservatives at the Imperial court were easily able to attribute this visitation to resentment on the part of the ancestral deities against the invasion of Japan by an alien creed. Thus the spread of Buddhism was checked; but only for a time. Thirty-five years after the coming of the Sutras, the first temple was erected to enshrine a wooden image of the Buddha 16 ft. high. It has often been alleged that the question between the imported and the indigenous cults had to be decided by the sword. The statement is misleading. That the final adoption of Buddhism resulted from a war is true, but its adoption or rejection did not constitute the motive of the combat. A contest for the succession to the throne at the opening of Sujun's reign (588-592) found the partisans of the Indian faith ranged on one side, its opponents on the other, and in a moment of stress the leaders of the former, Soma and Prince Umayado, vowed to erect Buddhist temples should victory rest on their arms. From that time the future of Buddhism was assured. In 588 Korea sent Buddhist relics, Buddhist priests, Buddhist ascetics, architects of Buddhist temples, and casters of Buddhist images. She had already sent men learned in divination, in medicine, and in the calendar. The building of temples began to be fashionable in the closing years of the 6th century, as did also abdication of the world by people of both sexes; and a census taken in 623, during the reign of the empress Suiko (583-628), showed that there were then 46 temples, 816 priests and 569 nuns in the empire. This rapid growth of the alien faith was due mainly to two causes: first, that the empress Suiko, being of the Soga family, naturally favoured a creed which had found its earliest Japanese patron in the great statesman and general, Soga no Umako; secondly, that one of the most illustrious scholars and philosophers ever possessed by Japan, Prince Shōtoku, devoted all his energies to fostering Buddhism.

The adoption of Buddhism meant to the Japanese much more than the acquisition of a practical religion with a code of clearly defined morality in place of the amorphous and jejune cult of Shintō. It meant the introduction of Chinese civilization. Priests and scholars crossed in numbers from China, and men passed over from Japan to study the Sutras at what was then regarded as the fountain-head of Buddhism. There was also a constant stream of immigrants from China and Korea, and the result may be gathered from the fact that a census taken of the Japanese nobility in 814 indicated 382 Korean and Chinese families against only 796 of pure Japanese origin. The records show that in costume and customs a signal advance was made towards refinement. Hair-ornaments of gold or silver chiselled in the form of flowers; caps of sarcenet in twelve special tints, each indicating a different grade; garments of brocade and embroidery with figured thin silks of various colours—all these were worn on ceremonial occasions; the art of painting was introduced; a recorder's office was established; perfumes were largely employed; court picnics to gather medicinal herbs were instituted, princes and princesses attending in brilliant raiment; Chinese music and dancing were introduced; cross bows and catapults were added to the weapons of war; domestic architecture made signal strides in obedience to the examples of Buddhist sacred edifices, which, from the first, showed magnificence of dimension and decoration hitherto unconceived in Japan; the arts of metal-casting and sculpture underwent great improvement; Prince Shōtoku compiled a code, commonly spoken of as the first written laws of Japan, but in reality a collection of maxims evincing a moral spirit of the highest type. In some respects, however, there was no improvement. The succession to the throne still tended to provoke disputes among the Imperial princes; the sword constituted the principal weapon of punishment, and torture the chief judicial device. Now, too, for the first time, a noble family is found seeking to usurp the Imperial authority. The head of the Soga house, Umako, having compassed the murder of the emperor Sujun and placed on the throne his own niece (Suiko), swept away all opposition to the latter's successor, Jomei, and controlled the administration of state affairs throughout two reigns. In all this he was strongly seconded by his son, Iruka, who even surpassed him in contumelious assumption of power and parade of dignity. Iruka was slain in the presence of the empress Kōgyoku by Prince Naka with the assistance of the minister of the interior, Kamako, and it is not surprising to find the empress (Kōgyoku) abdicating immediately afterwards in favour of Kamako's protégé, Prince Karu, who is known in history as Kōtoku. This Kamako, planner and leader of the conspiracy which overthrew the Soga, is remembered by posterity under the name of Kamatari and as the founder of the most illustrious of Japan's noble houses, the Fujiwara. At this time (645), a habit which afterwards contributed materially to the effacement of the Throne's practical authority was inaugurated. Prince Furubito, pressed by his brother, Prince Karu, to assume the sceptre in accordance with his right of primogeniture, made his refusal peremptory by abandoning the world and taking the tonsure. This retirement to a monastery was afterwards dictated to several sovereigns by ministers who found that an active occupant of the throne impeded their own exercise of administrative autocracy. Furubito's recourse to the tonsure proved, however, to be merely a cloak for ambitious designs. Before a year had passed he conspired to usurp the throne and was put to death with his children, his consorts strangling themselves. Suicide to escape the disgrace of defeat had now become a common practice. Another prominent feature of this epoch was the prevalence of superstition. The smallest incidents—the growing of two lotus flowers on one stem; a popular ballad; the reputed song of a sleeping monkey; the condition of the water in a pond; rain without clouds—all these and cognate trifles were regarded as omens; wizards and witches deluded the common people; a strange form of caterpillar was worshipped as the god of the everlasting world, and the peasants impoverished themselves by making sacrifices to it.

An interesting epoch is now reached, the first legislative era of early Japanese history. It commenced with the reign of the emperor Kōtoku (645), of whom the *Chronicles* say that he "honoured the religion of Buddha and despised *First Legislative Epoch.*Shintō"; that "he was of gentle disposition; loved men of learning; made no distinction of noble and mean, and continually dispensed beneficent edicts." The customs calling most loudly for reform in his time were abuse of the system of forced labour; corrupt administration of justice; spoliation of the peasant class; assumption of spurious titles to justify oppression; indiscriminate distribution of the families of slaves and serfs; diversion of taxes to the pockets of collectors; formation of great estates, and a general lack of administrative centralization. The first step of reform consisted in ordering the governors of provinces to prepare registers showing the numbers of freemen and serfs within their jurisdiction as well as the area of cultivated land. It was further ordained that the advantages of irrigation should be shared equally with the common people; that no local governor might try and decide criminal cases while in his province; that any one convicted of accepting bribes should be liable to a fine of double the amount as well as to other punishment; that in the Imperial court a box should be placed for receiving petitions and a bell hung to be sounded in the event of delay in answering them or unfairness in dealing with them; that all absorption of land into great estates should cease; that barriers, outposts, guards and post-horses should be 257provided; that high officials should be dowered with hereditary estates by way of emolument, the largest of such grants being 3000 homesteads; that men of unblemished character and proved capacity should be appointed aldermen for adjudicating criminal matters; that there should be chosen as clerks for governors and vice-governors of provinces men of solid competence "skilled in writing and arithmetic"; that the land should be parcelled out in fixed proportions to every adult unit of the population with right of tenure for a term of six years; that forced labour should be commuted for taxes of silk and cloth; and that for fiscal and administrative purposes households should be organized in groups of five, each group under an elder, and ten groups forming a township, which, again, should be governed by an elder. Incidentally to these reforms many of the evil customs of the time are exposed. Thus provincial governors when they visited the capital were accustomed to travel with great retinues who appear to have constituted a charge on the regions through which they passed. The law now limited the number of a chief governor's attendants to nine, and forbade him to use official houses or to fare at public cost unless journeying on public business. Again, men who had acquired some local distinction, though they did not belong to noble families, took advantage of the absence of historical records or official registers, and, representing themselves as descendants of magnates to whom the charge of public granaries had been entrusted, succeeded in usurping valuable privileges. The office of provincial governor had in many cases become hereditary, and not only were governors largely independent of Imperial control, but also, since every free man carried arms, there had grown up about these officials a population relying largely on the law of force.

Kōtoku's reforms sought to institute a system of temporary governors, and directed that all arms and armour should be stored in arsenals built in waste places, except in the case of provinces adjoining lands where unsubdued aborigines (Yemishi) dwelt. Punishments were drastic, and in the case of a man convicted of treason, all his children were executed with him, his wives and consorts committing suicide. From a much earlier age suicide had been freely resorted to as the most honourable exit from pending disgrace, but as yet the samurai's method of disembowelment was not employed, strangulation or cutting the throat being the regular practice. Torture was freely employed and men often died under it. Signal abuses prevailed in regions beyond the immediate range of the central government's observation. It has been shown that from early days the numerous scions of the Imperial family had generally been provided for by grants of provincial estates. Gradually the descendants of these men, and the representatives of great families who held hereditary rank, extended their domains unscrupulously, employing forced labour to reclaim lands, which they let to the peasants, not hesitating to appropriate large slices of public property, and remitting to the central treasury only such fractions of the taxes as they found convenient. So prevalent had the exaction of forced labour become that country-folk, repairing to the capital to seek redress of grievances, were often compelled to remain there for the purpose of carrying out some work in which dignitaries of state were interested. The removal of the capital to a new site on each change of sovereign involved a vast quantity of unproductive toil. It is recorded that in 656, when the empress Saimei occupied the throne, a canal was dug which required the work of 30,000 men and a wall was built which had employed 70,000 men before its completion. The construction of tombs for grandees was another heavy drain on the people's labour. Some of these sepulchres attained enormous dimensions—that of the emperor Ojin (270-310) measures 2312 yds. round the outer moat and is some 60 ft. high; the emperor Nintoku's (313-399) is still larger, and there is a tumulus in Kawachi on the flank of which a good-sized village has been built. Kōtoku's laws provided that the tomb of a prince should not be so large as to require the work of more than 1000 men for seven days, and that the grave of a petty official must be completed by 50 men in one day. Moreover, it was forbidden to bury with the body gold, silver, copper, iron, jewelled shirts, jade armour or silk brocade. It appears that the custom of suicide or sacrifice at the tomb of grandees still survived, and that people sometimes cut off their hair or stabbed their thighs preparatory to declaiming a threnody. All these practices were vetoed. Abuses had grown up even in connexion with the Shintō rite of purgation. This rite required not only the reading of rituals but also the offering of food and fruits. For the sake of these edibles the rite was often harshly enforced, especially in connexion with pollution from contact with corpses; and thus it fell out that when of two brothers, returning from a scene of forced labour, one lay down upon the road and died, the other, dreading the cost of compulsory purgation, refused to take up the body. Many other evil customs came into existence in connexion with this rite, and all were dealt with in the new laws. Not the least important of the reforms then introduced was the organization of the ministry after the model of the Tang dynasty of China. Eight departments of state were created, and several of them received names which are similarly used to this day. Not only the institutions of China were borrowed but also her official costumes. During Kōtoku's reign 19 grades of head-gear were instituted, and in the time of Tenchi (668-671) the number was increased to 26, with corresponding robes. Throughout this era intercourse was frequent with China, and the spread of Buddhism continued steadily. The empress Saimei (655-661), who succeeded Kōtoku, was an earnest patron of the faith. By her command several public expositions of the Sutras were given, and the building of temples went on in many districts, estates being liberally granted for the maintenance of these places of worship.

The Fujiwara Era.—In the *Chronicles of Japan* the year 672 is treated as a kind of interregnum. It was in truth a year of something like anarchy, a great part of it being occupied by a conflict of unparalleled magnitude between Prince Ōtomo (called in history Emperor Kōbun) and Prince Ōama, who emerged victorious and is historically entitled Temmu (673-686). The four centuries that followed are conveniently designated the Fujiwara era, because throughout that long interval affairs of state were controlled by the Fujiwara family, whose daughters were given as consorts to successive sovereigns and whose sons filled all the high administrative posts. It has been related above that Kamako, chief of the Shintō officials, inspired the assassination of the Soga chief, Iruka, and thus defeated the latter's designs upon the throne in the days of the empress Kōgyoku. Kamako, better known to subsequent generations as Kamatari, was thenceforth regarded with unlimited favour by successive sovereigns, and just before his death in 670, the family name of Fujiwara was bestowed on him by the emperor Tenchi. Kamatari himself deserved all the honour he received, but his descendants abused the high trust reposed in them, reduced the sovereign to a mere puppet, and exercised Imperial authority without openly usurping it. Much of this was due to the adoption of Chinese administrative systems, a process which may be said to have commenced during the reign of Kōtoku (645-654) and to have continued almost uninterruptedly until the 11th century. Under these systems the emperor ceased directly to exercise supreme civil or military power: he became merely the source of authority, not its wielder, the civil functions being delegated to a bureaucracy and the military to a soldier class. Possibly had the custom held of transferring the capital to a new site on each change of sovereign, and had the growth of luxurious habits been thus checked, the comparatively simple life of early times might have held the throne and the people in closer contact. But from the beginning of the 8th century a strong tendency to avoid these costly migrations developed itself. In 709 the court took up its residence at Nara, remaining there until 784; ten years after the latter date Kiōto became the permanent metropolis. The capital at Nara—established during the reign of the empress Gemmyō (708-715)—was built on the plan of the Chinese metropolis. It had nine gates and nine avenues, the palace being situated in the northern section and approached by a broad, straight avenue, which divided the city into two perfectly equal halves, all the other streets running parallel to this main 258avenue or at right angles to it. Seven sovereigns reigned at Heijō (castle of peace), as Nara is historically called, and, during this period of 75 years, seven of the grandest temples ever seen in Japan were erected; a multitude of idols were cast, among them a colossal bronze Daibutsu 53½ ft. high; large temple-bells were founded, and all the best artists and artisans of the era devoted their services to these works. This religious mania reached its acme in the reign of the emperor Shōmu (724-748), a man equally superstitious and addicted to display. In Temmu's time the custom had been introduced of compelling large numbers of persons to enter the Buddhist priesthood with the object of propitiating heaven's aid to heal the illness of an illustrious personage. In Shōmu's day every natural calamity or abnormal phenomenon was regarded as calling for religious services on a large scale, and the great expense involved in all these buildings and ceremonials, supplemented by lavish outlays on court pageants, was severely felt by the nation. The condition of the agricultural class, who were the chief tax-payers, was further aggravated by the operation of the emperor Kōtoku's land system, which rendered tenure so uncertain as to deter improvements. Therefore, in the Nara epoch, the principle of private ownership of land began to be recognized. Attention was also paid to road-making, bridge-building, river control and house construction, a special feature of this last being the use of tiles for roofing purposes in place of the shingles or thatch hitherto employed. In all these steps of progress Buddhist priests took an active part. Costumes were now governed by purely Chinese fashions. This change had been gradually introduced from the time of Kōtoku's legislative measures—generally called the Taikwa reforms after the name of the era (645-650) of their adoption—and was rendered more thorough by supplementary enactments in the period 701-703 while Mommu occupied the throne. Ladies seem by this time to have abandoned the strings of beads worn in early eras round the neck, wrists and ankles. They used ornaments of gold, silver or jade in their hair, but in other respects their habiliments closely resembled those of men, and to make the difference still less conspicuous they straddled their horses when riding. Attempts were made to facilitate travel by establishing stores of grain along the principal highways, but as yet there were no hostelries, and if a wayfarer did not find shelter in the house of a friend, he had to bivouac as best he could. Such a state of affairs in the provinces offered a marked contrast to the luxurious indulgence which had now begun to prevail in the capital. There festivals of various kinds, dancing, verse-composing, flower picnics, archery, polo, football—of a very refined nature—hawking, hunting and gambling absorbed the attention of the aristocracy. Nothing disturbed the serenity of the epoch except a revolt of the northern Yemishi, which was temporarily subdued by a Fujiwara general, for the Fujiwara had not yet laid aside the martial habits of their ancestors. In 794 the Imperial capital was transferred from Nara to Kiōto by order of the emperor Kwammu, one of the greatest of Japanese sovereigns. Education, the organization of the civil service, riparian works, irrigation improvements, the separation of religion from politics, the abolition of sinecure offices, devices for encouraging and assisting agriculture, all received attention from him. But a twenty-two years' campaign against the northern Yemishi; the building of numerous temples; the indulgence of such a passionate love of the chase that he organized 140 hunting excursions during his reign of 25 years; profuse extravagance on the part of the aristocracy in Kiōto and the exactions of provincial nobles, conspired to sink the working classes into greater depths of hardship than ever. Farmers had to borrow money and seed-rice from local officials or Buddhist temples, hypothecating their land as security; thus the temples and the nobles extended their already great estates, whilst the agricultural population gradually fell into a position of practical serfdom.

Meanwhile the Fujiwara family were steadily developing their influence in Kiōto. Their methods were simple but thoroughly effective. "By progressive exercises of arbitrariness they gradually contrived that the choice of a **Rise of the Fujiwara.**consort for the sovereign should be legally limited to a daughter of their family, five branches of which were specially designated to that honour through all ages. When a son was born to an emperor, the Fujiwara took the child into one of their palaces, and on his accession to the throne, the particular Fujiwara noble that happened to be his maternal grandfather became regent of the empire. This office of regent, created towards the close of the 9th century, was part of the scheme; for the Fujiwara did not allow the purple to be worn by a sovereign after he had attained his majority, or, if they suffered him to wield the sceptre during a few years of manhood, they compelled him to abdicate so soon as any independent aspirations began to impair his docility; and since for the purposes of administration in these constantly recurring minorities an office more powerful than that of prime minister (dajō daijin) was needed, they created that of regent (kwambaku), making it hereditary in their own family. In fact the history of Japan from the 9th to the 19th century may be described as the history of four families, the Fujiwara, the Taira, the Minamoto and the Tokugawa. The Fujiwara governed through the emperor; the Taira, the Minamoto and the Tokugawa governed in spite of the emperor. The Fujiwara based their power on matrimonial alliances with the Throne; the Taira, the Minamoto and the Tokugawa based theirs on the possession of armed strength which the throne had no competence to control. There another broad line of cleavage is seen. Throughout the Fujiwara era the centre of political gravity remained always in the court. Throughout the era of the Taira, the Minamoto and the Tokugawa the centre of political gravity was transferred to a point outside the court, the headquarters of a military feudalism." The process of transfer was of course gradual. It commenced with the granting of large tracts of tax-free lands to noblemen who had wrested them from the aborigines (Yemishi) or had reclaimed them by means of serf-labour. These tracts lay for the most part in the northern and eastern parts of the main island, at such a distance from the Capital that the writ of the central government did not run there; and since such lands could be rented at rates considerably less than the tax levied on farms belonging to the state, the peasants by degrees abandoned the latter and settled on the former, with the result that the revenues of the Throne steadily diminished, while those of the provincial magnates correspondingly increased. Moreover, in the 7th century, at the time of the adoption of Chinese models of administration and organization, the court began to rely for military protection on the services of guards temporarily drafted from the provincial troops, and, during the protracted struggle against the Yemishi in the north and east in the 8th century, the fact that the power of the sword lay with the provinces began to be noted.

Kiōto remained the source of authority. But with the growth of luxury and effeminacy in the capital the Fujiwara became more and more averse from the hardships of campaigning, and in the 9th and 10th centuries, respectively, **The Taira and the Minamoto.**the Taira and the Minamoto1 families came into prominence as military leaders, the field of the Taira operations being the south and west, that of the Minamoto the north and east. Had the court reserved to itself and munificently exercised the privilege of rewarding these services, it might still have retained power and wealth. But by a niggardly and contemptuous policy on the part of Kiōto not only were the Minamoto leaders estranged but also they assumed the right of recompensing their followers with tax-free estates, an example which the Taira leaders quickly followed. By the early years of the 12th century these estates had attracted the great majority of the farming class, whereas the public land was left wild and uncultivated. In a word, the court and the Fujiwara found themselves without revenue, while the coffers of the Taira and the Minamoto were full: the power of the purse and the power of the sword had passed effectually to the two military families. Prominent features of the moral condition of the capital at this era (12th century) were superstition, refinement and effeminacy. A belief was widely held that calamity 259could not be averted or success insured without recourse to Buddhist priests. Thus, during a reign of only 13 years at the close of the 11th century, the emperor Shirakawa caused 5420 religious pictures to be painted, ordered the casting of 127 statues of Buddha, each 11 ft. high, of 3150 life-sized images and of 2930 smaller idols, and constructed 21 large temples as well as 446,630 religious edifices of various kinds. Side by side with this faith in the supernatural, sexual immorality prevailed widely, never accompanied, however, by immodesty. Literary proficiency ranked as the be-all and end-all of existence. "A man estimated the conjugal qualities of a young lady by her skill in finding scholarly similes and by her perception of the cadence of words. If a woman was so fortunate as to acquire a reputation for learning, she possessed a certificate of universal virtue and amiability." All the pastimes of the Nara epoch were pursued with increased fervour and elaboration in the Heian (Kiōto) era. The building of fine dwelling-houses and the laying out of landscape gardens took place on a considerable scale, though in these respects the ideals of later ages were not yet reached. As to costume, the close-fitting, business-like and comparatively simple dress of the 8th century was exchanged for a much more elaborate style. During the Nara epoch the many-hued

29

hats of China had been abandoned for a sober head-gear of silk gauze covered with black lacquer, but in the Heian era this was replaced by an imposing structure glistening with jewels: the sleeves of the tunic grew so long that they hung to the knees when a man's arms were crossed, and the trowsers were made so full and baggy that they resembled a divided skirt. From this era may be said to have commenced the manufacture of the tasteful and gorgeous textile fabrics for which Japan afterwards became famous. "A fop's ideal was to wear several suits, one above the other, disposing them so that their various colours showed in harmoniously contrasting lines at the folds on the bosom and at the edges of the long sleeves. A successful costume created a sensation in court circles. Its wearer became the hero of the hour, and under the pernicious influence of such ambition men began even to powder their faces and rouge their cheeks like women. As for the fair sex, their costume reached the acme of unpracticality and extravagance in this epoch. Long flowing hair was essential, and what with developing the volume and multiplying the number of her robes, and wearing above her trowsers a many-plied train, a grand lady of the time always seemed to be struggling to emerge from a cataract of habiliments." It was fortunate for Japan that circumstances favoured the growth of a military class in this age of her career, for had the conditions existing in Kiōto during the Heian epoch spread throughout the whole country, the penalty never escaped by a demoralized nation must have overtaken her. But by the middle of the 12th century the pernicious influence of the Fujiwara had paled before that of the Taira and the Minamoto, and a question of succession to the throne marshalled the latter two families in opposite camps, thus inaugurating an era of civil war which held the country in the throes of almost continuous battle for 450 years, placed it under the administration of a military feudalism, and educated a nation of warriors. At first the Minamoto were vanquished and driven from the capital, Kiyomori, the Taira chief, being left complete master of the situation. He established his headquarters at Rokuharu, in Kiōto, appropriated the revenues of 30 out of the 66 provinces forming the empire, and filled all the high offices of state with his own relatives or connexions. But he made no radical change in the administrative system, preferring to follow the example of the Fujiwara by keeping the throne in the hands of minors. And he committed the blunder of sparing the lives of two youthful sons of his defeated rival, the Minamoto chief. They were Yoritomo and Yoshitsunē; the latter the greatest strategist Japan ever produced, with perhaps one exception; the former, one of her three greatest statesmen, the founder of military feudalism. By these two men the Taira were so completely overthrown that they never raised their heads again, a sea-fight at Dan-no-ura (1155) giving them the *coup de grâce*. Their supremacy had lasted 22 years.

The Feudal Era.—Yoritomo, acting largely under the advice of an astute counsellor, Oye no Hiromoto, established his seat of power at Kamakura, 300 m. from Kiōto. He saw that, effectively to utilize the strength of the military class, propinquity to the military centres in the provinces was essential. At Kamakura he organized an administrative body similar in mechanism to that of the metropolitan government but studiously differentiated in the matter of nomenclature. As to the country at large, he brought it effectually under the sway of Kamakura by placing the provinces under the direct control of military governors, chosen and appointed by himself. No attempt was made, however, to interfere in any way with the polity in Kiōto: it was left intact, and the nobles about the Throne—*kuge* (courtly houses), as they came to be called in contradistinction to the *buke* (military houses)—were placated by renewal of their property titles. The Buddhist priests, also, who had been treated most harshly during the Taira tenure of power, found their fortunes restored under Kamakura's sway. Subsequently Yoritomo obtained for himself the title of *sei-itai-shōgun* (barbarian-subduing generalissimo), and just as the office of regent (kwambaku) had long been hereditary in the Fujiwara family, so the office of shōgun became thenceforth hereditary in that of the Minamoto. These changes were radical. They signified a complete shifting of the centre of power. During eighteen centuries from the time of Jimmu's invasion—as Japanese historians reckon—the country had been ruled from the south; now the north became supreme, and for a civilian administration a purely military was substituted. But there was no contumely towards the court in Kiōto. Kamakura made a show of seeking Imperial sanction for every one of its acts, and the whole of the military administration was carried on in the name of the emperor by a shōgun who called himself the Imperial deputy. In this respect things changed materially after the death of Yoritomo (1198). Kamakura then became the scene of a drama analogous to that acted in Kiōto from the 10th century.

The Hōjō family, to which belonged Masa, Yoritomo's consort, assumed towards the Kamakura shōgun an attitude similar to that previously assumed by the Fujiwara family towards the emperor in Kiōto. A child, who on **Rule of the Hōjō.** state occasions was carried to the council chamber in Masa's arms, served as the nominal repository of the shōgun's power, the functions of administration being discharged in reality by the Hōjō family, whose successive heads took the name of *shikken*(constable). At first care was taken to have the shōgun's office filled by a near relative of Yoritomo; but after the death of that great statesman's two sons and his nephew, the puppet shōguns were taken from the ranks of the Fujiwara or of the Imperial princes, and were deposed so soon as they attempted to assert themselves. What this meant becomes apparent when we note that in the interval of 83 years between 1220 and 1308, there were six shōguns whose ages at the time of appointment ranged from 3 to 16. Whether, if events had not forced their hands, the Hōjō constables would have maintained towards the Throne the reverent demeanour adopted by Yoritomo must remain a matter of conjecture. What actually happened was that the ex-emperor, Go-Toba, made an ill-judged attempt (1221) to break the power of Kamakura. He issued a call to arms which was responded to by some thousands of cenobites and as many soldiers of Taira extraction. In the brief struggle that ensued the Imperial partisans were wholly shattered, and the direct consequences were the dethronement and exile of the reigning emperor, the banishment of his predecessor together with two princes of the blood, and the compulsory adoption of the tonsure by Go-Toba; while the indirect consequence was that the succession to the throne and the tenure of Imperial power fell under the dictation of the Hōjō as they had formerly fallen under the direction of the Fujiwara. Yoshitoki, then head of the Hōjō family, installed his brother, Tokifusa, as military governor of Kiōto, and confiscating about 3000 estates, the property of those who had espoused the Imperial cause, distributed these lands among the adherents of his own family, thus 260greatly strengthening the basis of the feudal system. "It fared with the Hōjō as it had fared with all the great families that preceded them: their own misrule ultimately wrought their ruin. Their first eight representatives were talented and upright administrators. They took justice, simplicity and truth for guiding principles; they despised luxury and pomp; they never aspired to high official rank; they were content with two provinces for estates, and they sternly repelled the effeminate, depraved customs of Kiōto." Thus the greater part of the 13th century was, on the whole, a golden era for Japan, and the lower orders learned to welcome feudalism. Nevertheless no century furnished more conspicuous illustrations of the peculiarly Japanese system of vicarious government. Children occupied the position of shōgun in Kamakura under authority emanating from children on the throne in Kiōto; and members of the Hōjō family as shikken administered affairs at the mandate of the child shōguns. Through all three stages in the dignities of mikado, shōgun and shikken, the strictly regulated principle of heredity was maintained, according to which no Hōjō shikken could ever become shōgun; no Minamoto or Fujiwara could occupy the throne. At the beginning of the 14th century, however, several causes combined to shake the supremacy of the Hōjō. Under the sway of the ninth shikken (Takatoki), the austere simplicity of life and earnest discharge of executive duties which had distinguished the early chiefs of the family were exchanged for luxury, debauchery and perfunctory government. Thus the management of fiscal affairs fell into the hands of Takasuke, a man of usurious instincts. It had been the wise custom of the Hōjō constables to store grain in seasons of plenty, and distribute it at low prices in times of dearth. There occurred at this epoch a succession of bad harvests, but instead of opening the state granaries with benevolent liberality, Takasuke sold their contents at the highest obtainable rates; and, by way of contrast to the prevailing indigence, the people saw the constable in Kamakura affecting the pomp and extravagance of a sovereign waited upon by 37 mistresses, supporting a band of 2000 dancers, and keeping a pack of 5000 fighting dogs. The throne happened to be then occupied (1310-1338) by an emperor, Go-Daigo, who had reached full maturity before his accession, and was correspondingly averse from acting the puppet part assigned to the sovereigns of his time. Female influence contributed to his impatience. One of his concubines bore a son for whom he sought to obtain nomination as prince imperial, in defiance of an arrangement made by the Hōjō that the succession should pass alternately to the senior and junior branches of the Imperial family. Kamakura refused to entertain Go-Daigo's project, and thenceforth the child's mother importuned her sovereign and lover to overthrow the Hōjō. The *entourage* of the throne in Kiōto at this time was a counterpart of former eras. The Fujiwara, indeed, wielded nothing of their ancient influence. They had been divided by the Hōjō into five branches, each endowed with an equal right to the office of regent, and their strength was thus dissipated in struggling among themselves for the possession of the prize. But what the Fujiwara had done in their days of greatness, what the Taira had done during their brief tenure of power, the Saionji were now doing, namely, aspiring to furnish prime ministers and empresses from their own family solely. They had already given consorts to five emperors in succession, and jealous rivals were watching keenly to attack this clan which threatened to usurp the place long held by the most illustrious family in the land. A petty incident disturbed this state of very tender equilibrium before the plan of the Hōjō's enemies had fully matured, and the emperor presently found himself an exile on the island of Oki. But there now appeared upon the scene three men of great prowess: Kusunoki

31

Masashige, Nitta Yoshisada and Ashikaga Takauji. The first espoused from the outset the cause of the Throne and, though commanding only a small force, held the Hōjō troops in check. The last two were both of Minamoto descent. Their common ancestor was Minamoto Yoshiiye, whose exploits against the northern Yemishi in the second half of the 11th century had so impressed his countrymen that they gave him the title of Hachiman Tarō (first-born of the god of war). Both men took the field originally in the cause of the Hōjō, but at heart they desired to be avenged upon the latter for disloyalty to the Minamoto. Nitta Yoshisada marched suddenly against Kamakura, carried it by storm and committed the city to the flames. Ashikaga Takauji occupied Kiōto, and with the suicide of Takatoki the Hōjō fell finally from rule after 115 years of supremacy (1219-1334). The emperor now returned from exile, and his son, Prince Moriyoshi, having been appointed to the office of shōgun at Kamakura, the restoration of the administrative power to the Throne seemed an accomplished fact.

Go-Daigo, however, was not in any sense a wise sovereign. The extermination of the Hōjō placed wide estates at his disposal, but instead of rewarding those who had deserved well of him, he used a great part of them to enrich *The Ashikaga Shoguns.* his favourites, the companions of his dissipation. Ashikaga Takauji sought just such an opportunity. The following year (1335) saw him proclaiming himself shōgun at Kamakura, and after a complicated pageant of incidents, the emperor Go-Daigo was obliged once more to fly from Kiōto. He carried the regalia with him, refused to submit to Takauji, and declined to recognize his usurped title of shōgun. The Ashikaga chief solved the situation by deposing Go-Daigo and placing upon the throne another scion of the imperial family who is known in history as Kōmyō (1336-1348), and who, of course, confirmed Takauji in the office of shōgun. Thus commenced the Ashikaga line of shōguns, and thus commenced also a fifty-six-year period of divided sovereignty, the emperor Go-Daigo and his descendants reigning in Yoshino as the southern court (*nanchō*), and the emperor Kōmyō and his descendants reigning in Kiōto as the northern court (*hokuchō*). It was by the efforts of the shōgun Yoshimitsu, one of the greatest of the Ashikaga potentates, that this quarrel was finally composed, but during its progress the country had fallen into a deplorable condition. "The constitutional powers had become completely disorganized, especially in regions at a distance from the chief towns. The peasant was impoverished, his spirit broken, his hope of better things completely gone. He dreamed away his miserable existence and left the fields untilled. Bands of robbers followed the armies through the interior of the country, and increased the feeling of lawlessness and insecurity. The coast population, especially that of the island of Kiūshiū, had given itself up in a great measure to piracy. Even on the shores of Korea and China these enterprising Japanese corsairs made their appearance." The shōgun Yoshimitsu checked piracy, and there ensued between Japan and China a renewal of cordial intercourse which, upon the part of the shōgun, developed phases plainly suggesting an admission of Chinese suzerainty.

For a brief moment during the sway of Yoshimitsu the country had rest from internecine war, but immediately after his death (1394) the struggle began afresh. Many of the great territorial lords had now grown too puissant to concern themselves about either mikado or shōgun. Each fought for his own hand, thinking only of extending his sway and his territories. By the middle of the 16th century Kiōto was in ruins, and little vitality remained in any trade or industry except those that ministered to the wants of the warrior. Again in the case of the Ashikaga shōguns the political tendency to exercise power vicariously was shown, as it had been shown in the case of the mikados in Kiōto and in the case of the Minamoto in Kamakura. What the regents had been to the emperors and the constables to the Minamoto shōguns, that the wardens (*kwanryō*) were to the Ashikaga shōguns. Therefore, for possession of this office of kwanryō vehement conflicts were waged, and at one time five rival shōguns were used as figure-heads by contending factions. Yoshimitsu had apportioned an ample allowance for the support of the Imperial court, but in the continuous warfare following his death the estates charged with the duty of paying this allowance ceased to return any revenue; the court nobles had to seek shelter and sustenance with one or other of the feudal chiefs in the provinces, and the court itself was reduced to such a state of indigence that when the emperor Go-Tsuchi died (1500), 261his corpse lay for forty days awaiting burial, no funds being available for purposes of sepulture.

Alone among the vicissitudes of these troublous times the strength and influence of Buddhism grew steadily. The great monasteries were military strongholds as well as places of worship. When the emperor Kwammu chose Kiōto for his capital, he established on the hill of Hiyei-zan, which lay north-east of the city, a magnificent temple to ward off the evil influences supposed to emanate from that quarter. Twenty years later, Kōbō, the most famous of all Japanese Buddhist saints, founded on Koyasan in Yamato a monastery not less important than that of Hiyei-zan. These and many other temples had large tax-free estates, and for the protection of their property they found it expedient to train and arm the cenobites as soldiers. From that to taking active part in the political struggles of the time was but a short step, especially as the great temples often became refuges of sovereigns and princes who, though nominally forsaking the world, retained all their interest, and even continued to take an active part, in its vicissitudes. It is recorded of the emperor Shirakawa (1073-1086) that the three things which he declared his total inability to control were the waters of the river Kamo, the fall of the dice, and the monks of Buddha. His successors might have confessed equal inability. Kiyōmori, the puissant chief of the Taira family, had fruitlessly essayed to defy the Buddhists; Yoritomo, in the hour of his most signal triumph, thought it wise to placate them. Where these representatives of centralized power found themselves impotent, it may well be supposed that the comparatively petty chieftains who fought each for his own hand in the 15th and 16th centuries were incapable of accomplishing anything. In fact, the task of centralizing the administrative power, and thus restoring peace and order to the distracted empire, seemed, at the middle of the 16th century, a task beyond achievement by human capacity.

But if ever events create the men to deal with them, such was the case in the second half of that century. Three of the greatest captains and statesmen in Japanese history appeared upon the stage simultaneously, and moreover *Nobunaga, Hideyoshi and Iyeyasu.*worked in union, an event altogether inconsistent with the nature of the age. They were Oda Nobunaga, Hideyoshi (the *taikō*) and Tokugawa Iyeyasu. Nobunaga belonged to the Taira family and was originally ruler of a small fief in the province of Owari. Iyeyasu, a sub-feudatory of Nobunaga's enemy, the powerful daimyō2 of Mikawa and two other provinces, was a scion of the Minamoto and therefore eligible for the shōgunate. Hideyoshi was a peasant's son, equally lacking in patrons and in personal attractions. No chance seemed more remote than that such men, above all Hideyoshi, could possibly rise to supreme power. On the other hand, one outcome of the commotion with which the country had seethed for more than four centuries was to give special effect to the principle of natural selection. The fittest alone surviving, the qualities that made for fitness came to take precedence of rank or station, and those qualities were prowess in the battlefield and wisdom in the statesman's closet. "Any plebeian that would prove himself a first-class fighting man was willingly received into the armed *comitatus* which every feudal potentate was eager to attach to himself and his flag." It was thus that Hideyoshi was originally enrolled in the ranks of Nobunaga's retainers.

Nobunaga, succeeding to his small fief in Owari in 1542, added to it six whole provinces within 25 years of continuous endeavour. Being finally invited by the emperor to undertake the pacification of the country, and appealed to by Yoshiaki, the last of the Ashikaga chiefs, to secure for him the shōgunate, he marched into Kiōto at the head of a powerful army (1568), and, having accomplished the latter purpose, was preparing to complete the former when he fell under the sword of a traitor. Throughout his brilliant career he had the invaluable assistance of Hideyoshi, who would have attained immortal fame on any stage in any era. Hideyoshi entered Nobunaga's service as a groom and ended by administering the whole empire. When he accompanied Nobunaga to Kiōto in obedience to the invitation of the mikado, Okimachi, order and tranquillity were quickly restored in the capital and its vicinity. But to extend this blessing to the whole country, four powerful daimyōs as well as the militant monks had still to be dealt with. The monks had from the outset sheltered and succoured Nobunaga's enemies, and one great prelate, Kenryō, hierarch of the Monto sect, whose headquarters were at Osaka, was believed to aspire to the throne itself. In 1571 Nobunaga attacked and gave to the flames the celebrated monastery of Hiyei-zan, established nearly eight centuries previously; and in 1580 he would have similarly served the splendid temple Hongwan-ji in Osaka, had not the mikado sought and obtained grace for it. The task then remained of subduing four powerful daimyōs, three in the south and one in the north-east, who continued to follow the bent of their own warlike ambitions without paying the least attention to either sovereign or shōgun. The task was commenced by sending an army under Hideyoshi against Mōri of Chōshū, whose fief lay on the northern shore of the Shimonoseki strait. This proved to be the last enterprise planned by Nobunaga. On a morning in June 1582 one of the corps intended to reinforce Hideyoshi's army marched out of Kameyama under the command of Akechi Mitsuhide, who either harboured a personal grudge against Nobunaga or was swayed by blind ambition. Mitsuhide suddenly changed the route of his troops, led them to Kiōto, and attacked the temple Honnō-ji where Nobunaga was sojourning all unsuspicious of treachery. Rescue and resistance being alike hopeless, the great soldier committed suicide. Thirteen days later, Hideyoshi, having concluded peace with Mōri of Chōshū, fell upon Mitsuhide's forces and shattered them, Mitsuhide himself being killed by a peasant as he fled from the field.

33

Nobunaga's removal at once made Hideyoshi the most conspicuous figure in the empire, the only man with any claim to dispute that title being Tokugawa Iyeyasu. These two had hitherto worked in concert. But the question *Hideyoshi.*of the succession to Nobunaga's estates threw the country once more into tumult. He left two grown-up sons and a baby grandson, whose father, Nobunaga's first-born, had perished in the holocaust at Honnō-ji. Hideyoshi, not unmindful, it may be assumed, of the privileges of a guardian, espoused the cause of the infant, and wrested from Nobunaga's three other great captains a reluctant endorsement of his choice. Nobutaka, third son of Nobunaga, at once drew the sword, which he presently had to turn against his own person; two years later (1584), his elder brother, Nobuo, took the field under the aegis of Tokugawa Iyeyasu. Hideyoshi and Iyeyasu, now pitted against each other for the first time, were found to be of equal prowess, and being too wise to prolong a useless war, they reverted to their old alliance, subsequently confirming it by a family union, the son of Iyeyasu being adopted by Hideyoshi and the latter's daughter being given in marriage to Iyeyasu. Hideyoshi had now been invested by the mikado with the post of regent, and his position in the capital was omnipotent. He organized in Kiōto a magnificent pageant, in which the principal figures were himself, Iyeyasu, Nobuo and twenty-seven daimyōs. The emperor was present. Hideyoshi sat on the right of the throne, and all the nobles did obeisance to the sovereign. Prior to this event Hideyoshi had conducted against the still defiant daimyōs of Kiūshiū, especially Shimazu of Satsuma, the greatest army ever massed by any Japanese general, and had reduced the island of the nine provinces, not by weight of armament only, but also by a signal exercise of the wise clemency which distinguished him from all the statesmen of his era.

The whole of Japan was now under Hideyoshi's sway except the fiefs in the extreme north and those in the region known as the Kwantō, namely, the eight provinces forming the eastern elbow of the main island. Seven of these provinces were virtually under the sway of Hōjō Ujimasa, fourth representative of a family established in 1476 by a brilliant adventurer of Ise, not related in any way to the great but then extinct house of Kamakura Hōjōs. The daimyōs in the north were comparatively powerless to resist Hideyoshi, but to reach them the Kwantō had 262to be reduced, and not only was its chief, Ujimasa, a formidable foe, but also the topographical features of the district represented fortifications of immense strength. After various unsuccessful overtures, having for their purpose to induce Ujimasa to visit the capital and pay homage to the emperor, Hideyoshi marched from Kiōto in the spring of 1590 at the head of 170,000 men, his colleagues Nobuo and Iyeyasu having under their orders 80,000 more. The campaign ended as did all Hideyoshi's enterprises, except that he treated his vanquished enemies with unusual severity. During the three months spent investing Odawara, the northern daimyōs surrendered, and thus the autumn of 1590 saw Hideyoshi master of Japan from end to end, and saw Tokugawa Iyeyasu established at Yedo as recognized ruler of the eight provinces of the Kwantō. These two facts should be bracketed together, because Japan's emergence from the deep gloom of long-continued civil strife was due not more to the brilliant qualities of Hideyoshi and Iyeyasu individually than to the fortunate synchronism of their careers, so that the one was able to carry the other's work to completion and permanence. The last eight years of Hideyoshi's life—he died in 1598—were chiefly remarkable for his attempt to invade China through Korea, and for his attitude towards Christianity (see § VIII.: FOREIGN INTERCOURSE).

The Tokugawa Era.—When Hideyoshi died he left a son, Hideyori, then only six years of age, and the problem of this child's future had naturally caused supreme solicitude to the peasant statesman. He finally entrusted the care of the boy and the management of state affairs to five regents, five ministers, and three intermediary councillors. But he placed chief reliance upon Iyeyasu, whom he appointed president of the board of regents. Among the latter was one, Ishida Mitsunari, who to insatiable ambition added an extraordinary faculty for intrigue and great personal magnetism. These qualities he utilized with such success that the dissensions among the daimyōs, which had been temporarily composed by Hideyoshi, broke out again, and the year 1600 saw Japan divided into two camps, one composed of Tokugawa Iyeyasu and his allies, the other of Ishida Mitsunari and his partisans.

The situation of Iyeyasu was eminently perilous. From his position in the east of the country, he found himself menaced by two powerful enemies on the north and on the south, respectively, the former barely contained by *Iyeyasu.*a greatly weaker force of his friends, and the latter moving up in seemingly overwhelming strength from Kiōto. He decided to hurl himself upon the southern army without awaiting the result of the conflict in the north. The encounter took place at Sekigahara in the province of Mino on the 21st of October 1600. The army of Iyeyasu had to move to the attack in such a manner that its left flank and its left rear were threatened by divisions of the enemy posted on commanding eminences. But with the leaders of these divisions Iyeyasu had come to an understanding by which they could be trusted to abide so long as victory did not declare against him. Such incidents were naturally common in an era when every man fought for his own hand. The southerners suffered a crushing defeat. The survivors fled pell-mell to Osaka, where in a colossal fortress, built by Hideyoshi, his son, Hideyori, and the latter's mother, Yodo, were sheltered behind ramparts held by 80,000 men. Hideyori's cause had been openly put forward by Ishida Mitsunari and his partisans, but Iyeyasu made no immediate attempt to visit the sin upon the head of his deceased benefactor's child. On the contrary, he sent word to the lady Yodo and her little boy that he absolved them of all complicity. The battle of Sekigahara is commonly spoken of as having terminated the civil war which had devastated Japan, with brief intervals, from the latter half of the 12th century to the beginning of the 17th. That is incorrect in view of the fact that Sekigahara was followed by other fighting, especially by the terrible conflict at Osaka in 1615 when Yodo and her son perished. But Sekigahara's importance cannot be over-rated. For had Iyeyasu been finally crushed there, the wave of internecine strife must have rolled again over the empire until providence provided another Hideyoshi and another Iyeyasu to stem it. Sekigahara, therefore, may be truly described as a turning-point in Japan's career and as one of the decisive battles of the world. As for the fact that the Tokugawa leader did not at once proceed to extremities in the case of the boy Hideyori, though the events of the Sekigahara campaign had made it quite plain that such a course would ultimately be inevitable, we have to remember that only two years had elapsed since Hideyoshi was laid in his grave. His memory was still green and the glory of his achievements still enveloped his family. Iyeyasu foresaw that to carry the tragedy to its bitter end at once must have forced into Hideyori's camp many puissant daimyōs whose sense of allegiance would grow less cogent with the lapse of time. When he did lay siege to the Osaka castle in 1615, the power of the Tokugawa was well-nigh shattered against its ramparts; had not the onset been aided by treachery, the stronghold would probably have proved impregnable.

But signal as were the triumphs of the Tokugawa chieftain in the field, what distinguishes him from all his predecessors is the ability he displayed in consolidating his conquests. The immense estates that fell into his hands he parcelled out in such a manner that all important strategical positions were held by daimyōs whose fidelity could be confidently trusted, and every feudatory of doubtful loyalty found his fief within touch of a Tokugawa partisan. This arrangement, supplemented by a system which required all the great daimyōs to have mansions in the shōgun's capital. Yedo, to keep their families there always and to reside there themselves in alternate years, proved so potent a check to disaffection that from 1615, when the castle of Osaka fell, until 1864, when the Chōshū rōnin attacked Kiōto, Japan remained entirely free from civil war.

It is possible to form a clear idea of the ethical and administrative principles by which Iyeyasu and the early Tokugawa chiefs were guided in elaborating the system which gave to Japan an unprecedented era of peace and prosperity. Evidence is furnished not only by the system itself but also by the contents of a document generally called the *Testament of Iyeyasu*, though probably it was not fully compiled until the time of his grandson, Iyemitsu (1623-1650). The great Tokugawa chief, though he munificently patronized Buddhism and though he carried constantly in his bosom a miniature Buddhist image to which he ascribed all his success in the field and his safety in battle, took his ethical code from Confucius. He held that the basis of all legislation and administration should be the five relations of sovereign and subject, parent and child, husband and wife, brother and sister, friend and friend. The family was, in his eyes, the essential foundation of society, to be maintained at all sacrifices. Beyond these broad outlines of moral duty it was not deemed necessary to instruct the people. Therefore out of the hundred chapters forming the *Testament* only 22 contain what can be called legal enactments, while 55 relate to administration and politics; 16 set forth moral maxims and reflections, and the remainder record illustrative episodes in the career of the author. No distinct line is drawn between law and morals, between the duty of a citizen and the virtues of a member of a family. Substantive law is entirely wanting, just as it was wanting in the so-called constitution of Prince Shōtoku. Custom, as sanctioned by public observance, must be complied with in the civil affairs of life. What required minute exposition was criminal law, the relations of social classes, etiquette, rank, precedence, administration and government.

Society under feudalism had been moulded into three sharply defined groups, namely, first, the Throne and the court nobles (*kuge*); secondly, the military class (*buke* or *samurai*); and thirdly, the common people (*heimin*). These lines **Social distinctions in the Tokugawa Era.** of cleavage were emphasized as much as possible by the Tokugawa rulers. The divine origin of the mikado was held to separate him from contact with mundane affairs, and he was therefore strictly secluded in the palace at Kiōto, his main function being to mediate between his heavenly ancestors and his subjects, entrusting to the shōgun and the samurai the duty of transacting all worldly business on behalf 263 of the state. In obedience to this principle the mikado became a kind of sacrosanct abstraction. No one except his consorts and his chief ministers ever saw his face. In the rare cases when he gave audience to a privileged subject, he sat behind a curtain, and when he went abroad, he rode in a closely shut car drawn by oxen. A revenue of ten thousand *koku* of rice—the equivalent of about as many guineas—was apportioned for his support, and the right was reserved to him of conferring empty titles upon the living and rank upon the dead. His majesty had one wife, the empress (*kōgō*), necessarily taken from one of the five chosen families (*go-sekke*) of the Fujiwara, but he might also have twelve consorts, and if direct issue failed, the succession passed to one of the two princely families of Arisugawa and Fushimi, adoption, however, being possible in the last resort. The *kuge* constituted the court nobility, consisting of 155 families all of whom traced their lineage to ancient mikados; they ranked far above the feudal chiefs, not excepting even the shōgun; filled by right of heredity nearly all the offices at the court, the emoluments attached being, however, a mere pittance; were entirely without the great estates which had belonged to them in ante-feudal times, and lived lives of proud poverty, occupying themselves with the study of literature and the practice of music and art. After the kuge and at a long distance below them in theoretical rank came the military families, who, as a class, were called *buke* or *samurai*. They had hereditary revenues, and they filled the administrative posts, these, too, being often hereditary. The third, and by far the most numerous, section of the nation were the commoners (*heimin*). They had no social status; were not allowed to carry swords, and possessed no income except what they could earn with their hands. About 55 in every 1000 units of the nation were samurai, the latter's wives and children being included in this estimate.

Under the Hōjō and the Ashikaga shōguns the holders of the great estates changed frequently according to the vicissitudes of those troublesome times, but under the Tokugawa no change took place, and there thus **Daimyōs.** grew up a landed nobility of the most permanent character. Every one of these estates was a feudal kingdom, large or small, with its own usages and its own laws, based on the general principles above indicated and liable to be judged according to those principles by the shōgun's government (*baku-fu*) in Yedo. A daimyō or feudal chief drew from the peasants on his estate the means of subsistence for himself and his retainers. For this purpose the produce of his estate was assessed by the shōgun's officials in *koku* (one *koku* = 180.39 litres, worth about £1), and about one-half of the assessed amount went to the feudatory, the other half to the tillers of the soil. The richest daimyō was Mayeda of Kaga, whose fief was assessed at a little over a million *koku*, his revenue thus being about half a million sterling. Just as an empress had to be taken from one of five families designated to that distinction for all time, so a successor to the shōgunate, failing direct heir, had to be selected from three families (*sanke*), namely, those of the daimyōs of Owari, Kii and Mito, whose first representatives were three sons of Iyeyasu. Out of the total body of 255 daimyōs existing in the year 1862, 141 were specially distinguished as *fudai*, or hereditary vassals of the Tokugawa house, and to 18 of these was strictly limited the perpetual privilege of filling all the high offices in the Yedo administration, while to 4 of them was reserved the special honour of supplying a regent (*go-tairō*) during the minority of the shōgun. Moreover, a *fudai* daimyō was of necessity appointed to the command of the fortress of Nijō in Kiōto as well as of the great castles of Osaka and Fushimi, which Iyeyasu designated the keys of the country. No intermarriage might take place between members of the court nobility and the feudal houses without the consent of Yedo; no daimyō might apply direct to the emperor for an official title, or might put foot within the imperial district of Kiōto without the shōgun's permit, and at all entrances to the region known as the Kwantō there were established guardhouses, where every one, of whatever rank, must submit to be examined, in order to prevent the wives and children of the daimyōs from secretly leaving Yedo for their own provinces. In their journeys to and from Yedo every second year the feudal chiefs had to travel by one of two great highways, the Tōkaidō or the Nakasendō, and as they moved with great retinues, these roads were provided with a number of inns and tea-houses equipped in a sumptuous manner, and having an abundance of female servants. A puissant daimyō's procession often numbered as many as 1000 retainers, and nothing illustrates more forcibly the wide interval that separated the soldier and the plebeian than the fact that at the appearance of the heralds who preceded these progresses all commoners who happened to be abroad had to kneel on the ground with bowed and uncovered heads; all wayside houses had to close the shutters of windows giving on the road, and none might venture to look down from a height on the passing magnate. Any violation of these rules of etiquette exposed the violator to instant death at the hands of the daimyō's retinue. Moreover, the samurai and the heimin lived strictly apart. A feudal chief had a castle which generally occupied a commanding position. It was surrounded by from one to three broad moats, the innermost crowned with a high wall of huge cut stones, its trace arranged so as to give flank defence, which was further provided by pagoda-like towers placed at the salient angles. Inside this wall stood the houses of the high officials on the outskirts of a park surrounding the residence of the daimyō himself, and from the scarps of the moats or in the intervals between them rose houses for the military retainers, barrack-like structures, provided, whenever possible, with small but artistically arranged and carefully tended gardens. All this domain of the military was called *yashiki* in distinction to the *machi* (streets) where the despised commoners had their habitat.

The general body of the samurai received stipends and lived frugally. Their pay was not reckoned in money: it took the form of so many rations of rice delivered from their chief's granaries. A few had landed estates, *Samurai.* usually bestowed in recognition of conspicuous merit. They were probably the finest type of hereditary soldiers the world ever produced. Money and all devices for earning it they profoundly despised. The right of wearing a sword was to them the highest conceivable privilege. They counted themselves the guardians of their fiefs' honour and of their country's welfare. At any moment they were prepared cheerfully to sacrifice their lives on the altar of loyalty. Their word, once given, must never be violated. The slightest insult to their honour might not be condoned. Stoicism was a quality which they esteemed next to courage: all outward display of emotion must be suppressed. The sword might never be drawn for a petty cause, but, if once drawn, must never be returned to its scabbard until it had done its duty. Martial exercises occupied much of their attention, but book learning also they esteemed highly. They were profoundly courteous towards each other, profoundly contemptuous towards the commoner, whatever his wealth. Filial piety ranked next to loyalty in their code of ethics. Thus the Confucian maxim, endorsed explicitly in the *Testament of Iyeyasu*, that a man must not live under the same sky with his father's murderer or his brother's slayer, received most literal obedience, and many instances occurred of vendettas pursued in the face of apparently insuperable difficulties and consummated after years of effort. By the standard of modern morality the Japanese samurai would be counted cruel. Holding that death was the natural sequel of defeat and the only certain way of avoiding disgrace, he did not seek quarter himself or think of extending it to an enemy. Yet in his treatment of the latter he loved to display courtesy until the supreme moment when all considerations of mercy were laid aside. It cannot be doubted that the practice of employing torture judicially tended to educate a mood of callousness towards suffering, or that the many idle hours of a military man's life in time of peace encouraged a measure of dissipation. But there does not seem to be any valid ground for concluding that either of these defects was conspicuous in the character of the Japanese samurai. Faithlessness towards women was the greatest fault that can be laid to his door. The 264 samurai lady claimed no privilege of timidity on account of her sex. She knew how to die in the cause of honour just as readily as her husband, her father or her brother died, and conjugal fidelity did not rank as a virtue in her eyes, being regarded as a simple duty. But her husband held marital faith in small esteem and ranked his wife far below his sword. It has to be remembered that when we speak of a samurai's suicide, there is no question of poison, the bullet, drowning or any comparatively painless manner of exit from the world. The invariable method was to cut open the abdomen (*hara-kiri* or *seppuku*) and afterwards, if strength remained, the sword was turned against the throat. To such endurance had the samurai trained himself that he went through this cruel ordeal without flinching in the smallest degree.

The heimin or commoners were divided into three classes—husbandmen, artisans and traders. The farmer, as the nation lived by his labour, was counted the most respectable among the bread-winners, and a cultivator *Heimin.* of his own estate might even carry one sword but never two, that privilege being strictly reserved to a samurai. The artisan, too, received much consideration, as is easily understood when we remember that included in his ranks were artists, sword-smiths, armourers, sculptors of sacred images or sword-furniture, ceramists and lacquerers. Many artisans were in the permanent service of feudal chiefs from whom they received fixed salaries. Tradesmen, however, were regarded with disdain and stood lowest of all in the social organization. Too much despised to be even included in that organization were the *eta* (defiled folks) and the *hinin* (outcasts). The exact origin of these latter pariahs is uncertain, but the ancestors of the eta would seem to have been prisoners of war or the enslaved families of criminals. To such people were assigned the defiling duties of tending tombs, disposing of the bodies of the dead, slaughtering animals or tanning hides. The hinin were mendicants. On them devolved the task of removing and burying the corpses of executed criminals. Living in segregated hamlets, forbidden to marry with heimin, still less with samurai, not allowed to eat, drink or associate with persons above their own class, the eta remained under the ban of ostracism from generation to generation, though many of them contrived to amass much wealth. They were governed by their own headmen, and they had three chiefs, one residing in each of the cities of Yedo, Osaka and Kiōto. All these members of the submerged classes were relieved from proscription and admitted to the ranks of the commoners under the enlightened system of Meiji. The 12th of October 1871 saw their enfranchisement, and at that date the census showed 287,111 eta and 695,689 hinin.

Naturally, as the unbroken peace of the Tokugawa régime became habitual, the mood of the nation underwent a change. The samurai, no longer required to lead the frugal life of camp or barracks, began to live beyond their *Decline and Fall of the Shōgunate.* incomes. "They found difficulty in meeting the pecuniary engagements of everyday existence, so that money acquired new importance in their eyes, and they gradually forfeited the respect which their traditional disinterestedness had won for them in the past." At the same time the abuses of feudalism were thrown into increased salience. A large body of hereditary soldiers become an anomaly when fighting has passed even out of memory. On the other hand, the agricultural and commercial classes acquired new importance. The enormous sums disbursed every year in Yedo, for the maintenance of the great establishments which the feudal chiefs vied with each other in keeping there, enriched the merchants and traders so greatly that their scale of living underwent radical change. Buddhism was a potent influence, but its ethical restraints were weakened by the conduct of its priests, who themselves often yielded to the temptation of the time. The aristocracy adhered to its refined pastimes—performances of the *No*; tea reunions; poem composing; polo; football; equestrian archery; fencing and gambling—but the commoner, being excluded from all this realm and, at the same time, emerging rapidly from his old position of penury and degradation, began to develop luxurious proclivities and to demand corresponding amusements. Thus the theatre came into existence; the dancing girl and the jester found lucrative employment; a popular school of art was founded and quickly carried to perfection; the *lupanar* assumed unprecedented dimensions; rich and costly costumes acquired wide vogue in despite of sumptuary laws enacted from time to time; wrestling became an important institution, and plutocracy asserted itself in the face of caste distinctions.

Simultaneously with the change of social conditions thus taking place, history repeated itself at the shōgun's court. The substance of administrative power passed into the hands of a minister, its shadow alone remaining to the shōgun. During only two generations were the successors of Iyeyasu able to resist this traditional tendency. The representative of the third—Iyetsuna (1661-1680)—succumbed to the machinations of an ambitious minister, Sakai Takakiyo, and it may be said that from that time the nominal repository of administrative authority in Yedo was generally a species of magnificent recluse, secluded from contact with the outer world and seeing and hearing only through the eyes and ears of the ladies of his household. In this respect the descendants of the great Tokugawa statesman found themselves reduced to a position precisely analogous to that of the emperor in Kiōto. Sovereign and shōgun were alike mere abstractions so far as the practical work of government was concerned. With the great mass of the feudal chiefs things fared similarly. These men who, in the days of Nobunaga, Hideyoshi and Iyeyasu, had directed the policies of their fiefs and led their armies in the field, were gradually transformed, during the long peace of the Tokugawa era, into voluptuous *fainéants* or, at best, thoughtless dilettanti, willing to abandon the direction of their affairs to seneschals and mayors, who, while on the whole their administration was able and loyal, found their account in contriving and perpetuating the effacement of their chiefs. Thus, in effect, the government of the country, taken out of the hands of the shōgun and the feudatories, fell into those of their vassals. There were exceptions, of course, but so rare as to be merely accidental.

Another important factor has to be noted. It has been shown above that Iyeyasu bestowed upon his three sons the rich fiefs of Owari, Kii (Kishū) and Mito, and that these three families exclusively enjoyed the privilege of furnishing an heir to the shōgun should the latter be without direct issue. Mito ought therefore to have been a most unlikely place for the conception and propagation of principles subversive of the shōgun's administrative autocracy. Nevertheless, in the days of the second of the Mito chiefs at the close of the 17th century, there arose in that province a school of thinkers who, revolting against the ascendancy of Chinese literature and of Buddhism, devoted themselves to compiling a history such as should recall the attention of the nation to its own annals and revive its allegiance to Shintō. It would seem that in patronizing the compilation of this great work the Mito chief was swayed by the spirit of pure patriotism and studentship, and that he discerned nothing of the goal to which the new researches must lead the litterati of his fief. "He and they, for the sake of history and without any thought of politics, undertook a retrospect of their country's annals, and their frank analysis furnished conclusive proof that the emperor was the prime source of administrative authority and that its independent exercise by a shōgun must be regarded as a usurpation. They did not attempt to give practical effect to their discoveries; the era was essentially academical. But this galaxy of scholars projected into the future a light which burned with growing force in each succeeding generation and ultimately burst into a flame which consumed feudalism and the shōgunate," fused the nation into one, and restored the governing authority to the emperor. Of course the Mito men were not alone in this matter: many students subsequently trod in their footsteps and many others sought to stem the tendency; but the net result was fatal to faith in the dual system of government. Possibly had nothing occurred to furnish signal proof of the system's practical defects, it might have long survived this theoretical disapproval. But the crisis caused by the advent of foreign ships and by the forceful renewal of foreign intercourse in the 19th century afforded convincing evidence of the shōgunate's incapacity to protect the state's supposed interests and to enforce the traditional policy of isolation which the nation had learned to consider essential to the empire's integrity.

Another important factor made for the fall of the shōgunate. That factor was the traditional disaffection of the two great southern fiefs, Satsuma and Chōshū. When Iyeyasu parcelled out the empire, he deemed it the wisest policy to leave these chieftains in full possession of their large estates. But this measure, construed as an evidence of weakness rather than a token of liberality, neither won the allegiance of the big feudatories nor cooled their ambition. Thus no sooner did the nation divide into two camps over the question of renewed foreign intercourse than men of the above clans, in concert with representatives of certain of the old court nobles, placed themselves at the head of a movement animated by two loudly proclaimed purposes: restoration of the administration to the emperor, and expulsion of aliens. This latter aspiration underwent a radical change when the bombardment of the Satsuma capital, Kagoshima, and the destruction of the Chōshū forts and ships at Shimonoseki proved conclusively to the Satsuma and Chōshū clans that Japan in her unequipped and backward condition could not hope to stand for a moment against the Occident in arms. But the unwelcome discovery was accompanied by a conviction that only a thoroughly united nation might aspire to preserve its independence, and thus the abolition of the dual form of government became more than ever an article of public faith. It is unnecessary to recount the successive incidents which conspired to undermine the shōgun's authority, and to destroy the prestige of the Yedo administration. Both had been reduced to vanishing quantities by the year 1866 when Keiki succeeded to the shōgunate.

Keiki, known historically as Yoshinobu, the last of the shōguns, was a man of matured intellect and high capacities. He had been put forward by the anti-foreign Conservatives for the succession to the shōgunate in 1857 when the complications of foreign intercourse were in their first stage of acuteness. But, like many other intelligent Japanese, he had learned, in the interval between 1857 and 1866, that to keep her doors closed was an impossible task for Japan, and very quickly after taking the reins of office he recognized that national union could never be achieved while power was divided between Kiōto and Yedo. At this juncture there was addressed to him by Yōdō, chief of the great Tosa fief, a memorial setting forth the hopelessness of the position in which the Yedo court now found itself, and urging that, in the interests of good government and in order that the nation's united strength might be available to meet the exigencies of its new career, the administration should be restored to the emperor. Keiki received this memorial in Kiōto. He immediately summoned a council of all the feudatories and high officials then in the Imperial city, announced to them his intention to lay down his office, and, the next day, presented his resignation to the sovereign. This happened on the 14th of October 1867. It must be ranked among the signal events of the world's history, for it signified the voluntary surrender of kingly authority wielded uninterruptedly for nearly three centuries. That the shōgun's resignation was tendered in good faith there can be no doubt, and had it been accepted in the same spirit, the great danger it involved might have been consummated without bloodshed or disorder. But the clansmen of Satsuma and Chōshū were distrustful. One of the shōgun's first acts after assuming office had been to obtain from the throne an edict for imposing penalties on Chōshū, and there was a precedent for suspecting that the renunciation of power by the shōgun might merely prelude its resumption on a firmer basis. Therefore steps were taken to induce the emperor, then a youth of fifteen, to issue a secret rescript to Satsuma and Chōshū, denouncing the shōgun as the nation's enemy and enjoining his destruction. At the same time all officials connected with the Tokugawa or suspected of sympathy with them were expelled from office in Kiōto, and the shōgun's troops were deprived of the custody of the palace gates by methods which verged upon the use of armed force. In the face of such provocation Keiki's earnest efforts to restrain the indignation of his vassals and adherents failed. They marched against Kiōto and were defeated, whereupon Keiki left his castle at Osaka and retired to Yedo, where he subsequently made unconditional surrender to the Imperial army. There is little more to be set down on this page of the history. The Yedo court consented to lay aside its dignities and be stripped of its administrative authority, but all the Tokugawa vassals and adherents did not prove equally placable. There was resistance in the northern provinces, where the Aizu feudatory

39

refused to abandon the Tokugawa cause; there was an attempt to set up a rival candidate for the throne in the person of an Imperial prince who presided over the Uyeno Monastery in Yedo; and there was a wild essay on the part of the admiral of the shōgun's fleet to establish a republic in the island of Yezo. But these were mere ripples on the surface of the broad stream which set towards the peaceful overthrow of the dual system of government and ultimately towards the fall of feudalism itself. That this system, the outcome of five centuries of nearly continuous warfare, was swept away in almost as many weeks with little loss of life or destruction of property constitutes, perhaps, the most striking incident, certainly the most momentous, in the history of the Japanese nation.

The Meiji Era.—It must be remembered that when reference is made to the Japanese nation in connexion with these radical changes, only the nobles and the samurai are indicated—in other words, a section of the population representing about one-sixteenth of the whole. The bulk of the people—the agricultural, the industrial and the mercantile classes—remained outside the sphere of politics, not sharing the anti-foreign prejudice, or taking any serious interest in the great questions of the time. Foreigners often noted with surprise the contrast between the fierce antipathy displayed towards them by certain samurai on the one hand, and the genial, hospitable reception given to them by the common people on the other. History teaches that the latter was the natural disposition of the Japanese, the former a mood educated by special experiences. Further, even the comparatively narrow statement that the restoration of the administrative power to the emperor was the work of the nobles and the samurai must be taken with limitations. A majority of the nobles entertained no idea of any necessity for change. They were either held fast in the vice of Tokugawa authority, or paralyzed by the sensuous seductions of the lives provided for them by the machinations of their retainers, who transferred the administrative authority of the fiefs to their own hands, leaving its shadow only to their lords. It was among the retainers that longings for a new order of things were generated. Some of these men were sincere disciples of progress—a small band of students and deep thinkers who, looking through the narrow Dutch window at Deshima, had caught a glimmering perception of the realities that lay beyond the horizon of their country's prejudices. But the influence of such Liberals was comparatively insignificant. Though they showed remarkable moral courage and tenacity of purpose, the age did not furnish any strong object lesson to enforce their propaganda of progress. The factors chiefly making for change were, first, the ambition of the southern clans to oust the Tokugawa, and, secondly, the samurai's loyal instinct, reinforced by the teachings of his country's history, by the revival of the Shintō cult, by the promptings of national enterprise, and by the object-lessons of foreign intercourse.

But though essentially imperialistic in its prime purposes, the revolution which involved the fall of the shōgunate, and ultimately of feudalism, may be called democratic with regard to the personnel of those who planned and *Character of the Revolution.* directed it. They were, for the most part, men without either official rank or social standing. That is a point essential 266to a clear understanding of the issue. Fifty-five individuals may be said to have planned and carried out the overthrow of the Yedo administration, and only five of them were territorial nobles. Eight, belonging to the court nobility, laboured under the traditional disadvantages of their class, poverty and political insignificance; and the remaining forty-two, the hearts and hands of the movement, may be described as ambitious youths, who sought to make a career for themselves in the first place, and for their country in the second. The average age of the whole did not exceed thirty. There was another element for which any student of Japanese history might have been prepared: the Satsuma samurai aimed originally not merely at overthrowing the Tokugawa but also at obtaining the shōgunate for their own chief. Possibly it would be unjust to say that all the leaders of the great southern clan harboured that idea. But some of them certainly did, and not until they had consented to abandon the project did their union with Chōshū, the other great southern clan, become possible—a union without which the revolution could scarcely have been accomplished. This ambition of the Satsuma clansmen deserves special mention, because it bore remarkable fruit; it may be said to have laid the foundation of constitutional government in Japan. For, in consequence of the distrust engendered by such aspirations, the authors of the Restoration agreed that when the emperor assumed the reins of power, he should solemnly pledge himself to convene a deliberative assembly, to appoint to administrative posts men of intellect and erudition wherever they might be found, and to decide all measures in accordance with public opinion. This promise, referred to frequently in later times as the Imperial oath at the Restoration, came to be accounted the basis of representative institutions, though in reality it was intended solely as a guarantee against the political ascendancy of any one clan.

At the outset the necessity of abolishing feudalism did not present itself clearly to the leaders of the revolution. Their sole idea was the unification of the nation. But when they came to consider closely the practical *The Anti-feudal Idea.* side of the problem, they understood how

40

far it would lead them. Evidently that one homogeneous system of law should replace the more or less heterogeneous systems operative in the various fiefs was essential, and such a substitution meant that the feudatories must be deprived of their local autonomy and, incidentally, of their control of local finances. That was a stupendous change. Hitherto each feudal chief had collected the revenues of his fief and had employed them at will, subject to the sole condition of maintaining a body of troops proportionate to his income. He had been, and was still, an autocrat within the limits of his territory. On the other hand, the active authors of the revolution were a small band of men mainly without prestige or territorial influence. It was impossible that they should dictate any measure sensibly impairing the local and fiscal autonomy of the feudatories. No power capable of enforcing such a measure existed at the time. All the great political changes in Japan had formerly been preceded by wars culminating in the accession of some strong clan to supreme authority, whereas in this case there had been a displacement without a substitution— the Tokugawa had been overthrown and no new administrators had been set up in their stead. It was, moreover, certain that an attempt on the part of any one clan to constitute itself executor of the sovereign's mandates would have stirred the other clans to vehement resistance. In short, the leaders of the revolution found themselves pledged to a new theory of government without any machinery for carrying it into effect, or any means of abolishing the old practice. An ingenious exit from this curious dilemma was devised by the young reformers. They induced the feudal chiefs of Satsuma, Chōshū, Tosa and Hizen, the four most powerful clans in the south, publicly to surrender their fiefs to the emperor, praying his majesty to reorganize them and to bring them all under the same system of law. In the case of Shimazu, chief of Satsuma, and Yōdō, chief of Tosa, this act must stand to their credit as a noble sacrifice. To them the exercise of power had been a reality and the effort of surrendering it must have been correspondingly costly. But the chiefs of Chōshū and Hizen obeyed the suggestions of their principal vassals with little, if any, sense of the probable cost of obedience. The same remark applies to all the other feudatories, with exceptions so rare as to emphasize the rule. They had long been accustomed to abandon the management of their affairs to their leading clansmen, and they allowed themselves to follow the same guidance at this crisis. Out of more than 250 feudatories, only 17 hesitated to imitate the example of the four southern fiefs.

An explanation of this remarkable incident has been sought by supposing that the samurai of the various clans, when they advised a course so inconsistent with fidelity to the interests of their feudal chiefs, were influenced *Motives of the Reformers.* by motives of personal ambition, imagining that they themselves might find great opportunities under the new régime. Some hope of that kind may fairly be assumed, and was certainly realized, in the case of the leading samurai of the four southern clans which headed the movement. But it is plain that no such expectations can have been generally entertained. The simplest explanation seems to be the true one: a certain course, indicated by the action of the four southern clans, was conceived to be in accord with the spirit of the Restoration, and not to adopt it would have been to shrink publicly from a sacrifice dictated by the principle of loyalty to the Throne—a principle which had acquired supreme sanctity in the eyes of the men of that era. There might have been some uncertainty about the initial step; but so soon as that was taken by the southern clans their example acquired compelling force. History shows that in political crises the Japanese samurai is generally ready to pay deference to certain canons of almost romantic morality. There was a fever of loyalty and of patriotism in the air of the year 1869. Any one hesitating, for obviously selfish reasons, to adopt a precedent such as that offered by the procedure of the great southern clans, would have seemed to forfeit the right of calling himself a samurai. But although the leaders of this remarkable movement now understood that they must contrive the total abolition of feudalism and build up a new administrative edifice on foundations of constitutional monarchy, they appreciated the necessity of advancing slowly towards a goal which still lay beyond the range of their followers' vision. Thus the first steps taken after the surrender of the fiefs were to appoint the feudatories to the position of governors in the districts over which they had previously ruled; to confirm the samurai in the possession of their incomes and official positions; to put an end to the distinction between court nobles and territorial nobles, and to organize in Kiōto a cabinet consisting of the leaders of the restoration. Each new governor received one-tenth of the income of the fief by way of emoluments; the pay of the officials and the samurai, as well as the administrative expenses of the district, was defrayed from the same source, and the residue, if any, was to pass into the treasury of the central government.

The defects of this system from a monarchical point of view soon became evident. It did not give the power of either the purse or the sword to the sovereign. The revenues of the administrative districts continued *Defects of the First Measures.* to be collected and disbursed by the former feudatories, who also retained the control of the troops, the right of appointing and dismissing officials, and almost complete local autonomy. A further radical step had to be taken, and the leaders of reform, seeing nothing better than to continue the method of procedure which had thus far proved so successful, contrived, first, that several of the administrative districts should send in petitions offering to surrender their local autonomy and be brought under the direct rule of the central government; secondly, that a number of samurai should apply for permission to lay aside their swords. While the nation was digesting the principles embodied in these petitions, the government made preparations for further measures of reform. The ex-chief of Satsuma, who showed some umbrage because the services of his clan in promoting the restoration had not been more fully recognized, was induced to take high ministerial office, as were also the ex-chiefs of Chōshū and Tosa. Each of the four 267 great clans had now three representatives in the ministry. These clans were further persuaded to send to Tōkyō—whither the emperor had moved his court—contingents of troops to form the nucleus of a national army. Importance attaches to these details because the principle of clan representation, illustrated in the organization of the cabinet of 1871, continued to be approximately observed for many years in forming ministries, and ultimately became a target for the attacks of party politicians.

On the 29th of August 1871 an Imperial decree announced the abolition of the system of local autonomy, and the removal of the territorial nobles from the posts of governor. The taxes of the former fiefs were to be paid thenceforth *Adoption of Radical Measures.* into the central treasury; all officials were to be appointed by the Imperial government, and the feudatories, retaining permanently an income of one-tenth of their original revenues, were to make Tōkyō their place of residence. As for the samurai, they remained for the moment in possession of their hereditary pensions. Radical as these changes seem, the disturbance caused by them was not great, since they left the incomes of the military class untouched. Some of the incomes were for life only, but the majority were hereditary, and all had been granted in consideration of their holders devoting themselves to military service. Four hundred thousand men approximately were in receipt of such emoluments, and the total amount annually taken from the tax-payers for this purpose was about £2,000,000. Plainly the nation would have to be relieved of this burden sooner or later. The samurai were essentially an element of the feudal system, and that they should survive the latter's fall would have been incongruous. On the other hand, suddenly and wholly to deprive these men and their families—a total of some two million persons—of the means of subsistence on which they had hitherto relied with absolute confidence, and in return for which they and their forefathers had rendered faithful service, would have been an act of inhumanity. It may easily be conceived that this problem caused extreme perplexity to the administrators of the new Japan. They left it unsolved for the moment, trusting that time and the loyalty of the samurai themselves would suggest some solution. As for the feudal chiefs, who had now been deprived of all official status and reduced to the position of private gentlemen, without even a patent of nobility to distinguish them from ordinary individuals, they did not find anything specially irksome or regrettable in their altered position. No scrutiny had been made into the contents of their treasuries. They were allowed to retain unquestioned possession of all the accumulated funds of their former fiefs, and they also became public creditors for annual allowances equal to one-tenth of their feudal revenues. They had never previously been so pleasantly circumstanced. It is true that they were entirely stripped of all administrative and military authority; but since their possession of such authority had been in most cases merely nominal, they only felt the change as a relief from responsibility.

By degrees public opinion began to declare itself with regard to the samurai. If they were to be absorbed into the bulk of the people and to lose their fixed revenues, some capital must be placed at their disposal to begin *Treatment of the Samurai.* the world again. The samurai themselves showed a noble faculty of resignation. They had been a privileged class, but they had purchased their privileges with their blood and by serving as patterns of all the qualities most prized among Japanese national characteristics. The record of their acts and the recognition of the people entitled them to look for munificent treatment at the hands of the government which they had been the means of setting up. Yet none of these considerations blinded them to the painful fact that the time had passed them by; that no place existed for them in the new polity. Many of them voluntarily stepped down into the company of the peasant or the tradesman, and many others signified their willingness to join the ranks of common bread-winners if some aid was given to equip them for such a career. After two years' consideration the government took action. A decree announced, in 1873, that the treasury was prepared to commute the pensions of the samurai at the rate of six years' purchase for hereditary pensions and four years for life pensions—one-half of the commutation to be paid in cash, and one-half in bonds bearing interest at the rate of 8%. It will be seen that a perpetual pension of £10 would be exchanged for a payment of £30 in cash, together with securities giving an income of £2, 8s.; and that a £10 life pensioner received £20 in cash and securities yielding £1, 12s. annually. It is scarcely credible that the samurai should have accepted such an arrangement. Something, perhaps, must be ascribed to their want of business knowledge, but the general explanation is that they made a large sacrifice in the interests of their country. Nothing in all their career as soldiers became them better than their manner of abandoning it. They were told that they might lay aside their swords, and many of them did so, though from time immemorial they had cherished the sword as the mark of a gentleman, the most precious possession of a warrior, and the one outward evidence that distinguished men of their order from common toilers after gain. They saw themselves deprived of their military employment, were invited to surrender more than one-half of the income it brought, and knew that they were unprepared alike by education and by tradition to earn bread in any calling save that of arms. Yet, at the invitation of a government which they had helped to establish, many of them bowed their heads quietly to this sharp reverse of fortune. It was certainly a striking instance of the fortitude and resignation which the creed of the samurai required him to display in the presence of adversity. As yet, however, the government's measures with regard to the samurai were not compulsory. Men laid aside their swords and commuted their pensions at their own option.

Meanwhile differences of opinion began to occur among the leaders of progress themselves. Coalitions formed for destructive purposes are often found unable to endure the strain of constructive efforts. Such lack of cohesion *Saigō Takamori.* might easily have been foreseen in the case of the Japanese reformers. Young men without experience of public affairs, or special education to fit them for responsible posts, found the duty suddenly imposed on them not only of devising administrative and fiscal systems universally applicable to a nation hitherto divided into a congeries of semi-independent principalities, but also of shaping the country's demeanour towards novel problems of foreign intercourse and alien civilization. So long as the heat of their assault upon the shōgunate fused them into a homogeneous party they worked together successfully. But when they had to build a brand-new edifice on the ruins of a still vivid past, it was inevitable that their opinions should vary as to the nature of the materials to be employed. In this divergence of views many of the capital incidents of Japan's modern history had their origin. Of the fifty-five men whose united efforts had compassed the fall of the shōgunate, five stood conspicuous above their colleagues. They were Iwakura and Sanjō, court nobles; Saigō and Okubo, samurai of Satsuma, and Kido, a samurai of Chōshū. In the second rank came many men of great gifts, whose youth alone disqualified them for prominence—Itō, the constructive statesman of the Meiji era, who inspired nearly all the important measures of the time, though he did not openly figure as their originator; Inouye, who never lacked a resource or swerved from the dictates of loyalty; Okuma, a politician of subtle, versatile and vigorous intellect; Itagaki, the Rousseau of his era; and a score of others created by the extraordinary circumstances with which they had to deal. But the five first mentioned were the captains, the rest only lieutenants. Among the five, four were sincere reformers—not free, of course, from selfish motives, but truthfully bent upon promoting the interests of their country before all other aims. The fifth, Saigō Takamori, was a man in whom boundless ambition lay concealed under qualities of the noblest and most enduring type. His absolute freedom from every trace of sordidness gave currency to a belief that his aims were of the simplest; the story of his career satisfied the highest canons of the samurai; his massive physique, commanding presence and sunny aspect impressed and attracted even those who had no opportunity of admiring his life of self-sacrificing effort or appreciating the remarkable military talent he possessed. In the first part of his career, the elevation of his clan to supreme power seems to have been his sole motive, but subsequently personal ambition appears to have swayed him. To the consummation of either object the preservation of the military class was essential. By the swords of the samurai alone could a new *imperium in imperio* be carved out. On the other hand, Saigō's colleagues in the ministry saw clearly not only that the samurai were an unwarrantable burden on the nation, but also that their continued existence after the fall of feudalism would be a menace to public peace as well as an anomaly. Therefore they took the steps already described, and followed them by a conscription law, making every adult male liable for military service without regard to his social standing. It is easy to conceive how painfully unwelcome this conscription law proved to the samurai. Many of them were not unwilling to commute their pensions, since their creed had always forbidden them to care for money. Many of them were not unwilling to abandon the habit of carrying swords, since the adoption of foreign costume rendered such a custom incongruous and inconvenient. But very few of them could readily consent to step down from their cherished position as the military class, and relinquish their traditional title to bear the whole responsibility and enjoy the whole honour of fighting their country's battles. They had supposed, not unreasonably, that service in the army and navy would be reserved exclusively for them and their sons, whereas now the commonest rustic, mechanic or tradesman would be equally eligible.

While the pain of this blow was still fresh there occurred a trouble with Korea. The little state had behaved with insulting contumely, and when Japan's course came to be debated in Tōkyō, a disruption resulted in the *Split among the Reformers.* ranks of the reformers. Saigō saw in a foreign war the sole remaining chance of achieving his ambition by lawful means. The government's conscription scheme, yet in its infancy, had not produced even the skeleton of an army. If Korea had to be conquered, the samurai must be employed; and their employment would mean, if not their rehabilitation, at least their organization into a force which, under Saigō's leadership, might dictate a new policy. Other members of the cabinet believed that the nation would be disgraced if it tamely endured Korea's insults. Thus several influential voices swelled the clamour for war. But a peace party offered strenuous opposition. Its members saw the collateral issues of the problem, and declared that the country must not think of taking up arms during a period of radical transition. The final discussion took place in the emperor's presence. The advocates of peace understood the national significance of the issue and perceived that they were debating, not merely whether there should be peace or war, but whether the country should halt or advance on its newly adopted path of progress. They prevailed, and four members of the cabinet, including Saigō, resigned. This rupture was destined to have far-reaching consequences. One of the seceders immediately raised the standard of revolt. Among the devices employed by him to win adherents was an attempt to fan into flame the dying embers of the anti-foreign sentiment. The government easily crushed the insurrection. Another seceder was Itagaki Taisuke. The third and most prominent was Saigō, who seems to have concluded from that moment that he must abandon his aims or achieve them by force. He retired to his native province of Satsuma, and applied his whole resources, his great reputation and the devoted loyalty of a number of able followers to organizing and equipping a strong body of samurai. Matters were facilitated for him by the conservatism of the celebrated Shimazu Saburō, former chief of Satsuma, who, though not opposed to foreign intercourse, had been revolted by the wholesale iconoclasm of the time, and by the indiscriminate rejection of Japanese customs in favour of foreign. He protested vehemently against what seemed to him a slavish abandonment of the nation's individuality, and finding his protest fruitless, he set himself to preserve in his own distant province, where the writ of the Yedo government had never run, the fashions, institutions and customs which his former colleagues in the administration were ruthlessly rejecting. Satsuma thus became a centre of conservative influences, among which Saigō and his constantly augmenting band of samurai found a congenial environment. During four years this breach between the central government and the southern clan grew constantly.

In the meanwhile (1876) two extreme measures were adopted by the government: a veto on the wearing of swords, and an edict ordering the compulsory commutation of the pensions and allowances received by the nobles and *Final Abolition of Sword-wearing and Pensions.* the samurai. Three years previously the discarding of swords had been declared optional, and a scheme of voluntary commutation had been announced. Many had bowed quietly to the spirit of these enactments. But many still retained their swords and drew their pensions as of old, obstructing, in the former respect, the government's projects for the reorganization of society, and imposing, in the latter, an intolerable burden on the resources of the treasury. The government thought that the time had come, and that its own strength sufficed, to substitute compulsion for persuasion. The financial measure—which was contrived so as to affect the smallest pension-holders least injuriously—evoked no complaint. The samurai remained faithful to the creed which forbade them to be concerned about money. But the veto against sword-wearing overtaxed the patience of the extreme Conservatives. It seemed to them that all the most honoured traditions of their country were being ruthlessly sacrificed on the altar of alien innovations. Armed protests ensued. A few score of samurai, equipping themselves with the hauberks and weapons of old times, fell upon the garrison of a castle, killed or wounded some 300, and then, retiring to an adjacent mountain, died by their own hands. Their example found imitators in two other places, and finally the Satsuma samurai rose in arms under Saigō.

This was an insurrection very different in dimensions and motives from the outbreaks that had preceded it. During four years the preparations of the Satsuma men had been unremitting. They were equipped with rifles and *Satsuma Insurrection.* cannon; they numbered some 30,000; they were all of the military class, and in addition to high training in western tactics and in the use of modern arms of precision, they knew how to wield that formidable weapon, the Japanese sword, of which their opponents were for the most part ignorant. Ostensibly their object was to restore the samurai to their old supremacy, and to secure for them all the posts in the army, the navy and the administration. But although they doubtless entertained that intention, it was put forward mainly with the hope of winning the co-operation of the military class throughout the empire. The real purpose of the revolt was to secure the governing power for Satsuma. A bitter struggle ensued. Beginning on the 29th of January 1877, it was brought to a close on the 24th of September by the death, voluntary or in battle, of all the rebel leaders. During that period the number of men engaged on the government's side had been 66,000 and the number on the side of the rebels 40,000, out of which total the killed and wounded aggregated 35,000, or 33% of the whole. Had the government's troops been finally defeated, there can be no doubt that the samurai's exclusive title to man and direct the army and navy would have been re-established, and Japan would have found herself permanently saddled with a military class, heavily burdening her finances, seriously impeding her progress towards constitutional government, and perpetuating all the abuses incidental to a policy in which the power of the sword rests entirely in the hands of one section of the people. The nation scarcely appreciated the great issues that were at stake. It found more interest in the struggle as furnishing a conclusive test of the efficiency of the new military system compared with the old. The army sent to quell the insurrection consisted of recruits drawn indiscriminately from every class of the people. Viewed in the light of history, it was an army of commoners, deficient in the fighting instinct, and traditionally 269demoralized for all purposes of resistance to the military class. The Satsuma insurgents, on the contrary, represented the flower of the samurai, long trained for this very struggle, and led by men whom the nation regarded as its bravest captains. The result dispelled all doubts about the fighting quality of the people at large.

Concurrently with these events the government diligently endeavoured to equip the country with all the paraphernalia of Occidental civilization. It is easy to understand that the master-minds of the era, who had planned and*Steps of Progress.*carried out the Restoration, continued to take the lead in all paths of progress. Their intellectual superiority entitled them to act as guides; they had enjoyed exceptional opportunities of acquiring enlightenment by visits to Europe and America, and the Japanese people had not yet lost the habit of looking to officialdom for every initiative. But the spectacle thus presented to foreign onlookers was not altogether without disquieting suggestions. The government's reforms seemed to outstrip the nation's readiness for them, and the results wore an air of some artificiality and confusion. Englishmen were employed to superintend the building of railways, the erection of telegraphs, the construction of lighthouses and the organization of a navy. To Frenchmen was entrusted the work of recasting the laws and training the army in strategy and tactics. Educational affairs, the organization of a postal service, the improvement of agriculture and the work of colonization were supervised by Americans. The teaching of medical science, the compilation of a commercial code, the elaboration of a system of local government, and ultimately the training of military officers were assigned to Germans. For instruction in sculpture and painting Italians were engaged. Was it possible that so many novelties should be successfully assimilated, or that the nation should adapt itself to systems planned by a motley band of aliens who knew nothing of its character and customs? These questions did not trouble the Japanese nearly so much as they troubled strangers. The truth is that conservatism was not really required to make the great sacrifices suggested by appearances. Among all the innovations of the era the only one that a Japanese could not lay aside at will was the new fashion of dressing the hair. He abandoned the *queue* irrevocably. But for the rest he lived a dual life. During hours of duty he wore a fine uniform, shaped and decorated in foreign style. But so soon as he stepped out of office or off parade, he reverted to his own comfortable and picturesque costume. Handsome houses were built and furnished according to Western models. But each had an annex where alcoves, verandas, matted floors and paper sliding doors continued to do traditional duty. Beefsteaks, beer, "grape-wine," knives and forks came into use on occasion. But rice-bowls and chopsticks held their everyday place as of old. In a word, though the Japanese adopted every convenient and serviceable attribute of foreign civilization, such as railways, steamships, telegraphs, post-offices, banks and machinery of all kinds; though they accepted Occidental sciences, and, to a large extent, Occidental philosophies; though they recognized the superiority of European jurisprudence and set themselves to bring their laws into accord with it, they nevertheless preserved the essentials of their own mode of life and never lost their individuality. A remarkable spirit of liberalism and a fine eclectic instinct were needed for the part they acted, but they did no radical violence to their own traditions, creeds and conventions. There was indeed a certain element of incongruity and even grotesqueness in the nation's doings. Old people cannot fit their feet to new roads without some clumsiness. The Japanese had grown very old in their special paths, and their novel departure was occasionally disfigured by solecisms. The refined taste that guided them unerringly in all the affairs of life as they had been accustomed to live it, seemed to fail them signally when they emerged into an alien atmosphere. They have given their proofs, however. It is now seen that the apparently excessive rapidity of their progress did not overtax their capacities; that they have emerged safely from their destructive era and carried their constructive career within reach of certain success, and that while they have still to develop some

45

of the traits of their new civilization, there is no prospect whatever of its proving ultimately unsuited to them.

After the Satsuma rebellion, nothing disturbed the even tenor of Japan's domestic politics except an attempt on the part of some of her people to force the growth of parliamentary government. It is evident that the united*Development of Representative Government.*effort made by the fiefs to overthrow the system of dual government and wrest the administrative power from the shōgun could have only one logical outcome: the combined exercise of the recovered power by those who had been instrumental in recovering it. That was the meaning of the oath taken by the emperor at the Restoration, when the youthful sovereign was made to say that wise counsels should be widely sought, and all things determined by public discussion. But the framers of the oath had the samurai alone in view. Into their consideration the common people—farmers, mechanics, tradesmen—did not enter at all, nor had the common people themselves any idea of advancing a claim to be considered. A voice in the administration would have been to them an embarrassing rather than a pleasing privilege. Thus the first deliberative assembly was composed of nobles and samurai only. A mere debating club without any legislative authority, it was permanently dissolved after two sessions. Possibly the problem of a parliament might have been long postponed after that fiasco, had it not found an ardent advocate in Itagaki Taisuke (afterwards Count Itagaki). A Tosa samurai conspicuous as a leader of the restoration movement, Itagaki was among the advocates of recourse to strong measures against Korea in 1873, and his failure to carry his point, supplemented by a belief that a large section of public opinion would have supported him had there been any machinery for appealing to it, gave fresh impetus to his faith in constitutional government. Resigning office on account of the Korean question, he became the nucleus of agitation in favour of a parliamentary system, and under his banner were enrolled not only discontented samurai but also many of the young men who, returning from direct observation of the working of constitutional systems in Europe or America, and failing to obtain official posts in Japan, attributed their failure to the oligarchical form of their country's polity. Thus in the interval between 1873 and 1877 there were two centres of disturbance in Japan: one in Satsuma, where Saigō figured as leader; the other in Tosa, under Itagaki's guidance. When the Satsuma men appealed to arms in 1877, a widespread apprehension prevailed lest the Tosa politicians should throw in their lot with the insurgents. Such a fear had its origin in failure to understand the object of the one side or to appreciate the sincerity of the other. Saigō and his adherents fought to substitute a Satsuma clique for the oligarchy already in power. Itagaki and his followers struggled for constitutional institutions. The two could not have anything in common. There was consequently no coalition. But the Tosa agitators did not neglect to make capital out of the embarrassment caused by the Satsuma rebellion. While the struggle was at its height, they addressed to the government a memorial, charging the administration with oppressive measures to restrain the voice of public opinion, with usurpation of power to the exclusion of the nation at large, and with levelling downwards instead of upwards, since the samurai had been reduced to the rank of commoners, whereas the commoners should have been educated up to the standard of the samurai. This memorial asked for a representative assembly and talked of popular rights. But since the document admitted that the people were uneducated, it is plain that there cannot have been any serious idea of giving them a share in the administration. In fact, the Tosa Liberals were not really contending for popular representation in the full sense of the term. What they wanted was the creation of some machinery for securing to the samurai at large a voice in the management of state affairs. They chafed against the fact that, whereas the efforts and sacrifices demanded by the Restoration had fallen 270 equally on the whole military class, the official prizes under the new system were monopolized by a small coterie of men belonging to the four principal clans. It is on record that Itagaki would have been content originally with an assembly consisting half of officials, half of non-official samurai, and not including any popular element whatever.

But the government did not believe that the time had come even for a measure such as the Tosa Liberals advocated. The statesmen in power conceived that the nation must be educated up to constitutional standards, and that the first step should be to provide an official model. Accordingly, in 1874, arrangements were made for periodically convening an assembly of prefectural governors, in order that they might act as channels of communication between the central authorities and the provincial population, and mutually exchange ideas as to the safest and most effective methods of encouraging progress within the limits of their jurisdictions. This was intended to be the embryo of representative institutions. But the governors, being officials appointed by the cabinet, did not bear in any sense the character of popular nominees, nor could it even be said that they reflected the public feeling of the districts they administered, for their habitual and natural tendency was to try, by means of heroic object lessons, to win the people's allegiance to the government's progressive policy, rather than to convince the government of the danger of overstepping the people's capacities.

These conventions of local officials had no legislative power whatever. The foundations of a body for discharging that function were laid in 1875, when a senate (*genro-in*) was organized. It consisted of official nominees, and its duty was to discuss and revise all laws and ordinances prior to their promulgation. It is to be noted, however, that expediency not less than a spirit of progress presided at the creation of the senate. Into its ranks were drafted a number of men for whom no places could be found in the executive, and who, without some official employment, would have been drawn into the current of disaffection. From that point of view the senate soon came to be regarded as a kind of hospital for administrative invalids, but undoubtedly its discharge of quasi-legislative functions proved suggestive, useful and instructive.

The second meeting of the provincial governors had just been prorogued when, in the spring of 1878, the great minister, Okubo Toshimitsu, was assassinated. Okubo, uniformly ready to bear the heaviest burden of responsibility *Assassination of Okubo.* in every political complication, had stood prominently before the nation as Saigō's opponent. He fell under the swords of Saigō's sympathizers. They immediately surrendered themselves to justice, having taken previous care to circulate a statement of motives, which showed that they ranked the government's failure to establish representative institutions as a sin scarcely less heinous than its alleged abuses of power. Well-informed followers of Saigō could never have been sincere believers in representative institutions. These men belonged to a province far removed from the scene of Saigō's desperate struggle. But the broad fact that they had sealed with their life-blood an appeal for a political change indicated the existence of a strong public conviction which would derive further strength from their act. The Japanese are essentially a brave people. Throughout the troublous events that preceded and followed the Restoration, it is not possible to point to one man whose obedience to duty or conviction was visibly weakened by prospects of personal peril. Okubo's assassination did not alarm any of his colleagues; but they understood its suggestiveness, and hastened to give effect to a previously formed resolve.

Two months after Okubo's death, an edict announced that elective assemblies should forthwith be established in various prefectures and cities. These assemblies were to consist of members having a high property qualification, **Local Government.** elected by voters having one-half of that qualification; the voting to be by signed ballot, and the session to last for one month in the spring of each year. As to their functions, they were to determine the method of levying and spending local taxes, subject to approval by the minister of state for home affairs; to scrutinize the accounts for the previous year, and, if necessary, to present petitions to the central government. Thus the foundations of genuine representative institutions were laid. It is true that legislative power was not vested in the local assemblies, but in all other important respects they discharged parliamentary duties. Their history need not be related at any length. Sometimes they came into violent collision with the governor of the prefecture, and unsightly struggles resulted. The governors were disposed to advocate public works which the people considered extravagant; and further, as years went by, and as political organizations grew stronger, there was found in each assembly a group of men ready to oppose the governor simply because of his official status. But on the whole the system worked well. The local assemblies served as training schools for the future parliament, and their members showed devotion to public duty as well as considerable aptitude for debate.

This was not what Itagaki and his followers wanted. Their purpose was to overthrow the clique of clansmen who, holding the reins of administrative power, monopolized the prizes of officialdom. Towards the consummation*The Liberal Party.* of such an aim the local assemblies helped little. Itagaki redoubled his agitation. He organized his fellow-thinkers into an association called *jiyūtō* (Liberals), the first political party in Japan, to whose ranks there very soon gravitated several men who had been in office and resented the loss of it; many that had never been in office and desired to be; and a still greater number who sincerely believed in the principles of political liberty, but had not yet considered the possibility of immediately adapting such principles to Japan's case. It was in the nature of things that an association of this kind, professing such doctrines, should present a picturesque aspect to the public, and that its collisions with the authorities should invite popular sympathy. Nor were collisions infrequent. For the government, arguing that if the nation was not ready for representative institutions, neither was it ready for full freedom of speech or of public meeting, legislated consistently with that theory, and entrusted to the police large powers of control over the press and the platform. The exercise of these powers often created situations in which the Liberals were able to pose as victims of official tyranny, so that they grew in popularity and the contagion of political agitation spread.

Three years later (1881) another split occurred in the ranks of the ruling oligarchy. Okuma Shigenobu (afterwards Count Okuma) seceded from the administration, and was followed by a number of able men who had owed *The Progressist Party.* their appointments to his patronage, or who, during his tenure of office as minister of finance, had passed under the influence of his powerful personality. If Itagaki be called the Rousseau of Japan, Okuma may be regarded as the Peel. To remarkable financial ability and a lucid, vigorous judgment he added the faculty of placing himself on the crest of any wave which a genuine *aura popularis* had begun to swell. He, too, inscribed on his banner of revolt against the oligarchy the motto "constitutional government," and it might have been expected that his followers would join hands with those of Itagaki, since the avowed political purpose of both was identical. They did nothing of the kind. Okuma organized an independent party, calling themselves Progressists (*shimpotō*), who not only stood aloof from the Liberals but even assumed an attitude hostile to them. This fact is eloquent. It shows that Japan's first political parties were grouped, not about principles, but about persons. Hence an inevitable lack of cohesion among their elements and a constant tendency to break up into caves and coteries. These are the characteristics that render the story of political evolution in Japan so perplexing to a foreign student. He looks for differences of platform and finds none. Just as a true Liberal must be a Progressist, and a true Progressist a Liberal, so, though each may cast his profession of faith in a mould of different phrases, the ultimate shape must be the same. The mainsprings of early political agitation in Japan were personal 271grievances and a desire to wrest the administrative power from the hands of the statesmen who had held it so long as to overtax the patience of their rivals. He that searches for profound moral or ethical bases will be disappointed. There were no Conservatives. Society was permeated with the spirit of progress. In a comparative sense the epithet "Conservative" might have been applied to the statesmen who proposed to defer parliamentary institutions until the people, as distinguished from the former samurai, had been in some measure prepared for such an innovation. But since these very statesmen were the guiding spirits of the whole Meiji revolution, it was plain that their convictions must be radical, and that, unless they did violence to their record, they must finally lead the country to representative institutions, the logical sequel of their own reforms.

Okubo's assassination had been followed, in 1878, by an edict announcing the establishment of local assemblies. Okuma's secession in 1881 was followed by an edict announcing that a national assembly would be convened in 1891.

The political parties, having now virtually attained their object, might have been expected to desist from further agitation. But they had another task to perform—that of disseminating anti-official prejudices among *Anti-Government Agitation.* the future electors. They worked diligently, and they had an undisputed field, for no one was put forward to champion the government's cause. The campaign was not always conducted on lawful lines. There were plots to assassinate ministers; there was an attempt to employ dynamite, and there was a scheme to foment an insurrection in Korea. On the other hand, dispersals of political meetings by order of police inspectors, and suspension or suppression of newspapers by the unchallengeable verdict of a minister for home affairs, were common occurrences. The breach widened steadily. It is true that Okuma rejoined the cabinet for a time in 1887, but he retired again in circumstances that aggravated his party's hostility to officialdom. In short, during the ten years immediately prior to the opening of the first parliament, an anti-government propaganda was incessantly preached from the platform and in the press.

Meanwhile the statesmen in power resolutely pursued their path of progressive reform. They codified the civil and penal laws, remodelling them on Western bases; they brought a vast number of affairs within the scope of minute regulations; they rescued the finances from confusion and restored them to a sound condition; they recast the whole framework of local government; they organized a great national bank, and established a network of subordinate institutions throughout the country; they pushed on the work of railway construction, and successfully enlisted private enterprise in its cause; they steadily extended the postal and telegraphic services; they economized public expenditures so that the state's income always exceeded its outlays; they laid the foundations of a strong mercantile marine; they instituted a system of postal savings-banks; they undertook large schemes of harbour improvement and road-making; they planned and put into operation an extensive programme of riparian improvement; they made civil service appointments depend on competitive examination; they sent numbers of students to Europe and America to complete their studies; and by tactful, persevering diplomacy they gradually introduced a new tone into the empire's relations with foreign powers. Japan's affairs were never better administered.

In 1890 the Constitution was promulgated. Imposing ceremonies marked the event. All the nation's notables were summoned to the palace to witness the delivery of the important document by the sovereign to the *The Constitution of 1890.* prime minister; salvos of artillery were fired; the cities were illuminated, and the people kept holiday. Marquis (afterwards Prince) Itō directed the framing of the Constitution. He had visited the Occident for the purpose of

48

investigating the development of parliamentary institutions and studying their practical working. His name is connected with nearly every great work of constructive statesmanship in the history of new Japan, and perhaps the crown of his legislative career was the drafting of the Constitution, to which the Japanese people point proudly as the only charter of the kind voluntarily given by a sovereign to his subjects. In other countries such concessions were always the outcome of long struggles between ruler and ruled. In Japan the emperor freely divested himself of a portion of his prerogatives and transferred them to the people. That view of the case, as may be seen from the story told above, is not untinged with romance; but in a general sense it is true.

No incident in Japan's modern career seemed more hazardous than this sudden plunge into parliamentary institutions. There had been some preparation. Provincial assemblies had partially familiarized the people with **Working of the System.** the methods of deliberative bodies. But provincial assemblies were at best petty arenas—places where the making or mending of roads, and the policing and sanitation of villages came up for discussion, and where political parties exercised no legislative function nor found any opportunity to attack the government or to debate problems of national interest. Thus the convening of a diet and the sudden transfer of financial and legislative authority from the throne and its entourage of tried statesmen to the hands of men whose qualifications for public life rested on the verdict of electors, themselves apparently devoid of all light to guide their choice—this sweeping innovation seemed likely to tax severely, if not to overtax completely, the progressive capacities of the nation. What enhanced the interest of the situation was that the oligarchs who held the administrative power had taken no pains to win a following in the political field. Knowing that the opening of the diet would be a veritable letting loose of the dogs of war, an unmuzzling of the agitators whose mouths had hitherto been partly closed by legal restrictions upon free speech, but who would now enjoy complete immunity within the walls of the assembly whatever the nature of their utterances—foreseeing all this, the statesmen of the day nevertheless stood severely aloof from alliances of every kind, and discharged their administrative functions with apparent indifference to the changes that popular representation could not fail to induce. This somewhat inexplicable display of unconcern became partially intelligible when the constitution was promulgated, for it then appeared that the cabinet's tenure of office was to depend solely on the emperor's will; that ministers were to take their mandate from the Throne, not from parliament. This fact was merely an outcome of the theory underlying every part of the Japanese polity. Laws might be redrafted, institutions remodelled, systems recast, but amid all changes and mutations one steady point must be carefully preserved, the Throne. The makers of new Japan understood that so long as the sanctity and inviolability of the imperial prerogatives could be preserved, the nation would be held by a strong anchor from drifting into dangerous waters. They laboured under no misapprehension about the inevitable issue of their work in framing the constitution. They knew very well that party cabinets are an essential outcome of representative institutions, and that to some kind of party cabinet Japan must come. But they regarded the Imperial mandate as a conservative safeguard, pending the organization and education of parties competent to form cabinets. Such parties did not yet exist, and until they came into unequivocal existence, the Restoration statesmen, who had so successfully managed the affairs of the nation during a quarter of a century, resolved that the steady point furnished by the throne must not be abandoned.

On the other hand, the agitators found here a new platform. They had obtained a constitution and a diet, but they had not obtained an instrument for pulling down the "clan" administrators, since these stood secure from attack under the aegis of the sovereign's mandate. They dared not raise their voices against the unfettered exercise of the mikado's prerogative. The nation, loyal to the core, would not have suffered such a protest, nor could the agitators themselves have found heart to formulate it. But they could read their own interpretation into the text of the Constitution, and they could demonstrate practically that a cabinet not acknowledging responsibility to the legislature was virtually impotent for law-making purposes.

272

These are the broad outlines of the contest that began in the first session of the Diet and continued for several years. It is unnecessary to speak of the special points of controversy. Just as the political parties had been formed on the **The Diet and the Government.** lines of persons, not principles, so the opposition in the Diet was directed against men, not measures. The struggle presented varying aspects at different times, but the fundamental question at issue never changed. Obstruction was the weapon of the political parties. They sought to render legislation and finance impossible for any ministry that refused to take its mandate from the majority in the lower house, and they imparted an air of respectability and even patriotism to their destructive campaign by making "anti-clannism" their war-cry, and industriously fostering the idea that the struggle lay between administration guided by public opinion and administration controlled by a clique of clansmen who separated the throne from the nation. Had not the House of Peers stood stanchly

49

by the government throughout this contest, it is possible that the nation might have suffered severely from the rashness of the political parties.

There was something melancholy in the spectacle. The Restoration statesmen were the men who had made Modern Japan; the men who had raised her, in the face of immense obstacles, from the position of an insignificant Oriental state to that of a formidable unit in the comity of nations; the men, finally, who had given to her a constitution and representative institutions. Yet these same men were now fiercely attacked by the arms which they had themselves nerved; were held up to public obloquy as self-seeking usurpers, and were declared to be impeding the people's constitutional route to administrative privileges, when in reality they were only holding the breach until the people should be able to march into the citadel with some show of orderly and competent organization. That there was no corruption, no abuse of position, is not to be pretended; but on the whole the conservatism of the clan statesmen had only one object—to provide that the newly constructed representative machine should not be set working until its parts were duly adjusted and brought into proper gear. On both sides the leaders understood the situation accurately. The heads of the parties, while publicly clamouring for parliamentary cabinets, privately confessed that they were not yet prepared to assume administrative responsibilities;3 and the so-called "clan statesmen," while refusing before the world to accept the Diet's mandates, admitted within official circles that the question was one of time only. The situation did not undergo any marked change until, the country becoming engaged in war with China (1894-95), domestic squabbles were forgotten in the presence of foreign danger. From that time an era of coalition commenced. Both the political parties joined hands to vote funds for the prosecution of the campaign, and one of them, the Liberals, subsequently gave support to a cabinet under the presidency of Marquis Itō, the purpose of the union being to carry through the diet an extensive scheme of enlarged armaments and public works planned in the sequel of the war. The Progressists, however, remained implacable, continuing their opposition to the thing called bureaucracy quite irrespective of its measures.

The next phase (1898) was a fusion of the two parties into one large organization which adopted the name "Constitutional Party" (kensei-tō). By this union the chief obstacles to parliamentary cabinets were removed.*Fusion of the Two Parties.*Not only did the Constitutionalists command a large majority in the lower house, but also they possessed a sufficiency of men who, although lacking ministerial experience, might still advance a reasonable title to be entrusted with portfolios. Immediately the emperor, acting on the advice of Marquis Itō, invited Counts Okuma and Itagaki to form a cabinet. It was essentially a trial. The party politicians were required to demonstrate in practice the justice of the claim they had been so long asserting in theory. They had worked in combination for the destructive purpose of pulling down the so-called "clan statesmen"; they had now to show whether they could work in combination for the constructive purposes of administration. Their heads, Counts Okuma and Itagaki, accepted the Imperial mandate, and the nation watched the result. There was no need to wait long. In less than six months these new links snapped under the tension of old enmities, and the coalition split up once more into its original elements. It had demonstrated that the sweets of power, which the "clan statesmen" had been so vehemently accused of coveting, possessed even greater attractions for their accusers. The issue of the experiment was such a palpable fiasco that it effectually rehabilitated the "clan statesmen," and finally proved, what had indeed been long evident to every close observer, that without the assistance of those statesmen no political party could hold office successfully.

Thenceforth it became the unique aim of Liberals and Progressists alike to join hands permanently with the men towards whom they had once displayed such implacable hostility. Prince Itō, the leader of the so-called *Enrolment of the Clan Statesmen in Political Associations.*"elder statesmen," received special solicitations, for it was plain that he would bring to any political party an overwhelming access of strength alike in his own person and in the number of friends and disciples certain to follow him. But Prince Itō declined to be absorbed into any existing party, or to adopt the principle of parliamentary cabinets. He would consent to form a new association, but it must consist of men sufficiently disciplined to obey him implicitly, and sufficiently docile to accept their programme from his hand. The Liberals agreed to these terms. They dissolved their party (August 1900) and enrolled themselves in the ranks of a new organization, which did not even call itself a party, its designation being *rikken seiyū-kai* (association of friends of the constitution), and which had for the cardinal plank in its platform a declaration of ministerial irresponsibility to the Diet. A singular page was thus added to the story of Japanese political development; for not merely did the Liberals enlist under the banner of the statesmen whom for twenty years they had fought to overthrow, but they also tacitly consented to erase from their profession of faith its essential article, parliamentary cabinets, and, by resigning that article to the Progressists, created for the first time an opposition with a solid and intelligible platform. Nevertheless the seiyū-kai grew steadily in strength whereas the number of its opponents declined correspondingly. At the general elections in May 1908 the former secured 195 seats, the four sections of the opposition winning only 184. Thus for the first time in Japanese parliamentary history a majority of the lower chamber found themselves marching under the same banner. Moreover, the four sections of the opposition were independently organized and differed nearly as much from one another as they all differed from the seiyū-kai. Their impotence to make head against the solid phalanx of the latter was thus conspicuous, especially during the 1908-1909 session of the Diet. Much talk then began to be heard about the necessity of coalition, and that this talk will materialize eventually cannot be doubted. Reduction of armaments, abolition of taxes specially imposed for belligerent purposes, and the substitution of a strictly constitutional system for the existing bureaucracy—these objects constitute a sufficiently solid platform, and nothing is wanted except that a body of proved administrators should join the opposition in occupying it. There were in 1909 no signs, however, that any such defection from the ranks of officialdom would take place. Deference is paid to public opinions inasmuch as even a seiyū-kai ministry will not remain in office after its popularity has begun to show signs of waning. But no deference is paid to the doctrine of party cabinets. Prince Itō did not continue to lead the seiyū-kai for more than three years. In July 1903 he delegated that function to Marquis Saionji, representative of one of the very oldest families of the court nobility and a personal friend of the emperor, as also was Prince Itō. The Imperial stamp is thus vicariously set upon the principle of 273political combinations for the better practical conduct of parliamentary business, but that the seiyū-kai, founded by Prince Itō and led by Marquis Saionji, should ever hold office in defiance of the sovereign's mandate is unthinkable. Constitutional institutions in Japan are therefore developing along lines entirely without precedent. The storm and stress of early parliamentary days have given place to comparative calm. During the first twelve sessions of the Diet, extending over 8 years, there were five dissolutions of the lower house. During the next thirteen sessions, extending over 11 years, there were two dissolutions. During the first 8 years of the Diet's existence there were six changes of cabinet; during the next 11 years there were five changes. Another healthy sign was that men of affairs were beginning to realize the importance of parliamentary representation. At first the constituencies were contested almost entirely by professional politicians, barristers and journalists. In 1909 there was a solid body (the *boshin* club) of business men commanding nearly 50 votes in the lower house; and as the upper chamber included 45 representatives of the highest tax-payers, the interests of commerce and industry were intelligently debated.

(F. BY.)

X.—THE CLAIM OF JAPAN: BY A JAPANESE STATESMAN4

It has been said that it is impossible for an Occidental to understand the Oriental, and vice versa; but, admitting that the mutual understanding of two different races or peoples is a difficult matter, why should Occidentals and Orientals be thus set in opposition? No doubt, different peoples of Europe understand each other better than they do the Asiatic; but can Asiatic peoples understand each other better than they can Europeans or than the Europeans can understand any of them? Do Japanese understand Persians or even Indians better than English or French? It is true perhaps that Japanese can and do understand the Chinese better than Europeans; but that is due not only to centuries of mutual intercourse, but to the wonderful and peculiar fact that they have adopted the old classical Chinese literature as their own, somewhat in the way, but in a much greater degree, in which the European nations have adopted the old Greek and Latin literatures. What is here contended for is that the mutual understanding of two peoples is not so much a matter of race, but of the knowledge of each other's history, traditions, literature, &c.

The Japanese have, they think, suffered much from the misunderstanding of their motives, feelings and ideas; what they want is to be understood fully and to be known for what they really are, be it good or bad. They desire, above all, not to be lumped as Oriental, but to be known and judged on their own account. In the latter half of the 19th century, in fact up to the Chinese War, it irritated Japanese travelling abroad more than anything else to be taken for Chinese. Then, after the Chinese War, the alarm about Japan leading Eastern Asia to make a general attack upon Europe—the so-called Yellow Peril—seemed so ridiculous to the Japanese that the bad effects of such wild talk were not quite appreciated by them. The aim of the Japanese nation, ever since, at the time of the Restoration (1868), they laid aside definitively all ideas of seclusion and entered into the comity of nations, has been that they should rise above the level of the Eastern peoples to an equality with the Western and should be in the foremost rank of the brotherhood of nations; it was not their ambition at all to be the champion of the East against the West, but rather to beat down the barriers between themselves and the West.

The intense pride of the Japanese in their nationality, their patriotism and loyalty, arise from their history, for what other nation can point to an Imperial family of one unbroken lineage

51

reigning over the land for twenty-five centuries? Is it not a glorious tradition for a nation, that its emperor should be descended directly from that grandson of "the great heaven-illuminating goddess," to whom she said, "This land (Japan) is the region over which my descendants shall be the lords. Do thou, my august child, proceed thither and govern it. Go! *The prosperity of thy dynasty shall be coeval with heaven and earth.*" Thus they call their country the land of *kami* (ancient gods of tradition). With this spirit, in the old days when China held the hegemony of the East, and all neighbouring peoples were regarded as its tributaries, Japan alone, largely no doubt on account of its insular position, held itself quite aloof; it set at defiance the power of Kublai and routed utterly the combined Chinese and Korean fleets with vast forces sent by him to conquer Japan, this being the only occasion that Japan was threatened with a foreign invasion.

With this spirit, as soon as they perceived the superiority of the Western civilization, they set to work to introduce it into their country, just as in the 7th and 8th centuries they had adopted and adapted the Chinese civilization. In 1868, the first year of the era of Meiji, the emperor swore solemnly the memorable oath of five articles, setting forth the policy that was to be and has been followed thereafter by the government. These five articles were:—

1. Deliberative assemblies shall be established and all measures of government shall be decided by public opinion.

2. All classes, high and low, shall unite in vigorously carrying out the plan of government.

3. Officials, civil and military, and all common people shall as far as possible be allowed to fulfil their just desires so that there may not be any discontent among them.

4. *Uncivilized customs of former times shall be broken through*, and everything shall be based upon just and equitable principles of heaven and earth (nature).

5. *Knowledge shall be sought for throughout the world*, so that the welfare of the empire may be promoted.

(Translation due to Prof. N. Hozumi of Tōkyō Imp. Univ.)

It is interesting, as showing the continuity of the policy of the empire, to place side by side with these articles the words of the Imperial rescript issued in 1908, which are as follows:—

"We are convinced that with the rapid and unceasing advance of civilization, the East and West, mutually dependent and helping each other, are bound by common interests. It is our sincere wish to continue to enjoy for ever its benefits in common with other powers by entering into closer and closer relations and strengthening our friendship with them. Now in order to be able to move onward along with the constant progress of the world and to share in the blessings of civilization, it is obvious that we must develop our internal resources; our nation, but recently emerged from an exhausting war, must put forth increased activity in every branch of administration. It therefore behoves our people to endeavour with one mind, from the highest to the lowest, to pursue their callings honestly and earnestly, to be industrious and thrifty, to abide in faith and righteousness, to be simple and warm-hearted, to put away ostentation and vanity and strive after the useful and solid, to avoid idleness and indulgence, and to apply themselves incessantly to strenuous and arduous tasks...."

The ambition of the Japanese people has been, as already stated, to be recognized as an equal by the Great Powers. With this object in view, they have spared no efforts to introduce what they considered superior in the Western civilization, although it may perhaps be doubted whether in their eagerness they have always been wise. *They have always resented any discrimination against them as an Asiatic people*, not merely protesting against it, knowing that such would not avail much, but making every endeavour to remove reasons or excuses for it. Formerly there were troops stationed to guard several legations; foreign postal service was not entirely in the hands of the Japanese government for a long time; these and other indignities against the sovereignty of the nation were gradually removed by proving that they were not necessary. Then there was the question of the extra-territorial jurisdiction; an embassy was sent to Europe and America as early as 1871 with a view to the revision of treaties in order to do away with this *imperium in imperio*, that being the date originally fixed for the revision; the embassy, however, failed in its object but was not altogether fruitless, for it was then clearly seen that it would be necessary to revise thoroughly the system of laws and entirely to reorganize the law courts before Occidental nations could be induced to forgo 274 this privilege. These measures were necessary in any case as a consequence of the introduction of the Western methods and ideas, but they were hastened by the fact of their being a necessary preliminary to the revision of treaties. When the new code of laws was brought before the Diet at its first session, and there was a great opposition against it in the House of Peers on account of its many defects and especially of its ignoring many established usages, the chief argument in its favour, or at least one that had a great influence with many who were unacquainted with technical points, was that it was necessary for the revision of treaties and that the defects, if any, could be afterwards amended at leisure. These preparations on the part of the government, however, took a long time, and in the meantime the whole nation, or at least the more intelligent part of it, was chafing impatiently under what was considered a national indignity. The United States, by being the first to agree to its abandonment, although this agreement was rendered nugatory by a conditional clause, added to the stock of goodwill with which the Japanese have always regarded the Americans on account of their attitude towards them. When at last the consummation so long and ardently desired was attained, great was the joy with which it was greeted, for now it was felt that Japan was indeed on terms of equality with Occidental nations. Great Britain, by being the first to conclude the revised treaty—an act due to the remarkable foresight of her statesmen in spite of the opposition of their countrymen in Japan—did much to bring about the cordial feeling of the Japanese towards the British, which made them welcome with such enthusiasm the Anglo-Japanese alliance. The importance of this last as a powerful instrument for the preservation of peace in the extreme East has been, and always will be, appreciated at its full value by the more intelligent and thoughtful among the Japanese; but by the mass of the people it was received with great acclamation, owing partly to the already existing good feeling towards the British, but also in a large measure because it was felt that the fact that Great Britain should leave its "splendid isolation" to enter into this alliance proclaimed in the clearest possible way that Japan had entered on terms of full equality among the brotherhood of nations, and that thenceforth there could be no ground for that discrimination against them as an Asiatic nation which had been so galling to the Japanese people.

There have been, and there still are being made, many charges against the Japanese government and people. While admitting that some of them may be founded on facts, it is permissible to point out that traits and acts of a few individuals have often been generalized to be the national characteristic or the result of a fixed policy, while in many cases such charges are due to misunderstandings arising from want of thorough knowledge of each other's language, customs, usages, ideas, &c. Take the principle of "the open door," for instance; the Japanese government has been charged in several instances with acting contrary to it. It is natural that where (as in China) competition is very keen between men of different nationalities, individuals should sometimes feel aggrieved and make complaints of unfairness against the government of their competitors; it is also natural that people at home should listen to and believe in those charges made against the Japanese by their countrymen in the East, while unfortunately the Japanese, being so far away and often unaware of them, have not a ready means of vindicating themselves; but subsequent investigations have always shown those charges to be either groundless or due to misunderstandings, and it may be asserted that in no case has the charge been substantiated that the Japanese government has knowingly, deliberately, of *malice prepense* been guilty of breach of faith in violating the principle of "the open door" to which it has solemnly pledged itself. That it has often been accused by the Japanese subjects of weakness *vis-à-vis* foreign powers to the detriment of their interests, is perhaps a good proof of its fairness.

The Japanese have often been charged with looseness of commercial morality. This charge is harder to answer than the last, for it cannot be denied that there have been many instances of dishonesty on the part of Japanese tradesmen or employees; *tu quoque* is never a valid argument, but there are black sheep everywhere, and there were special reasons why foreigners should have come in contact with many such in their dealings with the Japanese. In days before the Restoration, merchants and tradesmen were officially classed as the lowest of four classes, the samurai, the farmers, the artisans and the merchants; practically, however, rich merchants serving as bankers and employers of others were held in high esteem, even by the samurai. Yet it cannot be denied that the position of the last three was low compared with that of the samurai; their education was not so high, and although of course there was the same code of morality for them all, there was no such high standard of honour as was enjoined upon the samurai by the bushidō or "the way of samurai." Now, when foreign trade was first opened, it was naturally not firms with long-established credit and methods that first ventured upon the new field of business— some few that did failed owing to their want of experience—it was rather enterprising and adventurous spirits with little capital or credit who eagerly flocked to the newly opened ports to try their fortune. It was not to be expected that all or most of those should be very scrupulous in their dealings with the foreigners; the majority of those adventurers failed, while a few of the abler men, generally those who believed in and practised honesty as the best policy, succeeded and came to occupy an honourable position as business men. It is also asserted that foreigners, or at least some of them, did not scruple to take unfair advantage of the want of experience on the part of their Japanese customers to impose upon them methods which they would not have followed except in the East; it may be that such methods were necessary or were deemed so in dealing with those adventurers, but it is a fact that it afterwards took a long time and great effort on the part of Japanese traders to break through some usages and customs which were established in earlier days and which they deemed derogatory to their credit or injurious to their interests. Infringement of patent rights and fraudulent imitation of trade-marks have with some truth also been charged against the Japanese; about this it is to be remarked that although the principles of morality cannot change, their applications may be new; patents and trade-marks are something new to the Japanese, and it takes time to teach that their infringement should be regarded with the same moral censure as stealing. The government has done everything to prevent such practices by enacting and enforcing laws against them, and nowadays they are not so common. Be that as it may, such a state of affairs as that mentioned above is now passing away almost entirely; commerce and trade are now regarded as highly honourable professions, merchants and business men occupy the highest social positions, several of them having been lately raised to the peerage, and are as honourable a set of men as can be met anywhere. It is however to be regretted that in introducing Western business methods, it has not been quite possible to exclude some of their evils, such as promotion of swindling companies, tampering with members of legislature, and so forth.

The Japanese have also been considered in some quarters to be a bellicose nation. No sooner was the war with Russia over than they were said to be ready and eager to fight with the United States. This is another misrepresentation arising from want of proper knowledge of Japanese character and feelings. Although it is true that within the quarter of a century preceding 1909 Japan was engaged in two sanguinary wars, not to mention the Boxer affair, in which owing to her proximity to the scene of the disturbances she had to take a prominent part, yet neither of these was of her own seeking; in both cases she had to fight or else submit to become a mere cipher in the world, if indeed she could have preserved her existence as an independent state. The Japanese, far from being a bellicose people, deliberately cut off all intercourse with the outside world in order to avoid international troubles, and remained absolutely secluded from the world and at profound peace within their own territory for two centuries and a half. Besides, the Japanese have always regarded the Americans with a special goodwill, due no doubt to the steady liberal attitude of the American government and 275people towards Japan and Japanese, and they look upon the idea of war between Japan and the United States as ridiculous.

Restrictions upon Japanese emigrants to the United States and to Australia are irritating to the Japanese, because it is a discrimination against them as belonging to the "yellow" race, whereas it has been their ambition to raise themselves above the level of the Eastern nations to an equality with the Western nations, although they cannot change the colour of their skin. When a Japanese even of the highest rank and standing has to obtain a permit from an American immigrant officer before he can enter American territory, is it not natural that he and his countrymen should resent this discrimination as an indignity? But they have too much good sense to think or even dream of going to war upon such a matter; on the contrary, the Japanese government agreed in 1908 to limit the number of emigrants in order to avoid complications.

It may be repeated that it has ever been the ambition of the Japanese people to take rank with the Great Powers of the world, and to have a voice in the council of nations; they demand that they shall not be discriminated against because of the colour of their skin, but that they shall rather be judged by their deeds. With this aim, they have made great efforts: where charges brought against them have any foundation in fact, they have endeavoured to make reforms; where they are false or due to misunderstandings they have tried to live them down, trusting to time for their vindication. They are willing to be judged by the intelligent and impartial world: a fair field and no favour is what they claim, and think they have a right to claim, from the world.

(K.)

BIBLIOGRAPHY.—The latest edition of von Wemckstern's*Bibliography of the Japanese Empire* contains the names of all important books and publications relating to Japan, which have now become very numerous. A general reference must suffice here to Captain F. Brinkley's *Japan*(12 vols., 1904); the works of B. H. Chamberlain, *Things Japanese* (5th ed., 1905, &c.); W. G. Aston, *Hist. of Jap. Literature, &c.*, and Lafcadio Hearn, *Japan: an Interpretation* (1904), &c., as the European authors with intimate knowledge of the country who have done most to give accurate and illuminating expression to its development. See also *Fifty Years of New Japan*, an encyclopaedic account of the national development in all its aspects, compiled by Count Shigenobu Okuma (2 vols., 1907, 1908; Eng. ed. by Marcus B. Huish, 1909).

1The Taira and the Minamoto both traced their descent from imperial princes; the Tokugawa were a branch of the Minamoto.

2Daimyō ("great name") was the title given to a feudal chief.

3Neither the Liberals nor the Progressists had a working majority in the house of representatives, nor could the ranks of either have furnished men qualified to fill all the administrative posts.

4The following expression of the Japanese point of view, by a statesman of the writer's authority and experience, may well supplement the general account of the progress of Japan and its inclusion among the great civilized powers of the world.—(ED. E. B.)

JAPANNING, the art of coating surfaces of metal, wood, &c., with a variety of varnishes, which are dried and hardened on in stoves or hot chambers. These drying processes constitute the main distinguishing features of the art. The trade owes its name to the fact that it is an imitation of the famous lacquering of Japan (see JAPAN: *Art*), which, however, is prepared with entirely different materials and processes, and is in all respects much more brilliant, durable and beautiful than any ordinary japan work. Japanning is done in clear transparent varnishes, in black and in body colours; but black japan is the most characteristic and common style of work. The varnish for black japan consists essentially of pure natural asphaltum with a proportion of gum animé dissolved in linseed oil and thinned with turpentine. In thin layers such a japan has a rich dark brown colour; it only shows a brilliant black in thicker coatings. For fine work, which has to be smoothed and polished, several coats of black are applied in succession, each being separately dried in the stove at a heat which may rise to about 300° F. Body colours consist of a basis of transparent varnish mixed with the special mineral paints of the desired colours or with bronze powders. The transparent varnish used by japanners is a copal varnish which contains less drying oil and more turpentine than is contained in ordinary painters' oil varnish. Japanning produces a brilliant polished surface which is much more durable and less easily affected by heat, moisture or other influences than any ordinary painted and varnished work. It may be regarded as a process intermediate between ordinary painting and enamelling. It is very extensively applied in the finishing of ordinary iron-mongery goods and domestic iron-work, deed boxes, clock dials and papier-mâché articles. The process is also applied to blocks of slate for making imitation of black and other marbles for chimneypieces, &c., and in a modified form is employed for preparing enamelled, japan or patent leather.

JAPHETH (יפת), in the Bible, the youngest son of Noah1 according to the Priestly Code (*c.* 450 B.C.); but in the earlier tradition2 the second son, also the "father" of one of the three groups into which the nations of the world are divided.3In Gen. ix. 27, Noah pronounces the following blessing on Japheth—

"God enlarge (Heb. *yapht*) Japheth (Heb. *yepheth*),
And let him dwell in the tents of Shem;
And let Canaan be his servant."

This is probably an ancient oracle independent alike of the flood story and the genealogical scheme in Gen. x. Shem is probably Israel; Canaan, of course, the Canaanites; by analogy, Japheth should be some third element of the population of Palestine—the Philistines or the Phoenicians have been suggested. The sense of the second line is doubtful, it may be "let God dwell" or "let Japheth dwell"; on the latter view Japheth appears to be in friendly alliance with Shem. The words might mean that Japheth was an intruding invader, but this is not consonant with the tone of the oracle. Possibly Japheth is only present in Gen. ix. 20-27 through corruption of the text, Japheth may be an accidental repetition of yapht "may he enlarge," misread as a proper name.

In Gen. x. Japheth is the northern and western division of the nations; being perhaps used as a convenient title under which to group the more remote peoples who were not thought of as standing in ethnic or political connexion with Israel or Egypt. Thus of his descendants, Gomer, Magog,4 Tubal, Meshech, Ashkenaz, Riphath and Togarmah are peoples who are located with more or less certainty in N.E. Asia Minor, Armenia and the lands to the N.E. of the Black Sea; Javan is the Ionians, used loosely for the seafaring peoples of the West, including Tarshish (Tartessus in Spain), Kittim (Cyprus), Rodanim5(Rhodes). There is no certain identification of Tiras and Elishah.

The similarity of the name Japheth to the Titan Iapetos of Greek mythology is probably a mere accident. A place Japheth is mentioned in Judith ii. 25, but it is quite unknown.

In addition to commentaries and dictionary articles, see E. Meyer, *Die Israeliten und ihre Nachbarstämme*, pp. 219 sqq.

(W. H. BE.)

1Gen. v. 32, vi. 10, vii. 13, x. 1; cf. 1 Chron. i. 4.
2Gen. ix. 27, x. 2, J. *c.* 850-750 B.C. In ix. 18 Ham is an editorial addition.
3Gen. x. 1-5; cf. I Chron. i. 5-7. For the significance of the genealogies in Gen. x. see HAM.
4See GOMER, GOG.

So we should read with 1 Chron. i. 7 (LXX.) for Dodanim.

JAR, a vessel of simple form, made of earthenware, glass, &c., with a spoutless mouth, and usually without handles. The word came into English through Fr. *jarre* or Span, *jarra*, from Arab, *jarrah*, the earthenware vessel of Eastern countries, used to contain water, oil, wine, &c. The simple electrical condenser known as a *Leyden Jar* (*q.v.*) was so called because of the early experiments made in the science of electricity at Leiden. In the sense of a harsh vibrating sound, a sudden shock or vibrating movement, hence dissension, quarrel or petty strife, "jar" is onomatopoeic in origin; it is also seen in the name of the bird night-jar (also known as the goat-sucker). In the expression "on the jar" or "ajar," of a door or window partly open, the word is another form of *chare* or *char*, meaning turn or turning, which survives in charwoman, one who works at a turn, a job and *chore*, a job, spell of work.

JARGON, in its earliest use a term applied to the chirping and twittering of birds, but since the 15th century mainly confined to any language, spoken or written, which is either unintelligible to the user or to the hearer. It is particularly applied by uninstructed hearers or readers to the language full of technical terminology used by scientific, philosophic and other writers. The word is O. Fr., and Cotgrave defines it as "gibridge (gibberish), fustian language." It is cognate with Span. *gerigonza*, and Ital. *gergo, gergone*, and probably related to the onomatopoeic O. Fr. *jargouiller*, to chatter. The root is probably seen in Lat. *garrire*, to chatter.

JARGOON, or Jargon (occasionally in old writings *jargounce* and *jacounce*), a name applied by modern mineralogists to those zircons which are fine enough to be cut as gem-stones, but are not of the red colour which characterizes the hyacinth or jacinth. The word is related to Arab *zargun*(zircon). Some of the finest jargoons are green, others brown and yellow, whilst some are colourless. The colourless jargoon may be obtained by heating certain coloured stones. When zircon is heated it sometimes changes in colour, or altogether loses it, and at the same time usually increases in density and brilliancy. The so-called Matura diamonds, formerly sent from Matara (or Matura), in Ceylon, were decolorized zircons. The zircon has strong refractive power, and its lustre is almost adamantine, but it lacks the fire of the diamond. The specific gravity of zircon is subject to considerable variation in different varieties; thus Sir A. H. Church found the sp. gr. of a fine leaf-green jargoon to be as low as 3.982, and that of a pure white jargoon as high as 4.705. Jargoon and tourmaline, when cut as gems, are sometimes mistaken for each other, but the sp. gr. is distinctive, since that of tourmaline is only 3 to 3.2. Moreover, in tourmaline the dichroism is strongly marked, whereas in jargoon it is remarkably feeble. The refractive indices of jargoon are much higher than those of tourmaline (see ZIRCON).

(F. W. R.*)

JARĪR IBN 'ATĪYYA UL-KHATFĪ (d. 728), Arabian poet, was born in the reign of the caliph 'Ali, was a member of the tribe Kulaib, a part of the Tamīm, and lived in Irak. Of his early life little is known, but he succeeded in winning the favour of Hajjāj, the governor of Irak (see CALIPHATE). Already famous for his verse, he became more widely known by his feud with Farazdaq and Akhtal. Later he went to Damascus and visited the court of Abdalmalik ('Abd ul-Malik) and that of his successor, Walīd. From neither of these did he receive a warm welcome. He was, however, more successful with Omar II., and was the only poet received by the pious caliph.

His verse, which, like that of his contemporaries, is largely satire and eulogy, was published in 2 vols. (Cairo, 1896).

(G. W. T.)

JARKENT, a town of Russian Central Asia, in the province of Semiryechensk, 70 m. W.N.W. of Kulja and near to the Ili river. Pop. (1897), 16,372.

JARNAC, a town of western France in the department of Charente, on the right bank of the river Charente, and on the railway 23 m. W. of Angoulême, between that city and Cognac. Pop. (1906), 4493. The town is well built; and an avenue, planted with poplar trees, leads to a handsome suspension bridge. The church contains an interesting ogival crypt. There are communal colleges for both sexes. Brandy, wine and wine-casks are made in the town. Jarnac was in 1569 the scene of a battle in which the Catholics defeated the Protestants. A pyramid marks the spot where Louis, Prince de Condé, one of the Protestant generals, was slain. Jarnac gave its name to an old French family, of which the best known member is Gui Chabot, comte de Jarnac

(d. *c.* 1575), whose lucky backstroke in his famous duel with Châteigneraie gave rise to the proverbial phrase *coup de jarnac*, signifying an unexpected blow.

JARO, a town of the province of Iloílo, Panay, Philippine Islands, on the Jaro river, 2 m. N.W. of the town of Iloílo, the capital. Pop. (1903), 10,681. It lies on a plain in the midst of a rich agricultural district, has several fine residences, a cathedral, a curious three-tiered tower, a semi-weekly paper and a monthly periodical. Jaro was founded by the Spanish in 1584. From 1903 until February 1908 it was part of the town or municipality of Iloílo.

JAROSITE, a rare mineral species consisting of hydrous potassium and aluminium sulphate, and belonging to the group of isomorphous rhombohedral minerals enumerated below:—

Alunite	K$_2$	$[Al(OH)_2]_6(SO_4)_4$
Jarosite	K$_2$	$[Fe(OH)_2]_6(SO_4)_4$
Natrojarosite	Na$_2$	$[Fe(OH)_2]_6(SO_4)_4$
Plumbojarosite	Pb	$[Fe(OH)_2]_8(SO_4)_4$

Jarosite usually occurs as drusy incrustations of minute indistinct crystals with a yellowish-brown colour and brilliant lustre. Hardness 3; sp. gr. 3.15. The best specimens, consisting of crystalline crusts on limonite, are from the Jaroso ravine in the Sierra Almagrera, province of Almeria, Spain, from which locality the mineral receives its name. It has been also found, often in association with iron ores, at a few other localities. A variety occurring as concretionary or mulberry-like forms is known as moronolite (from Gr. μῶρον, "mulberry," andλίθος, "stone"); it is found at Monroe in Orange county, New York. The recently discovered species natrojarosite and plumbojarosite occur as yellowish-brown glistening powders consisting wholly of minute crystals, and are from Nevada and New Mexico respectively.

(L. J. S.)

JARRAH WOOD (an adaptation of the native name *Jerryhl*), the product of a large tree (*Eucalyptus marginata*) found in south-western Australia, where it is said to cover an area of 14,000 sq. m. The trees grow straight in the stem to a great size, and yield squared timber up to 40 ft. length and 24 in. diameter. The wood is very hard, heavy (sp. gr. 1.010) and close-grained, with a mahogany-red colour, and sometimes sufficient "figure" to render it suitable for cabinet-makers' use. The timber possesses several useful characteristics; and great expectations were at first formed as to its value for ship-building and general constructive purposes. These expectations have not, however, been realized, and the exclusive possession of the tree has not proved that source of wealth to western Australia which was at one time expected. Its greatest merit for ship-building and marine purposes is due to the fact that it resists, better than any other timber, the attacks of the *Teredo navalis* and other marine borers, and on land it is equally exempt, in tropical countries, from the ravages of white ants. When felled with the sap at its lowest point and well seasoned, the wood stands exposure in the air, earth or sea remarkably well, on which account it is in request for railway sleepers, telegraph poles and piles in the British colonies and India. The wood, however, frequently shows longitudinal blisters, or lacunae, filled with resin, the same as may be observed in spruce fir timber; and it is deficient in fibre, breaking with a short fracture under comparatively moderate pressure. It has been classed at Lloyds for ship-building purposes in line three, table A, of the registry rules.

JARROW, a port and municipal borough in the Jarrow parliamentary division of Durham, England, on the right bank of the Tyne, 6½ m. below Newcastle, and on a branch of the North-Eastern railway. Pop. (1901), 34,295. The parish church of St Paul was founded in 685, and retains portions of pre-Norman work. The central tower is Norman, and there are good Decorated and Perpendicular details in the body of the church. Close by are the scattered ruins of the monastery begun by the pious Biscop in 681, and consecrated with the church by Ceolfrid in 685. Within the walls of this monastery the Venerable Bede spent his life from childhood; and his body was at first buried within the church, whither, until it was removed under Edward the Confessor to Durham, it attracted many pilgrims. The town is wholly industrial, devoted to ship-building, chemical works, paper mills and the neighbouring collieries. It owes its development from a mere pit village very largely to the enterprise of Sir Charles Mark Palmer (*q.v.*). Jarrow Slake, a river bay, 1 m. long by ½ m. broad, contains the Tyne docks of the North-Eastern

57

railway company. A great quantity of coal is shipped. Jarrow was incorporated in 1875, and the corporation consists of a mayor, 6 aldermen and 18 councillors. Area, 783 acres.

JARRY, NICOLAS, one of the best-known 17th century French calligraphers. He was born at Paris about 1620, and was officially employed by Louis XIV. His most famous work is the *Guirlande de Julie* (1641). He died some time before 1674.

JARVIS, JOHN WESLEY (1780-1840), American artist, nephew of the great John Wesley, was born at South Shields, England, and was taken to the United States at the age of five. He was one of the earliest American painters to give serious attention to the study of anatomy. He lived at first in Philadelphia, afterwards establishing himself in New York, where he enjoyed great popularity, though his conviviality and eccentric mode of life affected his work. He visited Baltimore, Charleston and New Orleans, entertaining much and painting portraits of prominent people, particularly in New Orleans, where General Andrew Jackson was one of his sitters. He had for assistants at different times both Sully and Inman. He affected singularity in dress and manners, and his *mots* were the talk of the day. But his work deteriorated, and he died in great poverty in New York City. Examples of his painting are in the collection of the New York Historical Society.

JASHAR, BOOK OF, in Hebrew *Sepher ha-yashar*, a Hebrew composition mentioned as though well-known in Josh. x. 13 and 2 Sam. i. 18. From these two passages it seems to have been a book of songs relating to important events, but no early collection of the kind is now extant, nor is anything known of it. Various speculations have been put forward as to the name: (1) that it means the book of the upright, *i.e.* Israel or distinguished Israelites, the root being the same as in Jeshurun; (2) that Jashar (ישר) is a transposition of shîr (שיר, song); (3) that it should be pointed Yashir (ישר, sing; cf. Exod. xv. 1) and was so called after its first word. None of these is very convincing, though support may be found for them all in the versions. The Septuagint favours (1) by its rendering ἐπὶ βιβλίου τοῦ εὐθοῦς in Samuel (it omits the words in Joshua); the Vulgate has *in libro justorum* in both places; the Syriac in Samuel has *Ashîr*, which suggests a Hebrew reading *ha-shîr* (the song), and in Joshua it translates "book of praises." The Targum on both passages has "book of the law," an explanation which is followed by the chief Jewish commentators, making the incidents the fulfilment of passages in the Pentateuch. Since it contained the lament of David (2 Sam. i. 18) it cannot have been completed till after his time. If Wellhausen's restoration of 1 Kings viii. 12 be accepted (from Septuagint 1 Kings viii. 53, ἐν βιβλίῳ τῆς ᾠδῆς) where the reference is to the building of the Temple, the book must have been growing in the time of Solomon. The attempt of Donaldson1 to reconstruct it is largely subjective and uncritical.

In later times when it became customary to compose midrashic works under well-known names, a book of Jashar naturally made its appearance. It need hardly be remarked that this has nothing whatever to do with the older book. It is an anonymous elaboration in Hebrew of the early part of the biblical narrative, probably composed in the 12th century. The fact that its legendary material is drawn from Arabic sources, as well as from Talmud, Midrash and later Jewish works, would seem to show that the writer lived in Spain, or, according to others, in south Italy. The first edition appeared at Venice in 1625, and it has been frequently printed since. It was translated into English by (or for) M. M. Noah (New York, 1840). A work called *The Book of ... Jasher, translated ... by Alcuin* (1751; 2nd ed., Bristol, 1829), has nothing to do with this or with any Hebrew original, but is a mere fabrication by the printer, Jacob Hive, who put it forward as the book "mentioned in Holy Scripture."

BIBLIOGRAPHY.—M. Heilprin, *Historical Poetry of the Ancient Hebrews* (New York, 1879), i. 128-131; Mercati, "Una congettura sopra il libro del Giusto," in *Studi e Testi* (5, Roma, 1901). On the medieval work see Zunz,*Gottesdienstliche Vorträge der Juden* (Frankfurt a. M., 1892), 2nd ed., p. 162.

1*Jashar: fragmenta archetypa carminum Hebraicorum*(Berlin, 1854). Cf. Perowne's *Remarks* on it (Lond. 1855).

JASHPUR, a tributary state of India, in the Central Provinces, having been transferred from Bengal in 1905. The country is divided almost equally into high and low lands. The Uparghat plateau on the east rises 2200 ft. above sea-level, and the hills above it reach their highest point in Ranijula (3527 ft.). The only river of importance is the Ib, in the bed of which diamonds are found, while from time immemorial its sands have been washed for gold. Jashpur iron, smelted

58

by the Kols, is highly prized. Jungles of *sál* forests abound, harbouring elephant, bison and other wild beasts. Jungle products include lac, silk cocoons and beeswax, which are exported. Area 1948 sq. m.; pop. (1901), 132,114; estimated revenue £8000.

JASMIN, JACQUES (1798-1864), Provençal poet, was born at Agen on the 6th of March 1798, his family name being Boé. His father, who was a tailor, had a certain facility for making doggerel verses, which he sang or recited at fairs and such-like popular gatherings; and Jacques, who used generally to accompany him, was thus early familiarized with the part which he afterwards so successfully filled himself. When sixteen years of age he found employment at a hairdresser's shop, and subsequently started a similar business of his own on the Gravier at Agen. In 1825 he published his first volume of *Papillotos* ("Curl Papers"), containing poems in French (a language he used with a certain sense of restraint), and in the familiar Agen *patois*—the popular speech of the working classes—in which he was to achieve all his literary triumphs. Jasmin was the most famous forerunner in Provençal literature (*q.v.*) of Mistral and the *Félibrige*. His influence in rehabilitating, for literary purposes, his native dialect, was particularly exercised in the public recitals of his poems to which he devoted himself. His poetic gift, and his flexible voice and action, fitted him admirably for this double rôle of troubadour and jongleur. In 1835 he recited his "Blind Girl of Castel-Cuillé" at Bordeaux, in 1836 at Toulouse; and he met with an enthusiastic reception in both those important cities. Most of his public recitations were given for benevolent purposes, the proceeds being contributed by him to the restoration of the church of Vergt and other good works. Four successive volumes of *Papillotos* were published during his lifetime, and contained amongst others the following remarkable poems, quoted in order: "The Charivari," "My Recollections" (supplemented after an interval of many years), "The Blind Girl," "Françounetto," "Martha the Simple," and "The Twin Brothers." With the exception of "The Charivari," these are all touching pictures of humble life—in most cases real episodes—carefully elaborated by the poet till the graphic descriptions, full of light and colour, and the admirably varied and melodious verse, seem too spontaneous and easy to have cost an effort. Jasmin was not a prolific writer, and, in spite of his impetuous nature, would work a long time at one poem, striving to realize every feeling he wished to describe, and give it its most lucid and natural expression. A verse from his spirited poem, "The Third of May," written in honour of Henry IV., and published in the first volume of *Papillotos*, is engraved on the base of the statue erected to that king at Nérac. In 1852 Jasmin's works were crowned by the Académie Française, and a pension was awarded him. The medal struck on the occasion bore the inscription: *Au poëte moral et populaire*. His title of "Maistre ès Jeux" is a distinction only conferred by the academy of Toulouse on illustrious writers. Pius IX. sent him the insignia of a knight of St Gregory the Great, and he was made chevalier of the Legion of Honour. He spent the latter years of his life on a small estate which he had bought near Agen and named "Papillotos," and which he describes in *Ma Bigno* ("My Vine"). Though invited to represent his native city, he refused to do so, preferring the pleasures and leisure of a country life, and wisely judging that he was no really eligible candidate for electoral honours. He died on the 4th of October 1864. His last poem, an answer to Renan, was placed between his folded hands in his coffin.

JASMINE, or JESSAMINE, botanically *Jasminum*, a genus of shrubs or climbers constituting the principal part of the tribe Jasminoideae of the natural order Oleaceae, and comprising about 150 species, of which 40 or more occur in the gardens of Britain. The plants of the genus are mostly natives of the warmer regions of the Old World; there is one South American species. The leaves are pinnate or ternate, or sometimes apparently simple, consisting of one leaflet, articulated to the petiole. The flowers, usually white or yellow, are arranged in terminal or axillary panicles, and have a tubular 5- or 8-cleft calyx, a cylindrical corolla-tube, with a spreading limb, two included stamens and a two-celled ovary.

The name is derived from the Persian *yásmín*. Linnaeus obtained a fancied etymology from ἴα, violets, and ὀσμή, smell, but the odour of its flowers bears no resemblance to that of the violet. The common white jasmine, *Jasminum officinale*, one 278of the best known and most highly esteemed of British hardy ligneous climbers, is a native of northern India and Persia, introduced about the middle of the 16th century. In the centre and south of Europe it is thoroughly acclimatized. Although it grows to the height of 12 and sometimes 20 ft., its stem is feeble and requires support; its leaves are opposite, pinnate and dark green, the leaflets are in three pairs, with an odd one, and are pointed, the terminal one larger and with a tapering point. The fragrant white flowers bloom from June to October; and, as they are found chiefly on the young shoots, the plant should only be pruned in the autumn. Varieties with golden and silver-edged leaves and one with double flowers are known.

Jasminum grandiflorum; flower, natural
size.

The zambak or Arabian jasmine, *J. Sambac*, is an evergreen white-flowered climber, 6 or 8 ft. high, introduced into Britain in the latter part of the 17th century. Two varieties introduced somewhat later are respectively 3-leaved and double-flowered, and these, as well as that with normal flowers, bloom throughout the greater part of the year. On account of their exquisite fragrance the flowers are highly esteemed in the East, and are frequently referred to by the Persian and Arabian poets. An oil obtained by boiling the leaves is used to anoint the head for complaints of the eye, and an oil obtained from the roots is used medicinally to arrest the secretion of milk. The flowers of one of the double varieties are held sacred to Vishnu, and used as votive offerings in Hindu religious ceremonies. The Spanish, or Catalonian jasmine, *J. grandiflorum*, a native of the north-west Himalaya, and cultivated both in the old and new world, is very like *J. officinale*, but differs in the size of the leaflets; the branches are shorter and stouter, and the flowers very much larger, and reddish underneath. By grafting it on two-year-old plants of *J. officinale*, an erect bush about 3 ft. high is obtained, requiring no supports. In this way it is very extensively cultivated at Cannes and Grasse, in the south of France; the plants are set in rows, fully exposed to the sun; they come into full bearing the second year after grafting; the blossoms, which are very large and intensely fragrant, are produced from July till the end of October, but those of August and September are the most odoriferous.

The aroma is extracted by the process known as *enfleurage, i.e.* absorption by a fatty body, such as purified lard or olive oil. Square glass trays framed with wood about 3 in. deep are spread over with grease about half an inch thick, in which ridges are made to facilitate absorption, and sprinkled with freshly gathered flowers, which are renewed every morning during the whole time the plant remains in blossom; the trays are piled up in stacks to prevent the evaporation of the aroma; and finally the pomade is scraped off the glass, melted at as low a temperature as possible, and strained. When oil is employed as the absorbent, coarse cotton cloths previously saturated with the finest olive oil are laid on wire-gauze frames, and repeatedly covered in the same manner with fresh flowers; they are then squeezed under a press, yielding what is termed *huile antique au jasmin*. Three pounds of flowers will perfume 1 ℔ of grease—this is exhausted by maceration in 1 pt. of rectified spirit to form the "extract." An essential oil is distilled from jasmine in Tunis and Algeria, but its high price prevents its being used to any extent. The East Indian oil of jasmine is a compound largely contaminated with sandalwood-oil.

The distinguishing characters of *J. odoratissimum*, a native of the Canary Islands and Madeira, consist principally in the alternate, obtuse, ternate and pinnate leaves, the 3-flowered terminal peduncles and the 5-cleft yellow corolla with obtuse segments. The flowers have the advantage of retaining when dry their natural perfume, which is suggestive of a mixture of jasmine, jonquil and orange-blossom. In China *J. paniculatum* is cultivated as an erect shrub, known as *sieu-hing-hwa*; it is valued for its flowers, which are used with those of *J. Sambac*, in the proportion of 10 ℔ of the former to 30 ℔ of the latter, for scenting tea—40 ℔ of the mixture being required for 100 ℔ of tea. *J. angustifolium* is a beautiful evergreen climber 10 to 12 ft. high, found in the Coromandel forests, and introduced into Britain during the present century. Its leaves are of a bright shining green; its large terminal flowers are white with a faint tinge of red, fragrant and blooming throughout the year.

In Cochin China a decoction of the leaves and branches of *J. nervosum* is taken as a blood-purifier; and the bitter leaves of *J. floribundum* (called in Abyssinia *habbez-zelim*) mixed with kousso is considered a powerful anthelmintic, especially for tapeworm; the leaves and branches are added to some fermented liquors to increase their intoxicating quality. In Catalonia and in Turkey the wood of the jasmine is made into long, slender pipe-stems, highly prized by the Moors and Turks. Syrup of jasmine is made by placing in a jar alternate layers of the flowers and sugar, covering the whole with wet cloths and standing it in a cool place; the perfume is absorbed by the sugar, which is converted into a very palatable syrup. The important medicinal plant known in America as the "Carolina jasmine" is not a true jasmine (see GELSEMIUM).

Other hardy species commonly cultivated in gardens are the low or Italian yellow-flowered jasmine, *J. humile*, an East Indian species introduced and now found wild in the south of Europe, an erect shrub 3 or 4 ft. high, with angular branches, alternate and mostly ternate leaves, blossoming from June to September; the common yellow jasmine, *J. fruticans*, a native of southern

60

Europe and the Mediterranean region, a hardy evergreen shrub, 10 to 12 ft. high, with weak, slender stems requiring support, and bearing yellow, odourless flowers from spring to autumn; and *J. nudiflorum* (China), which bears its bright yellow flowers in winter before the leaves appear. It thrives in almost any situation and grows rapidly.

JASON (Ἰάσων), in Greek legend, son of Aeson, king of Iolcus in Thessaly. He was the leader of the Argonautic expedition (see ARGONAUTS). After he returned from it he lived at Corinth with his wife Medea (*q.v.*) for many years. At last he put away Medea, in order to marry Glauce (or Creusa), daughter of the Corinthian king Creon. To avenge herself, Medea presented the new bride with a robe and head-dress, by whose magic properties the wearer was burnt to death, and slew her children by Jason with her own hand. A later story represents Jason as reconciled to Medea (Justin, xlii. 2). His death was said to have been due to suicide through grief, caused by Medea's vengeance (Diod. Sic. iv. 55); or he was crushed by the fall of the poop of the ship "Argo," under which, on the advice of Medea, he had laid himself down to sleep (argument of Euripides' *Medea*). The name (more correctly Iason) means "healer," and Jason is possibly a local hero of Iolcus to whom healing powers were attributed. The ancients regarded him as the oldest navigator, and the patron of navigation. By the moderns he has been variously explained as a solar deity; a god of summer; a god of storm; a god of rain, who carries off the rain-giving cloud (the golden fleece) to refresh the earth after a long period of drought. Some regard the legend as a chthonian myth, Aea (Colchis) being the under-world in the Aeolic religious system from which Jason liberates himself and his betrothed; others, in view of certain resemblances between the story of Jason and that of Cadmus (the ploughing of the field, the sowing of the dragon's teeth, the fight with the Sparti, who are finally set fighting with one another by a stone hurled into their midst), associate both with Demeter the corn-goddess, and refer certain episodes to practices in use at country festivals, *e.g.* the stone throwing, which, like the βαλλητύς at the Eleusinia and theλιθοβολία at 279Troezen (Pausanias ii. 30, 4 with Frazer's note) was probably intended to secure a good harvest by driving away the evil spirits of unfruitfulness.

See articles by C. Seeliger in Roscher's *Lexikon der Mythologie* and by F. Durrbach in Daremberg and Saglio's*Dictionnaire des antiquités*; H. D. Müller, *Mythologie der griechischen Stämme* (1861), ii. 328, who explains the name Jason as "wanderer"; W. Mannhardt, *Mythologische Forschungen* (1884), pp. 75, 130; O. Crusius, *Beiträge zur griechischen Mythologie una Religionsgeschichte* (Leipzig, 1886).

Later Versions of the Legend.—*Les fais et prouesses du noble et vaillant chevalier Jason* was composed in the middle of the 15th century by Raoul Lefèvre on the basis of Benoît's*Roman de Troie*, and presented to Philip of Burgundy, founder of the order of the Golden Fleece. The manners and sentiments of the 15th century are made to harmonize with the classical legends after the fashion of the Italian pre-Raphaelite painters, who equipped Jewish warriors with knightly lance and armour. The story is well told; the digressions are few; and there are many touches of domestic life and natural sympathy. The first edition is believed to have been printed at Bruges in 1474.

Caxton translated the book under the title of *A Boke of the hoole Lyf of Jason*, at the command of the duchess of Burgundy. A Flemish translation appeared at Haarlem in 1495. The Benedictine Bernard de Montfaucon (1655-1741) refers to a MS. by Guido delle Colonne, *Historia Medeae et Jasonis* (unpublished).

The *Histoire de la Thoison d'Or* (Paris, 1516) by Guillaume Fillastre (1400-1473), written about 1440-1450, is an historical compilation dealing with the exploits of the*très chrétiennes maisons* of France, Burgundy and Flanders.

JASON OF CYRENE, a Hellenistic Jew, who lived about 100 B.C. and wrote a history of the times of the Maccabees down to the victory over Nicanor (175-161 B.C.). This work is said to have been in five books and formed the basis of the present 2 Macc. (see ch. ii. 19-32).

JASPER, an opaque compact variety of quartz, variously coloured and often containing argillaceous matter. The colours are usually red, brown, yellow or green, and are due to admixture with compounds of iron, either oxides or silicates. Although the term jasper is now restricted to opaque quartz it is certain that the ancient *jaspis* or ἴασπις was a stone of considerable translucency. The jasper of antiquity was in many cases distinctly green, for it is often compared with the emerald and other green objects. Jasper is referred to in the*Niebelungenlied* as being clear and green. Probably the jasper of the ancients included stones which would now be classed as chalcedony, and the emerald-like jasper may have been akin to our chrysoprase. The Hebrew word *yashefeh* may have designated a green jasper (cf. Assyrian *yashpu*). Professor Flinders Petrie has suggested that the *odem*, the first stone on the High Priest's breastplate, translated "sard," was a red jasper, whilst *tarshish*, the tenth stone, may have been a yellow jasper (Hastings's *Dict. Bible*, 1902).

Many varieties of jasper are recognized. Riband jasper is a form in which the colours are disposed in bands, as in the well-known ornamental stone from Siberia, which shows a regular alternation of dark red and green stripes. Egyptian jasper is a brown jasper, occurring as nodules in the Lybian desert and in the Nile valley, and characterized by a zonal arrangement of light and dark shades of colour. Agate-jasper is a variety intermediate between true jasper and chalcedony. Basanite, lydite, or Lydian stone, is a velvet-black flinty jasper, used as a touchstone for testing the purity of precious metals by their streak. Porcelain jasper is a clay indurated by natural calcination.

(F. W. R.*)

JASSY (*Iaşi*), also written JASII, JASCHI and YASSY, the capital of the department of Jassy, Rumania; situated on the left bank of the river Bahlui, an affluent of the Jijia, about 10 m. W. of the Pruth and the Russian frontier. Pop. (1900), 78,067. Jassy communicates by rail with Galatz on the Danube, Kishinev in Bessarabia, and Czernowitz in Bukowina. The surrounding country is one of uplands and woods, among which rise the monasteries of Cetaţuia, Frumoasa, and Galata with its mineral springs, the water-cure establishment of Rapide and the great seminary of Socola. Jassy itself stands pleasantly amid vineyards and gardens, partly on two hills, partly in the hollow between. Its primitive houses of timber and plaster were mostly swept away after 1860, when brick or stone came into general use, and good streets were cut among the network of narrow, insanitary lanes. Jassy is the seat of the metropolitan of Moldavia, and of a Roman Catholic archbishop. Synagogues and churches abound. The two oldest churches date from the reign of Stephen the Great (1458-1504); perhaps the finest, however, are the 17th-century metropolitan, St Spiridion and Trei Erarchi, the last a curious example of Byzantine art, erected in 1639 or 1640 by Basil the Wolf, and adorned with countless gilded carvings on its outer walls and twin towers. The St Spiridion Foundation (due to the liberality of Prince Gregory Ghika in 1727, and available for the sick of all countries and creeds) has an annual income of over £80,000, and maintains hospitals and churches in several towns of Moldavia, besides the baths at Slanic in Walachia. The main hospital in Jassy is a large building, and possesses a maternity institution, a midwifery school, a chemical institute, an inoculating establishment, &c. A society of physicians and naturalists has existed in Jassy since the early part of the 19th century, and a number of periodicals are published. Besides the university, founded by Prince Cuza in 1864, with faculties of literature, philosophy, law, science and medicine, there are a military academy and schools of art, music and commerce; a museum, a fine hall and a theatre; the state library, where the chief records of Rumanian history are preserved; an appeal court, a chamber of commerce and several banks. The city is the headquarters of the 4th army corps. It has an active trade in petroleum, salt, metals, timber, cereals, fruit, wine, spirits, preserved meat, textiles, clothing, leather, cardboard and cigarette paper.

The inscription by which the existence of a *Jassiorum municipium* in the time of the Roman Empire is sought to be proved, lies open to grave suspicion; but the city is mentioned as early as the 14th century, and probably does derive its name from the Jassians, or Jazygians, who accompanied the Cumanian invaders. It was often visited by the Moldavian court. About 1564, Prince Alexander Lapusneanu, after whom one of the chief streets is named, chose Jassy for the Moldavian capital, instead of Suceava (now Suczawa, in Bukowina). It was already famous as a centre of culture. Between 1561 and 1563 an excellent school and a Lutheran church were founded by the Greek adventurer, Jacob Basilicus (see RUMANIA:*History*). In 1643 the first printed book published in Moldavia was issued from a press established by Basil the Wolf. He also founded a school, the first in which the mother-tongue took the place of Greek. Jassy was burned by the Tatars in 1513, by the Turks in 1538, and by the Russians in 1686. By the Peace of Jassy the second Russo-Turkish War was brought to a close in 1792. A Greek insurrection under Ypsilanti in 1821 led to the storming of the city by the Turks in 1822. In 1844 there was a severe conflagration. For the loss caused to the city in 1861 by the removal of the seat of government to Bucharest the constituent assembly voted £148,150, to be paid in ten annual instalments, but no payment was ever made.

JĀTAKA, the technical name, in Buddhist literature, for a story of one or other of the previous births of the Buddha. The word is also used for the name of a collection of 547 of such stories included, by a most fortunate conjuncture of circumstances, in the Buddhist canon. This is the most ancient and the most complete collection of folk-lore now extant in any literature in the world. As it was made at latest in the 3rd century B.C., it can be trusted not to give any of that modern or European colouring which renders suspect much of the folk-lore collected by modern travellers.

Already in the oldest documents, drawn up by the disciples soon after the Buddha's death, he is identified with certain ancient sages of renown. That a religious teacher should claim to be successor of the prophets of old is not uncommon in the history of religions. But the current belief in metempsychosis led, or enabled, the early Buddhists to make a much wider claim. It was not very long before they gradually identified their master with the hero of each of the popular fables and stories of which 280they were so fond. The process must have been complete by the middle of the 3rd century B.C.; for we find at that date illustrations of the Jātakas in the bas-reliefs on the railing round the Bharahat tope with the titles of the Jātaka stories inscribed above them in the characters of that period.1The hero of each story is made into a Bodhisatta; that is, a being who is destined, after a number of subsequent births, to become a Buddha. This rapid development of the Bodhisatta theory is the distinguishing feature in the early history of Buddhism, and was both cause and effect of the simultaneous growth of the Jātaka book. In adopting the folk-lore and fables already current in India, the Buddhists did not change them very much. The stories as preserved to us, are for the most part Indian rather than Buddhist. The ethics they inculcate or suggest are milk for babes; very simple in character and referring almost exclusively to matters common to all schools of thought in India, and indeed elsewhere. Kindness, purity, honesty, generosity, worldly wisdom, perseverance, are the usual virtues praised; the higher ethics of the Path are scarcely mentioned. These stories, popular with all, were especially appreciated by that school of Buddhists that laid stress on the Bodhisatta theory—a school that obtained its chief support, and probably had its origin, in the extreme north-west of India and in the highlands of Asia. That school adopted, from the early centuries of our era, the use of Sanskrit, instead of Pali, as the means of literary expression. It is almost impossible, therefore, that they would have carried the canonical Pali book, voluminous as it is, into Central Asia. Shorter collections of the original stories, written in Sanskrit, were in vogue among them. One such collection, the Jātaka-mālā, by Ārya Sūra (6th century), is still extant. Of the existence of another collection, though the Sanskrit original has not yet been found, we have curious evidence. In the 6th century a book of Sanskrit fables was translated into Pahlavi, that is, old Persian (see Bidpai). In succeeding centuries this work was retranslated into Arabic and Hebrew, thence into Latin and Greek and all the modern languages of Europe. The book bears a close resemblance to the earlier chapters of a late Sanskrit fable book called, from its having five chapters, the *Pancha tantra*, or Pentateuch.

The introduction to the old Jātaka book gives the life of the historical Buddha. That introduction must also have reached Persia by the same route. For in the 8th century St John of Damascus put the story into Greek under the title of *Barlaam and Josaphat.* This story became very popular in the West. It was translated into Latin, into seven European languages, and even into Icelandic and the dialect of the Philippine Islands. Its hero, that is the Buddha, was canonized as a Christian saint; and the 27th of November was officially fixed as the date for his adoration as such.

The book popularly known in Europe as *Aesop's Fables*was not written by Aesop. It was put together in the 14th century at Constantinople by a monk named Planudes, and he drew largely for his stories upon those in the Jātaka book that had reached Europe along various channels. The fables of Babrius and Phaedrus, written respectively in the 1st century before, and in the 1st century after, the Christian era, also contain Jātaka stories known in India in the 4th century B.C. A great deal has been written on this curious question of the migration of fables. But we are still very far from being able to trace the complete history of each story in the Jātaka book, or in any one of the later collections. For India itself the record is most incomplete. We have the original Jātaka book in text and translation. The history of the text of the Pancha tantra, about a thousand years later, has been fairly well traced out. But for the intervening centuries scarcely anything has been done. There are illustrations, in the bas-reliefs of the 3rd century B.C., of Jātakas not contained in the Jātaka book. Another collection, the *Cariyā piṭaka*, of about the same date, has been edited, but not translated. Other collections both in Pali and Sanskrit are known to be extant in MS; and a large number of Jātaka stories, not included in any formal collection, are mentioned, or told in full, in other works.

AUTHORITIES.—V. Fausböll, *The Jataka*, Pali text (7 vols., London, 1877-1897), (Eng. trans., edited by E. B. Cowell, 6 vols., Cambridge, 1895-1907); *Cariyā piṭaka*, edited by R. Morris for the Pali Text Society (London, 1882); H. Kern,*Jātaka-mālā*, Sanskrit text (Cambridge, Mass., 1891), (Eng. trans. by J. S. Speyer, Oxford, 1895); Rhys Davids,*Buddhist Birth Stories* (with full bibliographical tables) (London, 1880); *Buddhist India* (chap. xi. on the Jātaka Book) (London,

1903); E. Kuhn, *Barlaam und Joasaph*(Munich, 1893); A. Cunningham, *The Stupa of Bharhut*(London, 1879).

(T. W. R. D.)

1A complete list of these inscriptions will be found in Rhys Davids's *Buddhist India*, p. 209.

JATH, a native state of India, in the Deccan division of Bombay, ranking as one of the southern Mahratta jagirs. With the small state of Daphlapur, which is an integral part of it, it forms the Bijapur Agency, under the collector of Bijapur district. Area, including Daphlapur, 980 sq. m. Pop. (1901), 68,665, showing a decline of 14% in the decade. Estimated revenue £24,000; tribute £700. Agriculture and cattle-breeding are carried on; there are no important manufactures. The chief, whose title is deshmukh, is a Mahratta of the Daphle family. The town of JATH is 92 m. S.E. of Satara. Pop. (1901), 5404.

JÁTIVA (formerly written XATIVA), or SAN FELIPE DE JÁTIVA, a town of eastern Spain, in the province of Valencia, on the right bank of the river Albaida, a tributary of the Júcar, and at the junction of the Valencia-Murcia and Valencia-Albacete railways. Pop. (1900), 12,600. Játiva is built on the margin of a fertile and beautiful plain, and on the southern slopes of the Monte Bernisa, a hill with two peaks, each surmounted by a castle. With its numerous fountains, and spacious avenues shaded with elms or cypresses, the town has a clean and attractive appearance. Its collegiate church, dating from 1414, but rebuilt about a century later in the Renaissance style, was formerly a cathedral, and is the chief among many churches and convents. The town-hall and a church on the castle hill are partly constructed of inscribed Roman masonry, and several houses date from the Moorish occupation. There is a brisk local trade in grain, fruit, wine, oil and rice.

Játiva was the Roman Saetabis, afterwards Valeria Augusta, of Carthaginian or Iberian origin. Pliny (23-79) and Martial (*c*.40-102) mention the excellence of its linen cloth. Under the Visigoths (*c*. 483-711) it became an episcopal see; but early in the 8th century it was captured by the Moors, under whom it attained great prosperity, and received its present name. It was reconquered by James I. of Aragon (1213-1276). During the 15th and 16th centuries, Játiva was the home of many members of the princely house of Borgia or Borja, who migrated hither from the town of Borja in the province of Saragossa. Alphonso Borgia, afterwards Pope Calixtus III., and Rodrigo Borgia, afterwards Pope Alexander VI., were natives of Játiva, born respectively in 1378 and 1431. The painter Jusepe Ribera was also born here in 1588. Owing to its gallant defence against the troops of the Archduke Charles in the war of the Spanish succession, Játiva received the additional name of San Felipe from Philip V. (1700-1746).

JÁTS, or JUTS, a people of north-western India, who numbered altogether more than 7 millions in 1901. They form a considerable proportion of the population in the Punjab, Rájputana and the adjoining districts of the United Provinces, and are also widely scattered through Sind and Baluchistan. Some writers have identified the Juts with the ancient Getae, and there is strong reason to believe them a degraded tribe of Rájputs, whose Scythic origin has also been maintained. Hindu legends point to a prehistoric occupation of the Indus valley by this people, and at the time of the Mahommedan conquest of Sind (712) they, with a cognate tribe called Meds, constituted the bulk of the population. They enlisted under the banner of Mahommed bin Kāsim, but at a later date offered a vigorous resistance to the Arab invaders. In 836 they were overthrown by Amran, who imposed on them a tribute of dogs, and used their arms to vanquish the Meds. In 1025, however, they had gathered audacity, not only to invade Mansura, and compel the abjuration of the Mussulman amir, but to attack the victorious army of Mahmūd, laden with the spoil of Somnāth. Chastisement duly ensued: a formidable flotilla, collected at Mūltān, shattered in thousands the comparatively defenceless Jāt boats on the Indus, and annihilated their national pretensions. It is not until the decay of the Mogul Empire that the Jāts again appear in history. One branch of them, settled 281south of Agra, mainly by bold plundering raids founded two dynasties which still exist at Bharatpur (*q.v.*) and Dholpur (*q.v.*). Another branch, settled north-west of Delhi, who adopted the Sikh religion, ultimately made themselves dominant throughout the Punjab (*q.v.*) under Ranjit Singh, and are now represented in their original home by the Phulkian houses of Patiala (*q.v.*), Jind (*q.v.*) and Nabha (*q.v.*). It is from this latter branch that the Sikh regiments of the Indian army are recruited. The Jāts are mainly agriculturists and cattle breeders. In their settlements on the Ganges and Jumna, extending as far east as Bareilly, they are divided into two great clans, the Dhe and the Hele; while in the Punjab there are said to be one hundred different sections. Their religion varies with locality. In the Punjab they have largely embraced Sikh tenets, while in Sind and Baluchistan they are

64

Mahommedans. In appearance they are not ill-favoured though extremely dark; they have good teeth, and large beards, sometimes stained with indigo. Their inferiority of social position, however, to some extent betrays itself in their aspect, and tends to be perpetuated by their intellectual apathy.

JAUBERT, PIERRE AMÉDÉE ÉMILIEN PROBE (1779-1847), French Orientalist, was born at Aix in Provence on the 3rd of June 1779. He was one of the most distinguished pupils of Silvestre de Sacy, whose funeral*Discours* he pronounced in 1838. Jaubert acted as interpreter to Napoleon in Egypt in 1798-1799, and on his return to Paris held various posts under government. In 1802 he accompanied Sebastiani on his Eastern mission; and in 1804 he was at Constantinople. Next year he was despatched to Persia to arrange an alliance with the shah; but on the way he was seized and imprisoned in a dry cistern for four months by the pasha of Bayazid. The pasha's death freed Jaubert, who successfully accomplished his mission, and rejoined Napoleon at Warsaw in 1807. On the eve of Napoleon's downfall he was appointed chargé d'affaires at Constantinople. The restoration ended his diplomatic career, but in 1818 he undertook a journey with government aid to Tibet, whence he succeeded in introducing into France 400 Kashmir goats. The rest of his life Jaubert spent in study, in writing and in teaching. He became professor of Persian in the collège de France, and director of the école des langues orientales, and in 1830 was elected member of the Académie des Inscriptions. In 1841 he was made a peer of France and councillor of state. He died in Paris on the 28th of January, 1847.

Besides articles in the *Journal asiatique*, he published*Voyage en Arménie et en Perse* (1821; the edition of 1860 has a notice of Jaubert, by M. Sédillot) and *Éléments de la grammaire turque* (1823-1834). See notices in the *Journal asiatique*, Jan. 1847, and the *Journal des débats*, Jan. 30, 1847.

JAUCOURT, ARNAIL FRANÇOIS,MARQUIS DE (1757-1852), French politician, was born on the 14th of November 1757 at Tournon (Seine-et-Marne) of a Protestant family, protected by the prince de Condé, whose regiment he entered. He adopted revolutionary ideas and became colonel of his regiment. In the Assembly, to which he was returned in 1791 by the department of Seine-et-Marne, he voted generally with the minority, and his views being obviously too moderate for his colleagues he resigned in 1792 and was soon after arrested on suspicion of being a reactionary. Mme de Staël procured his release from P. L. Manuel just before the September massacres. He accompanied Talleyrand on his mission to England, returning to France after the execution of Louis XVI. He lived in retirement until the establishment of the Consulate, when he entered the tribunate, of which he was for some time president. In 1803 he entered the senate, and next year became attached to the household of Joseph Bonaparte. Presently his imperialist views cooled, and at the Restoration he became minister of state and a peer of France. At the second Restoration he was for a brief period minister of marine, but held no further office. He devoted himself to the support of the Protestant interest in France. A member of the upper house throughout the reign of Louis Philippe, he was driven into private life by the establishment of the Second Republic, but lived to see the *Coup d'état* and to rally to the government of Louis Napoleon, dying in Paris on the 5th of February 1852.

JAUER, a town of Germany, in the Prussian province of Silesia, 13 m. by rail S. of Leignitz, on the Wüthende Neisse. Pop. (1900), 13,024. St Martin's (Roman Catholic) church dates from 1267-1290, and the Evangelical church from 1655. A new town-hall was erected in 1895-1898. Jauer manufactures leather, carpets, cigars, carriages and gloves, and is specially famous for its sausages. The town was first mentioned in 1242, and was formerly the capital of a principality embracing about 1200 sq. m., now occupied by the circles of Jauer, Bunzlau, Löweberg, Hirschberg and Schönau. From 1392 to 1741 it belonged to the kings of Bohemia, being taken from Maria Theresa by Frederick the Great. Jauer was formerly the prosperous seat of the Silesian linen trade, but the troubles of the Thirty Years' War, in the course of which it was burned down three times, permanently injured this.

See Schönaich, *Die alte Fürstentumshauptstadt Jauer*(Jauer, 1903).

JAUHARĪ (ABU NASR ISMAEIL IBN ḤAMMAD UL-JAUHARI) (d. 1002 or 1010), Arabian lexicographer, was born at Fārāb on the borders of Turkestan. He studied language in Fārāb and Bagdad, and later among the Arabs of the desert. He then settled in Damghan and afterwards at Nīshapūr, where he died by a fall from the roof of a house. His great work is the *Kitāb us-Ṣaḥāḥ fil-Lugha*, an Arabic dictionary, in which the words are arranged alphabetically according to the last letter of the root. He himself had only partially finished the last recension, but the work was completed by his pupil, Abū Isḥaq Ibrāhīm ibn Ṣāliḥ ul-Warrāq.

An edition was begun by E. Scheidius with a Latin translation, but one part only appeared at Harderwijk (1776). The whole has been published at Tebriz (1854) and at Cairo (1865), and many abridgments and Persian translations have appeared; cf. C. Brockelmann, *Geschichte der arabischen Literatur* (Weimar, 1898), i. 128 seq.

(G. W. T.)

JAUNDICE (Fr. *jaunisse*, from *jaune*, yellow), orICTERUS (from its resemblance to the colour of the golden oriole, of which Pliny relates that if a jaundiced person looks upon it he recovers but the bird dies), a term in medicine applied to a yellow coloration of the skin and other parts of the body, depending in most instances on some derangement affecting the liver. This yellow colour is due to the presence in the blood of bile or of some of the elements of that secretion. Jaundice, however, must be regarded more as a symptom of some morbid condition previously existing than as a disease *per se*.

Cases with jaundice may be divided into three groups.

1. *Obstructive Jaundice.*—Any obstruction of the passage of bile from the liver into the intestinal canal is sooner or later followed by the appearance of jaundice, which in such circumstances is due to the absorption of bile into the blood. The obstruction is due to one of the following causes: (1) Obstruction by foreign bodies within the bile duct, *e.g.*gallstones or parasites; (2) inflammation of the duodenum or the lining membrane of the duct; (3) stricture or obliteration of the duct; (4) a tumour growing from the duct; (5) pressure on the duct from without, from the liver or other organ, or tumours arising from them. Obstructions from these causes may be partial or complete, and the degree of jaundice will vary accordingly, but it is to be noted that extensive organic disease of the liver may exist without the evidence of obstructive jaundice.

The effect upon the liver of impediments to the outflow of bile such as those above indicated is in the first place an increase in its size, the whole biliary passages and the liver cells being distended with retained bile. This enlargement, however, speedily subsides when the obstruction is removed, but should it persist the liver ultimately shrinks and undergoes atrophy in its whole texture. The bile thus retained is absorbed into the system, and shows itself by the yellow staining seen to a greater or less extent in all the tissues and many of the fluids of the body. The kidneys, which in such circumstances act in some measure vicariously to the liver and excrete a portion of the 282retained bile, are apt to become affected in their structure by the long continuance of jaundice.

The symptoms of obstructive jaundice necessarily vary according to the nature of the exciting cause, but there generally exists evidence of some morbid condition before the yellow coloration appears. Thus, if the obstruction be due to an impacted gallstone in the common or hepatic duct, there will probably be the symptoms of intense suffering characterizing hepatic colic (see COLIC). In the cases most frequently seen—those, namely, arising from simple catarrh of the bile ducts due to gastro-duodenal irritation spreading through the common duct—the first sign to attract attention is the yellow appearance of the white of the eye, which is speedily followed by a similar colour on the skin over the body generally. The yellow tinge is most distinct where the skin is thin, as on the forehead, breast, elbows, &c. It may be also well seen in the roof of the mouth, but in the lips and gums the colour is not observed till the blood is first pressed from them. The tint varies, being in the milder cases faint, in the more severe a deep saffron yellow, while in extreme degrees of obstruction it may be of dark brown or greenish hue. The colour can scarcely, if at all, be observed in artificial light.

The urine exhibits well marked and characteristic changes in jaundice which exist even before any evidence can be detected on the skin or elsewhere. It is always of dark brown colour resembling porter, but after standing in the air it acquires a greenish tint. Its froth is greenish-yellow, and it stains with this colour any white substance. It contains not only the bile colouring matter but also the bile acids. The former is detected by the play of colours yielded on the addition of nitric acid, the latter by the purple colour, produced by placing a piece of lump sugar in the urine tested, and adding thereto a few drops of strong sulphuric acid.

The contents of the bowels also undergo changes, being characterized chiefly by their pale clay colour, which is in proportion to the amount of hepatic obstruction, and to their consequent want of admixture with bile. For the same reason they contain a large amount of unabsorbed fatty matter, and have an extremely offensive odour.

Constitutional symptoms always attend jaundice with obstruction. The patient becomes languid, drowsy and irritable, and has generally a slow pulse. The appetite is usually but not always diminished, a bitter taste in the mouth is complained of, while flatulent eructations arise from the stomach. Intolerable itching of the skin is a common accompaniment of jaundice, and cutaneous eruptions or boils are occasionally seen. Yellow vision appears to be present in some

66

very rare cases. Should the jaundice depend on advancing organic disease of the liver, such as cancer, the tinge becomes gradually deeper, and the emaciation and debility more marked towards the fatal termination, which in such cases is seldom long postponed. Apart from this, however, jaundice from obstruction may exist for many years, as in those instances where the walls of the bile ducts are thickened from chronic catarrh, but where they are only partially occluded. In the common cases of acute catarrhal jaundice recovery usually takes place in two or three weeks.

The treatment of this form of jaundice bears reference to the cause giving rise to the obstruction. In the ordinary cases of simple catarrhal jaundice, or that following the passing of gallstones, a light nutritious diet (milk, soups, &c., avoiding saccharine and farinaceous substances and alcoholic stimulants), along with counter-irritation applied over the right side and the use of laxatives and cholagogues, will be found to be advantageous. Diaphoretics and diuretics to promote the action of the skin and kidneys are useful in jaundice. In the more chronic forms, besides the remedies above named, the waters of Carlsbad are of special efficacy. In cases other than acute catarrhal, operative interference is often called for, to remove the gallstones, tumour, &c., causing the obstruction.

2. *Toxaemic Jaundice* is observed to occur as a symptom in certain fevers, *e.g.* yellow fever, ague, and in pyaemia also as the effect of certain poisons, such as phosphorus, and the venom of snake-bites. Jaundice of this kind is almost always slight, and neither the urine nor the discharges from the bowels exhibit changes in appearance to such a degree as in the obstructive variety. Grave constitutional symptoms are often present, but they are less to be ascribed to the jaundice than to the disease with which it is associated.

3. *Hereditary Jaundice.*—Under this group there are the jaundice of new-born infants, which varies enormously in severity; the cases in which a slight form of jaundice obtains in several members of the same family, without other symptoms, and which may persist for years; and lastly the group of cases with hypertrophic cirrhosis.

The name *malignant jaundice* is sometimes applied to that very fatal form of disease otherwise termed acute yellow atrophy of the liver (see ATROPHY).

JAUNPUR, a city and district of British India, in the Benares division of the United Provinces. The city is on the left bank of the river Gumti, 34 m. N.W. from Benares by rail. Pop. (1901), 42,771. Jaunpur is a very ancient city, the former capital of a Mahommedan kingdom which once extended from Budaun and Etawah to Behar. It abounds in splendid architectural monuments, most of which belong to the period when the rulers of Jaunpur were independent of Delhi. The fort of Feroz Shah is in great part completely ruined, but there remain a fine gateway of the 16th century, a mosque dating from 1376, and the *hammams* or baths of Ibrahim Shah. Among other buildings may be mentioned the Atala Masjid (1408) and the ruined Jinjiri Masjid, mosques built by Ibrahim, the first of which has a great cloistered court and a magnificent façade; the Dariba mosque constructed by two of Ibrahim's governors; the Lal Darwaza erected by the queen of Mahmud; the Jama Masjid (1438-1478) or great mosque of Husain, with court and cloisters, standing on a raised terrace, and in part restored in modern times; and finally the splendid bridge over the Gumti, erected by Munim Khan, Mogul governor in 1569-1573. During the Mutiny of 1857 Jaunpur formed a centre of disaffection. The city has now lost its importance, the only industries surviving being the manufacture of perfumes and papier-mâché articles.

The DISTRICT OF JAUNPUR has an area of 1551 sq. m. It forms part of the wide Gangetic plain, and its surface is accordingly composed of a thick alluvial deposit. The whole country is closely tilled, and no waste lands break the continuous prospect of cultivated fields. It is divided into two unequal parts by the sinuous channel of the Gumti, a tributary of the Ganges, which flows past the city of Jaunpur. Its total course within the district is about 90 m., and it is nowhere fordable. It is crossed by two bridges, one at Jaunpur and the other 2 m. lower down. The Gumti is liable to sudden inundations during the rainy season, owing to the high banks it has piled up at its entrance into the Ganges, which act as dams to prevent the prompt outflow of its flooded waters. These inundations extend to its tributary the Saī. Much damage was thus effected in 1774; but the greatest recorded flood took place in September 1871, when 4000 houses in the city were swept away, besides 9000 more in villages along its banks. The other rivers are the Saī, Barna, Pili and Basohi. Lakes are numerous in the north and south; the largest has a length of 8 m. Pop. (1901), 1,202,920, showing a decrease of 5% in the decade. Sugar-refining is the principal industry. The district is served by the line of the Oudh & Rohilkhand railway from Benares to Fyzabad, and by branches of this and of the Bengal & North-Western systems.

In prehistoric times Jaunpur seems to have formed a portion of the Ajodhya principality, and when it first makes an appearance in authentic history it was subject to the rulers of Benares. With the rest of their dominions it fell under the yoke of the Mussulman invaders in 1194. From that time the district appears to have been ruled by a prince of the Kanauj dynasty, as a tributary of the Mahommedan suzerain. In 1388 Mālik Sarwar Khwāja was sent by Mahommed Tughlak to govern the eastern province. He fixed his residence at Jaunpur, made himself independent of the Delhi court, and assumed the title of Sultan-us-Shark, or "eastern emperor." For nearly a century 283the Sharki dynasty ruled at Jaunpur, and proved formidable rivals to the sovereigns of Delhi. The last of the dynasty was Sultan Husain, who passed his life in a fierce and chequered struggle for supremacy with Bahlol Lodi, then actual emperor at Delhi. At length, in 1478, Bahlol succeeded in defeating his rival in a series of decisive engagements. He took the city of Jaunpur, but permitted the conquered Husain to reside there, and to complete the building of his great mosque, the Jama Masjid, which now forms the chief ornament of the town. Many other architectural works in the district still bear witness to its greatness under its independent Mussulman rulers. In 1775 the district was made over to the British by the Treaty of Lucknow. From that time nothing occurred which calls for notice till the Mutiny. On the 5th of June 1857, when the news of the Benares revolt reached Jaunpur, the sepoys mutinied. The district continued in a state of complete anarchy till the arrival of the Gurkha force from Azamgarh in September. In November the surrounding country was lost again, and it was not till May 1858 that the last smouldering embers of disaffection were stifled by the repulse of the insurgent leader at the hands of the people themselves.

See A. Führer, *The Shargi Architecture of Jaunpur*(1889).

JAUNTING-CAR, a light two-wheeled carriage for a single horse, in its commonest form with seats for four persons placed back to back, with the foot-boards projecting over the wheels. It is the typical conveyance for persons in Ireland (seeCAR). The first part of the word is generally taken to be identical with the verb "to jaunt," now only used in the sense of to go on a short pleasure excursion, but in its earliest uses meaning to make a horse caracole or prance, hence to jolt or bump up and down. It would apparently be a variant of "jaunce," of the same meaning, which is supposed to be taken from O. Fr. *jancer*. Skeat takes the origin of jaunt and jaunce to be Scandinavian, and connects them with the Swedish dialect word *ganta*, to romp; and he finds cognate bases in such words as "jump," "high jinks." The word "jaunty," sprightly, especially used of anything done with an easy nonchalant air, is a corruption of "janty," due to confusion with "jaunt." "Janty," often spelt in the 17th and 18th centuries "janté" or "jantee," represents the English pronunciation of Fr. *gentil*, well-bred, neat, spruce.

JAUREGUI, JUAN (1562-1582), a Biscayan by birth, was in 1582 in the service of a Spanish merchant, Gaspar d'Anastro, who was resident at Antwerp. Tempted by the reward of 80,000 ducats offered by Philip II. of Spain for the assassination of William the Silent, prince of Orange, but being himself without courage to undertake the task, d'Anastro, with the help of his cashier Venero, persuaded Jauregui to attempt the murder for the sum of 2877 crowns. On Sunday the 18th of March 1582, as the prince came out of his dining-room Jauregui offered him a petition, and William had no sooner taken it into his hand than Jauregui fired a pistol at his head. The ball pierced the neck below the right ear and passed out at the left jaw-bone; but William ultimately recovered. The assassin was killed on the spot.

JAURÉGUIBERRY, JEAN BERNARD(1815-1887), French admiral, was born at Bayonne on the 26th of August 1815. He entered the navy in 1831, was made a lieutenant in 1845, commander in 1856, and captain in 1860. After serving in the Crimea and in China, and being governor of Senegal, he was promoted to rear-admiral in 1869. He served on land during the second part of the Franco-German War of 1870-71, in the rank of auxiliary general of division. He was present at Coulmiers, Villépion and Loigny-Poupry, in command of a division, and in Chanzy's retreat upon Le Mans and the battle at that place in command of a corps. He was the most distinguished of the many naval officers who did good service in the military operations. On the 9th of December he had been made vice-admiral, and in 1871 he commanded the fleet at Toulon; in 1875 he was a member of the council of admiralty; and in October 1876 he was appointed to command the evolutionary squadron in the Mediterranean. In February 1879 he became minister of the navy in the Waddington cabinet, and on the 27th of May following was elected a senator for life. He was again minister of the navy in the Freycinet cabinet in 1880. A fine example of the fighting French seaman of his time, Jauréguiberry died at Paris on the 21st of October 1887.

JÁUREGUI Y AGUILAR, JUAN MARTÍNEZ DE (1583-1641), Spanish poet, was baptized at Seville on the 24th of November 1583. In due course he studied at Rome, returning to Spain shortly before 1610 with a double reputation as a painter and a poet. A reference in the preface to the *Novelas exemplares* has been taken to mean that he painted the portrait of Cervantes, who, in the second part of *Don Quixote*, praises the translation of Tasso's *Aminta* published at Rome in 1607. Jáuregui's *Rimas*(1618), a collection of graceful lyrics, is preceded by a controversial preface which attracted much attention on account of its outspoken declaration against *culteranismo*. Through the influence of Olivares, he was appointed groom of the chamber to Philip IV., and gave an elaborate exposition of his artistic doctrines in the *Discurso poético contra el hablar culto y oscuro* (1624), a skilful attack on the new theories, which procured for its author the order of Calatrava. It is plain, however, that the shock of controversy had shaken Jáuregui's convictions, and his poem *Orfeo* (1624) is visibly influenced by Góngora. Jáuregui died at Madrid on the 11th of January 1641, leaving behind him a translation of the *Pharsalia* which was not published till 1684. This rendering reveals Jáuregui as a complete convert to the new school, and it has been argued that, exaggerating the affinities between Lucan and Góngora—both of Cordovan descent—he deliberately translated the thought of the earlier poet into the vocabulary of the later master. This is possible; but it is at least as likely that Jáuregui unconsciously yielded to the current of popular taste, with no other intention than that of conciliating the public of his own day.

JAURÈS, JEAN LÉON (1859-   ), French Socialist leader, was born at Castres (Tarn) on the 3rd of September 1859. He was educated at the lycée Louis-le-Grand and the école normale supérieure, and took his degree as associate in philosophy in 1881. After teaching philosophy for two years at the lycée of Albi (Tarn), he lectured at the university of Toulouse. He was elected republican deputy for the department of Tarn in 1885. In 1889, after unsuccessfully contesting Castres, he returned to his professional duties at Toulouse, where he took an active interest in municipal affairs, and helped to found the medical faculty of the university. He also prepared two theses for his doctorate in philosophy, *De primis socialismi germanici lineamentis apud Lutherum, Kant, Fichte et Hegel* (1891), and *De la réalité du monde sensible*. In 1902 he gave energetic support to the miners of Carmaux who went out on strike in consequence of the dismissal of a socialist workman, Calvignac; and in the next year he was re-elected to the chamber as deputy for Albi. Although he was defeated at the elections of 1898 and was for four years outside the chamber, his eloquent speeches made him a force in politics as an intellectual champion of socialism. He edited the *Petite République*, and was one of the most energetic defenders of Captain Alfred Dreyfus. He approved of the inclusion of M. Millerand, the socialist, in the Waldeck-Rousseau ministry, though this led to a split with the more revolutionary section led by M. Guesde. In 1902 he was again returned as deputy for Albi, and during the Combes administration his influence secured the coherence of the radical-socialist coalition known as the *bloc*. In 1904 he founded the socialist paper,*L'Humanité*. The French socialist groups held a congress at Rouen in March 1905, which resulted in a new consolidation; the new party, headed by MM. Jaurès and Guesde, ceased to co-operate with the radicals and radical-socialists, and became known as the unified socialists, pledged to advance a collectivist programme. At the general elections of 1906 M. Jaurès was again elected for the Tarn. His ability and vigour were now generally recognized; but the strength of the socialist party, and the practical activity of its leader, still had to reckon with the equally practical and vigorous liberalism of M. Clemenceau. The latter was able to appeal to his countrymen (in a notable 284speech in the spring of 1906) to rally to a radical programme which had no socialist Utopia in view; and the appearance in him of a strong and practical radical leader had the result of considerably diminishing the effect of the socialist propaganda. M. Jaurès, in addition to his daily journalistic activity, published *Les preuves; affaire Dreyfus* (1900); *Action socialiste* (1899); *Études socialistes* (1902), and, with other collaborators, *Histoire socialiste* (1901), &c.

JAVA, one of the larger islands of that portion of the Malay Archipelago which is distinguished as the Sunda Islands. It lies between 105° 12' 40" (St Nicholas Point) and 114° 35' 38" E. (Cape Seloko) and between 5° 52' 34" and 8° 46' 46" S. It has a total length of 622 m. from Pepper Bay in the west to Banyuwangi in the east, and an extreme breadth of 121 m. from Cape Bugel in Japara to the coast of Jokjakarta, narrowing towards the middle to about 55 m. Politically and commercially it is important as the seat of the colonial government of the Dutch East Indies, all other parts of the Dutch territory being distinguished as the Outer Possessions (*Buitenbezittungens*). According to the triangulation survey (report published in 1901) the area of Java proper is 48,504 sq. m.; of Madura, the large adjacent and associated island, 1732; and of the smaller islands administratively included with Java and Madura 1416, thus making a total of 50,970 sq. m. The more important of these islands are the following: Pulau Panaitan or Princes Island (*Prinseneiland*), 47 sq. m., lies in the Sunda Strait, off the south-western peninsula of the main island, from which it is separated by the Behouden Passage. The Thousand Islands are situated almost due N. of Batavia. Of these five were inhabited in 1906 by about 1280 seafarers

69

from all parts and their descendants. The Karimon Java archipelago, to the north of Semarang, numbers twenty-seven islands with an area of 16 sq. m. and a population of about 800 (having one considerable village on the main island). Bavian1(Bawian), 100 m. N. of Surabaya, is a ruined volcano with an area of 73 sq. m. and a population of about 44,000. About a third of the men are generally absent as traders or coolies. In Singapore and Sumatra they are known as Boyans. They are devout Mahommedans and many of them make the pilgrimage to Mecca. The Sapudi and Kangean archipelagoes are eastward continuations of Madura. The former, thirteen in all, with an area of 58 sq. m. and 53,000 inhabitants, export cattle, dried fish and trepang; and many of the male population work as day labourers in Java or as lumbermen in Sumbawa, Flores, &c. The main island of the Kangians has an area of 19 sq. m.; the whole group 23 sq. m. It is best known for its limestone caves and its buffaloes. Along the south coast the islands are few and small— Klapper or Deli, Trouwers or Tingal, Nusa Kembangan, Sempu and Nusa Barung.

From Sumatra on the W., Java is separated by the Sunda Strait, which at the narrowest is only 14 m. broad, but widens elsewhere to about 50 m. On the E. the strait of Bali, which parts it from the island of that name, is at the northern end not more than 1½ m. across. Through the former strong currents run for the greater part of the day throughout the year, outwards from the Java Sea to the Indian Ocean. In the strait of Bali the currents are perhaps even stronger and are extremely irregular. Pilots with local knowledge are absolutely necessary for vessels attempting either passage. In spite of the strength of the currents the Sunda Strait is steadily being diminished in width, and the process if continued must result in a restoration of that junction of Sumatra and Java which according to some authorities formerly existed.2

In general terms Java may be described as one of the breakwater islands of the Indian Ocean—part of the mountainous rim (continuous more or less completely with Sumatra) of the partially submerged plateau which lies between the ocean on the S. and the Chinese Sea on the N., and has the massive island of Borneo as its chief subaerial portion. While the waves and currents of the ocean sweep away most of the products of denudation along the south coast or throw a small percentage back in the shape of sandy downs, the Java Sea on the north—not more than 50 fathoms deep—allows them to settle and to form sometimes with extraordinary rapidity broad alluvial tracts.3

It is customary and obvious to divide Java into three divisions, the middle part of the island narrowing into a kind of isthmus, and each of the divisions thus indicated having certain structural characteristics of its own. West Java, which consists of Bantam, Krawang and the Preanger Regencies, has an area of upwards of 18,000 sq. m. In this division the highlands lie for the most part in a compact mass to the south and the lowlands form a continuous tract to the north. The main portion of the uplands consists of the Preanger Mountains, with the plateaus of Bandong, Pekalongan, Tegal, Badung and Gurut, encircled with volcanic summits. On the borders of the Preanger, Batavia and Bantam are the Halimon Mountains (the Blue Mountains of the older travellers), reaching their greatest altitudes in the volcanic summits of Gedeh and Salak. To the west lie the highlands of Bantam, which extending northward cut off the northern lowlands from the Sunda Strait. Middle Java is the smallest of the three divisions, having an area of not much more than 13,200 sq. m. It comprises Tegal, Pekalongan, Banyumas, Bagelen, Kedu, Jokjakarta, Surakarta, and thus not only takes in the whole of the isthmus but encroaches on the broad eastern portion of the island. In the isthmus mountains are not so closely massed 285in the south nor the plains so continuous on the north. The watershed culminating in Slamet lies almost midway between the ocean and the Java Sea, and there are somewhat extensive lowlands in the south. In that part of middle Java which physically belongs to eastern Java there is a remarkable series of lowlands stretching almost right across the island from Semarang in the north to Jokjakarta in the south. Eastern Java comprises Rembang, Madiun, Kediri, Surabaya, Pasuruan and Besuki, and has an area of about 17,500 sq. m. In this division lowlands and highlands are intermingled in endless variety except along the south coast, where the watershed-range forms a continuous breakwater from Jokjakarta to Besuki. The volcanic eminences, instead of rising in lines or groups, are isolated.

For its area Java is one of the most distinctly volcanic regions of the world. Volcanic forces made it, and volcanic forces have continued to devastate and fertilize it. According to R. D. M. Verbeek about 125 volcanic centres can be distinguished, a number which may be increased or diminished by different methods of classification. It is usual to arrange the volcanoes in the following groups: westernmost Java 11 (all extinct); Preanger 50 (5 active); Cheribon 2 (both extinct); Slamet 2 (1 active); middle Java 16 (2 active); Murio 2 (both extinct); Lavu 2 (extinct); Wilis 2 (extinct); east Java 21 (5 active). The active volcanoes of the present time are Gedeh, Tangkuban, Prahu, Gutar, Papandayan, Galung-gung, Slamet, Sendor, Merapi,4 Kalut (or Klut),

Bromo, Semeru, Lamongan, Raung, but the activity of many of these is trifling, consisting of slight ejections of steam and scoriae.

The plains differ in surface and fertility, according to their geological formation. Built up of alluvium and diluvium, the plains of the north coast-lands in western and middle Java are at their lowest levels, near the mouths of rivers and the sea, in many cases marshy and abounding in lakes and coral remains, but for the rest they are fertile and available for culture. The plains, too, along the south coast of middle Java—of Banyumas and Bagelen—contain many morasses as well as sandy stretches and dunes impeding the outlet of the rivers. They are, nevertheless, available for the cultivation more particularly of rice, and are thickly peopled. In eastern Java, again, the narrow coast plains are to be distinguished from the wider plains lying between the parallel chains of limestone and between the volcanoes. The narrow plains of the north coast are constituted of yellow clay and tuffs containing chalk, washed down by the rivers from the mountain chains and volcanoes. Like the western plains, they, too, are in many cases low and marshy, and fringed with sand and dunes. The plains, on the other hand, at some distance from the sea, or lying in the interior of eastern Java, such as Surakarta, Madiun, Kediri, Pasuruan, Probolinggo and Besuki, owe their formation to the volcanoes at whose bases they lie, occupying levels as high as 1640 ft. down to 328 ft. above the sea, whence they decline to the lower plains of the coast. Lastly, the plains of Lusi, Solo and Brantas, lying between the parallel chains in Japara, Rembang and Surabaya, are in part the product of rivers formerly flowing at a higher level of 30 to 60 or 70 ft., in part the product of the sea, dating from a time when the northern part of the above-named residencies was an island, such as Madura, the mountains of which are the continuation of the north parallel chain, is still.

The considerable rivers of western Java all have their outlets on the north coast, the chief among them being the Chi (Dutch Tji) Tarum and the Chi Manuk. They are navigable for native boats and rafts, and are used for the transport of coffee and salt. On the south coast the Chi Tanduwi, on the east of the Preanger, is the only stream available as a waterway, and this only for a few miles above its mouth. In middle Java, also, the rivers discharging at the north coast—the Pamali, Chomal, &c.—are serviceable for the purposes of irrigation and cultivation, but are navigable only near their mouths. The rivers of the south coast—Progo, Serayu, Bogowonto, and Upak, enriched by rills from the volcanoes—serve abundantly to irrigate the plains of Bagelen, Banyumas, &c. Their stony beds, shallows and rapids, and the condition of their mouths lessen, however, their value as waterways. More navigable are the larger rivers of eastern Java. The Solo is navigable for large praus, or native boats, as far up as Surakarta, and above that town for lighter boats, as is also its affluent the Gentung. The canal constructed in 1893 at the lower part of this river, and alterations effected at its mouth, have proved of important service both in irrigating the plain and facilitating the river's outlet into the sea. The Brantas is also navigable in several parts. The smaller rivers of eastern Java are, however, much in the condition of those of western Java. They serve less as waterways than as reservoirs for the irrigation of the fertile plains through which they flow.

The north coast of Java presents everywhere a low strand covered with nipa or mangrove, morasses and fishponds, sandy stretches and low dunes, shifting river-mouths and coast-lines, ports and roads, demanding continual attention and regulation. The south coast is of a different make. The dunes of Banyumas, Bagelen, and Jokjakarta, ranged in three ridges, rising to 50 ft. high, and varying in breadth from 300 to over 1600 ft., liable, moreover, to transformation from tides and the east monsoon, oppose everywhere, also in Preanger and Besuki, a barrier to the discharge of the rivers and the drainage of the coast-lands. They assist the formation of lagoons and morasses. At intervals in the dune coast, running in the direction of the limestone mountains, there tower up steep inaccessible masses of land, showing neither ports nor bays, hollowed out by the sea, rising in perpendicular walls to a height of 160 ft. above sea-level. Sometimes two branches project at right angles from the chain on to the coast, forming a low bay between the capes or ends of the projecting branches, from 1000 to 1600 ft. high. Such a formation occurs frequently along the coast of Besuki, presenting a very irregular coast-line. Of course the north coast is of much greater commercial importance than the south coast.

Geology.—With the exception of a few small patches of schist, supposed to be Cretaceous, the whole island, so far as is known, is covered by deposits of Tertiary and Quaternary age. The ancient "schist formation," which occurs in Sumatra, Borneo, &c., does not rise to the surface anywhere in Java itself, but it is visible in the island of Karimon Java off the north coast. The Cretaceous schists have yielded fossils only at Banjarnegara, where a limestone with Orbitolina is interstratified with them. They are succeeded unconformably by Eocene deposits, consisting of sandstones with coal-seams and limestones containing Nummulites, Alveolina and Orthophragmina; and these beds are as limited in extent as the Cretaceous schists themselves. Sedimentary deposits of Upper Tertiary age are widely spread, covering about 38% of the surface.

71

They consist of breccias, marls and limestones containing numerous fossils, and are for the most part Miocene but probably include a part of the Pliocene also. They were laid down beneath the sea, but have since been folded and elevated to considerable heights. Fluviatile deposits of late Pliocene age have been found in the east of Java, and it was in these that the remarkable anthropoid ape or ape-like man,*Pithecanthropus erectus* of Dubois, was discovered. The Quaternary deposits lie horizontally upon the upturned edges of the Tertiary beds. They are partly marine and partly fluviatile, the marine deposits reaching to a height of some 350 ft. above the sea and thus indicating a considerable elevation of the island in recent times.

The volcanic rocks of Java are of great importance and cover about 28% of the island. The eruptions began in the middle of the Tertiary period, but did not attain their maximum until Quaternary times, and many of the volcanoes are still active. Most of the cones seem to lie along faults parallel to the axis of the island, or on short cross fractures. The lavas and ashes are almost everywhere andesites and basalts, with a little obsidian. Some of the volcanoes, however, have erupted leucite rocks. Similar rocks, together with phonolite, occur in the island of Bavian.5

Climate.—Our knowledge of the climate of Batavia, and thus of that of the lowlands of western Java, is almost perfect; but, rainfall excepted, our information as to the climate of Java as a whole is extremely defective. The dominant meteorological facts are simple and obvious: Java lies in the tropics, under an almost vertical sun, and thus has a day of almost uniform length throughout the year.6 It is also within the perpetual influence of the great atmospheric movements passing between Asia and Australia; and is affected by the neighbourhood of vast expanses of sea and land (Borneo and Sumatra). There are no such maxima of temperature as are recorded from the continents. The highest known at Batavia was 96° F. in 1877 and the lowest 66° in the same year. The mean annual temperature is 79°. The warmest months are May and October, registering 79.5° and 79.46° respectively; the coldest January and February with 77.63° and 77.7° respectively. The daily range is much greater; at one o'clock the thermometer has a mean height of 84°; after two o'clock it declines to about 73° at six o'clock; the greatest daily amplitude is in August and the least in January and February. Eastern Java and the inland plains of middle Java are said to be hotter, but scientific data are few. A very slight degree of elevation above the seaboard plains produces a remarkable difference in the climate, not so much in its mere temperature as in its influence on health. The dwellers in the coast towns are surprised at the invigorating effects of a change to health resorts from 300 to 1200 ft. above sea-level; and at greater elevations it may be uncomfortably cold at night, with chilly mists and occasional frosts. The year is divided into two seasons by the prevailing winds: the rainy season, that of the west monsoon, lasting from November to March, and the dry season, that of the east monsoon, during the rest of the year; the transition from one monsoon to another—the "canting" of the monsoons—being marked by 286irregularities. On the whole, the east monsoon blows steadily for a longer period than the west. The velocity of the wind is much less than in Europe—not more in the annual mean at Batavia than 3 ft. per second, against 12 to 18 ft. in Europe. The highest velocity ever observed at Batavia was 25 ft. Wind-storms are rare and hardly ever cyclonic. There are as a matter of course a large number of purely local winds, some of them of a very peculiar kind, but few of these have been scientifically dealt with. Thunder-storms are extremely frequent; but the loss of life from lightning is probably diminished by the fact that the palm-trees are excellent conductors. At night the air is almost invariably still. The average rainfall at Batavia is 72.28 in. per annum, of which 51.49 in. are contributed by the west monsoon. The amount varies considerably from year to year: in 1889, 1891 and 1897 there were about 47.24 in.; in 1868 and 1877 nearly 51.17, and in 1872 and 1882 no less than 94.8. There are no long tracts of unbroken rainfall and no long periods of continuous drought. The rainfall is heaviest in January, but it rains only for about one-seventh of the time. Next in order come February, March and December. August, the driest month, has from three to five days of rain, though the amount is usually less than an inch and not more than one and a half inches. The popular description of the rain falling not in drops but streams was proved erroneous by J. Wiesner's careful observations (see *Kais. Akad. d. Wiss. Math. Naturw. Cl.* Bd. xiv., Vienna, 1895), which have been confirmed by A. Woeikof ("Regensintensität und Regendauer in Batavia" in *Z. für Met.*, 1907). The greatest rainfall recorded in an hour (4.5 in.) is enormously exceeded by records even in Europe. From observations taken for the meteorological authorities at a very considerable number of stations, J. H. Boeseken constructed a map in 1900 (*Tijdschr. v. h. Kon. Ned. Aardr. Gen.*, 1900; reproduced in Veth, *Java*, iii. 1903). Among the outstanding facts are the following. The south coasts of both eastern and middle Java have a much heavier rainfall than the north. Majalenka has an annual fall of 175 in. In western Java the maximal district consists of a great ring of mountains from Salak and Gedeh in the west to Galung-gung in the east, while the enclosed plateau-region of Chanjur Bandung and Garut are not much different from the seaboard. The whole of middle Java, with the exception of the north coast, has a heavy rainfall.

72

At Chilachap the annual rainfall is 151.43 in., 87.8 in. of which is brought by the south-east monsoon. The great belt which includes the Slamet and the Dieng, and the country on the south coast between Chilachap and Parigi, are maximal. In comparison the whole of eastern Java, with the exception of the mountains from Wilis eastward to Ijen, has a low record which reaches its lowest along the north coast.7

Fauna.—In respect of its fauna Java differs from Borneo, Sumatra and the Malay Peninsula far more than these differ among themselves; and, at the same time, it shows a close resemblance to the Malay Peninsula, on the one hand, and to the Himalayas on the other. Of the 176 mammals of the whole Indo-Malayan region the greater number occur in Java. Of these 41 are found on the continent of Asia, 8 are common to Java and Borneo, and 6 are common to Java and Sumatra (see M. Weber, *Das Indo-Malay Archipelago und die Geschichte seiner Thierwelt,* Jena, 1902). No genus and only a few species are confined to the island. Of the land-birds only a small proportion are peculiar. The elephant, the tapir, the bear, and various other genera found in the rest of the region are altogether absent. The Javanese rhinoceros (*Rhinoceros sundaicus,* sarak in Javanese,*badak* in Sundanese), the largest of the mammals on the island, differs from that of Sumatra in having one horn instead of two. It ranges over the highest mountains, and its regular paths, worn into deep channels, may be traced up the steepest slopes and round the rims of even active volcanoes. Two species of wild swine, *Sus vittatus* and *Sus verrucosus,* are exceedingly abundant, the former in the hot, the latter in the temperate, region; and their depredations are the cause of much loss to the natives, who, however, being Mahommedans, to whom pork is abhorrent, do not hunt them for the sake of their flesh. Not much less than the rhinoceros is the banteng (*Bibos banteng* or*sundaicus*) found in all the uninhabited districts between 2000 and 7000 ft. of elevation. The kidang or muntjak (*Cervulus muntjac*) and the rusa or russa (*Rusa hippelaphus*or *Russa russa*) are the representatives of the deer kind. The former is a delicate little creature occurring singly or in pairs both in the mountains and in the coast districts; the latter lives in herds of fifty to a hundred in the grassy opens, giving excellent sport to the native hunters. Another species (*Russa kuhlii*) exists in Bavian. The kantjil (*Tragulus javanicus*) is a small creature allied to the musk-deer but forming a genus by itself. It lives in the high woods, for the most part singly, seldom in pairs. It is one of the most peculiar of the Javanese mammals. The royal tiger, the same species as that of India, is still common enough to make a tiger-hunt a characteristic Javanese scene. The leopard (*Felis pardus*) is frequent in the warm regions and often ascends to considerable altitudes. Black specimens occasionally occur, but the spots are visible on inspection; and the fact that in the Amsterdam zoological gardens a black leopard had one of its cubs black and the other normally spotted shows that this is only a case of melanism. In the tree-tops the birds find a dangerous enemy in the matjan rembak, or wild cat (*Felis minuta*), about the size of a common cat. The dog tribe is represented by the fox-like adjag (*Cuon* or *Canis sutilans*) which hunts in ferocious packs; and by a wild dog, *Canis tenggeranus,* if this is not now exterminated. The Cheiroptera hold a prominent place in the fauna, the principal genera being *Pteropus,Cynonycteris, Cynopterus* and *Macroglossus.* Remarkable especially for size is the kalong, or flying fox, *Pteropus edulis,* a fruit-eating bat, which may be seen hanging during the day in black clusters asleep on the trees, and in the evening hastening in long lines to the favourite feeding grounds in the forest. The damage these do to the young coco-nut trees, the maize and the sugar-palms leads the natives to snare and shoot them; and their flesh is a favourite food with Europeans, who prefer to shoot them by night as, if shot by day, they often cling after death to the branches. Smaller kinds of bats are most abundant, perhaps the commonest being *Scotophilus Temminckii.* In certain places they congregate in myriads, like sea-fowl on the cliffs, and their excrement produces extensive guano deposits utilized by the people of Surakarta and Madiun. The creature known to the Europeans as the flying-cat and to the natives as the kubin is the *Galeopithecus volans* or*variagatus*—a sort of transition from the bats to the lemuroids. Of these last Java has several species held in awe by the natives for their supposed power of fascination. The apes are represented by the wou-wou (*Hylobates leuciscus*), the lutung, and kowi (*Semnopithecus maurus*and *pyrrhus*), the surili (*Semnopithecus mitratus*), and the munyuk (*Cercocebus,* or *Macacus, cynamolgos*), the most generally distributed of all. From sunrise to sunset the wou-wou makes its presence known, especially in the second zone where it congregates in the trees, by its strange cry, at times harsh and cacophonous, at times weird and pathetic. The lutung or black ape also prefers the temperate region, though it is met with as high as 7000 ft. above the sea and as low as 2000. The *Cercocebus* or grey ape keeps for the most part to the warm coast lands. Rats (including the brown Norway rat, often called *Mus javanicus,* as if it were a native; a great plague); mice in great variety, porcupines (*Acanthion javanicum*); squirrels (five species) and flying squirrels (four species) represent the rodents. A hare, *Lepus nigricollis,* originally from Ceylon, has a very limited habitat; the Insectivora comprise a shrew-mouse (*Rachyura indica*), two species of tupaya and *Hylomys suillus* peculiar to Java and Sumatra. The nearest relation to the bears is*Arctictis*

73

binturong. Mydaus meliceps and *Helictis orientalis*represent the badgers. In the upper part of the mountains occurs *Mustela Henrici*, and an otter (*Aonyx leptonyx*) in the streams of the hot zone. The coffee rat (*Paradoxurus hermaphroditus*), a civet cat (*Viverricida indica*), the Javanese ichneumon (*Herpestes javanicus*), and *Priodon gracilis* may also be mentioned.

In 1820, 176 species of birds were known in Java; by 1900 Vorderman and O. Finsch knew 410. Many of these are, of course, rare and occupy a limited habitat far from the haunts of man. Others exist in myriads and are characteristic features in the landscape. Water-fowl of many kinds, ducks, geese, storks, pelicans, &c., give life to sea-shore and lake, river and marsh. Snipe-shooting is afavourite sport. Common night-birds are the owl (*Strix flammea*) and the goat-sucker (*Caprimulgus affinis*). Three species of hornbill, the year-bird of the older travellers (*Buceros plicatus, lunatus* and *albirostris*) live in the tall trees of the forest zone. The Javanese peacock is a distinct species (*Pavo muticus* or *spiciferus*), and even exceeds the well-known Indian species in the splendour of its plumage.*Gallus Bankiva* is famous as the reputed parent of all barn-door fowls; *Gallus furcatus* is an exquisitely beautiful bird and can be trained for cock-fighting. Of parrots two species only are known: *Palaeornis Alexandri* or *javanicus* and the pretty little grass-green *Curyllis pusilla*, peculiar to Java. As talkers and mimics they are beaten by the *Gracula javanensis*, a favourite cage-bird with the natives. A cuckoo, *Chrysococcyx basalis*, may be heard in the second zone. The grass-fields are the foraging-grounds of swarms of weaver-birds (*Plocula javanensis* and *Ploccus baya*). They lay nearly as heavy a toll on the rice-fields as the gelatiks (*Munia oryzivora*), which are everywhere the rice-growers' principal foe. Hawks and falcons make both an easy prey. The *Nictuarinas* or honey-birds (eight species) take the place of the humming-bird, which they rival in beauty and diminutiveness, ranging from the lowlands to an altitude of 4000 ft. In the upper regions the birds, like the plants, are more like those of Europe, and some of them—notably the kanchilan (*Hyloterpe Philomela*)—are remarkable for their song. The edible-nest swallow (*Collocalia fuciphaga*) builds in caves in many parts of the island.8

As far back as 1859 P. Bleeker credited Java with eleven hundred species of fish; and naturalists are perpetually adding to the number.9 In splendour and grotesqueness of colouring many kinds, as is well known, look rather like birds than fish. In the neighbourhood of Batavia about three hundred and eighty species are used as food by the natives and the Chinese, who have added to the number by the introduction of the goldfish, which reaches a great size. The sea fish most prized by Europeans is *Lates calcarifer* (a perch). Of more than one hundred species of snakes about twenty-four species 287(including the cobra di capella) are poisonous and these are responsible for the deaths of between one hundred and two hundred persons per annum. Adders and lizards are abundant. Geckos are familiar visitants in the houses of the natives. There are two species of crocodiles.

As in other tropical-rain forest lands the variety and abundance of insects are amazing. At sundown the air becomes resonant for hours with their myriad voices. The*Coleoptera* and the *Lepidoptera* form the glory of all great collections for their size and magnificence. Of butterflies proper five hundred species are known. Of the beetles one of the largest and handsomest is *Chalcosoma atlas*. Among the spiders (a numerously represented order) the most notable is a bird-killing species, *Selene scomia javanensis*. In many parts the island is plagued with ants, termites and mosquitoes. Crops of all kinds are subject to disastrous attacks of creeping and winged foes—many still unidentified (see especially Snellen van Hollenhoven, *Essai d'une faune entomologique de l'Archipel Indo-néerlandais*). Of still lower forms of life the profusion is no less perplexing. Among the worms the *Perichaeta musica*reaches a length of about twenty inches and produces musical sounds. The shell of the *Tridacna gigas* is the largest anywhere known.

Flora.—For the botanist Java is a natural paradise, affording him the means of studying the effects of moisture and heat, of air-currents and altitudes, without the interference of superincumbent arctic conditions. The botanic gardens of Buitenzorg have long been famous for their wealth of material, the ability with which their treasures have been accumulated and displayed, their value in connexion with the economic development of the island and the extensive scientific literature published by their directors.10 There is a special establishment at Chibodas open to students of all nations for the investigation on the spot of the conditions of the primeval forest. Hardly any similar area in the world has a flora of richer variety than Java. It is estimated that the total number of the species of plants is about 5000; but this is probably under the mark (De Candolle knew of 2605 phanerogamous species), and new genera and species of an unexpected character are from time to time discovered. The lower parts of the island are always in the height of summer. The villages and even the smaller towns are in great measure concealed by the abundant and abiding verdure; and their position in the landscape is to be recognized mainly by their groves, orchards and cultivated fields. The amount and distribution of heat and moisture at the various seasons of the year form the dominant factors in determining the character of the vegetation. Thus trees which are evergreen in west Java are deciduous in the east of the island, some dropping their leaves (*e.g. Tetrameles nudiflora*) at the very time they are in bloom or ripening their fruit. This and other contrasts are graphically described from personal observation by A. F. W. Schimper in his *Pflanzen-Geographie auf physiologischer Grundlage* (Jena, 1898). The abundance of epiphytes, orchids, pitcher-plants, mosses and fungi is a striking result of the prevalent humidity; and many trees and plants indeed, which in drier climates root in the soil, derive sufficient moisture from their stronger neighbours. Of orchids J. J. Smith records 562 species (100 genera), but the flowers of all except about a score are inconspicuous. This last fact is the more remarkable because, taken generally, the Javanese vegetation differs from that of many other tropical countries by being abundantly and often gorgeously floriferous. Many of the loftiest trees crown themselves with blossoms and require no assistance from the climbing plants that seek, as it were, to rival them in their display of colour. Shrubs, too, and herbaceous plants often give brilliant effects in the savannahs, the deserted clearings, the edges of the forest and the sides of the highways. The *lantana*, a verbenaceous alien introduced, it is said, from Jamaica by Lady Raffles, has made itself aggressively conspicuous in many parts of the island, more especially in the Preanger and middle Java, where it occupies areas of hundreds of acres.

The effect of mere altitude in the distribution of the flora was long ago emphasized by Friedrich Junghuhn, the Humboldt of Java, who divided the island into four vertical botanical zones—a division which has generally been accepted by his successors, though, like all such divisions, it is subject to many modifications and exceptions. The forest, or hot zone, extends to a height of 2000 ft. above the sea; the second, that of moderate heat, has its upper limit at about 4500; the third, or cool, zone reaches 7500; and the fourth, or coldest, comprises all that lies beyond. The lowest zone has, of course, the most extensive area; the second is only a fiftieth and the third a five-thousandth of the first; and the fourth is an insignificant remainder. The lowest is the region of the true tropical forest, of rice-fields and sugar-plantations, of coco-nut palms, cotton, sesamum, cinnamon and tobacco (though this last has a wide altitudinal range). Many parts of the coast (especially on the north) are fringed with mangrove (*Rhizophora mucronata*), &c., and species of *Bruguiera*; the downs have their characteristic flora—convolvulus and *Spinifex squarrosus* catching the eye for very different reasons. Farther inland along the seaboard appear the nipa dwarf palm (*Nipa fruticans*), the *Alsbonia scholaris* (the wood of which is lighter than cork), Cycadacea, tree-ferns, screw pines (*Pandanus*), &c. In west Java the gebang palm (*Corypha gebanga*) grows in clumps and belts not far from but never quite close to the coast; and in east Java a similar position is occupied by the lontar (*Borassus flabelliformis*), valuable for its timber, its sago and its sugar, and in former times for its leaves, which were used as a writing-material. The fresh-water lakes and ponds of this region are richly covered with Utricularia and various kinds of lotus (*Nymphaea lotus, N. stellata, Nelumbium speciosum*, &c.) interspersed with *Pista stratiotes* and other floating plants. Vast prairies are covered with the silvery alang-alang grass broken by bamboo thickets, clusters of trees and shrubs (*Butea frondosa,Emblica officinalis*, &c.) and islands of the taller erigedeh or glagah (*Saccharum spontaneum*). Alang-alang (*Imperata arundinacea*, Cyr. var. Bentham) grows from 1 to 4 ft. in height. It springs up wherever the ground is cleared of trees and is a perfect plague to the cultivator. It cannot hold its own, however, with the ananas, the kratok (*Phaseolus lunatus*) or the lantana; and, in the natural progress of events, the forest resumes its sway except where the natives encourage the young growth of the grass by annually setting the prairies on fire. The true forest, which occupies a great part of this region, changes its character as we proceed from west to east. In west Java it is a dense rain-forest in which the struggle of existence is maintained at high pressure by a host of lofty trees and parasitic plants in bewildering profusion. The preponderance of certain types is remarkable. Thus of the Moraceae there are in Java (and mostly here) seven genera with ninety-five species, eighty-three of which are *Ficus* (see S. H. Koorders and T. Valeton, "Boomsoorten op Java" in *Bijdr. Mede. Dep. Landbower* (1906). These include the so-called waringin, several kinds of figs planted as shade-trees in the parks of the nobles and officials. The Magnoliaceae and Anonaceae are both numerously represented. In middle Java the variety of trees is less, a large area being occupied by teak. In eastern Java the character of the forest is mainly determined by the abundance of the Casuarina or Chimoro (*C. montana* and *C. Junghuhniana*). Another species, *C. equisetifolia*, is planted in west Java as an ornamental tree. These trees are not crowded together and encumbered with the heavy parasitic growths of the rain-forest; but their tall stems are often covered with multitudes of small vermilion fungi. Wherever the local climate has sufficient humidity, the true rain-forest claims its own. The second of Junghuhn's zones is the region of, more especially, tea, cinchona and coffee plantations, of maize and the sugar palm (areng). In the forest the trees are richly clad with ferns and enormous fungi; there is a profusion of underwood (*Pavetta macrophylla Javanica* and *salicifolia*; several species of *Lasianthus, Boehmarias, Strobilanthus*, &c.), of woody lianas and ratans, of tree ferns (especially Alsophila). Between the bushes the ground is covered with ferns, lycopods, tradescantias, Bignoniaceae, species of *Aeschynanthus*. Of the lianas the largest is *Plectocomia elongata*;

one specimen of which was found to have a length of nearly 790 ft. One of the fungi, *Telephora princeps*, is more than a yard in diameter. The trees are of different species from those of the hot zone even when belonging to the same genus; and new types appear mostly in limited areas. The third zone, which consists mainly of the upper slopes of volcanic mountains, but also comprises several plateaus (the Dieng, parts of the Tengger, the Ijen) is a region of clouds and mists. There are a considerable number of lakes and swamps in several parts of the region, and these have a luxuriant environment of grasses, Cyperaceae, Characeae and similar forms. The taller trees of the region—oaks, chestnuts, various Lauraceae, and four or five species of *Podocarpus*—with some striking exceptions, *Astronia spectabilis*, &c., are less floriferous than those of the lower zones; but the shrubs (*Rhododendron javanicum,Ardisia javanica*, &c.), herbs and parasites more than make up for this defect. There is little cultivation, except in the Tengger, where the natives grow maize, rye and tobacco, and various European vegetables (cabbage, potatoes, &c.), with which they supply the lowland markets. In western Java one of the most striking features of the upper parts of this temperate region is what Schimper calls the "absolute dominion of mosses," associated with the "elfin forest," as he quaintly calls it, a perfect tangle of "low, thick, oblique or even horizontal stems," almost choked to leaflessness by their grey and ghostly burden. Much of the lower vegetation begins to have a European aspect; violets, primulas, thalictrums, ranunculus, vacciniums, equisetums, rhododendrons (*Rhod. retusum*). The *Primula imperialis*, found only on the Pangerango, is a handsome species, prized by specialists. In the fourth or alpine zone occur such distinctly European forms as *Artemisia vulgaris,Plantago major, Solanum nigrum, Stellaria media*; and altogether the alpine flora contains representatives of no fewer than thirty-three families. A characteristic shrub is*Anaphalis javanica*, popularly called the Javanese edelweiss, which "often entirely excludes all other woody plants."11 The tallest and noblest 288of all the trees in the island is the rasamala or liquid-ambar (*Altingia excelsa*), which, rising with a straight clean trunk, sometimes 6 ft. in diameter at the base, to a height of 100 to 130 ft., spreads out into a magnificent crown of branches and foliage. When by chance a climbing plant has joined partnership with it, the combination of blossoms at the top is one of the finest colour effects of the forest. The rasamala, however, occurs only in the Preanger and in the neighbouring parts of Bantam and Buitenzorg. Of the other trees that may be classified as timber—from 300 to 400 species—many attain noble proportions. It is sufficient to mention *Calophyllum inophyllum*, which forms fine woods in the south of Bantam, *Mimusops acuminata, Irna glabra, Dalbergia latifolia* (sun wood, English black-wood) in middle and east Java; the rare but splendid *Pithecolobium Junghuhnianum,Schima Noronhae, Bischofia javanica, Pterospermum javanicum* (greatly prized for ship-building), and the upas-tree. From the economic point of view all these hundreds of trees are of less importance than *Tectona grandis*, the jati or teak, which, almost to the exclusion of all others, occupies about a third of the government forest-lands. It grows best in middle and eastern Java, preferring the comparatively dry and hot climate of the plains and lower hills to a height of about 2000 ft. above the sea, and thriving best in more or less calciferous soils. In June it sheds its leaves and begins to bud again in October. Full-grown trees reach a height of 100 to 150 ft. In 1895 teak (with a very limited quantity of other timber) was felled to the value of about £101,800, and in 1904 the corresponding figure was about £119,935.

That an island which has for so long maintained a dense and growing population in its more cultivable regions should have such extensive tracts of primeval or quasi-primeval forest as have been above indicated would be matter of surprise to one who did not consider the simplicity of the life of the Javanese. They require but little fuel; and both their dwellings and their furniture are mostly constructed of bamboo supplemented with a palm or two. They destroy the forest mainly to get room for their rice-fields and pasture for their cattle. In doing this, however, they are often extremely reckless and wasteful; and if it had not been for the unusual humidity of the climate their annual fires would have resulted in widespread conflagrations. As it is, many mountains are now bare which within historic times were forested to the top; but the Dutch government has proved fully alive to the danger of denudation. The state has control of all the woods and forests of the island with the exception of those of the Preanger, the "particular lands," and Madura; and it has long been engaged in replanting with native trees and experimenting with aliens from other parts of the world—*Eucalyptus globulus*, the juar, *Cassia florida* from Sumatra, the surian (*Cedrela febrifuga*), &c. The greatest success has been with cinchona.

Left to itself Java would soon clothe itself again with even a richer natural vegetation than it had when it was first occupied by man. The open space left by the demolition of the fortifications on Nusa Kambangan was in twenty-eight years densely covered by thousands of shrubs and trees of about twenty varieties, many of the latter 80 ft. high. Resident Snijthoff succeeded about the close of the 19th century in re-afforesting a large part of Mount Muriâ by the simple expedient of protecting the territory he had to deal with from all encroachments by natives.12

Population.—The population of Java (including Madura, &c.) was 30,098,008 in 1905. In 1900 it was 28,746,688; in 1890, 23,912,564; and in 1880, 19,794,505. The natives consist of the Javanese proper, the Sundanese and the Madurese. All three belong to the Malay stock. Between Javanese and Sundanese the distinction is mainly due to the influence of the Hindus on the former and the absence of this on the latter. Between Javanese and Madurese the distinction is rather to be ascribed to difference of natural environment. The Sundanese have best retained the Malay type, both in physique and fashion of life. They occupy the west of the island. The Madurese area, besides the island of Madura and neighbouring isles, includes the eastern part of Java itself. The residencies of Tegal, Pekalongan, Banyumas, Bagelen, Kedu, Semarang, Japara, Surakarta, Jokjakarta, Rembang, Madiun, Kediri and Surabaya have an almost purely Javanese population. The Javanese are the most numerous and civilized of the three peoples.

The colour of the skin in all three cases presents various shades of yellowish-brown; and it is observed that, owing perhaps to the Hindu strain, the Javanese are generally darker than the Sundanese. The eyes are always brown or black, the hair of the head black, long, lank and coarse. Neither breast nor limbs are provided with hair, and there is hardly even the suggestion of a beard. In stature the Sundanese is less than the Javanese proper, being little over 5 ft. in average height, whereas the Javanese is nearly $5\frac{1}{2}$ ft.; at the same time the Sundanese is more stoutly built. The Madurese is as tall as the Javanese, and as stout as the Sundanese. The eye is usually set straight in the head in the Javanese and Madurese; among the Sundanese it is often oblique. The nose is generally flat and small, with wide nostrils, although among the Javanese it not infrequently becomes aquiline. The lips are thick, yet well formed; the teeth are naturally white, but often filed and stained. The cheek-bones are well developed, more particularly with the Madurese. In expressiveness of countenance the Javanese and Madurese are far in advance of the Sundanese. The women are not so well made as the men, and among the lower classes especially soon grow absolutely ugly. In the eyes of the Javanese a golden yellow complexion is the perfection of female beauty. To judge by their early history, the Javanese must have been a warlike and vigorous people, but now they are peaceable, docile, sober, simple and industrious.

One million only out of the twenty-six millions of natives are concentrated in towns, a fact readily explained by their sources of livelihood. The great bulk of the population is distributed over the country in villages usually called by Europeans dessas, from the Low Javanese word *désà* (High Javanese *dusun*). Every dessa, however small (and those containing from 100 to 1000 families are exceptionally large), forms an independent community; and no sooner does it attain to any considerable size than it sends off a score of families or so to form a new dessa. Each lies in the midst of its own area of cultivation. The general enceinte is formed by an impervious hedge of bamboos 40 to 70 ft. high. Within this lie the houses, each with its own enclosure, which, even when the fields are the communal property, belongs to the individual householder. The capital of a district is only a larger dessa, and that of a regency has the same general type, but includes several kampongs or villages. The bamboo houses in the strictly Javanese districts are always built on the ground; in the Sunda lands they are raised on piles. Some of the well-to-do, however, have stone houses. The principal article of food is rice; a considerable quantity of fish is eaten, but little meat. Family life is usually well ordered. The upper class practise polygamy, but among the common people a man has generally only one wife. The Javanese are nominally Mahommedans, as in former times they were Buddhists and Brahmins; but in reality, not only such exceptional groups as the Kalangs of Surakarta and Jokjakarta and the Baduwis or nomad tribes of Bantam, but the great mass of the people must be considered as believers rather in the primitive animism of their ancestors, for their belief in Islam is overlaid with superstition. As we ascend in the social scale, however, we find the name of Mahommedan more and more applicable; and consequently in spite of the paganism of the populace the influence of the Mahommedan "priests" (this is their official title in Dutch) is widespread and real. Great prestige attaches to the pilgrimage to Mecca, which was made by 5068 persons from Java in 1900. In every considerable town there is a mosque. Christian missionary work is not very widely spread.

Languages.—In spite of Sundanese, Madurese and the intrusive Malay, Javanese has a right to the name. It is a rich and cultivated language which has passed through many stages of development and, under peculiar influences, has become a linguistic complex of an almost unique kind. Though it is customary and convenient to distinguish New Javanese from Kavi or Old Javanese, just as it was customary to distinguish English from Anglo-Saxon, there is no break of historical continuity. Kavi (Basa Kavi, *i.e.* the language of poetry) may be defined as the form spoken and written before the founding of Majapahit; and middle Javanese, still represented by the dialect of Banyumas, north Cheribon, north Krawang and north Bantam, as the form the language assumed under the Majapahit court influence; while New Javanese is the language as it has developed since the fall of that kingdom. Kavi continued to be a literary language long after it had become archaic. It contains more Sanskrit than any other language of the archipelago. New Javanese breaks up into two great varieties, so different that sometimes they are regarded as two distinct languages. The nobility use one form, Krâmâ; the common people another, Ngoko, the "thouing" language (cf. Fr. *tutoyant*, Ger. *dutzend*); but each class understands the language of the other class. The aristocrat speaks 289to the commonalty in the language of the commoner; the commoner speaks to the aristocracy in the language of the aristocrat; and, according to clearly recognized etiquette, every Javanese plays the part of aristocrat or commoner towards those whom he addresses. To speak Ngoko to a superior is to insult him; to speak Krâmâ to an equal or inferior is a mark of respect. In this way Dipâ Negârâ showed his contempt for the Dutch General de Kock. The ordinary Javanese thinks in Ngoko; the children use it to each other, and so on. Between the two forms there is a kind of compromise, the Madya, or middle form of speech, employed by those who stand to each other on equal or friendly footing or by those who feel little constraint of etiquette. For every idea expressed in the language Krâmâ has one vocable, the Ngoko another, the two words being sometimes completely different and sometimes differing only in the termination, the beginning or the middle. Thus every Javanese uses, as it were, two or even three languages delicately differentiated from each other. How this state of affairs came about is matter of speculation. Almost certainly the existence side by side of two peoples, speaking each its own tongue, and occupying towards each other the position intellectually and politically of superior and inferior, had much to do with it. But Professor Kern thinks that some influence must also be assigned to *pamela* or *pantang*, word-taboo—certain words being in certain circumstances regarded as of evil omen—a superstition still lingering, *e.g.* even among the Shetland fishermen (see G. A. F. Hazeu, *De taal pantangs*). It has sometimes been asserted that Krâmâ contains more Sanskrit words than Ngoko does; but the total number in Krâmâ does not exceed 20; and sometimes there is a Sanskrit word in Ngoko which is not in Krâmâ. There is a village Krâmâ which is not recognized by the educated classes: Krâmâ inggil, with a vocabulary of about 300 words, is used in addressing the deity or persons of exalted rank. The Basa Kedaton or court language is a dialect used by all living at court except royalties, who use Ngoko. Among themselves the women of the court employ Krâmâ or Madya, but they address the men in Basa Kedaton.13

Literature.—Though a considerable body of Kavi literature is still extant, nothing like a history of it is possible. The date and authorship of most of the works are totally unknown. The first place may be assigned to the*Brata Yuda* (Sansk., *Bharata Yudha*, the conflict of the Bharatas), an epic poem dealing with the struggle between the Pandâwâs and the Korâwas for the throne of Ngastina celebrated in parwas 5-10 of the *Mahâbhârata*. To the conception, however, of the modern Javanese it is a purely native poem; its kings and heroes find their place in the native history and serve as ancestors to their noble families. (Cohen Stuart published the modern Javanese version with a Dutch translation and notes, *Brâtâ-Joedâ*, &c., Samarang, 1877. The Kavi text was lithographed at the Hague by S. Lankhout.) Of greater antiquity probably is the *Ardjunâ Wiwâhâ* (or marriage festival of Ardjuna), which Professor Kern thinks may be assigned to the first half of the 11th century of the Christian era. The name indicates its*Mahâbhârata* origin. (Friederich published the Kavi text from a Bali MS., and *Wiwâhâ Djarwa en Brâtâ Joedo Kawi*, lithographed facsimiles of two palm-leaf MSS., Batavia, 1878. Djarwa is the name of the poetic diction of modern Javanese.) The oldest poem of which any trace is preserved is probably the mythological *Kândâ* (*i.e.* tradition); the contents are to some extent known from the modern Javanese version. In the literature of modern Javanese there exists a great variety of so-called *babads* or chronicles. It is sufficient to mention the "history" of Baron Sakender, which appears to give an account—often hardly recognizable—of the settlement of Europeans in Java (Cohen Stuart published text and translation, Batavia, 1851; J. Veth gives an analysis of the contents), and the *Babad Tanah Djawi* (the Hague, 1874, 1877), giving the history of the island to 1647 of the Javanese era. Even more numerous are the *wayangs* or puppet-plays which usually take their subjects from the Hindu legends or from those relating to the kingdoms of Majapahit and Pajajaram (see*e.g.* H. C. Humme, *Abiâsâ, een Javaansche toneelstuk*, the Hague, 1878). In these plays grotesque figures of gilded leather are moved by the performer, who recites the appropriate speeches and, as occasion demands, plays the part of chorus.

Several Javanese specimens are also known of the beast fable, which plays so important a part in Sanskrit literature (W. Palmer van den Broek, *Javaansche Vertellingen, bevattende de lotgevallen van een kantjil, een reebok*, &c., the Hague, 1878). To the Hindu-Javanese literature there naturally succeeded a Mahommedan-Javanese literature consisting largely of translations or imitations of Arabic originals; it comprises religious romances, moral exhortations and mystical treatises in great variety.14

Arts.—In mechanic arts the Javanese are in advance of the other peoples of the archipelago. Of thirty different crafts practised among them, the most important are those of the blacksmith or cutler, the carpenter, the kris-sheath maker, the coppersmith, the goldsmith and the potter. Their skill in the working of the metals is the more noteworthy as they have to import the raw materials. The most esteemed product of the blacksmith's skill is the kris; every man and boy above the age of fourteen wears one at least as part of his ordinary dress, and men of rank two and sometimes four. In the finishing and adornment of the finer weapons no expense is spared; and ancient krises of good workmanship sometimes fetch enormous prices. The Javanese gold and silver work possesses considerable beauty, but there is nothing equal to the filigree of Sumatra; the brass musical instruments are of exceptional excellence. Both bricks and tiles are largely made, as well as a coarse unglazed pottery similar to that of Hindustan; but all the finer wares are imported from China. Cotton spinning, weaving and dyeing are carried on for the most part as purely domestic operations by the women. The usual mode of giving variety of colour is by weaving in stripes with a succession of different coloured yarns, but another mode is to cover with melted wax or damar the part of the cloth not intended to receive the dye. This process is naturally a slow one, and has to be repeated according to the number of colours required. As a consequence the *battiks*, as the cloths thus treated are called, are in request by the wealthier classes. For the most part quiet colours are preferred. To the Javanese of the present day the ancient buildings of the Hindu periods are the work of supernatural power. Except when employed by his European master he seldom builds anything more substantial than a bamboo or timber framework; but in the details of such erections he exhibits both skill and taste. When Europeans first came to the island they found native vessels of large size well entitled to the name of ships; and, though ship-building proper is now carried on only under the direction of Europeans, boat-building is a very extensive native industry along the whole of the north coast— the boats sometimes reaching a burden of 50 tons. The only one of the higher arts which the Javanese have carried to any degree of perfection is music; and in regard to the value of their efforts in this direction Europeans differ greatly. The orchestra (*gamelan*) consists of wind, string and percussion instruments, the latter being in preponderancy to the other two. (Details of the instruments will be found in Raffles' *Java*, and a description of a performance in the *Tour du monde*, 1880.)

Chief Towns and Places of Note.—The capital of Java and of the Dutch East India possessions is Batavia (*q.v.*), pop. 115,567. At Meester Cornelis (pop. 33,119), between 6 and 7 m. from Batavia on the railway to Buitenzorg, the battle was fought in 1811 which placed Java in the hands of the British. In the vicinity lies Depok, originally a Christian settlement of freed slaves, but now with about 3000 Mahommedan inhabitants and only 500 Christians. The other chief towns, from west to east through the island, are as follows: Serang (pop. 5600) bears the same relation to Bantam, about 6 m. distant, which New Batavia bears to Old Batavia, its slight elevation of 100 ft. above the sea making it fitter for European occupation. Anjer (Angerlor, Anger) lies 96 m. from Batavia by rail on the coast at the narrowest part of the Sunda Strait; formerly European vessels were wont to call there for fresh provisions and water. Pandeglang (pop. 3644), 787 ft. above sea-level, is known for its hot and cold sulphur springs. About 17 m. west of Batavia lies Tangerang (pop. 13,535), a busy place with about 2800 or 3000 Chinese among its inhabitants. Buitenzorg (*q.v.*) is the country-seat of the governor-general, and its botanic gardens are famous. Krawang, formerly chief town of the residency of that name—the least populous of all—has lost its importance since Purwakerta (pop. 6862) was made the administrative centre. At Wanyasa in the neighbourhood the first tea plantations were attempted on a large scale.

The Preanger regencies—Bandung, Chanjur, Sukabumi, Sumedang, Garut and Tasikmalaya—constitute the most important of all the residencies, though owing to their lack of harbour on the south and the intractable nature of much of their soil they have not shared in the prosperity enjoyed by many other parts of the island. Bandung, the chief town since 1864, lies 2300 ft. above sea-level, 109 m. south of Batavia by rail; it is a well-built and flourishing place (pop. 28,965; Europeans 1522, Chinese 2650) with a handsome resident's house (1867), a large mosque (1867), a school for the sons of native men of rank, the most important quinine factory in the island, and a race-course where in July a good opportunity is afforded of seeing both the life of fashionable and official Java and the customs and costumes of the common people. The district is famous for its waterfalls, one of the most remarkable of which is where the Chi Tarum rushes through a narrow gully to leap down from the Bandung plateau. In the neighbourhood is the great military camp of Chimahi. Chanjur, formerly the chief town, in spite of its loss of administrative position still has a population of 13,599. From Sukabumi (pop. 12,112; 569 Europeans), a pleasant health resort among the hills at an altitude of 1965 ft., tourists are accustomed to visit Wijnkoopers Bay for the sake of the picturesque shore scenery. Chichalengka became after 1870 one of the centres of the coffee industry. Sumedang has only 8013 inhabitants, having declined since the railway took away the highway traffic: it is exceeded both by Garut (10,647) and by Tasikmalaya (9196), but it is a beautiful place well known to sportsmen for its proximity to the Rancha Ekek swamp, where great snipe-shooting matches are 290held every year. For natural beauty few parts of Java can compare with the plain of Tasikmalaya, itself remarkable, in a country of trees, for its magnificent avenues. N.E. of the Preanger lies the residency of Cheribon15 (properly Chi Rebon, the shrimp river). The chief town (pop. 24,564) is one of the most important places on the north coast, though the unhealthiness of the site has caused Europeans to settle at Tangkil, 2 m. distant. The church (1842), the regent's residence, and the great prison are among the principal buildings; there are also extensive salt warehouses. The native part of the town is laid out more regularly than is usual, and the Chinese quarter (pop. 3352) has the finest Chinese temple in Java. The palaces of the old sultans of Cheribon are less extensive than those of Surakarta and Jokjakarta. Though the harbour has to be kept open by constant dredging the roadstead is good all the year round. A strange pleasure palace of Sultan Supeh, often described by travellers, lies about 2 m. off near Sunya Raja. Mundu, a village 4 m. south-east of Cheribon, is remarkable as the only spot on the north coast of the island visited by the ikan prut or belly-fish, a species about as large as a cod, caught in thousands and salted by the local fishermen. Indramayu, which lies on both banks of the Chi Manuk about 8 m. from the coast, is mentioned under the name of Dermayo as a port for the rice of the district and the coffee of the Preanger. The coffee trade is extinct but the rice trade is more flourishing than ever, and the town has 13,400 inhabitants, of whom 2200 are Chinese. It might have a great commercial future if money could be found for the works necessary to overcome the disadvantage of its position—the roads being safe only during the east monsoon and the river requiring to be deepened and regulated. Tegal has long been one of the chief towns of Java: commerce, native trade and industry, and fisheries are all well represented and the sugar factories give abundant employment to the inhabitants. The harbour has been the object of various improvements since 1871. The whole district is densely populated (3100 to the sq. m.) and the town proper with its 16,665 inhabitants is surrounded by extensive kampongs (Balapulang, Lebaksiu, &c.). In Pekalongan (pop. 38,211) and Batang (21,286) the most important industry is the production of battiks and stamped cloths; there are also iron-works and sugar factories. The two towns are only some 5 m. apart. The former has a large mosque, a Protestant church, an old fort and a large number of European houses. The Chinese quarters consist of neat stone or brick buildings. Pekalongan smoked ducks are well known. Brebes (13,474) on the Pamali is an important trade centre. Banyumas (5000) is the seat of a resident; it is exceeded by Purwokerto (12,610), Purbalinggo (12,094) and Chilachap (12,000). This last possesses the best harbour on the south coast, and but for malaria would have been an important place. It was chosen as the seat of a great military establishment but had to be abandoned, the fort being blown up in 1893. Semarang (pop. 89,286, of whom 4800 are Europeans and 12,372 Chinese) lies on the Kali Ngaran near the centre of the north coast. Up to 1824 the old European town was surrounded by a wall and ditch. It was almost the exact reproduction of a Dutch town without the slightest accommodation to the exigencies of the climate, the streets narrow and irregular. The modern town is well laid out. Among the more noteworthy buildings of Semarang are the old Prince of Orange fort, the resident's house, the Roman Catholic church, the Protestant church, the mosque, the military hospital. A new impulse to the growth of the town was given by the opening of the railway to Surakarta and Jokjakarta in 1875. As a seaport the place is unfortunately situated. The river has long been silted up; the roadstead is insecure in the west monsoon. After many delays an artificial canal, begun in 1858, became available as a substitute for the river; but further works are necessary. A second great canal to the east, begun in 1896, helps to prevent inundations and thus improve the healthiness of the town. Demak, 13 m. N.E. of Semarang, though situated in a wretched region of swamps and having only 5000 inhabitants, is famous in ancient Javanese history. The mosque, erected by the first sultan of Demak, was rebuilt in 1845; only a small part of the old structure has been preserved, but as a sanctuary it attracts 6000 or 7000 pilgrims annually. To visit Demak seven times has the same ceremonial value as the pilgrimage to Mecca. The tombs of several of the sultans are still extant. Salatiga ("three stones," with allusion to three temples now destroyed) was in early times one of the resting places of ambassadors proceeding to the court of Mataram, and in the European history of Java its name is associated with the peace of 1755 and the capitulation of 1811. It is the seat of a cavalry and artillery camp. Its population, about 10,000, seems to be declining. Ambarawa with its railway station is, on the other hand, rapidly increasing. Its population of 14,745 includes 459 Europeans. About a mile to the N. lies the fortress of Willem I. which Van den Bosch meant to make the centre of the Javanese system of defensive works; the Banyubiru military camp is in the neighbourhood. Kendal (15,000) is a centre of the sugar industry. Kudus (31,000; 4300 Chinese) has grown to be one of the most important inland towns. Its cloth and battik pedlars are known throughout the island and the success of their enterprise is evident in the style of their houses. A good trade is also carried on in cattle, kapok, copra, pottery and all sorts of small wares. The mosque in the old town has interesting remains of Majapahit architecture; and the tomb of Pangeran Kudus is a noted Mahommedan sanctuary. A steam tramway leads northward towards, but does not reach Japara, which in the 17th century was the chief port of the kingdom of Mataram and retained its commercial importance till the Dutch Company removed its establishment to Semarang. In 1818 Daendels transferred its resident to Pati. Ungaran, 1026 ft. above the sea, was a place of importance as early as the 17th century, and in modern times has become known as a sanatorium. Rembang, a well-built coast town and the seat of a resident, has grown rapidly to have a population of 29,538 with 210 Europeans. Very similar to each other are Surakarta or Solo and Jokjakarta, the chief towns of the quasi-independent states or Vorstenlanden. Surakarta (pop. 109,459; Chinese 5159, Europeans 1913) contains the palace (Kraton, locally called the Bata bumi) of the susuhunan (which the Dutch translated as emperor), the dalem of Prince Mangku Negârâ, the residences of the Solo nobles, a small Dutch fort (Vastenburg), a great mosque, an old Dutch settlement, and a Protestant church. Here the susuhunan lives in Oriental pomp and state. To visitors there are few more interesting entertainments than those afforded by the celebration of the 31st of August (the birthday of the queen of the Netherlands) or of the New Year and the Puasa festivals, with their wayungs, ballet-dancers, and so on. Jokjakarta (35 m. S.) has been a great city since Mangku Bumi settled there in 1755. The Kraton has a circuit of 3½ m., and is a little town in itself with the palace proper, the residences of the ladies of the court and kampongs for the hereditary smiths, carpenters, sculptors, masons, payong-makers, musical instrument makers, &c., &c., of his highness. The independent Prince Paku Alam has a palace of his own. As in Surakarta there are an old Dutch town and a fort. The Jogka market is one of the most important of all Java, especially for jewelry. The total population is 72,235 with 1424 Europeans. To the south-east lies Pasar Gedeh, a former capital of Mataram, with tombs of the ancient princes in the Kraton, a favourite residence of wealthy Javanese traders. Surabaya (*q.v.*), on the strait of Madura, is the largest commercial town in Java. Its population increased from 118,000 in 1890 to 146,944 in 1900 (8906 Europeans). To the north lies Grissee or Gresih (25,688 inhabitants) with a fairly good harbour and of special interest in the early European history of Java. Inland is the considerable town of Lamongan (12,485 inhabitants). Fifteen m. S. by rail lies Sidoarjo (10,207; 185 Europeans), the centre of one of the most densely populated districts and important as a railway junction. In the neighbourhood is the populous village of Mojosari. Pasuruan was until modern times one of the chief commercial towns in Java, the staple being sugar. Since the opening of the railway to Surabaya it has greatly declined, and its warehouses and dwelling-houses are largely deserted. The population is 27,152 with 663 Europeans. Probolinggo (called by the natives Banger) is a place of 13,240 inhabitants. The swampy tracts in the vicinity are full of fishponds. The baths of Banyubiru (blue water) to the south have Hindu remains much visited by devotees. Pasirian in the far south of the residency is a considerable market town and the terminus of a branch railway. Besuki, the easternmost of all the residencies, contains several places of some importance; the chief town Bondowoso (8289); Besuki, about the same size, but with no foreign trade; Jember, a small but rapidly increasing place, and Banyuwangi (17,559). This last was at one time the seat of the resident, now the eastern terminus of the railway system, and is a seaport on the Bali Strait with an important office of the telegraph company controlling communication with Port Darwin and Singapore. It has a very mingled population, besides Javanese and Madurese, Chinese and Arabs, Balinese, Buginese and Europeans. The chief town of Kediri (10,489) is the only residency town in the interior traversed by a navigable river, and is exceeded by Tulungagung; and the residency of Madiun has two considerable centres of population: Madiun (21,168) and Ponorogo (16,765).

Agriculture.—About 40% of the soil of Java is under cultivation. Bantam and Besuki have each 16% of land under cultivation; Krawang, 21%; Preanger, 23%; Rembang, 30%; Japara, 62%; Surabaya, 65%; Kedu, 66%; Samarang, 67%. Proceeding along the south coast from its west end, we find that in Bantam all the land cultivated on its south shore amounts to at most but 5% of that regency; in Preanger and Banyumas, as far as Chilachap, the land under cultivation amounts at a maximum to 20%. East of Surakarta the percentages of land on the south coast under cultivation decline from 30 to 20 and 10. East of the residency of Probolinggo the percentage of land cultivated on the south coast sinks to as low as 2. On the north coast, in Krawang and Rembang, with their morasses and double chains of chalk, there are districts with only 20% and 10% of the soil under cultivation. In the residencies, on the other hand, of Batavia, Cheribon, Tegal, Samarang, Japara, Surabaya and Pasuruan, there are districts having 80% to 90% of soil, and even more, under cultivation.

81

The agricultural products of Java must be distinguished into those raised by the natives for their own use and those raised for the government and private proprietors. The land assigned to the 291natives for their own culture and use amounts to about 9,625,000 acres. In western Java the prevailing crop is rice, less prominently cultivated in middle Java, while in eastern Java and Madura other articles of food take the first rank. The Javanese tell strange legends concerning the introduction of rice, and observe various ceremonies in connexion with its planting, paying more regard to them than to the proper cultivation of the cereal. The agricultural produce grown on the lands of the government and private proprietors, comprising an area of about 3½ million acres, consists of sugar, cinchona, coffee, tobacco, tea, indigo, &c. The Javanese possess buffaloes, ordinary cattle, horses, dogs and cats. The buffalo was probably introduced by the Hindus. As in agricultural products, so also in cattle-rearing, western Java is distinguished from middle and eastern Java. The average distribution of buffaloes is 106 per 1000 inhabitants, but it varies considerably in different districts, being greatest in western Java. The fact that rice is the prevailing culture in the west, while in eastern Java other plants constitute the chief produce, explains the larger number of buffaloes found in western Java, these animals being more in requisition in the culture of rice. The ordinary cattle are of mixed race; the Indian zebu having been crossed with the banting and with European cattle of miscellaneous origin. The horses, though small, are of excellent character, and their masters, according to their own ideas, are extremely particular in regard to purity of race. Riding comes naturally to the Javanese; horse-races and tournays have been in vogue among them from early times.

Coffee is an alien in Java. Specimens brought in 1696 from Cannanore on the Malabar coast perished in an earthquake and floods in 1699; the effective introduction of the precious shrub was due to Hendrik Zwaardekron (see N. P. van den Berg, "Voortbrenging en verbruck van koffie,"*Tijdschrift v. Nijverh. en Landb.* 1879; and the article "Koffie" in *Encyc. Ned. Ind.* Wiji kawih is mentioned in a Kavi inscription of A.D. 856, and the bean-broth in David Tappen's list of Javanese beverages, 1667-1682, may have been coffee). The first consignment of coffee (894 ℔) to the Netherlands was made in 1711-1712, but it was not till after 1721 that the yearly exports reached any considerable amount. The aggregate quantity sold in the home market from 1711 to 1791 was 2,036,437 piculs, or on an average about 143 tons per annum; and this probably represented nearly the whole production of the island. By the beginning of the 19th century the annual production was about 7143 tons and after the introduction of the Van den Bosch system of forced culture a further augmentation was effected. The forced culture system was, in 1909, however, of little importance. Official reports show that from 1840 to 1873 the amount ranged from 5226 tons to 7354. During the ten years 1869 to 1878 the average crop of the plantations under state control was 5226 tons, that of the private planters about 810. The government has shown a strange reluctance to surrender the old-fashioned monopoly, but the spirit of private enterprise has slowly gained the day. Though the appearance of the coffee blight (*Hemileia vastatrix*) almost ruined the industry the planters did not give in. An immune variety was introduced from Liberia, and scientific methods of treatment have been adopted in dealing with the plantations. In 1887, a record year, the value of the coffee crop reached £3,083,333, and at its average it was about £1,750,000 between 1886 and 1895. The value was only £1,166,666 in 1896. The greatest difficulties are the uncertainties both of the crop and of its marketable value. The former is well shown in the figures for 1903 to 1905; government 17,900, 3949 and 3511 tons, and private planters 22,395, 15,311 and 21,395 tons. Liberia coffee is still produced in much smaller quantity than Java coffee; the latter on an average of these three years 21,360 tons; the former 7409.

The cultivation of sugar has been long carried on in Java, and since the decline of the coffee plantations it has developed into the leading industry of the island. There are experimental stations at Pasuruan, Pekalongan and elsewhere, where attempts are made to overcome the many diseases to which the cane is subject. Many of the mills are equipped with high-class machinery and produce sugar of excellent colour and grain. In 1853-1857 the average crop was 98,094 tons; in 1869-1873, 170,831, and in 1875-1880, 204,678. By 1899-1900 the average had risen to 787,673 tons; and the crops for 1904 and 1905 were respectively 1,064,935 and 1,028,357 tons. Prices fluctuate, but the value of the harvest of 1905 was estimated at about £15,000,000.

The cultivation of indigo shows a strange vitality. Under the culture system the natives found this the most oppressive of all the state crops. The modern chemist at one time seemed to have killed the industry by his synthetic substitute, but in every year between 1899 and 1904 Java exported between one million and one and a half million pounds of the natural product. Japan and Russia were the largest buyers. As blue is a favourite colour with the Javanese proper a large quantity is used at home.

Tea was first introduced to Java by the Japanese scholar von Siebold in 1826. The culture was undertaken by the state in 1829 with plants from China, but in 1842 they handed it over to contractors, whose attempts to increase their profits by delivering an inferior article ultimately led to the abandonment of the contract system in 1860. In the meantime the basis of a better state of the industry had been laid by the Dutch tea-taster J. J. L. L. Jacobsen of the Nederlandsch Handel Maatschappij, who introduced not only fresh stock, but expert growers from China in 1852-1853. The tea-planters (often taking possession of the abandoned coffee-plantations) have greatly improved the quality of their products. Assam tea was introduced in 1878, and this has rapidly extended its area. The exports increased from 12,110,724 ℔ in 1898 to 25,772,564 in 1905. More than half the total goes to the Netherlands; the United Kingdom ranks next, and, far behind both, Russia.

In 1854 the government introduced the culture of cinchona with free labour, and it had considerable success under F. Junghuhn and his successors, though the varieties grown were of inferior quality. Later seed of the best cinchona was obtained, and under skilful management Java has become the chief producer of quinine in the world. Cacao is produced in the Preanger regencies, Pekalongan, Semarang, Pasuruan, Besuki, Kediri and Surakarta. In 1903, a record year, 1,101,835 piculs (about 6540 tons) were produced. *Broussonetia papyrifera* is grown for the sake of its bark, so well known in Japan (Jap. *kodsu*) as a paper material. The ground-nut (the widely spread *Arachis hypogaea* from South America), locally known as kachang china or tanah, is somewhat extensively grown. The oil is exported to Holland, where it is sold as Delft salad oil. Tapioca has long been cultivated, especially in the Preanger. The industry is mainly in the hands of the Chinese, and the principal foreign purchasers are English biscuit manufacturers. The kapok is a tree from tropical America which, growing freely in any soil, is extensively used throughout Java along the highways as a support for telegraph and telephone wires, and planted as a prop in pepper and cubeb plantations. The silky fibre contained in its long capsuloid fruits is known as cotton wool; and among other uses it serves almost as well as cork for filling life-belts; and the oil from its seed is employed to adulterate ground-nut oil. The quantity of wool exported nearly trebled between 1890 and 1896, in the latter year the total sent to Holland, Australia, Singapore, &c., amounting to 38,586 bales. The rapid exhaustion of the natural supply of india-rubber and gutta-percha began to attract the attention of government in the latter decades of the 19th century. Extensive experiments have been made in the cultivation of *Ficus elastica* (the karet of the natives), *Castilloa elastica*, and *Hevea brasiliensis*. The planting of gutta-percha trees was begun about 1886, and a regular system introduced in the Preanger in 1901. The *Palaquium oblongifolium* plantations at Blavan, Kemutuk and Sewang in Banyumas have also been brought under official control. Java tobacco, amounting to about 35,200,000 ℔ a year, is cultivated almost exclusively in eastern Java. Among other products which are of some importance as articles of export may be mentioned nutmegs, mace, pepper, hides, arrack and copra.

Particular Lands.—At different times down to 1830 the government disposed of its lands in full property to individuals who, acquiring complete control of the inhabitants as well as of the soil, continued down to the 19th century to act as if they were independent of all superior authority. In this way more than 1½ millions of the people were subject not to the state but to "stock companies, absentee landlords and Chinese." According to the *Regeerings Almanak* (1906) these "particular lands," as they are called, were distributed as follows: Bantam 21, Batavia 36, Meester Cornelis 163, Tangerang 80, Buitenzorg 61, Semarang 32, Surabaya 46, Krawang and Demak 3 each, Cheribon 2, and Pekalongan, Kendal and Pasuruan 1 each. In Meester Cornelis no fewer than 297,912 persons were returned in 1905 as living on these lands. Of the 168 estates there are not 20 that grow anything but grass, rice and coconuts. In Buitenzorg (thanks probably to the Botanic Gardens) matters are better: tea, coffee, cinchona and india-rubber appearing amongst the objects of cultivation; and, in general, it must be noted that these estates have often natural difficulties to contend against far beyond their financial strength.

Minerals.—Of all the great islands of the archipelago Java is the poorest in metallic ores. Gold and silver are practically nonexistent. Manganese is found in Jokjakarta and various other parts. A concession for working the magnetic iron sands in the neighbourhood of Chilachap was granted in 1904. Coal occurs in thin strata and small pockets in many parts (Bantam, Rembang, Jokjakarta, &c.); and in 1905 a concession was granted to a company to work the coal-beds at Bajah close to the harbour of Wijnkoopers Bay, a port of call of the Koninklijk Paketvaart Maatschappij. The discovery by De Groot in 1863 of petroleum added a most important industry to the list of the resources of Java. The great Dort Petroleum Company, now centred at Amsterdam, was founded in 1887. The production of this company alone rose from 79,179 *kisten* or cases (each 8.14 gall.) in 1891 to 1,642,780 in 1890, and to 1,967,124 in 1905. In 1904 there were no fewer than 36 concessions for petroleum. At the same time there is a larger importation of oil from Sumatra as well as from America and Russia. Sulphur is regularly worked in the Gunong Slamet, G. Sindoro, G. Sumbing, and in the crater of the Tangkuban Prahu as well as in other places in the Preanger regencies and in Pasuruan. Brine-wells exist in various parts. The bledegs (salt-mud wells) of Grobogan in the Solo Valley, Semarang, are best known. They rise from Miocene strata and yield iodine and bromine products as well as common salt. The natives of the district are allowed to extract the salt for their own use, but elsewhere (except in Jokjakarta) the manufacture 292of salt is a government monopoly and confined to the districts of Sumenep, Panekasan and Sampang in Madura, where from 3000 to 4000 people are hereditarily engaged in extracting salt from sea water, delivering it to the government at the rate of 10 fl. (nearly 17s.) per koyang (3700 ℔). The distribution of this salt (rough-grained, greyish and highly hygroscopic) is extremely unsatisfactory. The waste was so great that in 1901 the government paid a prize of about £835 (10,000 fl.) to Karl Boltz von Bolzberg for an improved method of packing. Between 1888 and 1892 the annual amount delivered was 71,405 tons; in the next five years it rose to 89,932; and between 1898 and 1902 sank again to 88,856. The evil effects of this monopoly have been investigated by J. E. de Meyer, "Zout als middel van belasting," De Ind. Gids. (1905). The scarcity of salt has led to a great importation of salted fish from Siam (upwards of 6600 tons in 1902).

Communications.—Roads and railways for the most part follow the fertile plains and table-lands along the coast and between the volcanic areas. The principal railways are the Semarang-Jokjakarta and Batavia-Buitenzorg lines of the Netherlands-Indian railway company, and the Surabaya-Pasuruan, Bangil-Mulang, Sidoarjo-Paron, Kertosono-Tulung Agung, Buitenzorg-Chianjur, Surakarta-Madiun, Pasuruan-Probolinggo, Jokjakarta-Chilachap and other lines of the government. The earliest lines, between Batavia and Buitenzorg and between Semarang and the capitals of the sultanates, were built about 1870 by a private company with a state guarantee. Since 1875, when Dr van Goltstein, then a cabinet minister and afterwards Dutch minister in London, had an act passed for the construction of state railways in Java, their progress has become much more rapid. In addition, several private companies have built either light railways or tramways, such as that between Semarang and Joana, and the total length of all lines was 2460 in 1905. There are some 3500 miles of telegraph line, and cables connect Java with Madura, Bali and Sumatra, and Port Darwin in Australia. Material welfare was promoted by the establishment of lines of steamships between Java and the other islands, all belonging to a Royal Packet Company, established in 1888 under a special statute, and virtually possessing a monopoly on account of the government mail contracts.

Administration.—Each village (dessa) forms an independent community, a group of dessas forms a district, a group of districts a department and a group of departments a residency, of which there are seventeen. At the head of each residency is a resident, with an assistant resident and a controller, all Dutch officials. The officials of the departments and districts are natives appointed by the government; those of the dessa are also natives, elected by the inhabitants and approved by the resident. In the two sultanates of Surakarta and Jokjakarta the native sultans govern under the supervision of the residents. (For the colonial administration of Netherlands India see MALAY ARCHIPELAGO.)

History.—The origin of the name Java is very doubtful. It is not improbable that it was first applied either to Sumatra or to what was known of the Indian Archipelago—the insular character of the several parts not being at once recognized. Jawa Dwipa, or "land of millet," may have been the original form and have given rise both to the Jaba diu of Ptolemy and to the Je-pho-thi of Fahien, the Chinese pilgrim of the 4th-5th century. The oldest form of the name in Arabic is apparently Zábej. The first epigraphic occurrence of Jawa is in an inscription of 1343. In Marco Polo the name is the common appellation of all the Sunda islands. The Jawa of Ibn Batuta is Sumatra; Java is his Mul Jáwa (*i.e.* possibly "original Java"). Jáwá is the modern Javanese name (in the court speech Jawi), sometimes with Nusa, "island," or Tanah, "country," prefixed.

It is impossible to extract a rational historical narrative from the earlier *babads* or native chronicles, and even the later are destitute of any satisfactory chronology. The first great era in the history is the ascendancy of the Hindus, and that breaks up into three periods—a period of Buddhism, a period of aggressive Sivaism, and a period of apparent compromise. Of the various Hindu states that were established in the island, that of Majapahit was the most widely dominant down to the end of the 15th century; its tributaries were many, and it even extended its sway into other parts of the archipelago. The second era of Javanese history is the invasion of Islam in the beginning of the 15th century; and the third is the establishment of European and more particularly of Dutch influence and authority in the island. About 1520 the Portuguese entered into commercial relationship with the natives, but at the close of the same century the Dutch began to establish themselves. At the time when the Dutch East India company began to fix its trading factories on the coast towns, the chief native state was Mataram, which had in the 16th century succeeded to the overlordship possessed by the house of Demak—one of the states that rose after the fall of Majapahit. The emperors of Java, as the princes of Mataram are called in the early accounts, had their capital at Kartasura, now an almost deserted place, 6 m. west of Surakarta. At first and for long the company had only forts and little fragments of territory at Jakatra (Batavia), &c.; but in 1705 it obtained definite possession of the Preanger by treaty with Mataram; and in 1745 its authority was extended over the whole north-east coast, from Cheribon to Banyuwangi. In 1755 the kingdom of Mataram was divided into the two states of Surakarta and Jokjakarta, which still retain a shadow of independence. The kingdom of Bantam was finally subjugated in 1808. By the English occupation of the island (1811-1818) the European ascendancy was rather strengthened than weakened; the great Java war (1825-1830), in which Dipå Negårå, the last Javanese prince, a clever, bold and unscrupulous leader, struggled to maintain his claim to the whole island, resulted in the complete success of the Dutch. To subdue him and his following, however, taxed all the resources of the Dutch Indian army for a period of five years, and cost it the loss of 15,000 officers and soldiers, besides millions of guilders. Nor did his great influence die with him when his adventurous career came to a close in 1855 at Macassar. Many Javanese, who dream of a restoration of their ancient empire, do not believe even yet that Dipå Negårå is dead. They are readily persuaded by fanatical hadjis that their hero will suddenly appear to drive away the Dutch and claim his rightful heritage. Several times there have been political troubles in the native states of central Java, in which Dipå Negårå's name was used, notably in 1883, when many rebellious chieftains were exiled. Similar attempts at revolt had been made before, mainly in 1865 and 1870, but none so serious perhaps as that in 1849, in which a son and a brother of Dipå Negårå were implicated, aiming to deliver and reinstate him. All such attempts proved as futile there as others in different parts of Java, especially in Bantam, where the trouble of 1850 and 1888 had a religious origin, and in the end they directly contributed to the consolidation of Dutch sway. Being the principal Dutch colony in the Malay Archipelago, Java was the first to benefit from the material change which resulted from the introduction of the Grondwet or Fundamental Law of 1848 in Holland. The main changes were of an economical character, but the political developments were also important. Since 1850 Dutch authority has steadily advanced, principally at the expense of the semi-independent sultanates in central Java, which had been allowed to remain after the capture and exile of Dipå Negårå. The power of the sultans of Jokjakarta and Surakarta has diminished; in 1863 Dutch authority was strengthened in the neighbouring island of Madura, and Bantam has lost every vestige of independence. The strengthening of the Dutch power has largely resulted from a more statesmanlike and more generous treatment of the natives, who have been educated to regard the *orang blanda*, or white man, as their protector against the native rulers. Thus, in 1866, passports for natives travelling in Java were abolished by the then governor-general, Dr Sloet van de Beele, who also introduced many reforms, reducing the *corvée* in the government plantations to a minimum, and doing away with the monopoly of fisheries. Six years later a primary education system for the natives, and a penal code, whose liberal provisions seemed framed for Europeans, were introduced.

Antiquities.—Ordinary traces of early human occupation are few in Java. The native bamboo buildings speedily perish. Stone weapons are occasionally found. But remains of the temples and monastic buildings of the Hindu period are numerous and splendid, and are remarkable as representing architecture which reached a high standard without the use of mortar, supporting columns or arches. Chandis (*i.e.* temples, though the word originally meant a depository for the ashes of a saint) are not found in western Java. They exist in two great zones: one in middle Java, one in eastern Java, each with its own distinguishing characteristics, both architectural and religious. The former begins in the Dyeng plateau, in the east of Banyumas, and extends into the east of Bagelen, Kedu and the neighbouring districts of Semarang, northern Jokjakarta, and the western corner of Surakarta. The latter lies mainly in Surabaya, Kediri and Pasuruan. A considerable number of 293ruins also exist in Probolinggo. Farther east they grow scarce. There is none in Madura. The remains of Macham Putih in Banyuwangi are possibly of non-Hindu origin. In the regency of Kendal (Semarang), to the north of Kedu, the place-names show that temples once existed.16 Some of them are Sivaite, some Buddhist, some astoundingly composite. None of the Buddhist buildings shows traces of the older Himaryana form of the creed. The greatest of all is a perfect sculptural exposition of the Mahayana doctrine. As to the period during which these temples were erected, authorities are not agreed. Ijzerman assigns the central Java groups to between the 8th and the 10th centuries. The seven-storeyed vihara (monastery) mentioned in the famous Menang-Kabu inscription (Sumatra) as founded by Maharaja Dhiraya Adityadharma in A.D. 656 is by some supposed to be Boro-Budur. A copper plate of 840 refers to Dyeng (Dehyang) as one of the sacred mountains of Java. One thing seems certain, that the temples of the eastern zone are of much more recent origin than most, at least, of the central zone. They are generally distinguished by the characteristics of a decadent and more voluptuous age, and show that the art of the time had become less Indian and more Javanese, with traces of influences derived from the more eastern East. At the same time it must be noted that even in

Boro Budur there are non-Indian elements in the decoration, indicating that the Hindu architect employed native artists and to some extent left them a free hand.

In his standard work on *Indian and Eastern Architecture*(London, 1876), James Fergusson asserted that the Javanese temples are in the Chalukyan style. But J. W. Ijzerman in an elaborate paper in the *Album-Kern* contends that the learned historian of architecture was misled by basing his opinion mainly on inaccurate drawings reproduced by Raffles. The Javanese temples, with the solitary exception of Chandi Bima in the Dyeng, are Dravidian and not Chalukyan. The very temples quoted by Fergusson, when more carefully examined, disprove his statement: a fact not without its bearing on the history of the Hindu immigration.

The wonderful scenery of the Dyeng plateau was already, in all probability, an object of superstitious awe to the aboriginal inhabitants of Java; and thus it would catch the attention of the earliest Hindu settlers. The old crater floor is full of traces of human occupation; though, in spite of the tradition of the existence of a considerable town, no sepulchral relics of the inhabitants have been discovered. There still remain five groups of temples—some well preserved, some mere heaps of stone—to prove the devotion their builders bore to Siva, his consort Durga, and Ganesha their son. The Arjuno group, in the middle of the plateau, consists of Chandi Arjuno (with its chapel or priests' residence, Ch. Semar), Ch. Srikahdi, Ch. Puntadeva and Ch. Sembadro, each a simple square chamber with a portico reached by a flight of steps. The second group, Ch. Daravati and Ch. Parakesit, lies to the north-east. The third, now a ruined mound, lies to the east. The fourth, to the north-west, is a group of seven small temples of which Ch. Sanchaki is the most important, with a square ground plan and an octagon roof with a second circular storey. Of the fifth group, in the south, only one temple remains—the Chandi Bima—a small, beautiful and exceptionally interesting building, in "the form of a pyramid, the ribs of which stand out much more prominently than the horizontal lines of the niche-shaped ornaments which rest each on its lotus cushion." How this happens to be the one Chalukyan temple amid hundreds is a problem to be solved. The plateau lies 6500 ft. above the sea, and roads and stairways, locally known as Buddha roads, lead up from the lowlands of Bagelen and Pekalongan. The stairway between Lake Menjur and Lake Chebong alone consisted of 4700 steps. The width of the roadway, however, is only some three or four feet. A remarkable subterranean tunnel still exists, which served to drain the plateau.

Of all the Hindu temples of Java the largest and most magnificent is Boro-Budur, which ranks among the architectural marvels of the world. It lies in the residency of Kedu, a little to the west of the Progo, a considerable stream flowing south to the Indian Ocean. The place is best reached by taking the steam-tram from Magelang or Jokjakarta to the village of Muntilam Passar, where a conveyance may be hired. Strictly speaking, Boro-Budur is not a temple but a hill, rising about 150 ft. above the plain, encased with imposing terraces constructed of hewn lava-blocks and crowded with sculptures. The lowest terrace now above ground forms a square, each side 497 ft. long. About 50 ft. higher there is another terrace of similar shape. Then follow four other terraces of more irregular contour. The structure is crowned by a dome or cupola 52 ft. in diameter surrounded by sixteen smaller bell-shaped cupolas. Regarded as a whole, the main design, to quote Mr Sewell, may be described as "an archaic Indian temple, considerably flattened and consisting of a series of terraces, surmounted by a quasi-stupa capped by a dagoba." It was discovered by the engineer J. W. Ijzerman in 1885 that the basement of the structure had been earthed up before the building was finished, and that the lowest retaining wall was completely concealed by the embankment. The architects had evidently found that their temple was threatened with a destructive subsidence; and, while the sculptors were still busy with the decoration of the lower façades, they had to abandon their work. But the unfinished bas-reliefs were carefully protected by clay and blocks of stone and left in position; and since 1896 they are gradually but systematically being exhumed and photographed by the Dutch archaeologists, who, however, have to proceed with caution, filling up one portion of the embankment before they go on to deal with another. The subjects treated in this lowest enceinte are of the most varied description, forming a picture-gallery of landscapes, scenes of outdoor and domestic life, mingled with mythological and religious designs. Among the genre class appear men shooting birds with blow-pipe or bow and arrow, fishermen with rod or net, a man playing a bagpipe, and so on. It would seem as if the architect had intended gradually to wean the devotees from the things of this world. When once they began to ascend from stage to stage of the temple-hill they were introduced to the realities of religion; and by the time they reached the dagoba they had passed through a process of instruction and were ready, with enlightened eyes, to enter and behold the image of Buddha, symbolically left imperfect, as beyond the power of human art to realize or portray. From basement to summit the whole hill is a great picture bible of the Mahayana creed.

If the statues and bas-reliefs of Boro-Budur were placed side by side they would extend for 3 m. The eye of the spectator, looking up from the present ground-level, is caught, says Mr Sewell, by the rows of life-size Buddhas that adorn the retaining walls of the several terraces and the cage-like shrines on the circular platforms. All the great figures on the east side represent Akshobhya, the Dhyani Buddha of the East. His right hand is in the Chumisparsa mudra (pose) touching the earth in front of the right knee—"I swear by the earth." All the statues on the south side are Ratnasam Chavu in the varada mudra—the right hand displayed upwards—"I give you all." On the west side the statues represent Amitabha in the dhyana or padinasama mudra, the right hand resting palm upwards on the left, both being on the lap—the attitude of meditation. Those on the north represent Amogasiddhi in the abhaya mudra, the right hand being raised and displayed, palm outwards—"Fear not, all is well."

Other remarkable groups of Hindu temples exist near the village of Prambanan17 (less correctly Brambanan) in Surakarta, but not far from the borders of Jokjakarta, with a station on the railway between the two chief towns. The village has been named after the temples, Prambanan signifying the place of teachers. The whole ecclesiastical settlement was surrounded by three lines of wall, of which only the inmost is now visible above ground. Between the second and third walls are 157 small temples, and in the central enclosure are the ruins of six larger temples in a double row with two smaller ones at the side. The middle temple of the western row is the main building, full of statues of purely Sivaite character—Siva as Guru or teacher, Siva as Kala or Time the Destroyer, Durga, Ganesha, and so on. But, just as many churches in Christendom are called not after the Christ but after the Virgin, so this is known as Lara (*i.e.* Virgin) Janggrang from the popular name of Durga. In the southern temple of the row is a very fine figure of a four-armed Brahma; in the northern there was a Vishnu with attendant figures. Of the other row the middle temple is again the largest, with Siva, his nandi or bull, and other symbolic sculptures. To the north lies the extraordinary cluster of temples which, though it does not deserve its popular name of Chandi Sewu, the thousand shrines, consists of at least 240 small buildings gathered round a great central temple, richly adorned, though roofless and partially ruined since the earthquake of 1867. Among the more noteworthy figures are those of the huge and ungainly guardians of the temple kneeling at the four main gateways of each of the principal buildings. Colonel Yule pointed out that there are distinct traces of a fine coat of stucco on the exterior and the interior of the buildings, and he compared in this respect "the cave walls of Ellora, the great idols at Bamian, and the Doric order at Selinus." Other temples in the same neighbourhood as Chandi Sewu are Ch. Lumbung, Ch. Kali Bening (Baneng), with a monstrous Kala head as the centre of the design on the southern side, Ch. Kalong and Ch. Plaosan. Tradition assigns these temples to 1266-1296.

Of the temples of the eastern zone the best known is Chandi Jago (or Tumpang), elaborately described in the Archaeological Commission's monograph. According to the *Pararaton*, a native chronicle (published in the *Verhand. v. h. Bat. Gen. v. K. en W.*, 1896), it belongs to the 13th century, containing the tomb of Rangavuni or Vishnuvardhana, who died in 1272-1273. The shrine proper occupies the third of three platforms, the lowest of which forms a 204 square of 45 to 46 ft. each side. The building fronts the west, and is constructed of an andesitic tuff of inferior quality and dark colour. Of distinctly Buddhistic influence there is no trace. The makara (elephant-fish head) is notably absent. The sculptures which run round the base and along the sides of the platforms or terraces are of the most elaborate and varied description—kings on thrones, dwarfs, elephants, supernatural beings, diabolical and grotesque, tree-monsters, palaces, temples, courtyards, lakes, gardens, forests—all are represented. In one place appears a Chinese—or Burmese-looking seven-roofed pagoda; in another, a tall temple strangely split down the centre, with a flight of steps running up the fissure. The inscriptions are in the Devanagari character. In the same neighbourhood are Ch. Singossari, Ch. Kidal, &c. Another of the most beautiful of the eastern temples is Ch. Jabung, mentioned in 1330. It is built of red brick; and its distinctly Javanese origin is suggested by the frequency of the snake-motif still characteristic of modern Javanese art. It may be added that a comparison of the several buildings of the zone affords an interesting study in the development of the pilaster as a decorative rather than structural element.

At Panabaram, near Blitar, Kediri, is another group of stone temples and other buildings. The chief temple is remarkable for the richness of its sculptures, which are peculiarly delicate and spirited in their details. The decoration of the mere robes of one of the free-standing stairway-guardians consists of scroll-work, interspersed with birds and animals rendered in a non-Indian style, reminiscent of Chinese or Japanese work. It has been described as one of the most beautiful pieces of sculpture in all the East.

Sculptures from the temples are scattered far and wide throughout Java, and it is one of the greatest difficulties of the archaeologist to determine the origin of many of the most interesting specimens. This, too, is often the case with those that have found their way to the museums of Java and Europe (Batavia, Leiden, Haarlem, Berlin, &c.). Minor relics of the past are to be found alike in the palaces of the nobles and the huts of the highland peasants. Zodiac cups of copper or

87

bronze dating from the 12th or 13th century are in daily use among the Tenggerese. The musical instruments used by the musicians of the native courts are often prized on account of their great antiquity.

As many of the Chinese came from China centuries ago and have not ceased to hold intercourse with their native country, the houses of the wealthier men among them are often rich in ancient specimens of Chinese art. The special exhibition organized by Henri Borel and other enthusiasts showed how much of value in this matter might be brought together in spite of the reluctance of the owners to commit the sacrilege of exposing to public gaze the images of their ancestral gods and heroes. Borel has given exquisite examples of images of Kwan-yin (the Chinese Virgin-Goddess), of Buddhas, of the ghoulish god of literature, of Lie-tai-Peh (the Chinese poet who has gone to live in the planet Venus), &c., in illustration of his papers in *L'Art flamand et hollandais*, pt. v. (1900), a translation of his monograph published at Batavia.

AUTHORITIES.—Besides the special works quoted *passim*, see Sir Stamford Raffles, *History of Java* (London, 1830); F. Junghuhn, *Java: seine Gestalt, Pflanzendecke, und innere Bauart* (Ger. trans. by J. K. Hasskarl, Leipzig, 1854-1857); P. J. Veth, *Java, Geographisch, ethnologisch, historisch* (2nd ed., Haarlem, 1896-1903), a masterly compendium originally based largely on Junghuhn's descriptions; L. van Deventer, *Geschiedenis der Nederlanders op Java* (2nd ed., Haarlem, 1895); L. W. C. van den Berg, *Le Hadhramout et les colonies arabes dans l'archipel indien* (Batavia, 1886); E. R. Scidmore, *Java, the Garden of the East* (New York, 1898); J. Chailley-Bert, *Java et ses habitants* (Paris, 1900); C. Day, *The Policy and Administration of the Dutch in Java* (London, 1904); E. S. de Klerck, *De Java-Oorlog van 1825-1830* (Batavia, 1905); *Encyclopaedie v. N. Indië*, art. "Java;" *Guide à travers l'Exposition de Paris* (The Hague, 1900), with articles by specialists on each department of the Dutch colonies, more particularly Java; *Koloniale Verslagen en Regeerings-almanak van N. Indië*, being official publications of the Dutch and Dutch East-Indian Government (see also MALAY ARCHIPELAGO).

(H. A. W.; O. J. R. H.)

1It must be observed that Bavian, &c., are mere conventional appendices to Java.

2H. B. Guppy (*R. S. G. Soc. Magazine*, 1889) holds that there is no sufficient proof of this connexion but gives interesting details of the present movement.

3See G. F. Tijdeman's map of the depths of the sea in the eastern part of the Indian archipelago in M. Weber's *Siboga Expedition*, 1903. The details of the coast forms of the island have been studied by J. F. Snelleman and J. F. Niermeyer in a paper in the Veth *Feestbundel*, utilizing *inter alia* Guppy's observations.

4This Merapi must be carefully distinguished from Merapi the Fire Mountain of Sumatra.

5R. D. M. Verbeek and R. Fennema, *Description géologique de Java et Madoura* (2 vols. and atlas, Amsterdam, 1896; also published in Dutch)—a summary with map was published by Verbeek in *Peterm. Mitt.* xliv. (1898), 24-33, pl. 3. Also K. Martin, *Die Eintheilung der versteinerungsführenden Sedimente von Java*, Samml. Geol. Reichsmus. Leiden, ser. i., vol. vi. (1899-1902), 135-245.

6On the 16th of November the sun rises at 5.32 and sets at 5.57; on the 16th of July it rises at 6.12 and sets at 5.57. The longest day is in December and the shortest in June, while on the other hand the sun is highest in February and October and lowest in June and December.

7S. Figei. *Regenwaarnemingen in Nederlandsch Indië* (1902).

8See J. C. Konigsberger, "De vogels Java en hunne oeconomische betukenis," *Med. int. s. Lands Plantentuin*.

9See especially M. Weber, *Siboga Expedition*.

10The *Annales de Buitenzorg*, with their *Icones bogorienses*, are universally known; the *Teysmannia* is named after a former director. A history of the gardens was published by Dr Treub, *Festboek van's Lands Plantentuin* (1891).

11Bertha Hoola van Nooten published *Fleurs, fruits et feuillages de la flore et de la pomone de l'île de Java* in 1863, but the book is difficult of access. Excellent views of characteristic aspects of the vegetation will be found in Karsten and Schenck, *Vegetationsbilder* (1903).

12It is interesting to compare this with the natural "reflorization" of Krakatoa. See Penzig, *Ann. jard. de Buitenzorg*, vol. viii. (1902); and W. Botting in *Nature* (1903).

13See Walbreken, *De Taalsvorten in het Javaansh*; and G. A. Wilken, *Handboek voor de vergelijkende Volkenkunde van Nederlandsch Indie*, edited by C. M. Pleyte (1893).

14See Van den Berg's account of the MSS. of the Batavian Society (the Hague, 1877); and a series of papers by C. Poensen in *Meded. van wege het Ned. Zendelinggenootschap* (1880).

15Cheriboh is the term employed by the Dutch: an exception to their usual system, in which Tj- takes the place of the Ch- used in this article.

16See R. Verbeek, "Liget der oudheden van Java," in *Verhand. v. h. Bat. Gen.*, xlvi., and his *Oudheidkundigekaart van Java*. R. Sewell's "Antiquarian notes in Java," in *Journal of the Royal*

Asiatic Society (1906), give the best conspectus available for English readers. W. B. Worsfold, *A Visit to Java* (London, 1893), has a good sketch of what was then known, revised by Professor W. Rhys Davids; but whoever wishes full information must refer to Dutch authorities. These are numerous but difficult of access.

17The chief authorities on Prambanan are J. W. Ijzerman,*Beschrijving der oudheden nabij de Grens der residenties Soerakarta en Djogjakarta* (Batavia, 1891, with photographs and atlas); and J. Groneman, *Tjandi Parambanan op Midden Java*; see also *Guide à travers l'exposition des Pays-Bas* (The Hague, 1900), No. 174, sqq.

JAVELIN, a spear, particularly one light enough to be thrown, a dart. The javelin was often provided with a thong to help in casting (see SPEAR). Javelin-throwing is one of the contests in the athletic section at the international Olympic games. Formerly the sheriff of a county or borough had a body of men armed with javelins, and known as javelin-men, who acted as a bodyguard for the judges when they went on assize. Their duties are now performed by the ordinary police. The word itself is an adaptation of Fr. *javeline*. There are several words in Celtic and Scandinavian languages and in Old English, meaning a spear or dart, that seem to be connected with *javel*, the base form in French; thus Welsh *gaflach*, Irish*gabhla*, O. Norwegian *gaflok*, O. E. *gafeluc*, later in the form*gavelock*, cf. O. Norman-Fr. *gavelot, javelot*, Ital. *giavelotto*. The origin seems to be Celtic, and the word is cognate with Ir.*gafa*, a hook, fork, gaff; the root is seen in "gable" (*q.v.*), and in the German *Gabel*, fork. The change in meaning from fork, forked end of a spear, to the spear itself is obscure.

JAW (Mid. Eng. *jawe, jowe* and*geowe*, O. Eng.*cheowan*, connected with "chaw" and "chew," and in form with "jowl"), in anatomy, the term for the upper maxillary bone, and the mandible or lower maxillary bone of the skull; it is sometimes loosely applied to all the lower front parts of the skull (*q.v.*).

JAWĀLĪQĪ, ABU MANṢŪR MAUHŪB UL-JAWĀLĪQĪ (1073-1145), Arabian grammarian, was born at Bagdad, where he studied philology under Tibrīzī and became famous for his handwriting. In his later years he acted as imam to the caliph Moqtafi. His chief work is the *Kitāb ul-Mu'arrab*, or "Explanation of Foreign Words used in Arabic."

The text was edited from an incomplete manuscript by E. Sachau (Leipzig, 1867). Many of the lacunae in this have been supplied from another manuscript by W. Spitta in the*Journal of the German Oriental Society*, xxxiii. 208 sqq. Another work, written as a supplement to the *Durrat ul-Ghawwās* of Harīrī (*q.v.*), has been published as "Le Livre des locutions vicieuses," by H. Derenbourg in*Morgenländische Forschungen* (Leipzig, 1875), pp. 107-166.

(G. W. T.)

JAWHAR, a native state of India, in the Konkan division of Bombay, situated among the lower ranges of the western Ghats. Area 310 sq. m. Pop. (1901), 47,538. The estimated revenue is £11,000; there is no tribute. The chief, who is a Koli by caste, traces back his descent to 1343. The leading exports are teak and rice. The principal village is that of Jawhar (pop. 3567).

JAWORÓW, a town in Galicia, Austria, 30 m. W. of Lemberg. Pop. (1900), 10,090. It has a pottery, a brewery, a distillery and some trade in agricultural produce. Not far from it is the watering-place of Szkto with sulphur springs. The town was a favourite residence of John Sobieski, who there received the congratulations of the pope and the Venetian republic on his success against the Turks at Vienna (1683). At Jaworów Peter the Great was betrothed to Catherine I.

JAY, JOHN (1745-1829), American statesman, the descendant of a Huguenot family, and son of Peter Jay, a successful New York merchant, was born in New York City on the 12th of December 1745. On graduating at King's College (now Columbia University) in 1764, Jay entered the office of Benjamin Kissam, an eminent New York lawyer. In 1768 he was admitted to the bar, and rapidly acquired a lucrative practice. In 1774 he married Sarah, youngest daughter of William Livingston, and was thus brought into close relations with one of the most influential families in New York. Like many other able young lawyers, Jay took an active part in the proceedings that resulted in the independence of the United States, identifying himself with the conservative element in the Whig or patriot party. He was sent as a delegate from New York City to the Continental Congress at Philadelphia in September 1774, and though almost the youngest member, was entrusted with drawing up the address to the people of Great Britain. Of the second congress, also, which met at Philadelphia on the 10th of May 1775, Jay was a member;

and on its behalf he prepared an address to the people of Canada and an address to the people of Jamaica and Ireland. In April 1776, while still retaining his seat in the Continental Congress, Jay was chosen as a member of the third provincial congress of New York; and his consequent absence from Philadelphia deprived him of the honour of affixing his signature to the Declaration of Independence. As a member of the fourth provincial congress he drafted a resolution by which the delegates of New York in the Continental Congress were authorized to sign the Declaration of Independence. In 1777 he was chairman of the committee of the convention which drafted the first New York state constitution. After acting for some time as one of the council of safety (which administered the state government until the new constitution came into effect), he was made chief justice of New York state, in September 1777. A clause in the state constitution prohibited any justice of the Supreme Court from holding any other post save that of delegate to Congress on a "special occasion," 295but in November 1778 the legislature pronounced the secession of what is now the state of Vermont from the jurisdiction of New Hampshire and New York to be such an occasion, and sent Jay to Congress charged with the duty of securing a settlement of the territorial claims of his state. He took his seat in congress on the 7th of December, and on the 10th was chosen president in succession to Henry Laurens.

On the 27th of September 1779 Jay was appointed minister plenipotentiary to negotiate a treaty between Spain and the United States. He was instructed to endeavour to bring Spain into the treaty already existing between France and the United States by a guarantee that Spain should have the Floridas in case of a successful issue of the war against Great Britain, reserving, however, to the United States the free navigation of the Mississippi. He was also to solicit a subsidy in consideration of the guarantee, and a loan of five million dollars. His task was one of extreme difficulty. Although Spain had joined France in the war against Great Britain, she feared to imperil her own colonial interests by directly encouraging and aiding the former British colonies in their revolt against their mother country, and she had refused to recognize the United States as an independent power. Jay landed at Cadiz on the 22nd of January 1780, but was told that he could not be received in a formally diplomatic character. In May the king's minister, Count de Florida Bianca, intimated to him that the one obstacle to a treaty was the question of the free navigation of the Mississippi, and for months following this interview the policy of the court was clearly one of delay. In February 1781 Congress instructed Jay that he might make concessions regarding the navigation of the Mississippi, if necessary; but further delays were interposed, the news of the surrender of Yorktown arrived, and Jay decided that any sacrifice to obtain a treaty was no longer advisable. His efforts to procure a loan were not much more successful, and he was seriously embarrassed by the action of Congress in drawing bills upon him for large sums. Although by importuning the Spanish minister, and by pledging his personal responsibility, Jay was able to meet some of the bills, he was at last forced to protest others; and the credit of the United States was saved only by a timely subsidy from France.

In 1781 Jay was commissioned to act with Franklin, John Adams, Jefferson and Henry Laurens in negotiating a peace with Great Britain. He arrived in Paris on the 23rd of June 1782, and jointly with Franklin had proceeded far with the negotiations when Adams arrived late in October. The instructions of the American negotiators were as follows:—

"You are to make the most candid and confidential communications upon all subjects to the ministers of our generous ally, the king of France; to undertake nothing in the negotiations for peace or truce without their knowledge and concurrence; and ultimately to govern yourselves by their advice and opinion, endeavouring in your whole conduct to make them sensible how much we rely on his majesty's influence for effectual support in every thing that may be necessary to the present security, or future prosperity, of the United States of America."

Jay, however, in a letter written to the president of Congress from Spain, had expressed in strong terms his disapproval of such dependence upon France, and, on arriving in Paris, he demanded that Great Britain should treat with his country on an equal footing by first recognizing its independence, although the French minister, Count de Vergennes, contended that an acknowledgment of independence as an effect of the treaty was as much as could reasonably be expected. Finally, owing largely to Jay, who suspected the good faith of France, the American negotiators decided to treat independently with Great Britain. The provisional articles, which were so favourable to the United States as to be a great surprise to the courts of France and Spain, were signed on the 30th of November 1782, and were adopted with no important change as the final treaty on the 3rd of September 1783.

On the 24th of July 1784 Jay landed in New York, where he was presented with the freedom of the city and elected a delegate to Congress. On the 7th of May Congress had already chosen him to be secretary for foreign affairs, and in December Jay resigned his seat in Congress and accepted the secretaryship. He continued to act in this capacity until 1790, when Jefferson became secretary of state under the new constitution. In the question of this constitution Jay had taken a keen interest, and as an advocate of its ratification he wrote over the name "Publius," five (Nos. 2, 3, 4, 5 and 64) of the famous series of papers known collectively as the *Federalist*(see HAMILTON, ALEXANDER). He published anonymously (though without succeeding in concealing the authorship) *An Address to the People of New York*, in vindication of the constitution; and in the state convention at Poughkeepsie he ably seconded Hamilton in securing its ratification by New York. In making his first appointments to federal offices President Washington asked Jay to take his choice; Jay chose that of chief justice of the Supreme Court, and held this position from September 1789 to June 1795. The most famous case that came before him was that of *Chisolm* v. *Georgia*, in which the question was, Can a state be sued by a citizen of another state? Georgia argued that it could not be so sued, on the ground that it was a sovereign state, but Jay decided against Georgia, on the ground that sovereignty in America resided with the people. This decision led to the adoption of the eleventh amendment to the federal constitution, which provides that no suit may be brought in the federal courts against any state by a citizen of another state or by a citizen or subject of any foreign state. In 1792 Jay consented to stand for the governorship of New York State, but a partisan returning-board found the returns of three counties technically defective, and though Jay had received an actual majority of votes, his opponent, George Clinton, was declared elected.

Ever since the War of Independence there had been friction between Great Britain and the United States. To the grievances of the United States, consisting principally of Great Britain's refusal to withdraw its troops from the forts on the north-western frontier, as was required by the peace treaty of 1783, her refusal to make compensation for negroes carried away by the British army at the close of the War of Independence, her restrictions on American commerce, and her refusal to enter into any commercial treaty with the United States, were added, after war broke out between France and Great Britain in 1793, the anti-neutral naval policy according to which British naval vessels were authorized to search American merchantmen and impress American seamen, provisions were treated as contraband of war, and American vessels were seized for no other reason than that they had on board goods which were the property of the enemy or were bound for a port which though not actually blockaded was declared to be blockaded. The anti-British feeling in the House of Representatives became so strong that on the 7th of April 1794 a resolution was introduced to prohibit commercial intercourse between the United States and Great Britain until the north-western posts should be evacuated and Great Britain's anti-neutral naval policy should be abandoned. Thereupon Washington, fearing that war might result, appointed Jay minister extraordinary to Great Britain to negotiate a new treaty, and the Senate confirmed the appointment by a vote of 18 to 8, although the non-intercourse resolution which came from the house a few days later was defeated in the senate only by the casting vote of Vice-President John Adams. Jay landed at Falmouth in June 1794, signed a treaty with Lord Grenville on the 19th of November, and disembarked again at New York on the 28th of May 1795. The treaty, known in history as Jay's Treaty, provided that the north-western posts should be evacuated by the 1st of June 1796, that commissioners should be appointed to settle the north-east and the north-west boundaries, and that the British claims for British debts as well as the American claims for compensation for illegal seizures should be referred to commissioners. More than one-half of the clauses in the treaty related to commerce, and although they contained rather small concessions to the United States, they were about as much as could reasonably have been expected in the circumstances. One clause, the operation of which was limited to two years from the close of the existing war, provided that American vessels not exceeding 70 tons burden 296might trade with the West Indies, but should carry only American products there and take away to American ports only West Indian products; moreover, the United States was to export in American vessels no molasses, sugar, coffee, cocoa or cotton to any part of the world. Jay consented to this prohibition under the impression that the articles named were peculiarly the products of the West Indies, not being aware that cotton was rapidly becoming an important export from the southern states. The operation of the other commercial clauses was limited to twelve years. By them the United States was granted limited privileges of trade with the British East Indies; some provisions were made for reciprocal freedom of trade between the United States and the British dominions in Europe; some articles were specified under the head of "contraband of war"; it was agreed that whenever provisions were seized as contraband they should be paid for, and that in cases of the capture of a vessel carrying contraband goods such goods only and not the whole cargo should be seized; it was also agreed that no vessel should be seized merely because it was bound for a blockaded port, unless it attempted to enter the port after receiving notice of the blockade. The treaty was laid before the Senate on the 8th of June 1795, and, with the exception of the clause relating to trade with the West Indies, was ratified on the 24th by a vote of 20 to 10. As yet the public was ignorant of its contents, and although the Senate had enjoined secrecy on its members even after the treaty had been ratified, Senator

Mason of Virginia gave out a copy for publication only a few days later. The Republican party, strongly sympathizing with France and strongly disliking Great Britain, had been opposed to Jay's mission, and had denounced Jay as a traitor and guillotined him in effigy when they heard that he was actually negotiating. The publication of the treaty only added to their fury. They filled newspapers with articles denouncing it, wrote virulent pamphlets against it, and burned Jay in effigy. The British flag was insulted. Hamilton was stoned at a public meeting in New York while speaking in defence of the treaty, and Washington was grossly abused for signing it. In the House of Representatives the Republicans endeavoured to prevent the execution of the treaty by refusing the necessary appropriations, and a vote (29th of April, 1795) on a resolution that it ought to be carried into effect stood 49 to 49; but on the next day the opposition was defeated by a vote of 51 to 48. Once in operation, the treaty grew in favour. Two days before landing on his return from the English mission, Jay had been elected governor of New York state; notwithstanding his temporary unpopularity, he was re-elected in April 1798. With the close of this second term of office in 1801, he ended his public career. Although not yet fifty-seven years old, he refused all offers of office and retiring to his estate near Bedford in Westchester county, N.Y., spent the rest of his life in rarely interrupted seclusion. In politics he was throughout inclined toward Conservatism, and after the rise of parties under the federal government he stood with Alexander Hamilton and John Adams as one of the foremost leaders of the Federalist party, as opposed to the Republicans or Democratic-Republicans. From 1821 until 1828 he was president of the American Bible Society. He died on the 17th of May 1829. The purity and integrity of his life are commemorated in a sentence by Daniel Webster: "When the spotless ermine of the judicial robe fell on John Jay, it touched nothing less spotless than itself."

See *The Correspondence and Public Papers of John Jay*(4 vols., New York, 1890-1893), edited by H. P. Johnston; William Jay, *Life of John Jay with Selections from his Correspondence and Miscellaneous Papers* (2 vols., New York, 1833); William Whitelocke, *Life and Times of John Jay* (New York, 1887); and George Pellew, *John Jay*(Boston, 1890), in the "American Statesmen Series."

John Jay's son, WILLIAM JAY (1789-1858), was born in New York City on the 16th of June 1789, graduated from Yale in 1807, and soon afterwards assumed the management of his father's large estate in Westchester county, N.Y. He was actively interested in peace, temperance and anti-slavery movements. He took a prominent part in 1816 in founding the American Bible Society; was a judge of Westchester county from 1818 to 1843, when he was removed from office by the party in power in New York, which hoped, by sacrificing an anti-slavery judge, to gain additional strength in the southern states; joined the American anti-slavery society in 1834, and held several important offices in this organization. In 1840, however, when it began to advocate measures which he deemed too radical, he withdrew his membership, but with his pen he continued his labours on behalf of the slave, urging emancipation in the district of Columbia and the exclusion of slavery from the Territories, though deprecating any attempt to interfere with slavery in the states. He was a member of the American peace society and was its president for several years. His pamphlet, *War and Peace: the Evils of the First with a Plan for Securing the Last*, advocating international arbitration, was published by the English Peace Society in 1842, and is said to have contributed to the promulgation, by the powers signing the Treaty of Paris in 1856, of a protocol expressing the wish that nations, before resorting to arms, should have recourse to the good offices of a friendly power. Among William Jay's other writings, the most important are *The Life of John Jay* (2 vols., 1833) and a *Review of the Causes and Consequences of the Mexican War* (1849). He died at Bedford on the 14th of October 1858.

See Bayard Tuckerman, *William Jay and the Constitutional Movement for the Abolition of Slavery* (New York, 1893).

William Jay's son, JOHN JAY (1817-1894), also took an active part in the anti-slavery movement. He was a prominent member of the free soil party, and was one of the organizers of the Republican party in New York. He was United States minister to Austria-Hungary in 1869-1875, and was a member, and for a time president, of the New York civil service commission appointed by Governor Cleveland in 1883.

JAY, WILLIAM (1769-1853), English Nonconformist divine, was born at Tisbury in Wiltshire on the 6th of May 1769. He adopted his father's trade of stone-mason, but gave it up in 1785 in order to enter the Rev. Cornelius Winter's school at Marlborough. During the three years that Jay spent there, his preaching powers were rapidly developed. Before he was twenty-one he had preached nearly a thousand times, and in 1788 he had for a while occupied Rowland Hill's pulpit in London. Wishing to continue his reading he accepted the humble pastorate of Christian Malford, near Chippenham, where he remained about two years. After one year at Hope chapel, Clifton, he was called to the ministry of Argyle Independent chapel in Bath; and on the 30th of January 1791 he began the work of his life there, attracting hearers of every religious denomination and of every rank, and winning for himself a wide reputation as a brilliant pulpit orator, an earnest religious author, and a friendly counsellor. Sheridan declared him to be the most manly orator he had ever heard. A long and honourable connexion of sixty-two years came to an end in January 1853, and he died on the 27th of December following.

The best-known of Jay's works are his *Morning and Evening Exercises*: The *Christian contemplated*: The *Domestic Minister's Assistant*; and his *Discourses*. He also wrote a *Life of Rev. Cornelius Winter*, and *Memoirs of Rev. John Clarke*. An edition of Jay's *Works* in 12 vols., 8vo, revised by himself, was issued in 1842-1844, and again in 1856. A new edition, in 8 vols., 8vo, was published in 1876. See *Autobiography* (1854); S. Wilson's *Memoir of Jay* (1854); S. Newth in *Pulpit Memorials* (1878).

JAY (Fr. *géai*), a well-known and very beautiful European bird, the *Corvus glandarius* of Linnaeus, the *Garrulus glandarius* of modern ornithologists. To this species are more or less closely allied numerous birds inhabiting the Palaearctic and Indian regions, as well as the greater part of America, but not occurring in the Antilles, in the southern portion of the Neotropical Region, or in the Ethiopian or Australian. All these birds are commonly called jays, and form a group of the crows or *Corvidae*, which may fairly be considered a sub-family,*Garrulinae*. Indeed there are, or have been, systematists who would elevate the jays to the rank of a family *Garrulidae*—a proceeding which seems unnecessary. Some of 297them have an unquestionable resemblance to the pies, if the group now known by that name can be satisfactorily severed from the true*Corvinae*. In structure the jays are not readily differentiated from the pies; but in habit they are much more arboreal, delighting in thick coverts, seldom appearing in the open, and seeking their food on or under trees. They seem also never to walk or run when on the ground, but always to hop. The body-feathers are commonly loose and soft; and, gaily coloured as are most of the species, in few of them has the plumage the metallic glossiness it generally presents in the pies, while the proverbial beauty of the "jay's wing" is due to the vivid tints of blue—turquoise and cobalt, heightened by bars of jet-black, an indication of the same style of ornament being observable in the greater number of the other forms of the group, and in some predominating over nearly the whole surface. Of the many genera that have been proposed by ornithologists, perhaps about nine may be deemed sufficiently well established.

FIG. 1—
European Jay.

The ordinary European jay, *Garrulus glandarius* (fig. 1), has suffered so much persecution in the British Islands as to have become in many districts a rare bird. In Ireland it seems now to be indigenous to the southern half of the island only; in England generally, it is far less numerous than formerly; and in Scotland its numbers have decreased with still greater rapidity. There is little doubt that it would have been exterminated but for its stock being supplied in autumn by immigration, and for its shy and wary behaviour, especially at the breeding-season, when it becomes almost wholly mute, and thereby often escapes detection. No truthful man, however much he may love the bird, will gainsay the depredations on fruit and eggs that it at times commits; but the gardeners and gamekeepers of Britain, instead of taking a few simple steps to guard their charge from injury, deliberately adopt methods of wholesale destruction—methods that in the case of this species are only too easy and too effectual—by proffering temptation to trespass which it is not in jay-nature to resist, and accordingly the bird runs great chance of total extirpation. Notwithstanding the war carried on against the jay, its varied cries and active gesticulations show it to be a sprightly bird, and at a distance that renders its beauty-spots invisible, it is yet rendered conspicuous by its cinnamon-coloured body and pure white tail-coverts, which contrast with the deep black and rich chestnut that otherwise mark its plumage, and even the young at once assume a dress closely resembling that of the adult. The nest, generally concealed in a leafy tree or bush, is carefully built, with a lining formed of fine roots neatly interwoven. Herein from four to seven eggs, of a greenish-white closely freckled, so as to seem suffused with light olive, are laid in March or April, and the young on quitting it accompany their parents for some weeks.

Though the common jay of Europe inhabits nearly the whole of this quarter of the globe south of 64° N. lat., its territory in the east of Russia is also occupied by *G. brandti*, a kindred form, which replaces it on the other side of the Ural, and ranges thence across Siberia to Japan; and again on the lower Danube and thence to Constantinople the nearly allied *G. krynicki*(which alone is found in southern Russia, Caucasia and Asia Minor) shares its haunts with it.1 It also crosses the Mediterranean to Algeria and Morocco; but there, as in southern Spain, it is probably but a winter immigrant. The three forms just named have the widest range of any of the genus. Next to them come G. *atricapillus*, reaching from Syria to Baluchistan, G. *japonicus*, the ordinary jay of southern Japan, and G. *sinensis*, the Chinese bird. Other forms have a much more limited area, as G. *cervicalis*, the local and resident jay of Algeria, G. *hyrcanus*, found on the southern shores of the Caspian Sea, and G. *taevanus*, confined to the island of Formosa. The most aberrant of the true jays is G. *lidthi*, a very rare species, which seems to come from some part of Japan (*vide* Salvadori, *Atti Accad. Torino*, vii. 474), though its exact locality is not known.

Leaving the true jays of the genus *Garrulus*, it is expedient next to consider those of a group named, in 1831, *Perisoreus*by Prince C. L. Bonaparte (*Saggio*, &c., *Anim. Vertebrati*, p. 43) and *Dysornithia* by Swainson (*F. B.-Americana*, ii. 495).2

FIG. 2.—American
Blue Jay.

This group contains two species—one the Lanius infaustus of Linnaeus and the Siberian jay of English writers, which ranges throughout the pine-forests of the north of Europe and Asia, and the second the *Corvus canadensis* of the same author, or Canada jay, occupying a similar station in America. The so-called Siberian jay is one of the most entertaining birds in the world. Its versatile cries and actions, as seen and heard by those who penetrate the solitude of the northern forests it inhabits, can never be forgotten by one who has had experience of them, any more than the pleasing sight of its rust-coloured tail, which an occasional gleam of sunshine will light up into a brilliancy quite unexpected by those who have only surveyed the bird's otherwise gloomy appearance in the glass-case of a museum. It seems scarcely to know fear, obtruding itself on the notice of any traveller who invades its haunts, and, should he halt, making itself at once a denizen of his bivouac. In confinement it speedily becomes friendly, but suitable food for it is not easily found. Linnaeus seems to have been under a misapprehension when he applied to it the trivial epithet it bears; for by none of his countrymen is it deemed an unlucky bird, but rather the reverse. In fact, no one can listen to the cheery sound of its ordinary calls with any but a hopeful feeling. The Canada jay, or "whisky-jack" (the corruption probably of a Cree name), seems to be of a similar nature, but it presents a still more sombre coloration, its nestling plumage,3indeed, being thoroughly corvine in appearance and suggestive of its being a pristine form.

As though to make amends for the dull plumage of the species last mentioned, North America offers some of the most brilliantly 298coloured of the sub-family, and the common blue jay4 of Canada and the eastern states of the Union, *Cyanurus cristatus* (fig. 2), is one of the most conspicuous birds of the Transatlantic woods. The account of its habits by Alexander Wilson is known to every student of ornithology, and Wilson's followers have had little to do but supplement his history with unimportant details. In this bird and its many allied forms, coloration, though almost confined to various tints of blue, seems to reach its climax, but want of space forbids more particular notice of them, or of the members of the other genera*Cyanocitta*, *Cyanocorax*, *Xanthura*, *Psilorhinus*, and more, which inhabit various parts of the Western continent. It remains, however, to mention the genus Cissa, including many beautiful forms belonging to the Indian region, and among them the C. *speciosa* and C. *sinensis*, so often represented in Oriental drawings, though doubts may be expressed whether these birds are not more nearly related to the pies than to the jays.

(A. N.)

1Further information will possibly show that these districts are not occupied at the same season of the year by the two forms.

2Recent writers have preferred the former name, though it was only used sub-generically by its author, who assigned to it no characters, which the inventor of the latter was careful to do, regarding it at the same time as a genus.

3In this it was described and figured (*F. B. Americana*, ii. 296, pl. 55) as a distinct species, G. *brachyrhynchus*.

4The birds known as blue jays in India and Africa are rollers (*q.v.*).

JEALOUSY (adapted from Fr. *jalousie*, formed from*jaloux*, jealous, Low Lat. *zelosus*, Gr. ζῆλος, ardour, zeal, from the root seen in ζέειν, to boil, ferment; cf. "yeast"), originally a condition of zealous emulation, and hence, in the usual modern sense, of resentment at being (or believing that one is or may be) supplanted or preferred in the love or affection of another, or in the enjoyment of some good regarded as properly one's own. Jealousy is really a form of envy, but implies a feeling of personal claim which in envy or covetousness is wanting. The jealousy of God, as in Exod. xx. 5, "For I, the Lord thy God, am a jealous God," has been defined by Pusey (*Minor Prophets*, 1860) as the attribute "whereby he does not endure the love of his creatures to be transferred from him." "Jealous," by etymology, is however, only another form of "zealous," and the identity is exemplified by such expressions as "I have been very jealous for the Lord God of Hosts" (1 Kings xix. 10). A kind of glass, thick, ribbed and non-transparent, was formerly known as "jealous-glass," and this application is seen in the borrowed French word *jalousie*, a blind or shutter, made of slats of wood, which slope in such a way as to admit air and a certain amount of light, while excluding rain and sun and inspection from without.

JEAN D'ARRAS, a 15th-century *trouvère*, about whose personal history nothing is known, was the collaborator with Antoine du Val and Fouquart de Cambrai in the authorship of a collection of stories entitled *Évangiles de quenouille*. They purport to record the narratives of a group of ladies at their spinning, who relate the current theories on a great variety of subjects. The work dates from the middle of the 15th century and is of considerable value for the light it throws on medieval manners.

There were many editions of this book in the 15th and 16th centuries, one of which was printed by Wynkyn de Worde in English, as *The Gospelles of Dystaves*. A modern edition (Collection Jannet) has a preface by Anatole France.

Another *trouvère*, JEAN D'ARRAS who flourished in the second half of the 14th century, wrote, at the request of John, duke of Berry, a long prose romance entitled *Chronique de la princesse*. It relates with many digressions the antecedents and life of the fairy Mélusine (*q.v.*).

JEAN DE MEUN, or DE MEUNG (*c.* 1250-*c.* 1305), whose original name was Jean Clopinel or Chopinel, was born at Meun-sur-Loire. Tradition asserts that he studied at the university of Paris. At any rate he was, like his contemporary, Rutebeuf, a defender of Guillaume de Saint-Amour and a bitter critic of the mendicant orders. Most of his life seems to have been spent in Paris, where he possessed, in the Rue Saint-Jacques, a house with a tower, court and garden, which was described in 1305 as the house of the late Jean de Meung, and was then bestowed by a certain Adam d'Andely on the Dominicans. Jean de Meun says that in his youth he composed songs that were sung in every public place and school in France. In the enumeration of his own works he places first his continuation of the *Roman de la rose* of Guillaume de Lorris (*q.v.*). The date of this second part is generally fixed between 1268 and 1285 by a reference in the poem to the death of Manfred and Conradin, executed (1268) by order of Charles of Anjou (d. 1285) who is described as the present king of Sicily. M. F. Guillon (*Jean Clopinel*, 1903), however, considering the poem primarily as a political satire, places it in the last five years of the 13th century. Jean de Meun doubtless edited the work of his predecessor, Guillaume de Lorris, before using it as the starting-point of his own vast poem, running to 19,000 lines. The continuation of Jean de Meun is a satire on the monastic orders, on celibacy, on the nobility, the papal see, the excessive pretensions of royalty, and especially on women and marriage. Guillaume had been the servant of love, and the exponent of the laws of "courtoisie"; Jean de Meun added an "art of love," exposing with brutality the vices of women, their arts of deception, and the means by which men may outwit them. Jean de Meun embodied the mocking, sceptical spirit of the *fabliaux*. He did not share in current superstitions, he had no respect for established institutions, and he scorned the conventions of feudalism and romance. His poem shows in the highest degree, in spite of the looseness of its plan, the faculty of keen observation, of lucid reasoning and exposition, and it entitles him to be considered the greatest of French medieval poets. He handled the French language with an ease and precision unknown to his predecessors, and the length of his poem was no bar to its popularity in the 13th and 14th centuries. Part of its vogue was no doubt due to the fact that the author, who had mastered practically all the scientific and literary knowledge of his contemporaries in France, had found room in his poem for a great amount of useful information and for numerous citations from classical authors. The book was attacked by Guillaume de Degulleville in his *Pèlerinage de la vie humaine* (*c.* 1330), long a favourite work both in England and France; by John Gerson, and by Christine de Pisan in her *Épître au dieu d'amour*; but it also found energetic defenders.

Jean de Meun translated in 1284 the treatise, *De re militari*, of Vegetius into French as *Le livre de Végèce de l'art de chevalerie*1 (ed. Ulysse Robert, *Soc. des anciens textes fr.*, 1897). He also produced a spirited version, the first in French, of the letters of Abelard and Hèloïse. A 14th-century MS. of this translation in the Bibliothèque Nationale has annotations by Petrarch. His translation of the*De consolatione philosophiae* of Boëtius is preceded by a letter to Philip IV. in which he enumerates his earlier works, two of which are lost—*De spirituelle amitié* from the *De spirituali amicitia* of Aelred of Rievaulx (d. 1166), and the*Livre des merveilles d'Hirlande* from the *Topographia Hibernica*, or *De Mirabilibus Hiberniae* of Giraldus Cambrensis (Giraud de Barry). His last poems are doubtless his *Testament* and *Codicille*. The *Testament* is written in quatrains in monorime, and contains advice to the different classes of the community.

See also Paulin Paris in *Hist. lit. de la France*, xxviii. 391-439, and E. Langlois in *Hist. de la langue et de la lit. française*, ed. L. Petit de Julleville, ii. 125-161 (1896); and editions of the *Roman de la rose* (*q.v.*).

1Jean de Meun's translation formed the basis of a rhymed version (1290) by Jean Priorat of Besançon, *Li abreyance de l'ordre de chevalerie.*

JEANNETTE, a borough of Westmoreland county, Pennsylvania, U.S.A., about 27 m. E. by S. of Pittsburg. Pop. (1890), 3296; (1900), 5865 (1340 foreign-born); (1910), 8077. It is served by the Pennsylvania railroad, and is connected with Pittsburg and Uniontown by electric railway. It is supplied with natural gas and is primarily a manufacturing centre, its principal manufactures being glass, table-ware and rubber goods. Jeannette was founded in 1888, and was incorporated as a borough in 1889.

JEANNIN, PIERRE (1540-1622), French statesman, was born at Autun. A pupil of the great jurist Jacques Cujas at Bourges, he was an advocate at Dijon in 1569 and became councillor and then president of the *parlement* of Burgundy. He opposed in vain the massacre of St Bartholomew in his province. As councillor to the duke of Mayenne he sought to reconcile him with Henry IV. After the victory of Fontaine-Française (1595), Henry took Jeannin into his council and in 1602 named him intendant of finances. He took part in the principal events of the reign, negotiated the treaty of Lyons with the duke of Savoy 299(see HENRY IV.), and the defensive alliance between France and the United Netherlands in 1608. As superintendent of finances under Louis XIII., he tried to establish harmony between the king and the queen-mother.

See Berger de Xivrey, *Lettres missives de Henri IV.* (in the *Collection inédite pour l'histoire de France*), t. v. (1850); P(ierre) S(aumaise), *Eloge sur la vie de Pierre Janin*(Dijon, 1623); Sainte-Beuve, *Causeries du lundi*, t. x. (May 1854).

JEBB, JOHN (1736-1786), English divine, was educated at Cambridge, where he was elected fellow of Peterhouse in 1761, having previously been second wrangler. He was a man of independent judgment and warmly supported the movement of 1771 for abolishing university and clerical subscription to the Thirty-nine Articles. In his lectures on the Greek Testament he is said to have expressed Socinian views. In 1775 he resigned his Suffolk church livings, and two years afterwards graduated M.D. at St Andrews. He practised medicine in London and was elected F.R.S. in 1779.

Another JOHN JEBB (1775-1833), bishop of Limerick, is best known as the author of *Sacred Literature* (London, 1820).

JEBB, SIR RICHARD CLAVERHOUSE(1841-1905), English classical scholar, was born at Dundee on the 27th of August 1841. His father was a well-known barrister, and his grandfather a judge. He was educated at Charterhouse and at Trinity College, Cambridge. He won the Porson and Craven scholarships, was senior classic in 1862, and became fellow and tutor of his college in 1863. From 1869 to 1875 he was public orator of the university; professor of Greek at Glasgow from 1875 to 1889, and at Cambridge from 1889 till his death on the 9th of December 1905. In 1891 he was elected member of parliament for Cambridge University; he was knighted in 1900. Jebb was acknowledged to be one of the most brilliant classical scholars of his time, a humanist in the best sense, and his powers of translation from and into the classical languages were unrivalled. A collected volume,*Translations into Greek and Latin*, appeared in 1873 (ed. 1909). He was the recipient of many honorary degrees from European and American universities, and in 1905 was made a member of the Order of Merit. He married in 1874 the widow of General A. J. Slemmer, of the United States army, who survived him.

Jebb was the author of numerous publications, of which the following are the most important: The *Characters* of Theophrastus (1870), text, introduction, English translation and commentary (re-edited by J. E. Sandys, 1909); *The Attic Orators from Antiphon to Isaeus* (2nd ed., 1893), with companion volume, *Selections from the Attic Orators* (2nd ed., 1888); *Bentley* (1882); *Sophocles* (3rd ed., 1893) the seven plays, text, English translation and notes, the promised edition of the fragments being prevented by his death; *Bacchylides* (1905), text, translation, and notes;*Homer* (3rd ed., 1888), an introduction to the *Iliad* and*Odyssey*; *Modern Greece* (1901); *The Growth and Influence of Classical Greek Poetry* (1893). His translation of the*Rhetoric* of Aristotle was published posthumously under the editorship of J. E. Sandys (1909). A selection from his*Essays and Addresses*, and a subsequent volume, *Life and Letters of Sir Richard Claverhouse Jebb* (with critical introduction by A. W. Verrall) were published by his widow in 1907; see also an appreciative notice by J. E. Sandys,*Hist. of Classical Scholarship*, iii. (1908).

JEBEIL (anc. *Gebal-Byblus*), a town of Syria pleasantly situated on a slight eminence near the sea, about 20 m. N. of Beirut. It is surrounded by a wall 1½ m. in circumference, with square towers at the angles, and a castle at the south-east corner. Numerous broken granite columns in the gardens and vineyards that surround the town, with the number of ruined houses within the walls, testify to its former importance. The stele of Jehawmelek, king of Gebal, found here, is one of the most important of Phoenician monuments. The small port is almost choked up with sand and ruins. Pop. 3000, all Moslems.

The inhabitants of the Phoenician Gebal and Greek Byblus were renowned as stonecutters and ship-builders. Arrian (ii. 20. 1) represents Enylus, king of Byblus, as joining Alexander with a fleet, after that monarch had captured the city. Philo of Byblus makes it the most ancient city of Phoenicia, founded by Cronus, *i.e.* the Moloch who appears from the stele of Jehawmelek to have been with Baalit the chief deity of the city. According to Plutarch (*Mor.* 357), the ark with the corpse of Osiris was cast ashore at Byblus, and there found by Isis. The orgies of Adonis in the temple of Baalit (Aphrodite Byblia) are described by Lucian, *De Dea Syr.*, cap. vi. The river Adonis is the Nahr al-Ibrahim, which flows near the town. The crusaders, after failing before it in 1099, captured "Giblet" in 1103, but lost it again to Saladin in 1189. Under Mahommedan rule it has gradually (D. G. H.) decayed.

JEBEL (plur. *jibāl*), also written GEBEL with hard *g* (plur.*gibāl*), an Arabic word meaning a mountain or a mountain chain. It is frequently used in place-names. The French transliteration of the word is *djebel. Jebeli* signifies a mountaineer. The pronunciation with a hard *g* sound is that used in the Egyptian dialect of Arabic.

JEDBURGH, a royal and police burgh and county-town of Roxburghshire, Scotland. Pop. of police burgh (1901), 3136. It is situated on Jed Water, a tributary of the Teviot, 56¼ m. S.E. of Edinburgh by the North British railway, via Roxburgh and St Boswells (49 m. by road), and 10 m. from the border at Catcleuch Shin, a peak of the Cheviots, 1742 ft. high. Of the name Jedburgh there have been many variants, the earliest being Gedwearde (800), Jedwarth (1251), and Geddart (1586), while locally the word is sometimes pronounced Jethart. The town is situated on the left bank of the Jed, the main streets running at right angles from each side of the central market-place. Of the renowned group of Border abbeys—Jedburgh, Melrose, Dryburgh and Kelso—that of Jedburgh is the stateliest. In 1118, according to tradition, but more probably as late as 1138, David, prince of Cumbria, here founded a priory for Augustinian monks from the abbey of St Quentin at Beauvais in France, and in 1147, after he had become king, erected it into an abbey dedicated to the Virgin. Repeatedly damaged in Border warfare, it was ruined in 1544-45 during the English invasion led by Sir Ralph Evers (or Eure). The establishment was suppressed in 1559, the revenues being temporarily annexed to the Crown. After changing owners more than once, the lands were purchased in 1637 by the 3rd earl of Lothian. Latterly five of the bays at the west end had been utilized as the parish church, but in 1873-1875 the 9th marquess of Lothian built a church for the service of the parish, and presented it to the heritors in exchange for the ruined abbey in order to prevent the latter from being injured by modern additions and alterations.

The abbey was built of Old Red sandstone, and belongs mostly to the end of the 12th and the beginning of the 13th centuries. The architecture is mixed, and the abbey is a beautiful example of the Norman and Transition styles. The total length is 235 ft., the nave being 133½ ft. long and 59½ ft. wide. The west front contains a great Norman porch and a fine wheel window. The nave, on each side, has nine pointed arches in the basement storey, nine round arches in the triforium, and thirty-six pointed arches in the clerestory, through which an arcade is carried on both sides. The tower, at the intersection of the nave and transepts, is of unusually massive proportions, being 30 ft. square and fully 100 ft. high; the network baluster round the top is modern. With the exception of the north piers and a small portion of the wall above, which are Norman, the tower dates from the end of the 15th century. The whole of the south transept has perished. The north transept, with early Decorated windows, has been covered in and walled off, and is the burial-ground of the Kerrs of Fernihirst, ancestors of the marquess of Lothian. The earliest tombstone is dated 1524; one of the latest is the recumbent effigy, by G. F. Watts, R.A., of the 8th marquess of Lothian (1832-1870). All that is left of the choir, which contains some very early Norman work, is two bays with three tiers on each side, corresponding to the design of the nave. It is supposed that the aisle, with Decorated window and groined roof, south of the chancel, formed the grammar school (removed from the abbey in 1751) in which Samuel Rutherford (1600-1661), principal of St Mary's College, St Andrews, and James Thomson, author of The *Seasons*, were educated. The door leading from the south aisle into a herbaceous garden, formerly the cloister, is an exquisite copy of one which had become greatly decayed. It was designed by Sir Rowand Anderson, under whose superintendence restoration in the abbey was carried out.

The castle stood on high ground at the south end of the burgh, or "town-head." Erected by David I., it was one of the strongholds ceded to England in 1174, under the treaty of Falaise, for the ransom of William the Lion. It was, however, so often captured by the English that it became a menace rather than a protection, and the townsfolk demolished it in 1409. It had 300occasionally been used as a royal residence, and was the scene, in November 1285, of the revels held in celebration of the marriage (solemnized in the abbey) of Alexander III. to Joleta, or Yolande, daughter of the count of Dreux. The site was occupied in 1823 by the county prison, now known as the castle, a castellated structure which gradually fell into disuse and was acquired by the corporation in 1890. A house exists in Backgate in which Mary Queen of Scots resided in 1566, and one in Castlegate which Prince Charles Edward occupied in 1745.

The public buildings include the grammar school (built in 1883 to replace the successor of the school in the abbey), founded by William Turnbull, bishop of Glasgow (d. 1454), the county buildings, the free library and the public hall, which succeeded to the corn exchange destroyed by fire in 1898, a loss that involved the museum and its contents, including the banners captured by the Jethart weavers at Bannockburn and Killiecrankie. The old market cross still exists, and there are two public parks. The chief industry is the manufacture of woollens (blankets, hosiery), but brewing, tanning and iron-founding are carried on, and fruit (especially pears) and garden produce are in repute. Jedburgh was made a royal burgh in the reign of David I., and received a charter from Robert I. and another, in 1566, from Mary Queen of Scots. Sacked and burned time after time during the Border strife, it was inevitable that the townsmen should become keen fighters. Their cry of "Jethart's here!" was heard wherever the fray waxed most fiercely, and the Jethart axe of their invention—a steel axe on a 4-ft. pole—wrought havoc in their hands.

"Jethart or Jeddart justice," according to which a man was hanged first and tried afterwards, seems to have been a hasty generalization from a solitary fact—the summary execution in James VI.'s reign of a gang of rogues at the instance of Sir George Home, but has nevertheless passed into a proverb.

Old Jeddart, 4 m. S. of the present town, the first site of the burgh, is now marked by a few grassy mounds, and of the great Jedburgh forest, only the venerable oaks, the "Capon Tree" and the "King of the Woods" remain. Dunion Hill (1095 ft.), about 2 m. south-west of Jedburgh, commands a fine view of the capital of the county.

JEEJEEBHOY (JIJIBHAI), SIR JAMSETJEE (JAMSETJI), Bart. (1783-1859), Indian merchant and philanthropist, was born in Bombay in 1783, of poor but respectable parents, and was left an orphan in early life. At the age of sixteen, with a smattering of mercantile education and a bare pittance, he commenced a series of business travels destined to lead him to fortune and fame. After a preliminary visit to Calcutta, he undertook a voyage to China, then fraught with so much difficulty and risk that it was regarded as a venture betokening considerable enterprise and courage; and he subsequently initiated a systematic trade with that country, being himself the carrier of his merchant wares on his passages to and fro between Bombay and Canton and Shanghai. His second return voyage from China was made in one of the East India Company's fleet, which, under the command of Sir Nathaniel Dance, defeated the French squadron under Admiral Linois (Feb. 15, 1804). On his fourth return voyage from China, the Indiaman in which he sailed was forced to surrender to the French, by whom he was carried as a prisoner to the Cape of Good Hope, then a neutral Dutch possession; and it was only after much delay, and with great difficulty, that he made his way to Calcutta in a Danish ship. Nothing daunted, he undertook yet another voyage to China, which was more successful than any of the previous ones. By this time he had fairly established his reputation as a merchant possessed of the highest spirit of enterprise and considerable wealth, and thenceforward he settled down in Bombay, where he directed his commercial operations on a widely extended scale. By 1836 his firm was large enough to engross the energies of his three sons and other relatives; and he had amassed what at that period of Indian mercantile history was regarded as fabulous wealth. An essentially self-made man, having experienced in early life the miseries of poverty and want, in his days of affluence Jamsetjee Jeejeebhoy developed an active instinct of sympathy with his poorer countrymen, and commenced that career of private and public philanthropy which is his chief title to the admiration of mankind. His liberality was unbounded, and the absorbing occupation of his later life was the alleviation of human distress. To his own community he gave lavishly, but his benevolence was mainly cosmopolitan. Hospitals, schools, homes of charity, pension funds, were founded or endowed by him, while numerous public works in the shape of wells, reservoirs, bridges, causeways, and the like, not only in Bombay, but in other parts of India, were the creation of his bounty. The total of his known benefactions amounted at the time of his death, which took place in 1859, to over £230,000. It was not, however, the amount of his charities so much as the period and circumstances in which they were performed that made his benevolent career worthy of the fame he won. In the first half of the 19th century the various communities of India were much more isolated in their habits and their sympathies than they are now. Jamsetjee Jeejeebhoy's unsectarian philanthropy awakened a common understanding and created a bond between them which has proved not only of domestic value but has had a national and political significance. His services were recognized first in 1842 by the bestowal of a knighthood upon him, and in 1858 by that of a baronetcy. These were the very first distinctions of their kind conferred by Queen Victoria upon a British subject in India.

His title devolved in 1859 on his eldest son CURSETJEE, who, by a special Act of the Viceroy's Council in pursuance of a provision in the letters-patent, took the name of Sir Jamsetjee Jeejeebhoy as second baronet. At his death in 1877 his eldest son, MENEKJEE, became Sir Jamsetjee Jeejeebhoy, the third baronet. Both had the advantage of a good English education, and continued the career of benevolent activity and devoted loyalty to British rule which had signalized the life-work of the founder of the family. They both visited England to do homage to their sovereign; and their public services were recognized by their nomination to the order of the Star of India, as well as by appointment to the Legislative Councils of Calcutta and Bombay.

On the death of the third baronet, the title devolved upon his brother, COWSAJEE (1853-1908), who became Sir Jamsetjee Jeejeebhoy, fourth baronet, and the recognized leader of the Parsee community all over the world. He was succeeded by his son RUSTOMJEE (b. 1878), who became Sir Jamsetjee Jeejeebhoy, fifth baronet.

Since their emigration from Persia, the Parsee community had never had a titular chief or head, its communal funds and affairs being managed by a public body, more or less democratic in its constitution, termed the Parsee panchayat. The first Sir Jamsetjee, by the hold that he established on the community, by his charities and public spirit, gradually came to be regarded in the light of its chief; and the recognition which he was the first in India to receive at the hands of the British sovereign finally fixed him and his successors in the baronetcy in the position and title of the official Parsee leader.

(M. M. BH.)

JEFFERIES, RICHARD (1848-1887), English naturalist and author, was born on the 6th of November 1848, at the farmhouse of Coate about 2½ m. from Swindon, on the road to Marlborough. He was sent to school, first at Sydenham and then at Swindon, till the age of fifteen or so, but his actual education was at the hands of his father, who gave him his love for Nature and taught him how to observe. For the faculty of observation, as Jefferies, Gilbert White, and H. D. Thoreau have remarked, several gifts are necessary, including the possession of long sight and quick sight, two things which do not always go together. To them must be joined trained sight and the knowledge of what to expect. The boy's father first showed him what there was to look for in the hedge, in the field, in the trees, and in the sky. This kind of training would in many cases be wasted: to one who can understand it, the book of Nature will by-and-by offer pages which are blurred and illegible to the city-bred lad, and even to the country lad the power of reading them must be maintained by constant practice. To live amid streets or in the working world destroys 301it. The observer must live alone and always in the country; he must not worry himself about the ways of the world; he must be always, from day to day, watching the infinite changes and variations of Nature. Perhaps, even when the observer can actually read this book of Nature, his power of articulate speech may prove inadequate for the expression of what he sees. But Jefferies, as a boy, was more than an observer of the fields; he was bookish, and read all the books that he could borrow or buy. And presently, as is apt to be the fate of a bookish boy who cannot enter a learned profession, he became a journalist and obtained a post on the local paper. He developed literary ambitions, but for a long time to come was as one beating the air. He tried local history and novels; but his early novels, which were published at his own risk and expense, were, deservedly, failures. In 1872, however, he published a remarkable letter in The Times, on "The Wiltshire Labourer," full of original ideas and of facts new to most readers. This was in reality the turning-point in his career. In 1873, after more false starts, Jefferies returned to his true field of work, the life of the country, and began to write for Fraser's Magazine on "Farming and

Farmers." He had now found himself. The rest of his history is that of continual advance, from close observation becoming daily more and more close, to that intimate communion with Nature with which his later pages are filled. The developments of the later period are throughout touched with the melancholy that belongs to ill-health. For, though in his prose poem called "The Pageant of Summer" the writer seems absolutely revelling in the strength of manhood that belongs to that pageant, yet, in the *Story of My Heart*, written about the same time, we detect the mind that is continually turned to death. He died at Goring, worn out with many ailments, on the 14th of August 1887. The best-known books of Richard Jefferies are: *The Gamekeeper at Home*(1878); *The Story of My Heart* (1883); *Life of the Fields*(1884), containing the best paper he ever wrote, "The Pageant of Summer"; *Amaryllis at the Fair* (1884), in which may be found the portraits of his own people; and *The Open Air*. He stands among the scanty company of men who address a small audience, for whom he read aloud these pages of Nature spoken of above, which only he, and the few like unto him, can decipher.

See Sir Walter Besant, *Eulogy of Richard Jefferies*(1888); H. S. Salt, *Richard Jefferies: a Study* (1894); Edward Thomas, *Richard Jefferies, his Life and Work*(1909).

(W. BE.)

JEFFERSON, JOSEPH (1820-1905), American actor, was born in Philadelphia on the 20th of February 1829. He was the third actor of this name in a family of actors and managers, and the most famous of all American comedians. At the age of three he appeared as the boy in Kotzebue's *Pizarro*, and throughout his youth he underwent all the hardships connected with theatrical touring in those early days. After a miscellaneous experience, partly as actor, partly as manager, he won his first pronounced success in 1858 as Asa Trenchard in Tom Taylor's *Our American Cousin* at Laura Keene's theatre in New York. This play was the turning-point of his career, as it was of Sothern's. The naturalness and spontaneity of humour with which he acted the love scenes revealed a spirit in comedy new to his contemporaries, long used to a more artificial convention; and the touch of pathos which the part required revealed no less to the actor an unexpected power in himself. Other early parts were Newman Noggs in *Nicholas Nickleby*, Caleb Plummer in *The Cricket on the Hearth*, Dr Pangloss in *The Heir at Law*, Salem Scudder in *The Octoroon*, and Bob Acres in *The Rivals*, the last being not so much an interpretation of the character as Sheridan sketched it as a creation of the actor's. In 1859 Jefferson made a dramatic version of the story of *Rip Van Winkle* on the basis of older plays, and acted it with success at Washington. The play was given its permanent form by Dion Boucicault in London, where (1865) it ran 170 nights, with Jefferson in the leading part. Jefferson continued to act with undiminished popularity in a limited number of parts in nearly every town in the United States, his Rip Van Winkle, Bob Acres, and Caleb Plummer being the most popular. He was one of the first to establish the travelling combinations which superseded the old system of local stock companies. With the exception of minor parts, such as the First Gravedigger in *Hamlet*, which he played in an "all star combination" headed by Edwin Booth, Jefferson created no new character after 1865; and the success of Rip Van Winkle was so pronounced that he has often been called a one-part actor. If this was a fault, it was the public's, who never wearied of his one masterpiece. Jefferson died on the 23rd of April 1905. No man in his profession was more honoured for his achievements or his character. He was the friend of many of the leading men in American politics, art and literature. He was an ardent fisherman and lover of nature, and devoted to painting. Jefferson was twice married: to an actress, Margaret Clements Lockyer (1832-1861), in 1850, and in 1867 to Sarah Warren, niece of William Warren the actor.

Jefferson's *Autobiography* (New York, 1889) is written with admirable spirit and humour, and its judgments with regard to the art of the actor and of the playwright entitle it to a place beside Cibber's *Apology*. See William Winter, *The Jeffersons* (1881), and *Life of Joseph Jefferson* (1894); Mrs. E. P. Jefferson, *Recollections of Joseph Jefferson*(1909).

JEFFERSON, THOMAS (1743-1826), third president of the United States of America, and the most conspicuous apostle of democracy in America, was born on the 13th of April 1743, at Shadwell, Albemarle county, Virginia. His father, Peter Jefferson (1707-1757), of early Virginian yeoman stock, was a civil engineer and a man of remarkable energy, who became a justice of the peace, a county surveyor and a burgess, served the Crown in inter-colonial boundary surveys, and married into one of the most prominent colonial families, the Randolphs. Albemarle county was then in the frontier wilderness of the Blue Ridge, and was very different, socially, from the lowland counties where a few broad-acred families dominated an open-handed, somewhat luxurious and assertive aristocracy. Unlike his Randolph connexions, Peter Jefferson was a whig and a thorough democrat; from him, and probably, too, from the Albemarle environment, his son came naturally by democratic inclinations.

Jefferson carried with him from the college of William and Mary at Williamsburg, in his twentieth year, a good knowledge of Latin, Greek and French (to which he soon added Spanish, Italian and Anglo-Saxon), and a familiarity with the higher mathematics and natural sciences only possessed, at his age, by men who have a rare natural taste and ability for those studies. He remained an ardent student throughout life, able to give and take in association with the many scholars, American and foreign, whom he numbered among his friends and correspondents. With a liberal Scotsman, Dr William Small, then of the faculty of William and Mary and later a friend of Erasmus Darwin, and George Wythe (1726-1806), a very accomplished scholar and leader of the Virginia bar, Jefferson was an habitual member, while still in college, of a *partie carrée* at the table of Francis Fauquier (*c.* 1720-1768), the accomplished lieutenant-governor of Virginia. Jefferson was an expert violinist, a good singer and dancer, proficient in outdoor sports, and an excellent horseman. Thorough-bred horses always remained to him a necessary luxury. When it is added that Fauquier was a passionate gambler, and that the gentry who gathered every winter at Williamsburg, the seat of government of the province, were ruinously addicted to the same weakness, and that Jefferson had a taste for racing, it does credit to his early strength of character that of his social opportunities he took only the better. He never used tobacco, never played cards, never gambled, and was never party to a personal quarrel.

Soon after leaving college he entered Wythe's law office, and in 1767, after five years of close study, was admitted to the bar. His thorough preparation enabled him to compete from the first with the leading lawyers of the colony, and his success shows that the bar had no rewards that were not fairly within his reach. As an advocate, however, he did not shine; a weakness of voice made continued speaking impossible, and he had neither the ability nor the temperament for oratory. To his legal scholarship and collecting zeal Virginia owed the preservation of a large part of her early statutes. He seems to have lacked interest in litigiousness, which was extraordinarily developed in colonial 302Virginia; and he saw and wished to reform the law's abuses. It is probable that he turned, therefore, the more willingly to politics; at any rate, soon after entering public life he abandoned practice (1774).

The death of his father had left him an estate of 1900 acres, the income from which (about £400) gave him the position of an independent country gentleman; and while engaged in the law he had added to his farms after the ambitious Virginia fashion, until, when he married in his thirtieth year, there were 5000 acres all paid for; and almost as much more1 came to him in 1773 on the death of his father-in-law. On the 1st of January 1772, Jefferson married Martha Wayles Skelton (1749-1782), a childless widow of twenty-three, very handsome, accomplished, and very fond of music. Their married life was exceedingly happy, and Jefferson never remarried after her early death. Of six children born from their union, two daughters alone survived infancy. Jefferson was emotional and very affectionate in his home, and his generous and devoted relations with his children and grandchildren are among the finest features of his character.

Jefferson began his public service as a justice of the peace and parish vestryman; he was chosen a member of the Virginia house of burgesses in 1769 and of every succeeding assembly and convention of the colony until he entered the Continental Congress in 1775. His forceful, facile pen gave him great influence from the first; but though a foremost member of several great deliberative bodies, he can fairly be said never to have made a speech. He hated the "morbid rage of debate" because he believed that men were never convinced by argument, but only by reflection, through reading or unprovocative conversation; and this belief guided him through life. Moreover it is very improbable that he could ever have shone as a public speaker, and to this fact unfriendly critics have attributed, at least in part, his abstention from debate. The house of burgesses of 1769, and its successors in 1773 and 1774, were dissolved by the governor (see VIRGINIA) for their action on the subject of colonial grievances and inter-colonial co-operation. Jefferson was prominent in all; was a signer of the Virginia agreement of non-importation and economy (1769); and was elected in 1774 to the first Virginia convention, called to consider the state of the colony and advance inter-colonial union. Prevented by illness from attending, Jefferson sent to the convention elaborate resolutions, which he proposed as instructions to the Virginia delegates to the Continental Congress that was to meet at Philadelphia in September. In the direct language of reproach and advice, with no disingenuous loading of the Crown's policy upon its agents, these resolutions attacked the errors of the king, and maintained that "the relation between Great Britain and these colonies was exactly the same as that of England and Scotland after the accession of James and until the Union; and that our emigration to this country gave England no more rights over us than the emigration of the Danes and Saxons gave to the present authorities of their mother country over England." This was cutting at the common root of allegiance, emigration and colonization; but such radicalism was too thorough-going for the immediate end. The resolutions were published, however, as a pamphlet, entitled *A Summary View of the Rights of America*, which was widely circulated. In

England, after receiving such modifications—attributed to Burke—as adapted it to the purposes of the opposition, this pamphlet ran through many editions, and procured for its author, as he said, "the honour of having his name inserted in a long list of proscriptions enrolled in a bill of attainder commenced in one of the two houses of parliament, but suppressed in embryo by the hasty course of events." It placed Jefferson among the foremost leaders of revolution, and procured for him the honour of drafting, later, the Declaration of Independence, whose historical portions were, in large part, only a revised transcript of the *Summary View*. In June 1775 he took his seat in the Continental Congress, taking with him fresh credentials of radicalism in the shape of Virginia's answer, which he had drafted, to Lord North's conciliatory propositions. Jefferson soon drafted the reply of Congress to the same propositions. Reappointed to the next Congress, he signalized his service by the authorship of the Declaration of Independence (*q.v.*). Again reappointed, he surrendered his seat, and after refusing a proffered election to serve as a commissioner with Benjamin Franklin and Silas Deane in France, he entered again, in October 1776, the Virginia legislature, where he considered his services most needed.

The local work to which Jefferson attributed such importance was a revision of Virginia's laws. Of the measures proposed to this end he says: "I considered four, passed or reported, as forming a system by which every trace would be eradicated of ancient or future aristocracy, and a foundation laid for a government truly republican"—the repeal of the laws of entail; the abolition of primogeniture and the unequal division of inheritances (Jefferson was himself an eldest son); the guarantee of freedom of conscience and relief of the people from supporting, by taxation, an established church; and a system of general education. The first object was embodied in law in 1776, the second in 1785, the third2 in 1786 (supplemented 1799, 1801). The last two were parts of a body of codified laws prepared (1776-1779) by Edmund Pendleton,3George Wythe, and Jefferson, and principally by Jefferson. Not so fortunate were Jefferson's ambitious schemes of education. District, grammar and classical schools, a free state library and a state college, were all included in his plan. He was the first American statesman to make education by the state a fundamental article of democratic faith. His bill for elementary education he regarded as the most important part of the code, but Virginia had no strong middle class, and the planters would not assume the burden of educating the poor. At this time Jefferson championed the natural right of expatriation, and gradual emancipation of the slaves. His earliest legislative effort, in the five-day session of 1769, had been marked by an effort to secure to masters freedom to manumit their slaves without removing them from the state. It was unsuccessful, and the more radical measure he now favoured was even more impossible of attainment; but a bill he introduced to prohibit the importation of slaves was passed in 1778—the only important change effected in the slave system of the state during the War of Independence. Finally he endeavoured, though unsuccessfully, to secure the introduction of juries into the courts of chancery, and—a generation and more before the fruition of the labours of Romilly and his co-workers in England—aided in securing a humanitarian revision of the penal code,4 which, though lost by one vote in 1785, was sustained by public sentiment, and was adopted in 1796. Jefferson is of course not entitled to the sole credit for all these services: Wythe, George Mason and James Madison, in particular, were his devoted lieutenants, and—after his departure for France—the principals in the struggle; moreover, an approving public opinion must receive large credit. But Jefferson was throughout the chief inspirer and foremost worker.

In 1779, at almost the gloomiest stage of the war in the southern states, Jefferson succeeded Patrick Henry as the governor of Virginia, being the second to hold that office after the organization of the state government. In his second term (1780-1781) the state was overrun by British expeditions, and Jefferson, a civilian, was blamed for the ineffectual resistance. Though he cannot be said to have been eminently fitted for the task that devolved upon him in such a crisis, most of the criticism of his 303administration was undoubtedly grossly unjust. His conduct being attacked, he declined renomination for the governorship, but was unanimously returned by Albemarle as a delegate to the state legislature; and on the day previously set for legislative inquiry on a resolution offered by an impulsive critic, he received, by unanimous vote of the house, a declaration of thanks and confidence. He wished however to retire permanently from public life, a wish strengthened by the illness and death of his wife. At this time he composed his*Notes on Virginia*, a semi-statistical work full of humanitarian liberalism. Congress twice offered him an appointment as one of the plenipotentiaries to negotiate peace with England, but, though he accepted the second offer, the business was so far advanced before he could sail that his appointment was recalled. During the following winter (1783) he was again in Congress, and headed the committee appointed to consider the treaty of peace. In the succeeding session his service was marked by a report, from which resulted the present monetary system of the United States (the fundamental idea of its decimal basis being due, however, to Gouverneur Morris); and by the honour of reporting the first definitely formulated plan for the government of the western territories,5 that embodied in the ordinance of 1784. He was already particularly associated with the great territory north-west of the Ohio; for Virginia had tendered to Congress in 1781, while Jefferson was governor, a cession of her claims to it, and now in 1784 formally transferred the territory by act of Jefferson and his fellow delegates in congress: a consummation for which he had laboured from the beginning. His anti-slavery opinions grew in strength with years (though he was somewhat inconsistent in his attitude on the Missouri question in 1820-1821). Not only justice but patriotism as well pleaded with him the cause of the negroes,6 for he foresaw the certainty that the race must some day, in some way, be freed, and the dire political dangers involved in the institution of slavery; and could any feasible plan of emancipation have been suggested he would have regarded its cost as a mere bagatelle.

From 1784 to 1789 Jefferson was in France, first under an appointment to assist Benjamin Franklin and John Adams in negotiating treaties of commerce with European states, and then as Franklin's successor (1785-1789) as minister to France.7 In these years he travelled widely in western Europe. Though the commercial principles of the United States were far too liberal for acceptance, as such, by powers holding colonies in America, Jefferson won some specific concessions to American trade. He was exceedingly popular as a minister. The criticism is even to-day current with the uninformed that Jefferson took his manners,8 morals, "irreligion" and political philosophy from his French residence; and it cannot be wholly ignored. It may therefore be said that there is nothing except unsubstantiated scandal to contradict the conclusion, which various evidence supports, that Jefferson's morals were pure. His religious views and political beliefs will be discussed later. His theories had a deep and broad basis in English whiggism; and though he may well have found at least confirmation of his own ideas in French writers—and notably in Condorcet—he did not read sympathetically the writers commonly named, Rousseau and Montesquieu; besides, his democracy was seasoned, and he was rather a teacher than a student of revolutionary politics when he went to Paris. The *Notes on Virginia* were widely read in Paris, and undoubtedly had some influence in forwarding the dissolution of the doctrines of divine rights and passive obedience among the cultivated classes of France. Jefferson was deeply interested in all the events leading up to the French Revolution, and all his ideas were coloured by his experience of the five seething years passed in Paris. On the 3rd of June 1789 he proposed to the leaders of the third estate a compromise between the king and the nation. In July he received the extraordinary honour of being invited to assist in the deliberations of the committee appointed by the national assembly to draft a constitution. This honour his official position compelled him, of course, to decline; for he sedulously observed official proprieties, and in no way gave offence to the government to which he was accredited.

When Jefferson left France it was with the intention of soon returning; but President Washington tendered him the secretaryship of state in the new federal government, and Jefferson reluctantly accepted. His only essential objection to the constitution—the absence of a bill of rights—was soon met, at least partially, by amendments. Alexander Hamilton (*q.v.*) was secretary of the treasury. These two men, antipodal in temperament and political belief, clashed in irreconcilable hostility, and in the conflict of public sentiment, first on the financial measures of Hamilton, and then on the questions with regard to France and Great Britain, Jefferson's sympathies being predominantly with the former, Hamilton's with the latter, they formed about themselves the two great parties of Democrats and Federalists. The schools of thought for which they stood have since contended for mastery in American politics: Hamilton's gradually strengthened by the necessities of stronger administration, as time gave widening amplitude and increasing weight to the specific powers—and so to Hamilton's great doctrine of the "implied powers"—of the general government of a growing country; Jefferson's rooted in colonial life, and buttressed by the hopes and convictions of democracy.

The most perplexing questions treated by Jefferson as secretary of state arose out of the policy of neutrality adopted by the United States toward France, to whom she was bound by treaties and by a heavy debt of gratitude. Separation from European politics—the doctrine of "America for Americans" that was embodied later in the Monroe declaration—was a tenet cherished by Jefferson as by other leaders (not, however, Hamilton) and by none cherished more firmly, for by nature he was peculiarly opposed to war, and peace was a fundamental part of his politics. However deep, therefore, his French sympathies, he drew the same safe line as did Washington between French politics and American politics,9 and handled the Genet complications to the satisfaction of even the most partisan Federalists. He expounded, as a very high authority has said, "with remarkable clearness and power the nature and scope of neutral duty," and gave a "classic" statement of the doctrine of recognition.10

But the French question had another side in its reaction on American parties.11 Jefferson did not read excesses in Paris as warnings against democracy, but as warnings against the abuses 304of monarchy; nor did he regard Bonaparte's *coup d'état* as revealing the weakness of republics, but rather as revealing the danger of standing armies; he did not look on the war of the coalitions against France as one of mere powers, but as one between forms of government; and though the immediate fruits of the Revolution belied his hopes, as they did those of ardent humanitarians the world over, he saw the broad trend of history, which vindicated his faith that a successful reformation of government in France would insure "a general reformation through Europe, and the resurrection to a new life of their people." Each of these statements could be reversed as regards Hamilton. It is the key to an understanding of the times to remember that the War of Independence had disjointed society; and democracy—which Jefferson had proclaimed in the Declaration of Independence, and enthroned in Virginia—after strengthening its rights by the sword, had run to excesses, particularly in the Shays' rebellion, that produced a conservative reaction. To this reaction Hamilton explicitly appealed in the convention of 1787; and of this reaction various features of the constitution, and Hamiltonian federalism generally, were direct fruits. Moreover, independently of special incentives to the alarmist and the man of property, the opinions of many Americans turned again, after the war, into a current of sympathy for England, as naturally as American commerce returned to English ports. Jefferson, however, far from America in these years and unexposed to reactionary influences, came back with undiminished fervour of democracy, and the talk he heard of praise for England, and fearful recoil before even the beginning of the revolution in France, disheartened him, and filled him with suspicion.12Hating as he did feudal class institutions and Tudor-Stuart traditions of arbitrary rule,13 his attitude can be imagined toward Hamilton's oft-avowed partialities—and Jefferson assumed, his intrigues—for British class-government with its eighteenth-century measure of corruption. In short, Hamilton took from recent years the lesson of the evils of lax government; whereas Jefferson clung to the other lesson, which crumbling colonial governments had illustrated, that governments derived their strength (and the Declaration had proclaimed that they derived their just rights) from the will of the governed. Each built his system accordingly: the one on the basis of order, the other on individualism—which led Jefferson to liberty alike in religion and in politics. The two men and the fate of the parties they led are understandable only by regarding one as the leader of reaction, the other as in line with the American tendencies. The educated classes characteristically furnished Federalism with a remarkable body of alarmist leaders; and thus it happened that Jefferson, because, with only a few of his great contemporaries, he had a thorough trust and confidence in the people, became the idol of American democracy.

As Hamilton was somewhat officious and very combative, and Jefferson, although uncontentious, very suspicious and quite independent, both men holding inflexibly to opinions, cabinet harmony became impossible when the two secretaries had formed parties about them and their differences were carried into the newspapers;14 and Washington abandoned perforce his idea "if parties did exist to reconcile them." Partly from discontent with a position in which he did not feel that he enjoyed the absolute confidence of the president,15 and partly because of the embarrassed condition of his private affairs, Jefferson repeatedly sought to resign, and finally on the 31st of December 1793, with Washington's reluctant consent, gave up his portfolio and retired to his home at Monticello, near Charlottesville.

Here he remained improving his estate (having refused a foreign mission) until elected vice-president in 1796. Jefferson was never truly happy except in the country. He loved gardening, experimented enthusiastically in varieties and rotations of crops and kept meteorological tables with diligence. For eight years he tabulated with painful accuracy the earliest and latest appearance of thirty-seven vegetables in the Washington market. When abroad he sought out varieties of grasses, trees, rice and olives for American experiment, and after his return from France received yearly for twenty-three years, from his old friend the superintendent of the *Jardin des plantes*, a box of seeds, which he distributed to public and private gardens throughout the United States. Jefferson seems to have been the first discoverer of an exact formula for the construction of mould-boards of least resistance for ploughs. He managed to make practical use of his calculus about his farms, and seems to have been remarkably apt in the practical application of mechanical principles.

In the presidential election of 1796 John Adams, the Federalist candidate, received the largest number of electoral votes, and Jefferson, the Republican candidate, the next largest number, and under the law as it then existed the former became president and the latter vice-president. Jefferson re-entered public life with reluctance, though doubtless with keen enough interest and resolution. He had rightly measured the strength of his followers, and was waiting for the government to "drift into unison" with the republican sense of its constituents, predicting that President Adams would be "overborne" thereby. This prediction was speedily fulfilled. At first the reign of terror and the X. Y. Z. disclosures strengthened the Federalists, until these, mistaking the popular resentment against France for a reaction against democracy—an equivalence in their own minds—passed the alien and sedition laws. In answer to those odious measures Jefferson and Madison prepared and procured the passage of the Kentucky and Virginia resolutions. These resolutions later acquired extraordinary and pernicious prominence in the historical elaboration of the states'-rights doctrine. It is, however, unquestionably true, that as a startling protest against measures "to silence," in Jefferson's words, "by force and not by reason the complaints or criticisms, just or unjust, of our citizens against the conduct of our agents," they served, in this respect, a useful purpose; and as a counterblast against Hamiltonian principles of centralization they were probably, at that moment, very salutary; while even as pieces of constitutional interpretation it is to be remembered that they did not contemplate nullification by any single state, and, moreover, are not to be judged by constitutional principles established later by courts and war. The Federalist party had ruined itself, and it lost the presidential election of 1800. The Republican candidates, Jefferson and Aaron Burr (*q.v.*), receiving equal votes, it devolved upon the House of Representatives, in accordance with the system which then obtained, to make one of the two president, the other vice-president. Party feeling in America has probably never been more dangerously impassioned than in the three years preceding 305this election; discount as one will the contrary obsessions of men like Fisher Ames, Hamilton and Jefferson, the time was fateful. Unable to induce Burr to avow Federalist principles, influential Federalists, in defiance of the constitution, contemplated the desperate alternative of preventing an election, and appointing an extra-constitutional (Federalist) president *pro tempore*. Better counsels, however, prevailed; Hamilton used his influence in favour of Jefferson as against Burr, and Jefferson became president, entering upon his duties on the 4th of March 1801. Republicans who had affiliated with the Federalists at the time of the X. Y. Z. disclosures returned; very many of the Federalists themselves Jefferson placated and drew over. "Believing," he wrote, "that (excepting the ardent monarchists) all our citizens agreed in ancient whig principles"—or, as he elsewhere expressed it, in "republican forms"—"I thought it advisable to define and declare them, and let them see the ground on which we can rally." This he did in his inaugural, which, though somewhat rhetorical, is a splendid and famous statement of democracy.16His conciliatory policy produced a mild schism in his own party, but proved eminently wise, and the state elections of 1801 fulfilled his prophecy of 1791 that the policy of the Federalists would leave them "all head and no body." In 1804 he was re-elected by 162 out of 176 votes.

Jefferson's administrations were distinguished by the simplicity that marked his conduct in private life. He eschewed the pomp and ceremonies, natural inheritances from English origins, that had been an innocent setting to the character of his two noble predecessors. His dress was of "plain cloth" on the day of his inauguration. Instead of driving to the Capitol in a coach and six, he walked without a guard or servant from his lodgings—or, as a rival tradition has it, he rode, and hitched his horse to a neighbouring fence—attended by a crowd of citizens. Instead of opening Congress with a speech to which a formal reply was expected, he sent in a written message by a private hand. He discontinued the practice of sending ministers abroad in public vessels. Between himself and the governors of states he recognized no difference in rank. He would not have his birthday celebrated by state balls. The weekly levée was practically abandoned. Even such titles as "Excellency," "Honourable," "Mr" were distasteful to him. It was formally agreed in cabinet meeting that "when brought together in society, all are perfectly equal, whether foreign or domestic, titled or untitled, in or out of office." Thus diplomatic grades were ignored in social precedence and foreign relations were seriously compromised by dinner-table complications. One minister who appeared in gold lace and dress sword for his first, and regularly appointed, official call on the president, was received—as he insisted with studied purpose—by Jefferson in negligent undress and slippers down at the heel. All this was in part premeditated system17—a part of Jefferson's purpose to republicanize the government and public opinion, which was the distinguishing feature of his administration; but it was also simply the nature of the man. In the company he chose by preference, honesty and knowledge were his only tests. He knew absolutely no social distinctions in his willingness to perform services for the deserving. He held up to his daughter as an especial model the family of a poor but gifted mechanic as one wherein she would see "the best examples of rational living." "If it be possible," he said, "to be certainly conscious of anything, I am conscious of feeling no difference between writing to the highest and lowest being on earth."

Jefferson's first administration was marked by a reduction of the army, navy, diplomatic establishment and, to the uttermost, of governmental expenses; some reduction of the civil service, accompanied by a large shifting of offices to Republicans; and, above all, by the Louisiana Purchase (*q.v.*), following which Meriwether Lewis and William Clark, sent by Jefferson, conducted that famous exploring expedition across the continent to the Pacific (see LEWIS, MERIWETHER). Early in his term he carried out a policy he had urged upon the government when minister to France and when vice-president, by dispatching naval forces to coerce Tripoli into a decent respect for the trade of his country—the first in Christendom to gain honourable immunity from tribute or piracy in the Mediterranean. The Louisiana Purchase, although the greatest "inconsistency" of his career, was also an illustration, in corresponding degree, of his essential practicality, and one of the greatest proofs of his statesmanship. It was the crowning achievement of his administration. It is often said that Jefferson established the "spoils system" by his changes in the civil service. He was the innovator, because for the first time there was opportunity for innovation. But mere justice requires attention to the fact that incentive to that innovation, and excuse for it, were found in the absolute one-party monopoly maintained by the Federalists. Moreover, Jefferson's ideals were high; his reasons for changes were in general excellent; he at least so far resisted the great pressure for office—producing by his resistance dissatisfaction within his party—as not to have lowered, apparently, the personnel of the service; and there were no such blots on his administration as President Adams's "midnight judges." Nevertheless, his record here was not clear of blots, showing a few regrettable inconsistencies.18Among important but secondary measures of his second administration were the extinguishment of Indian titles, and promotion of Indian emigration to lands beyond the Mississippi; reorganization of the militia; fortification of the seaports; reduction of the public debt; and a simultaneous reduction of taxes. But his second term derives most of its historical interest from the unsuccessful efforts to convict Aaron Burr of treasonable acts in the south-west, and from the efforts made to maintain, without war, the rights of neutrals on the high seas. In his diplomacy with Napoleon and Great Britain Jefferson betrayed a painful incorrigibility of optimism. A national policy of "growling before fighting"—later practised successfully enough by the United States—was not then possible; and one writer has very justly said that what chiefly affects one in the whole matter is the pathos of it—"a philosopher and a friend of peace struggling with a despot of superhuman genius, and a Tory cabinet of superhuman insolence and stolidity" (Trent). It is possible to regard the embargo policy dispassionately as an interesting illustration of Jefferson's love of peace. The idea—a very old one with Jefferson—was not entirely original; in essence it received other attempted applications in the Napoleonic period— and especially in the continental blockade. Jefferson's statesmanship had the limitations of an agrarian outlook. The extreme to which he carried his advocacy of diplomatic isolation, his opposition to the creation of an adequate navy,19his estimate of cities as "sores upon the body politic," his prejudice against manufactures, trust in farmers, and political distrust of the artisan class, all reflect them.

When, on the 4th of March 1809, Jefferson retired from the presidency, he had been almost continuously in the public service for forty years. He refused to be re-elected for a third time, though requested by the legislatures of five states to be a candidate; and thus, with Washington's prior example, helped 306to establish a precedent deemed by him to be of great importance under a democratic government. His influence seemed scarcely lessened in his retirement. Madison and Monroe, his immediate successors—neighbours and devoted friends, whom he had advised in their early education and led in their maturer years—consulted him on all great questions, and there was no break of principles in the twenty-four years of the "Jeffersonian system." Jefferson was one of the greatest political managers his country has known. He had a quick eye for character, was genuinely amiable, uncontentious, tactful, masterful; and it may be assumed from his success that he was wary or shrewd to a degree. It is true, moreover, that, unless tested by a few unchanging principles, his acts were often strikingly inconsistent; and even when so tested, not infrequently remain so in appearance. Full explanations do not remove from some important transactions in his political life an impression of indirectness. But reasonable judgment must find very unjust the stigma of duplicity put upon him by the Federalists. Measured by the records of other men equally successful as political leaders, there seems little of this nature to criticize severely. Jefferson had the full courage of his convictions. Extreme as were his principles, his pertinacity in adhering to them and his independence of expression were quite as extreme. There were philosophic and philanthropic elements in his political faith which will always lead some to class him as a visionary and fanatic; but although he certainly indulged at times in dreams at which one may still smile, he was not, properly speaking, a visionary; nor can he with justice be stigmatized as a fanatic. He felt fervently, was not afraid to risk all on the conclusions to which his heart and his mind led him, declared himself with openness and energy; and he spoke and even wrote his conclusions, how ever bold or abstract, without troubling to detail his reasoning or clip his off-hand speculations. Certain it is that there is much in his utterances for a less robust democracy than his own to cavil at.20 Soar, however, as he might, he was essentially not a doctrinaire, but an empiricist; his mind was objective. Though he remained, to the end, firm in his belief that there had been an active monarchist party,21 this obsession did not carry him out of touch with the realities of human nature and of his time. He built with surety on the colonial past, and had a better reasoned view of the actual future than had any of his contemporaries.

Events soon appraised the ultra-Federalist judgment of American democracy, so tersely expressed by Fisher Ames as "like death ... only the dismal passport to a more dismal hereafter"; and, with it, appraised Jefferson's word in his first inaugural for those who, "in the full tide of successful experiment," were ready to abandon a government that had so far kept them "free and firm, on the visionary fear that it might by possibility lack energy to preserve itself." Time soon tested, too, his principle that that government must prove the strongest on earth "where every man ... would meet invasions of the public order as his own personal concern." He summed up as follows the difference between himself and the Hamiltonian group: "One feared most the ignorance of the people; the other the selfishness of rulers independent of them." Jefferson, in short, had unlimited faith in the honesty of the people; a large faith in their common sense; believed that all is to be won by appealing to the reason of voters; that by education their ignorance can be eliminated; that human nature is indefinitely perfectible; that majorities rule, therefore, not only by virtue of force (which was Locke's ultimate justification of them), but of right.22 His importance as a maker of modern America can scarcely be overstated, for the ideas he advocated have become the very foundations of American republicanism. His administration ended the possibility, probability or certainty—measure it as one will—of the development of Federalism in the direction of class government; and the party he formed, inspired by the creed he gave it, fixed the democratic future of the nation. And by his own labours he had vindicated his faith in the experiment of self-government.

Jefferson's last years were devoted to the establishment of the university of Virginia at Charlottesville, near his home. He planned the buildings, gathered its faculty—mainly from abroad—and shaped its organization. Practically all the great ideas of aim, administration and curriculum that dominated American universities at the end of the 19th century were anticipated by him. He hoped that the university might be a dominant influence in national culture, but circumstances crippled it. His educational plans had been maturing in his mind since 1776. His financial affairs in these last years gave him grave concern. His fine library of over 10,000 volumes was purchased at a low price by Congress in 1815, and a national contribution ($16,500) just before his death enabled him to die in peace. Though not personally extravagant, his salary, and the small income from his large estates, never sufficed to meet his generous maintenance of his representative position; and after his retirement from public life the numerous visitors to Monticello consumed the remnants of his property. He died on the 4th of July 1826, the fiftieth anniversary of the Declaration of Independence, on the same day as John Adams. He chose for his tomb the epitaph: "Here was buried Thomas Jefferson, author of the Declaration of American Independence, of the statute of Virginia for religious freedom, and father of the university of Virginia."

Jefferson was about 6 ft. in height, large-boned, slim, erect and sinewy. He had angular features, a very ruddy complexion, sandy hair, and hazel-flecked, grey eyes. Age lessened the unattractiveness of his exterior. In later years he was negligent in dress and loose in bearing. There was grace, nevertheless, in his manners; and his frank and earnest address, his quick sympathy (yet he seemed cold to strangers), his vivacious, desultory, informing talk, gave him an engaging charm. Beneath a quiet surface he was fairly aglow with intense convictions and a very emotional temperament. Yet he seems to have acted habitually, in great and little things, on system. His mind, no less trenchant and subtle than Hamilton's, was the most impressible, the most receptive, mind of his time in America. The range of his interests is remarkable. For many years he was president of the American philosophical society. Though it is a biographical tradition that he lacked wit, Molière and Don Quixote seem to have been his favourites; and though the utilitarian wholly crowds romanticism out of his writings, he had enough of that quality in youth to prepare to learn Gaelic in order to translate Ossian, and sent to Macpherson for the originals! His interest in art was evidently intellectual. He was singularly sweet-tempered, and shrank from the impassioned political bitterness that raged about him; bore with relative equanimity a flood of coarse and malignant abuse of his motives, morals, religion,23 personal honesty and decency; cherished very few personal animosities; and better than any of his great antagonists cleared political opposition of ill-blooded personality. In short, his kindness of heart rose above all social, religious or political differences, and nothing destroyed his confidence in men and his sanguine views of life.

AUTHORITIES.—See the editions of Jefferson's *Writings* by H. A. Washington (9 vols., New York, 1853-1854), and—the best—by Paul 307Leicester Ford (10 vols., New York, 1892-1899); letters in Massachusetts Historical Society,*Collections*, series 7, vol. i.; S. E. Forman, *The Letters and Writings of Thomas Jefferson, including all his Important Utterances on Public Questions* (1900); J. P. Foley, *The Jefferson Cyclopaedia* (New York, 1900); the *Memoir, Correspondence*, &c., by T. J. Randolph (4 vols., Charlottesville, Va., 1829); biographies by James Schouler ("Makers of America Series," New York, 1893); John T. Morse ("American Statesmen Series," Boston, 1883); George Tucker

(2 vols., Philadelphia, 1837); James Parton (Boston, 1874); and especially that by Henry S. Randall (3 vols., New York, 1853), a monumental work, although marred by some special pleading, and sharing Jefferson's implacable opinions of the "Monocrats." See also Henry Adams, *History of the United States 1801-1817*, vols. 1-4 (New York, 1889-1890); Herbert B. Adams, *Thomas Jefferson and the University of Virginia* (U. S. bureau of education, Washington, 1888); Sarah N. Randolph,*Domestic Life of Thomas Jefferson* (New York, 1871); and an illuminating appreciation by W. P. Trent, in his *Southern Statesmen of the Old Régime* (New York, 1897); that by John Fiske, Essays, *Historical and Literary*, vol. i. (New York, 1902), has slighter merits.

(F. S. P.)

1It was embarrassed with a debt, however, of £3749, which, owing to conditions caused by the War of Independence, he really paid three times to his British creditors (not counting destruction on his estates, of equal amount, ordered by Lord Cornwallis). This greatly reduced his income for a number of years.

2The first law of its kind in Christendom, although not the earliest practice of such liberty in America.

3George Mason and Thomas L. Lee were members of the commission, but they were not lawyers, and did little actual work on the revision.

4Capital punishment was confined to treason and murder; the former was not to be attended by corruption of blood, drawing, or quartering; all other felonies were made punishable by confinement and hard labour, save a few to which was applied, against Jefferson's desire, the principle of retaliation.

5This plan applied to the south-western as well as to the north-western territory, and was notable for a provision that slavery should not exist therein after 1800. This provision was defeated in 1784, but was adopted in 1787 for the north-western territory—a step which is very often said to have saved the Union in the Civil War; the south-western territory (out of which were later formed Mississippi, Alabama, &c.) being given over to slavery. Thus the anti-slavery clause of the ordinance of 1784 was not adopted; and it was preceded by unofficial proposals to the same end; yet to it belongs rightly some special honour as blazoning the way for federal control of slavery in the territories, which later proved of such enormous consequence. Jefferson in the first draft of the Ordinance of 1784, suggested the names to be given to the states eventually to be formed out of the territory concerned. For his suggestions he has been much ridiculed. The names are as follows: Illinoia, Michigania, Sylvania, Polypotamia, Assenisipia, Charronesus, Pelisipia, Saratoga, Metropotamia and Washington.

6He owned at one time above 150 slaves. His overseers were under contract never to bleed them; but he manumitted only a few at his death.

7During this time he assisted in negotiating a treaty of amity and commerce with Prussia (1785) and one with Morocco (1789), and negotiated with France a "convention defining and establishing the functions and privileges of consuls and vice-consuls" (1788).

8Patrick Henry humorously declaimed before a popular audience that Jefferson, who favoured French wine and cookery, had "abjured his native victuals."

9Jefferson did not sympathize with the temper of his followers who condoned the zealous excesses of Genet, and in general with the "misbehaviour" of the democratic clubs; but, as a student of English liberties, he could not accept Washington's doctrine that for a self-created permanent body to declare "this act unconstitutional, and that act pregnant with mischiefs" was "a stretch of arrogant presumption" which would, if unchecked, "destroy the country."

10John Basset Moore, *American Diplomacy* (New York, 1905).

11Compare C. D. Hazen, *Contemporary American opinion of the French Revolution* (Johns Hopkins University, Baltimore, 1897).

12It was at this period of his life that Jefferson gave expression to some of the opinions for which he has been most severely criticized and ridiculed. For the Shays' rebellion he felt little abhorrence, and wrote: "A little rebellion now and then is a good thing ... an observation of this truth should render honest republican governors so mild in their punishment of rebellions as not to discourage them too much. It is a medicine necessary for the sound health of government" (*Writings*, Ford ed., iv. 362-363). Again, "Can history produce an instance of rebellion so honorably conducted?... God forbid that we should ever be twenty years without such a rebellion.... What signify a few lives lost in a century or two? The tree of liberty must be refreshed from time to time with the blood of patriots and tyrants. It is its natural manure" (Ibid. iv. 467). Again he says: "Societies exist under three forms—(1) without government, as among our Indians; (2) under governments wherein the will of every one has a just influence.... (3) under governments of force.... It is a problem not clear in my mind that the first condition is not the best." (Ibid. iv. 362.)

13He turned law students from Blackstone's toryism to Coke on Littleton; and he would not read Walter Scott, so strong was his aversion to that writer's predilection for class and feudalism.

14Hamilton wrote for the papers himself; Jefferson never did. A talented clerk in his department, however, Philip Freneau, set up an anti-administration paper. It was alleged that Jefferson appointed him for the purpose, and encouraged him. Undoubtedly there was nothing in the charge. The Federalist outcry could only have been silenced by removal of Freneau, or by disclaimers or admonitions, which Jefferson did not think it incumbent upon himself—or, since he thought Freneau was doing good, desirable for him—to make.

15Contrary to the general belief that Hamilton dominated Washington in the cabinet, there is the president's explicit statement that "there were as many instances" of his deciding against as in favour of the secretary of the treasury.

16See also Jefferson to E. Gerry, 26th of January 1799 (*Writings*, vii. 325), and to Dupont de Nemours (x. 23). Cf. Hamilton to J. Dayton, 1799 (*Works*, x. 329).

17In 1786 he suggested to James Monroe that the society of friends he hoped to gather in Albemarle might, in sumptuary matters, "set a good example" to a country (*i.e.*Virginia) that "needed" it.

18See C. R. Fish, *The Civil Service and the Patronage*(Harvard Historical Studies, New York, 1905), ch. 2.

19Jefferson's dislike of a navy was due to his desire for an economical administration and for peace. Shortly after his inauguration he expressed a desire to lay up the larger men of war in the eastern branch of the Potomac, where they would require only "one set of plunderers to take care of them." To Thomas Paine he wrote in 1807: "I believe that gunboats are the only *water* defence which can be useful to us and protect us from the ruinous folly of a navy." (*Works*, Ford ed., ix. 137.) The gunboats desired by Jefferson were small, cheap craft equipped with one or two guns and kept on shore under sheds until actually needed, when they were to be launched and manned by a sort of naval militia. A large number of these boats were constructed and they afforded some protection to coasting vessels against privateers, but in bad weather, or when employed against a frigate, they were worse than useless, and Jefferson's "gunboat system" was admittedly a failure.

20See *e.g.* his letters in 1787 on the Shays' rebellion, and his speculations on the doctrine that one generation may not bind another by paper documents. With the latter may be compared present-day movements like the initiative and referendum, and not a few discussions of national debts. Jefferson's distrust of governments was nothing exceptional for a consistent individualist.

21In his last years he carefully sifted and revised his contemporary notes evidencing, as he believed, the existence of such a party, and they remain as his *Ana*(chiefly Hamiltoniana). The only just judgment of these notes is to be obtained by looking at them, and by testing his suspicions with the letters of Hamilton, Ames, Oliver Wolcott, Theodore Sedgwick, George Cabot and the other Hamiltonians. Such a comparison measures also the relative judgment, temper and charity of these writers and Jefferson. It must still remain true, however, that Jefferson's *Ana*present him in a far from engaging light.

22"Jefferson, in 1789, wrote some such stuff about the will of majorities, as a New Englander would lose his rank among men of sense to avow."—Fisher Ames (Jan. 1800).

23He was classed as a "French infidel" and atheist. His attitude toward religion was in fact deeply reverent and sincere, but he insisted that religion was purely an individual matter, "evidenced, as concerns the world by each one's daily life," and demanded absolute freedom of private judgment. He looked on Unitarianism with much sympathy and desired its growth. "I am a Christian," he wrote in 1823, "in the only sense in which he (Jesus) wished any one to be; sincerely attached to his doctrines in preference to all others; ascribing to himself every human excellence, and believing he never claimed any other."

JEFFERSON CITY (legally and officially the City of Jefferson), the capital of Missouri, U.S.A., and the county-seat of Cole county, on the Missouri river, near the geographical centre of the state, about 125 m. W. of St Louis. Pop. (1890), 6742; (1900), 9664, of whom 786 were foreign-born and 1822 were negroes; (1910 census), 11,850. It is served by the Missouri Pacific, the Chicago & Alton, and the Missouri, Kansas & Texas railways. Its site is partly in the bottom-lands of the river and partly on the steep banks at an elevation of about 600 ft. above the sea. A steel bridge spans the river. The state capitol, an imposing structure built on a bluff above the river, was built in 1838-1842 and enlarged in 1887-1888; it was first occupied in 1840 by the legislature, which previously had met (after 1837) in the county court house. Other prominent buildings are the United States court house and post office, the state supreme court house, the county court house, the state penitentiary, the state armoury and the executive mansion. The penitentiary is to a large extent self-supporting; in 1903-1904 the earnings were $3493.80 in excess of the costs, but in 1904-1906 the costs exceeded the earnings by $9044. Employment is furnished for the convicts on the penitentiarypremises by incorporated companies. The state law library here is one of the best of the kind in the country, and the city has a public library. In the city is Lincoln Institute, a school for negroes, founded in 1866 by two regiments of negro infantry upon their discharge from the United States army, opened in 1868, taken over by the state in 1879, and having sub-normal, normal, college, industrial and agricultural courses. Coal and limestone are found near the city. In 1905 the total value of the factory product was $3,926,632, an increase of 28.2% since 1900. The original constitution of Missouri prescribed that the capital should be on the Missouri river within 40 m. of the mouth of the Osage, and a commission selected in 1821 the site of Jefferson City, on which a town was laid out in 1822, the name being adopted in honour of Thomas Jefferson. The legislature first met here in 1826; Jefferson City became the county-seat in 1828, and in 1839 was first chartered as a city. The constitutional conventions of 1845 and 1875, and the state convention which issued the call for the National Liberal Republican convention at Cincinnati in 1872, met here, and so for some of its sessions did the state convention of 1861-1863. In June 1861 Jefferson City was occupied by Union forces, and in September-October 1864 it was threatened by Confederate troops under General Sterling Price.

JEFFERSONVILLE, a city and the county-seat of Clark county, Indiana, U.S.A., situated on the N. bank of the Ohio river, opposite Louisville, Kentucky, with which it is connected by several bridges. Pop. (1890), 10,666; (1900), 10,774, of whom 1818 were of negro descent and 615 were foreign-born; (1910 census), 10,412. It is served by the Baltimore & Ohio South-western, the Cleveland, Cincinnati, Chicago & St Louis, and the Pittsburg, Cincinnati, Chicago & St Louis railways, and by three inter-urban electric lines. It is attractively situated on bluffs above the river, which at this point has a descent (known as the falls of the Ohio) of 26 ft. in 2 m. This furnishes good water power for manufacturing purposes both at Jeffersonville and at Louisville. The total value of the factory product in 1905 was $4,526,443, an increase of 20% since 1900. The Indiana reformatory (formerly the Southern Indiana penitentiary) and a large supply dépôt of the United States army are at Jeffersonville. General George Rogers Clark started (June 24, 1778) on his expedition against Kaskaskia and Vincennes from Corn Island (now completely washed away) opposite what is now Jeffersonville. In 1786 the United States government established Fort Finney (built by Captain Walter Finney), afterwards re-named Fort Steuben, on the site of the present city; but the fort was abandoned in 1791, and the actual beginning of Jeffersonville was in 1802, when a part of the Clark grant (the site of the present city) was transferred by its original owner, Lieut. Isaac Bowman, to three trustees, under whose direction a town was laid out. Jeffersonville was incorporated as a town in 1815, and was chartered as a city in 1839.

JEFFREY, FRANCIS JEFFREY, LORD (1773-1850), Scottish judge and literary critic, son of a depute-clerk in the Court of Session, was born at Edinburgh on the 23rd of October 1773. After attending the high school for six years, he studied at the university of Glasgow from 1787 to May 1789, and at Queen's College, Oxford, from September 1791 to June 1792. He had begun the study of law at Edinburgh before going to Oxford, and now resumed his studies there. He became a member of the speculative society, where he measured himself in debate with Scott, Brougham, Francis Horner, the marquess of Lansdowne, Lord Kinnaird and others. He was admitted to the Scotch bar in December 1794, but, having abandoned the Tory principles in which he had been educated, he found that his Whig politics seriously prejudiced his legal prospects. In consequence of his lack of success at the bar he went to London in 1798 to try his fortune as a journalist, but without success; he also made more than one vain attempt to obtain an office which would have secured him the advantage of a small but fixed salary. His marriage with Catherine Wilson in 1801 made the question of a settled income even more pressing. A project for a new review was brought forward by Sydney Smith in Jeffrey's flat in the presence of H. P. Brougham (afterwards Lord Brougham), Francis Horner and others; and the scheme resulted in the appearance on the 10th of October 1802 of the first number of the *Edinburgh Review*. At the outset the *Review* was not under the charge of any special editor. The first three numbers were, however, practically edited by Sydney Smith, and on his leaving for England the work devolved chiefly on Jeffrey, who, by an arrangement with Constable, the publisher, was eventually appointed editor at a fixed salary. Most of those associated in the undertaking were Whigs; but, although the general bias of the Review was towards social and political reforms, it was at first so little of a party organ that for a time it numbered Sir Walter Scott among its contributors; and no distinct emphasis was given to its political leanings until the publication in 1808 of an article by Jeffrey himself on the work of Don Pedro Cevallos on the *French Usurpation of Spain*. This article expressed despair of the success of the British arms in Spain, and Scott at once withdrew his subscription, the *Quarterly* being soon afterwards started in opposition.

According to Lord Cockburn the effect of the first number of the *Edinburgh Review* was "electrical." The English reviews were at that time practically publishers' organs, the articles in which were written by hackwriters instructed to praise or blame according to the publishers' interests. Few men of any standing consented to write for them. The *Edinburgh Review*, on the other hand, enlisted a brilliant and independent staff of contributors, guided by the editor, not the publisher. They received sixteen guineas a sheet (sixteen printed pages), increased subsequently to twenty-five guineas in many cases, instead of the two guineas which formed the ordinary London reviewer's fee. Further, the review was not limited to literary criticism. It constituted itself the accredited organ of moderate Whig public opinion. The particular work which provided the starting-point of an article was in many cases merely the occasion for the exposition, always 308brilliant and incisive, of the author's views on politics, social subjects, ethics or literature. These general principles and the novelty of the method ensured the success of the undertaking even after the original circle of exceptionally able men who founded it had been dispersed. It had a circulation, great for those days, of 12,000 copies. The period of Jeffrey's editorship extended to about twenty-six years, ceasing with the ninety-eighth number, published in June 1829, when he resigned in favour of Macvey Napier.

Jeffrey's own contributions, according to a list which has the sanction of his authority, numbered two hundred, all except six being written before his resignation of the editorship. Jeffrey wrote with great rapidity, at odd moments of leisure and with little special preparation. Great fluency and ease of diction, considerable warmth of imagination and moral sentiment, and a sharp eye to discover any oddity of style or violation of the accepted canons of good taste, made his criticisms pungent and effective. But the essential narrowness and timidity of his general outlook prevented him from detecting and estimating latent forces, either in politics or in matters strictly intellectual and moral; and this lack of understanding and sympathy accounts for his distrust and dislike of the passion and fancy of Shelley and Keats, and for his praise of the half-hearted and elegant romanticism of Rogers and Campbell. (For his treatment of the lake poets see WORDSWORTH, WILLIAM.)

A criticism in the fifteenth number of the *Review* on the morality of Moore's poems led in 1806 to a duel between the two authors at Chalk Farm. The proceedings were stopped by the police, and Jeffrey's pistol was found to contain no bullet. The affair led to a warm friendship, however, and Moore contributed to the *Review*, while Jeffrey made ample amends in a later article on *Lalla Rookh* (1817).

Jeffrey's wife had died in 1805, and in 1810 he became acquainted with Charlotte, daughter of Charles Wilkes of New York, and great-niece of John Wilkes. When she returned to America, Jeffrey followed her, and they were married in 1813. Before returning to England they visited several of the chief American cities, and his experience strengthened Jeffrey in the conciliatory policy he had before advocated towards the States. Notwithstanding the increasing success of the *Review*, Jeffrey always continued to look to the bar as the chief field of his ambition. As a matter of fact, his literary reputation helped his professional advancement. His practice extended rapidly in the civil and criminal courts, and he regularly appeared before the general assembly of the Church of Scotland, where his work, though not financially profitable, increased his reputation. As an advocate his sharpness and rapidity of insight gave him a formidable advantage in the detection of the weaknesses of a witness and the vulnerable points of his opponent's case, while he grouped his own arguments with an admirable eye to effect, especially excelling in eloquent closing appeals to a jury. Jeffrey was twice, in 1820 and 1822, elected lord rector of the university of Glasgow. In 1829 he was chosen dean of the faculty of advocates. On the return of the Whigs to power in 1830 he became lord advocate, and entered parliament as member for the Perth burghs. He was unseated, and afterwards returned for Malton, a borough in the interest of Lord Fitzwilliam. After the passing of the Scottish Reform Bill, which he introduced in parliament, he was returned for Edinburgh in December 1832. His parliamentary career, which, though not brilliantly successful, had won him high general esteem, was terminated by his elevation to the judicial bench as Lord Jeffrey in May 1834. In 1842 he was moved to the first division of the Court of Session. On the disruption of the Scottish Church he took the side of the seceders, giving a judicial opinion in their favour, afterwards reversed by the house of lords. He died at Edinburgh on the 26th of January 1850.

Some of his contributions to the *Edinburgh Review* appeared in four volumes in 1844 and 1845. This selection includes the essay on "Beauty" contributed to the *Ency. Brit.* The *Life of Lord Jeffrey, with a Selection from his Correspondence*, by Lord Cockburn, appeared in 1852 in 2 vols. See also the *Selected Correspondence of Macvey Napier* (1877); the sketch of Jeffrey in Carlyle's *Reminiscences*, vol. ii. (1881); and an essay by Lewis E. Gates in *Three Studies in Literature* (New York, 1899).

JEFFREYS, GEORGE JEFFREYS, 1ST BARON (1648-1689), lord chancellor of England, son of John Jeffreys, a Welsh country gentleman, was born at Acton Park, his father's seat in Denbighshire, in 1648. His family, though not wealthy, was of good social standing and repute in Wales; his mother, a daughter of Sir Thomas Ireland of Bewsey, Lancashire, was "a very pious good woman." He was educated at Shrewsbury, St Paul's and Westminster schools, at the last of which he was a pupil of Busby, and at Trinity College, Cambridge; but he left the university without taking a degree, and entered the Inner Temple as a student in May 1663. From his childhood Jeffreys displayed exceptional talent, but on coming to London he occupied himself more with the pleasures of conviviality than with serious study of the law. Though he never appears to have fallen into the licentious immorality prevalent at that period, he early became addicted to hard drinking and boisterous company. But as the records of his early years, and indeed of his whole life, are derived almost exclusively from vehemently hostile sources, the numerous anecdotes of his depravity cannot be accepted without a large measure of scepticism. He was a handsome, witty and attractive boon-companion, and in the taverns of the city he made friends among attorneys with practice in the criminal courts. Thus assisted he rose so rapidly in his profession that within three years of his call to the bar in 1668, he was elected common serjeant of the city of London. Such advancement, however, was not to be attained even in the reign of Charles II. solely by the aid of disreputable friendships. Jeffreys had remarkable aptitude for the profession of an advocate—quick intelligence, caustic humour, copious eloquence. His powers of cross-examination were masterly; and if he was insufficiently grounded in legal principles to become a profound lawyer, nothing but greater application was needed in the opinion of so hostile a critic as Lord Campbell, to have made him the rival of Nottingham and Hale. Jeffreys could count on the influence of respectable men of position in the city, such as Sir Robert Clayton and his own namesake Alderman Jeffreys; and he also enjoyed the personal friendship of the virtuous Sir Matthew Hale. In 1667 Jeffreys had married in circumstances which, if improvident, were creditable to his generosity and sense of honour; and his domestic life, so far as is known, was free from the scandal common among his contemporaries. While holding the judicial office of common serjeant, he pursued his practice at the bar. With a view to further preferment he now sought to ingratiate himself with the court party, to which he obtained an introduction possibly through William Chiffinch, the notorious keeper of the king's closet. He at once attached himself to the king's mistress, the duchess of Portsmouth; and as early as 1672 he was employed in confidential business by the court. His influence in the city of London, where opposition to the government of Charles II. was now becoming pronounced, enabled Jeffreys to make himself useful to Danby. In September 1677 he received a knighthood, and his growing favour with the court was further marked by his appointment as solicitor-general to James, duke of York; while the city showed its continued confidence in him by electing him to the post of recorder in October 1678.

In the previous month Titus Oates had made his first revelations of the alleged popish plot, and from this time forward Jeffreys was prominently identified, either as advocate or judge, with the memorable state trials by which the political conflict between the Crown and the people was waged during the remainder of the 17th century. The popish plot, followed by the growing agitation for the exclusion of the duke of York from the succession, widened the breach between the city and the court. Jeffreys threw in his lot with the latter, displaying his zeal by initiating the movement of the "abhorrers" (*q.v.*) against the "petitioners" who were giving voice to the popular demand for the summoning of parliament. He was rewarded with the coveted office of chief justice of Chester on the 30th 309of April 1680; but when parliament met in October the House of Commons passed a hostile resolution which induced him to resign his recordership, a piece of pusillanimity that drew from the king the remark that Jeffreys was "not parliament-proof." Jeffreys nevertheless received from the city aldermen a substantial token of appreciation for his past services. In 1681 he was created a baronet. In June 1683 the first of the Rye House conspirators were brought to trial. Jeffreys was briefed for the crown in the prosecution of Lord William Howard; and, having been raised to the bench as lord chief justice of the king's bench in September, he presided at the trials of Algernon Sidney in November 1683 and of Sir Thomas Armstrong in the following June. In the autumn of 1684 Jeffreys, who had been active in procuring the surrender of municipal charters to the crown, was called to the cabinet, having previously been sworn of the privy council. In May 1685 he had the satisfaction of passing sentence on Titus Oates for perjury in the plot trials; and about the same time James II. rewarded his zeal with a peerage as Baron Jeffreys of Wem, an honour never before conferred on a chief justice during his tenure of office. Jeffreys had for some time been suffering from stone, which aggravated the irritability of his naturally violent temper; and the malady probably was in some degree the cause of the unmeasured fury he displayed at the trial of Richard Baxter (*q.v.*) for seditious libel—if the unofficial *ex parte* report of the trial, which alone exists, is to be accepted as trustworthy.

In August 1685 Jeffreys opened at Winchester the commission known in history as the "bloody assizes," his conduct of which has branded his name with indelible infamy. The number of persons sentenced to death at these assizes for complicity in the duke of Monmouth's insurrection is uncertain. The official return of those actually executed was 320; many hundreds more were transported and sold into slavery in the West Indies. In all probability the great majority of those condemned were in fact concerned in the rising, but the trials were in many cases a mockery of the administration of justice. Numbers were cajoled into pleading guilty; the case for the prisoners seldom obtained a hearing. The merciless severity of the chief justice did not however exceed the wishes of James II.; for on his return to London Jeffreys received from the king the great seal with the title of lord chancellor. For the next two years he was a strenuous upholder of prerogative, though he was less abjectly pliant than has sometimes been represented. There is no reason to doubt the sincerity of his attachment to the Church of England; for although the king's favour was capricious Jeffreys never took the easy and certain path to secure it that lay through apostasy; and he even withstood James on occasion, when the latter pushed his Catholic zeal to extremes. Though it is true that he accepted the presidency of the ecclesiastical commission, Burnet's statement that it was Jeffreys who suggested that institution to James is probably incorrect; and he was so far from having instigated the prosecution of the seven bishops in 1688, as has been frequently alleged, that he disapproved of the proceedings and rejoiced secretly at the acquittal. But while he watched with misgiving the king's preferment of Roman Catholics, he made himself the masterful instrument of unconstitutional prerogative in coercing the authorities of Cambridge University, who in 1687 refused to confer degrees on a Benedictine monk, and the fellows of Magdalen College, Oxford, who declined to elect as their president a disreputable nominee of the king.

Being thus conspicuously identified with the most tyrannical measures of James II., Jeffreys found himself in a desperate plight when on the 11th of December 1688 the king fled from the country on the approach to London of William of Orange. The lord chancellor attempted to escape like his master; but in spite of his disguise as a common seaman he was recognized in a tavern at Wapping—possibly, as Roger North relates, by an attorney whom Jeffreys had terrified on some occasion in the court of chancery—and was arrested and conveyed to the Tower. The malady from which he had long suffered had recently made fatal progress, and he died in the Tower on the 18th of April 1689. He was succeeded in the peerage by his son, John (2nd Baron Jeffreys of Wem), who died without male issue in 1702, when the title became extinct.

It is impossible to determine precisely with what justice tradition has made the name of "Judge Jeffreys" a byword of infamy. The Revolution, which brought about his fall, handed over his reputation at the same time to the mercy of his bitterest enemies. They alone have recorded his actions and appraised his motives and character. Even the adherents of the deposed dynasty had no interest in finding excuse for one who served as a convenient scapegoat for the offences of his master. For at least half a century after his death no apology for Lord Jeffreys would have obtained a hearing; and none was attempted. With the exception therefore of what is to be gathered from the reports of the state trials, all knowledge of his conduct rests on testimony tainted by undisguised hostility. Innumerable scurrilous lampoons vilifying the hated instrument of James's tyranny, but without a pretence of historic value, flooded the country at the Revolution; and these, while they fanned the undiscriminating hatred of contemporaries who remembered the judge's severities, and perpetuated that hatred in tradition, have not been sufficiently discounted even by modern historians like Macaulay and Lord Campbell. The name of Jeffreys has therefore been handed down as that of a coarse, ignorant, dissolute, foul-mouthed, inhuman bully, who prostituted the seat of justice. That there was sufficient ground for the execration in which his memory was long held is not to be gainsaid. But the portrait has nevertheless been blackened overmuch. An occasional significant admission in his favour may be gleaned even from the writings of his enemies. Thus Roger North declares that "in matters indifferent," *i.e.* where politics were not concerned, Jeffreys became the seat of justice better than any other that author had seen in his place. Sir J. Jekyll, master of the rolls, told Speaker Onslow that Jeffreys "had great parts and made a great chancellor in the business of his court. In mere private matters he was thought an able and upright judge wherever he sat." His keen sense of humour, allied with a spirit of inveterate mockery and an exuberant command of pungent eloquence, led him to rail and storm at prisoners and witnesses in grossly unseemly fashion. But in this he did not greatly surpass most of his contemporaries on the judicial bench, and it was a failing from which even the dignified and virtuous Hale was not altogether exempt. The intemperance of Jeffreys which shocked North, certainly did not exceed that of Saunders; in violence he was rivalled by Scroggs; though accused of political apostasy, he was not a shameless

113

renegade like Williams; and there is no evidence that in pecuniary matters he was personally venal, or that in licentiousness he followed the example set by Charles II. and most of his courtiers. Some of his actions that have incurred the sternest reprobation of posterity were otherwise estimated by the best of his contemporaries. His trial of Algernon Sidney, described by Macaulay and Lord Campbell as one of the most heinous of his iniquities, was warmly commended by Dr William Lloyd, who was soon afterwards to become a popular idol as one of the illustrious seven bishops (see letter from the bishop of St Asaph in H. B. Irving's *Life of Judge Jeffreys*, p. 184). Nor was the habitual illegality of his procedure on the bench so unquestionable as many writers have assumed. Sir James Stephen inclined to the opinion that no actual abuse of law tainted the trials of the Rye House conspirators, or that of Alice Lisle, the most prominent victim of the "bloody assizes." The conduct of the judges in Russell's trial was, he thinks, "moderate and fair in general"; and the trial of Sidney "much resembled that of Russell." The same high authority pronounces that the trial of Lord Delamere in the House of Lords was conducted by Jeffreys "with propriety and dignity." And if Jeffreys judged political offenders with cruel severity, he also crushed some glaring abuses; conspicuous examples of which were the frauds of attorneys who infested Westminster Hall, and the systematic kidnapping practised by the municipal authorities of Bristol. Moreover, if any value is to be attached to the evidence of physiognomy, the traditional estimate of the character of Jeffreys obtains no confirmation from the refinement of his features and expression as depicted in Kneller's portrait in the National Portrait Gallery of London. But even though the popular notion requires to be thus modified in certain respects, it remains incontestable that Jeffreys was probably on the whole the worst example of a period when the administration of justice in England had sunk to the lowest degradation, and the judicial bench had become the too willing tool of an unconstitutional and unscrupulous executive.

BIBLIOGRAPHY.—The chief contemporary authorities for the life of Jeffreys are Bishop Burnet's *History of my own Time* (1724), and see especially the edition "with notes by the Earls of Dartmouth and Hardwick Speaker Onslow and Dean Swift" (Oxford Univ. Press, 1833); Roger North's *Life of the Right Hon. Francis North, Baron of Guildford* (1808) and *Autobiography* (ed. by Augustus Jessopp, 1887); *Ellis Correspondence, Verney Papers* (Hist. MSS. Comm.),*Hatton Correspondence* (Camden Soc. pub.); the earl of Ailesbury's *Memoirs*; Evelyn's *Diary*. The only trustworthy information as to the judicial conduct and capacity of Jeffreys is to be found in the reports of the *State Trials*, vols. vii.-xii.; and cf. Sir J. F. Stephen's *History of the Criminal Law of England* (1883). For details of the "bloody assizes," see *Harl. MSS.*, 4689; George Roberts, *The Life, Progresses and Rebellion of James Duke of Monmouth*, vol. ii. (1844); also many pamphlets, lampoons, &c., in the British Museum, as to which see the article on "Sources of History for Monmouth's Rebellion and the Bloody Assizes," by A. L. Humphreys, in *Proceedings of the Somersetshire Archaeological and Natural Hist. Soc.*(1892). Later accounts are by H. W. Woolrych, *Memoirs of the Life of Judge Jeffreys* (1827); Lord Campbell, *The Lives of the Lord Chancellors* (1845), 1st series, vol. iii.; E. Foss,*The Judges of England* (1864), vol. vii.; Henry Roscoe,*Lives of Eminent British Lawyers* (1830); Lord Macaulay,*History of England* (1848; and many subsequent editions). Most of these works, and especially those by Macaulay and Campbell, are uncritical in their hostility to Jeffreys, and are based for the most part on untrustworthy authorities. The best modern work on the subject, though unduly favourable to Jeffreys, is H. B. Irving's *Life of Judge Jeffreys* (1898), the appendix to which contains a full bibliography.

(R. J. M.)

JEHOIACHIN (Heb. "Yah[weh] establisheth"), in the Bible, son of Jehoiakim and king of Judah (2 Kings xxiv. 8 sqq.; 2 Chron, xxxvi. 9 seq.). He came to the throne at the age of eighteen in the midst of the Chaldean invasion of Judah, and is said to have reigned three months. He was compelled to surrender to Nebuchadrezzar and was carried off to Babylon (597 B.C.). This was the First Captivity, and from it Ezekiel (one of the exiles) dates his prophecies. Eight thousand people of the better class (including artisans, &c.) were removed, the Temple was partially despoiled (see Jer. xxvii. 18-20; xxiii.v. 3 seq.),1 and Jehoiachin's uncle Mattaniah (son of Josiah) was appointed king. Jehoiachin's fate is outlined in Jer. xxii. 20-30 (cf. xxvii. 20). Nearly forty years later, Nebuchadrezzar II. died (562 B.C.) and Evil-Merodach (Amil-Marduk) his successor released the unfortunate captive and gave him precedence over the other subjugated kings who were kept prisoners in Babylon. With this gleam of hope for the unhappy Judaeans both the book of Kings and the prophecies of Jeremiah conclude (2 Kings xxv. 27-30; Jer. lii. 31-34).

See, further, JEREMIAH (especially chaps. xxiv., xxvii. seq.), and JEWS, § 17.

1 2 Kings xxiv. 13 seq. gives other numbers and a view of the disaster which is more suitable for the Second Captivity. (See ZEDEKIAH.)

JEHOIAKIM (Heb. "Yah[weh] raiseth up"), in the Bible, son of Josiah (*q.v.*) and king of Judah (2 Kings xxiii. 34-xxiv. 6). On the defeat of Josiah at Megiddo his younger brother Jehoahaz (or Shallum) was chosen by the Judaeans, but the Egyptian conquerer Necho summoned him to his headquarters at Riblah (south of Hamath on the Orontes) and removed him to Egypt, appointing in his stead Eliakim, whose name ("El [God] raiseth up") was changed to its better-known synonym, Jehoiakim. For a time Jehoiakim remained under the protection of Necho and paid heavy tribute; but with the rise of the new Chaldean Empire under Nebuchadrezzar II., and the overthrow of Egypt at the battle of Carchemish (605 B.C.) a vital change occurred. After three years of allegiance the king revolted. Invasions followed by Chaldeans, Syrians, Moabites and Ammonites, perhaps the advance troops despatched by the Babylonian king; the power of Egypt was broken and the whole land came into the hands of Nebuchadrezzar. It was at the close of Jehoiakim's reign, apparently just before his death, that the enemy appeared at the gates of Jerusalem, and although he himself "slept with his fathers" his young son was destined to see the first captivity of the land of Judah (597 B.C.). (See JEHOIACHIN.)

Which "three years" (2 Kings xxiv. 1) are intended is disputed; it is uncertain whether Judah suffered in 605 B.C.(Berossus in Jos. *c. Ap.* i. 19) or was left unharmed (Jos.*Ant.* x. 6. 1); perhaps Nebuchadrezzar made his first inroad against Judah in 602 B.C. because of its intrigue with Egypt (H. Winckler, *Keilinschrift. u. d. alte Test.*, pp. 107 seq.), and the three years of allegiance extends to 599. The chronicler's tradition (2 Chron. xxxvi. 5-8) speaks of Jehoiakim's captivity, apparently confusing him with Jehoiachin. The Septuagint, however, still preserves there the record of his peaceful death, in agreement with the earlier source in 2 Kings, but against the prophecy of Jeremiah (xxii. 18 seq., xxxvi. 30), which is accepted by Jos. *Ant.* x. 6. 3. The different traditions can scarcely be reconciled. Nothing certain is known of the marauding bands sent against Jehoiakim; for Syrians (*Aram*) one would expect Edomites (*Edom*), but see Jer. xxxv. 11; some recensions of the Septuagint even include the "Samaritans"! (For further references to this reign see especially JEREMIAH; see also JEWS: *History*, § 17.)

(S. A. C.)

JEHOL ("hot stream"), or CH'ÊNG-TÊ-FU, a city of China, formerly the seat of the emperor's summer palace, near 118° E. and 41° N., about 140 m. N.E. of Peking, with which it is connected by an excellent road. Pop. (estimate), 10,000. It is a flourishing town, and consists of one great street, about 2 m. long, with smaller streets radiating in all directions. The people are well-to-do and there are some fine shops. The palace, called Pi-shu-shan-chuang, or "mountain lodge for avoiding heat," was built in 1703 on the plan of the palace of Yuen-ming-yuen near Peking. A substantial brick wall 6 m. in circuit encloses several well-wooded heights and extensive gardens, rockeries, pavilions, temples, &c. Jehol was visited by Lord Macartney on his celebrated mission to the emperor K'ienlung in 1793; and it was to Jehol that the emperor Hienfêng retired when the allied armies of England and France occupied Peking in 1860. In the vicinity of Jehol are numerous Lama monasteries and temples, the most remarkable being Potala-su, built on the model of the palace of the grand lama of Tibet at Potala.

JEHORAM, or JORAM (Heb. "Yah[weh] is high"), the name of two Biblical characters.

1. The son of Ahab, and king of Israel in succession to his brother Ahaziah.[1] He maintained close relations with Judah, whose king came to his assistance against Moab which had revolted after Ahab's death (2 Kings i. 1; iii.). The king in question is said to have been Jehoshaphat; but, according to Lucian's recension, it was Ahaziah, whilst i. 17 would show that it was Jehoram's namesake (see 2). The result of the campaign appears to have been a defeat for Israel (see on the incidents EDOM, ELISHA, MOAB). The prophetical party were throughout hostile to Jehoram (with his reform iii. 2 contrast x. 27), and the singular account of the war of Benhadad king of Syria against the king of Israel (vi. 24-vii.) shows the feeling against the reigning dynasty. But whether the incidents in which Elisha and the unnamed king of Israel appear originally belonged to the time of Jehoram is very doubtful, and in view of the part which Elisha took in securing the accession of Jehu, it has been urged with much force that they belong to the dynasty of the latter, when the high position of the prophet would be perfectly natural.[2] The briefest account is given of Jehoram's alliance with Ahaziah (son of 2 below) against Hazael of Syria, at Ramoth-Gilead 311(2 Kings viii. 25-29), and the incident—with the wounding of the Israelite king in or about the critical year 842 B.C.—finds a noteworthy parallel in the time of Jehoshaphat and Ahab (1 Kings xxii. 29-36) at the period of the equally momentous events in 854 (see AHAB). See further JEHU.

2. The son of Jehoshaphat and king of Judah. He married Athaliah the daughter of Ahab, and thus was brother-in-law of 1. above, and contemporary with him (2 Kings i. 17). In his days Edom revolted, and this with the mention of Libnah's revolt (2 Kings viii. 20 sqq.) suggests some common action on the part of Philistines and Edomites. The chronicler's account of his life (2 Chron. xxi-xxii. 1) presupposes this, but adds many remarkable details: he began his reign by massacring his brethren (cf. Jehu son of Jehoshaphat, and his bloodshed, 2 Kings ix. seq.); for his wickedness he received a communication from Elijah foretelling his death from disease (cf. Elijah and Ahaziah of Israel, 2 Kings i.); in a great invasion of Philistines and Arabian tribes he lost all his possessions and family, and only Jehoahaz (i.e. Ahaziah) was saved.[3] His son Ahaziah reigned only for a year (cf. his namesake of Israel); he is condemned for his Israelite sympathies, and met his end in the general butchery which attended the accession of Jehu (2 Kings viii. 25 sqq.; 2 Chron. xxii. 3 seq., 7; with 2 Kings ix. 27 seq., note the variant tradition in 2 Chron. xxii. 8 seq., and the details which the LXX. (Lucian) appends to 2 Kings x.).

(S. A. C.)

1 2 Kings i. 17 seq.; see Lucian's reading (cf. Vulg. and Pesh.). Apart from the allusion 1 Kings xxii. 49 (see 2 Chron. xx. 35), and the narrative in 2 Kings i. (see ELIJAH), nothing is known of this Ahaziah. Notwithstanding his very brief reign (1 Kings xxii. 51; 2 Kings iii. 1), the compiler passes the usual hostile judgment (1 Kings xxii. 52 seq.); see KINGS (BOOKS). The chronology in 1 Kings xxii. 51 is difficult; if Lucian's text (twenty-fourth year of Jehoshaphat) is correct, Jehoram 1 and 2 must have come to their respective thrones at almost the same time.

2 In vii. 6 the hostility of Hittites and Mizraim (q.v.) points to a period after 842 B.C. (See JEWS, § 10 seq.)

3 These details are scarcely the invention of the chronicler; see CHRONICLES, and EXPOSITOR, Aug. 1906, p. 191.

JEHOSHAPHAT (Heb. "Yahweh judges"), in the Bible, son of Asa, and king of Judah, in the 9th century B.C. During his period close relations subsisted between Israel and Judah; the two royal houses were connected by marriage (see ATHALIAH; JEHORAM, 2), and undertook joint enterprise in war and commerce. Jehoshaphat aided Ahab in the battle against Benhadad at Ramoth-Gilead in which Ahab was slain (1 Kings xxii.; 2 Chron. xviii.; cf. the parallel incident in 2 Kings viii. 25-29), and trading journeys to Ophir were undertaken by his fleet in conjunction no doubt with Ahab as well as with his son Ahaziah (2 Chron. xx. 35 sqq.; 1 Kings xxii. 47 sqq.). The chronicler's account of his war against Moab, Ammon and Edomite tribes (2 Chron. xx.), must rest ultimately upon a tradition which is presupposed in the earlier source (1 Kings xxii. 47), and the disaster to the ships at Ezion-Geber at the head of the Gulf of Aḳaba preceded, if it was not the introduction to, the great revolt in the days of Jehoshaphat's son Jehoram, where, again, the details in 2 Chron. xxi. must rely in the first instance upon an old source. Apart from what is said of Jehoshaphat's legislative measures (2 Chron. xix. 4 sqq.; cf. the meaning of his name above), an account is preserved of his alliance with Jehoram of Israel against Moab (2 Kings iii.), on which see JEHORAM; MOAB. The "valley of Jehoshaphat" (Joel iii. 12) has been identified by tradition (as old as Eusebius) with the valley between Jerusalem and the mount of Olives.

(S. A. C.)

JEHOVAH (YAHWEH1), in the Bible, the God of Israel. "Jehovah" is a modern mispronunciation of the Hebrew name, resulting from combining the consonants of that name, Jhvh, with the vowels of the word ădōnāy, "Lord," which the Jews substituted for the proper name in reading the scriptures. In such cases of substitution the vowels of the word which is to be read are written in the Hebrew text with the consonants of the word which is not to be read. The consonants of the word to be substituted are ordinarily written in the margin; but inasmuch as Adonay was regularly read instead of the ineffable name Jhvh, it was deemed unnecessary to note the fact at every occurrence. When Christian scholars began to study the Old Testament in Hebrew, if they were ignorant of this general rule or regarded the substitution as a piece of Jewish superstition, reading what actually stood in the text, they would inevitably pronounce the name Jĕhōvāh. It is an unprofitable inquiry who first made this blunder; probably many fell into it independently. The statement still commonly repeated that it originated with Petrus Galatinus (1518) is erroneous; Jehova occurs in manuscripts at least as early as the 14th century.

The form Jehovah was used in the 16th century by many authors, both Catholic and Protestant, and in the 17th was zealously defended by Fuller, Gataker, Leusden and others, against the criticisms of such scholars as Drusius, Cappellus and the elder Buxtorf. It appeared in the English Bible in Tyndale's translation of the Pentateuch (1530), and is found in all English

Protestant versions of the 16th century except that of Coverdale (1535). In the Authorized Version of 1611 it occurs in Exod. vi. 3; Ps. lxxxiii. 18; Isa. xii. 2; xxvi. 4, beside the compound names Jehovah-jireh, Jehovah-nissi, Jehovah-shalom; elsewhere, in accordance with the usage of the ancient versions, Jhvh is represented by Lord (distinguished by capitals from the title "Lord," Heb. *adonay*). In the Revised Version of 1885 Jehovah is retained in the places in which it stood in the A. V., and is introduced also in Exod. vi. 2, 6, 7, 8; Ps. lxviii. 20; Isa. xlix. 14; Jer. xvi. 21; Hab. iii. 19. The American committee which cooperated in the revision desired to employ the name Jehovah wherever Jhvh occurs in the original, and editions embodying their preferences are printed accordingly.

Several centuries before the Christian era the name Jhvh had ceased to be commonly used by the Jews. Some of the later writers in the Old Testament employ the appellative Elohim, God, prevailingly or exclusively; a collection of Psalms (Ps. xlii.-lxxxiii.) was revised by an editor who changed the Jhvh of the authors into Elohim (see *e.g.* xlv. 7; xlviii. 10; l. 7; li. 14); observe also the frequency of "the Most High," "the God of Heaven," "King of Heaven," in Daniel, and of "Heaven" in First Maccabees. The oldest Greek versions (Septuagint), from the third century B.C., consistently use Κύριος, "Lord," where the Hebrew has Jhvh, corresponding to the substitution of Adonay for Jhvh in reading the original; in books written in Greek in this period (*e.g.* Wisdom, 2 and 3 Maccabees), as in the New Testament, Κύριος takes the place of the name of God. Josephus, who as a priest knew the pronunciation of the name, declares that religion forbids him to divulge it; Philo calls it ineffable, and says that it is lawful for those only whose ears and tongues are purified by wisdom to hear and utter it in a holy place (that is, for priests in the Temple); and in another passage, commenting on Lev. xxiv. 15 seq.: "If anyone, I do not say should blaspheme against the Lord of men and gods, but should even dare to utter his name unseasonably, let him expect the penalty of death."2

Various motives may have concurred to bring about the suppression of the name. An instinctive feeling that a proper name for God implicitly recognizes the existence of other gods may have had some influence; reverence and the fear lest the holy name should be profaned among the heathen were potent reasons; but probably the most cogent motive was the desire to prevent the abuse of the name in magic. If so, the secrecy had the opposite effect; the name of the god of the Jews was one of the great names in magic, heathen as well as Jewish, and miraculous efficacy was attributed to the mere utterance of it.

In the liturgy of the Temple the name was pronounced in the priestly benediction (Num. vi. 27) after the regular daily sacrifice (in the synagogues a substitute—probably Adonay—was employed);3 on the Day of Atonement the High Priest uttered the name ten times in his prayers and benediction. In the last generations before the fall of Jerusalem, however, it was pronounced in a low tone so that the sounds were lost in the chant of the priests.4

312

After the destruction of the Temple (A.D. 70) the liturgical use of the name ceased, but the tradition was perpetuated in the schools of the rabbis.5 It was certainly known in Babylonia in the latter part of the 4th century,6 and not improbably much later. Nor was the knowledge confined to these pious circles; the name continued to be employed by healers, exorcists and magicians, and has been preserved in many places in magical papyri. The vehemence with which the utterance of the name is denounced in the Mishna—"He who pronounces the Name with its own letters has no part in the world to come!"7—suggests that this misuse of the name was not uncommon among Jews.

The Samaritans, who otherwise shared the scruples of the Jews about the utterance of the name, seem to have used it in judicial oaths to the scandal of the rabbis.8

The early Christian scholars, who inquired what was the true name of the God of the Old Testament, had therefore no great difficulty in getting the information they sought. Clement of Alexandria (d. *c.* 212) says that it was pronounced Ιαουε.9Epiphanius (d. 404), who was born in Palestine and spent a considerable part of his life there, gives Ιαβε (one cod.Ιαυε).10 Theodoret (d. *c.* 457),11 born in Antioch, writes that the Samaritans pronounced the name Ιαβε (in another passage,Ιαβαι), the Jews Αϊα.12 The latter is probably not Jhvh but*Ehyeh* (Exod. iii. 14), which the Jews counted among the names of God; there is no reason whatever to imagine that the Samaritans pronounced the name Jhvh differently from the Jews. This direct testimony is supplemented by that of the magical texts, in which Ιαβε Ζεβυθ (Jahveh Şebāōth), as well as Ιαβα, occurs frequently.13 In an Ethiopic list of magical names of Jesus, purporting to have been taught by him to his disciples, *Yāwē* is found.14 Finally, there is evidence from more than one source that the modern Samaritan priests pronounce the name *Yahweh* or *Yahwa*.15

There is no reason to impugn the soundness of this substantially consentient testimony to the pronunciation Yahweh or Jahveh, coming as it does through several independent channels. It

117

is confirmed by grammatical considerations. The name Jhvh enters into the composition of many proper names of persons in the Old Testament, either as the initial element, in the form Jeho- or Jo- (as in Jehoram, Joram), or as the final element, in the form -jahu or -jah (as in Adonijahu, Adonijah). These various forms are perfectly regular if the divine name was Yahweh, and, taken altogether, they cannot be explained on any other hypothesis. Recent scholars, accordingly, with but few exceptions, are agreed that the ancient pronunciation of the name was Yahweh (the first h sounded at the end of the syllable).

Genebrardus seems to have been the first to suggest the pronunciation *Iahué*,16 but it was not until the 19th century that it became generally accepted.

Jahveh or Yahweh is apparently an example of a common type of Hebrew proper names which have the form of the 3rd pers. sing, of the verb. *e.g.* Jabneh (name of a city), Jābīn, Jamlēk, Jiptāḥ (Jephthah), &c. Most of these really are verbs, the suppressed or implicit subject being *'ēl*, "*numen*, god," or the name of a god; cf. Jabneh and Jabnĕ-ēl, Jiptāḥ and Jiptaḥ-ēl.

The ancient explanations of the name proceed from Exod. iii. 14, 15, where "Yahweh17 hath sent me" in *v.* 15 corresponds to "Ehyeh hath sent me" in *v.* 14, thus seeming to connect the name Yahweh with the Hebrew verb *hāyāh*, "to become, to be." The Palestinian interpreters found in this the promise that God would be with his people (cf. *v.* 12) in future oppressions as he was in the present distress, or the assertion of his eternity, or eternal constancy; the Alexandrian translation Ἐγώ εἰμι ὁ ὤν ... Ὁ ὢν ἀπέσταλκέν με πρὸς ὑμᾶς, understands it in the more metaphysical sense of God's absolute being. Both interpretations, "He (who) is (always the same)," and "He (who) is (absolutely, the truly existent)," import into the name all that they profess to find in it; the one, the religious faith in God's unchanging fidelity to his people, the other, a philosophical conception of absolute being which is foreign both to the meaning of the Hebrew verb and to the force of the tense employed. Modern scholars have sometimes found in the name the expression of the aseity18 of God; sometimes of his reality, in contrast to the imaginary gods of the heathen. Another explanation, which appears first in Jewish authors of the middle ages and has found wide acceptance in recent times, derives the name from the causative of the verb; He (who) causes things to be, gives them being; or calls events into existence, brings them to pass; with many individual modifications of interpretation—creator, life-giver, fulfiller of promises. A serious objection to this theory in every form is that the verb *hāyāh*, "to be," has no causative stem in Hebrew; to express the ideas which these scholars find in the name Yahweh the language employs altogether different verbs.

This assumption that Yahweh is derived from the verb "to be," as seems to be implied in Exod. iii. 14 seq., is not, however, free from difficulty. "To be" in the Hebrew of the Old Testament is not *hāwāh*, as the derivation would require, but *hāyāh*; and we are thus driven to the further assumption that *hāwāh* belongs to an earlier stage of the language, or to some older speech of the forefathers of the Israelites. This hypothesis is not intrinsically improbable—and in Aramaic, a language closely related to Hebrew, "to be" actually is *hāwā*—but it should be noted that in adopting it we admit that, using the name Hebrew in the historical sense, Yahweh is not a Hebrew name. And, inasmuch as nowhere in the Old Testament, outside of Exod. iii., is there the slightest indication that the Israelites connected the name of their God with the idea of "being" in any sense, it may fairly be questioned whether, if the author of Exod. iii. 14 seq., intended to give an etymological interpretation of the name Yahweh,19 his etymology is any better than many other paronomastic explanations of proper names in the Old Testament, or than, say, the connexion of the name Ἀπόλλων with ἀπολούων, ἀπολύων in Plato's *Cratylus*, or the popular derivation from ἀπόλλυμι.

A root *hāwāh* is represented in Hebrew by the nouns *hōwāh* (Ezek., Isa. xlvii. 11) and *hawwāh* (Ps., Prov., Job) "disaster, calamity, ruin."20 The primary meaning is probably "sink down, fall," in which sense—common in Arabic—the verb appears in Job xxxvii. 6 (of snow falling to earth). A Catholic commentator of the 16th century, Hieronymus ab Oleastro, seems to have been the first to connect the name "Jehova" with *hōwāh* interpreting it *contritio, sive pernicies* (destruction of the Egyptians and Canaanites); Daumer, adopting the same etymology, took it in a more general sense: Yahweh, as well as Shaddai, meant "Destroyer," and fitly expressed the nature of the terrible god whom he identified with Moloch.

The derivation of Yahweh from *hāwāh* is formally unimpeachable, and is adopted by many recent scholars, who proceed, however, from the primary sense of the root rather than from the specific meaning of the nouns. The name is accordingly interpreted, He (who) falls (baetyl, βαίτυλος, meteorite); or causes (rain or lightning) to fall (storm god); or casts down (his foes, by his thunderbolts). It is obvious that if the derivation be correct, the significance of the name, which in itself denotes only "He falls" or "He fells," must be learned, if at all, from early Israelitish conceptions of the nature of Yahweh rather than from etymology.

118

A more fundamental question is whether the name Yahweh originated among the Israelites or was adopted by them from some other people and speech.21 The biblical author of the history of the sacred institutions (P) expressly declares that the name Yahweh was unknown to the patriarchs (Exod. vi. 3), and the much older Israelite historian (E) records the first revelation of the name to Moses (Exod. iii. 13-15), apparently following a tradition according to which the Israelites had not been worshippers of Yahweh before the time of Moses, or, as he conceived it, had not worshipped the god of their fathers under that name. The revelation of the name to Moses was made at a mountain sacred to Yahweh (the mountain of God) far to the south of Palestine, in a region where the forefathers of the Israelites had never roamed, and in the territory of other tribes; and long after the settlement in Canaan this region continued to be regarded as the abode of Yahweh (Judg. v. 4; Deut. xxxiii. 2 sqq.; 1 Kings xix. 8 sqq. &c.). Moses is closely connected with the tribes in the vicinity of the holy mountain; according to one account, he married a daughter of the priest of Midian (Exod. ii. 16 sqq.; iii. 1); to this mountain he led the Israelites after their deliverance from Egypt; there his father-in-law met him, and extolling Yahweh as "greater than all the gods," offered (in his capacity as priest of the place?) sacrifices, at which the chief men of the Israelites were his guests; there the religion of Yahweh was revealed through Moses, and the Israelites pledged themselves to serve God according to its prescriptions. It appears, therefore, that in the tradition followed by the Israelite historian the tribes within whose pasture lands the mountain of God stood were worshippers of Yahweh before the time of Moses; and the surmise that the name Yahweh belongs to their speech, rather than to that of Israel, has considerable probability. One of these tribes was Midian, in whose land the mountain of God lay. The Kenites also, with whom another tradition connects Moses, seem to have been worshippers of Yahweh. It is probable that Yahweh was at one time worshipped by various tribes south of Palestine, and that several places in that wide territory (Horeb, Sinai, Kadesh, &c.) were sacred to him; the oldest and most famous of these, the mountain of God, seems to have lain in Arabia, east of the Red Sea. From some of these peoples and at one of these holy places, a group of Israelite tribes adopted the religion of Yahweh, the God who, by the hand of Moses, had delivered them from Egypt.22

The tribes of this region probably belonged to some branch of the great Arab stock, and the name Yahweh has, accordingly, been connected with the Arabic *hawā*, "the void" (between heaven and earth), "the atmosphere," or with the verb*hawā*, cognate with Heb. *hāwāh*, "sink, glide down" (through space); *hawwā* "blow" (wind). "He rides through the air, He blows" (Wellhausen), would be a fit name for a god of wind and storm. There is, however, no certain evidence that the Israelites in historical times had any consciousness of the primitive significance of the name.

The attempts to connect the name Yahweh with that of an Indo-European deity (Jehovah-Jove, &c.), or to derive it from Egyptian or Chinese, may be passed over. But one theory which has had considerable currency requires notice, namely, that Yahweh, or Yahu, Yaho,23 is the name of a god worshipped throughout the whole, or a great part, of the area occupied by the Western Semites. In its earlier form this opinion rested chiefly on certain misinterpreted testimonies in Greek authors about a god Ἰάω, and was conclusively refuted by Baudissin; recent adherents of the theory build more largely on the occurrence in various parts of this territory of proper names of persons and places which they explain as compounds of Yahu or Yah.24 The explanation is in most cases simply an assumption of the point at issue; some of the names have been misread; others are undoubtedly the names of Jews. There remain, however, some cases in which it is highly probable that names of non-Israelites are really compounded with Yahweh. The most conspicuous of these is the king of Hamath who in the inscriptions of Sargon (722-705 B.C.) is called Yaubi'di and Ilubi'di (compare Jehoiakim-Eliakim). Azriyau of Jaudi, also, in inscriptions of Tiglath-Pileser (745-728 B.C.), who was formerly supposed to be Azariah (Uzziah) of Judah, is probably a king of the country in northern Syria known to us from the Zenjirli inscriptions as Ja'di.

Friedrich Delitzsch brought into notice three tablets, of the age of the first dynasty of Babylon, in which he read the names of *Ya-a'-ve-ilu*, *Ya-ve-ilu*, and *Ya-ū-um-ilu* ("Yahweh is God"), and which he regarded as conclusive proof that Yahweh was known in Babylonia before 2000 B.C.; he was a god of the Semitic invaders in the second wave of migration, who were, according to Winckler and Delitzsch, of North Semitic stock (Canaanites, in the linguistic sense).25 We should thus have in the tablets evidence of the worship of Yahweh among the Western Semites at a time long before the rise of Israel. The reading of the names is, however, extremely uncertain, not to say improbable, and the far-reaching inferences drawn from them carry no conviction. In a tablet attributed to the 14th century B.C. which Sellin found in the course of his excavations at Tell Ta'annuk (the Taanach of the O.T.) a name occurs which may be read Ahi-Yawi (equivalent to Hebrew Ahijah);26 if the reading be correct, this would show that Yahweh was worshipped in Central Palestine before the Israelite conquest. The reading is, however, only one of several possibilities. The fact that the full form Yahweh appears, whereas in Hebrew proper names only the shorter Yahu and Yah occur, weighs somewhat against the interpretation, as it does against Delitzsch's reading of his tablets.

It would not be at all surprising if, in the great movements of populations and shifting of ascendancy which lie beyond our historical horizon, the worship of Yahweh should have been established in regions remote from those which it occupied in historical times; but nothing which we now know warrants the opinion that his worship was ever general among the Western Semites.

Many attempts have been made to trace the West Semitic Yahu back to Babylonia. Thus Delitzsch formerly derived the name from an Akkadian god, I or Ia; or from the Semitic nominative ending, Yau;27 but this deity has since disappeared from the pantheon of Assyriologists. The combination of Yah with Ea, one of the great Babylonian gods, seems to have a peculiar fascination for amateurs, by whom it is periodically "discovered." Scholars are now agreed that, so far as Yahu or Yah occurs in Babylonian texts, it is as the name of a foreign god.

Assuming that Yahweh was primitively a nature god, scholars in the 19th century discussed the question over what sphere of nature he originally presided. According to some he was the god of consuming fire; others saw in him the bright sky, or the heaven; still others recognized in him a storm god, a theory with which the derivation of the name from Heb. *hāwāh*or Arab. *hawā* well accords. The association of Yahweh with storm and fire is frequent in the Old Testament; the thunder is the voice of Yahweh, the lightning his arrows, the rainbow his bow. The revelation at Sinai is amid the awe-inspiring phenomena of tempest. Yahweh leads Israel through the desert in a pillar of cloud and fire; he kindles Elijah's altar by lightning, and translates the prophet in a chariot of fire. See also Judg. v. 4 seq.; 314Deut. xxxiii. 1; Ps. xviii. 7-15; Hab. iii. 3-6. The cherub upon which he rides when he flies on the wings of the wind (Ps. xviii. 10) is not improbably an ancient mythological personification of the storm cloud, the genius of tempest (cf. Ps. civ. 3). In Ezekiel the throne of Yahweh is borne up on Cherubim, the noise of whose wings is like thunder. Though we may recognize in this poetical imagery the survival of ancient and, if we please, mythical notions, we should err if we inferred that Yahweh was originally a departmental god, presiding specifically over meteorological phenomena, and that this conception of him persisted among the Israelites till very late times. Rather, as the god—or the chief god—of a region and a people, the most sublime and impressive phenomena, the control of the mightiest forces of nature are attributed to him. As the God of Israel Yahweh becomes its leader and champion in war; he is a warrior, mighty in battle; but he is not a god of war in the specific sense.

In the inquiry concerning the nature of Yahweh the name Yahweh Sebaoth (E.V., The LORD of Hosts) has had an important place. The hosts have by some been interpreted of the armies of Israel (see 1 Sam. xvii. 45, and note the association of the name in the Books of Samuel, where it first appears, with the ark, or with war); by others, of the heavenly hosts, the stars conceived as living beings, later, perhaps, the angels as the court of Yahweh and the instruments of his will in nature and history (Ps. lxxxix.); or of the forces of the world in general which do his bidding, cf. the common Greek renderings, Κύριος τῶν δυνάμεων and Κ. παντοκράτωρ, (Universal Ruler). It is likely that the name was differently understood in different periods and circles; but in the prophets the hosts are clearly superhuman powers. In many passages the name seems to be only a more solemn substitute for the simple Yahweh, and as such it has probably often been inserted by scribes. Finally, Sebaoth came to be treated as a proper name (cf. Ps. lxxx. 5, 8, 20), and as such is very common in magical texts.

LITERATURE.—Reland, *Decas exercitationum philologicarum de vera pronuntiatione nominis Jehova*, 1707; Reinke, "Philologisch-historische Abhandlung über den Gottesnamen Jehova," in *Beiträge zur Erklärung des Alten Testaments*, III. (1855); Baudissin, "Der Ursprung des Gottesnamens Ἰάω," in *Studien zur semitischen Religionsgeschichte*, I. (1876); Driver, "Recent Theories on the Origin and Nature of the Tetragrammaton," in *Studia Biblica*, I. (1885), 1-20; Deissmann, "Griechische Transkriptionen des Tetragrammaton," in *Bibelstudien*(1895), 1-20; Blau, *Das altjüdische Zauberwesen*, 1898. See also HEBREW RELIGION.

(G. F. MO.)

1This form, *Yahweh*, as the correct one, is generally used in the separate articles throughout this work.

2See Josephus, Ant. ii. 12, 4; Philo, *Vita Mosis*, iii. 11 (ii. §114, ed. Cohn and Wendland); ib. iii. 27 (ii. §206). The Palestinian authorities more correctly interpreted Lev. xxiv. 15 seq., not of the mere utterance of the name, but of the use of the name of God in blaspheming God.

3*Siphrē*, Num. §§ 39, 43; *M. Sotah*, iii. 7; *Sotah*, 38a. The tradition that the utterance of the name in the daily benedictions ceased with the death of Simeon the Just, two centuries or more before the Christian era, perhaps arose from a misunderstanding of *Menaḥoth*, 109b; in any case it cannot stand against the testimony of older and more authoritative texts.

4*Yoma*, 39b; *Jer. Yoma*, iii. 7; *Kiddushin*, 71a.

5R. Johanan (second half of the 3rd century), *Kiddushin*, 71a.

6Kiddushin, l.c. = *Pesaḥim*, 50a.

7*M. Sanhedrin*, x. 1; Abba Saul, end of 2nd century.

8*Jer. Sanhedrin*, x. 1; R. Mana, 4th century.

9*Strom.* v. 6. Variants: Ια ουε, Ια ουαι; cod. L. Ιαου.

10*Panarion*, Haer. 40, 5; cf. Lagarde, *Psalter juxta Hebraeos*, 154.

11*Quaest.* 15 in Exod.; *Fab. haeret. compend.* v. 3, *sub fin.*

12Αϊα occurs also in the great magical papyrus of Paris, 1. 3020 (Wessely, *Denkschrift. Wien. Akad.*, Phil. Hist. Kl., XXXVI. p. 120), and in the Leiden Papyrus, xvii. 31.

13See Deissmann, *Bibelstudien*, 13 sqq.

14See Driver, *Studia Biblica*, I. 20.

15See Montgomery, *Journal of Biblical Literature*, xxv. (1906),49-51.

16*Chronographia*, Paris, 1567 (ed. Paris, 1600, p. 79 seq.).

17This transcription will be used henceforth.

18*A-se-itas*, a scholastic Latin expression for the quality of existing by oneself.

19The critical difficulties of these verses need not be discussed here. See W. R. Arnold, "The Divine Name in Exodus iii. 14," *Journal of Biblical Literature*, XXIV. (1905), 107-165.

20Cf. also *hawwāh*, "desire," Mic. vii. 3; Prov. x. 3.

21See HEBREW RELIGION.

22The divergent Judaean tradition, according to which the forefathers had worshipped Yahweh from time immemorial, may indicate that Judah and the kindred clans had in fact been worshippers of Yahweh before the time of Moses.

23The form *Yahu*, or *Yaho*, occurs not only in composition, but by itself; see *Aramaic Papyri discovered at Assuan*, B 4, 6, 11; E 14; J 6. This is doubtless the original of Ἰάω, frequently found in Greek authors and in magical texts as the name of the God of the Jews.

24See a collection and critical estimate of this evidence by Zimmern, *Die Keilinschriften und das Alte Testament*, 465 sqq.

25*Babel und Bibel*, 1902. The enormous, and for the most part ephemeral, literature provoked by Delitzsch's lecture cannot be cited here.

26*Denkschriften d. Wien. Akad.*, L. iv. p. 115 seq. (1904).

27*Wo lag das Paradies?* (1881), pp. 158-166.

JEHU, son of Jehoshaphat and grandson of Nimshi, in the Bible, a general of Ahab and Jehoram, and, later, king of Israel. Ahaziah son of Jehoram of Judah and Jehoram brother of Ahaziah of Israel had taken joint action against the Aramaeans of Damascus who were attacking Ramoth-Gilead under Hazael. Jehoram had returned wounded to his palace at Jezreel, whither Ahaziah had come down to visit him. Jehu, meanwhile, remained at the seat of war, and the prophet Elisha sent a messenger to anoint him king. The general at once acknowledged the call, "drove furiously" to Jezreel, and, having slain both kings, proceeded to exterminate the whole of the royal family (2 Kings ix., x.). A similar fate befell the royal princes of Judah (see ATHALIAH), and thus, for a time at least, the new king must have had complete control over the two kingdoms (cf. 2 Chron. xxii. 9). Israelite historians viewed these events as a great religious revolution inspired by Elijah and initiated by Elisha, as the overthrow of the worship of Baal, and as a retribution for the cruel murder of Naboth the Jezreelite (see JEZEBEL). A vivid description is given of the destruction of the prophets of Baal at the temple in Samaria (2 Kings x. 27; contrast iii. 2). While Jehu was supported by the Rechabites in his reforming zeal, a similar revolt against Baalism in Judah is ascribed to the priest Jehoiada (see JOASH). In the tragedies of the period it seems clear that Elisha's interest in both Jehu and the Syrian Hazael (2 Kings viii. 7 sqq.) had some political significance, and in opposition to the "Deuteronomic" the commendation in 2 Kings x. 28 sqq., Hosea's denunciation (i. 4) indicates the judgment which was passed upon Jehu's bloodshed in other circles.

In the course of an expedition against Hazael in 842 Shalmaneser II. of Assyria received tribute of silver and gold from Ya-u-a son of Omri,1 Tyre and Sidon; another attack followed in 839. For some years after this Assyria was unable to interfere, and war broke out between

121

Damascus and Israel. The Israelite story, which may perhaps be supplemented from Judaean sources (see JOASH), records a great loss of territory on the east of the Jordan (2 Kings x. 32 seq.). Under Jehu's successor Jehoahaz there was continual war with Hazael and his son Benhadad, but relief was obtained by his grandson Joash, and the land recovered complete independence under Jeroboam.

Jehu is also the name of a prophet of the time of Baasha and Jehoshaphat (1 Kings xvi.; 2 Chron. xix., xx.).

(S. A. C.)

1I.e. either descendant of, or from the same district as, Omri (see Hogg, *Ency. Bib.* col. 2291). The Assyrian king's sculpture, depicting the embassy and its gifts, is the so-called "black obelisk" now in the British Museum (Nimroud Central Gallery, No. 98; *Guide to Bab. and Ass. Antiq.*, 1900, p. 24 seq., pl. ii.).

JEKYLL, SIR JOSEPH (1663-1738), English lawyer and master of the rolls, son of John Jekyll, was born in London, and after studying at the Middle Temple was called to the bar in 1687. He rapidly rose to be chief justice of Chester (1697), serjeant-at-law and king's serjeant (1700), and a knight. In 1717 he was made master of the rolls. A Whig in politics, he sat in parliament for various constituencies from 1697 to the end of his life, and took an active part there in debating constitutional questions with much learning, though, according to Lord Hervey (*Mem.* 1, 474), with little "approbation." He was censured by the House of Commons for accepting a brief for the defence of Lord Halifax in a prosecution ordered by the house. He was one of the managers of the impeachment of the Jacobite earl of Wintoun in 1715, and of Harley (Lord Oxford) in 1717. In later years he supported Walpole. He became very unpopular in 1736 for his introduction of the "gin act," taxing the retailing of spirituous liquors, and his house had to be protected from the mob. Pope has an illusion to "Jekyll or some odd Whig, Who never changed his principle or wig" (*Epilogue to the Satires*). Jekyll was also responsible for the Mortmain Act of 1736, which was not superseded till 1888. He died without issue in 1738.

His great-nephew JOSEPH JEKYLL (d. 1837) was a lawyer, politician and wit, who excited a good deal of contemporary satire, and who wrote some *jeux d'esprit* which were well-known in his time. His *Letters of the late Ignatius Sancho, an African*, was published in 1782. In 1894 his correspondence was edited, with a memoir, by the Hon. Algernon Bourke.

JELLACHICH, JOSEF, COUNT (1801-1859), Croatian statesman, was born on the 16th of October 1801 at Pétervárad. He entered the Austrian army (1819), fought against the Bosnians in 1845, was made ban of Croatia, Slavonia and Dalmatia in 1848 on the petition of the Croatians, and was simultaneously raised to the rank of lieutenant-general by the emperor. As ban, Jellachich's policy was directed to preserving the Slav kingdoms for the Habsburg monarchy by identifying himself with the nationalist opposition to Magyar ascendancy, while at the same time discouraging the extreme "Illyrism" advocated by Lodovik Gáj (1809-1872). Though his separatist measures at first brought him into disfavour at the imperial court, their true objective was soon recognized, and, with the triumph of the more violent elements of the Hungarian revolution, he was hailed as the most conspicuous champion of the unity of the empire, and was able to bring about that union of the imperial army with the southern Slavs by which the revolution in Vienna and Budapest was overthrown (see AUSTRIA-HUNGARY: *History*). He began the war of independence in September 1848 by crossing the Drave at the head of 40,000 Croats. After the bloody battle of Buda he concluded a three days' truce with the Hungarians to enable him to assist Prince Windischgrätz to reduce Vienna, and subsequently fought against the Magyars at Schwechát. During the winter campaign of 1848-49 he commanded, under Windischgrätz, the Austrian right wing, capturing Magyar-Ovar and Raab, and defeating the Magyars at Mór. After the recapture of Buda he was made commander-in-chief of the southern army. 315At first he gained some successes against Bem (*q.v.*), but on the 14th of July 1849 was routed by the Hungarians at Hegyes and driven behind the Danube. He took no part in the remainder of the war, but returned to Agram to administer Croatia. In 1853 he was appointed commander-in-chief of the army sent against Montenegro, and in 1855 was created a count. He died on the 20th of May 1859. His *Gedichte* were published at Vienna in 1851.

See the anonymous *The Croatian Revolution* of the Year 1848 (Croat.), Agram, 1898.

(R. N. B.)

JELLINEK, ADOLF (1821-1893), Jewish preacher and scholar, was born in Moravia. After filling clerical posts in Leipzig, he became *Prediger* (preacher) in Vienna in 1856. He was associated with the promoters of the New Learning within Judaism, and wrote on the history of the

Kabbala. His bibliographies (each bearing the Hebrew title *Qontres*) were useful compilations. But his most important work lay in three other directions. (1) *Midrashic.* Jellinek published in the six parts of his *Beth ha-Midrasch* (1853-1878) a large number of smaller *Midrashi*, ancient and medieval homilies and folk-lore records, which have been of much service in the recent revival of interest in Jewish apocalyptic literature. A translation of these collections of Jellinek into German was undertaken by A. Wuensche, under the general title *Aus Israels Lehrhalle.* (2)*Psychological.* Before the study of ethnic psychology had become a science, Jellinek devoted attention to the subject. There is much keen analysis and original investigation in his two essays *Der jüdische Stamm* (1869) and *Der jüdische Stamm in nicht-jüdischen Sprüch-wörtern* (1881-1882). It is to Jellinek that we owe the oft-repeated comparison of the Jewish temperament to that of women in its quickness of perception, versatility and sensibility. (3) *Homiletic.* Jellinek was probably the greatest synagogue orator of the 19th century. He published some 200 sermons, in most of which are displayed unobtrusive learning, fresh application of old sayings, and a high conception of Judaism and its claims. Jellinek was a powerful apologist and an accomplished homilist, at once profound and ingenious.

His son, GEORGE JELLINEK, was appointed professor of international law at Heidelberg in 1891. Another son, MAX HERMANN JELLINEK, was made assistant professor of philology at Vienna in 1892.

A brother of Adolf, HERMANN JELLINEK (b. 1823), was executed at the age of 26 on account of his association with the Hungarian national movement of 1848. One of Hermann Jellinek's best-known works was *Uriel Acosta.* Another brother, MORITZ JELLINEK (1823-1883), was an accomplished economist, and contributed to the Academy of Sciences essays on the price of cereals and on the statistical organization of trade. He founded the Budapest tramway company (1864) and was also president of the corn exchange.

See *Jewish Encyclopedia*, vii. 92-94. For a character sketch of Adolf Jellinek see S. Singer, *Lectures and Addresses* (1908), pp. 88-93; Kohut, *Berühmte israelitische Männer und Frauen.*

(I. A.)

JEMAPPES, a town in the province of Hainaut, Belgium, near Mons, famous as the scene of the battle at which Dumouriez, at the head of the French Revolutionary Army, defeated the Austrian army (which was greatly outnumbered) under the duke of Saxe-Teschen and Clerfayt on the 6th of November 1792 (see FRENCH REVOLUTIONARY WARS).

JENA, a university town of Germany, in the grand duchy of Saxe-Weimar, on the left bank of the Saale, 56 m. S.W. from Leipzig by the Grossbergen-Saalfeld and 12 m. S.E. of Weimar by the Weimar-Gera lines of railway. Pop. (1905), 26,355. Its situation in a broad valley environed by limestone hills is somewhat dreary. To the north lies the plateau, descending steeply to the valley, famous as the scene of the battle of Jena. The town is surrounded by promenades occupying the site of the old fortifications; it contains in addition to the medieval market square, many old-fashioned houses and quaint narrow streets. Besides the old university buildings, the most interesting edifices are the 15th-century church of St Michael, with a tower 318 ft. high, containing an altar, beneath which is a doorway leading to a vault, and a bronze statue of Luther, originally destined for his tomb; the university library, in which is preserved a curious figure of a dragon; and the bridge across the Saale, as long as the church steeple is high, the centre arch of which is surmounted by a stone carved head of a malefactor. Across the river is the "mountain," or hill, whence a fine view is obtained of the town and surroundings, and hard by the Fuchs-Turm (Fox tower) celebrated for student orgies, while in the centre of the town is the house of an astronomer, Weigel, with a deep shaft through which the stars can be seen in the day time. Thus the seven marvels of Jena are summed up in the Latin lines:—

Ara, caput, draco, mons, pons, vulpecula
turris,
  Weigeliana domus; septem miracula
Jenae.

There must also be mentioned the university church, the new university buildings, which occupy the site of the ducal palace (Schloss) where Goethe wrote his *Hermann und Dorothea*, the Schwarzer Bär Hotel, where Luther spent the night after his flight from the Wartburg, and four towers and a gateway which now alone mark the position of the ancient walls. The town has of late years become a favourite residential resort and has greatly extended towards the west, where there is a colony of pleasant villas. Its chief prosperity centres, however, in the university. In 1547 the elector John Frederick the Magnanimous of Saxony, while a captive in the hands of the emperor Charles V., conceived the plan of founding a university at Jena, which was accordingly established by his three sons. After having obtained a charter from the emperor Ferdinand I., it was inaugurated on the 2nd of February 1558. It was most numerously attended about the middle of the 18th century; but the most brilliant professoriate was under the duke Charles Augustus, Goethe's patron (1787-1806), when Fichte, Hegel, Schelling, Schlegel and Schiller were on its teaching staff. Founded as a home for the new religious opinions of the 16th century, it has ever been in the forefront of German universities in liberally accepting new ideas. It distances perhaps every other German university in the extent to which it carries out what are popularly regarded as the characteristics of German student-life—duelling and the passion for *Freiheit*. At the end of the 18th and the beginning of the 19th century, the opening of new universities, co-operating with the suspicions of the various German governments as to the democratic opinions which obtained at Jena, militated against the university, which has never regained its former prosperity. In 1905 it was attended by about 1100 students, and its teaching staff (including *privatdocenten*) numbered 112. Amongst its numerous auxiliaries may be mentioned the library, with 200,000 volumes, the observatory, the meteorological institute, the botanical garden, seminaries of theology, philology and education, and well equipped clinical, anatomical and physical institutes. There are also veterinary and agricultural colleges in connexion with the university. The manufactures of Jena are not considerable. The book trade has of late years revived, and there are several printing establishments.

Jena appears to have possessed municipal rights in the 13th century. At the beginning of the 14th century it was in the possession of the margraves of Meissen, from whom it passed in 1423 to the elector of Saxony. Since 1485 it has remained in the Ernestine line of the house of Saxony. In 1662 it fell to Bernhard, youngest son of William duke of Weimar, and became the capital of a small separate duchy. Bernhard's line having become extinct in 1690, Jena was united with Eisenach, and in 1741 reverted with that duchy to Weimar. In more modern times Jena has been made famous by the defeat inflicted in the vicinity, on the 14th of October 1806, by Napoleon upon the Prussian army under the prince of Hohenlohe (see NAPOLEONIC CAMPAIGNS).

See Schreiber and Färber, *Jena von seinem Ursprung bis zur neuesten Zeit* (2nd ed., 1858); Ortloff, *Jena und Umgegend* (3rd ed., 1875); Leonhardt, *Jena als Universität und Stadt* (Jena, 1902); Ritter, *Führer durch Jena und Umgebung* (Jena, 1901); Biedermann, *Die Universität Jena* (Jena, 1858); and the *Urkundenbuch der Stadt Jena* edited by J. E. A. Martin and O. Devrient (1888-1903).

316

JENATSCH, GEORG (1596-1639), Swiss political leader, one of the most striking figures in the troubled history of the Grisons in the 17th century, was born at Samaden (capital of the Upper Engadine). He studied at Zürich and Basel, and in 1617 became the Protestant pastor of Scharans (near Thusis). But almost at once he plunged into active politics, taking the side of the Venetian and Protestant party of the Salis family, as against the Spanish and Romanist policy supported by the rival family, that of Planta. He headed the "preachers" who in 1618 tortured to death the arch-priest Rusca, of Sondrio, and outlawed the Plantas. As reprisals, a number of Protestants were massacred at Tirano (1620), in the Valtellina, a very fertile valley, of considerable strategical importance (for through it the Spaniards in Milan could communicate by the Umbrail Pass with the Austrians in Tirol), which then fell into the hands of the Spanish. Jenatsch took part in the murder (1621) of Pompey Planta, the head of the rival party, but later with his friends was compelled to fly the country, giving up his position as a pastor, and henceforth acting solely as a soldier. He helped in the revolt against the Austrians in the Prättigau (1622), and in the invasion of the Valtellina by a French army (1624), but the peace made (1626) between France and Spain left the Valtellina in the hands of the pope, and so destroyed Jenatsch's hopes. Having killed his colonel, Ruinelli, in a duel, Jenatsch had once more to leave his native land, and took service with the Venetians (1629-1630). In 1631 he went to Paris, and actively supported Richelieu's schemes for driving the Spaniards out of the Valtellina, which led to the successful campaign of Rohan (1635), one of whose firmest supporters was Jenatsch. But he soon saw that the French were as unwilling as the Spaniards to restore the Valtellina to the Grisons (which had seized it in 1512). So he became a Romanist (1635), and negotiated secretly with the Spaniards and Austrians. He was the leader of the conspiracy which broke out in 1637, and resulted in the expulsion of Rohan and the French from the Grisons. This treachery on Jenatsch's part did not, however, lead to the freeing of the Valtellina from the Spaniards, and once more he tried to get French support. But on the 24th of January 1639 he was assassinated at Coire by the Plantas; later in the same year the much coveted valley was restored by Spain to the Grisons, which held it till 1797. Jenatsch's career is of general historical importance by reason of the long conflict between France and Spain for the possession of the Valtellina, which forms one of the most bloody episodes in the Thirty Years' War.

(W. A. B. C.)

124

See biography by E. Haffter (Davos, 1894).

JENGHIZ KHAN (1162-1227), Mongol emperor, was born in a tent on the banks of the river Onon. His father Yesukai was absent at the time of his birth, in a campaign against a Tatar chieftain named Temuchin. The fortune of war favoured Yesukai, who having slain his enemy returned to his encampment in triumph. Here he was met by the news that his wife Yulun had given birth to a son. On examining the child heobserved in its clenched fist a clot of coagulated blood like a red stone. In the eyes of the superstitious Mongol this circumstance referred to his victory over the Tatar chieftain, and he therefore named the infant Temuchin. The death of Yesukai, which placed Temuchin at the age of thirteen on the Mongol throne, was the signal also for the dispersal of several tribes whose allegiance the old chieftain had retained by his iron rule. When remonstrated with by Temuchin, the rebels replied: "The deepest wells are sometimes dry, and the hardest stone is sometimes broken; why should we cling to thee?" But Yulun was by no means willing to see her son's power melt away; she led those retainers who remained faithful against the deserters, and succeeded in bringing back fully one half to their allegiance. With this doubtful material, Temuchin succeeded in holding his ground against the plots and open hostilities of the neighbouring tribes, more especially of the Naimans, Keraits and Merkits. With one or other of these he maintained an almost unceasing warfare until 1206, when he felt strong enough to proclaim himself the ruler of an empire. He therefore summoned the notables of his kingdom to an assembly on the banks of the Onon, and at their unanimous request adopted the name and title of Jenghiz Khan (Chinese, Chêng-sze, or "perfect warrior"). At this time there remained to him but one open enemy on the Mongolian steppes, Polo the Naiman khan. Against this chief he now led his troops, and in one battle so completely shattered his forces that Kushlek, the successor of Polo, who was left dead upon the field, fled with his ally Toto, the Merkit khan, to the river Irtysh.

Jenghiz Khan now meditated an invasion of the empire of the Kin Tatars, who had wrested northern China from the Sung dynasty. As a first step he invaded western Hia, and, having captured several strongholds, retired in the summer of 1208 to Lung-ting to escape the great heat of the plains. While there news reached him that Toto and Kushlek were preparing for war. In a pitched battle on the river Irtysh he overthrew them completely. Toto was amongst the slain, and Kushlek fled for refuge to the Khitan Tatars. Satisfied with his victory, Jenghiz again directed his forces against Hia. After having defeated the Kin army under the leadership of a son of the sovereign, he captured the Wu-liang-hai Pass in the Great Wall, and penetrated as far as Ning-sia Fu in Kansuh. With unceasing vigour he pushed on his troops, and even established his sway over the province of Liaotung. Several of the Kin commanders, seeing how persistently victory attended his banners, deserted to him, and garrisons surrendered at his bidding. Having thus secured a firm footing within the Great Wall, he despatched three armies in the autumn of 1213 to overrun the empire. The right wing, under his three sons, Juji, Jagatai and Ogotai, marched towards the south; the left wing, under his brothers Hochar, Kwang-tsin Noyen and Chow-tse-te-po-shi, advanced eastward towards the sea; while Jenghiz and his son Tulē with the centre directed their course in a south-easterly direction. Complete success attended all three expeditions. The right wing advanced as far as Honan, and after having captured upwards of twenty-eight cities rejoined headquarters by the great western road. Hochar made himself master of the country as far as Liao-si; and Jenghiz ceased his triumphal career only when he reached the cliffs of the Shantung promontory. But either because he was weary of the strife, or because it was necessary to revisit his Mongolian empire, he sent an envoy to the Kin emperor in the spring of the following year (1214), saying, "All your possessions in Shantung and the whole country north of the Yellow River are now mine with the solitary exception of Yenking (the modern Peking). By the decree of heaven you are now as weak as I am strong, but I am willing to retire from my conquests; as a condition of my doing so, however, it will be necessary that you distribute largess to my officers and men to appease their fierce hostility." These terms of safety the Kin emperor eagerly accepted, and as a peace offering he presented Jenghiz with a daughter of the late emperor, another princess of the imperial house, 500 youths and maidens, and 3000 horses. No sooner, however, had Jenghiz passed beyond the Great Wall than the Kin emperor, fearing to remain any longer so near the Mongol frontier, moved his court to K'ai-fêng Fu in Honan. This transfer of capital appearing to Jenghiz to indicate a hostile attitude, he once more marched his troops into the doomed empire.

While Jenghiz was thus adding city to city and province to province in China, Kushlek, the fugitive Naiman chief, was not idle. With characteristic treachery he requested permission from his host, the Khitan khan, to collect the fragments of his army which had been scattered by Jenghiz at the battle on the Irtysh, and thus having collected a considerable force he leagued himself with Mahommed, the shah of Khwārizm, against the confiding khan. After a short but decisive campaign the allies remained masters of the position, and the khan was compelled to abdicate the throne in favour of the late guest.

With the power and prestige thus acquired, Kushlek prepared once again to measure swords with the Mongol chief. On receiving the news of his hostile preparations, Jenghiz at once took the field, and in the first battle routed the Naiman troops and made Kushlek a prisoner. His ill-gotten kingdom became 317 an apanage of the Mongol Empire. Jenghiz now held sway up to the Khwārizm frontier. Beyond this he had no immediate desire to go, and he therefore sent envoys to Mahommed, the shah, with presents, saying, "I send thee greeting; I know thy power and the vast extent of thine empire; I regard thee as my most cherished son. On my part thou must know that I have conquered China and all the Turkish nations north of it; thou knowest that my country is a magazine of warriors, a mine of silver, and that I have no need of other lands. I take it that we have an equal interest in encouraging trade between our subjects." This peaceful message was well received by the shah, and in all probability the Mongol armies would never have appeared in Europe but for an unfortunate occurrence. Shortly after the despatch of this first mission Jenghiz sent a party of traders into Transoxiana who were seized and put to death as spies by Inaljuk, the governor of Otrar. As satisfaction for this outrage Jenghiz demanded the extradition of the offending governor. Far from yielding to this summons, however, Mahommed beheaded the chief of the Mongol envoys, and sent the others back without their beards. This insult made war inevitable, and in the spring of 1219 Jenghiz set out from Karakorum on a campaign which was destined to be as startling in its immediate results as its ulterior effects were far-reaching. The invading force was in the first instance divided into two armies: one commanded by Jenghiz's second son Jagatai was directed to march against the Kankalis, the northern defenders of the Khwārizm empire; and the other, led by Juji, his eldest son, advanced by way of Sighnak against Jand (Jend). Against this latter force Mahommed led an army of 400,000 men, who were completely routed, leaving it is said 160,000 dead upon the field. With the remnant of his host Mahommed fled to Samarkand. Meanwhile Jagatai marched down upon the Syr Daria (Jaxartes) by the pass of Taras and invested Otrar, the offending city. After a siege of five months the citadel was taken by assault, and Inaljuk and his followers were put to the sword. The conquerors levelled the walls with the ground, after having given the city over to pillage. At the same time a third army besieged and took Khojent on the Jaxartes; and yet a fourth, led by Jenghiz and his youngest son Tulē, advanced in the direction of Bokhara. Tashkent and Nur surrendered on their approach, and after a short siege Bokhara fell into their hands. On entering the town Jenghiz ascended the steps of the principal mosque, and shouted to his followers, "The hay is cut; give your horses fodder." No second invitation to plunder was needed; the city was sacked, and the inhabitants either escaped beyond the walls or were compelled to submit to infamies which were worse than death. As a final act of vengeance the town was fired, and before the last of the Mongols left the district, the great mosque and certain palaces were the only buildings left to mark the spot where the "centre of science" once stood. From the ruins of Bokhara Jenghiz advanced along the valley of the Sogd to Samarkand, which, weakened by treachery, surrendered to him, as did also Balkh. But in neither case did submission save either the inhabitants from slaughter or the city from pillage. Beyond this point Jenghiz went no farther westward, but sent Tulē, at the head of 70,000 men, to ravage Khorasan, and two flying columns under Chēpē and Sabutai Bahadar to pursue after Mahommed who had taken refuge in Nishapur. Defeated and almost alone, Mahommed fled before his pursuers to the village of Astara on the shore of the Caspian Sea, where he died of an attack of pleurisy, leaving his empire to his son Jelaleddīn (Jalāl ud-din). Meanwhile Tulē carried his arms into the fertile province of Khorasan, and after having captured Nessa by assault appeared before Merv. By an act of atrocious treachery the Mongols gained possession of the city, and, after their manner, sacked and burnt the town. From Merv Tulē marched upon Nishapur, where he met with a most determined resistance. For four days the garrison fought desperately on the walls and in the streets, but at length they were overpowered, and, with the exception of 400 artisans who were sent into Mongolia, every man, woman and child was slain. Herat escaped the fate which had overtaken Merv and Nishapur by opening its gates to the Mongols. At this point of his victorious career Tulē received an order to join Jenghiz before Talikhan in Badakshan, where that chieftain was preparing to renew his pursuit of Jelaleddīn, after a check he had sustained in an engagement fought before Ghazni. As soon as sufficient reinforcements arrived Jenghiz advanced against Jelaleddīn, who had taken up a position on the banks of the Indus. Here the Turks, though far outnumbered, defended their ground with undaunted courage, until, beaten at all points, they fled in confusion. Jelaleddīn, seeing that all was lost, mounted a fresh horse and jumped into the river, which flowed 20 ft. below. With admiring gaze Jenghiz watched the desperate venture of his enemy, and even saw without regret the dripping horseman mount the opposite bank. From the

Indus Jenghiz sent in pursuit of Jelaleddīn, who fled to Delhi, but failing to capture the fugitive the Mongols returned to Ghazni after having ravaged the provinces of Lahore, Peshawar and Melikpur. At this moment news reached Jenghiz that the inhabitants of Herat had deposed the governor whom Tulē had appointed over the city, and had placed one of their own choice in his room. To punish this act of rebellion Jenghiz sent an army of 80,000 men against the offending city, which after a siege of six months was taken by assault. For a whole week the Mongols ceased not to kill, burn and destroy, and 1,600,000 persons are said to have been massacred within the walls. Having consummated this act of vengeance, Jenghiz returned to Mongolia by way of Balkh, Bokhara and Samarkand.

Meanwhile Chēpē and Sabutai marched through Azerbeijan, and in the spring of 1222 advanced into Georgia. Here they defeated a combined force of Lesghians, Circassians and Kipchaks, and after taking Astrakhan followed the retreating Kipchaks to the Don. The news of the approach of the mysterious enemy of whose name even they were ignorant was received by the Russian princes at Kiev with dismay. At the instigation, however, of Mitislaf, prince of Galicia, they assembled an opposing force on the Dnieper. Here they received envoys from the Mongol camp, whom they barbarously put to death. "You have killed our envoys," was the answer made by the Mongols; "well, as you wish for war you shall have it. We have done you no harm. God is impartial; He will decide our quarrel." In the first battle, on the river Kaleza, the Russians were utterly routed, and fled before the invaders, who, after ravaging Great Bulgaria retired, gorged with booty, through the country of Saksin, along the river Aktuba, on their way to Mongolia.

In China the same success had attended the Mongol arms as in western Asia. The whole of the country north of the Yellow river, with the exception of one or two cities, was added to the Mongol rule, and, on the death of the Kin emperor Süan Tsung in 1223, the Kin empire virtually ceased to be, and Jenghiz's frontiers thus became conterminous with those of the Sung emperors who held sway over the whole of central and southern China. After his return from Central Asia, Jenghiz once more took the field in western China. While on this campaign the five planets appeared in a certain conjunction, which to the superstitiously minded Mongol chief foretold that evil was awaiting him. With this presentiment strongly impressed upon him he turned his face homewards, and had advanced no farther than the Si-Kiang river in Kansuh when he was seized with an illness of which he died a short time afterwards (1227) at his travelling palace at Ha-lao-tu, on the banks of the river Sale in Mongolia. By the terms of his will Ogotai was appointed his successor, but so essential was it considered to be that his death should remain a secret until Ogotai was proclaimed that, as the funeral procession moved northwards to the great ordu on the banks of the Kerulen, the escort killed every one they met. The body of Jenghiz was then carried successively to the ordus of his several wives, and was finally laid to rest in the valley of Kilien.

Thus ended the career of one of the greatest conquerors the world has ever seen. Born and nurtured as the chief of a petty Mongolian tribe, he lived to see his armies victorious from the China Sea to the banks of the Dnieper; and, though the empire 318which he created ultimately dwindled away under the hands of his degenerate descendants, leaving not a wrack behind, we have in the presence of the Turks in Europe a consequence of his rule, since it was the advance of his armies which drove their Osmanli ancestors from their original home in northern Asia, and thus led to their invasion of Bithynia under Othman, and finally their advance into Europe under Amurath I.

See Sir H. H. Howorth, *The History of the Mongols*; Sir Robert K. Douglas, *The Life of Jenghiz Khan*.

(R. K. D.)

JENKIN, HENRY CHARLES FLEEMING (1833-1885), British engineer, was born near Dungeness on the 25th of March 1833, his father (d. 1885) being a naval commander, and his mother (d. 1885) a novelist of some literary repute, her best books perhaps being *Cousin Stella* (1859) and *Who breaks, pays* (1861). Fleeming Jenkin was educated at first in Scotland, but in 1846 the family went to live abroad, owing to financial straits, and he studied at Genoa University, where he took a first-class degree in physical science. In 1851 he began his engineering career as apprentice in an establishment at Manchester, and subsequently he entered Newall's submarine cable works at Birkenhead. In 1859 he began, in concert with Sir William Thomson (afterwards Lord Kelvin), to work on problems respecting the making and use of cables, and the importance of his researches on the resistance of gutta-percha was at once recognized. From this time he was in constant request in connexion with submarine telegraphy, and he became known also as an inventor. In partnership with Thomson, he made a large income as a consulting telegraph engineer. In 1865 he was elected F.R.S., and was appointed professor of engineering at University College, London. In 1868 he obtained the same professorship at Edinburgh University, and in 1873 he published a textbook of *Magnetism and Electricity*, full of original work. He was author of the article "Bridges" in the ninth edition of this encyclopaedia. His influence among the Edinburgh students was pronounced, and R. L. Stevenson's well-known *Memoir* is a sympathetic tribute to his ability and character. The meteoric charm of his conversation is well described in Stevenson's essay on "Talk and Talkers," under the name of Cockshot. Jenkin's interests were by no means confined to engineering, but extended to the arts and literature; his miscellaneous papers, showing his critical and unconventional views, were issued posthumously in two volumes (1887). In 1882 Jenkin invented an automatic method of electric transport for goods—"telpherage"—but the completion of its details was prevented by his death on the 12th of June 1885. A telpher line on his system was subsequently erected at Glynde in Sussex. He was also well known as a sanitary reformer, and during the last ten years of his life he did much useful work in inculcating more enlightened ideas on the subject both in Edinburgh and other places.

JENKINS, SIR LEOLINE (1623-1685), English lawyer and diplomatist, was the son of a Welsh country gentleman. He was born in 1623 and was educated at Jesus College, Oxford, of which he was elected a fellow at the Restoration in 1660, having been an ardent royalist during the civil war and commonwealth; and in 1661 he became head of the college. In the same year he was made registrar of the consistory court of Westminster; in 1664 deputy judge of the court of arches; about a year later judge of the admiralty court; in 1689 judge of the prerogative court of Canterbury. In these offices Jenkins did enduring work in elucidating and establishing legal principles, especially in relation to international law and admiralty jurisdiction. He was selected to draw up the claim of Charles II. to succeed to the property of his mother, Henrietta Maria, on her death in August 1666, and while in Paris for this purpose he succeeded in defeating the rival claim of the duchess of Orleans, being rewarded by a knighthood on his return. In 1673, on being elected member for Hythe, Jenkins resigned the headship of Jesus College. He was one of the English representatives at the congress of Cologne in 1673, and at the more important congress of Nijmwegen in 1676-1679. He was made a privy councillor in February 1680 and became secretary of state in April of the same year, in which office he was the official leader of the opposition to the Exclusion Bill, though he was by no means a pliant tool in the hands of the court. He resigned office in 1684, and died on the 1st of September 1685. He left most of his property to Jesus College, Oxford, including his books, which he bequeathed to the college library, built by himself; and he left some important manuscripts to All Souls College, where they are preserved. Jenkins left his impress on the law of England in the Statute of Frauds, and the Statute of Distributions, of which he was the principal author, and of which the former profoundly affected the mercantile law of the country, while the latter regulated the inheritance of the personal property of intestates. He was never married.

See William Wynne, *Life of Sir Leoline Jenkins* (2 vols., London, 1724), which contains a number of his diplomatic despatches, letters, speeches and other papers. See also Sir William Temple, *Works*, vol. ii. (4 vols., 1770); Anthony à Wood, *Athenae Oxonienses* (Fasti) edited by P. Bliss (4 vols., London, 1813-1820), and *History and Antiquities of the University of Oxford*, edited by J. Gutch (Oxford, 1792-1796).

JENKINS, ROBERT (*fl.* 1731-1745), English master mariner, is known as the protagonist of the "Jenkins's ear" incident, which, magnified in England by the press and the opposition, became a contributory cause of the war between England and Spain (1739). Bringing home the brig "Rebecca" from the West Indies in 1731, Jenkins was boarded by a Spanish guarda-costa, whose commander rifled the holds and cut off one of his ears. On arriving in England Jenkins stated his grievance to the king, and a report was furnished by the commander-in-chief in the West Indies confirming his account. At first the case created no great stir, but in 1738 he repeated his story with dramatic detail before a committee of the House of Commons, producing what purported to be the ear that had been cut off. Afterwards it was suggested that he might have lost the ear in the pillory.

Jenkins was subsequently given the command of a ship in the East India Company's service, and later became supervisor of the company's affairs at St Helena. In 1741 he was sent from England to that island to investigate charges of corruption brought against the acting governor, and from May 1741 until March 1742 he administered the affairs of the island. Thereafter he resumed his naval career, and is stated in an action with a pirate vessel to have preserved his own vessel and three others under his care (see T. H. Brooke, *History of the Island of St Helena* (London, 2nd ed., 1824), and H. R. Janisch, *Extracts from the St Helena Records*, 1885).

JENKS, JEREMIAH WHIPPLE (1856-   ), American economist, was born in St Clair, Michigan, on the 2nd of September 1856. He graduated at the university of Michigan in 1878; taught Greek, Latin and German in Mt. Morris College, Illinois; studied in Germany, receiving the degree of Ph.D. from the university of Halle in 1885; taught political science and English literature at Knox College, Galesburg, Ill., in 1886-1889; was professor of political economy and social science at Indiana State University in 1889-1891; and was successively professor of political, municipal and social institutions (1891-1892), professor of political economy and civil and social institutions (1892-1901), and after 1901 professor of political economy and politics at Cornell University. In 1899-1901 he served as an expert agent of the United States industrial commission on investigation of trusts and industrial combinations in the United States and Europe, and contributed to vols. i., viii. and xiii. of this commission's report (1900 and 1901), vol. viii. being a report, written wholly by him, on industrial combinations in Europe. In 1901-1902 he was special commissioner of the United States war department on colonial administration, and wrote a *Report on Certain Economic Questions in the English and Dutch Colonies in the Orient*, published (1902) by the bureau of insular affairs; and in 1903 he was adviser to the Mexican ministry of finance on projected currency changes. In 1903-1904 he was a member of the United States commission on international exchange, in especial charge of the reform of currency in China; in 1905 he was special representative of the United States with the imperial Chinese special mission visiting the United States. In 1907 he became a member of the United States immigration commission. Best known as an expert on "trusts," he has written besides on elections, ballot reform, proportional representation, on education (especially as a training for citizenship), on legislation regarding highways, &c.

319

His principal published works are *Henry C. Carey als Nationalökonom* (Halle a. S., 1885); *The Trust Problem*(1900; revised 1903); *Great Fortunes* (1906); *Citizenship and the Schools* (1906); and *Principles of Politics* (1909).

JENNÉ, a city of West Africa, formerly the capital of the Songhoi empire, now included in the French colony of Upper Senegal and Niger. Jenné is situated on a marigot or natural canal connecting the Niger and its affluent the Bani or Mahel Balevel, and is within a few miles of the latter stream. It lies 250 m. S.W. of Timbuktu in a straight line. The city is surrounded by channels connected with the Bani but in the dry season it ceases to be an island. On the north is the Moorish quarter; on the north-west, the oldest part of the city, stood the citadel, converted by the French since 1893 into a modern fort. The market-place is midway between the fort and the commercial harbour. The old mosque, partially destroyed in 1830, covered a large area in the south-west portion of the city. It was built on the site of the ancient palace of the Songhoi kings. The architecture of many of the buildings bears a resemblance to Egyptian, the façades of the houses being adorned with great buttresses of pylonic form. There is little trace of the influence of Moorish or Arabian art. The buildings are mostly constructed of clay made into flat long bricks. Massive clay walls surround the city. The inhabitants are great traders and the principal merchants have representatives at Timbuktu and all the chief places on the Niger. The boats built at Jenné are famous throughout the western Sudan.

Jenné is believed to have been founded by the Songhoi in the 8th century, and though it has passed under the dominion of many races it has never been destroyed. Jenné seems to have been at the height of its power from the 12th to the 16th century, when its merchandise was found at every port along the west coast of Africa. From this circumstance it is conjectured that Jenné (Guinea) gave its name to the whole coast (see GUINEA). Subsequently, under the control of Moorish, Tuareg and Fula invaders, the importance of the city greatly declined. With the advent of the French, commerce again began to flourish.

See F. Dubois, *Tombouctou la mystérieuse* (Paris, 1897), in which several chapters are devoted to Jenné; alsoSONGHOI; TIMBUKTU; and SENEGAL.

JENNER, EDWARD (1749-1823), English physician and discoverer of vaccination, was born at Berkeley, Gloucestershire, on the 17th of May 1749. His father, the Rev. Stephen Jenner, rector of Rockhampton and vicar of Berkeley, came of a family that had been long established in that county, and was possessed of considerable landed property; he died when Edward was only six years old, but his eldest son, the Rev. Stephen Jenner, brought his brother up with paternal care and tenderness. Edward received his early education at Wotton-under-Edge and Cirencester, where he already showed a strong taste for natural history. The medical profession having been selected for him, he began his studies under Daniel Ludlow, a surgeon of Sodbury near Bristol; but in his twenty-first year he proceeded to London, where he became a favourite pupil of John Hunter, in whose house he resided for two years. During this period he was employed by Sir

Joseph Banks to arrange and prepare the valuable zoological specimens which he had brought back from Captain Cook's first voyage in 1771. He must have acquitted himself satisfactorily in this task, since he was offered the post of naturalist in the second expedition, but declined it as well as other advantageous offers, preferring rather to practise his profession in his native place, and near his eldest brother, to whom he was much attached. He was the principal founder of a local medical society, to which he contributed several papers of marked ability, in one of which he apparently anticipated later discoveries concerning rheumatic inflammations of the heart. He maintained a correspondence with John Hunter, under whose direction he investigated various points in biology, particularly the hibernation of hedgehogs and habits of the cuckoo; his paper on the latter subject was laid by Hunter before the Royal Society, and appeared in the *Phil. Trans.* for 1788. He also devoted considerable attention to the varied geological character of the district in which he lived, and constructed the first balloon seen in those parts. He was a great favourite in general society, from his agreeable and instructive conversation, and the many accomplishments he possessed. Thus he was a fair musician, both as a part singer and as a performer on the violin and flute, and a very successful writer, after the fashion of that time, of fugitive pieces of verse. In 1788 he married Catherine Kingscote, and in 1792 he obtained the degree of doctor of medicine from St Andrews.

Meanwhile the discovery that is associated with his name had been slowly maturing in his mind. When only an apprentice at Sodbury, his attention had been directed to the relations between cow-pox and small-pox in connexion with a popular belief which he found current in Gloucestershire, as to the antagonism between these two diseases. During his stay in London he appears to have mentioned the thing repeatedly to Hunter, who, being engrossed by other important pursuits, was not so strongly persuaded as Jenner was of its possible importance, yet spoke of it to his friends and in his lectures. After he began practice in Berkeley, Jenner was always accustomed to inquire what his professional brethren thought of it; but he found that, when medical men had noticed the popular report at all, they supposed it to be based on imperfect induction. His first careful investigation of the subject dated from about 1775, and five years elapsed before he had succeeded in clearing away the most perplexing difficulties by which it was surrounded. He first satisfied himself that two different forms of disease had been hitherto confounded under the term cow-pox, only one of which protected against small-pox, and that many of the cases of failure were to be thus accounted for; and his next step was to ascertain that the true cow-pox itself only protects when communicated at a particular stage of the disease. At the same time he came to the conclusion that "the grease" of horses is the same disease as cow-pox and small-pox, each being modified by the organism in which it was developed. For many years, cow-pox being scarce in his county, he had no opportunity of inoculating the disease, and so putting his discovery to the test, but he did all he could in the way of collecting information and communicating what he had ascertained. Thus in 1788 he carried a drawing of the cow-pox, as seen on the hands of a milkmaid, to London, and showed it to Sir E. Home and others, who agreed that it was "an interesting and curious subject." At length, on the 14th of May 1796, he was able to inoculate James Phipps, a boy about eight years old, with matter from cow-pox vesicles on the hand of Sarah Nelmes. On the 1st of the following July the boy was carefully inoculated with variolous matter, but (as Jenner had predicted) no small-pox followed. The discovery was now complete, but Jenner was unable to repeat his experiment until 1798, owing to the disappearance of cow-pox from the dairies. He then repeated his inoculations with the utmost care, and prepared a pamphlet (*Inquiry into the Cause and Effects of the Variolae Vaccinae*) which should announce his discovery to the world. Before publishing it, however, he thought it well to visit London, so as to demonstrate the truth of his assertions to his friends; but he remained in London nearly three months, without being able to find any person who would submit to be vaccinated. Soon after he had returned home, however, Henry Cline, surgeon of St Thomas's Hospital, inoculated some vaccine matter obtained from him over the diseased hip-joint of a child, thinking the counter-irritation might be useful, and found the patient afterwards incapable of acquiring small-pox. In the autumn of the same year, Jenner met with the first opposition to vaccination; and this was the more formidable because it proceeded from J. Ingenhousz, a celebrated physician and man of science. But meanwhile Cline's advocacy of vaccination brought it much more decidedly before the medical profession, of whom the majority were prudent enough to suspend their judgment until they had more ample information. But besides these there were two noisy and troublesome factions, one of which opposed vaccination as a useless and dangerous practice, while the other endangered its success much more by rash and self-seeking advocacy. At the head of the latter was George Pearson, 320who in November 1798 published a pamphlet speculating upon the subject, before even seeing a case of cow-pox, and afterwards endeavoured, by lecturing on the subject and supplying the virus, to put himself forward as the chief agent in the cause. The matter which he distributed, which had been derived from cows that were found to be infected in London, was found frequently to produce, not the slight disease described by Jenner, but more or less severe eruptions resembling small-pox. Jenner concluded at once that this was due to an accidental contamination of the vaccine with variolous matter, and a visit to London in the spring of 1799 convinced him that this was the case. In the course of this year the practice of vaccination spread over England, being urged principally by non-professional persons of position; and towards its close attempts were made to found institutions for gratuitous vaccination and for supplying lymph to all who might apply for it. Pearson proposed to establish one of these in London, without Jenner's knowledge, in which he offered him the post of honorary corresponding physician! On learning of this scheme to supplant him, and to carry on an institution for public vaccination on principles which he knew to be partly erroneous, Jenner once more visited London early in 1800, when he had influence enough to secure the abandonment of the project. He was afterwards presented to the king, the queen and the prince of Wales, whose encouragement materially aided the spread of vaccination in England. Meanwhile it had made rapid progress in the United States, where it was introduced by Benjamin Waterhouse, then professor of physic at Harvard, and on the continent of Europe, where it was at first diffused by De Carro of Vienna. In consequence of the war between England and France, the discovery was later in reaching Paris; but, its importance once realized, it spread rapidly over France, Spain and Italy.

A few of the incidents connected with its extension may be mentioned. Perhaps the most striking is the expedition which was sent out by the court of Spain in 1803, for the purpose of diffusing cow-pox through all the Spanish possessions in the Old and New Worlds, and which returned in three years, having circumnavigated the globe, and succeeded beyond its utmost expectations. Clergymen in Geneva and Holland urged vaccination upon their parishioners from the pulpit; in Sicily, South America and Naples religious processions were formed for the purpose of receiving it; the anniversary of Jenner's birthday, or of the successful vaccination of James Phipps, was for many years celebrated as a feast in Germany; and the empress of Russia caused the first child operated upon to receive the name of Vaccinov, and to be educated at the public expense. About the close of the year 1801 Jenner's friends in Gloucestershire presented him with a small service of plate as a testimonial of the esteem in which they held his discovery. This was intended merely as a preliminary to the presenting of a petition to parliament for a grant. The petition was presented in 1802, and was referred to a committee, of which the investigations resulted in a report in favour of the grant, and ultimately in a vote of £10,000.

Towards the end of 1802 steps were taken to form a society for the proper spread of vaccination in London, and the Royal Jennerian Society was finally established, Jenner returning to town to preside at the first meeting. This institution began very prosperously, more than twelve thousand persons having been inoculated in the first eighteen months, and with such effect that the deaths from small-pox, which for the latter half of the 18th century had averaged 2018 annually, fell in 1804 to 622. Unfortunately the chief resident inoculator soon set himself up as an authority opposed to Jenner, and this led to such dissensions as caused the society to die out in 1808.

Jenner was led, by the language of the chancellor of the exchequer when his grant was proposed, to attempt practice in London, but after a year's trial he returned to Berkeley. His grant was not paid until 1804, and then, after the deduction of about £1000 for fees, it did little more than pay the expenses attendant upon his discovery. For he was so thoroughly known everywhere as the discoverer of vaccination that, as he himself said, he was "the vaccine clerk of the whole world." At the same time he continued to vaccinate gratuitously all the poor who applied to him on certain days, so that he sometimes had as many as three hundred persons waiting at his door. Meanwhile honours began to shower upon him from abroad: he was elected a member of almost all the chief scientific societies on the continent of Europe, the first being that of Göttingen, where he was proposed by J. F. Blumenbach. But perhaps the most flattering proof of his influence was derived from France. On one occasion, when he was endeavouring to obtain the release of some of the unfortunate Englishmen who had been detained in France on the sudden termination of the Peace of Amiens, Napoleon was about to reject the petition, when Josephine uttered the name of Jenner. The emperor paused and exclaimed: "Ah, we can refuse nothing to that name." Somewhat later he did the same service to Englishmen confined in Mexico and in Austria; and during the latter part of the great war persons before leaving England would sometimes obtain certificates signed by him which served as passports. In his own country his merits were less recognized. His applications on behalf of French prisoners in England were less successful; he never shared in any of the patronage at the disposal of the government, and was even unable to obtain a living for his nephew George.

In 1806 Lord Henry Petty (afterwards the marquess of Lansdowne) became chancellor of the exchequer, and was so convinced of the inadequacy of the former parliamentary grant that he proposed an address to the Crown, praying that the college of physicians should be directed to report upon the success of vaccination. Their report being strongly in its favour, the then chancellor of the exchequer (Spencer Perceval) proposed that a sum of £10,000 without any deductions should be paid to Jenner. The anti-vaccinationists found but one advocate in the House of Commons; and finally the sum was raised to £20,000. Jenner, however, at the same time had the mortification of learning that government did not intend to take any steps towards checking small-pox inoculation, which so persistently kept up that disease. About the same time a subscription for his benefit was begun in India, where his discovery had been gratefully received, but the full amount of this (£7383) only reached him in 1812.

The Royal Jennerian Society having failed, the national vaccine establishment was founded, for the extension of vaccination, in 1808. Jenner spent five months in London for the purpose of organizing it, but was then obliged, by the dangerous illness of one of his sons, to return to Berkeley. He had been appointed director of the institution; but he had no sooner left London than Sir Lucas Pepys, president of the college of physicians, neglected his recommendations, and formed the board out of the officials of that college and the college of surgeons. Jenner at once resigned his post as director, though he continued to give the benefit of his advice whenever it was needed, and this resignation was a bitter mortification to him. In 1810 his eldest son died, and Jenner's grief at his loss, and his incessant labours, materially affected his health. In 1813 the university of Oxford conferred on him the degree of M.D. It was believed that this would lead to his election into the college of physicians, but that learned body decided that he could not be admitted until he had undergone an examination in classics. This Jenner at once refused; to brush up his classics would, he said, "be irksome beyond measure. I would not do it for a diadem. That indeed would be a bauble; I would not do it for John Hunter's museum."

He visited London for the last time in 1814, when he was presented to the Allied Sovereigns and to most of the principal personages who accompanied them. In the next year his wife's death was the signal for him to retire from public life: he never left Berkeley again, except for a day or two, as long as he lived. He found sufficient occupation for the remainder of his life in collecting further evidence on some points connected with his great discovery, and in his engagements as a physician, a naturalist and a magistrate. In 1818 a severe epidemic of small-pox prevailed, and fresh doubts were thrown on the 321efficacy of vaccination, in part apparently owing to the bad quality of the vaccine lymph employed. This caused Jenner much annoyance, which was relieved by an able defence of the practice, written by Sir Gilbert Blane. But this led him, in 1821, to send a circular letter to most of the medical men in the kingdom inquiring into the effect of other skin diseases in modifying the progress of cow-pox. A year later he published his last work, *On the Influence of Artificial Eruptions in Certain Diseases*; and in 1823 he presented his last paper—"On the Migration of Birds"—to the Royal Society. On the 24th of January 1823 he retired to rest apparently as well as usual, and next morning rose and came down to his library, where he was found insensible on the floor, in a state of apoplexy, and with the right side paralysed. He never rallied, and died on the following morning.

A public subscription was set on foot, shortly after his death, by the medical men of his county, for the purpose of erecting some memorial in his honour, and with much difficulty a sufficient sum was raised to enable a statue to be placed in Gloucester Cathedral. In 1850 another attempt was made to set up a monument to him; this appears to have failed, but at length, in 1858, a statue of him was erected by public subscription in London.

Jenner's life was written by the intimate friend of his later years, Dr John Baron of Gloucester (2 vols., 1827, 1838). See also Vaccination.

JENNER, SIR WILLIAM, BART. (1815-1898), English physician, was born at Chatham on the 30th of January 1815, and educated at University College, London. He became M.R.C.S. in 1837, and F.R.C.P. in 1852, and in 1844 took the London M.D. In 1847 he began at the London fever hospital investigations into cases of "continued" fever which enabled him finally to make the distinction between typhus and typhoid on which his reputation as a pathologist principally rests. In 1849 he was appointed professor of pathological anatomy at University College, and also assistant physician to University College Hospital, where he afterwards became physician (1854-1876) and consulting physician (1879), besides holding similar appointments at other hospitals. He was also successively Holme professor of clinical medicine and professor of the principles and practice of medicine at University College. He was president of the college of physicians (1881-1888); he was elected F.R.S. in 1864, and received honorary degrees from Oxford, Cambridge and Edinburgh. In 1861 he was appointed physician extraordinary, and in 1862 physician in ordinary, to Queen Victoria, and in 1863 physician in ordinary to the prince of Wales; he attended both the prince consort and the prince of Wales in their attacks of typhoid fever. In 1868 he was created a baronet. As a consultant Sir William Jenner had a great reputation, and he left a large fortune when he died, at Bishop's Waltham, Hants, on the 11th of December 1898, having then retired from practice for eight years owing to failing health.

JENNET, a small Spanish horse; the word is sometimes applied in English to a mule, the offspring of a she-ass and a stallion. Jennet comes, through Fr. *genet*, from Span, *jinete*, a light horseman who rides *à la gineta*, explained as "with his legs tucked up." The name is taken to be a corruption of the Arabic Zenāta, a Berber tribe famed for its cavalry. English and French transferred the word from the rider to his horse, a meaning which the word has only acquired in Spain in modern times.

JENOLAN CAVES, a series of remarkable caverns in Roxburgh county, New South Wales, Australia; 113 m. W. by N. of Sydney, and 36 m. from Tarana, which is served by railway. They are the most celebrated of several similar groups in the limestone of the country; they have not yielded fossils of great interest, but the stalactitic formations, sometimes pure white, are of extraordinary beauty. The caves have been rendered easily accessible to visitors and lighted by electricity.

JENSEN, WILHELM (1837-   ), German author, was born at Heiligenhafen in Holstein on the 15th of February 1837, the son of a local Danish magistrate, who came of old patrician Frisian stock. After attending the classical schools at Kiel and Lübeck, Jensen studied medicine at the universities of Kiel, Würzburg and Breslau. He, however, abandoned the medical profession for that of letters, and after engaging for some years in individual private study proceeded to Munich, where he associated with men of letters. After a residence in Stuttgart (1865-1869), where for a short time he conducted the *Schwäbische Volks-Zeitung*, he became editor in Flensburg of the *Norddeutsche Zeitung*. In 1872 he again returned to Kiel, lived from 1876 to 1888 in Freiburg im Breisgau, and since 1888 has been resident in Munich.

Jensen is perhaps the most fertile of modern German writers of fiction, more than one hundred works having proceeded from his pen; but only comparatively few of them have caught the public taste; such are the novels, *Karin von Schweden* (Berlin, 1878); *Die braune Erica* (Berlin, 1868); and the tale, *Die Pfeifer von Dusenbach, Eine Geschichte aus dem Elsass* (1884). Among others may be mentioned: *Barthenia* (Berlin, 1877); *Götz und Gisela* (Berlin, 1886); *Heimkunft* (Dresden, 1894); *Aus See und Sand* (Dresden, 1897); *Luv und Lee* (Berlin, 1897); and the narratives, *Aus den Tagen der Hansa* (Leipzig, 1885); *Aus stiller Zeit* (Berlin, 1881-1885); and *Heimath* (1901). Jensen also published some tragedies, among which *Dido* (Berlin, 1870) and *Der Kampf für's Reich* (Freiburg im Br., 1884) may be mentioned.

JENYNS, SOAME (1704-1787), English author, was born in London on the 1st of January 1704, and was educated at St John's College, Cambridge. In 1742 he was chosen M.P. for Cambridgeshire, in which his property lay, and he afterwards sat for the borough of Dunwich and the town of Cambridge. From 1755 to 1780 he was one of the commissioners of the board of trade. He died on the 18th of December 1787.

For the measure of literary repute which he enjoyed during his life Jenyns was indebted as much to his wealth and social standing as to his accomplishments and talents, though both were considerable. His poetical works, the *Art of Dancing* (1727) and *Miscellanies* (1770), contain many passages graceful and lively though occasionally verging on licence. The first of his prose works was his *Free Inquiry into the Nature and Origin of Evil* (1756). This essay was severely criticized on its appearance, especially by Samuel Johnson in the *Literary Magazine*. Johnson, in a slashing review—the best paper of the kind he ever wrote—condemned the book as a slight and shallow attempt to solve one of the most difficult of moral problems. Jenyns, a gentle and amiable man in the main, was extremely irritated by his failure. He put forth a second edition of his work, prefaced by a vindication, and tried to take vengeance on Johnson after his death by a sarcastic epitaph.[1] In 1776 Jenyns published his *View of the Internal Evidence of the Christian Religion*. Though at one period of his life he had affected a kind of deistic scepticism, he had now returned to orthodoxy, and there seems no reason to doubt his sincerity, questioned at the time, in defending Christianity on the ground of its total variance with the principles of human reason. The work was deservedly praised in its day for its literary merits, but is so plainly the production of an amateur in theology that as a scientific treatise it is valueless.

A collected edition of the works of Jenyns appeared in 1790, with a biography by Charles Nalson Cole. There are several references to him in Boswell's *Johnson*.

1Two lines will suffice:—

Boswell and Thrale, retailers of his wit,
Will tell you how he wrote, and talk'd, and cough'd, and
spit.

JEOPARDY, a term meaning risk or danger of death, loss or other injury. The word, in Mid. Eng. *juparti, jeupartie*, &c., was adapted from O. Fr. *ju*, later *jeu*, and *parti*, even game, in medieval Latin *jocus partitus*. This term was originally used of a problem in chess or of a stage in any other game at which the chances of success or failure are evenly divided between the players. It was thus early transformed to any state of uncertainty.

JEPHSON, ROBERT (1736-1803), British dramatist, was born in Ireland. After serving for some years in the British army, he retired with the rank of captain, and lived in England, where he was the friend of Garrick, Reynolds, Goldsmith, Johnson, Burke, Burney and Charles Townshend. His appointment as master of the horse to the lord-lieutenant of Ireland 322took him back to Dublin. He published, in the *Mercury*newspaper a series of articles in defence of the lord-lieutenant's administration which were afterwards collected and issued in book form under the title of *The Bachelor, or Speculations of Jeoffry Wagstaffe*. A pension of £300, afterwards doubled, was granted him, and he held his appointment under twelve succeeding viceroys. From 1775 he was engaged in the writing of plays. Among others, his tragedy *Braganza* was successfully performed at Drury Lane in 1775, *Conspiracy* in 1796, *The Law of Lombardy* in 1779, and *The Count of Narbonne* at Covent Garden in 1781. In 1794 he published an heroic poem*Roman Portraits*, and *The Confessions of Jacques Baptiste Couteau*, a satire on the excesses of the French Revolution. He died at Blackrock, near Dublin, on the 31st of May 1803.

JEPHTHAH, one of the judges of Israel, in the Bible, was an illegitimate son of Gilead, and, being expelled from his father's house by his lawful brethren, took refuge in the Syrian land of Tob, where he gathered around him a powerful band of homeless men like himself. The Ammonites pressing hard on his countrymen, the elders of Gilead called for his help, which he consented to give on condition that in the event of victory he should be made their head (Judg. xi. 1-xii. 7). His name is best known in history and literature in connexion with his vow, which led to the sacrifice of his daughter on his successful return. The reluctance shown by many writers in accepting the plain sense of the narrative on this point proceeds to a large extent on unwarranted assumptions as to the stage of ethical development which had been reached in Israel in the period of the judges, or at the time when the narrative took shape. The annual lamentation of the women for her death suggests a mythical origin (see Adonis). Attached to the narrative is an account of a quarrel between Jephthah and the Ephraimites. The latter were defeated, and their retreat was cut off by the Gileadites, who had seized the fords of the Jordan. As the fugitives attempted to cross they were bidden to say "shibbōleth" ("flood" or "ear of corn"), and those who said "sibbōleth" (the Ephraimites apparently being unused to *sh*), were at once put to death. In this way 42,000 of the tribe were killed.1
The loose connexion between this and the main narrative, as also the lengthy speech to the children of Ammon (xi. 14-27), which really relates to Moab, has led some writers to infer that two distinct heroes and situations have been combined. See further the commentaries on the Book of Judges (*q.v.*), and Cheyne, *Ency. Bib.*, art. "Jephthah."

(S. A. C.)

1Similarly a Syrian story tells how the Druses came to slay Ibrahim Pasha's troops, and desiring to spare the Syrians ordered the men to say *gamal* (camel). As the Syrians pronounce the *g* soft, and the Egyptians the *g*, hard, the former were easily identified. Other examples from the East will be found in H. C. Kay, *Yaman*, p. 36, and in S. Lane-Poole, *History of Egypt in the Middle Ages*, p. 300. Also, at the Sicilian Vespers (March 13, 1282) the French were made to betray themselves by their pronunciation of *ceci*and *ciceri* (Ital. *c* like *tch*; Fr. *c* like *s*).

JERAHMEEL, (Heb. "May God pity"), in the Bible, a clan which with Caleb, the Kenites and others, occupied the southern steppes of Palestine, probably in the district around Arad, about 17 m. S. of Hebron. It was on friendly terms with David during his residence at Ziklag (1 Sam. xxx. 29), and it was apparently in his reign that the various elements of the south were united and were reckoned to Israel. This is expressed in the chronicler's genealogies which make Jerahmeel and Caleb descendants of Judah (see DAVID; JUDAH).
On the names in 1 Chron. ii. see S. A. Cook, *Ency. Bib.*, col. 2363 seq. Peleth (*v.* 33) may be the origin of the Pelethites (2 Sam. viii. 18; xv. 18; xx. 7), and since the name occurs in the revolt

of Korah (Num. xvi. 1), it is possible that Jerahmeel, like Caleb and the Kenites, had moved northwards from Kadesh. Samuel (*q.v.*) was of Jerahmeel (1 Sam. i. 1; Septuagint), and the consecutive Jerahmeelite names Nathan and Zabad (1 Chron. ii. 36) have been associated with the prophet and officer (Zabud, 1 Kings iv. 5) of the times of David and Solomon respectively. The association of Samuel and Nathan with this clan, if correct, is a further illustration of the importance of the south for the growth of biblical history (see KENITESand RECHABITES). The *Chronicles of Jerahmeel* (M. Gaster,*Oriental Translation Fund*, 1899) is a late production containing a number of apocryphal Jewish legends of no historical value.

(S. A. C.)

JERBA, an island off the coast of North Africa in the Gulf of Gabes, forming part of the regency of Tunisia. It is separated from the mainland by two narrow straits, and save for these channels blocks the entrance to a large bight identified with the Lake Triton of the Romans. The western strait, opening into the Gulf of Gabes, is a mile and a half broad; the eastern strait is wider, but at low water it is possible to cross to the mainland by the Tarik-el-Jemil (road of the camel). The island is irregular in outline, its greatest length and breadth being some 20 m., and its area 425 sq. m. It contains neither rivers nor springs, but is supplied with water by wells and cisterns. It is flat and well wooded with date palms and olive trees. Pop. 35,000 to 40,000, the bulk of the inhabitants being Berbers. Though many of them have adopted Arabic a Berber idiom is commonly spoken. An affinity exists between the Berbers of Jerba and the Beni Mzab. About 3000 Jews live apart in villages of their own, and some 400 Europeans, chiefly Maltese and Greeks, are settled in the island. Jerba has a considerable reputation for the manufacture of the woollen tissues interwoven with silk which are known as burnous stuffs; a market for the sale of sponges is held from November till March; and there is a considerable export trade in olives, dates, figs and other fruits. The capital, trading centre and usual landing-place are at Haumt-es-Suk (market quarter) on the north side of the island (pop. 2500). Here are a medieval fort, built by the Spaniards in 1284, and a modern fort, garrisoned by the French. Gallala, to the south, is noted for the manufacture of a kind of white pottery, much prized. At El Kantara (the bridge) on the eastern strait, and formerly connected with the mainland by a causeway, are extensive ruins of a Roman city—probably those of Meninx, once a flourishing seaport.

Jerba is the Lotophagitis or Lotus-eaters' Island of the Greek and Roman geographers, and is also identified with the Brachion of Scylax. The modern name appears as early as the 4th century in Sextus Aurelius Victor. In the middle ages the possession of Jerba was contested by the Normans of Sicily, the Spaniards and the Turks, the Turks proving victorious. In 1560 after the destruction of the Spanish fleet off the coast of the island by Piali Pasha and the corsair Dragut the Spanish garrison at Haumt-es-Suk was exterminated, and a pyramid, 10 ft. broad at the base and 20 ft. high, was built of their skulls and other bones. In 1848 this pyramid was pulled down at the instance of the Christian community, and the bones were buried in the Catholic cemetery. In general, from the Arab invasion in the 7th century Jerba shared the fortunes of Tunisia.

See H. Barth, *Wanderungen durch die Küstenl. des Mittelmeeres* (Berlin, 1849); and H. von Maltzan, *Reise in Tunis und Tripolis* (Leipzig, 1870).

JERBOA, properly the name of an Arabian and North African jumping rodent mammal, *Jaculus aegyptius* (also known as *Jaculus*, or *Dipus, jaculus*) typifying the family*Jaculidae* (or *Dipodidae*), but in a wider sense applied to most of the representatives of that family, which are widely distributed over the desert and semi-desert tracts of the Old World, although unknown in Africa south of the Sahara. In all the more typical members of the family the three middle metatarsals of the long hind-legs are fused into a cannon-bone; and in the true jerboas of the genus *Jaculus* the two lateral toes, with their supporting metatarsals, are lost, although they are present in the alactagas (*Alactaga*), in which, however, as in certain allied genera, only the three middle toes are functional. As regards the true jerboas, there is a curious resemblance in the structure of their hind-legs to that obtaining among birds. In both groups, for instance, the lower part of the hind-leg is formed by a long, slender cannon-bone, or metatarsus, terminating inferiorly in triple condyles for the three long and sharply clawed toes, the resemblance being increased by the fact that in both cases the small bone of the leg (fibula) is fused with the large one (tibia). It may also be noticed that in mammals and birds which hop on two legs, such as jerboas, kangaroos, thrushes and 323finches, the proportionate length of the thigh-bone or femur to the tibia and foot (metatarsus and toes) is constant, being 2 to 5; in animals, on the other hand, such as hares, horses and frogs, which use all four feet, the corresponding lengths are 4 to 7. The resemblance between the jerboa's and the bird's skeleton is owing to adaptation to a similar mode of existence. In the young jerboa the proportion of the femur to the rest of the leg is the same as in ordinary running animals. Further, at an early stage of development the fibula is a complete and separate bone, while the three metatarsals, which subsequently fuse together to form the cannon-bone, are likewise separate. In addition to their long hind and short fore limbs, jerboas are mostly characterized by their silky coats—of a fawn colour to harmonize with their desert surroundings—their large eyes, and long tails and ears. As is always the case with large-eared animals, the tympanic bullae of the skull are of unusually large size; the size varying in the different genera according to that of the ears. (For the characteristics of the family and of its more important generic representatives, see RODENTIA.)

In the Egyptian jerboa the length of the body is 8 in., and that of the tail, which is long, cylindrical and covered with short hair terminated by a tuft, 10 in. The five-toed front limbs are extremely short, while the hind pair are six times as long. When about to spring, this jerboa raises its body by means of the hinder extremities, and supports itself at the same time upon its tail, while the fore-feet are so closely pressed to the breast as to be scarcely visible, which doubtless suggested the name *Dipus*, or two-footed. It then leaps into the air and alights upon its four feet, but instantaneously erecting itself, it makes another spring, and so on in such rapid succession as to appear as if rather flying than running. It is a gregarious animal, living in considerable colonies in burrows, which it excavates with its nails and teeth in the sandy soil of Egypt and Arabia. In these it remains during great part of the day, emerging at night in search of the herbs on which it feeds. It is exceedingly shy, and this, together with its extraordinary agility, renders it difficult to capture. The Arabs, however, succeed by closing up all the exits from the burrows with a single exception, by which the rodents are forced to escape, and over which a net is placed for their capture. When confined, they will gnaw through the hardest wood in order to make their escape. The Persian jerboa (*Alactaga indica*) is also a nocturnal burrowing animal, feeding chiefly on grain, which it stores up in underground repositories, closing these when full, and only drawing upon them when the supply of food above ground is exhausted (see also JUMPING MOUSE).

(R. L.*)

JERDAN, WILLIAM (1782-1869), Scottish journalist, was born on the 16th of April 1782, at Kelso, Scotland. During the years between 1799 and 1806 he spent short periods in a country lawyer's office, a London West India merchant's counting-house, an Edinburgh solicitor's chambers, and held the position of surgeon's mate on board H.M. guardship "Gladiator" in Portsmouth Harbour, under his uncle, who was surgeon. He went to London in 1806, and became a newspaper reporter. He was in the lobby of the House of Commons on the 11th of May 1812 when Spencer Perceval was shot, and was the first to seize the assassin. By 1812 he had become editor of *The Sun*, a semi-official Tory paper; he occasionally inserted literary articles, then quite an unusual proceeding; but a quarrel with the chief proprietor brought that engagement to a close in 1817. He passed next to the editor's chair of the *Literary Gazette*, which he conducted with success for thirty-four years. Jerdan's position as editor brought him into contact with many distinguished writers. An account of his friends, among whom Canning was a special intimate, is to be found in his *Men I have Known* (1866). When Jerdan retired in 1850 from the editorship of the *Literary Gazette* his pecuniary affairs were far from satisfactory. A testimonial of over £900 was subscribed by his friends; and in 1853 a government pension of 100 guineas was conferred on him by Lord Aberdeen. He published his *Autobiography* in 1852-1853, and died on the 11th of July 1869.

JEREMIAH, in the Bible, the last pre-exilic prophet (*fl.* 626-586 B.C.?), son of Hilkiah.

Early Days of Jeremiah.—There must anciently have existed one or more prose works on Jeremiah and his times, written partly to do honour to the prophet, partly to propagate those views respecting Israel's past with which the name of Jeremiah was associated. Some fragments of this work (or these works) have come down to us; they greatly add to the popularity of the Book of Jeremiah. Strict historical truth we must not ask of them, but they do give us what was believed concerning Jeremiah in the following age, and we must believe that the personality so honoured was an extraordinary one. We have also a number of genuine prophecies which admit us into Jeremiah's inner nature. These are our best authorities, but they are deficient in concrete facts. By birth Jeremiah was a countryman; he came of a priestly family whose estate lay at Anathoth "in the land of Benjamin" (xxxii. 3; cf. i. 1). He came forward as a prophet in the thirteenth year of Josiah (626 B.C.), still young but irresistibly impelled. Unfortunately the account of the call and of the object of the divine caller come to us from a later hand (ch. i.), but we can well believe that the concrete fact which the prophetic call illuminated was an impending blow to the state (i. 13-16; cf. ch. iv.). What the blow exactly was is disputed,1 but it is certain that Jeremiah saw the gathering storm and anticipated its result, while the statesmen were still wrapped in a false security. Five years later came the reform movement produced by the "finding" of the "book of the law" in the Temple in 621 B.C. (2 Kings xxii. 8), and some critics have gathered from Jer. xi. 1-8 that Jeremiah joined the ranks of those who publicly supported this book in Jerusalem and elsewhere. To others this view appears in itself improbable. How can a man like Jeremiah have advocated any such panacea? He was indeed not at first a complete pessimist, but to be a preacher of Deuteronomy required a sanguine temper which a prophet of the school of Isaiah could not possess. Besides, there is a famous passage (viii. 8, see R.V.) in which Jeremiah delivers a vehement attack upon the "scribes" (or, as we might render, "bookmen") and their "false pen." If, as Wellhausen and Duhm suppose, this refers to Deuteronomy (*i.e.* the original Deuteronomy), the incorrectness of the theory referred to is proved. And even if we think that the phraseology of viii. 8 applies rather to a body of writings than to a single book, yet there is no good ground (xi. 1-8 and xxxiv. 12 being of doubtful origin) for supposing that Jeremiah would have excepted Deuteronomy from his condemnation.

Stages of his Development.—At first our prophet was not altogether a pessimist. He aspired to convince the better minds that the only hope for Israelites, as well as for Israel, lay in "returning" to the true Yahweh, a deity who was no mere national god, and was not to be cajoled by the punctual offering of costly sacrifices. When Jeremiah wrote iv. 1-4 he evidently considered that the judgment could even then be averted. Afterwards he became less hopeful, and it was perhaps a closer acquaintance with the manners of the capital that served to disillusionize him. He began his work at Anathoth, but v. 1-5 (as Duhm points out) seems to come from one who has just now for the first time "run to and fro in the streets of Jerusalem," observing and observed. And what is the result of his expedition? That he cannot find a single just and honest man; that high and low, rich and poor, are all ignorant of the true method of worshipping God ("the way of Yahweh," v. 4). It would seem as if Anathoth were less corrupt than the capital, the moral state of which so shocked Jeremiah. And yet he does not really go beyond the great city-prophet Isaiah who calls the men of Jerusalem "a people of Gomorrah" (i. 10). With all reverence, an historical student has to deduct something from both these statements. It is true that commercial prosperity had put a severe strain on the old morality, and that contact with other 324peoples, as well as the course of political history, had appeared to lower the position of the God of Israel in relation to other gods. Still, some adherents of the old Israelitish moral and religious standards must have survived, only they were not to be found in the chief places of concourse, but as a rule in coteries which handed on the traditions of Amos and Isaiah in sorrowful retirement.

Danger of Book Religion.—Probably, too, even in the highest class there were some who had a moral sympathy with Jeremiah; otherwise we can hardly account for the contents of Deuteronomy, at least if the book "found" in the Temple at all resembled the central portion of our Deuteronomy. And the assumption seems to be confirmed by the respectful attitude of certain "elders of the land" in xxvi. 17 sqq., and of the "princes" in xxxvi. 19, 25, towards Jeremiah, which may, at any rate in part, have been due to the recent reform movement. If therefore Jeremiah aimed at Deuteronomy in the severe language of viii. 8, he went too far. History shows that book religion has special dangers of its own.2 Nevertheless the same incorruptible adviser also shows that book religion may be necessary as an educational instrument, and a compromise between the two types of religion is without historical precedent.

Reaction: Opposition to Jeremiah.—This, however, could not as yet be recognized by the friends of prophecy, even though it seemed for a time as if the claims of book religion were rebuffed by facts. The death of the pious king Josiah at Megiddo in 608 B.C. dashed the high hopes of the "book-men," but meant no victory for Jeremiah. Its only result for the majority was a falling back on the earlier popular cultus of the Baals, and on the heathen customs introduced, or reintroduced, by Josiah's grandfather, Manasseh. Would that we possessed the section of the prophet's biography which described his attitude immediately after the news of the battle of Megiddo! Let us, however, be thankful for what we have, and notably for the detailed narratives in chs. xxvi. and xxxvi. The former is dated in the beginning of the reign of Jehoiakim, though Wellhausen suspects that the date is a mistake, and that the real occasion was the death of Josiah. The one clear-sighted patriot saw the full meaning of the tragedy of Megiddo, and for "prophesying against this city"—secured, as men thought, by the Temple (vii. 4)—he was accused by "the priests, the prophets, and all the people" of high treason. But the divinity which hedged a prophet saved him. The "princes," supported by certain "elders" and by "the people" (quick to change their leaders), succeeded in quashing the accusation and setting the prophet free. No king, be it observed, is mentioned. The latter narrative is still more exciting. In the fourth year of Jehoiakim (= the first of Nebuchadrezzar, xxv. 1) Jeremiah was bidden to write down "all the words that Yahweh had spoken to him against Jerusalem (so LXX.), Judah and all the nations from the days of Josiah onwards" (xxxvi. 2). So at least the authors of Jeremiah's biography tell us. They add that in the next year Jeremiah's scribe Baruch read the prophecies of Jeremiah first to the people assembled in the Temple, then to the "princes," and then to the king, who decided his own future policy by burning Baruch's roll in the brazier. We cannot, however, bind ourselves to this tradition. Much more probably the prophecy was virtually a new one (*i.e.* even if some old passages were repeated yet the setting was new), and the burden of the prophecy was "The king of Babylon shall come and destroy this land."3 We cannot therefore assent to the judgment that "we have, at least as regards [the] oldest portions [of the book] information considerably more specific than is usual in the case of the writings of the prophets."4

Fall of the State.—Under Zedekiah the prophet was less fortunate. Such was the tension of feeling that the "princes," who were formerly friendly to Jeremiah, now took up an attitude of decided hostility to him. At last they had him consigned to a miry dungeon, and it was the king who (at the instance of the Cushite Ebed-melech) intervened for his relief, though he remained a prisoner in other quarters till the fall of Jerusalem (586 B.C.). Nebuchadrezzar, who is assumed to have heard of Jeremiah's constant recommendations of submission, gave him the choice either of going to Babylon or of remaining in the country (chs. xxxviii. seq.). He chose the latter and resided with Gedaliah, the native governor, at Mizpah. On the murder of Gedaliah he was carried to Mizraim or Egypt, or perhaps to the land of Mizrim in north Arabia—against his will (chs. xl.-xliii.). How far all this is correct we know not. The graphic style of a narrative is no sufficient proof of its truth. Conceivably enough the story of Jeremiah's journey to Egypt (or Mizrim) may have been imagined to supply a background for the artificial prophecies ascribed to Jeremiah in chs. xlvi.-li. A legend in Jerome and Epiphanius states that he was stoned to death at Daphnae, but the biography, though not averse from horrors, does not mention this.

A Patriot?—Was Jeremiah really a patriot? The question has been variously answered. He was not a Phocion, for he never became the tool of a foreign power. To say with Winckler5 that he was "a decided adherent of the Chaldean party" is to go beyond the evidence. He did indeed counsel submission, but only because his detachment from party gave him a clearness of vision (cf. xxxviii. 17, 18) which the politicians lacked. How he suffered in his uphill course he has told us himself (xv. 10-21). In after ages the oppressed people saw in his love for Israel and his patient resignation their own realized ideal. "And Onias said, This is the lover of the brethren, he who prayeth much for the people and the holy city, Jeremiah the prophet of God" (2 Macc. xv. 14). And in proportion as the popular belief in Jeremiah rose, fresh prophecies were added to the book (notably those of the new covenant and of the restoration of the people after seventy years) to justify it. Professor N. Schmidt has gone further into the character of this sympathetic prophet,*Ency. Bib.* "Jeremiah," § 5.

Jeremiah's Prophecies.—It has been said above that our best authorities are Jeremiah's own prophecies. Which may these be? Before answering we must again point out (see also ISAIAH) that the records of the pre-exilic prophets came down in a fragmentary form, and that these fragments needed much supplementing to adapt them to the use of post-exilic readers. In Jeremiah, as in Isaiah, we must constantly ask to what age do the phraseology, the ideas and the implied circumstances most naturally point? According to Duhm there are many passages in which metre (see also AMOS) may also be a factor in our critical conclusions. Jeremiah, he thinks, always uses the same metre. Giesebrecht, on the other hand, maintains that there are passages which are certainly Jeremiah's, but which are not in what Duhm calls Jeremiah's metre; Giesebrecht also, himself rather conservative, considers Duhm remarkably free with his emendations. There has also to be considered whether the text of the poetical passages has not often become corrupt, not only from ordinary causes but through the misunderstanding and misreading of north Arabian names on the part of late scribes and editors, the danger to Judah from north Arabia being (it is held) not less in pre-exilic times than the danger from Assyria and Babylonia, so that references to north Arabia are only to be expected. To bring educated readers into touch with critical workers it is needful to acquaint them with these various points, the neglect of any one of which may to some extent injure the results of criticism.

It is a new stage of criticism on which we have entered, so that no single critic can be reckoned as *the* authority on Jeremiah. But since the results of the higher criticism depend on the soundness and thoroughness of the criticism called "lower," and since Duhm has the advantage of being exceptionally free from that exaggerated respect for the letters of the traditional text which has survived the destruction of the old superstitious veneration for the vowel-points, it may be best to give the student his "higher critical" results, dated 1901. Let us premise, however, that the portions mentioned in the 9th edition of the *Ency. Brit.*as having been "entirely or in part denied," to Jeremiah, viz. x. 1-16; xxx.; xxxiii.; l.-li. and lii., are still regarded in their present form as non-Jeremianic. The question which next awaits decision is whether any part of the booklet on foreign nations (xxv., xlvi.-li.) can safely be regarded as Jeremianic. Giesebrecht still asserts the genuineness of xxv. 15-24 (apart from glosses), xlvii. (in the main) and xlix. 7, 8, 10, 11. Against these views see N. Schmidt, *Ency. Bib.*, col. 2384.

Let us now listen to Duhm, who analyses the book into six groups of passages. These are (a) i.-xxv., the "words of Jeremiah." (i. 1); (b) xxvi.-xxix., passages from Baruch's biography of Jeremiah; (c) xxx.-xxxi., the book of the future of Israel and Judah; (d) xxxii.-xlv., from Baruch; (e) xlvi.-li., the prophecies "concerning the nations";6 (f) lii., historical appendix. Upon examining these groups we find that besides a prose letter (ch. xxix.), about sixty poetical pieces may be Jeremiah's. A: Anathoth passages before 621, (a) ii. 2b, 3, 14-28; ii. 29-37; iii. 1-5; iii. 12b, 13, 19, 20; iii. 21-25; iv. i, 3, 4; these form a cycle, (b) xxxi. 2-6; 15-20; 21, 22; another cycle. (c) iv. 5-8; 11b, 12a, 13, 15-17a; 19-21; 23-26; 29-31; visions and "auditions" of the impending invasion. B: Jerusalem passages. (d) v. 1-6a; 6b-9; 10-17; vi. 1-5; 6b-8; 9-14; 16, 17, 20; 22-26a; 27-30; vii. 28, 29; viii. 4-7a; 8, 9, 13; 14-17; viii. 18-23; ix. 1-8; 9 (short song); 16-18; 19-21; x. 19, 20, 22; reign of Josiah, strong personal element. (e) xxii. 10 (Jehoahaz). xxii. 13-17; probably too xi. 15, 16; xii. 7-12 (Jehoiakim). xxii. 18, 19, perhaps too xxii. 6b, 7; 20-23; and the cycle xiii. 15, 16; 17; 18, 19; 20, 21a, 22-25a, 26, 27 (later, Jehoiakim). xxii. 24; xxii. 28 (Jehoiachin). (f) Later poems. xiv. 2-10; xv. 5-9; xvi. 5-7; xviii. 13-17; xxiii. 9-12; 13-15; xi. 18-20; xv. 10-12; 15-19a, and 20, 21; xvii. 9, 10, 14, 16, 17; xviii. 18-20; xx. 7-11; xx. 14-18; xiv. 17, 18; xvii. 1-4; xxxviii. 24; assigned to the close of Zedekiah's time.

Two Recensions of the Text.—It has often been said that we have virtually two recensions of the text, that represented by the Septuagint and the Massoretic text, and critics have taken different sides, some for one and some for the other. "Recension," however, is a bad term; it implies that the two texts which undeniably exist were the result of revising and editing according to definite critical principles. Such, however, is not the case. It is true that "there are (in the LXX.) many omissions of words, sentences, verses and whole passages, in fact, that altogether about 2700 words are wanting, or the eighth part of the Massoretic text" (Bleek). It may also be admitted that the scribes who produced the Hebrew basis of the Septuagint version, conscious of the unsettled state of the text, did not shrink from what they considered a justifiable simplification. But we must also grant that those from whom the "written" Hebrew text proceeds allowed themselves to fill up and to repeat without any sufficient warrant. In each case in which there is a genuine difference of reading between the two texts, it is for the critic to decide; often, however, he will have to seek to go behind what both the texts present in order to constitute a truer text than either. Here is the great difficulty of the future. We may add to the credit of the Septuagint that the position given to the prophecies on "the nations" (chs. xlvi.-li. in our Bible) in the Septuagint is probably more original than that in the Massoretic text. On this point see especially Schmidt,*Ency. Bib.* "Jeremiah (Book)" §§ 6 and 21; Davidson, Hastings's *Dict. Bible*, ii. 573b-575; Driver, *Introduction*(8th ed.), pp. 269, 270.

The best German commentary is that of Cornill (1905). A skilful translation by Driver, with notes intended for ordinary students (1906) should also be mentioned.

(T. K. C.)

1Davidson (Hast., *D.B.*; ii. 570 b) mentions two views. (1) The foe might be "a creation of his moral presentiment and assigned to the north as the cloudy region of mystery." (2) The more usual view is that the Scythians (see Herod, i. 76, 103-106; iv. 1) are meant. Neither of these views is satisfactory. The passage v. 15-17 is too definite for (1), and as for (2), the idea of a threatened Scythian invasion lacks a sufficient basis. Those who hold (2) have to suppose that original references to the Scythians were retouched under the impression of Chaldean invasions. Hence Cheyne's theory of a north Arabian invasion from the land of Zaphon = Zibeon (Gen. xxxvi. 2, 14), *i.e.* Ishmael. Cf. N. Schmidt, *Ency. Bib.*, Zibeon, "Scythians," § 8; Cheyne,*Critica Biblica*, part i. (Isaiah and Jeremiah).

2Cf. Ewald, *The Prophets*, Eng. trans., iii. 63, 64.

3Cheyne, *Ency. Brit.* (9th ed.,), "Jeremiah," suggests after Grätz that the roll simply contained ch. xxv., omitting the most obvious interpolations. Against this view see N. Schmidt, *Ency. Bib.*, "Jeremiah (Book)," § 8, who, however, accepts the negative part of Cheyne's arguments.

4Driver, *Introd. to the Lit. of the O.T.* (6), p. 249.

5In Helmolt's *Weltgeschichte*, iii. 211.

6li. 59-64a, however, is a specimen of imaginative "Midrashic" history. See Giesebrecht's monograph.

JEREMY, EPISTLE OF, an apocryphal book of the Old Testament. This letter purports to have been written by Jeremiah to the exiles who were already in Babylon or on the way thither. The author was a Hellenistic Jew, and not improbably a Jew of Alexandria. His work, which shows little literary skill, was written with a serious practical purpose. He veiled his fierce attack on the idol gods of Egypt by holding up to derision the idolatry of Babylon. The fact that Jeremiah (xxix. 1 sqq.) was known to have written a letter of this nature naturally suggested to a

Hellenist, possibly of the 1st centuryB.C. or earlier, the idea of a second epistolary undertaking, and other passages of Jeremiah's prophecy (x. 1-12; xxix. 4-23) may have determined also its general character and contents.

The writer warned the exiles that they were to remain in captivity for seven generations; that they would there see the worship paid to idols, from all participation in which they were to hold aloof; for that idols were nothing save the work of men's hands, without the powers of speech, hearing or self-preservation. They could not bless their worshippers even in the smallest concerns of life; they were indifferent to moral qualities, and were of less value than the commonest household objects, and finally, "with rare irony, the author compared an idol to a scarecrow (v. 70), impotent to protect, but deluding to the imagination" (MARSHALL).

The date of the epistle is uncertain. It is believed by some scholars to be referred to in 2 Macc. ii. 2, which says that Jeremiah charged the exiles "not to forget the statutes of the Lord, neither to be led astray in their minds when they saw images of gold and silver and the adornment thereof." But the reference is disputed by Fritzsche, Gifford, Shürer and others. The epistle was included in the Greek canon. There was no question of its canonicity till the time of Jerome, who termed it a pseudepigraph.

See Fritzsche, *Handb. zu den Apok.*, 1851; Gifford, in *Speaker's Apoc.* ii. 286-303; Marshall, in Hastings' *Dict. Bible*, ii. 578-579.

(R. H. C.)

JERÉZ DE LA FRONTERA (formerly XERES), a town of southern Spain, in the province of Cadiz, near the right bank of the river Guadalete, and on the Seville-Cadiz railway, about 7 m. from the Atlantic coast. Pop. (1900), 63,473. Jeréz is built in the midst of an undulating plain of great fertility. Its whitewashed houses, clean, broad streets, and squares planted with trees extend far beyond the limits formerly enclosed by the Moorish walls, almost entirely demolished. The principal buildings are the 15th-century church of San Miguel, the 17th-century collegiate church with its lofty bell-tower, the 16th-century town-hall, superseded, for official purposes, by a modern edifice, the bull-ring, and many hospitals, charitable institutions and schools, including academies of law, medicine and commerce. But the most characteristic features of Jeréz are the huge *bodegas*, or wine-lodges, for the manufacture and storage of sherry, and the vineyards, covering more than 150,000 acres, which surround it on all sides. The town is an important market for grain, fruit and livestock, but its staple trade is in wine. Sherry is also produced in other districts, but takes its name, formerly written in English as *sherris* or *xeres*, from Jeréz. The demand for sherry diminished very greatly during the last quarter of the 19th century, especially in England, which had been the chief consumer. In 1872 the sherry shipped from Cadiz to Great Britain alone was valued at £2,500,000; in 1902 the total export hardly amounted to one-fifth of this sum. The wine trade, however, still brings a considerable profit, and few towns of southern Spain display greater commercial activity than Jeréz. In the earlier part of the 18th century the neighbourhood suffered severely from yellow fever; but it was rendered comparatively healthy when in 1869 an aqueduct was opened to supply pure water. Strikes and revolutionary disturbances have frequently retarded business in more recent years.

Jeréz has been variously identified with the Roman Municipium Seriense; with Asido, perhaps the original of the Moorish Sherish; and with Hasta Regia, a name which may survive in the designation of La Mesa de Asta, a neighbouring hill. Jeréz was taken from the Moors by Ferdinand III. of Castile (1217-1252); but it was twice recaptured before Alphonso X. finally occupied it in 1264. Towards the close of the 14th century it received the title *de la Frontera, i.e.* "of the frontier," common to several towns on the Moorish border.

JERÉZ DE LOS CABALLEROS, a town of south-western Spain, in the province of Badajoz, picturesquely situated on two heights overlooking the river Ardila, a tributary of the Guadiana, 12 m. E. of the Portuguese frontier. Pop. (1900), 10,271. The old town is surrounded by a Moorish wall with six gates; the newer portion is well and regularly built, and planted with numerous orange and other fruit trees. Owing to the lack of railway communication Jeréz is of little commercial importance; its staple trade is in agricultural produce, especially in ham and bacon from the large herds of swine which are reared in the surrounding oak forests. The town is said to have been founded by Alphonso IX. of Leon in 1229; in 1232 it was extended by his son St Ferdinand, who gave it to the knights templar. Hence the name *Jeréz de los Caballeros*, "Jeréz of the knights."

JERICHO (יְרִחוֹ, יְרֵחוֹ, once יְרִיחֹה, a word of disputed meaning, whether "fragrant" or "moon [-god] city"), an important town in the Jordan valley some 5 m. N. of the Dead Sea. The references to it in the Pentateuch are confined to rough geographical indications of the latitude of the trans-Jordanic camp of the Israelites in Moab before their crossing of the river. This was the first Canaanite city to be attacked and reduced by the victorious Israelites. The story of its conquest is 326His Sundays were spent in the catacombs in discovering graves of the martyrs and deciphering inscriptions. Pope Liberius baptized him in 360; three years later the news of the death of the emperor Julian came to Rome, and Christians felt relieved from a great dread.

When his student days were over Jerome returned to Strido, but did not stay there long. His character was formed. He was a scholar, with a scholar's tastes and cravings for knowledge, easily excited, bent on scholarly discoveries. From Strido he went to Aquileia, where he formed some friendships among the monks of the large monastery, notably with Rufinus, with whom he was destined to quarrel bitterly over the question of Origen's orthodoxy and worth as a commentator; for Jerome was a man who always sacrificed a friend to an opinion, and when he changed sides in a controversy expected his acquaintances to follow him. From Aquileia he went to Gaul (366-370), visiting in turn the principal places in that country, from Narbonne and Toulouse in the south to Treves on the north-east frontier. He stayed some time at Treves studying and observing, and it was there that he first began to think seriously upon sacred things. From Treves he returned to Strido, and from Strido to Aquileia. He settled down to literary work in Aquileia (370-373) and composed there his first original tract,*De muliere septies percussa*, in the form of a letter to his friend Innocentius. Some dispute caused him to leave Aquileia suddenly; and with a few companions, Innocentius, Evagrius, and Heliodorus being among them, he started for a long tour in the East. The epistle to Rufinus (3rd in Vallarsi's enumeration) tells us the route. They went through Thrace, visiting Athens, Bithynia, Galatia, Pontus, Cappadocia and Cilicia, to Antioch, Jerome observing and making notes as they went. He was interested in the theological disputes and schisms in Galatia, in the two languages spoken in Cilicia, &c. At Antioch the party remained some time. Innocentius died of a fever, and Jerome was dangerously ill. This illness induced a spiritual change, and he resolved to renounce whatever kept him back from God. His greatest temptation was the study of the literature of pagan Rome. In a dream Christ reproached him with caring more to be a Ciceronian than a Christian. He disliked the uncouth style of the Scriptures. "O Lord," he prayed, "thou knowest that whenever I have and study secular MSS. I deny thee," and he made a resolve henceforth to devote his scholarship to the Holy Scripture. "David was to be henceforth his Simonides, Pindar and Alcaeus, his Flaccus, Catullus and Severus." Fortified by these resolves he betook himself to a hermit life in the wastes of Chalcis, S.E. from Antioch (373-379). Chalcis was the Thebaid of Syria. Great numbers of monks, each in solitary cell, spent lonely lives, scorched by the sun, ill-clad and scantily fed, pondering on portions of Scripture or copying MSS. to serve as objects of meditation. Jerome at once set himself to such scholarly work as the place afforded. He discovered and copied MSS., and began to study Hebrew. There also he wrote the life of St Paul of Thebes, probably an imaginary tale embodying the facts of the monkish life around him. Just then the Meletian schism, which arose over the relation of the orthodox to Arian bishops and to those baptized by Arians, distressed the church at Antioch (see MELETIUS OF ANTIOCH), and Jerome as usual eagerly joined the fray. Here as elsewhere he had but one rule to guide him in matters of doctrine and discipline—the practice of Rome and the West; for it is singular to see how Jerome, who is daringly original in points of scholarly criticism, was a ruthless partisan in all other matters; and, having discovered what was the Western practice, he set tongue and pen to work with his usual bitterness (*Altercatio luciferiani et orthodoxi*).

At Antioch in 379 he was ordained presbyter. From there he went to Constantinople, where he met with the great Eastern scholar and theologian Gregory of Nazianzus, and with his aid tried to perfect himself in Greek. The result of his studies there was the translation of the *Chronicon* of Eusebius, with a continuation1 of twenty-eight homilies of Origen on Jeremiah and Ezekiel, and of nine homilies of Origen on the visions of Isaiah.

In 381 Meletius died, and Pope Damasus interfered in the dispute at Antioch, hoping to end it. Jerome was called to Rome in 382 to give help in the matter, and was made secretary during the investigation. His work brought him into intercourse with this great pontiff, who soon saw what he could best do, and how his vast scholarship might be made of use to the church. Damasus suggested to him to revise the "Old Latin" translation of the Bible; and to this task he henceforth devoted his great abilities. At Rome were published the Gospels (with a dedication to Pope Damasus, an explanatory introduction, and the canons of Eusebius), the rest of the New Testament and the version of the Psalms from the Septuagint known as the*Psalterium romanum*, which was followed (*c.* 388) by the*Psalterium gallicanum*, based on the Hexaplar Greek text. These scholarly labours, however, did not take up his whole time, and it was almost impossible for Jerome to be long anywhere without getting into a dispute. He was a zealous defender of that monastic life which was beginning to take such a large place in the church of the 4th century, and he found enthusiastic disciples among the Roman ladies. A number of widows and maidens met together in the house of Marcella to study the Scriptures with him; he taught them Hebrew, and preached the virtues of the celibate life. His arguments and exhortations may be gathered from many of his epistles and from his tract *Adversus Helvidium*, in which he defends the perpetual virginity of Mary against Helvidius, who maintained that she bore children to Joseph. His influence over these ladies alarmed their relatives and excited the suspicions of the regular priesthood and of the populace, but while Pope Damasus lived Jerome remained secure. Damasus died, however, in 384, and was succeeded by Siricius, who did not show much friendship for Jerome. He found it expedient to leave Rome, and set out for the East in 385. His letters (especially Ep. 45) are full of outcries against his enemies and of indignant protestations that he had done nothing unbecoming a Christian, that he had taken no money, nor gifts great nor small, that he had no delight in silken attire, sparkling gems or gold ornaments, that no matron moved him unless by penitence and fasting, &c. His route is given in the third book*In Rufinum*; he went by Rhegium and Cyprus, where he was entertained by Bishop Epiphanius, to Antioch. There he was joined by two wealthy Roman ladies, Paula, a widow, and Eustochium, her daughter, one of Jerome's Hebrew students. They came accompanied by a band of Roman maidens vowed to live a celibate life in a nunnery in Palestine. Accompanied by these ladies Jerome made the tour of Palestine, carefully noting with a scholar's keenness the various places mentioned in Holy Scripture. The results of this journey may be traced in his translation with emendations of the book of Eusebius on the situation and names of Hebrew places, written probably three years afterwards, when he had settled down at Bethlehem. From Palestine Jerome and his companions went to Egypt, remaining some time in Alexandria, and they visited the convents of the Nitrian desert. Jerome's mind was evidently full of anxiety about his translation of the Old Testament, for we find him in his letters recording the conversations he had with learned men about disputed readings and doubtful renderings; the blind Didymus of Alexandria, whom he heard interpreting Hosea, appears to have been most useful. When they returned to Palestine they all settled at Bethlehem, where Paula built four monasteries, three for nuns and one for monks. She was at the head of the nunneries until her death in 404, when Eustochium succeeded her; Jerome presided over the fourth monastery. Here he did most of his literary work and, throwing aside his unfinished plan of a translation from Origen's Hexaplar text, translated the Old Testament directly from the Hebrew, with the aid of Jewish scholars. He mentions a rabbi from Lydda, a rabbi from Tiberias, and above all rabbi Ben Anina, who came to him by night secretly for fear of the Jews. Jerome was not familiar enough with Hebrew to be able to dispense with such assistance, and he makes the synagogue responsible for the 327fully narrated in the first seven chapters of Joshua. There must be some little exaggeration in the statement that Jericho was totally destroyed; a hamlet large enough to be enumerated among the towns of Benjamin (Josh. xviii. 21) must have remained; but that it was small is shown by the fact that it was deemed a suitable place for David's ambassadors to retire to after the indignities put upon them by Hanun (2 Sam. x. 5; 1 Chron. xix. 5). Its refortification was due to a Bethelite named Hiel, who endeavoured to avert the curse of Joshua by offering his sons as sacrifices at certain stages of the work (1 Kings xvi. 34). After this event it grew again into importance and became the site of a college of prophets (2 Kings ii. 4 sqq.) for whom Elisha "healed" its poisonous waters. The principal spring in the neighbourhood of Jericho still bears (among the foreign residents) the name of Elisha; the natives call it, Ain es-Sultan, or "Sultan's spring." To Jericho the victorious Israelite marauders magnanimously returned their Judahite captives at the bidding of the prophet Oded (2 Chron. xxviii. 15). Here was fought the last fight between the Babylonians and Zedekiah, wherein the kingdom of Judah came to an end (2 Kings xxv. 5; Jer. xxxix. 5, lii. 8). In the New Testament Jericho is connected with the well-known stories of Bar-Timaeus (Matt. xx. 29; Mark x. 46; Luke xviii. 35) and Zacchaeus (Luke xix. 1) and with the good Samaritan (Luke x. 30).

The extra-Biblical history of Jericho is as disastrous as are the records preserved in the Scriptures. Bacchides, the general of the Syrians, captured and fortified it (1. Macc. ix. 50), Aristobulus (Jos. *Ant.* XIV. i. 2) also took it, Pompey (ib. XIV. iv. 1) encamped here on his way to Jerusalem. Before Herod its inhabitants ran away (ib. XIV. xv. 3) as they did before Vespasian (*Wars*, IV. viii. 2). The reason of this lack of warlike quality was no doubt the enervating effect of the great heat of the depression in which the city lies, which has the same effect on the handful of degraded humanity that still occupies the ancient site.

Few places in Palestine are more fertile. It was the city of palm trees of the ancient record of the Israelite invasion preserved in part in Judg. i. 16; and Josephus speaks of its fruitfulness with enthusiasm (*Wars* IV. 8, 3). Even now with every possible hindrance in the way of cultivation it is an important centre of fruit-growing.

The modern er-Rīha is a poor squalid village of, it is estimated, about 300 inhabitants. It is not built exactly on the ancient site. Indeed, the site of Jericho has shifted several times. The mound of Tell es-Sultan, near "Elisha's Fountain," north of the modern village, no doubt covers the Canaanite town. There are two later sites, of Roman or Herodian date, one north, the other west, of this. It was probably the crusaders who established the modern site. An old tower attributed to them is to be seen in the village, and in the surrounding mountains are many remains of early monasticism. Aqueducts, ruined sugar-mills, and other remains of ancient industry abound in the neighbourhood. The whole district is the private property of the sultan of Turkey. In 1907-8 the Canaanite Jericho was excavated under the direction of Prof. Sellin of Vienna.

See "The German Excavations at Jericho," *Pal. Explor. Fund, Quart. Statem.* (1910), pp. 54-68.

1Cf. Schoene's critical edition (Berlin, 1866, 1875).

JERKIN, a short close-fitting jacket, made usually of leather, and without sleeves, the typical male upper garment of the 16th and 17th centuries. The origin of the word is unknown. The Dutch word *jurk*, a child's frock, often taken as the source, is modern, and represents neither the sound nor the sense of the English word. In architecture the term "jerkin-roofed" is applied, probably with some obscure connexion with the garment, to a particular form of gable end, the gable being cut off half way up the roof and sloping back like a "hipped roof" to the edge.

JEROBOAM (Heb. *yārob'ām*, apparently "Am ['the clan,' here perhaps a divine name] contends"; LXX.ιεροβοαμ), the name of two kings in the Bible.

1. The first king of (north) Israel after the disruption (seeSOLOMON). According to the traditions of his early life (1 Kings xi. 26 sqq. and LXX.), he was an Ephraimite who for his ability was placed over the forced levy of Ephraim and Manasseh. Having subsequently incurred Solomon's suspicions he fled to Shishak, king of Egypt, and remained with him until Rehoboam's accession. When the latter came to be made king at Shechem, the old religious centre (seeABIMELECH), hopes were entertained that a more lenient policy would be introduced. But Rehoboam refused to depart from Solomon's despotic rule, and was tactless enough to send Adoniram, the overseer of the *corvée*. He was stoned to death, and Rehoboam realizing the temper of the people fled to Jerusalem and prepared for war. Jeroboam became the recognized leader of the northern tribes.1 Conflicts occurred (1 Kings xiv. 30), but no details are preserved except the late story of Rehoboam's son Abijah in 2 Chron. xiii. Jeroboam's chief achievement was the fortification of Shechem (his new capital) and of Penuel in east Jordan. To counteract the influence of Jerusalem he established golden calves at Dan and Bethel, an act which to later ages was as gross a piece of wickedness as his rebellion against the legitimate dynasty of Judah. No notice has survived of Shishak's invasion of Israel (see REHOBOAM), and after a reign of twenty-two years Jeroboam was succeeded by Nadab, whose violent death two years later brought the whole house of Jeroboam to an end.

The history of the separation of Judah and Israel in the 10th century B.C. was written from a strong religious standpoint at a date considerably later than the event itself. The visit of Ahijah to Shiloh (xi. 29-39), to announce symbolically the rending of the kingdom, replaces some account of a rebellion in which Jeroboam "lifted up his hand" (*v.* 27) against Solomon. To such an account, not to the incident of Ahijah and the cloak, his flight (*v.* 40) is the natural sequel. The story of Ahijah's prophecy against Jeroboam (ch. xiv.) is not in the original LXX., but another version of the same narrative appears at xii. 24 (LXX.), in which there is no reference to a previous promise to Jeroboam through Ahijah, but the prophet is introduced as a new character. Further, in this version (xii. 24) the incident of the tearing of the cloak is related of Shemaiah and placed at the convention of Shechem. Shemaiah is the prophet who counselled Rehoboam to refrain from war (xii. 21-24); the injunction is opposed to xiv. 30, but appears to be intended to explain Rehoboam's failure to overcome north Israel. (See W. R. Smith, *Old Test. in Jewish Church* (2nd ed.), 117 sqq.; Winckler, *Alte Test. Untersuch.* 12 sqq., and J. Skinner, *Century Bible: Kings*, pp. 443 sqq.)

2. JEROBOAM, son of Joash (2) a contemporary of Azariah king of Judah. He was one of the greatest of the kings of Israel. He succeeded in breaking the power of Damascus, which had long been devastating his land, and extended his kingdom from Hamath on the Orontes to the Dead Sea. The brief summary of his achievements preserved in 2 Kings xiv. 23 sqq. may be supplemented by the original writings of Amos and Hosea.2There appears to be an allusion in Amos vi. 13 to the recovery of Ashteroth-Karnaim and Lodebar in E. Jordan, and the conquest of Moab (Isa. xv. seq.) is often ascribed to this reign. After a period of prosperity, internal disturbances broke out and the northern kingdom hastened to its fall. Jeroboam was succeeded by his son Zechariah, who after six months was killed at Ibleam (so read in 2 Kings xv. 10; cp. ix.

27, murder of Ahaziah) by Shallum the son of Jabesh—*i.e.* possibly of Jabesh-Gilead—who a month later fell to Menahem (*q.v.*).

(S. A. C.)

See, further, JEWS §§ 7, 9 and §§ 12, 13.

1On the variant traditions in the Hebrew text and the Septuagint, see the commentaries on Kings.

2See also JONAH. In 2 Kings xiv. 28, "Hamath, *which had belonged* to Judah" (R.V.) is incorrect; Winckler (*Keilinschrift. u. Alte Test.*, 2nd ed., 262) suspects a reference to Israel's overlordship in Judah; Burney (*Heb. Text of Kings*) reads: "how he fought with Damascus and how he turned away the wrath of Yahweh from Israel"; see also *Ency. Bib.* col. 2406 n. 4, and the commentaries.

JEROME, ST (HIERONYMUS, in full EUSEBIUS SOPHRONIUS HIERONYMUS) (*c.* 340-420), was born at Strido (modern Strigau?), a town on the border of Dalmatia fronting Pannonia, destroyed by the Goths in A.D. 377. What is known of Jerome has mostly been recovered from his own writings. He appears to have been born about 340; his parents were Christians, orthodox though living among people mostly Arians and wealthy. He was at first educated at home, Bonosus, a life-long friend, sharing his youthful studies, and was afterwards sent to Rome. Donatus taught him grammar and explained the Latin poets. Victorinus taught him rhetoric. He attended the law-courts, and listened to the Roman advocates pleading in the Forum. He went to the schools of philosophy, and heard lectures on Plato, Diogenes, Clitomachus and Carneades; the conjunction of names show how philosophy had become a dead tradition. 328accuracy of his version: "Let him who would challenge aught in this translation," he says, "ask the Jews." The result of all this labour was the Latin translation of the Scriptures which, in spite of much opposition from the more conservative party in the church, afterwards became the Vulgate or authorized version; but the Vulgate as we have it now is not exactly Jerome's Vulgate, for it suffered a good deal from changes made under the influence of the older translations; the text became very corrupt during the middle ages, and in particular all the Apocrypha, except Tobit and Judith, which Jerome translated from the Chaldee, were added from the older versions. (See BIBLE: *O.T. Versions.*)

Notwithstanding the labour involved in translating the Scriptures, Jerome found time to do a great deal of literary work, and also to indulge in violent controversy. Earlier in life he had a great admiration for Origen, and translated many of his works, and this lasted after he had settled at Bethlehem, for in 389 he translated Origen's homilies on Luke; but he came to change his opinion and wrote violently against two admirers of the great Alexandrian scholar, John, bishop of Jerusalem, and his own former friend Rufinus.

At Bethlehem also he found time to finish *Didymi de spiritu sancto liber*, a translation begun at Rome at the request of Pope Damasus, to denounce the revival of Gnostic heresies by Jovinianus and Vigilantius (*Adv. Jovinianum lib. II.* and*Contra Vigilantium liber*), and to repeat his admiration of the hermit life in his *Vita S. Hilarionis eremitae*, in his *Vita Malchi monachi captivi*, in his translations of the Rule of St Pachomius (the Benedict of Egypt), and in his *S. Pachomii et S. Theodorici epistolae et verba mystica*. He also wrote at Bethlehem *De viris illustribus sive de scriptoribus ecclesiasticis*, a church history in biographies, ending with the life of the author; *De nominibus Hebraicis*, compiled from Philo and Origen; and *De situ et nominibus locorum Hebraicorum*.1 At the same place, too, he wrote *Quaestiones Hebraicae* on Genesis,2 and a series of commentaries on Isaiah, Jeremiah, Ezekiel, Daniel, the Twelve Minor Prophets, Matthew and the Epistles of St Paul. About 394 Jerome came to know Augustine, for whom he held a high regard. He engaged in the Pelagian controversy with more than even his usual bitterness (*Dialogi contra pelagianos*); and it is said that the violence of his invective so provoked his opponents that an armed mob attacked the monastery, and that Jerome was forced to flee and to remain in concealment for nearly two years. He returned to Bethlehem in 418, and after a lingering illness died on the 30th of September 420.

Jerome "is one of the few Fathers to whom the title of Saint appears to have been given in recognition of services rendered to the Church rather than for eminent sanctity. He is the great Christian scholar of his age, rather than the profound theologian or the wise guide of souls." His great work was the Vulgate, but his achievements in other fields would have sufficed to distinguish him. His commentaries are valuable because of his knowledge of Greek and Hebrew, his varied interests, and his comparative freedom from allegory. To him we owe the distinction between canonical and apocryphal writings; in the *Prologus Galeatus* prefixed to his version of Samuel and Kings, he says that the church reads the Apocrypha "for the edification of the people, not for confirming the authority of ecclesiastical doctrines." He was a pioneer in the fields of patrology and of biblical archaeology. In controversy he was too fond of mingling personal abuse with legitimate argument, and this weakness mars his letters, which were held in high admiration in the early middle ages, and are valuable for their history of the man and his times. Luther in his *Table Talk* condemns them as dealing only with fasting, meats, virginity, &c. "If he only had insisted upon the works of faith and performed them! But he teaches nothing either about faith, or love, or hope, or the works of faith."

Editions of the complete works: Erasmus (9 vols., Basel, 1516-1520); Mar. Victorius, bishop of Rieti (9 vols., Rome, 1565-1572); F. Calixtus and A. Tribbechovius (12 vols., Frankfort and Leipzig, 1684-1690); J. Martianay (5 vols., incomplete Benedictine ed., Paris, 1693-1706); D. Vallarsi (11 vols., Verona, 1734-1742), the best; Migne, *Patrol. Ser. Lat.* (xxii.-xxix.). The *De viris illust.* was edited by Herding in 1879. A selection is given in translation by W. H. Fremantle, "Select Library of Nicene and Post Nicene Fathers," 2nd series, vol. vi. (New York, 1893). Biographies are prefixed to most of the above editions. See also lives by F. Z. Collombet (Paris and Lyons, 1844); O. Zöckler (Gotha, 1865); E. L. Cutts (London, 1878); C. Martin (London, 1888); P. Largent (Paris, 1898); F. W. Farrar, *Lives of the Fathers*, ii. 150-297 (Edinburgh, 1889). Additional literature is cited in Hauck-Herzog's *Realencyk. für prot. Theol.* viii. 42.

1Compare the critical edition of these two works in Lagarde's *Onomastica sacra* (Götting. 1870).

2See Lagarde's edition appended to his *Genesis Graece*(Leipzig, 1868).

JEROME, JEROME KLAPKA (1859-   ), English author, was born on the 2nd of May 1859. He was educated at the philological school, Marylebone, London; and was by turns clerk, schoolmaster and actor, before he settled down to journalism. He made his reputation as a humorist in 1889 with *Idle Thoughts of an Idle Fellow* and *Three Men in a Boat*, and from 1892 to 1897 he was co-editor of the *Idler* with Robert Barr. At the same time he was also the editor of *To-Day*. A one-act play of his, *Barbara*, was produced at the Globe theatre in 1886, and was followed by many others, among them *Sunset* (1888), *Wood Barrow Farm* (1891), *The Passing of the Third Floor Back* (1907). Among his later books are *Letters to Clorinda* (1898), *The Second Thoughts of an Idle Fellow* (1898), *Three Men on the Bummel* (1900),*Tommy and Co.* (1904), *They and I* (1909).

JEROME OF PRAGUE (d. 1416), an early Bohemian church-reformer and friend of John Hus. Jerome's part in the Hussite movement was formerly much over-rated. Very little is known of his early years. He is stated to have belonged to a noble Bohemian family1 and to have been a few years younger than Hus. After beginning his studies at the university of Prague, where he never attempted to obtain any ecclesiastical office, Jerome proceeded to Oxford in 1398. There he became greatly impressed by the writings of Wycliffe, of whose *Dialogus* and *Trialogus* he made copies. Always inclined to a roving life, he soon proceeded to the university of Paris and afterwards continued his studies at Cologne and Heidelberg, returning to Prague in 1407. In 1403 he is stated to have undertaken a journey to Jerusalem. At Paris his open advocacy of the views of Wycliffe brought him into conflict with John Gerson, chancellor of the university. In Prague Jerome soon attracted attention by his advanced and outspoken opinions. He gave great offence also by exhibiting a portrait of Wycliffe in his room. Jerome was soon on terms of friendship with Hus, and took part in all the controversies of the university. When in 1408 a French embassy arrived at Kutná Hora, the residence of King Wenceslaus of Bohemia, and proposed that the papal schism should be terminated by the refusal of the temporal authorities further to recognize either of the rival popes, Wenceslaus summoned to Kutná Hora the members of the university. The Bohemian *magistri* spoke strongly in favour of the French proposals, while the Germans maintained their allegiance to the Roman pope, Gregory XII. The reorganization of the university was also discussed, and as Wenceslaus for a time favoured the Germans, Hus and Jerome, as leaders of the Bohemians, incurred the anger of the king, who threatened them with death by fire should they oppose his will.

In 1410 Jerome, who had incurred the hostility of the archbishop of Prague by his speeches in favour of Wycliffe's teaching, went to Ofen, where King Sigismund of Hungary resided, and, though a layman, preached before the king denouncing strongly the rapacity and immorality of the clergy. Sigismund shortly afterwards received a letter from the archbishop of Prague containing accusations against Jerome. He was imprisoned by order of the king, but does not appear to have been detained long in Hungary. Appearing at Vienna, he was again brought 329before the ecclesiastical authorities. He was accused of spreading Wycliffe's doctrines, and his general conduct at Oxford, Paris, Cologne, Prague and Ofen was censured. Jerome vowed that he would not leave Vienna till he had cleared himself from the accusation of heresy. Shortly afterwards he secretly left Vienna, declaring that this promise had been forced on him. He went first to Vöttau in Moravia, and then to Prague. In 1412 the representatives of Pope

Gregory XII. publicly offered indulgences for sale at Prague, wishing to raise money for the pope's campaign against King Ladislaus of Naples, an adherent of the antipope of Avignon. Contrary to the wishes of the archbishop of Prague a meeting of the members of the university took place, at which both Hus and Jerome spoke strongly against the sale of indulgences. The fiery eloquence of Jerome, which is noted by all contemporary writers, obtained for him greater success even than that of Hus, particularly among the younger students, who conducted him in triumph to his dwelling-place. Shortly afterwards Jerome proceeded to Poland—it is said on the invitation of King Wladislaus. His courtly manners and his eloquence here also caused him to become very popular, but he again met with strong opposition from the Roman Church. While travelling with the grand-duke Lithold of Lithuania Jerome took part in the religious services of the Greek Orthodox Church.

During his stay in northern Europe Jerome received the news that Hus had been summoned to appear before the council of Constance. He wrote to his friend advising him to do so and adding that he would also proceed there to afford him assistance. Contrary to the advice of Hus he arrived at Constance on the 4th of April 1415. Advised to fly immediately to Bohemia, he succeeded in reaching Hirschau, only 25 m. from the Bohemian frontier. He was here arrested and brought back in chains to Constance, where he was examined by judges appointed by the council. His courage failed him in prison and, to regain his freedom, he renounced the doctrines of Wycliffe and Hus. He declared that Hus had been justly executed and stated in a letter addressed on the 12th of August 1415 to Lacek, lord of Kravař—the only literary document of Jerome that has been preserved—that "the dead man (Hus) had written many false and harmful things." Full confidence was not placed in Jerome's recantation. He claimed to be heard at a general meeting of the council, and this was granted to him. He now again maintained all the theories which he had formerly advocated, and, after a trial that lasted only one day, he was condemned to be burnt as a heretic. The sentence was immediately carried out on the 30th of May 1416, and he met his death with fortitude. As Poggio Bracciolini writes, "none of the Stoics with so constant and brave a soul endured death, which he (Jerome) seemed rather to long for." The eloquence of the Italian humanist has bestowed a not entirely merited aureole on the memory of Jerome of Prague.

See all works dealing with Hus; and indeed all histories of Bohemia contain detailed accounts of the career of Jerome. *The Lives of John Wicliffe, Lord Cobham, John Huss, Jerome of Prague and Žižka* by William Gilpin (London, 1765) still has a certain value. (L.)

1The statement that Jerome's family name was Faulfiss, is founded on a misunderstood passage of Aeneas Sylvius,*Historica Bohemica.* Aeneas Sylvius names as one of the early Bohemian reformers a man *"genere nobilis, ex domo quam Putridi Piscis vacant."* This was erroneously believed to refer to Jerome.

JERROLD, DOUGLAS WILLIAM (1803-1857), English dramatist and man of letters, was born in London on the 3rd of January 1803. His father, Samuel Jerrold, actor, was at that time lessee of the little theatre of Wilsby near Cranbrook in Kent, but in 1807 he removed to Sheerness. There, among the bluejackets who swarmed in the port during the war with France, Douglas grew into boyhood. He occasionally took a child's part on the stage, but his father's profession had little attraction for the boy. In December 1813 he joined the guardship "Namur," where he had Jane Austen's brother as captain, and he served as a midshipman until the peace of 1815. He saw nothing of the war save a number of wounded soldiers from Waterloo; but till his dying day there lingered traces of his early passion for the sea. The peace of 1815 ruined Samuel Jerrold; there was no more prize money. On the 1st of January 1816 he removed with his family to London, where the ex-midshipman began the world again as a printer's apprentice, and in 1819 became a compositor in the printing-office of the *Sunday Monitor.* Several short papers and copies of verses by him had already appeared in the sixpenny magazines, and one evening he dropped into the editor's box a criticism of the opera *Der Freischütz.* Next morning he received his own copy to set up, together with a flattering note from the editor, requesting further contributions from the anonymous author. Thenceforward Jerrold was engaged in journalism. In 1821 a comedy that he had composed in his fifteenth year was brought out at Sadler's Wells theatre, under the title *More Frightened than Hurt.* Other pieces followed, and in 1825 he was engaged for a few pounds weekly to produce dramas and farces to the order of Davidge of the Coburg theatre. In the autumn of 1824 the "little Shakespeare in a camlet cloak," as he was called, married Mary Swann; and, while he was engaged with the drama at night, he was steadily pushing his way as a journalist. For a short while he was part proprietor of a small Sunday newspaper. In 1829, through a quarrel with the exacting Davidge, Jerrold left the Coburg; and his three-act melodrama, *Black-eyed Susan; or, All in the Downs,* was brought out by R. W. Elliston at the Surrey theatre. The success of the piece was enormous. With its free gallant sea-flavour, it took the town by storm, and "all London went over the water to see it." Elliston made a fortune by the piece; T. P. Cooke, who played William, made his reputation; Jerrold received about £60 and was engaged as dramatic author at five pounds a week. But his fame as a dramatist was achieved. In 1830 it was proposed that he should adapt something from the French for Drury Lane. "No," was his reply, "I shall come into this theatre as an original dramatist or not at all." *The Bride of Ludgate* (December 8, 1831) was the first of a number of his plays produced at Drury Lane. The other patent houses threw their doors open to him also (the Adelphi had already done so); and in 1836 Jerrold became co-manager of the Strand theatre with W. J. Hammond, his brother-in-law. The venture was not successful, and the partnership was dissolved. While it lasted Jerrold wrote his only tragedy, *The Painter of Ghent*, and himself appeared in the title-rôle, without any very marked success. He continued to write sparkling comedies till 1854, the date of his last piece, *The Heart of Gold*.

Meanwhile he had won his way to the pages of numerous periodicals—before 1830 of the second-rate magazines only, but after that to those of more importance. He was a contributor to the *Monthly Magazine, Blackwood's*, the *New Monthly*, and the *Athenaeum*. To *Punch*, the publication which of all others is associated with his name, he contributed from its second number in 1841 till within a few days of his death. He founded and edited for some time, though with indifferent success, the *Illuminated Magazine, Jerrold's Shilling Magazine*, and *Douglas Jerrold's Weekly Newspaper;* and under his editorship *Lloyd's Weekly Newspaper* rose from almost nonentity to a circulation of 182,000. The history of his later years is little more than a catalogue of his literary productions, interrupted now and again by brief visits to the Continent or to the country. Douglas Jerrold died at his house, Kilburn Priory, in London, on the 8th of June 1857.

Jerrold's figure was small and spare, and in later years bowed almost to deformity. His features were strongly marked and expressive from the thin humorous lips to the keen blue eyes gleaming from beneath the shaggy eyebrows. He was brisk and active, with the careless bluffness of a sailor. Open and sincere, he concealed neither his anger nor his pleasure; to his simple frankness all polite duplicity was distasteful. The cynical side of his nature he kept for his writings; in private life his hand was always open. In politics Jerrold was a Liberal, and he gave eager sympathy to Kossuth, Mazzini and Louis Blanc. In social politics especially he took an eager part; he never tired of declaiming against the horrors of war, the luxury of bishops, and the iniquity of capital punishment.

Douglas Jerrold is now perhaps better known from his reputation as a brilliant wit in conversation than from his writings. As a dramatist he was very popular, though his plays have not kept the stage. He dealt with rather humbler forms of social life than had commonly been represented on the boards. He was one of the first and certainly one of the most successful of those 330 who in defence of the native English drama endeavoured to stem the tide of translation from the French, which threatened early in the 19th century altogether to drown original native talent. His skill in construction and his mastery of epigram and brilliant dialogue are well exemplified in his comedy, *Time Works Wonders* (Haymarket, April 26, 1845). The tales and sketches which form the bulk of Jerrold's collected works vary much in skill and interest; but, although there are evident traces of their having been composed from week to week, they are always marked by keen satirical observation and pungent wit.

Among the best known of his numerous works are: *Men of Character* (1838), including "Job Pippin: The man who couldn't help it," and other sketches of the same kind; *Cakes and Ale* (2 vols., 1842), a collection of short papers and whimsical stories; some more serious novels—*The Story of a Feather* (1844), *The Chronicles of Clovernook*(1846), *A Man made of Money* (1849); and *St Giles and St James* (1851); and various series of papers reprinted from *Punch—Punch's Letters to his Son* (1843), *Punch's Complete Letter-writer* (1845), and the famous *Mrs Caudle's Curtain Lectures* (1846).

See W. B. Jerrold, *Life and Remains of Douglas Jerrold*(1859). A collected edition of his writings appeared in 1851-1854, and *The Works of Douglas Jerrold*, with a memoir by his son, W. B. Jerrold, in 1863-1864; but neither is complete. Among the numerous selections from his tales and witticisms are two edited by his grandson, Walter Jerrold, *Bons Mots of Charles Dickens and Douglas Jerrold*(new ed. 1904), and *The Essays of Douglas Jerrold* (1903), illustrated by H. M. Brock. See also *The Wit and Opinions of Douglas Jerrold* (1858), edited by W. B. Jerrold.

His eldest son, WILLIAM BLANCHARD JERROLD (1826-1884), English journalist and author, was born in London on the 23rd of December 1826, and abandoning the artistic career for which he was educated, began newspaper work at an early age there. He was appointed Crystal Palace commissioner to Sweden in 1853, and wrote *A Brage-Beaker with the Swedes*(1854) on his return. In 1855 he was sent to the Paris exhibition as correspondent for several London papers, and from that time he lived much in Paris. In 1857 he succeeded his father as editor of *Lloyd's Weekly Newspaper*, a post which he held for twenty-six years. During the Civil War in America he strongly supported the North, and several of his leading articles were reprinted and placarded in New York by the federal government. He was the founder and president of the English branch of the international literary association for the assimilation of copyright laws. Four of his plays were successfully produced on the London stage, the popular farce *Cool as a Cucumber* (Lyceum 1851) being the best known. His French experiences resulted in a number of books, most important of which is his *Life of Napoleon III.* (1874). He was occupied in writing the biography of Gustave Doré, who had illustrated several of his books, when he died on the 10th of March 1884.

Among his books are *A Story of Social Distinction*(1848), *Life and Remains of Douglas Jerrold* (1859), *Up and Down in the World* (1863), *The Children of Lutetia*(1864), *Cent per Cent* (1871), *At Home in Paris* (1871), *The Best of all Good Company* (1871-1873), and *The Life of George Cruikshank* (1882).

JERRY, a short form of the name Jeremiah, applied to various common objects, and more particularly to a machine for finishing cloth. The expression "jerry-built" is applied to houses built badly and of inferior materials, and run up by a speculative builder. There seems to be no foundation for the assertion that this expression was occasioned by the work of a firm of Liverpool builders named Jerry.

JERSEY, EARLS OF. Sir Edward Villiers (*c.*1656-1711), son of Sir Edward Villiers (1620-1689), of Richmond, Surrey, was created Baron Villiers and Viscount Villiers in 1691 and earl of Jersey in 1697. His grandfather, Sir Edward Villiers (*c.* 1585-1626), master of the mint and president of Munster, was half-brother of George Villiers, 1st duke of Buckingham, and of Christopher Villiers, 1st earl of Anglesey; his sister was Elizabeth Villiers, the mistress of William III., and afterwards countess of Orkney. Villiers was knight-marshal of the royal household in succession to his father; master of the horse to Queen Mary; and lord chamberlain to William III. and Queen Anne. In 1696 he represented his country at the congress of Ryswick; he was ambassador at the Hague, and after becoming an earl was ambassador in Paris. In 1699 he was made secretary of state for the southern department, and on three occasions he was one of the lords justices of England. In 1704 he was dismissed from office by Anne, and after this event he was concerned in some of the Jacobite schemes. He died on the 25th of August 1711. The 2nd earl was his son William (*c.* 1682-1721), an adherent of the exiled house of Stuart, and the 3rd earl was the latter's son William (d. 1769), who succeeded his kinsman John Fitzgerald (*c.* 1692-1766) as 6th Viscount Grandison. The 3rd earl's son, George Bussy, the 4th earl (1735-1805), held several positions at the court of George III., and on account of his courtly manners was called the "prince of Maccaronies." The 4th earl's son, George, 5th earl of Jersey (1773-1859), one of the most celebrated fox-hunters of his time and a successful owner of racehorses, married Sarah Sophia (1785-1867), daughter of John Fane, 10th earl of Westmorland, and granddaughter of Robert Child, the banker. She inherited her grandfather's great wealth, including his interest in Child's bank, and with her husband took the name of Child-Villiers. Since this time the connexions of the earls of Jersey with Child's bank has been maintained. Victor Albert George Child-Villiers (b. 1845) succeeded his father George Augustus (1808-1859), 6th earl, who had only held the title for three weeks, as 7th earl of Jersey in 1859. This nobleman was governor of New South Wales from 1890 to 1893.

JERSEY, the largest of the Channel Islands, belonging to Great Britain. Its chief town, St Helier, on the south coast of the island, is in 49° 12' N., 2° 7' W., 105 m. S. by E. of Portland Bill on the English coast, and 24 m. from the French coast to the east. Jersey is the southernmost of the more important islands of the group. It is of oblong form with a length of 10 m. from east to west and an extreme breadth of 6¼ m. The area is 28,717 acres, or 45 sq. m. Pop. (1901), 52,576.

The island reaches its greatest elevation (nearly 500 ft.) in the north, the land rising sharply from the north coast, and displaying bold and picturesque cliffs towards the sea. The east, south and west coasts consist of a succession of large open bays, shallow and rocky, with marshy or sandy shores separated by rocky headlands. The principal bays are Grève au Lançons, Grève de Lecq, St John's and Bouley Bays on the north coast; St Catherine's and Grouville Bays on the east; St Clement's, St Aubin's and St Brelade's Bays on the south; and St Ouen's Bay, the wide sweep of which occupies nearly the whole of the west coast. The sea in many places has encroached greatly on the land, and sand drifts have been found troublesome, especially on the west coast. The surface of the country is broken by winding valleys having a general direction from north to south, and as they approach the south uniting so as to form small plains. The lofty hedges which bound the small enclosures into which Jersey is divided, the trees and shrubberies which line the roads and cluster round the uplands and in almost every nook of the valleys unutilized for pasturage or tillage, give the island a luxuriant appearance, neutralizing the bare effect of the few sandy plains and sand-covered hills. Fruits and flowers indigenous to warm climates grow freely in the open air. The land, under careful cultivation, is rich and productive, the soil being generally a deep loam, especially in the valleys, but in the west shallow, light and sandy. The subsoil is usually gravel, but in some parts an unfertile clay. Some two-thirds of the total area is under cultivation, great numbers of cattle being pastured, and much market gardening practised. The potato crop is very large. The peasants take advantage of every bit of wall and every isolated nook of ground for growing fruit trees. Grapes are ripened under glass; oranges can be grown in sheltered situations, but the most common fruits are apples, which are used for cider, and pears. A manure of burnt sea-weed (**vraic**) is generally used. The pasturage is very rich, and is much improved by the application of this manure to the surface. The breed of cattle is kept pure by stringent laws against the importation of foreign animals. The milk is used almost exclusively to manufacture butter. The cattle are always housed in winter, but remain out 331at night from May till October. There was formerly a small black breed of horses peculiar to the island, but horses are now chiefly imported from France or England. Pigs are kept principally for local consumption, and only a few sheep are reared. Fish are not so plentiful as round the shores of Guernsey, but mackerel, turbot, cod, mullet and especially the conger eel are abundant at the Minquiers. There is a large oyster bed between Jersey and France, but partly on account of over-dredging the supply is not so abundant as formerly. There is a great variety of other shell fish. The fisheries, ship-building and boat-building employ many of the inhabitants. Kelp and iodine are manufactured from sea-weed. The principal exports are granite, fruit and vegetables (especially potatoes), butter and cattle; and the chief imports coal and articles of human consumption. Communications with England are maintained principally from Southampton and Weymouth, and there are regular steamship services from Granville and St Malo on the French coast. The Jersey railway runs west from St Helier round St Aubin's Bay to St Aubin, and continues to Corbière at the south-western extremity of the island; and the Jersey eastern railway follows the southern and eastern coasts to Gorey. The island is intersected with a network of good roads.

Jersey is under a distinct and in several respects different form of administrative government from Guernsey and the smaller islands included in the bailiwick of Guernsey. For its peculiar constitution, system of justice, ecclesiastical arrangements and finance, see CHANNEL ISLANDS. There are twelve parishes, namely St Helier, Grouville, St Brelade, St Clement, St John, St Laurence, St Martin, St Mary, St Ouen, St Peter, St Saviour and Trinity. The population of the island nearly doubled between 1821 and 1901, but decreased from 54,518 to 52,576 between 1891 and 1901.

The history of Jersey is treated under CHANNEL ISLANDS. Among objects of antiquarian interest, a cromlech near Mont Orgueil is the finest of several examples. St Brelade's church, probably the oldest in the island, dates from the 12th century; among the later churches St Helier's, of the 14th century, may be mentioned. There are also some very early chapels, considered to date from the 10th century or earlier; among these may be noted the Chapelle-ès-Pêcheurs at St Brelade's, and the picturesque chapel in the grounds of the manor of Rozel. The castle of Mont Orgueil, of which there are considerable remains, is believed to be founded upon the site of a Roman stronghold, and a "Caesar's fort" still forms a part of it.

JERSEY CITY, a city and the county-seat of Hudson county, New Jersey, U.S.A., on a peninsula between the Hudson and Hackensack rivers at the N. and between New York and Newark bays at the S., opposite lower Manhattan Island. Pop. (1890), 163,003; (1900), 206,433, of whom 58,424 were foreign-born (19,314 Irish, 17,375 German, 4642 English, 3832 Italian, 1694 Russian, 1690 Scottish, 1643 Russian Poles, 1445 Austrian) and 3704 were negroes; (1910 census) 267,779. It is the eastern terminus of the Pennsylvania, the Lehigh Valley, the West Shore, the Central of New Jersey, the Baltimore & Ohio, the Northern of New Jersey (operated by the Erie), the Erie, the New York, Susquehanna & Western, and the New Jersey & New York (controlled by the Erie) railways, the first three using the Pennsylvania station; and of the little-used Morris canal. Jersey City is served by several inter-urban electric railways and by the tunnels of the Hudson & Manhattan railroad company to Dey St. and to 33rd St. and 6th Ave., New York City, and it also has docks of several lines of Transatlantic and coast steamers. The city occupies a land area of 14.3 sq. m. and has a water-front of about 12 m. Bergen Hill, a southerly extension of the Palisades, extends longitudinally through it from north to south. At the north end this hill rises on the east side precipitously to a height of nearly 200 ft.; on the west and south sides the slope is gradual. On the crest of the hill is the fine Hudson County Boulevard, about 19 m. long and 100 ft. wide, extending through the city and county from north to south and passing through West Side Park, a splendid county park containing lakes and a 70-acre playground. The water-front, especially on the east side, is given up to manufacturing and shipping establishments. In the hill section are the better residences, most of which are wooden and detached.

The principal buildings are the city hall and the court house. There are nine small city parks with an aggregate area of 39.1 acres. The city has a public library containing (1907) 107,600 volumes and an historical museum. At the corner of Bergen Ave. and Forrest St. is the People's Palace, given in 1904 by Joseph Milbank to the First Congregational church and containing a library and reading-room, a gymnasium, bowling alleys, a billiard-room, a rifle-range, a roof-garden, and an auditorium and theatre; kindergarten classes are held and an employment bureau is maintained. Among the educational institutions are the German American school, Hasbrouck institute, St Aloysius academy (Roman Catholic) and St Peter's college (Roman Catholic); and there are good public schools. Grain is shipped to and from Jersey City in large quantities, and in general the city is an important shipping port; being included, however, in the port of New York, no separate statistics are available. There are large slaughtering establishments, and factories for the refining of sugar and for the manufacture of tobacco goods, soap and perfumery, lead pencils, iron and steel, railway cars, chemicals, rubber goods, silk goods, dressed lumber, and malt liquors. The value of the city's manufactured products increased from $37,376,322 in 1890 to $77,225,116 in 1900, or 106.6%; in 1905 the factory product alone was valued at $75,740,934, an increase of only 3.9% over the factory product in 1900, this small rate of increase being due very largely to a decline in the value of the products of the sugar and molasses refining industry. The value of the wholesale slaughtering and meat-packing product decreased from $18,551,783 in 1880 and $11,356,511 in 1890 to $6,243,217 in 1900—of this $5,708,763 represented wholesale slaughtering alone; in 1905 the wholesale slaughtering product was valued at $7,568,739.

In 1908 the assessed valuation of the city was $267,039,754. The city is governed by a board of aldermen and a mayor (elected biennially), who appoints most of the officials, the street and water board being the principal exception.

Jersey City when first incorporated was a small sandy peninsula (an island at high tide) known as Paulus Hook, directly opposite the lower end of Manhattan Island. It had been a part of the Dutch patroonship of Pavonia granted to Michael Pauw in 1630. In 1633 the first buildings were erected, and for more than a century the Hook was occupied by a small agricultural and trading community. In 1764 a new post route between New York and Philadelphia passed through what is now the city, and direct ferry communication began with New York. Early in the War of Independence Paulus Hook was fortified by the Americans, but soon after the battle of Long Island they abandoned it, and on the 23rd of September 1776 it was occupied by the British. On the morning of the 19th of August 1779 the British garrison was surprised by Major Henry Lee ("Light Horse Harry"), who with about 500 men took 159 prisoners and lost only 2 killed and 3 wounded, one of the most brilliant exploits during the War of Independence. In 1804 Paulus Hook, containing 117 acres and having about 15 inhabitants, passed into the possession of three enterprising New York lawyers, who laid it out as a town and formed an association for its government, which was incorporated as the "associates of the Jersey company." In 1820 the town was incorporated as the City of Jersey, but it remained a part of the township of Bergen until 1838, when it was reincorporated as a distinct municipality. In 1851 the township of Van Vorst, founded in 1804 between Paulus Hook and Hoboken, was annexed. In 1870 there were two annexations: to the south, the town of Bergen, the county-seat, which was founded in 1660; to the north-west, Hudson City, which had been separated from the township of North Bergen in 1852 and incorporated as a city in 1855. The town of Greenville, to the south, was annexed in 1873.

JERUSALEM (Heb. ירושלים *Yerushalaïm*, pronounced as a dual), the chief city of Palestine. Letters found at Tell el-Amarna in Egypt, written by an early ruler of Jerusalem, show that the name existed under the form*Urusalim, i.e.* "City of Salim" or "City of Peace," many years before the Israelites under Joshua entered Canaan. The emperor Hadrian, when he rebuilt the city, changed the name to Aelia Capitolina. The Arabs usually designate Jerusalem by names expressive of 332holiness, such as Beit el Maḳdis and El Muḳaddis or briefly El Ḳuds, *i.e.* the Sanctuary.

Natural Topography.—Jerusalem is situated in 31° 47′ N. and 35° 15′ E., in the hill country of southern Palestine, close to the watershed, at an average altitude of 2500 ft. above the Mediterranean, and 3800 ft. above the level of the Dead Sea. The city stands on a rocky plateau, which projects southwards from the main line of hills. On the east the valley of the Kidron separates this plateau from the ridge of the Mount of Olives, which is 100 to 200 ft. higher, while the Wadi Er Rababi bounds Jerusalem on the west and south, meeting the Valley of Kidron near the lower pool of Siloam. Both valleys fall rapidly as they approach the point of junction, which lies at a depth of more than 600 ft. below the general valley of the plateau. The latter, which covers an area of about 1000 acres, has at the present time a fairly uniform surface and slopes gradually from the north to the south and east. Originally, however, its formation was very different, as it was intersected by a deep valley, called Tyropoeon by Josephus, which, starting from a point N.W. of the Damascus gate, followed a course first south-east and then west of south, and joined the two main valleys of Kidron and Er Rababi at Siloam. Another shorter valley began near the present Jaffa gate and, taking an easterly direction, joined the Tyropoeon; while a third ravine passed across what is now the northern part of the Haram enclosure and fell into the valley of the Kidron. The exact form of these three interior valleys, which had an important influence on the construction and history of the city, is still imperfectly known, as they are to a great extent obliterated by vast accumulations of rubbish, which has filled them up in some places to a depth of more than 100 ft. Their approximate form was only arrived at by excavations made during the later years of the 19th century. The limited knowledge which we possess of the original features of the ground within the area of the city makes a reconstruction of the topographical history of the latter a difficult task; and, as a natural result, many irreconcilable theories have been suggested. The difficulty is increased by the fact that the geographical descriptions given in the Old Testament the Apocrypha and the writings of Josephus are very short, and, having been written for those who were acquainted with the places, convey insufficient information to historians of the present day, when the sites are so greatly altered. All that can be done is to form a continuous account in accord with the ancient histories, and with the original formation of the ground, so far as this has been identified by modern exploration. But the progress of exploration and excavation may render this subject to further modification.

The geological formation of the plateau consists of thin beds of hard silicious chalk, locally called *misse*, which overlie a thick bed of soft white limestone, known by the name of *meleke*. Both descriptions of rock yielded good material for building; while in the soft *meleke* tanks, underground chambers, tombs, &c., were easily excavated. In ancient times a brook flowed down the valley of the Kidron, and it is possible that a stream flowed also through the Tyropoeon valley. The only known spring existing at present within the limits of the city is the "fountain of the Virgin," on the western side of the Kidron valley, but there may have been others which are now concealed by the accumulations of rubbish. Cisterns were also used for the storage of rain water, and aqueducts, of which the remains still exist (see AQUEDUCTS *ad init.*), were constructed for the conveyance of water from a distance. Speaking generally, it is probable that the water supply of Jerusalem in ancient times was better than it is at present.

History.—The early history of Jerusalem is very obscure. The Tell el-Amarna letters show that, long before the invasion by Joshua, it was occupied by the Egyptians, and was probably a stronghold of considerable importance, as it formed a good strategical position in the hill country of southern Palestine. We do not know how the Egyptians were forced to abandon Jerusalem; but, at the time of the Israelite conquest, it was undoubtedly in the hands of the Jebusites, the native inhabitants of the country. The exact position of the Jebusite city is unknown; some authorities locate it on the western hill, now known as Zion; some on the eastern hill, afterwards occupied by the Temple and the city of David; while others consider it was a double settlement, one part being on the western, and the other on the eastern hill, separated from one another by the Tyropoeon valley. The latter view appears to be the most probable, as, according to the Biblical accounts, Jerusalem was partly in Judah and partly in Benjamin, the line of demarcation between the two tribes passing through the city. According to this theory, the part of Jerusalem known as Jebus was situated on the western hill, and the outlying fort of Zion on the eastern hill. The men of Judah and Benjamin did not succeed in getting full possession of the place, and the Jebusites still held it when David became king of Israel. Some years after his accession David succeeded after some difficulty in taking Jerusalem. He established his royal city on the eastern hill close to the site of the Jebusite Zion, while Jebus, the town on the western side of the Tyropoeon valley, became the civil city, of which Joab, David's leading general, was appointed governor. David surrounded the royal city with a wall and built a citadel, probably on the site of the Jebusite fort of Zion, while Joab fortified the western town. North of the city of David, the king, acting under divine guidance, chose a site for the Temple of Jehovah, which was erected with great magnificence by Solomon. The actual site occupied by this building has given rise to much controversy, though all authorities are agreed that it must have stood on some part of the area now known as the Haram. James Fergusson was of opinion that the Temple stood near the south-western corner. As, however, it was proved by the explorations of Sir Charles Warren in 1869-1870 that the Tyropoeon valley passed under this corner, and that the foundations must have been of enormous depth, Fergusson's theory must be regarded as untenable (see also SEPULCHRE, HOLY). On the whole it is most likely that the Temple was erected by Solomon on the same spot as is now occupied by the Dome of the Rock, commonly known as the Mosque of Omar, and, regard being had to the levels of the ground, it is possible that the Holy of Holies, the most sacred chamber of the Temple, stood over the rock which is still regarded with veneration by the Mahommedans. Solomon greatly strengthened the fortifications of Jerusalem, and was probably the builder of the line of defence, called by Josephus the first or old wall, which united the cities on the eastern and western hills. The kingdom reached its highest point of importance during the reign of Solomon, but, shortly after his death, it was broken up by the rebellion of Jeroboam, who founded the separate kingdom of Israel with its capital at Shechem. Two tribes only, Judah and Benjamin, with the descendants of Levi, remained faithful to Rehoboam, the son of Solomon. Jerusalem thus lost much of its importance, especially after it was forced to surrender to Shishak, king of Egypt, who carried off a great part of the riches which had been accumulated by Solomon. The history of Jerusalem during the succeeding three centuries consists for the most part of a succession of wars against the kingdom of Israel, the Moabites and the Syrians. Joash, king of Israel, captured the city from Amaziah, king of Judah, and destroyed part of the fortifications, but these were rebuilt by Uzziah, the son of Amaziah, who did much to restore the city to its original prosperity. In the reign of Hezekiah, the kingdom of Judah became tributary to the Assyrians, who attempted the capture of Jerusalem. Hezekiah improved the defences and arranged for a good water supply, preparatory to the siege by Sennacherib, the Assyrian general. The siege failed and the Assyrians retired. Some years later Syria was again invaded by the Egyptians, who reduced Judah to the position of a tributary state. In the reign of Zedekiah, the last of the line of kings, Jerusalem was captured by Nebuchadrezzar, king of Babylon, who pillaged the city, destroyed the Temple, and ruined the fortifications (see JEWS, § 17). A number of the principal inhabitants were carried captive to Babylon, and Jerusalem was reduced to the position of an insignificant town. Nebuchadrezzar placed in the city a garrison which appears to have been quartered on the western hill, while the eastern hill on which were the Temple and the city of David was left more or less desolate. We have no information regarding Jerusalem during the period of the captivity, but fortunately Nehemiah, who was permitted to return and rebuild the defences about 445 B.C., has given a fairly clear description of the line of the wall which enables us to obtain a good idea of the extent of the city at this period. The Temple had already been partially rebuilt by Zedekiah and his companions, but on a scale far inferior to the magnificent building of King Solomon, and Nehemiah devoted his attention to the reconstruction of the walls. Before beginning the work, he made a preliminary reconnaissance of the fortifications on the south of the town from the Valley Gate, which was near the S.E. corner, to the pool of Siloam and valley of the Kidron. He then allotted the reconstruction of wall and gates to different parties of workmen, and 333his narrative describes the portion of wall upon which each of these was employed.1

It is clear from his account that the lines of fortifications included both the eastern and western hills. North of the Temple enclosure there was a gate, known as the Sheep Gate, which must have opened into the third valley mentioned above, and stood somewhere near what is now the north side of the Haram enclosure, but considerably south of the present north wall of the latter. To the west of the Sheep Gate there were two important towers in the wall, called respectively Meah and Hananeel. The tower Hananeel is specially worthy of notice as it stood N.W. of the Temple and probably formed the basis of the citadel built by Simon Maccabaeus, which again was succeeded by the fortress of Antonia, constructed by Herod the Great, and one of the most important positions at the time of the siege by Titus. At or near the tower Hananeel the wall turned south along the east side of the Tyropoeon valley, and then again westward, crossing the valley at a point probably near the remarkable construction known as Wilson's arch. A gate in the valley, known as the Fish Gate, opened on a road which, leading from the north, went down the Tyropoeon valley to the southern part of the city. Westward of this gate the wall followed the south side of the valley which joined the Tyropoeon from the west as far as the north-western corner of the city at the site of the present Jaffa Gate and the so-called tower of David. In this part of the wall there were apparently two gates facing north, i.e. the Old Gate and the Gate of Ephraim, 400 cubits from the corner.2 At the corner stood the residence of the Babylonian governor, near the site upon which King Herod afterwards built his magnificent palace. From the corner at the governor's house, the wall went in a southerly direction and turned south-east to the Valley Gate, remains of which were discovered by F. J. Bliss and fully described in his *Excavations in Jerusalem in 1894-1897*. From the Valley Gate the wall took an easterly course for a distance of 1000 cubits to the Dung Gate, near which on the east was the Fountain Gate, not far from the lower pool of Siloam. Here was the most southerly point of Jerusalem, and the wall turning hence to the north followed the west side of the valley of the Kidron, enclosing the city of David and the Temple enclosure, and finally turning west at some point near the site of the Golden Gate joined the wall, already described, at the Sheep Gate. Nehemiah mentions a number of places on the eastern hill, including the tomb of David, the positions of which cannot with our present knowledge be fixed with any certainty.

152

After the restoration of the walls of Jerusalem by Nehemiah, a considerable number of Jews returned to the city, but we know practically nothing of its history for more than a century until, in 332 B.C., Alexander the Great conquered Syria. The gates of Jerusalem were opened to him and he left the Jews in peaceful occupation. But his successors did not act with similar leniency; when the city was captured by Ptolemy I., king of Egypt, twelve years later, the fortifications were partially demolished and apparently not again restored until the period of the high priest Simon II., who repaired the defences and also the Temple buildings. In 168 B.C. Antiochus Epiphanes captured Jerusalem, destroyed the walls, and devastated the Temple, reducing the city to a worse position than it had occupied since the time of the captivity. He built a citadel called the Acra to dominate the town and placed in it a strong garrison of Greeks. The position of the Acra is doubtful, but it appears most probable that it stood on the eastern hill between the Temple and the city of David, both of which it commanded. Some writers place it north of the Temple on the site afterwards occupied by the fortress of Antonia, but such a position is not in accord with the descriptions either in Josephus or in the books of the Maccabees, which are quite consistent with each other. Other writers again have placed the Acra on the eastern side of the hill upon which the church of the Holy Sepulchre now stands, but as this point was probably quite outside the city at the time of Antiochus Epiphanes, and is at too great a distance from the Temple, it can hardly be accepted. But the site which has been already indicated at the N.E. corner of the present Mosque el Aksa meets the accounts of the ancient authorities better than any other. At this point in the Haram enclosure there is an enormous underground cistern, known as the Great Sea, and this may possibly have been the source of water supply for the Greek garrison. The oppression of Antiochus led to a revolt of the Jews under the leadership of the Maccabees, and Judas Maccabaeus succeeded in capturing Jerusalem after severe fighting, but could not get possession of the Acra, which caused much trouble to the Jews, who erected a wall between it and the Temple, and another wall to cut it off from the city. The Greeks held out for a considerable time, but had finally to surrender, probably from want of food, to Simon Maccabaeus, who demolished the Acra and cut down the hill upon which it stood so that it might no longer be higher than the Temple, and that there should be no separation between the latter and the city. Simon then constructed a new citadel, north of the Temple, to take the place of the Acra, and established in Judaea the Asmonean dynasty, which lasted for nearly a century, when the Roman republic began to make its influence felt in Syria. In 65 B.C. Jerusalem was captured by Pompey after a difficult siege. The Asmonean dynasty lasted a few years longer, but finally came to an end when Herod the Great, with the aid of the Romans, took possession of Jerusalem and became the first king of the Idumaean dynasty. Herod again raised the city to the position of an important capital, restoring the fortifications, and rebuilding the Temple from its foundations. He also built the great fortress of Antonia, N.W. of the Temple, on the site of the citadel of the Asmoneans, and constructed a magnificent palace for himself on the western hill, defended by three great towers, which he named Mariamne, Hippicus and Phasaelus. At some period between the time of the Maccabees and of Herod, a second or outer wall had been built outside and north of the first wall, but it is not possible to fix an accurate date to this line of defence, as the references to it in Josephus are obscure. Herod adorned the town with other buildings and constructed a theatre and gymnasium. He doubled the area of the enclosure round the Temple, and there can be little doubt that a great part of the walls of the Haram area date from the time of Herod, while probably the tower of David, which still exists near the Jaffa Gate, is on the same foundation as one of the towers adjoining his palace. Archelaus, Herod's successor, had far less authority than Herod, and the real power of government at Jerusalem was assumed by the Roman procurators, in the time of one of whom, Pontius Pilate, Jesus Christ was condemned to death and crucified outside Jerusalem. The places of his execution and burial are not certainly known (see SEPULCHRE, HOLY).

Herod Agrippa, who succeeded to the kingdom, built a third or outer wall on the north side of Jerusalem in order to enclose and defend the buildings which had gradually been constructed outside the old fortifications. The exact line of this third wall is not known with certainty, but it probably followed approximately the same line as the existing north wall of Jerusalem. Some writers have considered that it extended a considerable distance farther to the north, but of this there is no proof, and no remains have as yet been found which would support the opinion. The wall of Herod Agrippa was planned on a grand scale, but its execution was stopped by the Romans, so that it was not completed at the time of the siege of Jerusalem by Titus. The writings of Josephus give a good idea of the fortifications and buildings of Jerusalem at the time of the siege, and his accurate personal knowledge makes his account worthy of the most careful perusal. He explains clearly how Titus, beginning his attack from the north, captured the third or outer wall, then the second wall, and finally the fortress of Antonia, the Temple, and the upper city. After the capture, Titus ordered the Temple to be demolished and the fortifications to be

153

levelled, with the exception of the three great towers at Herod's palace. It is, however, uncertain how far the order was carried out, and it is probable that the outer walls of the Temple enclosure were left partially standing and that the defences on the west and south of the city were not completely levelled. When Titus and his army withdrew from Jerusalem, the 10th legion was left as a permanent Roman garrison, and a fortified camp for their occupation was established on the western hill. We have no account of the size or position of this camp, but a consideration of the site, and a comparison with other Roman camps in various parts of Europe, make it probable that it occupied an area of about 50 acres, extending over what is now known as the Armenian quarter of the town, and that it was bounded on the north by the 334old or first wall, on the west also by the old wall, on the south by a line of defence somewhat in the same position as the present south wall where it passes the Zion Gate, and on the east by an entrenchment running north and south parallel to the existing thoroughfare known as David Street. For sixty years the Roman garrison were left in undisturbed occupation, but in 132 the Jews rose in revolt under the leadership of Bar-Cochebas or Barcochba, and took possession of Jerusalem. After a severe struggle, the revolt was suppressed by the Roman general, Julius Severus, and Jerusalem was recaptured and again destroyed. According to some writers, this devastation was even more complete than after the siege by Titus. About 130 the emperor Hadrian decided to rebuild Jerusalem, and make it a Roman colony. The new city was called Aelia Capitolina. The exact size of the city is not known, but it probably extended as far as the present north wall of Jerusalem and included the northern part of the western hill. A temple dedicated to Jupiter Capitolinus was erected on the site of the Temple, and other buildings were constructed, known as the Theatre, the Demosia, the Tetranymphon, the Dodecapylon and the Codra. The Jews were forbidden to reside in the city, but Christians were freely admitted. The history of Jerusalem during the period between the foundation of the city of Aelia by the emperor Hadrian and the accession of Constantine the Great in 306 is obscure, but no important change appears to have been made in the size or fortifications of the city, which continued as a Roman colony. In 326 Constantine, after his conversion to Christianity, issued orders to the bishop Macarius to recover the site of the crucifixion of Jesus Christ, and the tomb in which his body was laid (see SEPULCHRE, HOLY). After the holy sites had been determined, Constantine gave orders for the construction of two magnificent churches, the one over the tomb and the other over the place where the cross was discovered. The present church of the Holy Sepulchre stands on the site upon which one of the churches of Constantine was built, but the second church, the Basilica of the Cross, has completely disappeared. The next important epoch in building construction at Jerusalem was about 460, when the empress Eudocia visited Palestine and expended large sums oh the improvement of the city. The walls were repaired by her orders, and the line of fortifications appears to have been extended on the south so as to include the pool of Siloam. A church was built above the pool, probably at the same time, and, after having completely disappeared for many centuries, it was recovered by F. J. Bliss when making his exploration of Jerusalem. The empress also erected a large church in honour of St Stephen north of the Damascus Gate, and is believed to have been buried therein. The site of this church was discovered in 1874, and it has since been rebuilt. In the 6th century the emperor Justinian erected a magnificent basilica at Jerusalem, in honour of the Virgin Mary, and attached to it two hospitals, one for the reception of pilgrims and one for the accommodation of the sick poor. The description given by Procopius does not indicate clearly where this church was situated. A theory frequently put forward is that it stood within the Haram area near the Mosque of el Aksa, but it is more probable that it was on Zion, near the traditional place of the Coenaculum or last supper, where the Mahommedan building known as the tomb of David now stands. In 614 Chosroes II., the king of Persia, captured Jerusalem, devastated many of the buildings, and massacred a great number of the inhabitants. The churches at the Holy Sepulchre were much damaged, but were partially restored by the monk Modestus, who devoted himself with great energy to the work. After a severe struggle the Persians were defeated by the emperor Heraclius, who entered Jerusalem in triumph in 629 bringing with him the holy cross, which had been carried off by Chosroes. At this period the religion of Mahomet was spreading over the east, and in 637 the caliph Omar marched on Jerusalem, which capitulated after a siege of four months. Omar behaved with great moderation, restraining his troops from pillage and leaving the Christians in possession of their churches. A wooden mosque was erected near the site of the Temple, which was replaced by the Mosque of Aksa, built by the amir Abdalmalik (Abd el Malek), who also constructed the Dome of the Rock, known as the Mosque of Omar, in 688. The Mahommedans held Jerusalem until 1099, when it was captured by the crusaders under Godfrey of Bouillon, and became the capital of the Latin Kingdom of Jerusalem (see CRUSADES, vol. viii. p. 401) until 1187, when Saladin reconquered it, and rebuilt the walls. Since that time, except from 1229 to 1239, and from 1243 to 1244, the city has been held by the Mahommedans. It was occupied by the Egyptian sultans until 1517, when the Turks under Selim I. occupied Syria. Selim's successor, Suleiman the Magnificent, restored the fortifications, which since that time have been little altered.

Modern Jerusalem.—Jerusalem is the chief town of a sanjak, governed by a *mutessarif*, who reports directly to the Porte. It has the usual executive and town councils, upon which the recognized religious communities, or*millets*, have representatives; and it is garrisoned by infantry of the V. army corps. The city is connected with its port, Jaffa, by a carriage road, 41 m., and by a metre-gauge railway, 54 m., which was completed in 1892, and is worked by a French company. There are also carriage roads to Bethlehem, Hebron and Jericho, and a road to Nablus was in course of construction in 1909. Prior to 1858, when the modern building period commenced, Jerusalem lay wholly within its 16th-century walls, and even as late as 1875 there were few private residences beyond their limits. At present Jerusalem without the walls covers a larger area than that within them. The growth has been chiefly towards the north and north-west; but there are large suburbs on the west, and on the south-west near the railway station on the plain of Rephaim. The village of Siloam has also increased in size, and the western slopes of Olivet are being covered with churches, monasteries and houses. Amongst the most marked features of the change that has taken place since 1875 are the growth of religious and philanthropic establishments; the settlement of Jewish colonies from Bokhara, Yemen and Europe; the migration of Europeans, old Moslem families, and Jews from the city to the suburbs; the increased vegetation, due to the numerous gardens and improved methods of cultivation; the substitution of timber and red tiles for the vaulted stone roofs which were so characteristic of the old city; the striking want of beauty, grandeur, and harmony with their environment exhibited by most of the new buildings; and the introduction of wheeled transport, which, cutting into the soft limestone, has produced mud and dust to an extent previously unknown. To facilitate communication between the city and its suburbs, the Bab ez-Zāhire, or Herod's Gate, and a new gate, near the north-west angle of the walls, have been opened; and a portion of the wall, adjoining the Jaffa Gate, has been thrown down, to allow free access for carriages. Within the city the principal streets have been roughly paved, and iron bars placed across the narrow alleys to prevent the passage of camels. Without the walls carriage roads have been made to the mount of Olives, the railway station, and various parts of the suburbs, but they are kept in bad repair. Little effort has been made to meet the increased sanitary requirements of the larger population and wider inhabited area. There is no municipal water-supply, and the main drain of the city discharges into the lower pool of Siloam, which has become an open cesspit. In several places the débris within the walls is saturated with sewage, and the water of the Fountain of the Virgin, and of many of the old cisterns, is unfit for drinking. Amongst the more important buildings for ecclesiastical and philanthropic purposes erected to the north of the city since 1860 are the Russian cathedral, hospice and hospital; the French hospital of St Louis, and hospice and church of St Augustine; the German schools, orphanages and hospitals; the new hospital and industrial school of the London mission to the Jews; the Abyssinian church; the church and schools of the Church missionary society; the Anglican church, college and bishop's house; the Dominican monastery, seminary and church of St Stephen; the Rothschild hospital and girls' school; and the industrial school and workshops of the Alliance Israélite. On the mount of Olives are the Russian church, tower and hospice, near the chapel of the Ascension; the French Paternoster church; the Carmelite nunnery; and the Russian church of St Mary Magdalene, near Gethsemane. South of the city are the Armenian monastery of Mount Zion and Bishop Gobat's school. On the west side are the institution of the sisters of St Vincent; the Ratisbon school; the Montefiore hospice; the British ophthalmic hospital of the knights of St John; the convent and church of the Clarisses; and the Moravian leper hospital. Within the city walls are the Latin Patriarchal church and residence; the school of the Frères de la Doctrine Chrétienne; the schools and printing house of the Franciscans; the Coptic monastery; the German church of the Redeemer, and hospice; the United Armenian church of the Spasm; the convent and school of the Sœurs de Zion; the Austrian hospice; the Turkish school and museum; the monastery and seminary of the Frères de la Mission Algérienne, with the restored church of St Anne, the church, schools and hospital of the London mission to the Jews; the Armenian seminary and Patriarchal buildings; the Rothschild hospital; and Jewish hospices and synagogues. 335The climate is naturally good, but continued neglect of sanitary precautions has made the city unhealthy. During the summer months the heat is tempered by a fresh sea-breeze, and there is usually a sharp fall of temperature at night; but in spring and autumn the east and south-east winds, which blow across the heated depression of the Ghor, are enervating and oppressive. A dry season, which lasts from May to October, is followed by a rainy season, divided into the early winter and latter rains. Snow falls two years out of three, but soon melts. The mean annual temperature is 62.8° F., the maximum 112°, and the minimum 25°. The mean monthly temperature is lowest (47.2°) in February, and highest (76.3°) in August. The mean annual rainfall (1861 to 1899) is 26.06 in. The most unhealthy period is from 1st May to 31st October, when there are, from time to time, outbreaks of typhoid, small-pox, diphtheria and other epidemics. The unhealthiness of the city is chiefly due to want of proper drainage, impure drinking-water, miasma from the disturbed rubbish heaps, and contaminated dust from the uncleansed roads and streets. The only industry is the manufacture of olive-wood and mother-of-pearl goods for sale to pilgrims and for export. The imports (see Joppa) are chiefly food, clothing and building material. The population in 1905 was about 60,000 (Moslems 7000, Christians 13,000, Jews 40,000). During the pilgrimage season it is increased by about 15,000 travellers and pilgrims.

AUTHORITIES.—Pal. Exp. Fund Publications—Sir C. Warren, *Jerusalem, Memoir* (1884); Clermont-Ganneau,*Archaeol. Researches* (vol. i., 1899); Bliss, *Excavns.* at *Jerusalem* (1898); Conder, *Latin Kingdom of Jerusalem*(1897), and *The City of Jerusalem* (1909), an historical survey over 4000 years; Le Strange, *Pal. under the Moslems* (1890); Fergusson, *Temples of the Jews* (1878); Hayter Lewis, *Holy Places of Jerusalem*(1888); *Churches of Constantine at Jerusalem* (1891); Guthe, "Ausgrabungen in Jer.," in *Zeitschrift d. D. Pal. Vereins* (vol. v.); Tobler,*Topographie von Jerusalem* (Berlin, 1854); Dritte Wanderung (1859); Sepp, *Jerusalem und das heilige Land*(1873); Röhricht, *Regesta Regni Hierosolymitani; Bibliotheca Geographica Palaestinae* (1890); De Vogüé, *Le Temple de Jérusalem* (1864); Sir C. W. Wilson, *Golgotha and the Holy Sepulchre* (1906); publications of the Pal. Pilgrims' Text Society and of the *Société de l'Orient latin*; papers in *Quarterly Statements* of the P. E. Fund, the*Zeitschrift d. D. Pal. Vereins*, Clermont-Ganneau's *Recueil d'archéologie orientale and Études d'arch. orientale*, and the *Revue Biblique*; Baedeker's *Handbook to Palestine and Syria* (1906); Mommert, *Die hl. Grabeskirche zu Jerusalem*(1898); *Golgotha und das hl. Grab zu Jerusalem* (1900); Couret, *La Prise de Jérusm. par les Perses, 614.* (Orléans, 1896—Plans, Ordnance Survey, revised ed.; Ordnance Survey revised by Dr Schick in *Z.D.P.V.* xviii., 1895).

(C. W. W.; C. M. W.)

1The sites shown on the plan are tentative, and cannot be regarded as certain; see Nehemiah ii. 12-15, iii. 1-32, xii. 37-39.

2See 2 Kings xiv. 13.

JERUSALEM, SYNOD OF (1672). By far the most important of the many synods held at Jerusalem (see Wetzer and Welte, *Kirchenlexikon*, 2nd ed., vi. 1357 sqq.) is that of 1672; and its confession is the most vital statement of faith made in the Greek Church during the past thousand years. It refutes article by article the confession of Cyril Lucaris, which appeared in Latin at Geneva in 1629, and in Greek, with the addition of four "questions," in 1633. Lucaris, who died in 1638 as patriarch of Constantinople, had corresponded with Western scholars and had imbibed Calvinistic views. The great opposition which arose during his lifetime continued after his death, and found classic expression in the highly venerated confession of Petrus Mogilas, metropolitan of Kiev (1643). Though this was intended as a barrier against Calvinistic influences, certain Reformed writers, as well as Roman Catholics, persisted in claiming the support of the Greek Church for sundry of their own positions. Against the Calvinists the synod of 1672 therefore aimed its rejection of unconditional predestination and of justification by faith alone, also its advocacy of what are substantially the Roman doctrines of transubstantiation and of purgatory; the Oriental hostility to Calvinism had been fanned by the Jesuits. Against the Church of Rome, however, there was directed the affirmation that the Holy Ghost proceeds from the Father and not from both Father and Son; this rejection of the *filioque* was not unwelcome to the Turks. Curiously enough, the synod refused to believe that the heretical confession it refuted was actually by a former patriarch of Constantinople; yet the proofs of its genuineness seem to most scholars overwhelming. In negotiations between Anglican and Russian churchmen the confession of Dositheus1usually comes to the front.

TEXTS.—The confession of Dositheus, or the eighteen decrees of the Synod of Jerusalem, appeared in 1676 at Paris as *Synodus Bethlehemitica*; a revised text in 1678 as*Synodus Jerosolymitana*; Hardouin, *Acta conciliorum*, vol. xi.; Kimmel, *Monumenta fidei ecclesiae orientalis* (Jena, 1850; critical edition); P. Schaff, *The Creeds of Christendom*, vol. ii. (text after Hardouin and Kimmel, with Latin translation); *The Acts and Decrees of the Synod of Jerusalem translated from the Greek, with notes*, by J. N. W. B. Robertson (London, 1899); J. Michalcescu, *Die Bekenntnisse und die wichtigsten Glaubenszeugnisse der griechisch-orientalischen Kirche* (Leipzig, 1904; Kimmel's text with introductions). LITERATURE.—*The Doctrine of the Russian Church* ... translated by R. W. Blackmore (Aberdeen, 1845), p. xxv. sqq.; Schaff, i. § 17; Wetzer and Welte, *Kirchenlexikon* (2nd ed.) vi. 1359 seq.; Herzog-Hauck, *Realencyklopädie* (3rd ed.), viii. 703-705; Michalcescu, 123 sqq. (See COUNCILS.)

(W. W. R.*)

JESI (anc. *Aesis*), a town and episcopal see of the Marches, Italy, in the province of Ancona, from which it is 17 m. W. by S. by rail, 318 ft. above sea-level. Pop. (1901), 23,285. The place took its ancient name from the river Aesis (mod. Esino), upon the left bank of which it lies. It still retains its picturesque medieval town walls. The Palazzo del Comune is a fine, simple, early Renaissance building (1487-1503) by Francesco di Giorgio Martini; the walls are of brick and the window and door-frames of stone, with severely restrained ornamentation. The courtyard with its loggie was built by Andrea Sansovino in 1519. The library contains some good pictures by Lorenzo Lotto. The castle was built by Baccio Pontelli (1488), designer of the castle at Ostia (1483-1486). Jesi was the birthplace of the emperor Frederic II. (1194), and also of the musical composer, Giovanni Battista Pergolesi (1710-1736). The river Aesis formed the boundary of Italy proper from about 250 B.C. to the time of Sulla (*c.* 82 B.C.); and, in Augustus' division of Italy, that between Umbria (the 6th region) and Picenum (the 5th). The town itself was a colony, of little importance, except, apparently, as a recruiting ground for the Roman army.

JESSE, in the Bible, the father of David (*q.v.*), and as such often regarded as the first in the genealogy of Jesus Christ (cf. Isa. xi. 1, 10). Hence the phrase "tree of Jesse" is applied to a design representing the descent of Jesus from the royal line of David, formerly a favourite ecclesiastical ornament. From a recumbent figure of Jesse springs a tree bearing in its branches the chief figures in the line of descent, and terminating in the figure of Jesus, or of the Virgin and Child. There are remains of such a tree in the church of St Mary at Abergavenny, carved in wood, and supposed to have once stood behind the high altar. Jesse candelabra were also made. At Laon and Amiens there are sculptured Jesses over the central west doorways of the cathedrals. The design was chiefly used in windows. The great east window at Wells and the window at the west end of the nave at Chartres are fine examples. There is a 16th-century Jesse window from Mechlin in St George's, Hanover Square, London. The Jesse window in the choir of Dorchester Abbey, Oxfordshire, is remarkable in that the tree forms the central mullion, and many of the figures are represented as statuettes on the branches of the upper tracery; other figures are in the stained glass; the whole gives a beautiful example of the combination of glass and carved stonework in one design.

JESSE, EDWARD (1780-1868), English writer on natural history, was born on the 14th of January 1780, at Hutton Cranswick, Yorkshire, where his father was vicar of the parish. He became clerk in a government office in 1798, and for a time was secretary to Lord Dartmouth, when president of the Board of Control. In 1812 he was appointed commissioner of hackney coaches, and later he became deputy surveyor-general of the royal parks and palaces. On the abolition of this office he retired on a pension, and he died at Brighton on the 28th of March 1868.

The result of his interest in the habits and characteristics of animals was a series of pleasant and popular books on natural history, the principal of which are *Gleanings in Natural History* (1832-1835); *An Angler's Rambles* (1836);*Anecdotes of Dogs* (1846); and *Lectures on Natural History*(1863). He also edited Izaak Walton's *Compleat Angler*, Gilbert White's *Selborne*, and L. Ritchie's *Windsor Castle*, and wrote a number of handbooks to places of interest, including Windsor and Hampton Court.

JESSE, JOHN HENEAGE (1815-1874), English historian, son of Edward Jesse, was educated at Eton, and afterwards 336became a clerk in the secretary's department of the admiralty. He died in London on the 7th of July 1874. His poem on Mary Queen of Scots was published about 1831, and was followed by a collection of poems entitled *Tales of the Dead*. He also wrote a drama, *Richard III.*, and a fragmentary poem entitled *London*. None of these ventures achieved any success, but his numerous historical works are written with vivacity and interest, and, in their own style, are an important contribution to the history of England. They include *Memoirs of the Court of England during the Reign of the Stuarts* (1840),*Memoirs of the Court of England from the Revolution of 1688 to the Death of George II.* (1843), *George Selwyn and his Contemporaries* (1843, new ed. 1882), *Memoirs of the Pretenders and their Adherents* (1845), *Memoirs of Richard the Third and his Contemporaries* (1861), and *Memoirs of the Life and Reign of King George the Third* (1867). The titles of these works are sufficiently indicative of their character. They are sketches of the principal personages and of the social details of various periods in the history of England rather than complete and comprehensive historical narratives. In addition to these works Jesse wrote *Literary and Historical Memorials of London* (1847), *London and its Celebrities* (1850), and a new edition of this work as *London: its Celebrated Characters and Remarkable Places* (1871). His *Memoirs of Celebrated Etonians* appeared in 1875.

A collected edition containing most of his works in thirty volumes was published in London in 1901.

JESSEL, SIR GEORGE (1824-1883), English judge, was born in London on the 13th of February 1824. He was the son of Zadok Aaron Jessel, a Jewish coral merchant. George Jessel was educated at a school for Jews at Kew, and being prevented by then existing religious disabilities from proceeding to Oxford or Cambridge, went to University College, London. He entered as a student at Lincoln's Inn in 1842, and a year later took his B.A. degree at the university of London, becoming M.A. and gold medallist in mathematics and natural philosophy in 1844. In 1846 he became a fellow of University College, and in 1847 he was called to the bar at Lincoln's Inn. His earnings during his first three years at the bar were 52, 346, and 795 guineas, from which it will be seen that his rise to a tolerably large practice was rapid. His work, however, was mainly conveyancing, and for long his income remained almost stationary. By degrees, however, he got more work, and was called within the bar in 1865, becoming a bencher of his Inn in the same year and practising in the Rolls Court. Jessel entered parliament as Liberal member for Dover in 1868, and although neither his intellect nor his oratory was of a class likely to commend itself to his fellow-members, he attracted Gladstone's attention by two learned speeches on the Bankruptcy Bill which was before the house in 1869, with the result that in 1871 he was appointed solicitor-general. His reputation at this time stood high in the chancery courts; on the common law side he was unknown, and on the first occasion upon which he came into the court of Queen's bench to move on behalf of the Crown, there was very nearly a collision between him and the bench. His forceful and direct method of bringing his arguments home to the bench was not modified in his subsequent practice before it. His great powers were fully recognized; his business in addition to that on behalf of the Crown became very large, and his income for three years before he was raised to the bench amounted to nearly £25,000 per annum. In 1873 Jessel succeeded Lord Romilly as master of the rolls. From 1873 to 1881 Jessel sat as a judge of first instance in the rolls court, being also a member of the court of appeal. In November 1874 the first Judicature Act came into effect, and in 1881 the Judicature Act of that year made the master of the rolls the ordinary president of the first court of appeal, relieving him of his duties as a judge of first instance. In the court of appeal Jessel presided almost to the day of his death. For some time before 1883 he suffered from diabetes with chronic disorder of the heart and liver, but struggled against it; on the 16th of March 1883 he sat in court for the last time, and on the 21st of March he died at his residence in London, the immediate cause of death being cardiac syncope.

As a judge of first instance Jessel was a revelation to those accustomed to the proverbial slowness of the chancery courts and of the master of the rolls who preceded him. He disposed of the business before him with rapidity combined with correctness of judgment, and he not only had no arrears himself, but was frequently able to help other judges to clear their lists. His knowledge of law and equity was wide and accurate, and his memory for cases and command of the principles laid down in them extraordinary. In the rolls court he never reserved a judgment, not even in the Epping Forest case (*Commissioners of Sewers* v. *Glasse*, L.R. 19 Eq.; *The Times*, 11th November 1874), in which the evidence and arguments lasted twenty-two days (150 witnesses being examined in court, while the documents went back to the days of King John), and in the court of appeal he did so only twice, and then in deference to the wishes of his colleagues. The second of these two occasions was the case of *Robarts* v. *The Corporation of London* (49 *Law Times* 455; *The Times*, 10th March 1883), and those who may read Jessel's judgment should remember that, reviewing as it does the law and custom on the subject, and the records of the city with regard to the appointment of a remembrancer from the 16th century, together with the facts of the case before the court, it occupied nearly an hour to deliver, but was nevertheless delivered without notes—this, too, on the 9th of March 1883, when the judge who uttered it was within a fortnight of his death. Never during the 19th century was the business of any court performed so rapidly, punctually, and satisfactorily as it was when Jessel presided. He was master of the rolls at a momentous period of legal history. The Judicature Acts, completing the fusion of law and equity, were passed while he was judge of first instance, and were still new to the courts when he died. His knowledge and power of assimilating knowledge of all subjects, his mastery of every branch of law with which he had to concern himself, as well as of equity, together with his willingness to give effect to the new system, caused it to be said when he died that the success of the Judicature Acts would have been impossible without him. His faults as a judge lay in his disposition to be intolerant of those who, not able to follow the rapidity of his judgment, endeavoured to persist in argument after he had made up his mind; but though he was peremptory with the most eminent counsel, young men had no cause to complain of his treatment of them.

Jessel sat on the royal commission for the amendment of the Medical Acts, taking an active part in the preparation of its report. He actively interested himself in the management of London University, of which he was a fellow from 1861, and of which he was elected vice-chancellor in 1880. He was one of the commissioners of patents, and trustee of the British Museum. He was also chairman of the committee of judges which drafted the new rules rendered necessary by the Judicature Acts. He was treasurer of Lincoln's Inn in 1883, and vice-president of the council of legal education. He was also a fellow of the Royal Society. Jessel's career marks an epoch on the bench, owing to the active part taken by him in rendering the Judicature Acts effective, and also because he was the last judge capable of sitting in the House of Commons, a privilege of which he did not avail himself. He was the first Jew who, as solicitor-general, took a share in the executive government of his country, the first Jew who was sworn a regular member of the privy council, and the first Jew who took a seat on the judicial bench of Great Britain; he was also, for many years after being called to the bar, so situated that any one might have driven him from it, because, being a Jew, he was not qualified to be a member of the bar. In person Jessel was a stoutish, square-built man of middle height, with dark hair, somewhat heavy features, a fresh ruddy complexion, and a large mouth. He married in 1856 Amelia, daughter of Joseph Moses, who survived him together with three daughters and two sons, the elder of whom, Charles James (b. 1860), was made a baronet shortly after the death of his distinguished father and in recognition of his services.

See *The Times*, March 23, 1883; E. Manson, *Builders of our Law* (1904).

JESSORE, a town and district of British India, in the Presidency division of Bengal. The town is on the Bhairab river, with a railway station 75 m. N.E. of Calcutta. Pop. (1901), 8054.

337

The DISTRICT OF JESSORE has an area of 2925 sq. m. Pop. (1901), 1,813,155, showing a decrease of 4% in the decade. The district forms the central portion of the delta between the Hugli and the united Ganges and Brahmaputra. It is a vast alluvial plain intersected by rivers and watercourses, which in the southern portion spread out into large marshes. The northern part is verdant, with extensive groves of date-palms; villages are numerous and large; and the people are prosperous. In the central portion the population is sparse, the only part suitable for dwellings being the high land on the banks of rivers. The principal rivers are the Madhumati or Haringhata (which forms the eastern boundary of the district), with its tributaries the Nabaganga, Chitra, and Bhairab; the Kumar, Kabadak, Katki, Harihar, Bhadra and Atharabanka. Within the last century the rivers in the interior of Jessore have ceased to be true deltaic rivers; and, whereas the northern portion of the district formerly lay under water for several months every year, it is now reached only by unusual inundations. The tide reaches as far north as the latitude of Jessore town. Jessore is the centre of sugar manufacture from date palms. The exports are sugar, rice, pulse, timber, honey, shells, &c.; the imports are salt, English goods, and cloth. The district is crossed by the Eastern Bengal railway, but the chief means of communication are waterways.

British administration was completely established in the district in 1781, when the governor-general ordered the opening of a court at Murali near Jessore. Before that, however, the fiscal administration had been in the hands of the English, having been transferred to the East India company with that of the rest of Bengal in 1765. The changes in jurisdiction in Jessore have been very numerous. After many transfers and rectifications, the district was in 1863 finally constituted as it at present stands. The rajas of Jessore or Chanchra trace their origin to Bhabeswar Rai, a soldier in the army of Khan-i-Azam, an imperial general, who deprived Raja Pratapaditya, the popular hero of the Sundarbans, of several fiscal divisions, and conferred them on Bhabeswar. But Manohar Rai (1649-1705) is regarded as the principal founder of the family. The estate when he inherited it was of moderate size, but he acquired one *pargana* after another, until, at his death, the property was by far the largest in the neighbourhood.

JESTER, a provider of "jests" or amusements, a buffoon, especially a professional fool at a royal court or in a nobleman's household (see FOOL). The word "jest," from which "jester" is formed, is used from the 16th century for the earlier "gest," Lat. *gesta*, or *res gestae*, things done, from *gerere*, to do, hence deeds, exploits, especially as told in history, and so used of the metrical and prose romances and chronicles of the middle ages. The word became applied to satirical writings and to any long-winded empty tale, and thence to a joke or piece of fun, the current meaning of the word.

JESUATI, a religious order founded by Giovanni Colombini of Siena in 1360. Colombini had been a prosperous merchant and a senator in his native city, but, coming under ecstatic religious influences, abandoned secular affairs and his wife and daughter (after making provision

159

for them), and with a friend of like temperament, Francesco Miani, gave himself to a life of apostolic poverty, penitential discipline, hospital service and public preaching. The name Jesuati was given to Colombini and his disciples from the habit of calling loudly on the name of Jesus at the beginning and end of their ecstatic sermons. The senate banished Colombini from Siena for imparting foolish ideas to the young men of the city, and he continued his mission in Arezzo and other places, only to be honourably recalled home on the outbreak of a devastating pestilence. He went out to meet Urban V. on his return from Avignon to Rome in 1367, and craved his sanction for the new order and a distinctive habit. Before this was granted Colombini had to clear the movement of a suspicion that it was connected with the heretical sect of Fraticelli, and he died on the 31st of July 1367, soon after the papal approval had been given. The guidance of the new order, whose members (all lay brothers) gave themselves entirely to works of mercy, devolved upon Miani. Their rule of life, originally a compound of Benedictine and Franciscan elements, was later modified on Augustinian lines, but traces of the early penitential idea persisted, e.g. the wearing of sandals and a daily flagellation. Paul V. in 1606 arranged for a small proportion of clerical members, and later in the 17th century the Jesuati became so secularized that the members were known as the Aquavitae Fathers, and the order was dissolved by Clement IX. in 1668. The female branch of the order, the Jesuati sisters, founded by Caterina Colombini (d. 1387) in Siena, and thence widely dispersed, more consistently maintained the primitive strictness of the society and survived the male branch by 200 years, existing until 1872 in small communities in Italy.

JESUITS, the name generally given to the members of the Society of Jesus, a religious order in the Roman Catholic Church, founded in 1539. This Society may be defined, in its original conception and well-avowed object, as a body of highly trained religious men of various degrees, bound by the three personal vows of poverty, chastity and obedience, together with, in some cases, a special vow to the pope's service, with the object of labouring for the spiritual good of themselves and their neighbours. They are declared to be mendicants and enjoy all the privileges of the other mendicant orders. They are governed and live by constitutions and rules, mostly drawn up by their founder, St Ignatius of Loyola, and approved by the popes. Their proper title is "Clerks Regulars of the Society of Jesus," the word *Societas* being taken as synonymous with the original Spanish term, *Compañia*; perhaps the military term *Cohors* might more fully have expressed the original idea of a band of spiritual soldiers living under martial law and discipline. The ordinary term "Jesuit" was given to the Society by its avowed opponents; it is first found in the writings of Calvin and in the registers of the Parlement of Paris as early as 1552.

Constitution and Character.—The formation of the Society was a masterpiece of genius on the part of a man (see LOYOLA) who was quick to realize the necessity of the moment. Just before Ignatius was experiencing the call to conversion, Luther had begun his revolt against the Roman Church by burning the papal bull of excommunication on the 10th of December 1520. But while Luther's most formidable opponent was thus being prepared in Spain, the actual formation of the Society was not to take place for eighteen years. Its conception seems to have developed very slowly in the mind of Ignatius. It introduced a new idea into the Church. Hitherto all regulars made a point of the choral office in choir. But as Ignatius conceived the Church to be in a state of war, what was desirable in days of peace ceased when the life of the cloister had to be exchanged for the discipline of the camp; so in the sketch of the new society which he laid before Paul III., Ignatius laid down the principle that the obligation of the breviary should be fulfilled privately and separately and not in choir. The other orders, too, were bound by the idea of a constitutional monarchy based on the democratic spirit. Not so with the Society. The founder placed the general for life in an almost uncontrolled position of authority, giving him the faculty of dispensing individuals from the decrees of the highest legislative body, the general congregations. Thus the principle of military obedience was exalted to a degree higher than that existing in the older orders, which preserved to their members certain constitutional rights.

The soldier-mind of Ignatius can be seen throughout the constitutions. Even in the spiritual labours which the Society shares with the other orders, its own ways of dealing with persons and things result from the system of training which succeeds in forming men to a type that is considered desirable. But it must not be thought that in practice the rule of the Society and the high degree of obedience demanded result in mere mechanism. By a system of check and counter check devised in the constitutions the power of local superiors is modified, so that in practice the working is smooth. Ignatius knew that while a high ideal was necessary for every society, his followers were flesh and blood, not machines. He made it clear from the first that the Society was everything and the individual nothing, except so far as he might prove a useful instrument for carrying out the Society's objects. Ignatius said to his 338secretary Polanco that "in those who offered themselves he looked less to purely natural goodness than to firmness of character and ability for business, for he was of opinion that those who were not fit for public business were not adapted for filling offices in the Society." He further declared that even exceptional qualities and endowments in a candidate were valuable in his eyes only on the condition of their being brought into play, or held in abeyance, strictly at the command of a superior. Hence his teaching on obedience. His letter on this subject, addressed to the Jesuits of Coimbra in 1553, is still one of the standard formularies of the Society, ranking with those other products of his pen, the *Spiritual Exercises* and the *Constitutions*. In this letter Ignatius clothes the general with the powers of a commander-in-chief in time of war, giving him the absolute disposal of all members of the Society in every place and for every purpose. He pushes the claim even further, requiring, besides entire outward submission to command, also the complete identification of the inferior's will with that of the superior. He lays down that the superior is to be obeyed simply as such and as standing in the place of God, without reference to his personal wisdom, piety or discretion; that any obedience which falls short of making the superior's will one's own, in inward affection as well as in outward effect, is lax and imperfect; that going beyond the letter of command, even in things abstractly good and praiseworthy, is disobedience, and that the "sacrifice of the intellect" is the third and highest grade of obedience, well pleasing to God, when the inferior not only wills what the superior wills, but thinks what he thinks, submitting his judgment, so far as it is possible for the will to influence and lead the judgment. This *Letter on Obedience* was written for the guidance and formation of Ignatius's own followers; it was an entirely domestic affair. But when it became known beyond the Society the teaching met with great opposition, especially from members of other orders whose institutes represented the normal days of peace rather than those of war. The letter was condemned by the Inquisitions of Spain and Portugal; and it tasked all the skill and learning of Bellarmine as its apologist, together with the whole influence of the Society, to avert what seemed to be a probable condemnation at Rome.

The teaching of the *Letter* must be understood in the living spirit of the Society. Ignatius himself lays down the rule that an inferior is bound to make all necessary representations to his superior so as to guide him in imposing a precept of obedience. When a superior knows the views of his inferior and still commands, it is because he is aware of other sides of the question which appear of greater importance than those that the inferior has brought forward. Ignatius distinctly excepts the case where obedience in itself would be sinful: "In all things *except sin* I ought to do the will of my superior and not my own." There may be cases where an inferior judges that what is commanded is sinful. What is to be done? Ignatius says: "When it seems to me that I am commanded by my superior to do a thing against which my conscience revolts as sinful and my superior judges otherwise, it is my duty to yield my doubts to him unless I am otherwise constrained by evident reasons. ... If submissions do not appease my conscience I must impart my doubts to two or three persons of discretion and abide by their decision." From this it is clear that only in *doubtful* cases concerning sin should an inferior try to submit his judgment to that of his superior, who *ex officio* is held to be not only one who would not order what is clearly sinful, but also a competent judge who knows and understands, better than the inferior, the nature and aspect of the command. As the Jesuit obedience is based on the law of God, it is clearly impossible that he should be bound to obey in what is directly opposed to the divine service. A Jesuit lives in obedience all his life, though the yoke is not galling nor always felt. He can accept no dignity or office which will make him independent of the Society; and even if ordered by the pope to accept the cardinalate or the episcopate, he is still bound, if not to obey, yet to listen to the advice of those whom the general deputes to counsel him in important matters.

The Jesuits had to find their principal work in the world and in direct and immediate contact with mankind. To seek spiritual perfection in a retired life of contemplation and prayer did not seem to Ignatius to be the best way of reforming the evils which had brought about the revolt from Rome. He withdrew his followers from this sort of retirement, except as a mere temporary preparation for later activity; he made habitual intercourse with the world a prime duty; and to this end he rigidly suppressed all such external peculiarities of dress or rule as tended to put obstacles in the way of his followers acting freely as emissaries, agents or missionaries in the most various places and circumstances. Another change he introduced even more completely than did the founders of the Friars. The Jesuit has no home: the whole world is his parish. Mobility and cosmopolitanism are of the very essence of the Society. As Ignatius said, the ancient monastic communities were the infantry of the Church, whose duty was to stand firmly in one place on the battlefield; the Jesuits were to be her light horse, capable of going anywhere at a moment's notice, but especially apt and designed for scouting and skirmishing. To carry out this view, it was one of his plans to send foreigners as superiors or officers to the Jesuit houses in each country, requiring of these envoys, however, invariably to use the language of their new place of residence and to study it both in speaking and writing till entire mastery of it had been acquired—thus by degrees making all the parts of his system mutually interchangeable, and so largely increasing the number of persons eligible to fill any given post without reference to locality. But subsequent experience has, in practice, modified this interchange, as far as local government goes, though the central government of the Society is always cosmopolitan.

Next we must consider the machinery by which the Society is constituted and governed so as to make its spirit a living energy and not a mere abstract theory. The Society is distributed into six grades: novices, scholastics, temporal coadjutors (lay brothers), spiritual coadjutors, professed of the three vows, and professed of the four vows. No one can become a postulant for admission to the Society until fourteen years old, unless by special dispensation. The novice is classified according as his destination is the priesthood or lay brotherhood, while a third class of "indifferents" receives such as are reserved for further inquiry before a decision of this kind is made. The novice has first to undergo a strict retreat, practically in solitary confinement, during which he receives from a director the *Spiritual Exercises* and makes a general confession of his whole life; after which the first novitiate of two years' duration begins. In this period of trial the real character of the man is discerned, his weak points are noted and his will is tested. Prayer and the practices of asceticism, as means to an end, are the chief occupations of the novice. He may leave or be dismissed at any time during the two years; but at the end of the period if he is approved and destined for the priesthood, he is advanced to the grade of scholastic and takes the following simple vows in the presence of certain witnesses, but not to any person:—

"Almighty Everlasting God, albeit everyway most unworthy in Thy holy sight, yet relying on Thine infinite kindness and mercy and impelled by the desire of serving Thee, before the Most Holy Virgin Mary and all Thy heavenly host, I, N., vow to Thy divine Majesty Poverty, Chastity and Perpetual Obedience to the Society of Jesus, and promise that I will enter the same Society to live in it perpetually, understanding all things according to the Constitutions of the Society. I humbly pray from Thine immense goodness and clemency, through the Blood of Jesus Christ, that Thou wilt deign to accept this sacrifice in the odour of sweetness; and as Thou hast granted me to desire and to offer this, so wilt Thou bestow abundant grace to fulfil it."

The scholastic then follows the ordinary course of an undergraduate at a university. After passing five years in arts he has, while still keeping up his own studies, to devote five or six years more to teaching the junior classes in various Jesuit schools or colleges. About this period he takes his simple vows in the following terms:—

"I, N., promise to Almighty God, before His Virgin Mother and the whole heavenly host, and to thee, Reverend Father General of the Society of Jesus, holding the place of God, and to thy successors (or to thee, Reverend Father M.in place of the General of the Society of Jesus and his successors holding the place of God), Perpetual Poverty, Chastity and Obedience; and according to it a peculiar care in the education of boys, according to the manner expressed in the Apostolic Letter and Constitutions of the said Society."

The lay brothers leave out the clause concerning education. The scholastic does not begin the study of theology until he is twenty-eight or thirty, and then passes through a four or six years' course. Only when he is thirty-four or thirty-six can he be ordained a priest and enter on the grade of a spiritual coadjutor. A lay brother, before he can become a temporal coadjutor for the discharge of domestic duties, must pass ten years before he is admitted to vows. Sometimes after ordination the priest, in the midst of his work, is again called away to a third year's novitiate, called the tertianship, as a preparation for his solemn profession of the three vows. His former vows were simple and the Society was at liberty to dismiss him for any canonical reason. The formula of the famous Jesuit vow is as follows:—

"I, N., promise to Almighty God, before His Virgin Mother and the whole heavenly host, and to all standing by; and to thee, Reverend Father General of the Society of Jesus, holding the place of God, and to thy successors (or to thee, Reverend Father M. in place of the General of the Society of Jesus and his successors holding the place of God), Perpetual Poverty, Chastity and Obedience; and according to it a peculiar care in the education of boys according to 339the form of life contained in the Apostolic Letters of the Society of Jesus and in its Constitutions."

Immediately after the vows the Jesuit adds the following simple vows: (1) that he will never act nor consent that the provisions in the constitutions concerning poverty should be changed; (2) that he will not directly nor indirectly procure election or promotion for himself to any prelacy or dignity in the Society; (3) that he will not accept or consent to his election to any dignity or prelacy outside the Society unless forced thereunto by obedience; (4) that if he knows of others doing these things he will denounce them to the superiors; (5) that if elected to a bishopric he will never refuse to hear such advice as the general may deign to send him and will follow it if he judges it is better than his own opinion. The professed is now eligible to certain offices in the Society, and he may remain as a professed father of the three vows for the rest of his life. The highest class, who constitute the real core of the Society, whence all its chief officers are taken, are the professed of the four vows. This grade can seldom be reached until the candidate is in his forty-fifth year, which involves a probation of thirty-one years in the case of those who have entered on the novitiate at the earliest legal age. The number of these select members is small in comparison with the whole Society; the exact proportion varies from time to time, the present tendency being to increase the number. The vows of this grade are the same as the last formula, with the addition of the following important clause:—

"Moreover I promise the special obedience to the Sovereign Pontiff concerning missions, as is contained in the same Apostolic Letter and Constitutions."

These various members of the Society are distributed in its novitiate houses, its colleges, its professed houses and its mission residences. The question has been hotly debated whether, in addition to these six grades, there be not a seventh answering in some degree to the tertiaries of the Franciscan and Dominican orders, but secretly affiliated to the Society and acting as its emissaries in various lay positions. This class was styled in France "Jesuits of the short robe," and there is some evidence in support of its actual existence under Louis XV. The Jesuits themselves deny the existence of any such body, and are able to adduce the negative disproof that no provision for it is to be found in their constitutions. On the other hand there are clauses therein which make the creation of such a class perfectly feasible if thought expedient. An admitted instance is the case of Francisco Borgia, who in 1548, while still duke of Gandia, was received into the Society. What has given colour to the idea is that certain persons have made vows of obedience to individual Jesuits; as Thomas Worthington, rector of the Douai seminary, to Father Robert Parsons; Ann Vaux to Fr. Henry Garnet, who told her that he was not indeed allowed to receive her vows, but that she might make them if she wished and then receive his direction. The archaeologist George Oliver of Exeter was, according to Foley's *Records of the English Province*, the last of the secular priests of England who vowed obedience to the Society before its suppression.

The general lives permanently at Rome and holds in his hands the right to appoint, not only to the office of provincial over each of the head districts into which the Society is mapped, but to the offices of each house in particular. There is no standard of electoral right in the Society except in the election of the general himself. By a minute and frequent system of official and private reports he is informed of the doings and progress of every member of the Society and of everything that concerns it throughout the world. Every Jesuit has not only the right but the duty in certain cases of communicating, directly and privately, with his general. While the general thus controls everything, he himself is not exempt from supervision on the part of the Society. A consultative council is imposed upon him by the general congregation, consisting of the assistants of the various nations, a *socius*, or adviser, to warn him of mistakes, and a confessor. These he cannot remove nor select; and he is bound, in certain circumstances, to listen to their advice, although he is not obliged to follow it. Once elected the general may not refuse the office, nor abdicate, nor accept any dignity or office outside of the Society; on the other hand, for certain definite reasons, he may be suspended or even deposed by the authority of the Society, which can thus preserve itself from destruction. No such instance has occurred, although steps were once taken in this direction in the case of a general who had set himself against the current feeling.

It is said that the general of the Jesuits is independent of the pope; and his popular name, "the black pope," has gone to confirm this idea. But it is based on an entirely wrong conception of the two offices. The suppression of the Society by Clement XIV. in 1773 was an object-lesson in the supremacy of the pope. The Society became very numerous and, from time to time, received extraordinary privileges from popes, who were warranted by the necessities of the times in granting them. A great number of influential friends, also, gathered round the fathers who, naturally, sought in every way to retain what had been granted. Popes who thought it well to bring about certain changes, or to withdraw privileges that were found to have passed their intentions or to interfere unduly with the rights of other bodies, often met with loyal resistances against their proposed measures. Resistance up to a certain point is lawful and is not disobedience, for every society has the right of self-preservation. In cases where the popes insisted, in spite of the representations of the Jesuits, their commands were obeyed. Many of the popes were distinctly unfavourable to the Society, while others were as friendly, and often what one pope did against them the next pope withdrew. Whatever was done in times when strong divergence of opinion existed, and whatever may have been the actions of individuals who, even in so highly organized a body as the Society of Jesus, cannot always be successfully controlled by their superiors, yet the ultimate result on the part of the Society has always been obedience to the pope, who authorized, protected and privileged them, and on whom they ultimately depend for their very existence.

Thus constituted, with a skilful union of strictness and freedom, of complex organization with a minimum of friction in working, the Society was admirably devised for its purpose of introducing a new power into the Church and the world. Its immediate services to the Church were great. The Society did much, single-handed, to roll back the tide of Protestant advance when half of Europe, which had not already shaken off its allegiance to the papacy, was threatening to do so. The honours of the reaction belong to the Jesuits, and the reactionary spirit has become their tradition. They had the wisdom to see and to admit, in their correspondence with their superiors, that the real cause of the Reformation was the ignorance, neglect and vicious lives of so many priests. They recognized, as most earnest men did, that the difficulty was in the higher places, and that these could best be touched by indirect methods. At a time when primary or even secondary education had in most places become a mere effete and pedantic adherence to obsolete methods, they were bold enough to innovate, both in system and material. Putting fresh spirit and devotion into the work, they not merely taught and catechized in a new, fresh and attractive manner, besides establishing free schools of good quality, but provided new school books for their pupils which were an enormous advance on those they found in use; so that for nearly three centuries the Jesuits were accounted the best schoolmasters in Europe, as they were, till their forcible suppression in 1901, confessedly the best in France. The Jesuit teachers conciliated the goodwill of their pupils by mingled firmness and gentleness. Although the method of the *Ratio Studiorum* has ceased to be acceptable, yet it played in its time as serious a part in the intellectual development of Europe as did the method of Frederick the Great in modern warfare. Bacon succinctly gives his opinion of the Jesuit teaching in these words: "As for the pedagogical part, the shortest rule would be, Consult the schools of the Jesuits; for nothing better has been put in practice" (*De Augmentis*, vi. 4). In instruction they were excellent; but in education, or formation of character, deficient. Again, when most of the continental clergy had sunk, more or less, into the moral and intellectual slough which is pictured for us in the writings of Erasmus and the *Epistolae obscurorum virorum* (see HUTTEN, ULRICH VON), the Jesuits won back respect for the clerical calling by their personal culture 340and the unimpeachable purity of their lives. These qualities they have carefully maintained; and probably no large body of men in the world has been so free from the reproach of discreditable members or has kept up, on the whole, an equally high average of intelligence and conduct. As preachers, too, they delivered the pulpit from the bondage of an effete scholasticism and reached at once a clearness and simplicity of treatment such as the English pulpit scarcely begins to exhibit till after the days of Tillotson; while in literature and theology they count a far larger number of respectable writers than any other religious society can boast. It is in the mission field, however, that their achievements have been most remarkable. Whether toiling among the teeming millions in Hindustan and China, labouring amongst the Hurons and Iroquois of North America, governing and civilizing the natives of Brazil and Paraguay in the missions and "reductions," or ministering, at the hourly risk of his life to his fellow-Catholics in England under Elizabeth and the Stuarts, the Jesuit appears alike devoted, indefatigable, cheerful and worthy of hearty admiration and respect.

Nevertheless, two startling and indisputable facts meet the student who pursues the history of the Society. The first is the universal suspicion and hostility it has incurred—not merely from the Protestants whose avowed foe it has been, not yet from the enemies of all clericalism and dogma, but from every Catholic state and nation in the world. Its chief enemies have been those of the household of the Roman Catholic faith. The second fact is the ultimate failure which seems to dog all its most promising schemes and efforts. These two results are to be observed alike in the provinces of morals and politics. The first cause of the opposition indeed redounds to the Jesuits' credit, for it was largely due to their success. Their pulpits rang with a studied eloquence; their churches, sumptuous and attractive, were crowded; and in the confessional their advice was eagerly sought in all kinds of difficulties, for they were the fashionable professors of the art of direction. Full of enthusiasm and zeal, devoted wholly to their Society, they were able to bring in numbers of rich and influential persons to their ranks; for, with a clear understanding of the power of wealth, they became, of set purpose, the apostles of the rich and influential. The Jesuits felt that they were the new men, the men of the time; so with a perfect confidence in themselves they went out to set the Church to rights. It was no wonder that success, so well worked for and so well deserved, failed to win the approval or sympathy of those who found themselves supplanted. Old-fashioned men, to whom the apostles' advice to "do all to the glory of God" seemed sufficient, mistrusted those who professed to go beyond all others and adopted as their motto the famous *Ad majorem Dei gloriam*, "To the greater glory of God." But, besides this, the *esprit de corps* which is necessary for every body of men was, it was held, carried to an excess and made the Jesuits intolerant of any one or anything if not of "ours." The novelties too which they introduced into the conception of the religious life, naturally, were displeasing to the older orders, who felt like old aristocratic families towards a newly rich or purse-proud upstart. The Society, or rather its members, were too aggressive and self-assertive to be welcomed; and a certain characteristic, which soon began to manifest itself in an impatience of episcopal control, showed that the quality of "Jesuitry," usually associated with the Society, was singularly lacking in their dealings with opponents. Their political attitude also alienated many. Many of the Jesuits could not separate religion from politics. To say this is only to assert that they were not clearer-minded than most men of their age. But unfortunately they invariably took the wrong side and allowed themselves to be made the tools of men who saw farther and more clearly than they did. They had their share, direct or indirect, in the embroiling of states, in concocting conspiracies and in kindling wars. They were also responsible by their theoretical teachings in theological schools, where cases were considered and treated in the abstract, for not a few assassinations of the enemies of the cause. Weak minds heard tyrannicide discussed and defended in the abstract; and it was no wonder that, when opportunity served, the train that had been heedlessly laid by speculative professors was fired by rash hands. What professors like Suarez taught in the calm atmosphere of the lecture hall, what writers like Mariana upheld and praised, practical men took as justification for deeds of blood. There is no evidence that any Jesuit took a direct part in political assassinations; however, indirectly, they may have been morally responsible. They were playing with edged tools and often got wounded through their own carelessness. Other grievances were raised by their perpetual meddling in politics,*e.g.* their large share in fanning the flames of political hatred against the Huguenots under the last two Valois kings; their perpetual plotting against England in the reign of Elizabeth; their share in the Thirty Years' War and in the religious miseries of Bohemia; their decisive influence in causing the revocation of the edict of Nantes and the expulsion of the Protestants from France; the ruin of the Stuart cause under James II., and the establishment of the Protestant succession. In a number of cases where the evidence against them is defective, it is at least an unfortunate coincidence that there is always direct proof of some Jesuit having been in communication with the actual agents engaged. They were the stormy petrels of politics. Yet the Jesuits, as a body, should not be made responsible for the doings of men who, in their political intrigues, were going directly against the distinct law of the Society, which in strict terms, and under heavy penalties, forbade them to have anything to do with such matters. The politicians were comparatively few in number, though unfortunately they held high rank; and their disobedience to the rule besmirched the name of the society and destroyed the good work of the other Jesuits who were faithfully carrying out their own proper duties.

A far graver cause for uneasiness was given by the Jesuits' activity in the region of doctrine and morals. Here the charges against them are precise, early, numerous and weighty. Their founder himself was arrested, more than once, by the Inquisition and required to give account of his belief and conduct. But St Ignatius, with all his powerful gifts of intellect, was entirely practical and ethical in his range, and had no turn whatever for speculation, nor desire to discuss, much less to question, any of the received dogmas of the Church. He gives it as a rule of orthodoxy to be ready to say that black is white if the Church says so. He was therefore acquitted on every occasion, and applied each time for a formally attested certificate of his orthodoxy, knowing well that, in default of such documents, the fact of his arrest as a suspected heretic would be more distinctly recollected by opponents than that of his honourable dismissal from custody. His followers, however, have not been so fortunate. On doctrinal questions indeed, though their teaching on grace, especially in the form given to it by Molina (*q.v.*), ran contrary to the accepted teaching on the subject by the Augustinians, Dominicans and other representative schools; yet by their pertinacity they gained for their views a recognized and established position. A special congregation of cardinals and theologians known as *de auxiliis* was summoned by the pope to settle the dispute, for the *odium theologicum* had risen to a desperate height between the representatives of the old and the new theology; but after many years they failed to arrive at any satisfactory conclusion, and the pope, instead of settling the dispute, was only able to impose mutual silence on all opponents. Among those who held out stiffly against the Jesuits on the subject of grace were the Jansenists, who held that they were following the special teaching of St Augustine, known *par excellence* as the doctor of grace. The Jesuits and the Jansenists soon became deadly enemies; and in the ensuing conflict both parties accused each other of flinging scruples to the wind. (See JANSENISM.)

But the accusations against the Jesuit system of moral theology and their action as guides of conduct have had a more serious effect on their reputation. It is undeniable that some of their moral writers were lax in their teaching; and conscience was strained to the snapping point. The Society was trying to make itself all things to all men. Propositions extracted from 341 Jesuit moral theologians have again and again been condemned by the pope and declared untenable. Many of these can be found in Viva's *Condemned Propositions*. As early as 1554 the Jesuits were censured by the Sorbonne, chiefly at the instance of Eustache de Bellay, bishop of Paris, as being dangerous in matters of faith. Melchor Cano, a Dominican, one of the ablest divines of the 16th century, never ceased to lift up his testimony against them, from their first beginnings till his own death in 1560; and, unmollified by the bribe of the bishopric of the Canaries, which their interest procured for him, he succeeded in banishing them from the university of Salamanca. Carlo Borromeo, to whose original advocacy they owed much, especially in the council of Trent, found himself attacked in his own cathedral pulpit and interfered with in his jurisdiction. He withdrew his protection and expelled them from his colleges and churches; and he was followed in 1604 in this policy by his cousin and successor Cardinal Federigo Borromeo. St Theresa learnt, in after years, to mistrust their methods, although she was grateful to them for much assistance in the first years of her work. The credit of the Society was seriously damaged by the publication, at Cracow, in 1612, of the *Monita Secreta*. This book, which is undoubtedly a forgery, professes to contain the authoritative secret instructions drawn up by the general Acquaviva and given by the superiors of the Society to its various officers and members. A bold caricature of Jesuit methods, the book has been ascribed to John Zaorowsky or to Cambilone and Schloss, all ex-Jesuits, and it is stated to have been discovered in manuscript by Christian of Brunswick in the Jesuit college at Prague. It consists of suggestions and methods for extending the influence of the Jesuits in various ways, for securing a footing in fresh places, for acquiring wealth, for creeping into households and leading silly rich widows captive and so forth, all marked with ambition, craft and unscrupulousness. It had a wide success and popularity, passing through several editions, and even to this day it is used by controversialists as unscrupulous as the original writers. It may, perhaps, represent the actions of some individuals who allowed their zeal to outrun their discretion, but surely no society which exists for good and is marked by so many worthy men could systematically have conducted its operations in such a manner. Later on a formidable assault was made on Jesuit moral theology in the famous *Provincial Letters* of Blaise Pascal (*q.v.*), eighteen in number, issued under the pen-name of Louis de Montalte, from January 1656 to March 1657. Their wit, irony, eloquence and finished style have kept them alive as one of the great French classics—a destiny more fortunate than that of the kindred works by Antoine Arnauld, *Théologie morale des Jésuites*, consisting of extracts from writings of members of the Society, and *Morale pratique des Jésuites*, made up of narratives professing to set forth the manner in which they carried out their own maxims. But, like most controversial writers, the authors were not scrupulous in their quotations, and by giving passages divorced from their contexts often entirely misrepresented their opponents. The immediate reply on the part of the Jesuits, *The Discourses of Cleander and Eudoxus* by Père Daniel, could not compete with Pascal's work in brilliancy, wit or style; moreover, it was unfortunate enough to be put upon the Index of prohibited books in 1701. The reply on behalf of the Society to Pascal's charges of lax morality, apart from mere general denials, is broadly as follows:—

(1) St Ignatius himself, the founder of the Society, had a special aversion from untruthfulness in all its forms, from quibbling, equivocation or even studied obscurity of language, and it would be contrary to the spirit of conformity with his example and institutions for his followers to think and act otherwise. Hence, any who practised equivocation were, so far, unfaithful to the Society. (2) Several of the cases cited by Pascal are mere abstract hypotheses, many of them now obsolete, argued simply as intellectual exercises, but having no practical bearing whatever. (3) Even such as do belong to the sphere of actual life are of the nature of counsel to spiritual physicians, how to deal with exceptional maladies; and were never intended to fix the standard of moral obligation for the general public. (4) The theory that they were intended for this latter purpose and do represent the normal teaching of the Society becomes more untenable in exact proportion as this immorality is insisted on, because it is a matter of notoriety that the Jesuits themselves have been singularly free from personal, as distinguished from corporate, evil repute; and no one pretends that the large number of lay-folk whom they have educated or influenced exhibit greater moral inferiority than others.

The third of these replies is the most cogent as regards Pascal, but the real weakness of his attack lies in that nervous dread of appeal to first principles and their logical result which has been the besetting snare of Gallicanism. Pascal, at his best, has mistaken the part for the whole; he charges to the Society what, at the most, are the doings of individuals; and from these he asserts the degeneration of the body from its original standard; whereas the stronger the life and the more extensive the natural development, side by side will exist marks of degeneration; and a society like the Jesuits has no difficulty in asserting its life independently of such excrescences or, in time, in freeing itself from them.

A charge persistently made against the Society is that it teaches that the end justifies the means. And the words of Busembaum, whose *Medulla theologiae* has gone through more than fifty editions, are quoted in proof. True it is that Busembaum uses these words: *Cui licitus est finis etiam licent media*. But on turning to his work (ed. Paris 1729, p. 584, or Lib. vi. Tract vi. cap. ii., *De sacramentis*, dubium ii.) it will be found that the author is making no universal application of an old legal maxim; but is treating of a particular subject (concerning certain lawful liberties in the marital relation) beyond which his words cannot be forced. The sense in which other Jesuit

166

theologians—*e.g.* Paul Laymann (1575-1635), in his *Theologia moralis* (Munich, 1625), and Ludwig Wagemann (1713-1792), in his *Synopsis theologiae moralis* (Innsbruck, 1762)—quote the axiom is an equally harmless piece of common sense. For instance, if it is lawful to go on a journey by railway it is lawful to take a ticket. No one who put forth that proposition would be thought to mean that it is lawful to defraud the company by stealing a ticket; for the *proviso* is always to be understood, that the means employed should, in themselves, not be bad but good or at least indifferent. So when Wagemann says tersely *Finis determinat probitatem actus* he is clearly referring to acts which in themselves are indifferent, *i.e.* indeterminate. For instance: shooting is an indifferent act, neither good nor bad in itself. The morality of any specified shooting depends upon what is shot, and the circumstances attending that act: shooting a man in self-defence is, as a moral act, on an entirely different plane to shooting a man in murder. It has never been proved, and never can be proved, although the attempt has frequently been made, that the Jesuits ever taught the nefarious proposition ascribed to them, which would be entirely subversive of all morality. Again, the doctrine of probabilism is utterly misunderstood. It is based on an accurate conception of law. Law to bind must be clear and definite; if it be not so, its obligation ceases and liberty of action remains. No probable opinion can stand against a clear and definite law; but when a law is doubtful in its application, in certain circumstances, so is the obligation of obedience: and as a doubtful law is, for practical purposes, no law at all, so it superinduces no obligation. Hence a probable opinion is one, founded on reason and held on serious grounds, that the law does not apply to certain specified cases; and that the law-giver therefore did not intend to bind. It is the principle of equity applied to law. In moral matters a probable opinion, that is one held on no trivial grounds but by unprejudiced and solid thinkers, has no place where the voice of conscience is clear, distinct and formed.

Two causes have been at work to produce the universal failure of the great Society in all its plans and efforts. First stands its lack of really great intellects. It has had its golden age. No society can keep up to its highest level. Nothing can be wider of the truth than the popular conception of the ordinary Jesuit as a being of almost superhuman abilities and universal knowledge. The Society, numbering as it does so many thousands, and with abundant means of devoting men to special branches of study, has, without doubt, produced men of great intelligence and solid learning. The average member, too, on account of his long and systematic training, is always equal and often superior to the average member of any other equally large body, besides being disciplined by a far more perfect drill. But it takes great men to carry out great plans; and of really great men, as the outside world knows and judges, the Society has been markedly barren from almost the first. Apart from its founder and his early companion, St Francis Xavier, there is none who stands in the very first rank. Laynez and Acquaviva were able administrators and politicians; the Bollandists (*q.v.*) were industrious workers and have developed a critical spirit from which much good can be expected; Francisco Suarez, 342Leonhard Lessius and Cardinal Franzelin were some of the leading Jesuit theologians; Cornelius a Lapide (1567-1637) represents their old school of scriptural studies, while their new German writers are the most advanced of all orthodox higher critics; the French Louis Bourdaloue (*q.v.*), the Italian Paolo Segneri (1624-1694), and the Portuguese Antonio Vieyra (1608-1697) represent their best pulpit orators; while of the many mathematicians and astronomers produced by the Society Angelo Secchi, Ruggiero Giuseppe Boscovich and G. B. Beccaria are conspicuous, and in modern times Stephen Joseph Perry (1833-1889), director of the Stonyhurst College observatory, took a high rank among men of science. Their boldest and most original thinker, Denis Petau, so many years neglected, is now, by inspiring Cardinal Newman's *Essay on the Development of Christian Doctrine*, producing a permanent influence over the current of human thought. The Jesuits have produced no Aquinas, no Anselm, no Bacon, no Richelieu. Men whom they trained, and who broke loose from their teaching, Pascal, Descartes, Voltaire, have powerfully affected the philosophical and religious beliefs of great masses of mankind; but respectable mediocrity is the brand on the long list of Jesuit names in the catalogues of Alegambe and De Backer. This is doubtless due in great measure to the destructive process of scooping out the will of the Jesuit novice, to replace it with that of his superior (as a watchmaker might fit a new movement into a case), and thereby tending, in most cases, to annihilate those subtle qualities of individuality and originality which are essential to genius. Men of the higher stamp will either refuse to submit to the process and leave the Society, or run the danger of coming forth from the mill with their finest qualities pulverized and useless. In accordance with the spirit of its founder, who wished to secure uniformity in the judgment of his followers even in points left open by the Church ("Let us all think the same way, let us all speak in the same manner if possible"), the Society has shown itself to be impatient of those who think or write in a way different from what is current in its ranks.

Nor is this all. The *Ratio Studiorum*, devised by Acquaviva and still obligatory in the colleges of the Society, lays down rules which are incompatible with all breadth and progress in the higher forms of education. True to the anti-speculative and traditional side of the founder's mind, it prescribes that, even where religious topics are not in question, the teacher is not to permit any novel opinions or discussions to be mooted; nor to cite or allow others to cite the opinions of an author not of known repute; nor to teach or suffer to be taught anything contrary to the prevalent opinions of acknowledged doctors current in the schools. Obsolete and false opinions are not to be mentioned at all, even for refutation, nor are objections to received teaching to be dwelt on at any length. The result is that the Jesuit emerges from his schools without any real knowledge of any other method of thought than that which his professors have instilled into him. The professor of Biblical Literature is always to support and defend the Vulgate and can never prefer the marginal readings from the Hebrew and Greek. The Septuagint, as far as it is incorrupt, is to be held not less authentic than the Vulgate. In philosophy Aristotle is always to be followed, and St Thomas Aquinas generally, care being taken to speak respectfully of him even when abandoning his opinions, though now it is customary for the Jesuit teachers to explain him in their own sense. *De vera mente D. Thomas* is no unfamiliar expression in their books. It is not wonderful, under such a method of training, fixed as it has been in minute detail for more than three hundred years, that highly cultivated commonplaces should be the inevitable average result; and that in proportion as Jesuit power has become dominant in Christendom, especially in ecclesiastical circles, the same doom of intellectual sterility and consequent loss of influence with the higher and thoughtful classes, has separated the part from the whole. The initial mistake in the formation of character is that the Jesuits have aimed at educating lay boys in the same manner as they consider advisable for their own novices, for whom obedience and direction is the one thing necessary; whereas for lay people the right use of liberty and initiative are to be desired.

The second cause which has blighted the efforts of the Society is the lesson, too faithfully learnt and practised, of making its corporate interests the first object at all times and in all places. Men were quick to see that Jesuits did not aim at co-operation with the other members of the Church but directly or indirectly at mastery. The most brilliant exception to this rule is found in some of the missions of the Society and notably in that of St Francis Xavier (*q.v.*). But he quitted Europe in 1541 before the new society, especially under Laynez, had hardened into its final mould; and he never returned. His work, so far as can be gathered from contemporary accounts, was not done on true Jesuit lines as they afterwards developed, though the Society has reaped all the credit; and it is even possible that, had he succeeded the founder as general, the institute might not have received that political and self-seeking turn which Laynez, as second general, gave at the critical moment.

It would almost seem that careful selection was made of the men of the greatest piety and enthusiasm, whose unworldliness made them less apt for diplomatic intrigues, to break new ground in the various missions where their success would throw lustre on the Society and their scruples need never come into play. But such men are not to be found easily; and, as they died off, the tendency was to fill their places with more ordinary characters, whose aim was to increase the power and resources of the body. Hence the condescension to heathen rites in Hindustan and China, and the attempted subjugation of the English Catholic clergy. The first successes of the Indian mission were entirely among the lower classes; but when in Madura, in 1606, Robert de Nobili, a nephew of Bellarmine, to win the Brahmins, adopted their dress and mode of life—a step sanctioned by Gregory XV. in 1623 and by Clement XI. in 1707—the fathers who followed his example pushed the new caste-feeling so far as absolutely to refuse the ministrations and sacraments to the pariahs, lest the Brahmin converts should take offence—an attempt which was reported to Rome and was vainly censured by the breves of Innocent X. in 1645, Clement IX. in 1669, Clement XII. in 1734 and 1739, and Benedict XIV. in 1745. The Chinese rites, assailed with equal unsuccess by one pope after another, were not finally put down until 1744 by a bull of Benedict XIV. For Japan, where their side of the story is that best known, we have a remarkable letter, printed by Lucas Wadding in the *Annales minorum*, addressed to Paul V. by Soleto, a Franciscan missionary, who was martyred in 1624, in which he complains to the pope that the Jesuits systematically postponed the spiritual welfare of the native Christians to their own convenience and advantage; while as regards the test of martyrdom, no such result had followed on their teaching, but only on that of the other orders who had undertaken missionary work in Japan. Yet soon many Jesuit martyrs in Japan were to shed a new glory on the Society (see JAPAN: *Foreign Intercourse*). Again, even in Paraguay, the most promising of all Jesuit undertakings, the evidence shows that the fathers, though civilizing the Guarani population just sufficiently to make them useful and docile servants, happier no doubt than they were before or after, stopped there. While the mission was begun on the rational principle of governing races still in their childhood by methods adapted to that stage in their mental development, yet for one

168

hundred and fifty years the "reductions" were conducted in the same manner, and when the hour of trial came the Jesuit civilization fell like a house of cards.

These examples are sufficient to explain the final collapse of so many promising efforts. The individual Jesuit might be, and often was, a hero, saint and martyr, but the system which he was obliged to administer was foredoomed to failure; and the suppression which came in 1773 was the natural result of forces and elements they had set in antagonism without the power of controlling.

The influence of the Society since its restoration in 1814 has not been marked with greater success than in its previous history. It was natural after the restoration that an attempt should be made to pick up again the threads that were dropped; but soon they came to realize the truth of the saying of St Ignatius: "The Society shall adapt itself to the times and not the times to the Society." The political conditions of Europe have completely changed, and constitutionalism is unfavourable to that personal influence which, in former times, the Jesuits were able to bring to bear upon the heads of states. In Europe they confine themselves mainly to educational and ecclesiastical politics, although both Germany and France have followed the example of Portugal and refuse, on political grounds, to allow them to be in these countries. It would appear as though some of the Jesuits had not, even yet, learnt the lesson that meddling with politics has always been their ruin. The main cause of any difficulty that may exist to-day with the Society is that the Jesuits are true to the teaching of that remarkable panegyric, the*Imago primi saeculi Societatis* (probably written by John Tollenarius in 1640), by identifying the Church with their own body, and being intolerant of all who will not share this view. Their power is still large in certain sections of the ecclesiastical 343world, but in secular affairs it is small. Moreover within the church itself there is a strong and growing feeling that the interests of Catholicism may necessitate a second and final suppression of the Society. Cardinal Manning, a keen observer of times and influences, was wont to say:—"The work of 1773 was the work of God: and there is another 1773 coming." But, if this come, it will be due not to the pressure of secular governments, as in the 18th century, but to the action of the Church itself. The very nations which have cast out the Society have shown no disposition to accept its own estimate and identify it with the Church; while the Church itself is not conscious of depending upon the Society. To the Church the Jesuits have been what the Janissaries were to the Ottoman Empire, at first its defenders and its champions, but in the end its taskmasters.

History.—The separate article on Loyola tells of his early years, his conversion, and his first gathering of companions. It was not until November 1537, when all hope of going to the Holy Land was given up, that any outward steps were taken to form these companions into an organized body. It was on the eve of their going to Rome, for the second time, that the fathers met Ignatius at Vicenza and it was determined to adopt a common rule and, at the suggestion of Ignatius, the name of the Company of Jesus. Whatever may have been his private hopes and intentions, it was not until he, Laynez and Faber (Pierre Lefevre), in the name of their companions, were sent to lay their services at the feet of the pope that the history of the Society really begins.

On their arrival at Rome the three Jesuits were favourably received by Paul III., who at once appointed Faber to the chair of scripture and Laynez to that of scholastic theology in the university of the Sapienza. But they encountered much opposition and were even charged with heresy; when this accusation had been disposed of, there were still difficulties in the way of starting any new order. Despite the approval of Cardinal Contarini and the goodwill of the pope (who is said to have exclaimed on perusing the scheme of Ignatius, "The finger of God is here"), there was a strong and general feeling that the regular system had broken down and could not be wisely developed farther. Cardinal Guidiccioni, one of the commission of three appointed to examine the draft constitution, was known to advocate the abolition of all existing orders, save four which were to be remodelled and put under strict control. That very year, 1538, a commission of cardinals, including Reginald Pole, Contarini, Sadolet, Caraffa (afterwards Paul IV.), Fregoso and others, had reported that the conventual orders, which they had to deal with, had drifted into such a state that they should all be abolished. Not only so, but, when greater strictness of rule and of enclosure seemed the most needful reforms in communities that had become too secular in tone, the proposal of Ignatius, to make it a first principle that the members of his institute should mix freely in the world and be as little marked off as possible externally from secular clerical life and usages, ran counter to all tradition and prejudice, save that Caraffa's then recent order of Theatines, which had some analogy with the proposed Society, had taken some steps in the same direction.

Ignatius and his companions, however, had but little doubt of ultimate success, and so bound themselves, on the 15th of April 1539, to obey any superior chosen from amongst their body, and added on the 4th of May certain other rules, the most important of which was a vow of special allegiance to the pope for mission purposes to be taken by all the members of the society. But Guidiccioni, on a careful study of the papers, changed his mind; it is supposed that the cause of this change was in large measure the strong interest in the new scheme exhibited by John III., king of Portugal, who instructed his ambassador to press it on the pope and to ask Ignatius to send some priests of his Society for mission work in Portugal and its Indian possessions. Francis Xavier and Simon Rodriguez were sent to the king in March 1540. Obstacles being cleared away, Paul III., on the 27th of September 1540, issued his bull*Regimini militantis ecclesiae*, by which he confirmed the new Society (the term "order" does not belong to it), but limited the members to sixty, a restriction which was removed by the same pope in the bull *Injunctum nobis* of the 14th of March 1543. In the former bull, the pope gives the text of the formula submitted by Ignatius as the scheme of the proposed society, and in it we get the founder's own ideas: "... This Society, instituted to this special end, namely, to offer spiritual consolation for the advancement of souls in life and Christian doctrine, for the propagation of the faith by public preaching and the ministry of the word of God, spiritual exercises and works of charity and, especially, by the instruction of children and ignorant people in Christianity, and by the spiritual consolation of the faithful in Christ in hearing confessions...." In this original scheme it is clearly marked out "that this entire Society and all its members fight for God under the faithful obedience of the most sacred lord, the pope, and the other Roman pontiffs his successors"; and Ignatius makes particular mention that each member should "be bound by a special vow," beyond that formal obligation under which all Christians are of obeying the pope, "so that whatsoever the present and other Roman pontiffs for the time being shall ordain, pertaining to the advancement of souls and the propagation of the faith, to whatever provinces he shall resolve to send us, we are straightway bound to obey, as far as in us lies, without any tergiversation or excuse, whether he send us among the Turks or to any other unbelievers in being, even to those parts called India, or to any heretics or schismatics or likewise to any believers." Obedience to the general is enjoined "in all things pertaining to the institute of the Society ... and in him they shall acknowledge Christ as though present, and as far as is becoming shall venerate him"; poverty is enjoined, and this rule affects not only the individual but the common sustentation or care of the Society, except that in the case of colleges revenues are allowed "to be applied to the wants and necessities of the students"; and the private recitation of the Office is distinctly mentioned. On the other hand, the perpetuity of the general's office during his life was no part of the original scheme.

On the 7th of April 1541, Ignatius was unanimously chosen general. His refusal of this post was overruled, so he entered on his office on the 13th of April; and two days after, the newly constituted Society took its formal corporate vows in the basilica of San Paolo *fuori le mura*. Scarcely was the Society launched when its members dispersed in various directions to their new tasks. Alfonso Salmeron and Pasquier-Brouet, as papal delegates, were sent on a secret mission to Ireland to encourage the native clergy and people to resist the religious changes introduced by Henry VIII.; Nicholas Bobadilla went to Naples; Faber, first to the diet of Worms and then to Spain; Laynez and Claude le Jay to Germany, while Ignatius busied himself at Rome in good works and in drawing up the constitutions and completing the *Spiritual Exercises*. Success crowned these first efforts; and the Society began to win golden opinions. The first college was founded at Coimbra in 1542 by John III. of Portugal and put under the rectorship of Rodriguez. It was designed as a training school to feed the Indian mission of which Francis Xavier had already taken the oversight, while a seminary at Goa was the second institution founded outside Rome in connexion with the Society. Both from the original scheme and from the foundation at Coimbra it is clear that the original idea of the colleges was to provide for the education of future Jesuits. In Spain, national pride in the founder aided the Society's cause almost as much as royal patronage did in Portugal; and the third house was opened in Gandia under the protection of its duke, Francisco Borgia, a grandson of Alexander VI. In Germany, the Jesuits were eagerly welcomed as the only persons able to meet the Lutherans on equal terms. Only in France, among the countries which still were united with the Roman Church, was their advance checked, owing to political distrust of their Spanish origin, together with the hostility of the Sorbonne and the bishop of Paris. However, after many difficulties, they succeeded in getting a footing through the help of Guillaume du Prat, bishop of Clermont (d. 1560), who founded a college for them in 1545 in the town of Billom, besides making over to them his house at Paris, the hôtel de Clermont, which became the nucleus of the afterwards famous college of Louis-le-Grand, while a formal legalization was granted to them by the states-general at Poissy in 1561. In Rome, Paul III.'s favour did not lessen. He bestowed on them the church of St Andrea and conferred at the same time the valuable privilege of making and altering their own statutes; besides the other points, in 1546, which Ignatius had still more at heart, as touching the very essence of his institute, namely, exemption from ecclesiastical offices and dignities and from the task of acting as directors and confessors to convents of women. The former of these measures effectually stopped any drain of the best members away from the society and limited their hopes within its bounds, by putting them more freely at the general's disposal, especially as it was provided that the final vows could not be annulled, nor could a professed member be dismissed, save by the joint action of the general and the pope. The regulation as to convents seems partly due to a desire to avoid the worry and expenditure of time involved in the discharge of such offices 344and partly to a conviction that penitents living in enclosure, as all religious persons then were, would be of no effective use to the Society; whereas the founder, against the wishes of several of his companions, laid much stress on the duty of accepting the post of confessor to kings, queens and women of high rank when opportunity presented itself. And the year 1546 is notable in the annals of the Society as that in which it embarked on its great educational career, especially by the annexation of free day-schools to all its colleges.

The council of Trent, in its first period, seemed to increase the reputation of the Society; for the pope chose Laynez, Faber and Salmeron to act as his theologians in that assembly, and in this capacity they had no little influence in framing its decrees. When the council reassembled under Pius IV., Laynez and Salmeron again attended in the same capacity. It is sometimes said that the council formally approved of the Society. This is impossible; for as the Society had received the papal approval, that of the council would have been impertinent as well as unnecessary. St Charles Borromeo wrote to the presiding cardinals, on the 11th of May 1562, saying that, as France was disaffected to the Jesuits whom the pope wished to see established in every country, Pius IV. desired, when the council was occupying itself about regulars, that it should make some honourable mention of the Society in order to recommend it. This was done in the twenty-fifth session (cap. XVI., d.r.) when the decree was passed that at the end of the time of probation novices should either be professed or dismissed; and the words of the council are: "By these things, however, the Synod does not intend to make any innovation or prohibition, so as to hinder the religious order of Clerks of the Society of Jesus from being able to serve God and His Church, in accordance with their pious institute approved of by the Holy Apostolic See."

In 1548 the Society received a valuable recruit in the person of Francisco Borgia, duke of Gandia, afterwards thrice general, while two important events marked 1550—the foundation of the Collegio Romano and a fresh confirmation of the Society by Julius III. The German college, for the children of poor nobles, was founded in 1552; and in the same year Ignatius firmly settled the discipline of the Society by putting down, with promptness and severity, some attempts at independent action on the part of Rodriguez at Coimbra—this being the occasion of the famous letter on obedience; while 1553 saw the despatch of a mission to Abyssinia with one of the fathers as patriarch, and the first rift within the lute when the pope thought that the Spanish Jesuits were taking part with the emperor against the Holy See. Paul IV. (whose election alarmed the Jesuits, for they had not found him very friendly as cardinal) was for a time managed with supreme tact by Ignatius, whom he respected personally. In 1556, the founder died and left the Society consisting of forty-five professed fathers and two thousand ordinary members, distributed over twelve provinces, with more than a hundred colleges and houses.

After the death of the first general there was an interregnum of two years, with Laynez as vicar. During this long period he occupied himself with completing the constitutions by incorporating certain declarations, said to be Ignatian, which explained and sometimes completely altered the meaning of the original text. Laynez was an astute politician and saw the vast capabilities of the Society over a far wider field than the founder contemplated; and he prepared to give it the direction that it has since followed. In some senses, this learned and consummately clever man may be looked upon as the real founder of the Society as history knows it. Having carefully prepared the way, he summoned the general congregation from which he emerged as second general in 1556. As soon as Ignatius had died Paul IV. announced his intention of instituting reforms in the Society, especially in two points: the public recitation of the office in choir and the limitation of the general's office to a term of three years. Despite all the protests and negotiations of Laynez, the pope remained obstinate; and there was nothing but to submit. On the 8th of September 1558, two points were added to the constitutions: that the generalship should be triennial and not perpetual, although after the three years the general might be confirmed; and that the canonical hours should be observed in choir after the manner of the other orders, but with that moderation which should seem expedient to the general. Taking advantage of this last clause, Laynez applied the new law to two houses only, namely, Rome and Lisbon, the other houses contenting themselves with singing vespers on feast days; and as soon as Paul IV. died, Laynez, acting on advice, quietly ignored for the future the orders of the late pope. He also succeeded in increasing further the already enormous powers of the general. Laynez took a leading part in the colloquy of Poissy in 1561 between the Catholics and Huguenots; and obtained a legal footing from the states-general for colleges of the Society in

France. He died in 1564, leaving the Society increased to eighteen provinces with a hundred and thirty colleges, and was succeeded by Francisco Borgia. During the third generalate, Pius V. confirmed all the former privileges, and in the amplest form extended to the Society, as being a mendicant institute, all favours that had been or might afterwards be granted to such mendicant bodies. It was a trifling set-off that in 1567 the pope again enjoined the fathers to keep choir and to admit only the professed to priests' orders, especially as Gregory XIII. rescinded both these injunctions in 1573; and indeed, as regards the hours, all that Pius V. was able to obtain was the nominal concession that the breviary should be recited in choir in the professed houses only, and that not of necessity by more than two persons at a time. Everard Mercurian, a Fleming, and a subject of Spain, succeeded Borgia in 1573, being forced on the Society by the pope, in preference to Polanco, Ignatius's secretary and the vicar-general, who was rejected partly as a Spaniard and still more because he was a "New Christian" of Jewish origin and therefore objected to in Spain itself. During his term of office there took place the troubles in Rome concerning the English college and the subsequent Jesuit rule over that institution; and in 1580 the first Jesuit mission, headed by the redoubtable Robert Parsons and the saintly Edmund Campion, set out for England. This mission, on one side, carried on an active propaganda against Elizabeth in favour of Spain; and on the other, among the true missionaries, was marked with devoted zeal and heroism even to the ghastly death of traitors. Claude Acquaviva, the fifth general, held office from 1581 to 1615, a time almost coinciding with the high tide of the successful reaction, chiefly due to the Jesuits. He was an able, strong-willed man, and crushed what was tantamount to a rebellion in Spain. It was during this struggle that Mariana, the historian and the author of the famous *De rege* in which he defends tyrannicide, wrote his treatise *On the Defects in the Government of the Society*. He confessed freely that the Society had faults and that there was a great deal of unrest among the members; and he mentioned among the various points calling for reform the education of the novices and students; the state of the lay brother and the possessions of the Society; the spying system, which he declared to be carried so far that, if the general's archives at Rome should be searched, not one Jesuit's character would be found to escape; the monopoly of the higher offices by a small clique; and the absence of all encouragement and recompense for the best men of the Society.

It was chiefly during the generalship of Acquaviva that the Society began to gain an evil reputation which eclipsed its good report. In France the Jesuits joined, if they did not originate, the league against Henry of Navarre. Absolution was refused by them to those who would not join in the Guise rebellion, and Acquaviva is said to have tried to stop them, but in vain. The assassination of Henry III. in the interests of the league and the wounding of Henry IV. in 1594 by Chastel, a pupil of theirs, revealed the danger that the whole Society was running by the intrigues of a few men. The Jesuits were banished from France in 1594, but were allowed to return by Henry IV. under conditions; as Sully has recorded, the king declared his only motive to be the expediency of not driving them into a corner with possible disastrous results to his life, and because his only hope of tranquillity lay in appeasing them and their powerful friends. In England the political schemings of Parsons were no small factors in the odium which fell on the Society at large; and his determination to capture the English Catholics as an apanage of the Society, to the exclusion of all else, was an object lesson to the rest of Europe of a restless ambition and lust of domination which were to find many imitators. The political turn which was being given by some to the Society, to the detriment of its real spiritual work, evoked the fears of the wiser heads of the body; and in the fifth general congregation held in 1593-1594 it was decreed: "Whereas in these times of difficulty and danger it has happened through the fault of certain individuals, through ambition and intemperate zeal, that our institute has been ill spoken of in divers places and before divers sovereigns ... it is severely and strictly forbidden to all members of the Society to interfere in any manner whatever in public affairs even though they be thereto invited; or to deviate from the institute through entreaty, persuasion or any other motive whatever." It would have been well had Acquaviva enforced this decree; but Parsons was allowed to keep on with his work, and other Jesuits in France for many years after directed, to the loss of religion, affairs of state. In 1605 took place in England the Gunpowder Plot, in which Henry Garnet, the superior of the Society in 345England, was implicated. That the Jesuits were the instigators of the plot there is no evidence, but they were in close touch with the conspirators, of whose designs Garnet had a general knowledge. There is now no reasonable doubt that he and other Jesuits were legally accessories, and that the condemnation of Garnet as a traitor was substantially just (seeGARNET, HENRY).

It was during Acquaviva's generalship that Philip II. of Spain complained bitterly of the Society to Sixtus V., and encouraged him in those plans of reform (even to changing the name) which were only cut short by the pope's death in 1590, and also that the long protracted discussions on grace, wherein the Dominicans contended against the Jesuits, were carried on at

Rome with little practical result, by the Congregation *de auxiliis*, which sat from 1598 till 1607. The *Ratio Studiorum* took its shape during this time. The Jesuit influence at Rome was supported by the Spanish ambassador; but when Henry IV. "went to Mass," the balance inclined to the side of France, and the Spanish monopoly became a thing of the past. Acquaviva saw the expulsion of the Jesuits from Venice in 1606 for siding with Paul V. when he placed the republic under interdict, but did not live to see their recall, which took place at the intercession of Louis XIV. in 1657. He also had to banish Parsons from Rome, by order of Clement VIII., who was wearied with the perpetual complaints made against that intriguer. Gregory XIV., by the bull *Ecclesiae Christi* (July 28, 1591), again confirmed the Society, and granted that Jesuits might, for true cause, be expelled from the body without any form of trial or even documentary procedure, besides denouncing excommunications against every one, save the pope or his legates, who directly or indirectly infringed the constitutions of the Society or attempted to bring about any change therein.

Under Vitelleschi, the next general, the Society celebrated its first centenary on the 25th of September 1639, the hundredth anniversary of the verbal approbation given to the scheme by Paul III. During this hundred years the Society had grown to thirty-six provinces, with eight hundred houses containing some fifteen thousand members. In 1640 broke out the great Jansenist controversy, in which the Society took the leading part on one side and finally secured the victory. In this same year, considering themselves ill-used by Olivarez, prime minister of Philip IV. of Spain, the Jesuits powerfully aided the revolution which placed the duke of Braganza on the throne of Portugal; and their services were rewarded for nearly one hundred years with the practical control of ecclesiastical and almost of civil affairs in that kingdom.

The Society also gained ground steadily in France; for, though held in check by Richelieu and little more favoured by Mazarin, yet from the moment that Louis XIV. took the reins, their star was in the ascendant, and Jesuit confessors, the most celebrated of whom were François de La Chaise (*q.v.*) and Michel Le Tellier (1643-1719), guided the policy of the king, not hesitating to take his side in his quarrel with the Holy See, which nearly resulted in a schism, nor to sign the Gallican articles. Their hostility to the Huguenots forced on the revocation of the Edict of Nantes in 1685, and their war against their Jansenist opponents did not cease till the very walls of Port Royal were demolished in 1710, even to the very abbey church itself, and the bodies of the dead taken with every mark of insult from their graves and literally flung to the dogs to devour. But while thus gaining power in one direction, the Society was losing it in another. The Japanese mission had vanished in blood in 1651; and though many Jesuits died with their converts bravely as martyrs for the faith, yet it is impossible to acquit them of a large share in the causes of that overthrow. It was also about this same period that the grave scandal of the Chinese and Malabar rites began to attract attention in Europe, and to make thinking men ask seriously whether the Jesuit missionaries in those parts taught anything which could fairly be called Christianity at all. When it was remembered, too, that they had decided, at a council held at Lima, that it was inexpedient to impose any act of Christian devotion except baptism, on the South American converts, without the greatest precautions, on the ground of intellectual difficulties, it is not wonderful that this doubt was not satisfactorily cleared up, notably in face of the charges brought against the Society by Bernardin de Cardonas, bishop of Paraguay, and the saintly Juan de Palafox (*q.v.*), bishop of Angelopolis in Mexico.

But "the terrible power in the universal church, the great riches and the extraordinary prestige" of the Society, which Palafox complained had raised it "above all dignities, laws, councils and apostolic constitutions," carried with them the seeds of rapid and inevitable decay. A succession of devout but incapable generals, after the death of Acquaviva, saw the gradual secularization of tone by the flocking in of recruits of rank and wealth desirous to share in the glories and influence of the Society, but not well adapted to increase them. The general's supremacy received a shock when the eleventh general congregation appointed Oliva as vicar, with the right of succession and powers that practically superseded those of the general Goswin Nickel, whose infirmities, it is said, did not permit him to govern with the necessary application and vigour; and an attempt was made to depose Tirso Gonzalez, the thirteenth general, whose views on probabilism diverged from those favoured by the rest of the Jesuits. Though the political weight of the Society continued to increase in the cabinets of Europe, it was being steadily weakened internally. The Jesuits abandoned the system of free education which had won them so much influence and honour; by attaching themselves exclusively to the interests of courts, they lost favour with the middle and lower classes; and above all, their monopoly of power and patronage in France, with the fatal use they had made of it, drew down the bitterest hostility upon them. It was to their credit, indeed, that the encyclopaedists attacked them as the foremost representatives of Christianity, but they are accountable in no small degree in France, as in England, for alienating the minds of men from the religion for which they professed to work.

But the most fatal part of the policy of the Society was its activity, wealth and importance as a great trading firm with branch houses scattered over the richest countries of the world. Its founder, with a wise instinct, had forbidden the accumulation of wealth; its own constitutions, as revised in the 84th decree of the sixth general congregation, had forbidden all pursuits of a commercial nature, as also had various popes; but nevertheless the trade went on unceasingly, necessarily with the full knowledge of the general, unless it be pleaded that the system of obligatory espionage had completely broken down. The first muttering of the storm which was soon to break was heard in a breve issued in 1741 by Benedict XIV., wherein he denounced the Jesuit offenders as "disobedient, contumacious, captious and reprobate persons," and enacted many stringent regulations for their better government. The first serious attack came from a country where they had been long dominant. In 1753 Spain and Portugal exchanged certain American provinces with each other, which involved a transfer of sovereign rights over Paraguay; but it was also provided that the populations should severally migrate also, that the subjects of each crown might remain the same as before. The inhabitants of the "reductions," whom the Jesuits had trained in the use of European arms and discipline, naturally rose in defence of their homes, and attacked the troops and authorities. Their previous docility and their entire submission to the Jesuits left no possible doubt as to the source of the rebellion, and gave the enemies of the Jesuits a handle against them that was not forgotten. In 1757 Carvalho, marquis of Pombal, prime minister of Joseph I. of Portugal, and an old pupil of the Jesuits at Coimbra, dismissed the three Jesuit chaplains of the king and named three secular priests in their stead. He next complained to Benedict XIV. that the trading operations of the Society hampered the commercial prosperity of the nation, and asked for remedial measures. The pope, who knew the situation, committed a visitation of the Society to Cardinal Saldanha, an intimate friend of Pombal, who issued a severe decree against the Jesuits and ordered the confiscation of all their merchandise. But at this juncture Benedict XIV., the most learned and able pope of the period, was succeeded by a pope strongly in favour of the Jesuits, Clement XIII. Pombal, finding no help from Rome, adopted other means. The king was fired at and wounded on returning from a visit to his mistress on the 3rd of September 1758. The duke of Aveiro and other high personages were tried and executed for conspiracy; while some of the Jesuits, who had undoubtedly been in communication with them, were charged, on doubtful evidence, with complicity in the attempted assassination. Pombal charged the whole Society with the possible guilt of a few, and, unwilling to wait the dubious issue of an application to the pope for licence to try them in the civil courts, whence they were exempt, issued on the 1st of September 1759 a decree ordering the immediate deportation of every Jesuit from Portugal and all its dependencies and their suppression by the bishops in the schools and universities. Those in Portugal were at once shipped, in great misery, to the papal states, and were soon followed by those in the colonies. In France, Madame de Pompadour was their enemy because they had refused her absolution while she remained the king's mistress; but the immediate cause of their ruin was the bankruptcy of Father Lavalette, the Jesuit superior in Martinique, a daring speculator, who failed, after trading for some years, for 2,400,000 francs and brought ruin upon some French commercial houses of note. Lorenzo Ricci, then general of the Society, repudiated the debt, alleging lack of authority on Lavalette's part to pledge 346the credit of the Society, and he was sued by the creditors. Losing his cause, he appealed to the parlement of Paris, and it, to decide the issue raised by Ricci, required the constitutions of the Jesuits to be produced in evidence, and affirmed the judgment of the courts below. But the publicity given to a document scarcely known till then raised the utmost indignation against the Society. A royal commission, appointed by the duc de Choiseul to examine the constitutions, convoked a private assembly of fifty-one archbishops and bishops under the presidency of Cardinal de Luynes, all of whom except six voted that the unlimited authority of the general was incompatible with the laws of France, and that the appointment of a resident vicar, subject to those laws, was the only solution of the question fair on all sides. Ricci replied with the historical answer, *Sint ut sunt, aut non sint*; and after some further delay, during which much interest was exerted in their favour, the Jesuits were suppressed by an edict in November 1764, but suffered to remain on the footing of secular priests, a grace withdrawn in 1767, when they were expelled from the kingdom. In the very same year, Charles III. of Spain, a monarch known for personal devoutness, convinced, on evidence not now forthcoming, that the Jesuits were plotting against his authority, prepared, through his minister D'Aranda, a decree suppressing the Society in every part of his dominions. Sealed despatches were sent to every Spanish colony, to be opened on the same day, the 2nd of April 1767, when the measure was to take effect in Spain itself, and the expulsion was relentlessly carried out, nearly six thousand priests being deported from Spain alone, and sent to the Italian coast, whence, however, they were repelled by the orders of the pope and Ricci himself, finding a refuge at Corte in Corsica, after some months' suffering in overcrowded vessels at sea. The general's object may probably have been to accentuate the harshness with which the fathers had been treated, and so to increase public sympathy, but the actual result of his policy was blame for the cruelty with which he enhanced their misfortunes, for the poverty of Corsica made even a bare subsistence scarcely procurable for them there. The Bourbon courts of Naples and Parma followed the example of France and Spain; Clement XIII. retorted with a bull launched at the weakest adversary, and declaring the rank and title of the duke of Parma forfeit. The Bourbon sovereigns threatened to make war on the pope in return (France, indeed, seizing on the county of Avignon), and a joint note demanding a retractation, and the abolition of the Jesuits, was presented by the French ambassador at Rome on the 10th of December 1768 in the name of France, Spain and the two Sicilies. The pope, a man of eighty-two, died of apoplexy, brought on by the shock, early in 1769. Cardinal Lorenzo Ganganelli, a conventual Franciscan, was chosen to succeed him, and took the name of Clement XIV. He endeavoured to avert the decision forced upon him, but, as Portugal joined the Bourbon league, and Maria Theresa with her son the emperor Joseph II. ceased to protect the Jesuits, there remained only the petty kingdom of Sardinia in their favour, though the fall of Choiseul in France raised the hopes of the Society for a time. The pope began with some preliminary measures, permitting first the renewal of lawsuits against the Society, which had been suspended by papal authority, and which, indeed, had in no case been ever successful at Rome. He then closed the Collegio Romano, on the plea of its insolvency, seized the houses at Frascati and Tivoli, and broke up the establishments in Bologna and the Legations. Finally on the 21st of July 1773 the famous breve*Dominus ac Redemptor* appeared, suppressing the Society of Jesus. This remarkable document opens by citing a long series of precedents for the suppression of religious orders by the Holy See, amongst which occurs the ill-omened instance of the Templars. It then briefly sketches the objects and history of the Jesuits themselves. It speaks of their defiance of their own constitution, expressly revived by Paul V., forbidding them to meddle in politics; of the great ruin to souls caused by their quarrels with local ordinaries and the other religious orders, their condescension to heathen usages in the East, and the disturbances, resulting in persecutions of the Church, which they had stirred up even in Catholic countries, so that several popes had been obliged to punish them. Seeing then that the Catholic sovereigns had been forced to expel them, that many bishops and other eminent persons demanded their extinction, and that the Society had ceased to fulfil the intention of its institute, the pope declares it necessary for the peace of the Church that it should be suppressed, extinguished, abolished and abrogated for ever, with all its houses, colleges, schools and hospitals; transfers all the authority of its general or officers to the local ordinaries; forbids the reception of any more novices, directing that such as were actually in probation should be dismissed, and declaring that profession in the Society should not serve as a title to holy orders. Priests of the Society are given the option of either joining other orders or remaining as secular clergy, under obedience to the ordinaries, who are empowered to grant or withhold from them licences to hear confessions. Such of the fathers as are engaged in the work of education are permitted to continue, on condition of abstaining from lax and questionable doctrines apt to cause strife and trouble. The question of missions is reserved, and the relaxations granted to the Society in such matters as fasting, reciting the hours and reading heretical books, are withdrawn; while the breve ends with clauses carefully drawn to bar any legal exceptions that might be taken against its full validity and obligation. It has been necessary to cite these heads of the breve because the apologists of the Society allege that no motive influenced the pope save the desire of peace at any price, and that he did not believe in the culpability of the fathers. The categorical charges made in the document rebut this plea. The pope followed up this breve by appointing a congregation of cardinals to take possession of the temporalities of the Society, and armed it with summary powers against all who should attempt to retain or conceal any of the property. He also threw Lorenzo Ricci, the general, into prison, first in the English college and then in the castle of St Angelo, where he died in 1775, under the pontificate of Pius VI., who, though not unfavourable to the Society, and owing his own advancement to it, dared not release him, probably because his continued imprisonment was made a condition by the powers who enjoyed a right of veto in papal elections. In September 1774 Clement XIV. died after much suffering, and the question has been hotly debated ever since whether poison was the cause of his death. But the latest researches have shown that there is no evidence to support the theory of poison. Salicetti, the pope's physician, denied that the body showed signs of poisoning, and Tanucci, Neapolitan ambassador at Rome, who had a large share in procuring the breve of suppression, entirely acquits the Jesuits, while F. Theiner, no friend to the Society, does the like.

At the date of this suppression, the Society had 41 provinces and 22,589 members, of whom 11,295 were priests. Far from submitting to the papal breve, the ex-Jesuits, after some ineffectual attempts at direct resistance, withdrew into the territories of the free-thinking sovereigns of Russia and Prussia, Frederick II. and Catherine II., who became their active friends and protectors; and the fathers alleged as a principle, in so far as their theology is concerned, that no papal bull is binding in a state whose sovereign has not approved and authorized its publication and execution. Russia formed the headquarters of the Society, and two forged breves were speedily circulated, being dated June 9 and June 29, 1774, approving their establishment in Russia, and implying the repeal of the breve of suppression. But these are contradicted by the tenor of five genuine breves issued in September 1774 to the archbishop of Gnesen, and making certain assurances to the ex-Jesuits, on condition of their complete obedience to the injunctions already laid on them. The Jesuits also pleaded a verbal approbation by Pius VI., technically known as an *Oraculum vivae vocis*, but this is invalid for purposes of law unless reduced to writing and duly authenticated.

They elected three Poles successively as generals, taking, however, only the title of vicars, till on the 7th of March 1801 Pius VII. granted them liberty to reconstitute themselves in north Russia, and permitted Kareu, then vicar, to exercise full authority as general. On the 30th of July 1804 a similar breve restored the Jesuits in the Two Sicilies, at the express desire of Ferdinand IV., 347the pope thus anticipating the further action of 1814, when, by the constitution *Sollicitudo omnium Ecclesiarum*, he revoked the action of Clement XIV., and formally restored the Society to corporate legal existence, yet not only omitted any censure of his predecessor's conduct, but all vindication of the Jesuits from the heavy charges in the breve *Dominus ac Redemptor*. In France, even after their expulsion in 1765, they had maintained a precarious footing in the country under the partial disguise and names of "Fathers of the Faith" or "Clerks of the Sacred Heart," but were obliged by Napoleon I. to retire in 1804. They reappeared under their true name in 1814, and obtained formal licence in 1822, but became the objects of so much hostility that Charles X. deprived them by ordinance of the right of instruction, and obliged all applicants for licences as teachers to make oath that they did not belong to any community unrecognized by the laws. They were dispersed again by the revolution of July 1830, but soon reappeared and, though put to much inconvenience during the latter years of Louis Philippe's reign, notably in 1845, maintained their footing, recovered the right to teach freely after the revolution of 1848, and gradually became the leading educational and ecclesiastical power in France, notably under the Second Empire, till they were once more expelled by the Ferry laws of 1880, though they quietly returned since the execution of those measures. They were again expelled by the Law of Associations of 1901. In Spain they came back with Ferdinand VII., but were expelled at the constitutional rising in 1820, returning in 1823, when the duke of Angoulême's army replaced Ferdinand on his throne; they were driven out once more by Espartero in 1835, and have had no legal position since, though their presence is openly tolerated. In Portugal, ranging themselves on the side of Dom Miguel, they fell with his cause, and were exiled in 1834. There are some to this day in Lisbon under the name of "Fathers of the Faith." Russia, which had been their warmest patron, drove them from St Petersburg and Moscow in 1813, and from the whole empire in 1820, mainly on the plea of attempted proselytizing in the imperial army. Holland drove them out in 1816, and, by giving them thus a valid excuse for aiding the Belgian revolution of 1830, secured them the strong position they have ever since held in Belgium; but they have succeeded in returning to Holland. They were expelled from Switzerland in 1847-1848 for the part they were charged with in exciting the war of the Sonderbund. In south Germany, inclusive of Austria and Bavaria, their annals since their restoration have been uneventful; but in north Germany, owing to the footing Frederick II. had given them in Prussia, they became very powerful, especially in the Rhine provinces, and, gradually moulding the younger generation of clergy after the close of the War of Liberation, succeeded in spreading Ultramontane views amongst them, and so leading up to the difficulties with the civil government which issued in the Falk laws, and their own expulsion by decree of the German parliament (June 19, 1872). Since then many attempts have been made to procure the recall of the Society to the German Empire, but without success, although as individuals they are now allowed in the country. In Great Britain, whither they began to straggle over during the revolutionary troubles at the close of the 18th century, and where, practically unaffected by the clause directed against them in the Emancipation Act of 1829, their chief settlement has been at Stonyhurst in Lancashire, an estate conferred on them by Thomas Weld in 1795, they have been unmolested; but there has been little affinity to the order in the British temperament, and the English province has consequently never risen to numerical or intellectual importance in the Society. In Rome itself, its progress after the restoration was at first slow, and it was not till the reign of Leo XII. (1823-1829) that it recovered its place as the chief educational body there. It advanced steadily under Gregory XVI., and, though it was at first shunned by Pius IX., it secured his entire confidence after his return from Gaeta in 1849, and obtained from him a special breve erecting the staff of its literary journal, the *Civiltà Cattolica*, into a perpetual college under the general of the Jesuits, for the purpose of teaching and propagating the faith in its pages. How, with this pope's support throughout his long reign, the gradual filling of nearly all the sees of Latin Christendom with bishops of their own selection, and their practical capture, directly or indirectly, of the education of the clergy in seminaries, they contrived to stamp out the last remains of independence everywhere, and to crown the Ultramontane triumph with the Vatican Decrees, is matter of familiar knowledge. Leo XIII., while favouring them somewhat, never gave them his full confidence; and by his adhesion to the Thomist philosophy and theology, and his active work for the regeneration and progress of the older orders, he made another suppression possible by destroying much of their prestige. But the usual sequence has been observed under Pius X., who appeared to be greatly in favour of the Society and to rely upon them for many of the measures of his pontificate.

The Society has been ruled by twenty-five generals and four vicars from its foundation to the present day (1910). Of all the various nationalities represented in the Society, neither France, its original cradle, nor England, has ever given it a head, while Spain, Italy, Holland, Belgium, Germany and Poland, were all represented. The numbers of the Society are not accurately known, but are estimated at about 20,000, in all parts of the world; and of these the English, Irish and American Jesuits are under 3000.

The generals of the Jesuits have been as follow:—

	Ignatius de Loyola (Spaniard)	1541-1556
	Diego Laynez (Spaniard)	1558-1565
	Francisco Borgia (Spaniard)	1565-1572
	Everard Mercurian (Belgian)	1573-1580
	Claudio Acquaviva (Neapolitan)	1581-1615
	Mutio Vitelleschi (Roman)	1615-1645
	Vincenzio Caraffa (Neapolitan)	1646-1649
	Francesco Piccolomini (Florentine)	1649-1651
	Alessandro Gottofredi (Roman)	1652
0.	Goswin Nickel (German)	1652-1664
1.	Giovanni Paolo Oliva (Genoese) vicar-general and coadjutor, 1661; general	1664-1681
2.	Charles de Noyelle (Belgian)	1682-1686
3.	Tirso Gonzalez (Spaniard)	1687-1705
4.	Michele Angelo Tamburini (Modenese)	1706-1730
5.	Franz Retz (Bohemian)	1730-1750
6.	Ignazio Visconti (Milanese)	1751-1755
7.	Alessandro Centurioni (Genoese)	1755-1757
8.	Lorenzo Ricci (Florentine)	1758-1775
	a. Stanislaus Czerniewicz (Pole), vicar-general	1782-1785
	b. Gabriel Lienkiewicz (Pole), vicar-general	1785-1798
	c. Franciscus Xavier Kareu (Pole), (general in Russia, 7th March 1801)	1799-1802

	d. Gabriel Gruber (German)	1802-1805
9.	Thaddaeus Brzozowski (Pole)	1805-1820
0.	⁚ Aloysio Fortis (Veronese)	1820-1829
1.	⁚ Johannes Roothaan (Dutchman)	1829-1853
2.	⁚ Peter Johannes Beckx (Belgian)	1853-1884
3.	⁚ Antoine Anderledy (Swiss)	1884-1892
4.	⁚ Luis Martin (Spanish)	1892-1906
5.	⁚ Francis Xavier Wernz (German)	1906-

The bibliography of Jesuitism is of enormous extent, and it is impracticable to cite more than a few of the most important works. They are as follows: *Institutum Societatis Jesu* (7 vols., Avignon, 1830-1838); Orlandini, *Historia Societatis Jesu* (Antwerp, 1620); *Imago primi saeculi Societatis Jesu* (Antwerp, 1640); Nieremberg, *Vida de San Ignacio de Loyola* (9 vols., fol., Madrid, 1645-1736); Genelli, *Life of St Ignatius of Loyola* (London, 1872); Backer, *Bibliothèque des écrivains de la Compagnie de Jésus* (7 vols., Paris, 1853-1861); Crétineau Joly, *Histoire de la Compagnie de Jésus* (6 vols., Paris, 1844); Guettée,*Histoire des Jésuites* (3 vols., Paris, 1858-1859); Wolff,*Allgemeine Geschichte der Jesuiten* (4 vols., Zürich, 1789-1792); Gioberti, *Il Gesuita moderno* (Lausanne, 1846); F. Parkman, *Pioneers of France in the New World* and *The Jesuits in North America* (Boston, 1868); *Lettres édifiantes et curieuses, écrites des missions étrangères, avec les Annales de la propagation de la foi* (40 vols., Lyons, 1819-1854); Saint-Priest, *Histoire de la chute des Jésuites au XVIIIe Siècle* (Paris, 1844); Ranke, *Römische Päpste* (3 vols., Berlin, 1838); E. Taunton, *History of the Jesuits in England* (London, 1901); Thomas Hughes, S.J., *History of the Society of Jesus in North America* (London and New York, 1907); R. G. Thwaites, *Jesuit Relations and Allied Documents* (73 vols. Cleveland, 1896-1901).

(R. F. L.; E. TN.)

JESUP, MORRIS KETCHUM (1830-1908), American banker and philanthropist, was born at Westport, Connecticut, on the 21st of June 1830. In 1842 he went to New York City, where after some experience in business he established a banking house 348in 1852. In 1856 he organized the banking firm of M. K. Jesup & Company, which after two reorganizations became Cuyler, Morgan & Jesup. He became widely known as a financier, retiring from active business in 1884. He was best known, however, as a munificent patron of scientific research, a large contributor to the needs of education, and a public-spirited citizen of wide interests, who did much for the betterment of social conditions in New York. He contributed largely to the funds for the Arctic expeditions of Commander Robert E. Peary, becoming president of the Peary Arctic Club in 1899. To the American museum of natural history, in New York City, he gave large sums in his lifetime and bequeathed $1,000,000. He was president of the New York chamber of commerce from 1899 until 1907, and was the largest subscriber to its new building. To his native town he gave a fine public library. He died in New York City on the 22nd of January 1908.

JESUS CHRIST. To write a summary account of the life of Christ, though always involving a grave responsibility, was until recent years a comparatively straightforward task; for it was assumed that all that was needed, or could be offered, was a chronological outline based on a harmony of the four canonical Gospels. But to-day history is not satisfied by this simple procedure. Literary criticism has analysed the documents, and has already established some important results; and many questions are still in debate, the answers to which must affect our judgment of the historical value of the existing narratives. It seems therefore consonant alike with prudence and reverence to refrain from attempting to combine afresh into a single picture the materials derivable from the various documents, and to endeavour instead to describe the main contents of the sources from which our knowledge of the Lord Jesus Christ as an historical personage is ultimately drawn, and to observe the picture of Him which each writer in turn has offered to us.

The chief elements of the evidence with which we shall deal are the following:—

1. First, because earliest in point of time, the references to the Lord Jesus Christ in the earliest Epistles of St Paul.

2. The Gospel according to St Mark.

3. A document, no longer extant, which was partially incorporated into the Gospels of St Matthew and St Luke.

4. Further information added by St Matthew's Gospel.

5. Further information added by St Luke's Gospel.

6. The Gospel according to St John.

With regard to traditional sayings or doings of our Lord, which were only written down at a later period, it will suffice to say that those which have any claim to be genuine are very scanty, and that their genuineness has to be tested by their correspondence with the great bulk of information which is derived from the sources already enumerated. The fictitious literature of the second and third centuries, known as the Apocryphal Gospels, offers no direct evidence of any historical value at all: it is chiefly valuable for the contrast which it presents to the grave simplicity of the canonical Gospels, and as showing how incapable a later age was of adding anything to the Gospel history which was not palpably absurd.

1. *Letters of St Paul.*—In the order of chronology we must give the first place to the earliest letters of St Paul. The first piece of Christian literature which has an independent existence and to which we can fix a date is St Paul's first Epistle to the Thessalonians. Lightfoot dates it in 52 or 53; Harnack places it five years earlier. We may say, then, that it was written some twenty years after the Crucifixion. St Paul is not an historian; he is not attempting to describe what Jesus Christ said or did. He is writing a letter to encourage a little Christian society which he, a Jew, had founded in a distant Greek city; and he reminds his readers of many things which he had told them when he was with them. The evidence, to be collected from his epistles generally must not detain us here, but we may glance for a moment at this one letter, because it contains what appears to be the first mention of Jesus Christ in the literature of the world. Those who would get a true history cannot afford to neglect their earliest documents. Now the opening sentence of this letter is as follows: "Paul and Silvanus and Timothy to the Church of the Thessalonians in God the Father and the Lord Jesus Christ: Grace to you, and peace." Three men with Greek or Latin names are writing to some kind of assembly in a city of Macedonia. The writers are Jews, to judge by their salutation of "peace," and by their mention of "God the Father," and of the assembly or society as being "in" Him. But what is this new name which is placed side by side with the Divine Name—"in God the Father and the Lord Jesus Christ"? An educated Greek, who knew something (as many at that time did) of the Greek translation of the ancient Hebrew Scriptures, if he had picked up this letter before he had ever heard the name of Jesus Christ, would have been deeply interested in these opening words. He would have known that "Jesus" was the Greek form of Joshua; that "Christ" was the Greek rendering of Messiah, or Anointed, the title of the great King for whom the Jews were looking; he might further have remembered that "the Lord" is the expression which the Greek Old Testament constantly uses instead of the ineffable name of God, which we now call "Jehovah" (*q.v.*). Who, then, he might well ask is this Jesus Christ who is lifted to this unexampled height? For it is plain that Jesus Christ stands in some close relation to "God the Father," and that on the ground of that relation a society has been built up, apparently by Jews, in a Greek city far distant from Palestine. He would learn something as he read on; for the letter makes a passing reference to the foundation of the society, and to the expansion of its influence in other parts of Greece; to the conversion of its members from heathenism, and to the consequent sufferings at the hands of their heathen neighbours. The writers speak of themselves as "apostles," or messengers, of Christ; they refer to similar societies "in Christ Jesus," which they call "churches of God," in Judaea, and they say that these also suffer from the Jews there, who had "killed the Lord Jesus" some time before. But they further speak of Jesus as "raised from the dead," and they refer to the belief which they had led the society to entertain, that He would come again "from heaven to deliver them from the coming wrath." Moreover, they urge them not to grieve for certain members of the society who have already died, saying that, "if we believe that Jesus died and rose again," we may also be assured that "the dead in Christ will rise" and will live for ever with Him. Thus the letter assumes that its readers already have considerable knowledge as to "the Lord Jesus Christ," and as to His relation to "God the Father," a knowledge derived from teaching given in person on a former visit. The purpose of the letter is not to give information as to the past, but to stimulate its readers to perseverance by giving fresh teaching as to the future. Historically it is of great value as showing how widely within twenty or twenty-five years of the Crucifixion a religion which proclaimed developed theological teaching as to "the Lord Jesus Christ" had spread in the Roman Empire. We may draw a further conclusion from this and other letters of St Paul before we go on. St Paul's missionary work must have created a demand. Those who had heard him and read his

letters would want to know more than he had told them of the earthly life of the Lord Jesus. They would wish to be able to picture Him to their minds; and especially to understand what could have led to His being put to death by the Romans at the requisition of the Jews. St Paul had not been one of his personal disciples in Galilee or Jerusalem; he had no memories to relate of His miracles and teaching. Some written account of these was an obvious need. And we may be sure that any such narrative concerning One who was so deeply reverenced would be most carefully scrutinized at a time when many were still living whose memories went back to the period of Our Lord's public ministry. One such narrative we now proceed to describe.

2. *St Mark's Gospel.*—The Gospel according to St Mark was written within fifteen years of the first letter of St Paul to the Thessalonians—*i.e.* about 65. It seems designed to meet the requirements of Christians living far away from Palestine. The author was not an eye-witness of what he relates, but he writes with the firm security of a man who has the best authority behind him. The characteristics of his work confirm the early belief that St Mark wrote this Gospel for the Christians of Rome under the guidance of St Peter. It is of the first importance that 349we should endeavour to see this book as a whole; to gain the total impression which it makes on the mind; to look at the picture of Jesus Christ which it offers. That picture must inevitably be an incomplete representation of Him; it will need to be supplemented by other pictures which other writers have drawn. But it is important to consider it by itself, as showing us what impress the Master had made on the memory of one disciple who had been almost constantly by His side.

The book opens thus: "The beginning of the Gospel of Jesus Christ." This "beginning" is shown to be itself rooted in the past. Hebrew prophets had foretold that God would send a "messenger"; that a voice ***Beginning of Christ's Mission.***would be heard saying, "Prepare the way of the Lord." And so, in fact, John came, baptizing in the wilderness and turning the heart of the nation back to God. But John was only a forerunner. He was himself a prophet, and his prophecy was this, "He that is stronger than I am is coming after me." Then, we read, "Jesus came." St Mark introduces Him quite abruptly, just as he had introduced John; for he is writing for those who already know the outlines of the story. "Jesus came from Nazareth of Galilee." He was baptized by John, and as He came out of the water He had a vision of the opened heavens and the Holy Spirit, like a dove, descending upon Him; and He heard a Voice saying, "Thou art My Son, the Beloved: in Thee I am well pleased." He then passed away into the wilderness, where He was tempted by Satan and fed by angels. Then He begins His work; and from the very first we feel that He fulfils John's sign: He is strong. His first words are words of strength; "the time is fulfilled"—that is to say, all the past has been leading up to this great moment; "the kingdom of God is at hand"—that is to say, all your best hopes are on the point of being fulfilled; "repent, and believe the Gospel"—that is to say, turn from your sins and accept the tidings which I bring you. It is but a brief summary of what He must have said; but we feel its strength. He does not hesitate to fix all eyes upon Himself. Then we see Him call two brothers who are fishermen. "Come after Me," He says, "and I will make you fishers of men." They dropped their nets and went after Him, and so did two other brothers, their partners; for they all felt the power of this Master of men: He was strong. He began to teach in the synagogue; they were astonished at His teaching, for he spoke with authority. He was interrupted by a demoniac, but He quelled the evil spirit by a word; He was stronger than the power of evil. When the sun set the Sabbath was at an end, and the people could carry out their sick into the street where He was; and He came forth and healed them all. The demoniacs showed a strange faculty of recognition, and cried that He was "the holy one of God," and "the Christ," but He silenced them at once. The next morning He was gone. He had sought a quiet spot for prayer. Peter, one of those fishermen whom He had called, whose wife's mother had been healed the day before, found Him and tried to bring Him back. "All men are seeking Thee," he pleaded. "Let us go elsewhere" was the quiet reply of one who could not be moved by popular enthusiasm. Once again, we observe, He fulfils John's sign: He is strong. This is our first sight of Jesus Christ. The next shows us that this great strength is united to a most tender sympathy. To touch a leper was forbidden, and the offence involved ceremonial defilement. Yet when a leper declared that Jesus could heal him, if only He would, "He put forth His hand and touched him." The act perfected the leper's faith, and he was healed immediately. But he disobeyed the command to be silent about the matter, and the result was that Jesus could not openly enter into the town, but remained outside in the country. It is the first shadow that falls across His path; His power finds a check in human wilfulness. Presently He is in Capernaum again. He heals a paralysed man, but not until He has come into touch, as we say, with him also, by reaching his deepest need and declaring the forgiveness of his sins. This declaration disturbs the rabbis, who regard it as a blasphemous usurpation of Divine authority. But He claims that "the Son of Man hath authority on earth to forgive sins." The title which He thus adopts must be considered later.

We may note, as we pass on, that He has again, in the exercise of His power and His sympathy, come into conflict with the established religious tradition. This freedom from the trammels of convention appears yet *Attitude towards Religious Tradition.* again when he claims as a new disciple a publican, a man whose calling as a tax-gatherer for the Roman government made him odious to every patriotic Jew. Publicans were classed with open sinners; and when Jesus went to this man's house and met a company of his fellows the rabbis were scandalized: "Why eateth your Master with publicans and sinners?" The gentle answer of Jesus showed His sympathy even with those who opposed Him: "The doctor," He said, "must go to the sick." And again, when they challenged His disciples for not observing the regular fasts, He gently reminded them that they themselves relaxed the discipline of fasting for a bridegroom's friends. And He added, in picturesque and pregnant sayings, that an old garment could not bear a new patch, and that old wine-skins could not take new wine. Such language was at once gentle and strong; without condemning the old, it claimed liberty for the new. To what lengths would this liberty go? The sacred badge of the Jews' religion, which marked them off from other men all the world over, was their observance of the Sabbath. It was a national emblem, the test of religion and patriotism. The rabbis had fenced the Sabbath round with minute commands, lest any Jews should even seem to work on the Sabbath day. Thus, plucking and rubbing the ears of corn was counted a form of reaping and threshing. The hungry disciples had so transgressed as they walked through the fields of ripe corn. Jesus defended them by the example of David, who had eaten the shewbread, which only priests might eat, and had given it to his hungry men. Necessity absolves from ritual restrictions. And he went farther, and proclaimed a principle: "The Sabbath was made for man, and not man for the Sabbath, so that the Son of Man is lord even of the Sabbath." For a second time, in justifying His position, He used the expression "the Son of Man." The words might sound to Jewish ears merely as a synonym for "man." For Himself, and possibly for some others, they involved a reference, as appears later, to the "one like to a son of man" in Daniel's prophecy of the coming kingdom. They emphasized His relation to humanity as a whole, in contrast to such narrower titles as "Son of Abraham" or "Son of David." They were fitted to express a wider mission than that of a merely Jewish Messiah: He stood and spoke for mankind. The controversy was renewed when a man with a withered hand appeared in the synagogue on the Sabbath, and the rabbis watched to see whether Jesus would heal him. For the first time, we read that Jesus was angry. They were wilfully blind, and they would rather not see good done than see it done in a way that contradicted their teachings and undermined their influence. After a sharp remonstrance, He healed the man by a mere word. And they went out to make a compact with the followers of the worldly Herod to kill Him, and so to stave off a religious revolution which might easily have been followed by political trouble.

Up to this point what have we seen? On the stage of Palestine, an outlying district of the Roman Empire, the home of the Jewish nation, now subject but still fired with the hope of freedom and even of universal domination *Recapitulation.* under the leadership of a divinely anointed King, a new figure has appeared. His appearance has been announced by a reforming prophet, who has summoned the nation to return to its God, and promised that a stronger than himself is to follow. In fulfilment of this promise, who is it that has come? Not a rough prophet in the desert like John, not a leader striking for political freedom, not a pretender aiming at the petty throne of the Herods, not even a great rabbi, building on the patriotic foundation of the Pharisees who had secured the national life by a new devotion to the ancient law. None of these, but, on the contrary, an unknown figure from the remote hills of Galilee, standing on the populous shores of its lake, proclaiming as a message from God that the highest hopes were about to be fulfilled, fastening attention on Himself by speaking with authority and attaching a few followers to His person, exhibiting wonderful powers of healing as a sign that He has come to fulfil all needs, manifesting at the same time an unparalleled sympathy, and setting quietly aside every religious convention which limited the outflow of this sympathy; and as the result of all this arousing the enthusiasm of astonished multitudes and evoking the opposition and even the murderous resentment of the religious guides of the nation. Of His teaching we have heard nothing, except in the occasional sentences by which He justified some of His unexpected actions. No party is formed, no programme is announced, no doctrine is formulated; without assuming the title of Messiah, He offers Himself as the centre of expectation, and seems to invite an unlimited confidence in His person. This, then, in brief summary, is what we have seen: the natural development of an historical situation, a march of events leading rapidly to a climax; an unexampled strength and an unexampled sympathy issuing inevitably in an unexampled liberty; and then the forces of orthodox religion combining with the forces of worldly indifference in order to suppress a dangerous innovator. Yet the writer who in a few pages presents us with so remarkable a representation shows no consciousness at all of artistic treatment. He tells a simple tale in the plainest words: he never stops to offer a comment or to point a moral. The wonder of it all is not in the writing, but in the subject itself. We feel that we have here no skilful composition, but a bare transcript of what occurred. And we feel besides that such a narrative as this is the worthy commencement of an answer to the question with which its readers would have come to it: What was the beginning of the Gospel? How did the Lord Jesus speak and act? and why did He arouse such malignant enmity amongst His own people?

We have followed St Mark's narrative up to the point at which it became clear that conciliatory argument could have no effect upon the Jewish religious leaders. The controversy about the Sabbath had brought their dissatisfaction to a climax. Henceforth Jesus was to them a revolutionary, who must, by any means, be suppressed. After this decisive breach a new period opens. Jesus leaves Capernaum, never again, it would seem, to appear in its synagogue. Henceforward He was to be found, with His disciples, on the shore of the lake, where vast multitudes gathered round Him, drawn not only from Galilee and Judaea, but also from the farther districts north and east of these. He would take refuge from the crowds in a boat, which carried Him from shore to shore; and His healing activity was now at its height. Yet in the midst of this popular enthusiasm He knew that the time had come to prepare for a very different future, and accordingly a fresh departure was made when He selected twelve of His disciples for a more intimate companionship, with a view to a special mission: "He appointed twelve that they might be with Him, and that He might send them forth to preach and to have power to cast out the devils." The excitement and pressure of the crowds was at this time almost overwhelming, and the relatives of Jesus endeavoured to restrain Him; "for they said, He is mad." The scribes from Jerusalem offered a more sinister explanation, saying that He was possessed by the prince of the devils, and that this was why He was able to control all the evil spirits. He answered them first in figurative language, speaking of the certain downfall of a kingdom or a family divided against itself, and of the strong man's house which could not be looted unless the strong man were first bound. Then followed the tremendous warning, that to assign His work to Satan, and so to call good evil, was to blaspheme against the Holy Spirit—the one sin which admitted of no forgiveness. Presently, when He was told that His mother and brethren were calling for Him, He disclaimed their interference by pointing to a new circle of family relationship, consisting of all those who "do the will of God."

Again we find Him teaching by the lake, and the pressure of the multitude is still so great that He sits in a boat while they line the shore. For the first time we are allowed to hear how He taught them. He gives them a parable from nature—the **Christ's Teaching.** sower's three kinds of failure, compensated by the rich produce of the good soil. At the close He utters the pregnant saying: "He that hath ears to hear let him hear." When His disciples afterwards asked for an explanation, He prefaced it by saying that the inner circle only were intended to understand. The disciples might learn that the message would often prove fruitless, but that nevertheless an abundant harvest would result. For the light was intended to shine, and the hidden was meant to be revealed. Another parable compared the kingdom of God to seed which, when once planted, must inevitably germinate; the process was secret and slow, but the harvest was certain. Again, it was like the tiny mustard-seed which grew out of all proportion to its original size, till the birds could shelter in its great branches. These enigmatic speeches were all that the multitudes got, but the disciples in private were taught their lesson of hope. As we review this teaching it is very remarkable. The world of common things is seen to be a lesson-book of the kingdom of God to those who have eyes to read it. What that kingdom is to be we are not told; we are only taught that its coming is secret, slow and certain. If nature in its ordinary processes was thus seen to be full of significance, the disciples were also to learn that it was under His control. As the boat from which He had been teaching passed to the other side, the tired Teacher slept. A sudden storm terrified the disciples, and they roused Him in alarm. He stilled the storm with a word and rebuked their want of faith. "Who then is this," they whispered with awe, "that even the wind and the sea obey Him?" On the opposite hills a solitary spectator had watched the rise and the lull of the tempest, a fierce demoniac who dwelt among the tombs on the mountain-side. He believed himself to be possessed by a regiment of demons. When Jesus bade them go forth, he begged that they might be allowed to enter into a herd of swine which was hard by. His request was granted, and the swine rushed over a steep place into the lake. It is worth while to note that while most of the cures which Jesus had performed appear to have belonged to this class, this particular case is described as an exceptionally severe one, and the visible effect of the removal of his tormentors may have greatly helped to restore the man's shattered personality.

We must not attempt to trace in detail the whole of St Mark's story. We have followed it long enough to see its directness and simplicity, to observe the naturalness with which one incident succeeds another, and to watch the gradual manifestation of a personality at once strong and sympathetic, wielding extraordinary powers, which are placed wholly at the service of others, and refusing to be hindered from helping men by the ordinary restrictions of social or religious custom. And we have seen as the consequence of all this the development of an historical situation in which the leaders of current orthodoxy ally themselves with the indifferentism which accepts existing political conditions in order to put down a disturber of the peace. We must now be content with a broader survey of the course of events.

Two notable cures were wrought on the western side of the lake—the healing of the woman with the issue and the raising of Jairus's daughter. In each of these cures prominence is given to the requirement and the reward of faith—that *Healing Powers.* is to say, of personal confidence in the Healer: "Thy faith hath made thee whole." "Fear not, only believe." After this Jesus passed away from the enthusiastic crowds by the lake to visit His own Nazareth, and to find there a strange incredulity in regard to one whom the villagers knew as the carpenter. Once more we come across a mysterious limitation of His powers: "He could not do there any miracle," save the cure of a few sick folk; and He marvelled because of their want of faith. The moment had now come when the twelve disciples were to be entrusted with a share of His healing power and with the proclamation of repentance. While they are journeying two and two in various directions St Mark takes occasion to tell us the current conjectures as to who Jesus really was. Some 351 thought him Elijah or one of the ancient prophets returned to earth—a suggestion based on popular tradition; others said He was John the Baptist risen from the dead—the superstition of Herod who had put him to death. When the disciples returned, Jesus took them apart for rest; but the crowds reassembled when they found Him again near the lake, and His yearning compassion for these shepherdless sheep led Him to give them an impressive sign that He had indeed come to supply all human needs. Hitherto His power had gone forth to individuals, but now He fed five thousand men from the scanty stock of five loaves and two fishes. That night He came to His disciples walking upon the waters, and in the period which immediately followed there was once more a great manifestation of healing power.

We have heard nothing for some time of any opposition; but now a fresh conflict arose with certain scribes who had come down from Jerusalem, and who complained that the disciples neglected the ceremonial washing of their *Opposition of the Scribes.* hands before meals. Jesus replied with a stern rebuke, addressing the questioners as hypocrites, and exposing the falsity of a system which allowed the breach of fundamental commandments in order that traditional regulations might be observed. He then turned from them to the multitude, and uttered a saying which in effect annulled the Jewish distinction between clean and unclean meats. This was a direct attack on the whole Pharisaic position. The controversy was plainly irreconcilable, and Jesus withdrew to the north, actually passing outside the limits of the Holy Land. He desired to remain unknown, and not to extend His mission to the heathen population, but the extraordinary faith and the modest importunity of a Syrophenician woman induced Him to heal her daughter. Then He returned by a circuitous route to the Sea of Galilee. His return was marked by another miraculous feeding of the multitude, and also by two healing miracles which present unusual features. In both the patient was withdrawn from the multitude and the cure was wrought with the accompaniment of symbolic actions. Moreover, in one case Jesus is described as groaning before He spoke; in the other the cure was at first incomplete; and both of the men were strictly charged to observe silence afterwards. It cannot be a mere coincidence that these are the last cures which St Mark records as performed in Galilee.

In fact the Galilean ministry is now closed. Jesus retires northwards to Caesarea Philippi, and appears henceforth to devote Himself entirely to the instruction of his disciples, who needed to be prepared for the fatal issue *Messianic Teaching.* which could not long be delayed. He begins by asking them the popular opinion as to His Person. The suggestions are still the same—John the Baptist, or Elijah, or some other of the prophets. But when He asked their own belief, Peter replied, "Thou art the Christ." He warned them not to make this known; and He proceeded to give them the wholly new teaching that the Son of Man must suffer and be killed, adding that after three days He must rise again. Peter took Him aside and urged Him not to speak so. But He turned to the other disciples and openly rebuked Peter. And then, addressing a yet wider circle, He demanded of those who should follow Him a self-sacrifice like His own. He even used the metaphor of the cross which was carried by the sufferer to the place of execution. Life, he declared, could only be saved by voluntary death. He went on to demand an unswerving loyalty to Himself and His teaching in the face of a threatening world; and then He promised that some of those who were present should not die before they had seen the coming of the kingdom of God. We have had no hint of such teaching as this in the whole of the Galilean ministry. Jesus had stood forth as the strong healer and helper of men; it was bewildering to hear Him speak of dying. He had promised to fulfil men's highest expectations, if only they would not doubt His willingness and power. He had been enthusiastically reverenced by the common people, though suspected and attacked by the religious leaders. He had spoken of "the will of God" as supreme, and had set aside ceremonial traditions. He had announced the nearness of the kingdom of God,

183

but had described it only in parables from nature. He had adopted the vague title of the "Son of Man," but had refrained from proclaiming Himself as the expected Messiah. At last the disciples had expressed their conviction that He was the Christ, and immediately He tells them that He goes to meet humiliation and death as the necessary steps to a resurrection and a coming of the Son of Man in the glory of His Father. It was an amazing announcement and He plainly added that their path like His own lay through death to life. The dark shadows of this picture of the future alone could impress their minds, but a week later three of them were allowed a momentary vision of the light which should overcome the darkness. They saw Jesus transfigured in a radiance of glory: Elijah appeared with Moses, and they talked with Jesus. A cloud came over them, and a Voice, like that of the Baptism, proclaimed "This is My Son, the Beloved: hear ye Him." They were bidden to keep the vision secret till the Son of Man should have risen from the dead. It was in itself a foretaste of resurrection, and the puzzled disciples remembered that the scribes declared that before the resurrection Elijah would appear. Their minds were confused as to what resurrection was meant. Jesus told them that Elijah had in fact come; and He also said that the Scriptures foretold the sufferings of the Son of Man. But the situation was wholly beyond their grasp, and the very language of St Mark at this point seems to reflect the confusion of their minds.

The other disciples, in the meantime, had been vainly endeavouring to cure a peculiarly violent case of demoniacal possession. Jesus Himself cast out the demon, but not before the suffering child had been rendered seemingly lifeless by a final assault. Then they journeyed secretly through Galilee towards Judaea and the eastern side of the Jordan. On the way Jesus reinforced the new lesson of self-renunciation. He offered the little children as the type of those to whom the kingdom of God belonged; and He disappointed a young and wealthy aspirant to His favour, amazing His disciples by saying that the kingdom of God could hardly be entered by the rich; he who forsook all should have all, and more than all; the world's estimates were to be reversed—the first should be last and the last first. They were now journeying towards Jerusalem, and the prediction of the Passion was repeated. James and John, who had witnessed the Transfiguration, and who were confident of the coming glory, asked for the places nearest to their Master, and professed their readiness to share His sufferings. When the other ten were aggrieved Jesus declared that greatness was measured by service, not by rank; and that the Son of Man had come not to be served but to serve, and to give His life to ransom many other lives. As they came up from the Jordan valley and passed through Jericho, an incident occurred which signalized the beginning of the final period. A blind man appealed to Jesus as "the Son of David," and was answered by the restoration of his sight; and when, a little later, Jesus fulfilled an ancient prophecy by mounting an ass and riding into Jerusalem, the multitudes snouted their welcome to the returning "kingdom of David." Hitherto He had not permitted any public recognition of His Messiahship, but now He entered David's city in lowly but significant pomp as David's promised heir.

Two incidents illustrate the spirit of judgment with which He approached the splendid but apostate city. On His arrival He had carefully observed the condition of the Temple, and had retired to sleep outside the city. On the *Entry into Jerusalem.* following morning, finding no fruit on a fig-tree in full leaf, He said, "Let no man eat fruit of thee henceforth for ever." It was a parable of impending doom. Then, when He entered the Temple, He swept away with a fiery zeal the merchants and merchandise which had turned God's House into "a robbers' den." The act was at once an assertion of commanding authority and an open condemnation of the religious rulers who had permitted the desecration. Its immediate effect was to make new and powerful enemies; for the chief priests, as well as their rivals the scribes, were now inflamed against Him. At the moment they could do nothing, but the next day they formally 352demanded whence He derived His right so to act. When they refused to answer His question as to the authority of John the Baptist, He in turn refused to tell them His own. But He uttered a parable which more than answered them. The owner of the vineyard, who had sent his servants and last of all his only son, would visit their rejection and murder on the wicked husbandmen. He added a reminder that the stone which the builders refused was, after all, the Divine choice. They were restrained from arresting Him by fear of the people, to whom the meaning of the parable was plain. They therefore sent a joint deputation of Pharisees and Herodians to entrap Him with a question as to the Roman tribute, in answering which He must either lose His influence with the people or else lay Himself open to a charge of treason. When they were baffled, the Sadducees, to whose party the chief priests belonged, sought in vain to pose Him with a problem as to the resurrection of the dead; and after that a more honest scribe confessed the truth of His teaching as to the supremacy of love to God and man over all the sacrificial worship of the Temple, and was told in reply that he was not far from the kingdom of God. Jesus Himself now put a question as to the teaching of the scribes which identified the Messiah with "the Son of David"; and then He denounced those scribes whose pride and extortion and hypocrisy were preparing for them a terrible doom. Before He left the Temple, never to return, one incident gave Him pure satisfaction. His own teaching that all must be given for God was illustrated by the devotion of a poor widow who cast into the treasury the two tiny coins which were all that she had. As He passed out He foretold, in words which corresponded to the doom of the fig-tree, the utter demolition of the imposing but profitless Temple; and presently He opened up to four of His disciples a vision of the future, warning them against false Christs, bidding them expect great sorrows, national and personal, declaring that the gospel must be proclaimed to all the nations, and that after a great tribulation the Son of Man should appear, "coming with the clouds of heaven." The day and the hour none knew, neither the angels nor the Son, but only the Father: it was the duty of all to watch.

We now come to the final scenes. The passover was approaching, and plots were being laid for His destruction. He Himself spoke mysteriously of His burial, when a woman poured a vase of costly ointment upon His head. *Final Scenes.* To some this seemed a wasteful act; but He accepted it as a token of the love which gave all that was in its power, and He promised that it should never cease to illustrate His Gospel. Two of the disciples were sent into Jerusalem to prepare the Passover meal. During the meal Jesus declared that He should be betrayed by one of their number. Later in the evening He gave them bread and wine, proclaiming that these were His body and His blood—the tokens of His giving Himself to them, and of a new covenant with God through His death. As they withdrew to the Mount of Olives He foretold their general flight, but promised that when He was risen He would go before them into Galilee. Peter protested faithfulness unto death, but was told that he would deny his Master three times that very night. Then coming to a place called Gethsemane, He bade the disciples wait while He should pray; and taking the three who had been with Him at the Transfiguration He told them to tarry near Him and to watch. He went forward, and fell on the ground, praying that "the cup might be taken away" from Him, but resigning Himself to His Father's will. Presently Judas arrived with a band of armed men, and greeted his Master with a kiss—the signal for His arrest. The disciples fled in panic, after one of them had wounded the high priest's servant. Only a nameless young man tried to follow, but he too fled when hands were laid upon him. Before the high priest Jesus was charged, among other accusations, with threatening to destroy the Temple; but the matter was brought to an issue when He was plainly asked if He were "the Christ, the Son of the Blessed One." He answered that He was, and He predicted that they should see the fulfilment of Daniel's vision of the Son of Man sitting on the right hand of power. Thereupon He was condemned to death for manifest blasphemy, and a scene of cruel mockery followed. Meanwhile Peter in the court below had been sitting with the servants, and in his anxiety to escape recognition had thrice declared that he did not know Jesus. Thus the night passed, and in the morning Jesus was taken to Pilate, for the Jewish council had no power to execute their decree of death. Pilate's question, "Art Thou the King of the Jews?" shows the nature of the accusation which was thought likely to tell with the Roman governor. He had already in bonds one leader of revolution, whose hands were stained with blood—a striking contrast to the calm and silent figure who stood before him. At this moment a crowd came up to ask the fulfilment of his annual act of grace, the pardon of a prisoner at the Passover. Pilate, discerning that it was the envy of the rulers which sought to destroy an inconvenient rival, offered "the King of the Jews" as the prisoner to be released. But the chief priests succeeded in making the people ask for Barabbas and demand the crucifixion of Jesus. Pilate fulfilled his pledge by giving them the man of their choice, and Jesus, whom he had vainly hoped to release on a satisfactory pretext, he now condemned to the shameful punishments of scourging and crucifixion; for the cross, as Jesus had foreseen, was the inevitable fate of a Jewish pretender to sovereignty. The Roman soldiers mocked "the King of the Jews" with a purple robe and a crown of thorns. As they led Him out they forced the cross, which the sufferer commonly carried, upon the shoulders of one Simon of Cyrene, whose son's Alexander and Rufus are here mentioned—probably as being known to St Mark's readers; at any rate, it is interesting to note that, in writing to the Christians at Rome, St Paul a few years earlier had sent a greeting to "Rufus and his mother." Over the cross, which stood between two others, was the condemnatory inscription, "The King of the Jews." This was the Roman designation of Him whom the Jewish rulers tauntingly addressed as "the King of Israel." The same revilers, with a deeper truth than they knew, summed up the mystery of His life and death when they said, "He saved others, Himself He cannot save."

A great darkness shrouded the scene for three hours, and then, in His native Aramaic, Jesus cried in the words of the Psalm, "My God, My God, why has Thou forsaken Me?" One other cry He uttered, and the end came, and at that moment the veil of the Temple was rent from top to bottom—an omen of fearful import to those who had mocked Him, even on the cross, as the destroyer of the Temple, who in three days should build it anew. The disciples of Jesus do not appear as spectators of the end, but only a group of women who had ministered to His needs in Galilee, and had followed Him up to Jerusalem. These women watched His burial, which was performed by a Jewish councillor, to whom Pilate had granted the body after the centurion had certified the reality of the unexpectedly early death. The body was placed in a rock-hewn tomb, and a great stone was rolled against the entrance. Sunset brought on the Jewish sabbath, but the next evening the women brought spices to anoint the body, and at sunrise on the third day they arrived at the tomb, and saw that the stone was rolled away. They entered and found a young man in a white robe, who said, "He is risen, He is not here," and bade them say to His disciples and Peter, "He goeth before you into Galilee; there ye shall see Him, as He said unto you." In terror they fled from the tomb, "and they said nothing to any man, for they feared...."

So with a broken sentence the narrative ends. The document is imperfect, owing probably to the accidental loss of its last leaf. In very early times attempts were made to furnish it with a fitting close; but neither of the supplements which we find in manuscripts can be regarded as coming from the original writer. If we ask what must, on grounds of literary probability, have been added before the record was closed, we may content ourselves here with saying that some incident must certainly have been narrated which should have realized the twice-repeated promise that Jesus would be seen by His disciples in Galilee.

3. *Document used by St Matthew and St Luke.*—We pass on now to compare with this narrative of St Mark another very early 353document which no longer exists in an independent form, but which can be partially reconstructed from the portions of it which have been embodied in the Gospels of St Matthew and St Luke.

When we review St Mark's narrative as a whole we are struck, first of all, with its directness and simplicity. It moves straightforward upon a well-defined path. It shows us the Lord Jesus entering on the mission predicted by the Baptist without declaring Himself to be the Messiah; attracting the multitudes in Galilee by His healing power and His unbounded sympathy, and at the same time awakening the envy and suspicion of the leaders of religion; training a few disciples till they reach the conviction that He is the Christ, and then, but not till then, admitting them into the secret of His coming sufferings, and preparing them for a mission in which they also must sacrifice themselves; then journeying to Jerusalem to fulfil the destiny which He foresaw, accepting the responsibility of the Messianic title, only to be condemned by the religious authorities as a blasphemer and handed over to the Roman power as a pretender to the Jewish throne. That is the story in its barest outline. It is adequate to its presumed purpose of offering to distant Gentile converts a clear account of their Master's earthly work, and of the causes which led to His rejection by His own people and to His death by Roman crucifixion. The writer makes no comment on the wonderful story which he tells. Allusions to Jewish customs are, indeed, explained as they occur, but apart from this the narrative appears to be a mere transcript of remembered facts. The actors are never characterized; their actions are simply noted down; there is no praise and no blame. To this simplicity and directness of narrative we may in large measure attribute the fact that when two later evangelists desired to give fuller accounts of our Lord's life they both made this early book the basis of their work. In those days there was no sense of unfairness in using up existing materials in order to make a more complete treatise. Accordingly so much of St Mark's Gospel has been taken over word for word in the Gospels of St Luke and St Matthew that, if every copy of it had perished, we could still reconstruct large portions of it by carefully comparing their narratives. They did not hesitate, however, to alter St Mark's language where it seemed to them rough or obscure, for each of them had a distinctive style of his own, and St Luke was a literary artist of a high order. Moreover, though they both accepted the general scheme of St Mark's narrative, each of them was obliged to omit many incidents in order to find room for other material which was at their disposal, by which they were able to supplement the deficiencies of the earlier book. The most conspicuous deficiency was in regard to our Lord's teaching, of which, as we have seen, St Mark had given surprisingly little. Here they were happily in a position to make a very important contribution.

For side by side with St Mark's Gospel there was current in the earliest times another account of the doings and sayings of Jesus Christ. Our knowledge of it to-day is entirely derived from a comparison of the two later evangelists who embodied large portions of it, working it in and out of the general scheme which they derived from St Mark, according as each of them thought most appropriate. St Luke appears to have taken it over in sections for the most part without much modification; but in St Matthew's Gospel its incidents seldom find an independent place; the sayings to which they gave rise are often detached from their context and grouped with sayings of a similar character so as to form considerable discourses, or else they are linked on to sayings which were uttered on other occasions recorded by St Mark. It is probable that many passages of St Luke's Gospel which have no parallel in St Matthew were also derived from this early source; but this is not easily capable of distinct proof; and, therefore, in order to gain a secure conception of the document we must confine ourselves at first to those parts of it which were borrowed by both writers. We shall, however, look to St Luke in the main as preserving for us the more nearly its original form.

We proceed now to give an outline of the contents of this document. To begin with, it contained a fuller account of the teaching of John the Baptist. St Mark tells us only his message of hope; but here we read the severer language with which he called men to repentance. We hear his warning of "the coming wrath": his mighty Successor will baptize with fire; the fruitless tree will be cast into the fire; the chaff will be separated from the wheat and burned with unquenchable fire; the claim to be children of Abraham will not avail, for God can raise up other children to Abraham, if it be from the stones of the desert. Next, we have a narrative of the Temptation, of which St Mark had but recorded the bare fact. It was grounded on the Divine sonship, which we already know was proclaimed at the Baptism. In a threefold vision Jesus is invited to enter upon His inheritance at once; to satisfy His own needs, to accept of earthly dominion, to presume on the Divine protection. The passage stands almost alone as a revelation of inner conflict in a life which outwardly was marked by unusual calm.

Not far from the beginning of the document there stood a remarkable discourse delivered among the hills above the lake. It opens with a startling reversal of the common estimates of happiness and misery. In the light of the *The Sermon on the Mount.* coming kingdom it proclaims the blessedness of the poor, the hungry, the sad and the maligned; and the woefulness of the rich, the full, the merry and the popular. It goes on to reverse the ordinary maxims of conduct. Enemies are to be loved, helped, blessed, prayed for. No blow is to be returned; every demand, just or unjust, is to be granted: in short, "as ye desire that men should do to you, do in like manner to them." Then the motive and the model of this conduct are adduced: "Love your enemies ... and ye shall be sons of the Highest; for He is kind to the thankless and wicked. Be merciful, as your Father is merciful; and judge not, and ye shall not be judged." We note in passing that this is the first introduction of our Lord's teaching of the fatherhood of God. God is your Father, He says in effect; you will be His sons if like Him you will refuse to make distinctions, loving without looking for a return, sure that in the end love will not be wholly lost. Then follow grave warnings—generous towards others, you must be strict with yourselves; only the good can truly do good; hearers of these words must be doers also, if they would build on the rock and not on the sand. So, with the parable of the two builders, the discourse reached its formal close.

It was followed by the entry of Jesus into Capernaum, where He was asked to heal the servant of a Roman officer. This man's unusual faith, based on his soldierly sense of discipline, surprised the Lord, who declared that it had no equal in Israel itself. Somewhat later messengers arrived from the imprisoned Baptist, who asked if Jesus were indeed "the coming One" of whom he had spoken. Jesus pointed to His acts of healing the sick, raising the dead and proclaiming good news for the poor; thereby suggesting to those who could understand that He fulfilled the ancient prophecy of the Messiah. He then declared the greatness of John in exalted terms, adding, however, that the least in the kingdom of God was John's superior. Then He complained of the unreasonableness of an age which refused John as too austere and Himself as too lax and as being "the friend of publicans and sinners." This narrative clearly presupposes a series of miracles already performed, and also such a conflict with the Pharisees as we have seen recorded by St Mark. Presently we find an offer of discipleship met by the warning that "the Son of Man" is a homeless wanderer; and then the stern refusal of a request for leave to perform a father's funeral rites.

Close upon these incidents follows a special mission of disciples, introduced by the saying: "The harvest is great, but the labourers are few." The disciples as they journey are to take no provisions, but to throw themselves *Other Sayings of Jesus.* on the bounty of their hearers; they are to heal the sick and to proclaim the nearness of the kingdom of God. The city that rejects them shall have a less lenient judgment than Sodom; Tyre and Sidon shall be better off than cities like Chorazin and Bethsaida which have seen His miracles; 354 Capernaum, favoured above all, shall sink to the deepest depth. If words could be sterner than these, they are those which follow: "He that heareth you heareth Me; and he that rejecteth you rejecteth Me; but He that rejecteth Me rejecteth Him that sent Me." This reference to His own personal mission is strikingly expanded in words which He uttered on the return of the disciples. After thanking the Father for revealing to babes what He hides from the wise, He continued in mysterious language: "All things are delivered to Me by My Father; and none knoweth who the Son is but the Father; and who the Father is but the Son, and he to whom the Son chooseth to reveal Him." Happy were the disciples in seeing and hearing what prophets and kings had looked for in vain.

When His disciples, having watched Him at prayer, desired to be taught how to pray, they were bidden to address God as "Father"; to ask first for the hallowing of the Father's name, and the coming of His kingdom; then for their daily food, for the pardon of their sins and for freedom from temptation. It was the prayer of a family—that the sons might be true to the Father, and the Father true to the sons; and they were further encouraged by a parable of the family: "Ask and ye shall receive.... Every one that asketh receiveth": for the heavenly Father will do more, not less, than an earthly father would do for his children. After He had cast out a dumb demon, some said that His power was due to Beelzebub. He accordingly asked them by whom the Jews themselves cast out demons; and He claimed that His power was a sign that the kingdom of God was come. But He warned them that demons cast out once might return in greater force. When they asked for a sign from heaven, He would give them no more than the sign of Jonah, explaining that the repentant Ninevites should condemn the present generation: so, too, should the queen of Sheba; for that which they were now rejecting was more than Jonah and more than Solomon. Yet further warnings were given when a Pharisee invited Him to his table, and expressed surprise that He did not wash His hands before the meal. The cleansing of externals and the tithing of garden-produce, He declares, have usurped the place of judgment and the love of God. Woe is pronounced upon the Pharisees: they are successors to the murderers of the prophets. Then citing from Genesis and 2 Chronicles, the first and last books in the order of the Jewish Bible, He declared that all righteous blood from that of Abel to that of Zachariah should be required of that generation. After this the disciples are encouraged not to fear their murderous opponents. The very sparrows are God's care—much more shall they be; the hairs of their head are all counted. In the end the Son of Man will openly own those who have owned Him before men. For earthly needs no thought is to be taken: the birds and the flowers make no provision for their life and beauty. God will give food and raiment to those who are seeking His kingdom. Earthly goods should be given away in exchange for the imperishable treasures. Suddenly will the Son of Man come: happy the servant whom His Master finds at his appointed task. In brief parables the kingdom of God is likened to a mustard-seed and to leaven. When Jesus is asked if the saved shall be few, He replies that the door is a narrow one. Then, changing His illustration, He says that many shall seek entrance in vain; for the master of the house will refuse to recognize them. But while they are excluded, a multitude from all quarters of the earth shall sit down with Abraham, Isaac and Jacob, and the prophets in the kingdom of God.

His eyes are now fixed on Jerusalem, where, like the prophets, He must die. "Jerusalem, Jerusalem, how often have I desired to gather thy children together, as a bird her brood beneath her wings, but ye refused." "Ye shall not see Me, until ye shall say, Blessed is He that cometh in the name of the Lord." After this we have the healing of a dropsical man on the Sabbath, with a reply to the murmuring Pharisees; and then a parable of the failure of invited guests and the filling of their places from the streets. A few fragmentary passages remain, of which it will be sufficient to cite a word or two to call them to remembrance. There is a warning that he who forsakes not father and mother cannot be a disciple, nor he who does not bear his cross. Savourless salt is fit for nothing. The lost sheep is brought home with a special joy. "Ye cannot serve God and Mammon." Scandals must arise, but woe to him through whom they arise. The Son of Man will come with the suddenness of lightning; the days of Noah and the days of Lot will find a parallel in their blind gaiety and their inevitable disaster. He who seeks to gain his life will lose it. "One shall be taken, and the other left." "Where the carcase is, the vultures will gather." Then, lastly, we have a parable of the servant who failed to employ the money entrusted to him; and a promise that the disciples shall sit on twelve thrones to judge the twelve tribes of Israel. We cannot say by our present method of determination, how this document closed; for in the narratives of the Passion and the Resurrection St Matthew and St Luke only coincide in passages which they have taken from St Mark.

Now that we have reconstructed in outline this early account of the Lord Jesus, so far as it has been used by both the later evangelists, we may attempt to compare the picture which it presents to us with that which was offered **Comparison with St Mark.** by St Mark. But in doing so we must remember that we know it only in fragments. There can be little doubt that much more of it is embedded in St Luke's Gospel, and something more also in St Matthew's; but in order to stand on firm ground we have considered thus far only those portions which both of these writers elected to use in composing their later narratives. To go beyond this is a work of delicate discrimination. It can only be effected by a close examination of the style and language of the document, which may enable us in some instances to identify with comparative security certain passages which are found in St Luke, but which St Matthew did not regard as suitable for his purpose. Among these we may venture, quite tentatively, to mention the sermon at Nazareth which opened with a passage from the Book of Isaiah, the raising of the widow's son at Nain, and the parable of the good Samaritan. These are found in St Luke, but not in St Matthew. On the other hand, it is not improbable that the wonderful words which begin, "Come unto Me all ye that labour," were drawn by St Matthew from the same document, though they are not recorded by St Luke. But here we have entered upon a region of less certainty, in which critical scholarship has still much to do; and these passages are mentioned here only as a reminder that the document must have contained more than what St Matthew and St Luke each independently determined to borrow from it. Looking, then, at the portions which we have indicated as having this two-fold testimony, we see that in their fragmentary condition we cannot trace the clear historical development which was so conspicuous a feature of St Mark's Gospel; yet we need not conclude that in its complete form it failed to present an orderly narrative. Next, we see that wherever we are able to observe its method of relating an incident, as in the case of the healing of the centurion's servant, we have the same characteristics of brevity and simplicity which we admired in St Mark. No comment is made by the narrator; he tells his tale in the fewest words and passes on. Again, we note that it supplies just what we feel we most need when we have reached the end of St Mark's story, a fuller account of the teaching which Jesus gave to His disciples and to the people at large. And we see that the substance of that teaching is in complete harmony with the scattered hints that we found in St Mark. If the fatherhood of God stands out clearly, we may remember a passage of St Mark also which speaks of "the Heavenly Father" as forgiving those who forgive. If prayer is encouraged, we may also remember that the same passage of St Mark records the saying: "All things whatsoever ye pray for and ask, believe that ye have received them and ye shall have them." If in one mysterious passage Jesus speaks of "the Father" and "the Son"—terms with which the Gospel of St John has made us familiar—St Mark also in one passage uses the same impressive terms—"the Son" and "the Father." There are, of course, many other parallels with St Mark, and at some points the two documents seem to overlap and to relate the same incidents in 355somewhat different forms. There is the same use of parables from nature, the same incisiveness of speech and employment of paradox, the same demand to sacrifice all to Him and for His cause, the same importunate claim made by Him on the human soul.

But the contrast between the two writers is even more important for our purpose. No one can read through the passages to which we have pointed without feeling the solemn sternness of the great Teacher, a sternness which can *The Element of Warning.*indeed be traced here and there in St Mark, but which does not give its tone to the whole of his picture. Here we see Christ standing forth in solitary grandeur, looking with the eyes of another world on a society which is blindly hastening to its dissolution. It may be that if this document had come down to us in its entirety, we should have gathered from it an exaggerated idea of the severity of our Lord's character. Certain it is that as we read over these fragments we are somewhat startled by the predominance of the element of warning, and by the assertion of rules of conduct which seem almost inconsistent with a normal condition of settled social life. The warning to the nation sounded by the Baptist, that God could raise up a new family for Abraham, is heard again and again in our Lord's teaching. Gentile faith puts Israel to shame. The sons of the kingdom will be left outside, while strangers feast with Abraham. Capernaum shall go to perdition; Jerusalem shall be a desolate ruin. The doom of the nation is pronounced; its fate is imminent; there is no ray of hope for the existing constitution of religion and society. As to individuals within the nation, the despised publicans and sinners will find God's favour before the self-satisfied representatives of the national religion. In such a condition of affairs it is hardly surprising to find that the great and stern Teacher congratulates the poor and has nothing but pity for the rich; that He has no interest at all in comfort or property. If a man asks you for anything, give it him; if he takes it without asking, do not seek to recover it. Nothing material is worth a thought; anxiety is folly; your Father, who feeds His birds and clothes His flowers, will feed and clothe you. Rise to the height of your sonship to God; love your enemies even as God loves His; and if they kill you, God will care for you still; fear them not, fear only Him who loves you all.

Here is a new philosophy of life, offering solid consolation amid the ruin of a world. We have no idea who the disciple may have been who thus seized upon the sadder elements of the teaching of Jesus; but we may well think of him as one of those who were living in Palestine in the dark and threatening years of internecine strife, when the Roman eagles were gathering round their prey, and the first thunder was muttering of the storm which was to leave Jerusalem a heap of stones. At such a moment the warnings of our Lord would claim a large place in a record of His teaching, and the strange comfort which He had offered would be the only hope which it would seem possible to entertain.

4. *Additions by the Gospel according to St Matthew.*—We have now examined in turn the two earliest pictures which have been preserved to us of the life of Jesus Christ. The first portrays Him chiefly by a record of His actions, *The Earlier Narratives.*and illustrates His strength, His sympathy, and His freedom from conventional restraints. It shows the disturbing forces of these characteristics, which aroused the envy and apprehension of the leaders of religion. The first bright days of welcome and popularity are soon clouded: the storm begins to lower. More and

more the Master devotes Himself to the little circle of His disciples, who are taught that they, as well as He, can only triumph through defeat, succeed by failure, and find their life in giving it away. At length, in fear of religious innovations and pretending that He is a political usurper, the Jews deliver Him up to die on a Roman cross. The last page of the story is torn away, just at the point when it has been declared that He is alive again and about to show Himself to His disciples. The second picture has a somewhat different tone. It is mainly a record of teaching, and the teaching is for the most part stern and paradoxical. It might be described as revolutionary. It is good tidings to the poor: it sets no store on property and material comfort: it pities the wealthy and congratulates the needy. It reverses ordinary judgments and conventional maxims of conduct. It proclaims the downfall of institutions, and compares the present blind security to the days of Noah and of Lot: a few only shall escape the coming overthrow. Yet even in this sterner setting the figure portrayed is unmistakably the same. There is the same strength, the same tender sympathy, the same freedom from convention: there is the same promise to fulfil the highest hopes, the same surrender of life, and the same imperious demand on the lives of others. No thoughtful man who examines and compares these pictures can doubt that they are genuine historical portraits of a figure wholly different from any which had hitherto appeared on the world's stage. They are beyond the power of human invention. They are drawn with a simplicity which is their own guarantee. If we had these, and these only, we should have an adequate explanation of the beginnings of Christianity. There would still be a great gap to be filled before we reached the earliest letters of St Paul; but yet we should know what the Apostle meant when he wrote to "the Church of the Thessalonians in God the Father and the Lord Jesus Christ," and reminded them how they had "turned from idols to serve the living and true God, and to wait for His Son from heaven, whom He raised from the dead, even Jesus who delivereth us from the wrath to come."

If these two narratives served the first needs of Christian believers, it is easy to see that they would presently stimulate further activity in the same direction. For, to begin with, they were obviously incomplete: many incidents and teachings known to the earliest disciples found no place in them; and they contained no account of the life of Jesus Christ before His public ministry, no record of His pedigree, His birth or His childhood. Secondly, their form left much to be desired; for one of them at least was rude in style, sometimes needlessly repetitive and sometimes brief to obscurity. Moreover the very fact that there were two challenged a new and combined work which perhaps should supersede both.

Accordingly, some years after the fall of Jerusalem—we cannot tell the exact date or the author's name—the book which we call the Gospel according to St Matthew was written to give the Palestinian Christians a *The Gospel of St Matthew.* full account of Jesus Christ, which should present Him as the promised Messiah, fulfilling the ancient Hebrew prophecies, proclaiming the kingdom of heaven, and founding the Christian society. The writer takes St Mark as his basis, but he incorporates into the story large portions of the teaching which he has found in the other document. He groups his materials with small regard to chronological order; and he fashions out of the many scattered sayings of our Lord continuous discourses, everywhere bringing like to like, with considerable literary art. A wide knowledge of the Old Testament supplies him with a text to illustrate one incident after another; and so deeply is he impressed with the correspondence between the life of Christ and the words of ancient prophecy, that he does not hesitate to introduce his quotations by the formula "that it might be fulfilled which was spoken by the prophet."

His Hebrew instinct leads him to begin with a table of genealogy, artificially constructed in groups of fourteen generations—from Abraham to David, from David to the Captivity, and from the Captivity to the Christ. The royal descent of the Messiah is thus declared, and from the outset His figure is set against the background of the Old Testament. He then proceeds to show that, though His lineage is traced through Joseph's ancestors, He was but the adopted son of Joseph, and he tells the story of the Virgin-birth. The coming of the Child draws Eastern sages to his cradle and fills the court of Herod with suspicious fears. The cruel tyrant kills the babes of Bethlehem, but the Child has been withdrawn by a secret flight into Egypt, whence he presently returns to the family home at Nazareth in Galilee. All this is necessarily fresh material, for the other records had dealt only with the period of public ministry. We have no knowledge of the source from which it was drawn. From the historical standpoint its value must be appraised by the estimate which is formed of the writer's general trustworthiness as a narrator, and by the extent to which the incidents receive confirmation from other quarters. The central fact of the Virgin-birth, as we shall presently see, has high attestation from another early writer.

The next addition which St Matthew's Gospel makes to our knowledge is of a different kind. It consists of various important sayings of our Lord, which are combined with discourses found in the second document and are worked *Discourses and Parables.* up into the great utterance

190

which we call the Sermon on the Mount. Such grouping of materials is a feature of this Gospel, and was possibly designed for purposes of public instruction; so that continuous passages might be read aloud in the services of the Church, just as passages from the Old Testament were read in the Jewish synagogues. This motive would account not only for the arrangement of the material, but also for certain changes in the language which seem intended to remove difficulties, and to interpret what is ambiguous or obscure. An example of such interpretation meets us at the outset. The startling saying, "Blessed are ye poor," followed by the woe pronounced upon the rich, might seem like a condemnation of the very principle of property; and when the Christian Church had come to be organized as a society containing rich and poor, the heart of the saying was felt to be more truly and clearly expressed in the words, "Blessed are the poor in spirit." This interpretative process may be traced again and again in this Gospel, which frequently seems to reflect the definite tradition of a settled Church.

Apart from the important parables of the tares, the pearl and the net, the writer adds little to his sources until we come to the remarkable passage in ch. xvi., in which Peter the Rock is declared to be the foundation of the future Church, and is entrusted with the keys of the kingdom of heaven. The function of "binding and loosing," here assigned to him, is in identical terms assigned to the disciples generally in a passage in ch. xviii. in which for the second time we meet with the word "Church"—a word not found elsewhere in the Gospels. There is no sufficient ground for denying that these sayings were uttered by our Lord, but the fact that they were now first placed upon record harmonizes with what has been said already as to the more settled condition of the Christian society which this Gospel appears to reflect.

The parables of the two debtors, the labourers in the vineyard, the two sons, the ten virgins, the sheep and goats, are recorded only by this evangelist. But by way of incident he has almost nothing to add till we come to the closing scenes. The earthquake at the moment of our Lord's death and the subsequent appearance of departed saints are strange traditions unattested by other writers. The same is to be said of the soldiers placed to guard the tomb, and of the story that they had been bribed to say that the sacred body had been stolen while they slept. On the other hand, the appearance of the risen Christ to the women may have been taken from the lost pages of St Mark, being the sequel to the narrative which is broken off abruptly in this Gospel: and it is not improbable that St Mark's Gospel was the source of the great commission to preach and baptize with which St Matthew closes, though the wording of it has probably been modified in accordance with a settled tradition.

The work which the writer of this Gospel thus performed received the immediate sanction of a wide acceptance. It met a definite spiritual need. It presented the Gospel in a suitable form for the edification of the Church; and it confirmed its truth by constant appeals to the Old Testament scriptures, thus manifesting its intimate relation with the past as the outcome of a long preparation and as the fulfilment of a Divine purpose. No Gospel is so frequently quoted by the early post-apostolic writers: none has exercised a greater influence upon Christianity, and consequently upon the history of the world.

Yet from the purely historical point of view its evidential value is not the same as that of St Mark. Its facts for the most part are simply taken over from the earlier evangelist, and the historian must obviously prefer the primary source. Its true importance lies in its attestation of the genuineness of the earlier portraits to which it has so little to add, in its recognition of the relation of Christ to the whole purpose of God as revealed in the Old Testament, and in its interpretation of the Gospel message in its bearing on the living Church of the primitive days.

5. *Additions by St Luke.*—While the needs of Jewish believers were amply met by St Matthew's Gospel, a like service was rendered to Gentile converts by a very different writer. St Luke was a physician who had accompanied St Paul on his missionary journeys. He undertook a history of the beginnings of Christianity, two volumes of which have come down to us, entitled the Gospel and the Acts of the Apostles. His Gospel, like St Matthew's, is founded on St Mark, with the incorporation of large portions of the second document of which we have spoken above. But the way in which the two writers have used the same materials is strikingly different. In St Matthew's Gospel the original sources are frequently blended: the incidents of St Mark are rearranged and often grouped afresh according to subject matter: harsh and ambiguous sentences of both documents are toned down or interpreted. St Luke, on the contrary, chooses between parallel stories of his two sources, preferring neither to duplicate nor to combine: he incorporates St Mark in continuous sections, following him alone for a time, then leaving him entirely, and then returning to introduce a new block of his narrative. He modifies St Mark's style very freely, but he makes less change in the recorded words of our Lord, and he adheres more closely to the original language of the second document.

In his first two chapters he gives an account of the birth and childhood of St John the Baptist and of our Lord Himself, gathered perhaps directly from the traditions of the Holy

Family, and written in close imitation of the sacred stories of the Old Testament which were familiar to him in their Greek translation. The whole series of incidents differ from that which we find in St Matthew's Gospel, but there is no direct variance between them. The two narratives are in agreement as to the central fact of the Virgin-birth. St Luke gives a table of genealogy which is irreconcilable with the artificial table of St Matthew's Gospel, and which traces our Lord's ancestry up to Adam, "which was the son of God."

The opening scene of the Galilean ministry is the discourse at Nazareth, in which our Lord claims to fulfil Isaiah's prophecy of the proclamation of good tidings to the poor. The same prophecy is alluded to in His reply to the Baptist's messengers which is incorporated subsequently from the second document. The scene ends with the rejection of Christ by His own townsfolk, as in the parallel story of St Mark which St Luke does not give. It is probable that St Luke found this narrative in the second document, and chose it after his manner in preference to the less instructive story in St Mark. He similarly omits the Marcan account of the call of the fishermen, substituting the story of the miraculous draught. After that he follows St Mark alone, until he introduces after the call of the twelve apostles the sermon which begins with the beatitudes and woes. This is from the second document, which he continues to use, and that without interruption (if we may venture to assign to it the raising of the widow's son at Nain and the anointing by the sinful woman in the Pharisee's house), until he returns to incorporate another section from St Mark.

This in turn is followed by the most characteristic section of his Gospel (ix. 51-xviii. 14), a long series of incidents wholly independent of St Mark, and introduced as belonging to the period of the final journey from Galilee to *Characteristic Section of St. Luke's Gospel.* Jerusalem. Much of this material is demonstrably derived from the second document; and it is quite possible that the whole of it may come from that source. There are special reasons for thinking so in regard to certain passages, as for example the mission of the seventy disciples and the parable of the good Samaritan, although they are not contained in St Matthew's Gospel.

For the closing scenes at Jerusalem St Luke makes considerable additions to St Mark's narrative: he gives a different account of the Last Supper, and he adds the trial before Herod and the 357incident of the penitent robber. He appears to have had no information as to the appearance of the risen Lord in Galilee, and he accordingly omits from his reproduction of St Mark's narrative the twice-repeated promise of a meeting with the disciples there. He supplies, however, an account of the appearance to the two disciples at Emmaus and to the whole body of the apostles in Jerusalem.

St Luke's use of his two main sources has preserved the characteristics of both of them. The sternness of certain passages, which has led some critics to imagine that he was an Ebionite, is mainly, if not entirely, due to his faithful reproduction of the language of the second document. The key-note of his Gospel is universality: the mission of the Christ embraces the poor, the weak, the despised, the heretic and the sinful: it is good tidings to all mankind. He tells of the devotion of Mary and Martha, and of the band of women who ministered to our Lord's needs and followed Him to Jerusalem: he tells also of His kindness to more than one sinful woman. Zacchaeus the publican and the grateful Samaritan leper further illustrate this characteristic. Writing as he does for Gentile believers he omits many details which from their strongly Jewish cast might be unintelligible or uninteresting. He also modifies the harshness of St Mark's style, and frequently recasts his language in reference to diseases. From an historical point of view his Gospel is of high value. The proved accuracy of detail elsewhere, as in his narration of events which he witnessed in company with St Paul, enhances our general estimation of his work. A trustworthy observer and a literary artist, the one non-Jewish evangelist has given us—to use M. Renan's words—"the most beautiful book in the world."

6. *Additions by St John.*—We come lastly to consider what addition to our knowledge of Christ's life and work is made by the Fourth Gospel. St Mark's narrative of our Lord's ministry and passion is so simple and straightforward that it satisfies our historical sense. We trace a natural development in it: we seem to see why with such power and such sympathy He necessarily came into conflict with the religious leaders of the people, who were jealous of the influence which He gained and were scandalized by His refusal to be hindered in His mission of mercy by rules and conventions to which they attached the highest importance. The issue is fought out in Galilee, and when our Lord finally journeys to Jerusalem He knows that He goes there to die. The story is so plain and convincing in itself that it gives at first sight an impression of completeness. This impression is confirmed by the Gospels of St Matthew and St Luke, which though they add much fresh material do not disturb the general scheme presented by St Mark. But on reflection we are led to question the sufficiency of the account thus offered to us. Is it probable, we ask, that our Lord should have neglected the sacred custom in accordance with which the pious Jew visited Jerusalem several times each year for the observance of the divinely

appointed feasts? It is true that St Mark does not break his narrative of the Galilean ministry to record such visits: but this does not prove that such visits were not made. Again, is it probable that He should have so far neglected Jerusalem as to give it no opportunity of seeing Him and hearing His message until the last week of His life? If the writers of the other two Gospels had no means at their disposal for enlarging the narrow framework of St Mark's narrative by recording definite visits to Jerusalem, at least they preserve to us words from the second document which seem to imply such visits: for how else are we to explain the pathetic complaint, "Jerusalem, Jerusalem, how often would I have gathered thee, as a hen gathereth her chickens under her wings; but ye would not"?

St John's Gospel meets our questionings by a wholly new series of incidents and by an account of a ministry which is concerned mainly not with Galileans but with Judaeans, and which centres in Jerusalem. It is carried on to a large extent concurrently with the Galilean ministry: it is not continuous, but is taken up from feast to feast as our Lord visits the sacred city at the times of its greatest religious activity. It differs in character from the Galilean ministry: for among the simple, unsophisticated folk of Galilee Jesus presents Himself as a healer and helper and teacher, keeping in the background as far as possible His claim to be the Messiah; whereas in Jerusalem His authority is challenged at His first appearance, the element of controversy is never absent, His relation to God is from the outset the vital issue, and consequently His Divine claim is of necessity made explicit. Time after time His life is threatened before the feast is ended, and when the last passover has come we can well understand, what was not made sufficiently clear in the brief Marcan narrative, why Jerusalem proved so fatally hostile to His Messianic claim.

The Fourth Gospel thus offers us a most important supplement to the limited sketch of our Lord's life which we find in the Synoptic Gospels. Yet this was not the purpose which led to its composition. That purpose is plainly stated *The Purpose of St John's Gospel.* by the author himself: "These things have been written that ye may believe that Jesus Christ is the Son of God, and that believing ye may have life in His name." His avowed aim is, not to write history, but to produce conviction. He desires to interpret the coming of Jesus Christ into the world, to declare whence and why He came, and to explain how His coming, as light in the midst of darkness, brought a crisis into the lives of all with whom He came in contact. The issue of this crisis in His rejection by the Jews at Jerusalem is the main theme of the book.

St John's prologue prepares us to find that he is not writing for persons who require a succinct narrative of facts, but for those who having such already in familiar use are asking deep questions as to our Lord's mission. It goes back far behind human birth or lines of ancestry. It begins, like the sacred story of creation, "In the beginning." The Book of Genesis had told how all things were called into existence by a Divine utterance: "God said, Let there be ... and there was." The creative Word had been long personified by Jewish thought, especially in connexion with the prophets to whom "the Word of the Lord" came. "In the beginning," then, St John tells us, the Word was—was with God—yea, was God. He was the medium of creation, the source of its light and its life—especially of that higher life which finds its manifestation in men. So He was in the world, and the world was made by Him, and yet the world knew Him not. At length He came, came to the home which had been prepared for Him, but His own people rejected Him. But such as did receive Him found a new birth, beyond their birth of flesh and blood: they became children of God, were born of God. In order thus to manifest Himself He had undergone a human birth: "the Word was made flesh, and dwelt among us, and we beheld His glory"—the glory, as the evangelist has learned to see, of the Father's only-begotten Son, who has come into the world to reveal to men that God whom "no man hath ever seen." In these opening words we are invited to study the life of Christ from a new point of view, to observe His self-manifestation and its issue. The evangelist looks back across a period of half a century, and writes of Christ not merely as he saw Him in those far-off days, but as he has come by long experience to think and speak of Him. The past is now filled with a glory which could not be so fully perceived at the time, but which, as St John tells, it was the function of the Holy Spirit to reveal to Christ's disciples.

The first name which occurs in this Gospel is that of John the Baptist. He is even introduced into the prologue which sketches in general terms the manifestation of the Divine Word: "There was a man sent from God, whose name was John: he came for witness, to witness to the Light, that through him all might believe." This witness of John holds a position of high importance in this Gospel. His mission is described as running on for a while concurrently with that of our Lord, whereas in the other Gospels we have no record of our Lord's work until John is cast into prison. It is among the disciples of the Baptist on the banks of the Jordan that Jesus finds His first disciples. The Baptist has pointed Him out to them in striking language, which recalls at once the symbolic ritual of the law and the spiritual lessons of the prophets: "Behold, the Lamb of God, which taketh away the sin of the world."

Soon afterwards at Cana of Galilee Jesus gives His first "sign," as the evangelist calls it, in the change of water into wine to supply the deficiency at a marriage feast. This scene has all the happy brightness of the early Galilean ministry which St Mark records. It stands in sharp contrast with the subsequent appearance of Jesus in Jerusalem at the Passover, when His first act is to drive the traders from the Temple courts. In this He seems to be carrying the Baptist's stern mission of purification from the desert into the heart of the sacred city, and so fulfilling, perhaps consciously, the solemn prophecy of Malachi which opens with the words: "Behold, I will send My Messenger, and He shall prepare the way before Me; and the Lord whom ye seek shall suddenly come to His Temple" (Mal. iii. 1-5). This significant action provokes a challenge of His authority, which is answered by a mysterious saying, not understood at the time, but interpreted afterwards as referring to the Resurrection. After this our Lord was visited secretly by a Pharisee named Nicodemus, whose advances were severely met by the words, "Except a man be born again, he cannot see the kingdom of God." When Nicodemus objected that this was to demand a physical impossibility, he was answered that the new birth was "of water and spirit"—words which doubtless contained a reference to the mission of the Baptist and to his prophecy of One who should baptize with the Holy Spirit. Towards the end of this conversation the evangelist passes imperceptibly from reporting the words of the Lord into an interpretation or amplification of them, and in language which recalls the prologue he unfolds the meaning of Christ's mission and indicates the crisis of self-judgment which necessarily accompanies the manifestation of the Light to each individual. When he resumes his narrative the Lord has left Jerusalem, and is found baptizing disciples, in even greater numbers than the Baptist himself. Though Jesus did not personally perform the rite, it is plain once again that in this early period He closely linked His own mission with that of John the Baptist. When men hinted at a rivalry between them, John plainly declared "He must increase, and I must decrease": and the reply of Jesus was to leave Judaea for Galilee.

Away from the atmosphere of contention we find Him manifesting the same broad sympathy and freedom from convention which we have noted in the other Gospels, especially in that of St Luke. He converses with a woman, with a woman moreover who is a Samaritan, and who is of unchaste life. He offers her the "living water" which shall supply all her needs: she readily accepts Him as the expected Messiah, and He receives a welcome from the Samaritans. He passes on to Galilee, where also He is welcomed, and where He performs His second "sign," healing the son of one of Herod's courtiers.

But St John's interest does not lie in Galilee, and he soon brings our Lord back to Jerusalem on the occasion of a feast. The Baptist's work is now ended; and, though Jesus still appeals to the testimony of John, the new conflict **The Ministry at Jerusalem.** with the Jewish authorities shows that He is moving now on His own independent and characteristic lines. In cleansing the Temple He had given offence by what might seem an excess of rigour: now, by healing a sick man and bidding him carry his bed on the Sabbath, He offended by His laxity. He answered His accusers by the brief but pregnant sentence: "My Father worketh even until now, and I work." They at once understood that He thus claimed a unique relation to God, and their antagonism became the more intense: "the Jews therefore sought the more to kill Him, because He had not only broken the Sabbath, but had also said that God was His own Father, making Himself equal to God." His first reply is then expanded to cover the whole region of life. The Son beholds the Father at work, and works concurrently, doing nothing of Himself. He does the Father's will. The very principle of life is entrusted to Him. He quickens, and He judges. As Son of Man He judges man.

The next incident is the feeding of the five thousand, which belongs to the Galilean ministry and is recorded by the three other evangelists. St John's purpose in introducing it is not historical but didactic. It is made the occasion of instruction as to the heavenly food, the flesh and blood of Him who came down from heaven. This teaching leads to a conflict with certain Judaeans who seem to have come from Jerusalem, and it proves a severe test even to the faith of disciples.

The feast of tabernacles brings fresh disputes in Jerusalem, and an attempt is made to arrest Jesus. A climax of indignation is reached when a blind man is healed at the pool of Siloam on the sabbath day. At the feast of the dedication a fresh effort at arrest was made, and Jesus then withdrew beyond the Jordan. Here He learned of the sickness of Lazarus, and presently He returned and came to Bethany to raise him from the dead. The excitement produced by this miracle led to yet another attack, destined this time to be successful, on the life of Jesus. The Passover was at hand, and the last supper of our Lord with His disciples on the evening before the Passover lamb was killed is made the occasion of the most inspiring consolations. Our Lord interprets His relation to the disciples by the figure of a tree and its branches—He is the whole of which they are the parts; He promises the mission of the Holy Spirit to continue His work in the world; and He solemnly commends to His Father the disciples whom He is about to leave.

The account of the trial and the crucifixion differs considerably from the accounts given in the other Gospels. St John's narratives are in large part personal memories, and in more than one incident he himself figures as the unnamed disciple "whom Jesus loved." In the Resurrection scenes he also gives incidents in which he has played a part; and the appearances of the risen Lord are not confined either to Jerusalem or to Galilee, but occur in both localities.

If we ask what is the special contribution to history, apart from theology, which St John's Gospel makes, the answer would seem to be this—that beside the Galilean ministry reported by St Mark there was a ministry to "Jews" (Judaeans) in Jerusalem, not continuous, but occasional, taken up from time to time as the great feasts came round; that its teaching was widely different from that which was given to Galileans, and that the situation created was wholly unlike that which arose out of the Galilean ministry. The Galilean ministry opens with enthusiasm, ripening into a popularity which even endangers a satisfactory result. Where opposition manifests itself, it is not native opposition, but comes from religious teachers who are parts of a system which centres in Jerusalem, and who are sometimes expressly noted as having come from Jerusalem. The Jerusalem ministry on the contrary is never welcomed with enthusiasm. It has to do with those who challenge it from the first. There is no atmosphere of simplicity and teachableness which rejoices in the manifestation of power and sympathy and liberty. It is a witness delivered to a hostile audience, whether they will hear or no. Ultimate issues are quickly raised: keen critics see at once the claims which underlie deeds and words, and the claims in consequence become explicit: the relation of the teacher to God Himself is the vital interest. The conflict which thus arose explains what St Mark's succinct narrative had left unexplained—the fatal hostility of Jerusalem. It may have been a part of St John's purpose to give this explanation, and to make other supplements or corrections where earlier narratives appeared to him incomplete or misleading. But he says nothing to indicate this, while on the other hand he distinctly proclaims that his purpose is to produce and confirm conviction of the divine claims of Jesus Christ.

For bibliography see BIBLE; CHRISTIANITY; CHURCH HISTORY; and the articles on the separate Gospels.

(J. A. R.)

JET (Fr. *jais*, Ger. *Gagat*), a substance which seems to be a peculiar kind of lignite or anthracite; often cut and polished for ornaments. The word "jet" probably comes, through O. Fr.*jaiet*, from the classical *gagates*, a word which was derived, according to Pliny, from Gagas, in Lycia, where jet, or a similar substance, was originally found. Jet was used in Britain in prehistoric times; many round barrows of the Bronze age have yielded jet beads, buttons, rings, armlets and other ornaments. The abundance of jet in Britain is alluded to by Caius Julius 359Solinus (*fl.* 3rd century) and jet ornaments are found with Roman relics in Britain. Probably the supply was obtained from the coast of Yorkshire, especially near Whitby, where nodules of jet were formerly picked up on the shore. Caedmon refers to this jet, and at a later date it was used for rosary beads by the monks of Whitby Abbey.

The Whitby jet occurs in irregular masses, often of lenticular shape, embedded in hard shales known as jet-rock. The jet-rock series belongs to that division of the Upper Lias which is termed the zone of *Ammonites serpentinus*. Microscopic examination of jet occasionally reveals the structure of coniferous wood, which A. C. Seward has shown to be araucarian. Probably masses of wood were brought down by a river, and drifted out to sea, where becoming water-logged they sank, and became gradually buried in a deposit of fine mud, which eventually hardened into shale. Under pressure, perhaps assisted by heat, and with exclusion of air, the wood suffered a peculiar kind of decomposition, probably modified by the presence of salt water, as suggested by Percy E. Spielmann. Scales of fish and other fossils of the jet-rock are frequently impregnated with bituminous products, which may replace the original tissues. Drops of liquid bitumen occur in the cavities of some fossils, whilst inflammable gas is not uncommon in the jet-workings, and petroleum may be detected by its smell. Iron pyrites is often associated with the jet.

Formerly sufficient jet was found in loose pieces on the shore, set free by the disintegration of the cliffs, or washed up from a submarine source. When this supply became insufficient, the rock was attacked by the jet-workers; ultimately the workings took the form of true mines, levels being driven into the shales not only at their outcrop in the cliffs but in some of the inland dales of the Yorkshire moorlands, such as Eskdale. The best jet has a uniform black colour, and is hard, compact and homogeneous in texture, breaking with a conchoidal fracture. It must be tough enough to be readily carved or turned on the lathe, and sufficiently compact in texture to receive a high polish. The final polish was formerly given by means of rouge, which produces a beautiful velvety surface, but rotten-stone and lampblack are often employed instead. The softer kinds, not capable of being freely worked, are known as bastard jet. A soft jet is obtained from the estuarine series of the Lower Oolites of Yorkshire.

Much jet is imported from Spain, but it is generally less hard and lustrous than true Whitby jet. In Spain the chief locality is Villaviciosa, in the province of Asturias. France furnishes jet, especially in the department of the Aude. Much jet, too, occurs in the Lias of Württemberg, and works have been established for its utilization. In the United States jet is known at many localities but is not systematically worked. Pennsylvanian anthracite, however, has been occasionally employed as a substitute. In like manner Scotch cannel coal has been sometimes used at Whitby. Imitations of jet, or substitutes for it, are furnished by vulcanite, glass, black obsidian and black onyx, or stained chalcedony. Jet is sometimes improperly termed black amber, because like amber, though in less degree, it becomes electric by friction.

See P. E. Spielmann, "On the Origin of Jet," *Chemical News* (Dec. 14, 1906); C. Fox-Strangways, "The Jurassic Rocks of Britain, Vol. I. Yorkshire," *Mem. Geol. Surv.* (1892); J. A. Bower, "Whitby Jet and its Manufacture," *Journ. Soc. Arts* (1874, vol. xxii. p. 80).

JETHRO (or JETHER, Exod. iv. 18), the priest of Midian, in the Bible, whose daughter Zipporah became the wife of Moses. He is known as Hobab the son of Reuel the Kenite (Num. x. 29; Judg. iv. 11), and once as Reuel (Exod. ii. 18); and if Zipporah is the wife of Moses referred to in Num. xii. 1, the family could be regarded as Cushite (see Cush). Jethro was the priest of Yahweh, and resided at the sacred mountain where the deity commissioned Moses to deliver the Israelites from Egypt. Subsequently Jethro came to Moses (probably at Kadesh), a great sacrificial feast was held, and the priest instructed Moses in legislative procedure; Exod. xviii. 27 (seeEXODUS) and Num. x. 30 imply that the scene was not Sinai. Jethro was invited to accompany the people into the promised land, and later, we find his clan settling in the south of Judah (Judg. i. 16); see KENITES. The traditions agree in representing the kin of Moses as related to the mixed tribes of the south of Palestine (see EDOM) and in ascribing to the family an important share in the early development of the worship of Yahweh. Cheyne suggests that the names of Hobab and of Jonadab the father of the Rechabites (*q.v.*) were originally identical (*Ency. Bib.* ii. col. 2101).

JETTY. The term jetty, derived from Fr. *jetée*, and therefore signifying something "thrown out," is applied to a variety of structures employed in river, dock and maritime works, which are generally carried out in pairs from river banks, or in continuation of river channels at their outlets into deep water; or out into docks, and outside their entrances; or for forming basins along the sea-coast for ports in tideless seas. The forms and construction of these jetties are as varied as their uses; for though they invariably extend out into water, and serve either for directing a current or for accommodating vessels, they are sometimes formed of high open timber-work, sometimes of low solid projections, and occasionally only differ from breakwaters in their object.

Jetties for regulating Rivers.—Formerly jetties of timber-work were very commonly extended out, opposite one another, from each bank of a river, at intervals, to contract a wide channel, and by concentration of the current to produce a deepening of the central channel; or sometimes mounds of rubble stone, stretching down the foreshore from each bank, served the same purpose. As, however, this system occasioned a greater scour between the ends of the jetties than in the intervening channels, and consequently produced an irregular depth, it has to a great extent been superseded by longitudinal training works, or by dipping cross dikes pointing somewhat upstream (see RIVER ENGINEERING).

FIG 1.—Timber Jetty across Dock
Slope.

Jetties at Docks.—Where docks are given sloping sides, openwork timber jetties are generally carried across the slope, at the ends of which vessels can lie in deep water (fig. 1); or more solid structures are erected over the slope for supporting coal-tips. Pilework jetties are also constructed in the water outside the entrances to docks on each side, so as to form an enlarging trumpet-shaped channel between the entrance, lock or tidal basin and the approach channel, in order to guide vessels in entering or leaving the docks. Solid jetties, moreover, lined with quay walls, are sometimes carried out into a wide dock, at right angles to the line of quays at the side, to enlarge the accommodation; and they also serve, when extended on a large scale from the coast of a tideless sea under shelter of an outlying breakwater, to form the basins in which vessels lie when discharging and taking in cargoes in such a port as Marseilles (see DOCK).

Jetties at Entrances to Jetty Harbours.—The approach channel to some ports situated on sandy coasts is guided and protected across the beach by parallel jetties, made solid up to a little above low water of neap tides, on which open timber-work is erected, provided with a planked platform at the top raised above the highest tides. The channel between the jetties was originally maintained by tidal scour from low-lying areas close to the coast, and subsequently by the current from sluicing basins; but it is now often considerably deepened by sand-pump dredging. It is protected to some extent by the solid portion of the jetties from the inroad of sand from the adjacent beach, and from the levelling action of the waves; whilst the upper open portion serves to indicate the channel, and to guide the vessels if necessary (see HARBOUR). The bottom part of the older jetties, in such long-established jetty ports as Calais, Dunkirk and Ostend, was composed of clay or rubble stone, covered on the top by fascine-work or pitching; but the deepening of the jetty channel by dredging, and the need which arose for its enlargement, led to the reconstruction of the jetties at these ports. The new jetties at Dunkirk were founded in the sandy beach, by the aid of compressed air, at a depth of 22¾ ft. below low water of spring tides; and their solid masonry portion, on a concrete foundation, was raised 53⁄5 ft. above low water of neap tides (fig. 2).

FIG. 2.—Dunkirk East Jetty.

Jetties at Lagoon Outlets.—A small tidal rise spreading tidal water over a large expanse of lagoon or inland back-water causes the influx and efflux of the tide to maintain a deep channel through a narrow outlet; but the issuing current on emerging from the outlet, being no longer confined by a bank on each side, becomes dispersed, and owing to the reduction of its scouring force, is no longer able at a moderate distance from the shore effectually to resist the action of the waves and littoral currents tending to form a continuous beach in front of the outlet. Hence a bar is produced which diminishes the available depth in the approach channel. By carrying out a solid jetty over the bar, however, on each side of the outlet, the tidal currents are concentrated in the channel across the bar, and lower it by scour. Thus the available depth of the approach channels to Venice through the Malamocco and Lido outlets from the Venetian lagoon have been deepened several feet over their bars by jetties of rubble stone surmounted by a small superstructure (fig. 3), carried out across the foreshore into deep water on both sides of the channel. Other examples are provided by the long jetties extended into the sea in front of the entrance to Charleston harbour, formerly constructed of fascines, weighted with stone and logs, but subsequently of rubble stone, and by the two converging rubble jetties carried out from each shore of Dublin bay for deepening the approach to Dublin harbour.

FIG. 3.—Lido Outlet Jetty,
Venice.

FIG. 4.—Mississippi South Pass Outlet Jetty.

Jetties at the Outlet of Tideless Rivers.—Jetties have been constructed on each side of the outlet of some of the rivers flowing into the Baltic, with the objects of prolonging the scour of the river and protecting the channel from being shoaled by the littoral drift along the shore. The most interesting application of parallel jetties is in lowering the bar in front of one of the mouths of a deltaic river flowing into a tideless sea, by extending the scour of the river out to the bar by a virtual prolongation of its banks. Jetties prolonging the Sulina branch of the Danube into the Black Sea, and the south pass of the Mississippi into the Gulf of Mexico (fig. 4), formed of rubble stone and concrete blocks, and fascine mattresses weighted with stone and surmounted with large concrete blocks respectively, have enabled the discharge of these rivers to scour away the bars obstructing the access to them; and they have also carried the sediment-bearing waters sufficiently far out to come under the influence of littoral currents, which, by conveying away some of the sediment, postpone the eventual formation of a fresh bar farther out (see RIVER ENGINEERING).

FIG. 5.—River Maas Outlet, North Jetty.

FIG. 6.—River Nervion Outlet, Western Jetty.

Jetties at the Mouth of Tidal Rivers.—Where a river is narrow near its mouth, and its discharge is generally feeble, the sea is liable on an exposed coast, when the tidal range is small, to block up its outlet during severe storms. The river is thus forced to seek another exit at a weak spot of the beach, which along a low coast may be at some distance off; and this new outlet in its turn may be blocked up, so that the river from time to time shifts the position of its mouth. This inconvenient cycle of changes may be stopped by fixing the outlet of the river at a suitable site, by carrying a jetty on each side of this outlet across the beach, thereby concentrating its discharge in a definite channel and protecting the mouth from being blocked up by littoral drift. This system was long ago applied to the shifting outlet of the river Yare to the south of Yarmouth, and has also been successfully employed for fixing the wandering mouth of the Adur near Shoreham, and of the Adour flowing into the Bay of Biscay below Bayonne. When a new channel was cut across the Hook of Holland to provide a straighter and deeper outlet channel for the river Maas, forming the approach channel to Rotterdam, low, broad, parallel jetties, composed of fascine mattresses weighted with stone (fig. 5), were carried across the foreshore into the sea on either side of the new mouth of the river, to protect the jetty channel from littoral drift, and cause the discharge of the river to maintain it out to deep water (see RIVER ENGINEERING). The channel, also, beyond the outlet of the river Nervion into the Bay of Biscay has been regulated by jetties; and by extending the south-west jetty out for nearly half a mile with a curve concave towards the channel the outlet has not only been protected to some extent from the easterly drift, but the bar in front has been lowered by the scour produced by the discharge of the river following the concave bend of the south-west jetty. As the outer portion of this jetty was exposed to westerly storms from the Bay of Biscay before the outer harbour was constructed, it has been given the form and strength of a breakwater situated in shallow water (fig. 6).

(L. F. V.-H.)

JEVER, a town of Germany, in the grand-duchy of Oldenburg, 13 m. by rail N.W. of Wilhelmshaven, and connected with the North Sea by a navigable canal. Pop. (1901), 5486. The chief industries are weaving, spinning, dyeing, brewing and milling; there is also a trade in horses and cattle. The fathers (*Die Getreuen*) of the town used to send an annual birthday present of 101 plovers' eggs to Bismarck, with a dedication in verse.

The castle of Jever was built by Prince Edo Wiemken (d. 1410), the ruler of Jeverland, a populous district which in 1575 came under the rule of the dukes of Oldenburg. In 1603 it passed to the house of Anhalt and was later the property of the empress Catherine II. of Russia, a member of this family. In 1814 it came again into the possession of Oldenburg.

See D. Hohnholz, *Aus Jevers Vorgangenheit* (Jever, 1886); Hagena, *Jeverland bis zum Jahr* 1500 (Oldenburg, 1902); and F. W. Riemann, *Geschichte des Jeverlandes*(Jever, 1896).

JEVEROS (JEBEROS, JIBAROS, JIVAROS or GIVAROS), a tribe of South American Indians on the upper Marañon, Peru, where they wander in the forests. The tribe has many branches and there are frequent tribal wars, but they have always united against a common enemy. Juan de Velasco declares them to be faithful, noble and amiable. They are brave and warlike, and though upon the conquest of Peru they temporarily submitted, a general insurrection in 1599 won them back their liberty. Curious dried human heads, supposed to have been objects of worship, have been found among the Jeveros (see *Ethnol. Soc. Trans.* 1862, W. Bollaert).